MICRO

THE CANADIAN CONTEXT

ECONOMICS

THIRD
EDITION

ALEXANDER MacMILLAN

Queen's University
and St. Lawrence College

BOHUMÍR PAZDERKA

Queen's University

Prentice-Hall Canada Inc.,
Scarborough, Ontario

Canadian Cataloguing in Publication Data

MacMillan, Alexander, 1942–
   Microeconomics: the Canadian context

3rd ed.
Includes bibliographical references and index.
ISBN 0-13-582032-4

1. Microeconomics.   I. Pazderka, Bohumír, 1941–
II.   Title.

HB172.M25 1989   338.5   C87-094588-2

Prentice-Hall, Inc., Englewood Cliffs, New Jersey
Prentice-Hall International, Inc., London
Prentice-Hall of Australia, Pty., Ltd., Sydney
Prentice-Hall of India, Pvt., Ltd., New Delhi
Prentice-Hall of Japan, Inc., Tokyo
Prentice-Hall of Southeast Asia (Pte.) Ltd., Singapore
Editora Prentice-Hall do Brasil Ltda., Rio de Janeiro
Prentice-Hall Hispanoamericana, S.A., Mexico

ISBN 0-13-582032-4

Production Editor: Maurice Esses
Copy Editor: Maura Brown
Designer: Cedric Hefkie/Martin Zibauer
Cover Designer: Bill Fox
Production Coordinator: Matt Lumsdon
Typesetting: Vellum Print & Graphic Services Inc.

1 2 3 4 5 JD 92 91 90 89

Printed and bound in Canada by John Deyell Company

CONTENTS

PREFACE

Micro and *Macro* Texts

The *Micro* and *Macro* volumes are designed for courses in introductory microeconomics and macroeconomics. The approach is *analytical*: it attempts to explain economic events in terms of cause and effect. A most important characteristic of both books is the strong practical linkage we make between economic theory and economic realities. We have taken considerable pains to show the reader the connection between the study of economics and observable daily events. For this purpose, we have included numerous press articles and cases for analysis, along with the more standard problem sets.

The texts contain the fundamental concepts necessary for the study of most economic issues. However, when faced with a tradeoff between maintaining the reader's perspective on the one hand and further complexity (or theoretical intricacy) on the other, we have generally opted for perspective. It is our desire to evoke and maintain the reader's interest and at the same time to make a large number of elaborations accessible in the appendices to various chapters. The appendices are, of course, entirely optional, and their complete omission does not affect textual continuity in any way.

We have made a conscious effort to de-emphasize the use of specialized terminology and technical tools of analysis. Where economic terms are employed, alternative expressions are suggested (unless the economists' jargon has become part of everyday discourse among the general public or business community). Furthermore, readers are encouraged not to rely upon any particular analytical tool, but to use whatever method they feel most comfortable with in order to examine the substantive issue at hand. The primary objective of these books is to discuss economic principles and their application, not to teach new vocabulary, geometry or algebra. In fact, the mathematical prerequisites for all the material are considerably below the level of senior high school.

The first two editions of these books have been found useful for teaching students majoring in economics as well as those specializing in other disciplines. The texts have been successfully used in courses at the high school, college and undergraduate university levels as well as in graduate programs in both Canada and the United States. The *Micro* volume has been translated by the Chinese for teaching their students how market economies function, and the *Macro* volume has been adapted for the Australian market.

Micro Text

The original edition of *Micro* emphasized the practical applications of the material by drawing on the Canadian microeconomic experience. We have enhanced this flavour in the third edition by distributing the Canadian illustrations more thoroughly throughout the text.

Users of the first and second editions informed us that the blend of verbal exposition, diagrams and numerical examples was very helpful. Thus, we have prepared the third edition along similar lines.

The beginning chapters of the book provide the essential concepts for the study of microeconomics. These chapters we call the *prerequisite group*. To provide flexibility, we have kept their number to a minimum: they consist simply of Chapters 2 through 6. For the other chapters, this group is a sufficient prerequisite. Because of this arrangement, certain chapters may be skipped without inhibiting the treatment of later ones. Thus, a shorter course could consist of Chapters 2 through 6 and selected topics from various other chapters.

Most economists would agree that there are some topics in microeconomics that involve more difficult concepts than others, or that by their very nature, require more detail than others. These concepts (such as price and output decisions of firms, elasticity, and government intervention in the economy) we have intentionally broken down into simpler components. The components are sometimes treated within a particular chapter and its appendix, while at other times they are spread over two or more chapters. The rationale for this may be illustrated with reference to the concept of elasticity.

Elasticity is a topic that can appear difficult to students. They often become so preoccupied with the formulas for calculating *arc* or *point elasticity* that they lose sight of the basic concept. Therefore, we have given a straightforward presentation of *elasticity* in Section 4-6 and relegated the algebraic mechanics of its measurement to a supplementary position in Appendix 4A. Some instructors may wish to skip this appendix entirely.

Changes to the Third Edition of *Micro*

In the previous edition of *Micro*, two chapters were devoted to the microeconomics of selected Canadian industries. For the third edition, we have decided to reorganize the book by eliminating these chapters. We have updated the material on Canadian industries and distributed it throughout the text. Thus, it serves to illustrate more effectively the application of theoretical concepts. We have also repositioned the appendices. Each now appears at the end of the appropriate chapter rather than at the end of the book.

Among the new theoretical developments discussed in the third edition are *economies of scope* (Chapter 9), *contestable markets* (Chapter 9) and the industrial organization approach to *free trade* (Chapter 11). Furthermore, three new sections have been added: Section 1-4 on the history of economics, Appendix 9B on Canadian competition legislation and Section 11-8 on freer trade between the U.S. and Canada. We have also chosen to discuss many legislative and policy developments that have recently taken place in Canada. Thus, we have included material on the Competition Act, 1986 (Appendix 9B); the Investment Canada Act, 1985 (Chapter 11); the Freedom to Move legislation on deregulation of transportation, January 1988 (Chapter 1); the modification of legislation on Compulsory Licensing of pharmaceuticals, 1987 (Chapter 7); and the signing of the Canada-U.S. Free Trade Agreement, October 1987 (Chapter 7).

We have updated and expanded the problem sets and cases at the ends of the chapters. In particular, we have introduced fifteen new cases covering a wide range of topics, such as experiments in economics, the excess supply of doctors, the Pepsi-Coke war, and the stock market crash on "Black Monday."

We have also made some significant changes of a pedagogical nature. The text now includes brief summaries of almost all diagrams and tables. As well, the important concepts of each section are highlighted in summary form. Key terms are also highlighted in the body of the text and are listed at the end of each chapter. We believe that these changes will make comprehension easier and facilitate the student's review for assignments and tests.

Acknowledgements

We would like to thank all those instructors who used the previous two editions of *Microeconomics* and took the time to send in useful comments and suggestions for improvement, especially Professors J. Hughes, W. L. Marr and R. L. Canon. For the third edition, we would particularly like to thank Professors Har Kang and Chuck Casson for their helpful remarks as reviewers of the manuscript.

We would also like to extend a special thanks to all those at Prentice-Hall Canada Inc. who have worked on this third edition — in particular, Don Bettger, Rich Ludlow, Monica Schwalbe, and especially Maurice Esses.

To the Student

We hope that this book will continue to be enjoyable and will help you gain some important insights into how the Canadian economy functions. We would like to encourage suggestions and comments from your perspective that might improve the explanation of any topic or that would better illustrate the application of particular economic principles. Please address your letters to either of us.

Alex MacMillan
School of Business
Queen's University
Kingston, Ontario
Canada K7L 1N6

Bohumír Pazderka
School of Business
Queen's University
Kingston, Ontario
Canada K7L 1N6

SYMBOLS AND ABBREVIATIONS

↑	an increase in an economic variable *or* an upward shift in a demand or supply curve
↓	a decrease in an economic variable *or* a downward shift in a demand or supply curve
→	a causal relationship between two variables (for example, $y\uparrow \rightarrow u\downarrow$ means that an increase in real gross domestic product causes a decrease in unemployment)
Δ	a change in an economic variable (for example, ΔW represents a change in nominal wage rates)
% Δ	a percentage change in an economic variable, usually with respect to time (for example, $\% \Delta W$ represents a percentage change in nominal wage rates over a certain period of time, such as a year)
π	price of foreign exchange
AC	average cost
AD	aggregate demand
AFC	average fixed cost
AP	average product
apc	average propensity to consume
APL	average productivity of labour
AS	aggregate supply
AS_{LR}	long-run aggregate supply curve
c	real consumption
C	nominal consumption
CCA	capital consumption allowances
CPI	consumer price index

D	demand *or* depreciation
e	elasticity
E	equilibrium
FC	fixed cost
g	real government expenditure
G	nominal government expenditure
GATT	The General Agreement on Tariffs and Trade
GDP	gross domestic product
GNI	gross national income
GNP	gross national product
i	real investment demand
I	nominal investment demand *or* indifference curve
I^g	nominal gross investment before depreciation
I^n	nominal net investment after depreciation (thus, $I^n = I^g - D$)
im	real import demand
IM	nominal import demand
$(IM - X)_{GNP}$	domestic borrowing from abroad
IMF	International Monetary Fund
IRP	interest rate parity
k	real capital stock
ℓ	labour
ℓ_d	labour demand
ℓ_f	labour force
ℓ_s	labour supply
L	labour
LAC	long-run average cost
LMC	long-run marginal cost

M_d	money demand
M_s	money supply
$M1$	narrowly defined money supply
$M2$	$M1$ plus personal notice deposits
$M3$	$M2$ plus nonpersonal notice deposits
MC	marginal cost
MES	minimum efficient scale
MLC	marginal labour cost
MMP	modified marginal product
$MMRP$	modified marginal revenue product
MP	marginal product
mpc	marginal propensity to consume
MPL	marginal productivity of labour
MR	marginal revenue
MRP	marginal revenue product
NNP	net national product
NPV	net present value
OECD	Organization for Economic Cooperation and Development
OPEC	Organization of Petroleum Exporting Countries
P	price level
P_E	equilibrium price level
PPP	purchasing power parity
pr	productivity
PROF	profit
Q	quantity
r	real interest rate
R	nominal interest rate
RP	retained profits
s	aggregate annual real savings
S	saving or supply
S_1	saving of sector I (household)
S_2	saving of sector II (business)
S_2^g	gross saving of sector II (thus, $S_2^g = RP + D$)
S_2^n	net saving of sector II (thus, $S_2^n = RP$)
S_3	saving of sector III (government)
S_4	saving of sector IV (foreign)
S_g	gross aggregate saving
SAC	short-run average cost
$SAVC$	short-run average variable cost
SDR	Special Drawing Right

SMC	short-run marginal cost
SP	stock prices
t	real taxes
T	nominal taxes
TC	total cost
TR	total revenue
u	unemployment rate
u_n	natural unemployment rate
v	vacancy rate
VC	variable cost
w	real wage rate
w_e	equilibrium real wage rate
W	nominal wage rate
x	real export demand
X	nominal export demand
$(x - im)$	real net foreign demand (i.e. real net exports)
$(X - IM)$	nominal net foreign demand (i.e. nominal net exports)
$(x - im)_{GDP}$	real net foreign demand (i.e. excluding net payments of interest and dividends abroad)
$(X - IM)_{GDP}$	nominal net foreign demand (i.e. excluding net payments of interest and dividends abroad)
$(x - im)_{GNP}$	real all-inclusive net foreign demand (i.e. including net payments of interest and dividends abroad)
$(X - IM)_{GNP}$	nominal all-inclusive net foreign demand (i.e. including net payments of interest and dividends abroad)
y	real GDP or real GNP
Y	nominal GDP or nominal GNP
y_{disp}	real disposable income
Y_{disp}	nominal disposable income
y_E	short-run equilibrium level of real GDP (or of real GNP)
Y_E	short-run equilibrium level of nominal GDP (or of nominal GNP)
y_F	full-employment level of real GDP (or of real GNP)
Y_F	full-employment level of nominal GDP (or of nominal GNP)
y_P	potential level of real GDP (or of real GNP)
Y_P	potential level of nominal GDP (or of nominal GNP)

CHAPTER 1

Economics: Purpose and Method

LEARNING OBJECTIVES

After reading this chapter you should be able to explain:

1. The subject of economics as a scientific discipline and the tasks performed by economists.
2. The general methodology of economics, including the testing of hypotheses and theories.

3. The use of diagrams in economic analysis.
4. The concept of opportunity cost and its use in economic reasoning.

1-1 THE PURPOSE OF ECONOMICS

Economics is most often defined as a social science dealing with the allocation of scarce resources among competing ends. This definition is certainly general, compact and accurate, but like many definitions it may be best understood only after one has studied the subject. More simply put, economics is a systematic investigation of such questions as:

(1) How do people decide what goods and services to produce (how many cars, shirts, theatre performances, eggs and taxi rides) and what the selling prices will be?

(2) Who gets the output that is produced and how is this determined — in other words, why do people earn the incomes that they do?

(3) What determines the general level of stock prices, interest rates, unemployment, inflation and foreign exchange rates (and what do these terms mean precisely)?

Traditionally, the study of economics is subdivided into two major subject areas: **microeconomics** and **macroeconomics**. Microeconomics focuses primarily on markets for particular goods or services and on actions of such economic agents as consumers and business firms. Macroeconomics comprises concepts that concern the economy as a whole. For example, questions (1) and (2) above are microeconomic concerns while question (3) is macroeconomic. This micro-macro division has rather fuzzy boundaries but is a traditional way of categorizing economic topics.

For purposes of further analysis, economists sometimes divide the economy into four sectors: households (consumers, workers), business firms, government (all levels) and the rest of the world (foreign sector). From the above list of economic concerns it is clear that almost everyone is interested in at least some aspect of economics as it affects daily life. Typically, though, direct interest in economics — a person's economic perspective — will depend upon the sector to which the individual belongs. Also, many people are in two sectors at once. For example, corporate business managers are in the business sector as producers and in the household sector as consumers. Members of Parliament are in the government sector as legislators and in the household sector as consumers.

Decision Making and Scarcity

Some people pursue economic inquiry to gain economic understanding. For most of us, however, the incentive for engaging in economic analysis is to enable us to make decisions as consumers, workers, business managers or government officials so that we may become better off than we otherwise might be. In making decisions that will improve our *welfare* (well-being), we should define our objectives, know what instruments and resources we have to achieve these objectives and understand how the instruments within our control are linked through the economic system to our objectives.

Economic decisions involve choice among scarcity. As a nation we have limited human resources, as well as limited numbers of machines and finite quantities of natural resources. If we want more of one good or service, we have to sacrifice some other good or service. As workers we may want more goods and services and therefore work hard and long hours. Since time is limited, we have to sacrifice leisure time. As consumers with limited wealth and income potential we may want to take a trip to Europe and thus have to forego the purchase of a new car.

Most economic decisions are concerned with the acquisition of some benefit at some cost. In fact, economic decision making is sometimes called **cost-benefit analysis**. Conceptually, economic decision making is straightforward. If the decision is between all or nothing, for instance whether or not to go to Europe next summer, the decision maker will attempt to evaluate the costs and benefits of the trip and decide to go only if the benefits seem to exceed the costs. If, on the other hand, a decision involves steps (or degrees) rather than "all or nothing," another step should be taken only if the additional benefit is thought to outweigh the additional cost. For example, a group that has decided to go bowling one evening will presumably continue to bowl only as long as the bowlers judge the additional pleasure from one more game to be

greater than the extra cost (which would include not only the price of the game, but getting home later and perhaps being more tired the next day).

Most decisions have step-by-step elements. For example, even a trip to Europe can be arranged for two weeks, four weeks, or other lengths of time.

Economics is the study of the allocation of scarce resources among competing ends. Much of economic decision making consists of comparing the additional benefits of an action with the additional costs.

Framework for Analysis

The most general framework for economic analysis is that of **supply and demand**. Supply considerations capture the cost side of any market, and demand considerations characterize the perceived benefit or value of the particular good or service in question. The principles behind supply and demand apply whether or not an economy operates under a free market system. It may be shown that these concepts are as relevant for countries like the USSR and Yugoslavia as they are for North America.

Uncertainty and Economic Forecasting

Because all economic decisions depend on and affect the future, the actual costs and benefits of any action will not be known with certainty until after the decision has been made. Consequently, decisions have to be made on the basis of *estimated* or *expected* costs and benefits. Though good economic analysis of these factors may have been carried out with the best information available at the time, the costs and benefits that actually occur may prove in hindsight that the decision was incorrect. In fact, the acquisition of reliable information concerning costs and benefits is a prime source of difficulty in economic decision making. This point is emphasized many times and in many different contexts in this book. The problem affects consumers, workers, business managers and government decision makers alike.

The outcome of economic decisions in terms of costs and benefits depends critically on what happens in the future. In attempting to estimate potential costs and benefits, many decision makers have to engage in **economic forecasting**. For example, we may be contemplating buying a house for which we have to borrow heavily. If we know that interest rates (the cost of borrowing) are on their way up, we may be wise to acquire the loan as soon as possible. If interest rates will be significantly lower in the near future, we may be better off to wait. Bank managers are often deluged with questions concerning the future course of interest rates.

It may be natural to think that if economists really do understand how the economy works, then they should also be able to predict reasonably accurately at least a year or two ahead what will happen to interest rates and other important economic variables. Unfortunately, the problem is not quite as straightforward as that. Economic units are dynamic because they are continually reacting to internal and external **shocks** of an economic, social, political, biological, psychological and even a meteorological nature. To expect economists to predict with some degree of accuracy how the economy will behave would be reasonable if the size and number of specific shocks which can have an impact on the economy were known. However, economists cannot predict these shocks. For example, how can an economist know well in advance that the government will change tax rates, or that the Prairies will have weather conducive to a good grain crop? Yet these factors affect prices, interest rates and other things that people expect economists to forecast. Therefore, even though a good understanding of the economic system may enable economists to forecast better than noneconomists, their predictions may still not be as accurate as many decision makers would like.

1-2 FUNCTIONS OF AN ECONOMIST

The main function of an economist is to seek out the economic goals of various groups within society or of society as a whole and to perform analyses that result in advice on how best to achieve these goals.

For example, if the main goal of a business is to maximize profit, the job of the economist is three-fold: (i) Identify those factors that influence profit and are within the firm's control (perhaps price, advertising and product quality), (ii) Analyze the connection between the firm's decisions and the firm's profit (for instance, predict how a price increase or additional advertising may be expected to influence the firm's costs, sales and hence profit) and (iii) Advise the firm (based on the analysis in the second step) on the appropriate price level, advertising and product quality that would be expected to maximize profit.

Suppose, from an aggregate standpoint, that society wished to achieve a faster rate of growth in the standard of living or a lower rate of unemployment. It is the function of the economist to explain whether these goals are possible, and if they are, to determine how they may be achieved and at what cost. For example, economic analysis may show that one cost of attempting to achieve a lower rate of unemployment within a particular year may be a higher rate of inflation in the same year or in future years. It would then be the economist's task to search out the nature and magnitude of such inflation costs and inform the public of them. The public may then have to choose between the goal of lower unemployment and the goal of lower inflation.

Another goal of society may be a redistribution of income among various groups within society. It would then be the economist's task to explain the best way of attaining this goal.

Economics and Philosophy

An economist shows whether and at what costs various economic goals may be achieved. It is not the function of economics to formulate these goals or judge them as being good or bad in an ethical sense. An economist is not specially trained in moral philosophy and is therefore no better qualified to judge good or bad than the average citizen. An economist has neither more nor less responsibility than the average citizen to comment on the desirability of various societal goals. An economist does, however, have a responsibility to inform fellow citizens of the economic consequences of the use of specific methods to pursue particular goals.

Economics is not philosophy, and it is not the business of economists to promote various moral principles, though they may wish to do so and even feel it their duty to do so as citizens. Some famous economists of the past have also been moral philosophers, including Adam Smith, and John Stuart Mill. Consequently, some of their works appear as a mix of ethics and economic principles. Statements about what should be in a moral value sense are referred to as **normative**. **Positive** economic statements are about cause and effect relationships. They suggest how to achieve particular goals and describe how individuals and institutions behave, without judging whether such goals or behaviour are good or bad.

Disagreement concerning positive statements may potentially be settled by an empirical study (a study of facts) whereas disagreement concerning normative statements cannot. For example, consider the following four statements:

(1) The circumference of the earth at the equator is approximately 40 000 kilometres.

(2) Increases in consumer income cause increases in consumer spending.

(3) It is wrong to look for life on other planets.

(4) Firms should attempt to maximize profit.

Statements (1) and (2) are positive statements, whose truth or falsity may be settled by factual study. For example, the circumference of the earth may be measured and actual data on consumer incomes and consumption may be examined. Statements (3) and (4) are normative statements about what ought to be. No factual studies can prove or disprove them. Instead, whether or not we agree with normative issues depends largely on our ethical perspective. Furthermore, although it is theoretically possible to verify or disprove positive statements, it may sometimes be very difficult or costly to do so. Consider, for example, the cost of disproving the statement, "Common forms of life exist on Venus."

In this book, we are for the most part concerned with describing how the economy works and how individuals and institutions act and react, and what courses of action are best to achieve the desired goals — that is, positive economics. In many different contexts, we try to point out where positive economics ends and normative discussions begin. We certainly do not mean to imply, however, that discussions should end when moral value judgements must be made. Often these value judgements may be the most important considerations of all. Nevertheless, economic principles and morality are separate. For instance, economic principles shed light on the means by which certain goals

may best be attained but have nothing to say about the desirability of the ends (or goals) themselves.

Conflicting Goals

Following is a short list of various **goals** which different groups of Canadians, at one time or another, have suggested we as a nation should strive for. Some are purely economic, some are more social than economic, and some are a socio-economic mixture. They are not listed in any particular order of priority.

(1) Efficiency (that is, obtaining the most output with the least economic input wastage)

(2) Limited inflation

(3) Minimum unemployment

(4) Increased income per capita

(5) Freedom of choice

(6) Fair distribution of income across age groups, sex and geographic regions

(7) Protection of the environment

(8) Control over our economy and a low degree of foreign ownership

It is often quite difficult for various groups to specify their economic goals, other than to say that they would like to be better off. If specific goals emerge — for example, lower inflation, lower unemployment and greater regional equality — these goals are likely to be conflicting with each other at some level or over some period of time. If so, how much weight should be placed on each one? Because of circumstances, one group may desire greater regional equality at all costs. Others, though, may be totally unconcerned with this goal and instead be more interested in lower unemployment regardless of inflationary consequences. Still others (for example, pensioners) may want as little inflation as possible. It is a source of frustration to economists, as well as to the public, that there often is no action that can make everyone better off at once.

Goals and Government Policy

To a significant extent, each country's unique geographical position and social, economic and cultural history influence its economic and noneconomic goals as well as the strategies used to achieve them.

Canada is a country of enormous land area inhabited by a small and widely dispersed population. Canada is also a land of relatively abundant natural resources distributed rather unevenly across the country. The relative abundance of natural resources has meant that, in the past, it has been most profitable for Canada to concentrate much of its effort on the extraction of these resources. Early in Canada's history, fish, fur and timber were the **staple** (most important) **commodities** on which much of its economy was based. Later these products were supplemented by grain and meat production, pulp and paper, minerals and petroleum. Many of these products have traditionally been sold abroad (exported) in return for purchases (imports) of foreign machinery and manufactured consumer goods.

To rely so heavily on natural resource and agricultural production has been distasteful to some Canadians who wish to be known as more than "hewers of wood and drawers of water." A narrow concentration of economic activity is also risky because a sudden drop in world demand for one or more of our staple exports can have a serious adverse effect on the economy.

Shortly after Confederation (1867), the *National Policy* was formulated by the Conservative government. The National Policy had three prongs: (i) Develop and protect a Canadian manufacturing base in central Canada, (ii) Subsidize the construction of a transcontinental railway system and (iii) Encourage immigration to the West. The programs of welfare assistance and income sharing across the regions of Canada through federal-provincial agreements, which grew up in the 1930s and the following years, could be said to have had their roots in the National Policy of the 1800s. These programs have not always been formed with the objective of maximizing national economic wealth but instead have often been concerned largely with the regional distribution of such wealth.

Other government policies deal with such noneconomic concerns as human rights and culture. Most citizens are willing to pay some economic cost to achieve goals in these areas. It is important to recognize that economic goals are not the only worthy objectives in society. In instances where a choice must be made between pursuit of an economic goal and an alternative objective, society may, in fact, choose the alternative objective in a perfectly rational manner. To make a wise choice, though, the total costs and benefits involved must be understood.

Since choices among competing societal goals are often made by the government, political considerations may significantly influence the outcome.

Positive economics analyzes the cause-and-effect relationship among economic variables. Normative economics evaluates the desirability of a particular economic outcome. Policy considerations determine the priorities assigned to the competing economic goals.

Economics and Politics

Economists in some instances are able to identify specific nonconflicting goals, perform excellent analysis that evaluates all relevant economic costs and benefits and prescribe a specific course of action, only to be thwarted by political considerations. Time and again, we see apparent contradictions between what economic analysis demonstrates to be the best way to achieve certain stated goals and the actions taken by particular governments. This happens despite the fact that governments are the largest single employer of economists.

This paradox is understood, however, once we consider the fact that many economic decisions lead to unequal spreading of costs and benefits. Consider, for example, a certain course of action *A*. We assume that each member of society is to be considered equal. Table 1-1 contains the relevant cost-benefit data including the distribution of these costs and benefits.

The costs to society of action *A* are expected to exceed the benefits by $20 000 000 a year. On this basis, the economic decision would be to forego action *A*. However, suppose the 80 000 people who would be favourably affected by the decision to go ahead were a well organized group with considerable political influence, whereas the 25 000 000 people consisted of the general population. Each member of the general population would be hurt by only $4 a year, which loss (if it is noticed at all) may be worth grumbling about but

Table 1-1 Cost-benefit analysis of action A

	Totals	No. of people affected	Per capita effect
Costs			
(per annum)	$100 000 000	25 000 000	$ 4
Benefits			
(per annum)	80 000 000	80 000	1000

The total costs of this policy action are larger than the total benefits. Since the cost per citizen (voter) is negligible, the politicians need not fear a strong electoral opposition. Benefits are, however, highly visible to those affected, who will presumably support the politicians if they implement the action.

hardly worth a letter to a Member of Parliament. On the other hand, each member of the group to benefit by the action would receive the significant sum of $1000 a year. The population at large would be unlikely to organize a lobby against this $4-a-year issue whereas the well organized group, seeing it as a $1000-a-year issue, will probably lobby for it. This sort of *political pressure* may certainly make it difficult for politicians to carry out the advice of economic studies. It is a great source of frustration to economists for two reasons: first, because many good economic studies go to waste; and second, because the structure of markets and government economic actions are often attributed by the general public to the advice of the economist when they may instead be the result of political compromise and bear little relation to the conclusions of economic analysis.

1-3 THE METHOD OF ECONOMIC ANALYSIS

The purpose of positive economics is to explain relations among phenomena that affect our material well-being (such things as: prices, output, employment, profits, wealth and income). We hope that through gaining a better understanding of these relations we will discover ways to enhance our material well-being.

A **theory** or **model** is an explanation of observed facts, whether they are crime rates, heart failures, weather patterns or inflation. Economists use the scientific method to develop explanations of relationships among economic phenomena. By and

large, the **scientific method** consists of the following four steps:

(1) Formulating a hypothesis concerning an observed phenomenon
(2) Constructing an experiment to test the hypothesis
(3) Evaluating statistical evidence from the experiment
(4) Accepting, rejecting or modifying the hypothesis in light of statistical evidence

Formulating a Hypothesis

In formulating a hypothesis concerning a particular phenomenon, economists may have either of two basic purposes: (i) to forecast or predict the phenomenon, or (ii) to provide policy advice on how to alter the phenomenon. If we only want to forecast the phenomenon, we may or may not particularly care about precise causal connections. On the other hand, if we want to influence the phenomenon we must be interested in causal connections.

For example, some information concerning profitability performance of most large corporations is generally perceived by the stock market before the companies' financial statements are published. Rumours in the stock market that the companies will report higher profits lead to increases in the prices of the firms' listed stocks. Similarly, rumours concerning possible lower profits to be reported in the near future lead to depressed stock prices. For purposes of forecasting reported profits, we could therefore construct a hypothesis that would connect a company's stock price to future actual reported profits. For instance, perhaps stock prices in the third quarter may be used as a reasonable predictor of a company's year-end reported profits. However, even though stock prices could be used to predict reported profits, one should certainly not manipulate stock prices (if it were possible) in an attempt to raise future reported profits. Such antics would be completely ineffective.

Economic forecasters sometimes construct and test predictive hypotheses without any thought to causal connections. If the hypotheses produce good predictions, they are useful; if they do not, they are, of course, pointless. If the height of women's skirt hemlines could be used as a predictor of stock market performance, few market participants would lose sleep worrying about the causal nature of the process. In fact, this hemline theory has in the past been mentioned half jokingly as such a stock market indicator. Figure 1-1 shows the apparent correspondence between women's hemlines and stock market performance. Notice for example, the short skirt "flapper" era of the late 1920s, and that of the mini-skirt in the late 1960s and early 1970s. During the market doldrums of the 1930s, late 1970s and early 1980s, skirts were relatively long.

Most economic hypotheses, though, are formulated to deal with cause and effect relationships, not only because they are expected to yield good predictions. In our example directly above, because there is no causal connection between women's hemlines and stock market performance, attempting to increase the value of stock portfolios by encouraging women to wear shorter skirts would be silly. On the other hand, higher income may cause higher consumer purchases of a particular good, while a price rise may have the opposite effect; higher interest rates may cause lower borrowing and reduced investment, and so forth. Causal analysis can help explain how to change the volume of output produced or the level of investment. These changes may be desired in order to achieve certain economic goals.

Constructing an Experiment and Evaluating the Evidence

The hypothesis must be put into a form amenable to experimentation. Relevant variables within the particular phenomenon must be identified and defined in measurable terms. This task requires setting up an economic model designed to represent the significant elements of the phenomenon under study and omitting most of the real world details whose total net effect is thought to be insignificant.

Usually the hypothesis is of the type that says A causes (or influences) B, or perhaps that W, X and Y cause (or influence) Z. In these instances, B and Z are dependent variables whereas A and W, X and Y are independent variables — or better still, *explanatory variables*. There are various possible ways of representing the hypothesis in a shorthand manner. One method is the following:

(1) $A \longrightarrow B$ (1)′ $W \longrightarrow Z$
                           $X \nearrow$
                           $Y \nearrow$

where the arrows indicate the hypothesized direction of causation, that is, A causes B. Such representations as (1) and (1)′ are called **causal network diagrams** or **flow charts** and are often a very convenient way of representing expected causal linkages.

A second way of representing the above hypotheses is as follows:

(2) $B = f(A)$ (2)′ $Z = g(W, X, Y)$

Here the statements are read: B is a function of A; Z is a function of W, X and Y. Another way of phrasing this is to say B is related to (or caused by) A; Z is related to (or caused by) W, X and Y. An example of relationship (2)′ is the hypothesis that the sales of chewing gum (Z) are related to (or caused by or determined by) its price (W), its advertising (X), and the advertising of competing products (Y).

Good theories or hypotheses explain a large amount of the movement in the dependent variable (or phenomenon being explained) with a small number of explanatory variables.

At this stage economists are sometimes criticized by those who would argue that all economic models are abstract and unrealistic. This idea is certainly correct, but it should not be expressed as a negative criticism. If a model has all the detail that a real world phenomenon has, it ceases to be a model and it no longer provides a viable means of investigation into the nature of the phenomenon.

For instance, compare the following two models. Model 1 — The sales of lemonade in a particular city in a given month are a function of its price; the price of other soft drinks; the price of beer; temperature; advertising; the number, location and opening hours of fast-food outlets, restaurants and corner stores; age structure of the population; disposable income; and the number of football games and similar activities taking place. Model 2 — The sales of lemonade go up as its price goes down and vice versa (other things being equal).

To be sure, all of the variables listed in Model 1 are relevant. (Many others are as well.) However, for many practical purposes it is sufficient to concentrate on only one or a few explanatory variables and measure their influence on the dependent variable.

A model that has a single explanatory variable explaining 95% of a phenomenon will probably

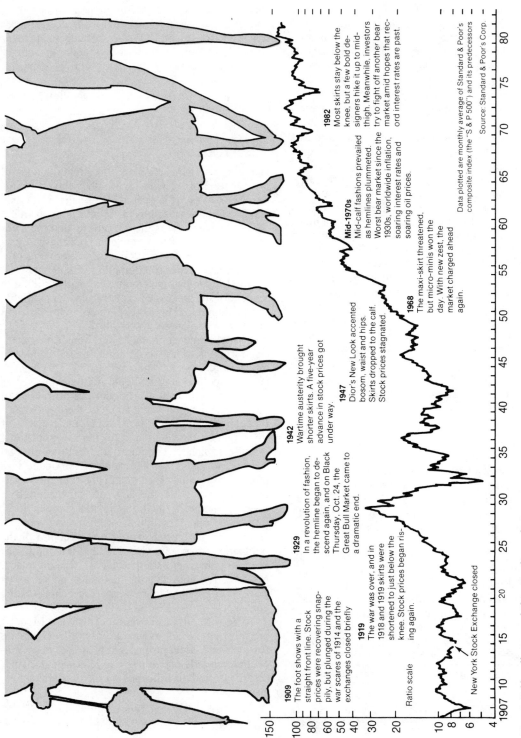

1909
The foot shows with a straight front line. Stock prices were recovering snappily, but plunged during the war scares of 1914 and the exchanges closed briefly

1919
The war was over, and in 1918 and 1919 skirts were shortened to just below the knee. Stock prices began rising again.

1929
In a revolution of fashion, the hemline began to descend again, and on Black Thursday, Oct. 24, the Great Bull Market came to a dramatic end.

1942
Wartime austerity brought shorter skirts. A five-year advance in stock prices got under way.

1947
Dior's New Look accented bosom, waist and hips. Skirts dropped to the calf. Stock prices stagnated.

1968
The maxi-skirt threatened, but micro-minis won the day. With new zest, the market charged ahead again.

Mid-1970s
Mid-calf fashions prevailed as hemlines plummeted. Worst bear market since the 1930s, worldwide inflation, soaring interest rates and soaring oil prices.

1982
Most skirts stay below the knee, but a few bold designers hike it up to mid-thigh. Meanwhile, investors try to fight off another bear market amid hopes that record interest rates are past.

Ratio scale

New York Stock Exchange closed

Data plotted are monthly average of Standard & Poor's composite index (the "S & P 500") and its predecessors

Source: Standard & Poor's Corp.

150
100
80
60
50
40
30
20
10
8
6
4

1907 10 15 20 25 30 35 40 45 50 55 60 65 70 75 80

Fig. 1-1 Hemlines and the stock market

The graph suggests a correlation between the height of the hemlines and stock market performance. However, no plausible causal relationship between the two has been formulated.

provide more insight and be more useful than a model that explains 97% of the same phenomenon but uses 100 explanatory variables as part of the explanation. The test of when to stop adding explanatory variables to make a model more realistic (i.e., more in keeping with the details of the real world) is to see whether the extra cost of adding one more explanatory variable exceeds the extra value gained in terms of better predictions or better understanding. If it does, then the simpler, more abstract model is to be preferred. Indeed, Milton Friedman, one of the winners of the Nobel Prize in Economics, argues in a classic essay on the methodology of economics that "the more significant the theory, the more unrealistic the assumptions (in this sense) ... [and] a hypothesis is important if it 'explains' much by little, that is, if it abstracts the common and crucial elements from the mass of complex and detailed circumstances ..."[1]

Once a model is formulated and all economic variables are defined in measurable terms, the hypothesis can be tested. Unfortunately, economists can seldom hold *controlled experiments* to test hypotheses in the same way as researchers can in the physical sciences. This is a serious drawback. For example, suppose that X causes Z. It may be that X and Z are observed to move up and down together, thereby providing some evidence that X causes Z. Often, however, alternative hypotheses can explain the observations equally well. Thus the data may also support the hypothesis that it is really Z which causes X, instead of the other way round. Further, in all probability hundreds of other variables, such as U, V, W and Y will also have been changing along with X and Z. Perhaps, therefore, the data equally well indicate that W causes both X and Z to move together, with no direct link between X and Z.

In the physical sciences, controlled experiments may be carried out in which, by careful design, the researcher can more easily discard alternative hypotheses. For instance, the following experiment may help to discern whether X causes Z or Z causes X. First, the researcher actively varies X and examines whether Z responds. Then, he varies Z and examines whether X responds. To see whether X and Z move together only because variable W influences them both, the researcher can carry out an experiment whereby W is held constant and then observe whether X and Z still vary together.

An economist may sometimes find it possible to design experiments along the same lines, but it is generally very difficult to control for other influences. Consider, for example, the task of measuring the effect of advertising on sales of chewing gum. A market experiment can be designed where advertising may be doubled in one region (city) and kept constant elsewhere. The change in sales in the experimental area as compared to the control area would then indicate the effect of advertising on sales. Unfortunately, competitors can (and do) confound the measurement by changing their advertising in the same two areas at the same time. Also, the price of another product (chocolate bars) may change at the same time in one of the areas.

More often than not, experiments in economics are not feasible. For example, it would be impractical and politically unacceptable to analyze the relationship between tax structure and consumer spending by means of an experiment. The Minister of Finance would have to agree to employ one set of taxes one year, another set the following year, and so on. The disruptions in financial planning by businesses, households and the government itself would likely be very costly.

In place of experiments, economists frequently test their hypotheses with the help of past data which contain information on the extraneous variables that have to be controlled for. An economist measuring the effect of advertising on sales of chewing gum would need data for many months of the product's history. This would likely include information on sales, advertising, price, in-store promotion and other important influences on sales. Similar information would be required also for competing products. Statistical (econometric) techniques would then be used, with varying degrees of success, to disentangle the relationship between sales of the product and the many variables listed above.

Accepting, Modifying, Rejecting the Hypothesis

Depending on the results of the previous step, an economist will do one of three things: (i) Accept the original hypothesis, (ii) Modify and retest it or

1. Milton Friedman, "The Methodology of Positive Economics," in *Essays in Positive Economics* (Chicago: University of Chicago Press, 1953), p. 14.

(iii) Reject it completely. As with all statistical results, there may emerge a difference of opinion about the meaning of the data. Some economists may feel the original hypothesis is supported by the statistical results; others may dispute such an interpretation. This is the nature of any science: questions easily answered are often not worth asking in the first place, and important issues are often difficult to resolve.

The purpose of economic models or theories is to explain the relationship among economic phenomena. When developing a theory, an economist begins with a hypothesis and tests its validity by evaluating its logical consistency and by statistically analyzing its conformity with real life data. Experimental testing of economic theories is possible only rarely.

Theory versus Practice

In economics, the statement "good in theory but no good in practice" is self-contradictory. A theory is only as good as its value in practice. A theory that is no good in practice is a bad theory and should be replaced by a better one if possible. A good theory is one that is useful and valuable to society or particular groups within it for the achievement of their goals.

Usually "good in theory but no good in practice" means that the theory itself is no good. The practical test of a theory is whether we are better off with it than without it.

1-4 A HISTORICAL NOTE

It is not too surprising that some economic theorizing can be found in the writings of Greek and other ancient philosophers. Aristotle, for example, argued that *exchange of equivalents* is required to guarantee contractual justice. Later, St. Thomas Aquinas and other medieval theologians debated the notion of *just price* as well as the propriety of charging interest on loans and similar issues of an economic nature. These writings, however, produce only a few insights into the functioning of modern economies and contribute very little to the method of economic reasoning.

Theoreticians of the Merchant Class

The newly developing capitalist system became the subject of a much higher level of economic theorizing. For example, the **mercantilist thinkers**, writing during the 17th and first half of the 18th centuries, tackled a whole range of problems which economists and politicians debate to this day.

A central notion of their theories was that a favourable balance of trade should be the objective of economic policy. The underlying reason was that a nation with a surplus received gold from the nations in deficit, and gold was viewed as the essence of national wealth. The purpose of this theorizing was to support a policy of national autarky (self-sufficiency), as practiced, for example, in France by Colbert during the reign of King Louis XIV. Together with national autarky went, of course, an expansion of the power of the state. Some of the government policies advocated by mercantilists sound rather familiar to a modern reader: government regulation of foreign trade to enhance inflow of gold, the promotion of industrial development by inducing imports of cheap raw materials, protective tariffs on imported manufactured goods and the promotion of exports of finished products.

A competing French group of writers, the **physiocrats**, objected to many of the mercantilist policies, especially trade protectionism and the neglect of agriculture. The place of the physiocrats in the history of economics, however, is associated mainly with their attempt to construct a model of the economic system divided into three sectors and to describe the interactions (flows) among them. The formal representation of such intersectoral flows — the *Tableau Economique* — was published in 1759. It is, in a sense, the forerunner of the *input-output table* developed by Leontief almost two hundred years later (see our Microeconomics Volume, Chapter 16, for a brief discussion).

Classical "Political Economy"

The first truly comprehensive book on economics, encompassing production and distribution theory as well as a whole range of economic policy, was written by **Adam Smith** (1723–1790). The book, entitled *An Inquiry into the Nature and Causes of* *the Wealth of Nations*, was published in 1776. Many historians of economic thought consider this date to be the beginning of economics as a scientific discipline.

The most famous concept developed in the *Wealth of Nations* is probably that of the *invisible hand*. Adam Smith observed that each individual — producer or consumer — is driven by the desire to maximize his or her own gain. Yet, under certain conditions (described in modern economic terminology as *perfect competition*) this pursuit of private benefits means that individuals contribute to the welfare of society at large "as if led by an invisible hand."

Nevertheless, Adam Smith did realize that the market mechanism if left alone would not always guarantee the best possible outcome. He therefore discussed the various economic functions a government should play. In spite of his awareness of the role of government intervention, his name is generally associated with the economic philosophy of *laissez-faire* (let people do as they please, especially in commerce). Closely linked to Adam Smith's praise of the free market is his opposition to all forms of monopoly. He wrote that "people of the same trade seldom meet together, even for merriment and diversion, but the conversation ends in a conspiracy against the public, or in some contrivance to raise prices."[2] This observation initiated a long tradition in economics and underlies much of the thinking embodied in *antitrust laws* or *competition policy* (discussed in our Microeconomics Volume, Chapter 9).

The classical economist who contributed more than any other to the development of the analytical apparatus of economics is **David Ricardo** (1772–1823). His theoretical model revolves around the notion that the economic growth of nations must eventually slow down as the less productive resources are utilized and *diminishing returns* set in. This, of course, has rather serious consequences not only for the level of output, but also for its distribution among landowners, capitalists and workers.

Ricardo developed a highly sophisticated *theory of distribution* in order to analyze how the changes in relative shares of land, labour and capital are connected with the rate of capital accumulation (to use the modern terms). His model is rather complicated and his argument is difficult to follow. In many respects his theory is inadequate by modern standards. Nevertheless, many of the analytical concepts from Ricardo's theory of distribution will be encountered throughout our study of both micro and macroeconomics (especially in our Microeconomics Volume, Chapters 5 and 10).

Ricardo also rigorously demonstrated the benefits of international trade. His *theory of comparative advantage* remains one of the cornerstones of the modern theory of international trade and its modernized version is presented in our Microeconomics Volume, Chapter 11.

Classical economists like Adam Smith, David Ricardo, Thomas Malthus (1766–1834), John Stuart Mill (1806–1873) and others understood the key purpose of their discipline in a rather similar way. It was an investigation of the "nature and causes of the wealth of nations" or "the laws which regulate the distribution of the produce on the earth" or "the laws of motion of capitalism."

In the writings of **Karl Marx** (1818–1883) the investigation of the "laws of motion of capitalism" was pushed to its limits. Marx set out to prove that the capitalist system — whose productive potential he greatly admired — must collapse from within. His argument is discussed in our Microeconomics Volume, Chapter 14.

Modern Economics

After two centuries of concern with the trends in growth of resources and with the "laws of motion" of society, the focus of the discipline has gradually shifted. By about 1870 the subject of mainstream economics became first and foremost the *allocation of scarce resources among alternative uses*. The relationship between consumer satisfaction and demand on the one hand and producer behaviour and supply on the other hand provided a new approach to the study of market prices. The analytical tools of modern economists include mathematics and diagrammatical analysis.

Among the pioneers of modern economics are Karl Menger (1840–1921), William Stanley Jevons

---

2. Adam Smith, *An Inquiry into the Nature and Causes of the Wealth of Nations* (New York: Random House, Modern Library Edition, 1937), bk. I, chap. 10, p. 128.

(1835–1882), Leon Walras (1834–1910) and Vilfredo Pareto (1848–1923). In 1890 Alfred Marshall (1842–1924) published his *Principles of Economics* — a book with terminology and diagrams much like those found throughout this textbook. In the 1930s Edward Chamberlin (1899–1967) and Joan Robinson (1903–1983) developed the theory of imperfect competition (discussed in our Microeconomics Volume, Chapter 7). One of the most important modern economists is **John Maynard Keynes** (1883–1946). His macroeconomic theory implies that a central government should actively use its powers of taxation and spending to manipulate the economy in a desired direction. On the other hand, another modern economist, **Milton Friedman** (b. 1912), argues that active government spending and taxation policies designed to manipulate an economy will be largely ineffective. These two opposing theories provide for a rich and interesting debate, which we will examine in some detail in our study of macroeconomics.

Modern microeconomics has developed from writings preoccupied with the fairness of distribution of wealth, the long-term trends in population growth and the use of resources, and the proper role of the state in the economy. Its development as a full-fledged scientific discipline began over two hundred years ago. In its present form, economics employs verbal, graphical and mathematical approaches to analyze economic phenomena.

1-5 TOOLS OF ECONOMIC ANALYSIS

Economics studies cause and effect relations within phenomena that may have an impact on material welfare. Such cause and effect relations are formulated by economic theory according to the scientific method. Expression of economic theory may take the form of *verbal, graphical* or *algebraic* representation. The verbal mode is the most useful form of analysis for those who wish to communicate their method and findings to the public or at least to those who may have had no specialized training in economics. Graphs are sometimes useful visual aids in a discussion. Finally, algebraic analysis provides the most compact form of discussion. In this book we shall concentrate on the first two simpler means of analysis.

The Use of Graphs

We economists are very fond of graphs. However, graphs are only a means to an end. They are at best an aid to the understanding of logical argument, which can usually be stated verbally. When some arguments become detailed and require more than just one or two steps, it is often useful to have a shorthand representation of outcomes.

Graphs are used in economics (i) as pictorial representations of actual data whose significance may be more easily seen when graphed than, say, when put into tabular form, and (ii) as shorthand devices in logical argument. Let us now describe each of these uses of graphs by means of a numerical example.

(i) A Pictorial Representation

Suppose we have the following information concerning how much ice cream would be sold at various prices in a particular store (Table 1-2).

If we look at Table 1-2 carefully we can see exactly how the volume of ice cream sold varies with the price per litre. This relation may be more readily appreciated, however, if we plot the information on a graph. Quantity sold could go on the horizontal axis and price per litre on the vertical axis (as in Fig. 1-2a). Each of the five points represents an observation of ice cream price and quantity sold from Table 1-2. For example, point *d* represents a price of $2.50 per litre, at which 250 litres would be sold. There is no information on the graph which is not also in the table but pictorially it may be easier to comprehend. For example, we can see from a glance at the graph not only that the volume sold increases as the price is lowered but also how fast the volume increases as the price is lowered.

Table 1-2 Ice cream sales related to price

Observation	Price ($ per litre)	Ice cream sold (litres per week)
a	4.00	25
b	3.50	125
c	3.00	200
d	2.50	250
e	2.00	263

One of the many possible sets of combinations of price and quantity. As price per litre declines, quantity sold increases.

This latter piece of information can also be found in the table, but not without closer scrutiny.

Also, though no information is given concerning how much ice cream would be purchased each week at prices between those shown in Table 1-2, if we take the liberty of joining the five graphed dots with a smooth curve we may approximate these amounts by reading them off the graph. This has been done in Figure 1-2b. One might expect, for example, that the volume of ice cream sold at a price of $3.75 per litre would be roughly 75 litres per week.

(ii) Shorthand for Logical Argument

Even though actual tabular data may not be available to plot in a graphical form, a graph may still be useful as a shorthand representation of an analytical discussion. For example, suppose someone asks what will happen if the price of ice cream is lowered. Also, suppose that although we do not have the precise quantitative data of Table 1-2 or Figure 1-2, we have seen such studies in the past and are convinced that if the price were lowered the volume sold would increase.

We could either relate this conviction verbally or convey precisely the same information graphically, by the curve (or line) labelled D in Figure 1-3. If we employ the shorthand symbols P and Q for price per litre of ice cream and quantity sold per week respectively, it could easily be inferred from

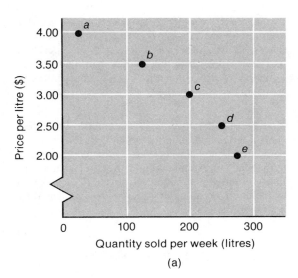

(a)

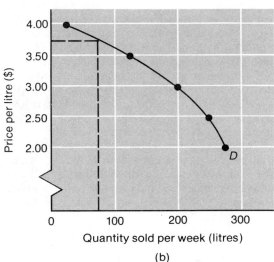

(b)

Fig. 1-2 Ice cream sales related to price

(a) The exact plot of information from Table 1-2.
(b) Prices and quantities other than those indicated in Table 1-2 are approximated by a smooth curve.

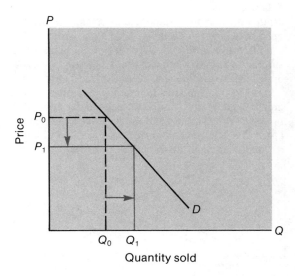

Quantity sold

Fig. 1-3 Ice cream sales related to price

A graphical representation of the relationship between prices and quantities of ice cream sold: lower prices cause higher ice cream sales.

the D curve that we expect a reduction in price to be accompanied by an increase in volume sold. For example, if the price were reduced from any price (P_0) to any lower price (P_1), the curve indicates that the quantity sold would increase from whatever the initial quantity (Q_0) was to some larger quantity (Q_1). This information would be conveyed regardless of exactly where we placed the curve on the plane of the graph as long as we made it slope downward to the right (and in fact we would not know precisely where to draw it unless we had quantitative information such as that of Table 1-2).

Here, it might be argued that it would be easier to say, "If the price is lowered we will sell more" than to draw a picture (sometimes a picture is not worth a thousand words). However, for more complex questions such as, "What will happen to the volume sold if the sales tax on ice cream is raised?" or, "What will happen to interest rates in the economy if wage rates increase?" a diagrammatic representation of the situation is helpful.

Curves: Movements versus Shifts

When graphs are used as shorthand aids to logical argument, it is important to understand the difference between *a movement along* a particular curve (or line) and *a shift* in the entire curve. This consideration arises whenever the economic variable under study is influenced by two or more other variables. For instance, suppose the quantity of ice cream sold (Q) is really influenced by both the price (P) of ice cream and the weather temperature (T). The cause and effect process could be summarized by a flow chart as follows:

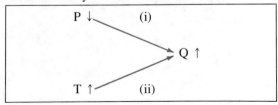

To be more specific, our argument would be (i) that lower prices cause higher ice cream sales and (ii) that higher temperatures cause higher ice cream sales.

In economics we emphasize price-quantity relations. It would be usual therefore to represent causal connection (i) by a curve such as D in Figure 1-4a. We can see (as we did in Figure 1-3)

that the effect of a price change on volume sold is reflected or captured by moving along the D curve. But can we adapt Figure 1-4a to show the effect of a temperature change on quantity sold? In fact, we can. The effect of a temperature change on ice cream sales would be reflected by a shift in the D curve, as shown in Figure 1-4b. For instance, suppose the temperature rises. This event means that at any price level (P_0, for example), a greater volume of ice cream ($Q'_0 > Q_0$) would be sold than would have been the case if the temperature had not risen. In other words, an increase in temperature *shifts* the entire price-quantity curve to the right.

A relationship between any economic variables, such as price and quantity demanded, may be conveniently depicted as a curve. A change in quantity demanded in response to a change in price is captured by movement along the curve. A response to a change in variable other than price is reflected by a shift in the curve.

1-6 OPPORTUNITY COST

Every economic action has its costs and benefits. An action is worthwhile if the benefits exceed the costs. A popular expression for economic cost is **opportunity cost**. The word "opportunity" implies that for every economic action contemplated there are alternative actions or opportunities that the decision maker must forgo. The real economic cost associated with any action is therefore the benefit that the decision maker could have attained by taking the best alternative course of action.

The cost of a trip to Europe can be calculated in dollar terms at perhaps $3500. However, behind the money, the cost of a trip to Europe is really the alternative goods we could have purchased instead (perhaps a colour television set and a small sailboat) or future consumption which we could have prepared for by saving the money. Of course, we could have purchased $3500 worth of gumdrops instead of going to Europe, but obviously this action would not be viewed as our best alternative. If the TV and sailboat combination is the alternative course of action which would have given us the most pleasure, the loss of these items becomes the real sacrifice or opportunity cost of the trip to Europe.

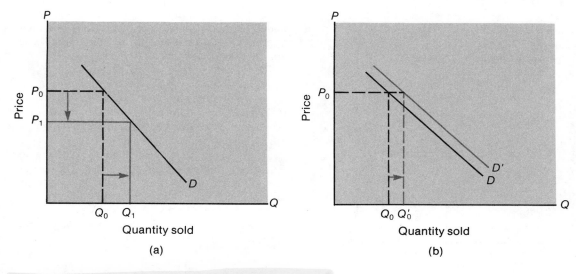

Fig. 1-4 Ice cream sales related to price and weather

(a) The D curve correctly describes the price and quantity combinations only if all other circumstances remain unchanged.

(b) Circumstances have changed: warmer weather causes higher ice cream sales. The D curve shifts to the right (to D').

As another example, consider the cost of keeping our savings under a mattress. Here we would be forgoing the opportunity to earn a rate of interest by depositing our funds in a bank or perhaps by buying Canada Savings Bonds. The opportunity cost of keeping our savings under a mattress would therefore be the dollar interest we could earn if the funds were invested — or more accurately, the goods and services that could be bought with the interest so earned.

Production Possibilities Curves

We might also examine opportunity cost from a more macro standpoint. Through individual market decisions and government actions, society chooses the quantity of various types of goods and services that will be produced. The real cost of producing any particular good or service is the amount of alternative goods and services society had the opportunity to produce but did not.

For example, southern Alberta farmers may have a choice of whether to produce livestock or grain. Since the total amount of land available in southern Alberta is fixed, more farmland devoted to grain means less farmland devoted to livestock.

Consequently, at any given time, more grain production means less livestock production, as Figure 1-5 illustrates. The curve on this diagram is designed to show the maximum possible quantities of both grain and livestock which could be produced with our given know-how (or state of technology) within southern Alberta during a particular period of time (say, a year). Such a curve is called a **production possibilities curve** (boundary or frontier) and is frequently utilized to illustrate society's available choices between alternative types of goods or services. Figure 1-5 indicates that if all southern Alberta farmland were devoted to grain production, 12 units of grain could be produced, but of course, no livestock. At the other extreme, if all land were devoted to the raising of livestock, 14 units could be produced, but no grain. Point A represents an intermediate possibility where most but not all land is devoted to livestock production. In this case, 12 units of livestock and 5 units of grain could be produced.[3]

---

3. The numbers in Figure 1-5 are for illustration purposes only. Actual units of measurement might be "millions of head per year" for livestock and "millions of tonnes per year" for grain.

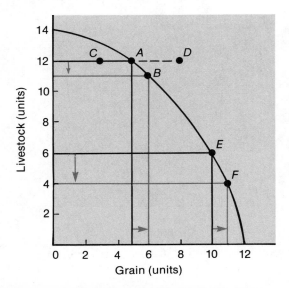

Fig. 1-5 Production possibilities curve for grain and livestock

It costs more to produce an extra tonne of grain when moving from E to F than it does when moving from A to B. The opportunity costs of grain rise as its production is expanded.

Since a production possibilities curve represents *maximum* possible production combinations, it is assumed that we are operating at *full employment* and using the most efficient means of production available within our given state of technical know-how. Point A indicates that with full employment of resources, 5 units of grain and 12 units of live-stock could be produced. Point C represents the same amount of livestock production as point A but less grain production. Point C is a *production possibility point* which represents an output loss due to *underutilization* of resources (land, labour and capital). Point D represents the same amount of livestock as point A but more grain. Point D, therefore, represents the utilization of more resources than are available and is a *production impossibility point*.

Suppose, in fact, that initially the region fully employs its input resources at point A. If one more unit of grain production is desired (6 units in total), more of the available (but limited or scarce) inputs will have to be devoted to grain production. This concentration leaves fewer inputs for livestock

production (which falls to 11 units). The real economic (or opportunity) cost of the additional unit of grain production is thus the resulting loss of one unit of livestock production.

The fact that the production possibilities curve of Figure 1-5 is bowed away from the origin (0) implies an *increasing cost* of grain production as more and more inputs are shifted out of livestock production. For example, when grain production is relatively low (as it is at point A) there will be a relatively large amount of land available that would be suitable for grain production. The expansion of grain output from 5 units to 6 units by utilizing such grain-suitable land will thus entail a relatively small sacrifice of livestock output (from 12 units to 11 units). However, at point E most farmland would already be devoted to grain production. The high-yielding grain-land would already be producing grain and the remaining land would be relatively more suitable to livestock. Consequently, going from point E to F, which describes the same expansion in grain output as going from point A to B (namely one unit), requires a greater drop in livestock production (2 units as opposed to one unit).

The whole analysis can, of course, be done in reverse. The opportunity costs of producing livestock, in terms of lost grain production, increase as more livestock is produced.

As a final example of opportunity cost, consider society's choice (at point A in Figure 1-6) between government-provided goods and services and goods and services produced in the private sector. As the production possibilities curve illustrates, with a given state of technology and a limited amount of input resources, the provision of more government goods and services implies the sacrifice of some privately produced goods and services. The real economic (or opportunity) cost of additional schools, roads, military and police protection, government buildings or civil servants is fewer televisions, private automobiles, skiing vacations and children's skates. One way in which the government can bring about this result is by raising taxes to finance the increased expenditure on government goods, an action that reduces the income citizens have available to spend on private goods.

In subsequent chapters, we shall seldom refer specifically to the phrase *opportunity cost*; instead

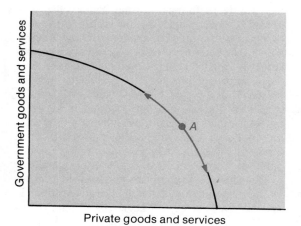

Fig. 1-6 Choice between private and government production

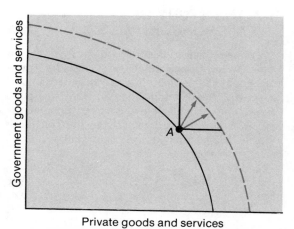

Fig. 1-7 The effect of growth on economic choice

Economic growth makes it possible for society to have more of both types of goods and services than at point A.

Moving left along the curve from point A, we find that more government-provided goods and services can be obtained only if the quantity of goods and services produced in the private sector is reduced. Moving in the opposite direction along the curve, we find that more private goods and services can be obtained only if the quantity of government goods and services is reduced.

we shall measure cost in customary dollar terms. Yet, it should always be remembered that real costs are forgone benefits from the best alternative action. This point will be emphasized repeatedly.

The production possibilities curve describes the maximum possible combinations of goods and services that an economy can produce with a given amount of resources. Its shape is concave (bowed away from the origin), because the opportunity costs of producing a good or a service increase as resources best suited for its production are used up.

Economic Growth

Since outputs require inputs, limited input resources generally imply that more of any particular good or service may be produced only at a cost of not being able to produce as many other goods and services. The only escape from this constraint is via economic growth. **Economic growth** means an increased capability of an economy to produce. Such increased capability may arise either from an

increased availability of inputs (for example, increased amounts of available labour or more factories, machinery and equipment) or from productivity improvements, that is to say, an increase in the amount of output possible from any given amount of inputs. This latter source of economic growth may result from technological developments, from improvements in the level of worker education and skills, or from improved organization of production and distribution.

Since economic growth expands the capability of an economy to produce, economic growth causes an economy's production possibilities curve to shift outward. Figure 1-7 illustrates economic growth in the context of the choice between private and government goods and services. Without growth (but at full employment), an increase in government-produced goods and services means a reduction in private goods and services. Economic growth allows for an expansion in government goods and services without necessarily a reduction in private goods and services. For example, as growth shifts the production possibilities curve outward, every point in the triangular region represents a higher possible production level of government goods and services and private goods and services than was experienced at point A.

1-7 THE STUDY OF MICROECONOMICS

Microeconomics is that part of the discipline in which we investigate individual markets for particular goods and services. Whereas macroeconomics deals with the determination of the average price levels, outputs and employment throughout the entire economy, microeconomics focuses on those factors that determine prices, outputs and employment within particular markets.

The two main groups of participants within any market are consumers and producers. It is their actions that determine whether a market price will rise or fall, and whether sales will increase or decline. Microeconomics, therefore, examines the motivating forces behind the actions of consumers and producers.

Although consumers and producers are the two main groups of market participants, the government often interferes significantly with the market process. In some markets, the government sees fit to establish certain rules of the game — for example, minimum product standards, maximum or minimum prices or volumes, and market entry or exit requirements. These rules have a profound influence on market outcomes and individual welfare. Therefore, it is important that we examine the rationale for such intervention and the type of results it produces.

Most people are interested in microeconomic causal dynamics; that is, the factors that cause market prices and outputs to *change*. For this reason, we shall emphasize causal relationships in our study of microeconomics. In order to proceed from cause to effect, it is necessary to formulate a logical chain of reasoning. The chain can be simple or complex depending on the required depth of analysis. First, we shall start with a skeletal form of analysis in Chapter 2. Then, in Chapters 3 through 7 we shall gradually flesh out the details of the analytical tools and methods. Finally, in the later chapters, we shall turn our attention to the various applications of the cause and effect analysis. Specifically, Chapter 8 focuses on the relationship

between the performance of the firm and the stock market. Chapter 9 discusses the scale of operations of business firms and the market adjustment mechanism. The determination of wage and property incomes is the subject of Chapter 9. A brief sketch of the microeconomics of international trade is presented in Chapter 11. In Chapters 12 and 13, we outline the rationale for government intervention in the market economy and the various regulatory policies, taxes and expenditures the three levels of government in Canada employ for this purpose. Selected alternative theoretical approaches to economic analysis are reviewed in Chapter 14, and the working of some alternative economic systems is evaluated in Chapter 15. Lastly, Chapter 16 briefly looks at the relationship between various industries (markets) and regions in the Canadian economy.

Our intention is to simplify the analysis at the start in order to gain a few key insights into the workings of the microeconomy. Gradually, we shall remove these simplifications and investigate the ramifications of particular market shocks more widely. In order to gain the most from this approach, you should practise our methods by analyzing the study problems and cases (provided at the end of each chapter), as well as other interesting microeconomic events (reported in the media).

CONCLUDING REMARKS

Economics is a set of concepts, principles and tools designed to give useful insights into the workings of the economy. Economics is useful because we may utilize such insights to achieve a higher level of material well-being than we might otherwise attain. We must never forget, however, that the world is more than dollars and cents. The use of economic criteria is often tempered with a consideration of social and political goals. Remembering this fact is important if we are to understand fully the workings of the real world.

KEY TERMS AND CONCEPTS

economics	flow chart
microeconomics	mercantilists
macroeconomics	physiocrats
cost-benefit analysis	Adam Smith
supply and demand	David Ricardo
economic forecasting	Karl Marx
economic shock	John Maynard Keynes
normative statement	Milton Friedman
positive statement	movement along curves
economic goals	curve shift
staple commodity	opportunity cost
economic model	production possibility curve
scientific method	economic growth

PROBLEMS

Problem 1

a) Suppose you have a voluntary expenditure decision to make which involves a considerable amount of money. How would you decide whether or not to undertake the expenditure?

b) For everyday minor expenditures, do you undertake the same sort of analysis? Explain. (Consider the purchase of individual items at a supermarket.)

Problem 2

In what sense might an economic decision which turns out to have disastrous consequences nevertheless have been a "good" decision at the time it was made?

Problem 3

Jones is an experienced bowler. Before leaving for the bowling alley she is asked about the equivalent dollar value to her of each of one to six games which might be played that evening. After thinking a while, she writes down the following figures:

Game	Perceived Value
1	$3.00
2	2.00
3	1.00
4	0.85
5	0.50
6	0.25

a) Does the fact that she anticipates each game bowled to yield less satisfaction than the one preceding surprise you, or does it fit in with your expectations? Why?

b) Everything else being equal, if the price per game were $1.50, how many games would she be planning on bowling? Explain.

c) How might the following events affect her evaluation of the costs and benefits from bowling the fourth game: (i) an extraordinarily poor performance in the third game? (ii) Jones suddenly remembers after the third game that a special TV program would have to be missed by her bowling the fourth game?

Problem 4

Explain the main functions of an economist and the sort of frustrations that some economists face.

Problem 5

a) What would be your priority ranking of the societal goals listed in Section 1-2 of the text?

b) What other Canadian goals do you feel are important?

c) Which goals in this listing (or goals of your own) may be conflicting in practice and how might such conflict be handled?

Problem 6

Senator Snort appears to have his hand on the political pulse of the country. Or has he?

"I say import more beef. . . . There are more voters out there who eat hamburger than those who grow it!"

GRIN AND BEAR IT by George Lichty: © 1978 Field Enterprises, Inc.
Courtesy of Field Newspaper Syndicate.

a) Explain how an economist might judge whether to allow more beef imports into the country.

b) From a political standpoint attempt to argue against Senator Snort (attempt to argue why it might be better, from a political standpoint, to help beef producers rather than beef consumers).

Problem 7

A taxi company has obtained the following data on the relationship between its fares and volume of business:

Price of taxi service ($ per kilometre)	Fare-kilometres sold per cab per day
1.00	60
0.80	80
0.60	90
0.40	95
0.20	97

a) Plot the above information on a graph like the one below and join the points with a smooth curve.

b) Approximate from your graph how many fare-kilometres would be sold per cab per day if the fare were 50¢ per km.

c) Though we do not have enough information to decide on the most profitable price for the cab company to charge, why, in view of the above data, would 80¢ per km be more profitable than 20¢ per km?

d) Suppose there is a day when the weather is particularly nasty. Explain briefly in words how you think such bad weather would influence the amount of taxi service sold at each possible price. (A numerical answer is not required.)

e) By sketching a new curve on the graph of part (a), show diagrammatically the sort of influence you would expect bad weather to have on the amount of taxi service sold at various possible prices.

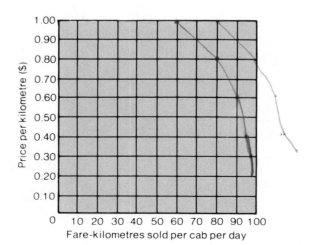

Problem 8

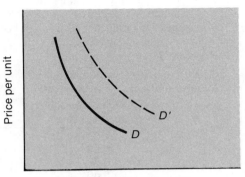

Volume (units per week)

The above graph, drawn by an economist, is designed to reflect the relation between the volume of a particular good that would be purchased each week at various possible market prices and under two different sets of general economic conditions. The curve D is related to a poor economic environment (for example, consumers have low incomes). The curve D' is related to a good economic environment (for example, consumers have high incomes).

a) What belief does the economist have concerning the effect of price on the volume of the particular good that would be purchased each week by consumers? Does this belief hold under both possible sets of economic circumstances?

b) What message is conveyed by the graph concerning the effect of a better set of economic circumstances on the volume demanded at each possible price?

c) The graph reflects a theory concerning the demand for the particular good in question. Representing the volume demanded by Q_0, price by P and economic circumstances by EC, rewrite the economic theory (i) in causal network format and (ii) in functional form. Identify separately the dependent and explanatory variables.

Problem 9

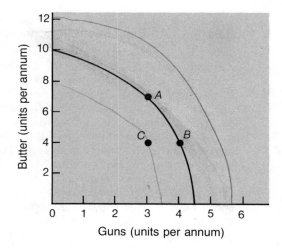

Suppose the production possibilities curve above represents the maximum potential yearly output combinations for defence goods (guns) and civilian goods (butter) within a particular economy.

a)   If the economy is initially fully utilizing its input resources and producing at point A, what annual quantity of guns and butter are currently being produced?

b)   What would be the opportunity (real economic) cost to the economy of expanding production of guns to 4 units per year? Describe what actions in practice might typically go on in an economy to cause production to move from point A to point B?

c)   Next, suppose that the economy was originally producing at point C. What employment situation is represented by point C? What now would be the cost to the economy of expanding guns production and moving from point C to point B?

d)   By roughly sketching in a new production possibilities curve illustrate how economic growth could allow an increase of one unit of defence production relative to point A, with no reduction of civilian goods.

CASES

Case 1-1: An Experiment in Economics*

Conducting experiments in economics is less common than in, say, physics or chemistry, but it is not unheard of. Consider the following example. In the U.S. a variety of programs have been initiated during the past two decades to improve the job prospects of long-term unemployed welfare recipients. In one such program, it was proposed that the welfare recipients seeking jobs should be given vouchers, entitling the prospective employers to a government subsidy for a portion of their wage costs (50% of the applicant's wage in the first year and 25% in the second year). The hypothesis was that employers would be willing to hire subsidized workers in order to enhance profits.

An experiment was conducted by the U.S. Department of Labor in Dayton, Ohio, in 1980–81 to establish exactly how employers would respond to such a policy measure. The 900 eligible applicants for the program were randomly assigned to three groups: (i) holders of vouchers entitling the employer to a direct cash-rebate subsidy, (ii) holders of vouchers entitling the employer to a tax credit and (iii) a control group consisting of individuals with no vouchers. All participants were given two weeks of job-search training, with instruction for the first two groups on how to use the vouchers. After the training period, all participants were required to spend six to eight weeks in intensive, structured job search.

Only about 15% of the participants landed a job. Unexpectedly, however, the two groups with vouchers achieved significantly lower placement rates than the control group (12.8% versus 20.6%). The lesson derived from this experiment was that employers used the information provided by the existence of vouchers as a reason to discriminate against the voucher holders. They may have been biased against welfare recipients in general or they may have believed that any applicant who required a wage subsidy would be a poor hiring and training prospect.

a) What are the benefits of experiments of this type?
b) If you were asked to comment on the validity of this experiment, what sort of questions would you ask?
c) Based on this example, do you think experiments in economics are as reliable as those in physics, chemistry or biology?
d) Does the outcome of the experiment surprise you? What might be some of the additional (alternative) explanations for this particular result? In your opinion, would the outcome be the same if the experiment were conducted in Canada? Discuss.

---

*Based on Gary Burtless, "Are targeted wage subsidies harmful? Evidence from a wage voucher experiment," *Industrial and Labor Relations Review* 39 (1985), pp. 105–114.

CHAPTER 2

Basic Demand and Supply

LEARNING OBJECTIVES

After reading this chapter you should be able to explain:

1. Supply and demand diagrams and the market equilibrium.

2. Why rent controls are an example of interference with the market mechanism.

3. Changing market supply and demand conditions and their representation in economic analysis.

2-1 INTRODUCTION AND PURPOSE

This chapter provides a simple framework within which to study the microeconomy. The primary concern of microeconomics is to explain what determines the level of, and changes in, prices and volumes of output. While macroeconomics attempts to explain movements in such economic variables as the general price level and the total volume of goods and services produced in the entire economy, microeconomics restricts its attention to prices and volumes of a single good or service.

The price and quantity of any particular good or service are determined neither by demand nor supply alone, but jointly, by both demand and supply. This is easily forgotten yet very important when we are performing any type of economic analysis. Let us begin by describing the basic determinants of market demand and supply, leaving details to later chapters.

2-2 FRAMEWORK FOR ANALYSIS

Market Demand

Market demand refers to the total quantity of a good or service that consumers are willing to purchase per unit of time at various market prices. In order to be as concrete as possible, let us define a particular product, geographical area for our market, and unit of time. For instance, suppose that the product is athletic shoes, the location is Canada and the unit of time is one year. Specifically, then, we are speaking of the total (market) annual demand for athletic shoes in Canada.

As can be seen, we are still not taking as micro an approach as we could. We might, for example, consider the demand for athletic shoes by the Smith family, 138 King Street, Regina. Later on we shall get down to this most micro of all analytical levels.

Since most people have limited incomes, the

higher the price for athletic shoes, the more of life's other luxuries a family has to sacrifice in order to make a purchase. Therefore, it seems reasonable to suppose that the higher the market price of athletic shoes, the lower the volume demanded.

For example, if the price is $20 per pair, some 10 million pairs per year will be bought; as the price rises to $30 per pair, the quantity demanded drops to 9 million pairs per year; when the price is $35 per pair, only 8 million pairs will be bought; at $45 per pair only 6 million, and so on.

We may depict this quantity demanded-market price relation in a shorthand graphical fashion, though in many instances this is not absolutely necessary for a complete analysis. We suppose in Figure 2-1 that the relation between market prices and quantities which would be demanded at these prices may be depicted by the *D* curve.

Other Demand Influences

Actually, the total volume of athletic shoes that consumers would be willing to purchase in 19X1 depends on a number of factors besides price. Among the most important of these would be *consumer tastes* (that is, how much consumers like such athletic shoes), *consumer incomes, prices of other goods and services* and *population* (the number of potential consumers in a given area). Often, though, when economists speak of "the demand" for a product they refer to the connection between the quantities that consumers are willing to buy and various possible market prices of the good *when all other demand factors are held constant*.

With reference to Figure 2-1, we can see that the quantity of athletic shoes demanded by consumers would increase from about six million pairs per year to seven million pairs per year if the price of such shoes was to drop from $45 per pair to $40 per pair — but only if people's tastes and incomes, the prices of other goods and all other demand influences remained unchanged.

It is often difficult to measure with precision this separate connection between price and quantity demanded. For example, we may observe a 10% decrease in a product's price combined with a 20% drop in its quantity demanded. But there may also have been a concurrent 5% decrease in people's incomes and a 15% decrease in the price of compet-

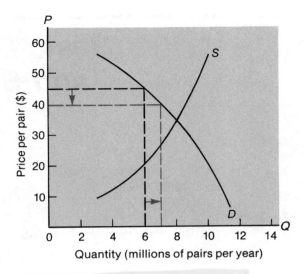

Fig. 2-1 Market demand and supply for athletic shoes, 19X1

The *D* curve depicts the relationship between market prices and quantities demanded at these prices. The *S* curve depicts the relationship between market prices and quantities offered for sale at these prices.

ing goods. Obviously, these last two factors also affected the quantity demanded. How, then, can we isolate the influence that price change alone would have had on quantity demanded? As it turns out, there are statistical techniques that can aid in this process. The estimation of demand relations in which the separate contributions of price, income and other factors are approximated is practised both by business and government.

A given relation between price and quantity demanded depicts a causal connection in which all other demand factors are constant. We must, of course, still analyze the effect on quantity demanded of changes in demand factors other than price. In fact, it will be a prime concern of this and subsequent chapters to do just that.

There are many different brands of athletic shoes, each of which may be considered by the consumer to be a slightly different product. Not having differentiated between different brands, we have not yet restricted our microanalysis as narrowly as we could. Specification of the market in terms of the product is sometimes difficult. We shall return to this problem later.

Market Supply

Market supply refers to the total quantity of athletic shoes that producers are willing to supply at various market prices.

Supply depends on unit costs. For example, if it costs a particular company $30 to produce one more pair of athletic shoes in a given year, the company would not produce that pair unless the market price was at least $30. High market prices allow costly (and otherwise unprofitable) ways of increasing output to become profitable. Hence, higher market prices induce greater market supply. In the short run, higher prices make it profitable for producers to employ additional labour within existing physical plant facilities and possibly speed up the production process, or even reduce the machine down-time required for normal maintenance and overhaul work. In the long run, higher prices may make it profitable for new producers to enter the market and for existing producers to expand their physical facilities.[1]

Suppose there are many producers in the market. Some are capable of producing at lower cost than others. For example, if the price is $20 per pair, only 6 million pairs will be supplied; at $35 per pair, supply will increase to 8 million pairs; at $45 per pair it will increase to 9 million pairs, and so on.

As in the case of market demand, we may represent on a graph the connection between market price and the volume of output that would be offered at these prices. This relation appears as the *S* curve in Figure 2-1.

A comment is warranted here about possible complications concerning a product's *channel of distribution*. Using the athletic shoe market as an example, manufacturers, wholesalers and retailers will be involved in transforming raw materials into a finished product on the feet of consumers. For each pair of shoes bought by the consumer there may be three prices charged along the way. A wholesaler may buy the shoes from the manufacturer at a manufacturing price and then sell them to a retailer at a wholesale price. Finally, the consumer pays a retail price when he purchases the shoes from the store. Because additional costs are incurred at each stage within the channel of dis-

tribution, each successive price is usually higher than the preceeding one.

In all our discussions, "price" will refer to a **final price** — including sales taxes and product-specific taxes. Any less inclusive definition would leave out part of the cost of purchase to the ultimate consumer and part of the gross receipts to the firm.

When we speak of producing a good for ultimate consumption, we must consider the total process, from transforming the raw material at the manufacturing level to wrapping, or delivery and installation of the good at the retail level. Production costs in this context correspondingly include all manufacturing, transportation, wholesaling and retailing costs. Production costs in this definition therefore cover much more than just manufacturing costs.

Most likely, athletic shoes are sold through retail stores across the country, in department stores and specialty shoe stores, and perhaps even through discount outlets. For now, though, it will simplify things if we assume that the manufacturers sell the shoes through their own retail outlets. Later we shall remove this assumption and consider the more typical situation.

In microeconomics, demand refers to the quantity of a particular good or service that consumers in a well-defined market are willing to purchase over a specified period of time at various market prices. Supply refers to the quantity of the same product that producers in the same market are willing to supply at these prices over the same period of time.

2-3 MARKET EQUILIBRIUM

The interaction of market demand and supply determines both the market price and the volume of actual production. For instance, suppose the market situation for athletic shoes during 19X1 is the one illustrated in Figure 2-2. It will now be shown that the market price and volume sold will move toward those levels designated by the intersection point (*E*) of market demand and supply. This is commonly known as the **market equilibrium** point. The market supply curve indicates the quantity which producers will produce at various prices. Thus, we assume the market outcome is always on the supply curve. Market demand, however, determines where on the supply curve the

---

1. In the long run, if significant *economies of scale* exist, higher volumes of output may mean lower costs per unit of output. For now it will be convenient to disregard this possibility. Economies of scale are discussed in some detail in Chapter 9.

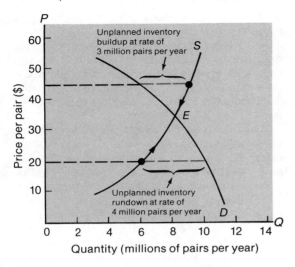

Fig. 2-2 Inventory pressures and market movement toward equilibrium

When the price is set at $45 a pair, 9 million pairs will be supplied, but only 6 million pairs will be bought. Unplanned inventory buildup of 3 million pairs will result. When the price is set at $20 a pair, only 6 million pairs will be supplied, but 10 million pairs will be demanded. Unplanned inventory rundown of 4 million pairs will occur.

market outcome will be during any given period of time. Both market supply and demand play a part in determining prices actually charged by sellers and volumes actually sold.

Market Pressures toward Equilibrium

At any point in time and in any particular industry, no one knows exactly where the market supply and demand curves are. Why, then, would a given market move toward this unknown equilibrium point? One reason is the pressures caused by *unplanned inventory buildups and rundowns*.

For example, suppose the shoe manufacturers wished to produce and sell a total of 9 million pairs of athletic shoes during 19X1. Given their profit objectives and costs per pair, Figure 2-2 indicates that they would price the shoes at $45 a pair. At this high price, all Canadian families combined would not be willing to purchase 9 million pairs. In fact, Figure 2-2 indicates that only about 6 million

pairs would be bought. Thus, inventories of athletic shoes would begin to pile up beyond desired levels.[2] Based on 300 operating days per year, production at a level that causes an annual surplus of 3 million pairs (9 million − 6 million) would build up inventories at the rate of 10 000 pairs per day. This buildup would provide the manufacturers with information that they had overestimated demand. It would begin to look very unlikely that, at $45 per pair, the 9 million pairs could be sold during the year.

To prevent a continual unwanted buildup of finished goods inventory, the manufacturers would begin to lower their production rate and possibly reduce prices to help eliminate unwanted inventory. For example, we might see "Reduced to Clear" advertisements for athletic shoes, and possibly some "Going Out of Business" sales.

As we saw in the previous section, the market supply curve is sloped upward because higher output volumes are asssociated with higher unit costs of production. Consequently, a reduction in output volume in the face of unwanted inventory will reduce the industry's unit costs. These lower unit costs will in turn induce producers to accept prices below the original $45 level (although perhaps not as low as the clearance prices used to dump unwanted stock).

In summary, inventory pressures caused by the above-equilibrium price of $45 cause producers in the aggregate to reduce output volume and accept lower prices. In other words, the market moves down the supply curve toward *E*.

On the other hand, suppose that during 19X1 producers attempted to sell only 6 million pairs, at $20 a pair. At this price demand would be brisk and, in fact, greater than supply by approximately 4 million pairs (10 million − 6 million) for the whole year. Retailers would very quickly run out of popular sizes and colours. Attempting to keep pace with demand, stores would order greater quantities from the factories and at more frequent intervals. The manufacturers, not having planned on so high a sales volume, would find their finished goods inventories quickly depleting below desired levels.

---

2. Most producers wish to carry certain inventory stocks of their own finished products. For simplicity's sake, therefore, suppose that producers were already operating with the desired inventory levels at the beginning of the year.

This unplanned inventory rundown would therefore make it profitable for manufacturers to step up their production rates. If, as is quite likely, per unit production costs increase as volume is stepped up, such cost increases would be passed on to retail outlets, which would in turn raise their prices. Producers would move along the supply curve toward *E*.

Although unplanned inventory buildups or rundowns occur only in goods-producing industries, service industries also experience pressures that move the market toward equilibrium. Service industries do not, of course, carry inventories of their services, which are only produced when demanded. For example, haircuts cannot be produced unless customers come in and ask to have their hair cut. But this does not mean that service industries are always in equilibrium in the sense that demand for their services is continually equal to the volume that the firms would like to supply at the prevailing level of prices. In periods when the prevailing price levels are too high (above equilibrium), suppliers of services also receive information in this regard. Their staff will be idle a great deal of the time. When the price levels are below equilibrium, the staff becomes overworked, and sales are missed because there are too many potential customers to handle. Therefore, in the service industries prices which are temporarily either above or below equilibrium levels create pressures — albeit not inventory pressures — that move the market toward equilibrium.

Frequent Price Adjustment

Producers may be unwilling to adjust their prices frequently if it is costly to do so. For example, retail outlets may have catalogue sales of athletic shoes. Because main catalogues are printed in advance for each season, it may be difficult and costly to change these prices until the next catalogue comes out. Also, firms may fear customer irritation at frequently changing prices. Nevertheless, even stores that use catalogues commonly issue smaller "Sale" catalogues in which the price tags of a number of overpriced items have been lowered. These prices then override those of the main catalogues.

If it is too costly to adjust prices when inventory

pressures dictate, movement toward market equilibrium will be slow. When prices are below equilibrium consumers suffer a goods shortage, and producers suffer the lost profit on the extra volume they could have sold. If the market price is too high and cannot easily be lowered, firms suffer inventory buildups and hope to sell them off perhaps in some foreign market or wait and sell them in the Canadian market early next season, possibly on a "Clearance Price" basis.

When quantity supplied exceeds quantity bought, the suppliers experience unplanned inventory buildup. When quantity bought exceeds quantity supplied, there is an unplanned inventory rundown. In both cases, an adjustment of prices or quantities supplied, or both, is needed in order to restore the market equilibrium.

2-4 DEFINING A FREE MARKET

The term **free market** is generally applied to a market in which there are no artificial blockages preventing the establishment of an equilibrium price or stopping entry into and exit out of the industry by producers. We emphasize here that "free" has no moral connotation. It does not necessarily mean "good," though a free market has several desirable features. One such feature is that shortages or surpluses of products are temporary, because producer adjustments correct these imbalances.

Most of us can think of examples of free market situations that we would regard as bad — a free market in heroin, for instance. Of course, many people would argue that a free market for a particular good or service is a beneficial thing, while others, given their tastes and moral convictions, would argue that it is not.

Equilibrium

Several points concerning market equilibrium should be made. First of all, market equilibrium is not necessarily "*best*" for either the consumer or the producer alone. For example, the consumer no doubt would prefer lower prices, and the producer higher ones. Yet, the equilibrium price is the only price possible without the emergence of market shortages or surpluses. In this sense, the equi-

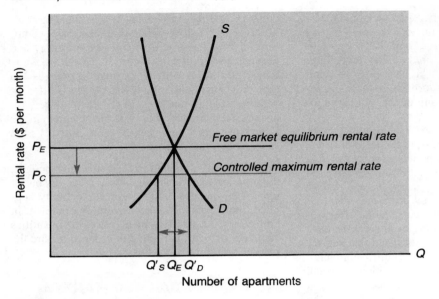

Fig. 2-3 Effect of rent control

With the controlled maximum rental rate (price ceiling) P_C in effect, the number of apartments people wish to rent (Q'_D) exceeds the number of apartments supplied (Q'_S).

librium price is usually the only *feasible price* maintainable for a prolonged period of time. This point is often brought home to those who wish to control certain market prices at levels different from those that supply and demand would otherwise determine.

The apartment rental market illustrates the predictive power of supply and demand analysis and the difficulties in attempting to replace market-determined prices with arbitrarily administered ones. Figure 2-3 illustrates the supply and demand for apartments within a given year. At lower rents, more apartments are demanded. Young singles and married couples can afford to move out of their parents' homes. On the other hand, at higher rents more apartments are offered (supplied). For example, at higher rents some people would convert their basement suites or attics to rental accommodation.

The market equilibrium average rental rate for apartments according to Figure 2-3 would be P_E. At this price, the number of apartments demanded each year (Q_D) would be equal to the number offered (Q_S), both represented by Q_E.

Now, suppose a government thinks that rents are too high and consequently legislates a lower, controlled maximum rental rate, a **price ceiling**. In response to the lower rent, the volume of apartments demanded would increase (to Q'_D) and the volume of apartments supplied would decrease (to Q'_S). As a result there would appear on the market a shortage of apartments ($Q'_D - Q'_S$).

A predicted consequence of **rent control** is, therefore, a shortage of rental accommodations. This fact has been borne out by statistical evidence from many countries, including Canada, which have attempted to implement such a housing policy. This evidence does not necessarily mean that rent control should never be implemented, but that the resulting accommodation shortage is a cost that must be taken into consideration.[3]

An interference with the market mechanism, such as imposition of a price ceiling, will prevent the equilibrating mechanism from functioning. As a result, there will be shortages at the controlled price.

2-5 MARKET OUTPUT, LABOUR AND CAPITAL

Within any given year, the greater the volume of production in a particular market, the greater will be the demand for labour and capital (both real capital such as factories and machines, and capital funds to finance the real capital) in that particular industry. The amount that firms are willing to pay for their labour, capital and capital funds borrowed depends on the *value of output* generated.

The Value of Labour

Suppose that hiring an additional hour of labour (having an employee work one more hour) is estimated to increase athletic shoe production by five pairs, which, after deduction of the extra expense for the materials needed, yields an extra $10 to a firm. The firm would then be willing to pay up to $10 for this extra hour of labour. If the market price of the shoes had been higher, or the productivity of the extra hour of labour greater, the producer would have been willing to pay a higher wage rate.

The Value of Capital

Capital funds are not classified as an input to the production process. They are, nevertheless, an important aspect of business. All financial and physical assets of the firm must be financed. Capital funds may be raised by business in many forms (for example, bank loans, bonds and common stocks). The financial instruments, which are the paper receipts given by a business for the funds

received (for example, bond and stock certificates), are held by the lenders to, and the owners of, the business. These people are entitled to all the revenue of the business firm in excess of all nonfinancial operating expenses: payments for labour, materials, taxes, heat, light and so forth.

When a firm thinks about adding new capital to its production process (i.e. when a firm thinks about building a new factory or adding some machinery or equipment), it realizes that it must first acquire the necessary capital funds. The physical investment and the capital funds are inseparable. We may speak of the value or worth to the firm of a $1 000 000 factory expansion and emphasize the physical part of the investment. Alternatively, we may speak of the value to the firm of borrowing an additional $1 000 000, and emphasize the financial part of the investment. In both instances we would be referring to the same project, namely a $1 000 000 acquisition entailing the borrowing of $1 000 000 in capital funds.

In general, the costs connected with any investment include both the purchase price of the physical capital and the cost the firm must pay for the use of borrowed or invested funds. The estimated worth of a particular investment project can be calculated as follows. Suppose that a business could invest in a new plant or equipment that would provide an increase in net annual operating earnings (*net* meaning after all nonfinancial expenses have been deducted), of 18% of the dollar amount invested. If the business could borrow capital funds to finance the project for an annual cost of less than 18%, the capital expansion would be worthwhile.

Free Market and Fair Payment

There is no guarantee that the market place will give people *fair incomes* for either their work or their invested funds. To begin with, what may seem fair to one person is not necessarily fair to another. The criteria for judging what is or is not fair are a matter for considerable argument. Businesses pay people for their funds and labour according to what these are worth to the firm. This worth in turn depends on the output which the capital equipment (bought with the invested funds)

---

3. See, for instance, F.A. Hayek, M. Friedman et al., *Rent Control, Myths and Realities* (Vancouver: The Fraser Institute, 1981).

Table 2-1 Shifts of market supply and demand, and their effects

Cause	Effects		
	P	Q	E
$D \rightarrow$	↑	↑	↑
$D \leftarrow$	↓	↓	↓
$S \uparrow$	↑	↓	↓
$S \downarrow$	↓	↑	↑

D and S represent the market demand and supply curves respectively. E stands for employment in the industry. The arrows ← and → represent a shift in the demand curve to the left and right respectively. The arrows ↑ and ↓ represent either a shift upward and downward of the supply curve, or an increase and decrease in the price per unit, volume of sales, or the industry employment level. Note therefore that S ↑ indicates an upward shift in the supply curve and not an increase in the volume of output supplied.

and labour can produce. It also depends on the amount consumers are willing to pay for the goods and services so produced. If the results of this arrangement turn out to be fair for all concerned, it is by chance rather than by design. Most people can point to certain inequities within the market system. Some people argue for government action to remedy these inequities, while more radical voices call for an end to the market system itself. These suggestions are considered in some detail in later chapters.

The market mechanism determines prices for the output sold by a particular firm. These prices, in turn, influence the magnitude of the payments the firm makes to its workers and to those who invest in or lend funds to the firm.

2-6 CAUSE AND EFFECT

If market demand and supply conditions remained fixed in reaction to inventory pressures, producers would, through trial-and-error production and pricing decisions, eventually arrive at the stationary market equilibrium price and output level, and remain there. However, the economy is not static. There is continual movement of prices, output and employment within almost all markets for goods

and services. From our discussion above, these market dynamics can be broadly explained in terms of changing supply and demand conditions (*shifting market supply and demand curves*).

A brief summary of a free market's cause and effect implications is given in Table 2-1. We should verify that the entries result directly from our preceding market supply-demand considerations. This may be done by drawing a market supply and demand diagram and shifting the curves in the direction indicated by each particular *cause*. Notice that change in supply or demand conditions may make market prices rise or fall. Consumers sometimes get the feeling that prices only rise and never fall. This feeling is understandable, because many demand and supply influences have an upward influence on market prices, and favourable price influences are swamped more often that not by larger unfavourable ones. Nevertheless, across all markets for goods and services there is a considerable variation in the direction and magnitude of price movements over time as may be seen in Figure 2-4. Notice, for example, the continual rise in the price of gasoline and health care and the almost continual fall in the price of television sets over the 20-year period from 1967 to 1985. The price of gasoline, for example, was about five times higher in 1985 than in 1967; it dropped considerably in 1986, largely as a result of weakening of the international oil cartel, OPEC (see Chapter 7 for a more detailed analysis).

CONCLUDING REMARKS

Both price and output levels for any good or service in a market economy are determined by the joint interaction of supply and demand. Apart from the product's price itself, important determinants of market demand are consumer tastes, income, prices of other goods and population within the market area, whereas the most important determinant of market supply is per unit production cost. In the absence of artificial impediment, a free market will generally move toward equilibrium, the point where supply equals demand. External interference with the market price (for example, government-imposed minimum or maximum prices) may result in prolonged market surpluses or shortages.

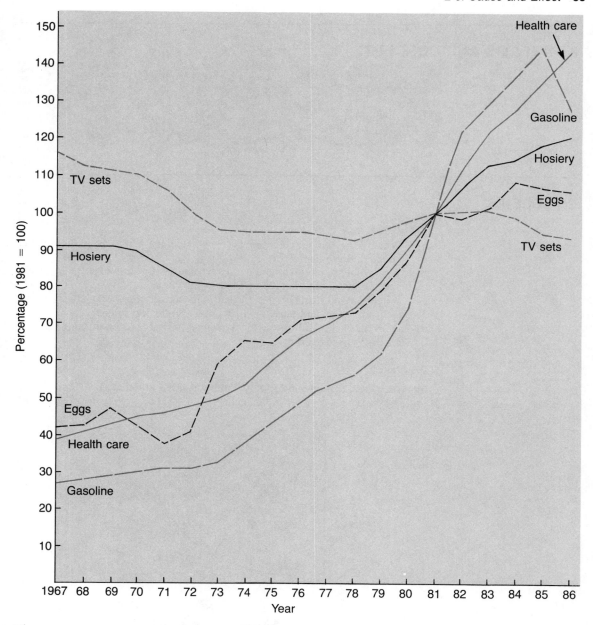

Fig. 2-4 Price indexes of various goods and services

Source: Statistics Canada 62-010

The plots in this figure represent four components of the Consumer Price Index. They were generated by tracing the prices of the selected goods and services over the period indicated on the horizontal axis.

KEY TERMS AND CONCEPTS

market demand	price ceiling
market supply	rent control
final price	value of labour
market equilibrium	value of capital
free market	fair payment

PROBLEMS

Problem 1

a) What does the market supply curve depict? What does the market demand curve depict?

b) Why would market demand curves normally slope downward to the right and market supply curves upward to the right?

c) What is market equilibrium? What is its connection to unplanned inventory rundowns and buildups in a goods-producing industry?

d) Does market equilibrium always give desirable economic and social results? Discuss briefly.

Problem 2

Suppose actual demand and supply conditions for a given market are as shown in this figure.

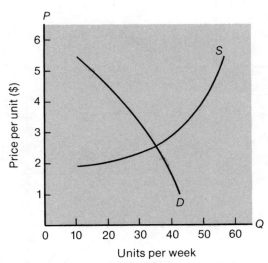

a) What would be the weekly demand for the product at a price of $2 per unit? What would be the amount produced each week at this price? At a price of $5 per unit?

b) In connection with part (a), at a price of $2 per unit, would there be a shortage of the commodity in question, or would there be a surplus? How much? At $5 per unit?

c) If producers usually carried very low inventories, at $2 per unit how would the shortage or surplus show up in the market place?

d) How would your answer to the previous question differ if producers typically carried large inventories?

e) If market demand and supply conditions remained unchanged, at what levels would you expect the market price and weekly sales to settle eventually?

Problem 3

a) If a shortage exists in a particular market, is the price temporarily too high or too low? What if a surplus exists?

b) Why is the use of the word "temporarily" appropriate in a free market?

c) Can you think of a good or service you personally would not like to see sold in a free market? Why do you feel this way?

CASES

Case 2-1

The Wall Street Journal

GM Plans to Halve Its Production Rate for Chevette Model

DETROIT — General Motors Corp. said it plans to halve the output rate for its new Chevette minicar, whose sales have consistently lagged the auto maker's expectations.

GM said the cut will take effect Monday with the elimination of the second work turn at the company's Wilmington, Del., assembly plant. The facility will continue to produce the Chevrolet division's sub-compact at the rate of 65 units hourly, but only on one work turn, GM explained. About 1,625 employees at the plant will be indefinitely laid off because of the change, the company added.

The cutback is GM's second such change of plans for the little car. In February, GM announced it was deferring addition of Chevette production to its South Gate, Calif., plant because of lower-than-expected sales, then estimated at some 250,000 units for the current model year.

Yesterday, a GM spokesman said the company currently expects sales of about 200,000 Chevettes in it first year. As of April 10, the spokesman added, about 78,330 Chevettes had been sold since the beginning of the current model year last Oct. 1.

• • •

GM's latest action is an attempt to prevent inventories of the Chevette from rising further. Based on daily selling rates, for instance, there was 123 days' supply of the Chevette on April 1, according to Automotive News, a trade publication. By contrast, the inventory of all GM models on April 1 was only 45 days's supply, the publication reported.

But by eliminating a work turn, rather than adopting a temporary plant closedown to cut these inventories, GM is also indicating it doesn't expect a quick upturn in Chevette demand. The company's new production rate works out to only about 130,000 units annually.

In this chapter we emphasized that there are no unplanned inventory buildups or rundowns in a product market equilibrium situation. Unplanned inventory movement informs business firms that they have incorrectly estimated demand, and they are thereby led to take corrective action.

a) What evidence is presented in the article to indicate that the market for Chevettes is in disequilibrium?

b) Did General Motors overestimate or underestimate market demand for Chevettes? What corrective action are they taking?

c) Which of the two diagrams (i) and (ii) reflects the current position of General Motors with respect to its Chevette market?

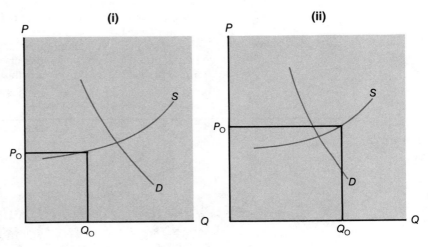

P_0 — Current GM price for Chevettes
Q_0 — Yearly output of Chevettes at current production rates

Indicate on the diagram this year's surplus or shortage, which is now anticipated to occur at current prices and unchanged production levels. What would be more likely — that GM would offer a price rebate scheme, or that it would increase prices on the Chevette model, in combination with production cutbacks?

d) From the numbers given in the article show that GM's new production schedule and inventory are roughly consistent with the revised sales estimate.

Case 2-2

The Financial Post

Rent curbs upheaval
The growing case against controls
- *Little construction*
- *Tight vacancies*
- *Upkeep falls down*

By CAROLYN GREEN

FOR-RENT signs are a rare sight in most Canadian cities these days as apartment vacancy rates plummet to abnormally low levels. And there's little hope an adequate supply of new apartments will magically appear in the next couple of years.

As Canada's real estate developers see it, rent controls are clearly the chief culprit. Instituted in 1975, curbs on rents are still in force a decade later in seven provinces, including Ontario where one third of all rental accommodation is located.

And controls — at least in Ontario — may be here to stay.

Bernard Ghert, president of Cadillac Fairview Corp., Toronto, says former Ontario Premier Bill Davis "always made promises" but "found the political expediency was to keep rent controls." He says new Ontario Premier David Peterson "is no different."

Peterson's "first job is to maintain himself in power. [The government] knows it's a problem. They'd like to get rid of [rent controls] but everybody's saying it just can't be done," says Ghert, who is also president of the Canadian Institute of Public Real Estate Companies, a group of developers.

Once a developer and landlord of thousands of apartment units in Ontario, Cadillac Fairview sold off its residential interests in the early 1980s. It has no intention of returning.

Indeed, a number of disturbing facts emerge from an analysis of Canada's rental market:

☐ In many areas, vacancies are well below the 3% level considered adequate to provide enough supply at various rental rates. And they're getting tighter all the time.

Nationally, the vacancy rate fell in October to 1.5% from 2.1% in April. Of the 24 communities surveyed by Canada Mortgage & Housing Corp., only three had vacancy rates above 3%. Six months earlier, rates in seven cities were above 3%.

Starts down

☐ New apartment construction is next to nil. From a high of 90,000 apartment units in 1977, starts last year totaled 37,000. For 1985, Clayton Research Associates estimates they'll move up slightly to about 45,000. However, condominium apartments — of which there are a fair number — are lumped into this category.

With rent controls intact in all provinces except British Columbia, Alberta and New Brunswick, developers are staying away from apartment construction. Most of the rental building these days is being done with help from municipal and federal subsidies. Generally, this aid is geared to low-income housing.

☐ Proposals to tighten the rent review system in Ontario are scaring off the few daring builders with rental schemes on the drawing board.

Bramalea Ltd., for example, shelved plans after the province announced its intentions to lower the annual rent increase ceiling to 4% from 6% and to include all units in the rent review system. Till now, only units built before 1976 have been under control.

☐ Rent control is primarily a political issue and any decision to remove it is made on that basis. In Ontario, a very large and powerful tenant lobby has emerged in recent years, calling for the maintenance of rent controls. Because of the tight supply, tenants fear rent-gouging by landlords should controls be removed.

☐ Controls, while protecting the tenant from excessive increases, have indirectly hurt the people they were intended to assist. Because of shortages, a number of unsavory rental practices have developed in many cities. These include: key money — upfront payments by tenants which are not considered rent — and discrimination against families or singles with children, and ethnic groups.

☐ Since rent controls seem here to stay, solutions to severe apartment shortages must be found within that framework.

The modern-day version of rent controls is only a decade old. However, Canada's first experience with them began in 1941 when the federal government imposed a nationwide rent freeze as part of the war effort. Later, modest increases were permitted and, in 1951, Ottawa relinquished authority of rents to the provinces. Between 1951–54, all provinces, except Quebec and Newfoundland, abolished controls.

In 1975, the provinces were asked by Ottawa to impose rent controls as part of the general wage and price policy. Alberta, New Brunswick and Manitoba got rid of them in 1980, but both New Brunswick and Manitoba reinstated them in 1982.

Manitoba's are still in place while New Brunswick dropped them (again) in August. After a phase-out period, British Columbia removed controls in 1983. All other provinces have kept them in some form or another.

Unlike Ontario's constant ceiling, some provinces have annually-determined increases, while others provide a more relaxed system, allowing the tenant and landlord to negotiate a fair rent. The province steps in if no agreement is reached.

Although rent review has always been a contentious issue, it's gained momentum in recent years, particularly in provinces where some units are under control and others are exempt. In Ontario, for example, all units built after 1976 have been out of the system, meaning landlords can increase rents to whatever level they want. (Plans call for control of all units, new and old, and legislation is expected before the end of the year.)

With a two-tier system, builders have long claimed that rents charged for new uncontrolled units can't compete with those regulated by the system — so they wouldn't build.

Until 1983, Ottawa was the white knight in shining armor, doling out tax breaks and grants to help close the gap.

With interest rates down to more affordable levels, some developers say they can get a reasonable rate of return without government aid.

Says Peter Goring, senior vice-president, corporate finance and treasury, Bramalea Ltd.:

"We think in the lower luxury class, we probably could have done it without subsidy. That would have meant putting a fair amount of equity in and a low return on equity, but people do that in a low inflation environment."

So why isn't there any private construction being planned?

Some projects might have gone ahead if Ontario had not indicated its plans to tighten controls. But by extending controls to cover all rental units, the system is felt to be too rigid should the developer misjudge future profits.

The proposed system, says Goring, "doesn't allow you to increase your return on equity."

Maintenance an issue

Clearly, there are no easy answers. Even if a perfect system were introduced today and developers started new projects, the lead time necessary before new units were available is one–two years.

In addition to the absence of new construction, one of the prime issues that must be addressed is the maintenance of existing buildings. Because of a restriction on rent increases, landlords have kept repairs to a minimum.

Cadillac's Ghert says the process works this way: The original owner reduces maintenance to allow some profit. When it no longer makes sense financially, he'll sell it to someone willing to cut back more, and this cycle will continue.

Recognizing the problems with upkeep, the Ontario government has announced plans to establish a rehabilitation assistance program. Housing Minister Alvin Curling, in a recent speech, said the rehab plan would be designed to assist 25% of the present rental stock which needs repairs and upgrading.

Curling also called for an end to adversarial tenant/landlord relations and announced plans to establish an advisory committee composed of tenant and landlord representatives. Its mandate would be to foster better relations between the two groups and to advise the minister on short- and long-term housing policy.

According to Bramalea's Goring, who is a director of a recently established landlord's group — Fair Rental Policy Organization — one of the first things necessary to get the ball rolling is public education.

For example, says Goring, home owners must recognize their taxes are used, in part, to assist with new apartment construction through grant programs.

As well, says Ghert, prospective home buyers are affected through higher house prices. Because rental accommodation is scarce, there's a large group of buyers, therefore pushing up prices.

Environmentalists also should be concerned, says Ghert. Single-family house construction means greater land use. "If highrise rental apartments aren't available, you've got to push out the urban fringes and it uses up more land."

This article describes the state of rent control policies across Canada as of late 1985. It is only one of thousands of newspaper articles, studies and books written on the subject. As a small sample of this literature, the following are perhaps the two most often quoted remarks concerning the issue of rent control.

> "If educated people can't or won't see that fixing a price below the market level inevitably creates a shortage (and one above a surplus), it is hard to believe in the usefulness of telling them anything whatever in this field of discourse [economics]."

> "In many cases rent control appears to be the most efficient means presently known to destroy a city — except for bombing."

The quotations are from famous economists of different political persuasions. The first quotation is from Frank H. Knight of the University of Chicago, and the second is from Assar Lindbeck of the University of Stockholm.* Knight would be regarded as a conservative and Lindbeck, a socialist. Regardless of philosophical or political outlook, there is almost universal agreement among economists that rent controls are a most inappropriate tool for the purpose of creating affordable housing for low income groups. There is wide agreement among economists that the exact opposite is true: effective rent controls cause a reduction in the volume of affordable housing.

If economists are generally against rent controls, why, then, have rent controls been imposed at various times and in various countries, including Britain, Sweden, France, the United States and Canada? In most instances, the answer appears to be political. Tenants are an easily identifiable block of potential voters. Rent controls bring immediate and highly visible benefits to this group. The resulting accommodation shortage initially affects a much smaller group of people searching for living quarters. Also, these and other costs dealt with below tend to appear only after a time lag; election or re-election may be a more immediate concern.

Drawing upon the article and the material in this chapter, discuss the following:

a) Often rent controls are initially imposed because there exists a shortage of rental accommodation. Usually the government argues that the con-

---

* Frank H. Knight, "Truth and relevance at bay," *American Economic Review* (1949), p. 1274. Assar Lindbeck, *The Political Economy of the New Left. An Outsider's View* (New York: Harper & Row, 1971), p. 39.

trols themselves are only temporary in nature until the shortage of accommodation is eliminated. Explain how within a free market a shortage of rental accommodation could only be *temporary*. Explain (with the aid of a diagram if you like) how a controlled rent below the equilibrium market rate guarantees a rental shortage as long as the controls are effective.

b) The "units out of the system" referred to in the article means the newer units which are without rent ceilings. Explain briefly why rent controls for the controlled sector would lead to higher demand for the uncontrolled apartment units. Since new (uncontrolled) units eventually become old (controlled) units, explain the effect of rent controls on the supply of new rental units, even if new units are initially exempt. From your previous analysis, explain how rent controls mean that rents in the uncontrolled sector are generally higher than they would have been in the absence of controls.

c) Families with several children are typically perceived by landlords as causing greater wear and tear on apartments and other forms of rental housing than smaller families. Under rent controls, explain why larger families would have greater difficulty finding rental accommodation than smaller families.

d) One of the consequences of rent controls is that landlords reduce maintenance services and let their buildings fall into disrepair. In cities like New York and London, England, which have had some of the strictest forms of rent control, some landlords have eventually abandoned their buildings altogether to escape paying municipal taxes. Can you explain why rent controls would lead to "problems with upkeep"?

e) What sort of government administrative costs and private administrative costs are necessary under a program of rent controls? Recognizing that municipal taxes are paid roughly according to the value of property and buildings, explain briefly how rent controls cause lost taxes on rental properties which have to be made up by either less government services or more taxes collected from home owners. Part of the government costs of rent controls are the subsidies (grants) given to developers and additional government spending programs designed to stimulate construction of new accommodation. What political pressures would tend to cause the government to carry out this sort of expenditure? (In other words, what groups would we expect to see complaining to the government to do something in the presence of rent controls?)

f) Suggest an alternate policy to help low income people that does not involve tampering with the housing market.

CHAPTER 3

Cause and Effect in a Market Supply-Demand Framework

LEARNING OBJECTIVES

After reading this chapter you should be able to explain:

1. Changes in consumer tastes, incomes, prices and population, and their impact on market demand.

2. Changes in wage rates, productivity, taxes and prices of raw materials, and their impact on market supply.

3. The length of the time period as a factor determining market outcome.

3-1 INTRODUCTION AND PURPOSE

It is important for economic policymakers to identify, as precisely as possible, the root causes of economic events. Because micro analysis has more narrowly defined boundaries than macro analysis, it is generally easier to identify **external shocks** (exogenous influences). This chapter pinpoints some of these shocks and examines how they work their way through the supply or the demand side of the market to influence prices and output. In this chapter, we attempt to gain an overall view of those factors which influence both demand and supply, relying to a certain extent on intuitive reasoning. As far as the graphical analysis is concerned, the important feature of the chapter is the distinction between movements along and shifts in demand and supply curves.

Chapters 4 through 7 continue the theme of market demand and supply analysis in considerably greater detail.

3-2 SHIFTS IN MARKET DEMAND

We must distinguish between a change in quantity demanded as a result of a change in the price of the particular good in question, and a change or **shift in market demand**. A change in quantity demanded in response to a change in market price is reflected by moving *along* a given market demand curve. A demand curve is typically downward sloping to the right, as in the athletic shoes example of Figure 2-1 which has been reproduced for convenience as Figure 3-1. The athletic shoes demand curve reflects the fact that as the price of shoes falls, consumers need to spend less money on shoes, and do not have to cut back so much on purchases of other goods to buy each pair. Therefore, consumers would be expected to buy more shoes at lower prices. A given fixed demand curve thus illustrates the normal case, in which the lower the price of a good (or service), the greater will be the quantity bought by consumers.

A *shift* in market demand is something completely different from the preceding example. Such a shift for athletic shoes indicates that for some reason a different volume of these shoes is demanded (than was previously demanded) *at each and every price level*. Therefore, a shift in market demand occurs only as a result of a changing demand factor *other than the price level*. This is a very important point.

Some examples may help in distinguishing

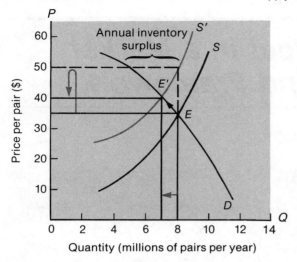

**Fig. 3-1 Movement along a given
demand curve**

At the price of $35 a pair, the market is in equilibrium at 8 million pairs per year. The supply curve shifts upward from *S* to *S'* as a result of a unit cost increase. If the producers keep output constant at 8 million pairs, the supply price rises to $50 a pair and unplanned inventory buildup develops. The adjustment process will result in a new equilibrium at 7 million pairs and $40 a pair.

between a movement along a given demand relation (along a given demand curve) and a change in the relation itself (a shift in the demand curve). Suppose something happens on the supply side of the athletic shoe market. Perhaps a sudden increase in the wage rates of employees is bargained for, which in turn forces unit production costs upward. Firms will respond by requiring higher prices for every possible output level produced (supplied).

For example, in order to supply 6 million pairs, the shoe producers originally required a price of no less than $20 per pair, but after the cost increase they will need $35 per pair to produce the same quantity. Similarly, to produce 7 million pairs originally required a price of $25 per pair, but after the cost increase will require $40 per pair, and so on. That is, there is a shift upward in the market supply curve (see Figure 3-1). The producers may react by merely raising their prices from $35 to $50, while holding their production level constant

at 8 million pairs per year. This action is unlikely to be permanent, though, because the quantity demanded would fall to about 4.5 million pairs in reaction to the price increase (as shown in Figure 3-1).

Families would now shy away from athletic shoes and instead purchase cheaper running shoes, or perhaps even sandals or some other substitute footwear. The tendency to turn toward substitutes as prices increase is reflected by the given demand curve (*D*), which shows that the volume of athletic shoes demanded at $50 per pair is only 4.5 million pairs per year. To escape the continual unwanted buildup of inventories which results from firms producing or supplying more than is demanded at $50, prices and production levels would be rolled back to roughly $40 per pair and 7 million pairs per year respectively. The net result, then, is a new equilibrium price that is higher than the original price ($40 as compared with $35), with the quantity demanded falling to 7 million pairs per year from the original 8 million pairs per year but with no shift in the demand relation (curve).

Market demand may shift for several reasons, however, and we now consider the four most important of these **demand shocks**.

Change in Tastes

Consider a sudden change of consumer tastes, in favour of athletic shoes. This change may be induced by TV advertising aimed at children, who then pester their parents until athletic shoes suddenly appear to the parents to be a better buy than before.[1] Therefore, at any given price level, more athletic shoes would be demanded than before.

For example, at $20 per pair, the original quantity demanded is 10 million pairs, but after the change in tastes, it may be about 13 million pairs. At $35 per pair, the change in tastes raises the quantity demanded from the original 8 million pairs to 11 million; at $45 per pair, the quantity demanded increases from 6 million pairs to

---

1. Some may not like referring to this as a change in tastes. The point is that the perceived value of running shoes has increased in the minds of the parents (the purchasers) not only because the child's feet will be covered, but also because the pestering will stop (or so the parents think).

9 million, and so on. This is a shift in demand and is represented graphically by Figure 3-2.

The firms will feel an increase in consumer demand by an increase in sales and a reduction in inventories. (After the demand shift, at the old price level demand is now greater than supply.) The firms will know that they have underestimated demand and that they should increase production. As they do, per unit production costs for the extra volume may rise, causing producers to require higher prices. Now two factors are working to remove the inventory shortages: (i) firms are producing more (moving from *E* toward *E'*) and (ii) firms are increasing their prices. The higher prices for athletic shoes will dampen the quantity of such shoes demanded (consumers are moving up the new market demand curve from *A* toward *E'*). Market demand and supply quantities therefore converge toward 9 million pairs per year at a price of $45 per pair.

Change in Income

Suppose that family incomes in Canada rise. This event makes athletic shoes at any price level more affordable to more people. Hence, at any given price level, the market quantity demanded will be greater than it was before the income rise. In other words an income rise can be expected to shift the market demand curve to the right.[2]

Change in Prices of Related Goods

Suppose the price of ordinary running shoes suddenly increases. This rise would cause some consumers who were previously wavering between fancy athletic shoes and ordinary shoes to decide in favour of the athletic shoes. Therefore, the market demand curve for the latter would shift to the right.

Change in Population

Changing population is perhaps the most obvious reason for a shift in market demand. For example, as the population increases, the market demand for athletic shoes will also increase at each and every price level. The demand curve will shift to the right.

---

2. An exception to this rule occurs for so-called *inferior goods*. It is discussed in Chapter 4.

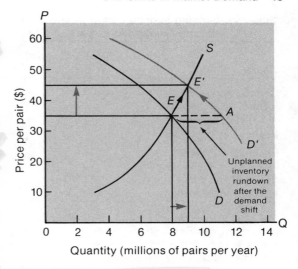

Fig. 3-2 Shift in market demand

At the price of $35 a pair, the market is in equilibrium at 8 million pairs per year. The demand curve shifts upward from *D* to *D'* because of a change in consumer tastes. If the producers maintain the price constant at $35 a pair, an unplanned inventory rundown develops. The adjustment process will result in a new equilibrium at 9 million pairs and $45 a pair.

"Sales have really soared since we posted a warning that our lemonade may be hazardous to your health!"

Table 3-1 **Demand shocks and their effects in shifting the market demand curve**

Cause	Effect on market demand curve
Change in tastes toward the particular product (or service)	→
Increase in incomes	→
Increase in price of substitute products (or services)	→
Increase in population	→

Changes in these four exogenous variables (factors other than the price of the product in question) cause a shift in the market demand curve in the direction indicated by the arrows.

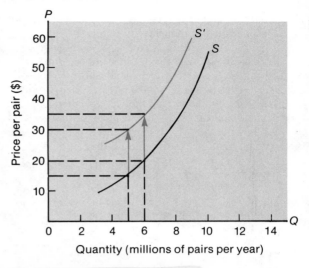

Fig. 3-3 Shift in market supply

The supply curve shifts upwards (to the left) from *S* to *S'* as a result of an increase in wages of workers producing the product.

Table 3-1 lists a number of causes of shifts in market demand and the direction of their effects. Only increases in these particular shocks are shown, but decreases would produce symmetrically opposite results.

The market demand curve may shift to the right or to the left because of changes in economic circumstances. Among the most important reasons are changes in tastes, changes in income, changes in the price of related goods or services, and changes in population.

3-3 SHIFTS IN MARKET SUPPLY

The market supply curve indicates the minimum price levels that the producing sector will require in order to produce various amounts of output. For example, according to Figure 3-3 (with reference to the solid *S* curve) producers would be satisfied with $20 per pair to produce the 6 millionth pair of athletic shoes for the Canadian market. This is the minimum price per unit that would induce them to produce the 6 millionth pair. If, on the other hand, prices were lower, say $15 per pair, producers would not be willing to produce 6 million pairs per

year. They would, however, be willing to produce and sell, for $15 per pair, a lower volume, one at which unit costs are lower. In Figure 3-3, this is shown to be 5 million pairs per year. This change in price represents a movement along a given supply relation (supply curve), not a shift in the relation itself.

A **shift in the market supply** curve would occur, for example, if something happened to cause firms to require higher prices than before to produce *at each and every volume of output*. Let us now consider four types of **supply shocks**.

Change in Wage Rates

If the wage rate of shoe workers was raised, it would cost more to produce the 5 millionth or the 6 millionth pair of athletic shoes than before. If producers were previously willing to accept $15 per pair for a level of production of 5 million pairs and $20 per pair for a level of production of 6 million pairs, now they would produce at either of these levels only if prices were raised — perhaps to $30 and $35 per pair, respectively, as shown in Figure 3-3. In other words, the supply curve would shift upward from *S* to *S'*.

Change in Productivity

Productivity relates output produced to inputs used. For instance, labour productivity is often measured by output per unit of labour. An increase in output per unit of labour causes unit production costs to fall. If a firm pays $10 per hour for labour that produces 10 units of output per hour, labour cost per unit of output is $1. If productivity was instead 20 units per worker-hour, unit labour costs would be only $0.50. Therefore, an increase in productivity has the opposite effect on unit costs to an increase in wage rates. Consequently, an increase in productivity causes the supply curve to shift downward.

Change in Excise Taxes[3]

Excise taxes are government taxes placed on some goods but not on others. They may be levied at the wholesale or manufacturing level, but they have the same effect on the retail price. To understand what happens when an excise tax is changed, let us look at the situation from the standpoint of the athletic shoe market.

Figure 3-4 indicates that at $35 per pair, total market demand is 8 million pairs per year — which is also the amount of production (amount supplied). Presumably the consumer does not care what portions of the $35 price the firm and the government each receives. Demand would be 8 million pairs per year for a final price of $35 regardless of whether the price included a $0.05 or a $5 excise tax.

Though the consumer may not care what portion of any final price goes to the government, the firm certainly does. To remit part of the money collected from each sale to the government in the form of an excise tax is a cost of doing business just like all other production costs — labour, heat, light and power, materials and so forth.

Suppose, then, that there is an increase in the excise tax of $10 per pair on each pair of athletic shoes produced (or perhaps an excise tax of $10 imposed on each pair produced where there was none originally) but no corresponding increase in the excise tax on plain footwear. With this increased cost of producing and selling each pair, athletic shoe suppliers would not act passively,

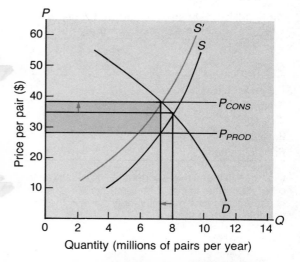

Fig. 3-4 Effect of an excise tax increase

Imposition of an excise tax causes a shift upwards (to the left) of the supply curve from *S* to *S′*. The equilibrium quantity decreases, the price paid by the consumer increases above the original equilibrium price and the price received by the producer decreases below the original equilibrium price. The government tax revenue is indicated by the shaded rectangle.

leaving the final prices asked from consumers unchanged. Instead, they would ask for higher prices for each possible level of output. That is, the supply curve would shift upward (as shown in Figure 3-4).

Several things happen as a result of imposition of the tax. With retailers asking for a higher final price (which includes the higher tax) more families would opt for cheaper running shoes, thereby reducing the quantity of athletic shoes demanded to about 7.2 million pairs. This latter effect represents a movement along the given demand curve for athletic shoes, and not a shift in demand. Moreover, the tax has driven a "wedge" between the price paid by the consumer and the price received by the producer. The former pays P_{CONS} or $38 per pair, but the latter receives P_{PROD} or $28 per pair. The government receives the difference between the two prices times the new (after-tax) equilibrium quantity sold. The amount of the tax proceeds in this case is $72 million (i.e. 7.2 million pairs times $10 per pair) and is indicated by the shaded area in Figure 3-4.

---

3. A tax on foreign, imported goods (a tax known as a *duty* or *tariff*) would be expected to exert a similar effect on the market as an excise tax.

Table 3-2 Supply shocks and their effects in shifting the market supply curve

Cause		Effect on market supply curve
Wage rates ($/hr.)	↑	↑
Productivity (output/worker)	↑	↓
Excise taxes	↑	↑
Price of materials	↑	↑

Changes in these four exogenous variables (factors other than the price of the product in question) cause a shift in the market supply curve in the direction indicated by the arrows.

Change in Materials Price

A change in the price of materials used in manufacturing a product affects the cost of production and hence the market supply curve, in the same way that changes in wage rates do. Higher materials costs per unit of output increase the per unit costs of production, thereby causing firms to require higher prices for each volume of output. The supply curve in this case would again shift upward.

The causes and effects of shifts in the market supply curve are summarized in Table 3-2.

The market supply curve may shift to the right or to the left because of changes in economic circumstances. Among the most important reasons are changes in wage rates, changes in productivity, changes in excise taxes, and changes in the price of raw materials.

3-4 CAUSE AND EFFECT ANALYSIS

Table 3-3 lists all the market demand-and-supply factors discussed above together with their ultimate effects on price, volume of sales and employment within a particular industry. This is not an exhaustive list. For example, we have not yet considered the effect of an increase in the cost of capital funds to the firm, an aspect we will discuss later. However, these shocks account for a large percentage of important market events. Understanding the connection between these shocks and market prices, sales, and industrial employment

means that we have gone a considerable way toward understanding how the economy works at the microeconomic level.

As can be seen, the effect on employment (E) of an increase in productivity is ambiguous. Even though output (Q) increases, it is not clear whether more or less labour would be required to produce the extra output, since productivity (output per unit of labour) has increased.

3-5 TIME ANALYSIS

We must establish the time period to which we shall limit our anaysis. In microeconomics it is often useful to divide analyses into either two or three time frames. When a microeconomic shock occurs, we may wish to analyze the *immediate effects* — those within a day, week or month (the time depends on the nature of the market in question). Instead of, or perhaps in addition to, the immediate effects, *short-run effects* may be of interest — which take place, say, within a year after the shock. Finally, it may be important to round out our investigation of the events by examining *long-run effects*.[4]

The importance of specifying the time span of analysis cannot be overemphasized. For example, diametrically opposite conclusions are often reached concerning the effect of a market shock on a product's price in the long run (when economies of scale may be present) as compared with the short run. Our choice of a time span to be used in our analysis of microeconomic events depends on the particular interest we may have in the problem at hand.

3-6 SHORTHAND AIDS TO ECONOMIC ANALYSIS

Graphical representations of particular market phenomena have been used liberally in this chapter. One purpose is to supplement written descriptions of the subject under study with illustrations so that a better feel for each particular situation can be gained. Further, various tabular summaries of cause and effect arguments are presented.

---

4. This one-year borderline between short run and long run should not be taken literally. In some markets the borderline may be much less than one year, while in other markets it may be much more. More precise definitions of short run and long run are provided in Chapter 9.

Table 3-3 Microeconomic shocks and their effects on markets

Market shocks (causes)		Effect on market supply curve	Effect on market demand curve	Effects on P	Q	E
Wage rates	↑	↑		↑	↓	↓
Productivity	↑	↓		↓	↑	?
Excise taxes	↑	↑		↑	↓	↓
Price of materials	↑	↑		↑	↓	↓
Change in tastes (toward the product)	↑		→	↑	↑	↑
Income	↑		→	↑	↑	↑
Price of substitutes	↑		→	↑	↑	↑
Population	↑		→	↑	↑	↑

The upper half of the table lists supply shocks, the lower half demand shocks. The second and third columns indicate the direction of shifts in the relevant curves. The last column indicates the impact of each shock on equilibrium price (*P*), quantity (*Q*) and employment (*E*).

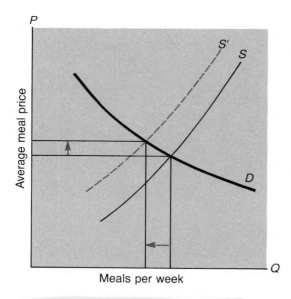

Fig. 3-5 Effect of wage increases in the restaurant business

An increase in wages of restaurant personnel shifts the supply curve upwards (to the left) from *S* to *S'*. The average meal price rises, and output level declines.

To simplify our diagrammatic presentations we typically proceed as follows:

(1) All original (before shock) demand and supply curves are drawn with solid lines.

(2) Any shift in demand or supply curves is indicated by broken lines representing the final (after shock) curves.

(3) Original (before shock) and final (after shock) prices and quantities are depicted by solid lines to the axes.

(4) The direction of change in market prices and volumes is indicated by small arrows.

Mathematics and graphical shorthand analysis may be useful in describing complex problems, but to some people these tools only get in the way. For example, suppose there is an increase in the wage rates of personnel within the restaurant industry. Figure 3-5 graphically illustrates the effect on restaurant prices, volume of business and, indirectly, employment. From studying the diagram, we conclude that restaurant meal prices would rise, there would be a dropoff in restaurant business and hence fewer waiters and other personnel would be required. However, this is a greatly summarized argument.

Many people would prefer a written or verbal explanation. Such an explanation might stress that the higher wage rates for restaurant personnel will increase the per meal cost. In response, restaurants will raise their prices. The higher prices will cause some people to eat out less frequently, and will thereby reduce the volume of restaurant business and perhaps also reduce the required number of restaurant personnel.

We encourage you to use graphical techniques in your analyses, but when doing the economic problems at the end of each chapter you should also try to describe in writing exactly what is going on.

CONCLUDING REMARKS

Any change in the demand or supply determinants for a particular good will also change both the market price and output levels of that good. Analysis of market shocks therefore proceeds as follows:

(1) Decide whether the shock is of a demand or a supply nature. A rule of thumb is to ask yourself whether the shock affects cost per unit of ouptut. If so, it is a supply shock; if not, in all probability it operates through the demand side of the market.

(2a) If the event is a demand shock, ask yourself whether the change at the existing price and output level before the shock will lead to a temporary surplus or shortage of goods on the market. Depending on your answer to this question, you should be able to see which way output and market price will move.

(2b) If the event is a supply shock, ask yourself whether firms will be inclined to raise or lower prices as a result, and then whether (at the original output level) this action will cause a surplus or shortage of goods on the market. From your answer to this, you should be able to tell which way the resulting shortage or surplus will lead market production volume.

A market shock or event more often than not causes a shift in either the demand or the supply curve and a movement along the other.

KEY TERMS AND CONCEPTS

external shocks	supply shocks
shift in market demand	excise tax
demand shocks	cause and effect analysis
shift in market supply	time analysis

PROBLEMS

Problem 1

In Chapter 3, we focused on cause-and-effect analysis within the framework of market demand and supply. Our primary interest was in examining how market shocks could affect changes in market price (*P*) and volume of output (*Q*) within any particular industry. To be able to use the tools of demand and supply it is important to distinguish between demand and supply curve shifts and movements along given curves.

a) For each of the market shocks listed below describe the effects in terms of shifts in market demand or supply curves and movements along such curves. (Hint: each market shock usually involves a shift in either the demand curve or the supply curve and a movement along the other.)

(i) Reduction in the population

(ii) Increase in the price of a product that is similar to the product being sold in this industry

(iii) Increase in the excise tax on this particular item alone

(iv) Increase in productivity

(v) Increase in the wage rates paid to the workers of this industry

b) Show the effects of each of the above shocks on a market demand and supply diagram.

c) For each of the above shocks state the effect on market price, volume of output sold and employment within the industry.

Problem 2

Goods and services that are typically consumed along with other goods and services are called "complementary" items. Gasoline is a complementary product for automobiles. When something affects the price of a product, repercussions are felt in complementary markets.

For each part below signify the most appropriate answer from the following list: increase substantially, increase slightly, no effect, decrease slightly, decrease substantially.

a) What would you expect to happen to the number of larger automobiles sold if the price of gasoline suddenly increased by 25%? By 1000%?

b) What would happen to the price of motel accommodation in Florida if the price of transportation in Florida increased by 20%? By 200%?

c) What would happen to the volume of tea consumed if the price of sugar increased by 10%? By 100%?

Problem 3

a) Suppose the inventory of unsold new houses is at historically high levels in a particular geographical area. Depict the situation on a demand and supply diagram. What would you expect (everything else being equal) to happen to new-house prices in the near future?

b) Goods and services that satisfy consumer needs are called *substitutes*. For example, second-hand houses are for many families a similar or substitute good for new houses. Depict diagrammatically the effect of the change in new-house prices on the second-hand housing market. What would likely happen to second-hand house prices?

c) What would be the likely effect of the extraordinarily high new-house inventory on residential construction activity and on employment within the construction industry?

d) What would be the effect on the housing market and the apartment rental market of (i) an increase in population? (ii) a general increase in incomes? (iii) an increase in mortgage interest rates? (Mortgages are loans for the purchase of real estate.)

Problem 4

Suppose the Canadian dollar appreciates against the U.S. dollar (it will cost more U.S. dollars to buy one Canadian dollar). Explain, with the help of a supply-demand diagram, why the Canadian producers of such exportables as lumber will experience lower output prices.

Alternatively, suppose productivity in the Canadian lumber industry improves. Explain, with the help of a supply-demand diagram, what will happen to the output price of the Canadian lumber industry.

What is the difference between the two cases as far as the welfare of the Canadian lumber industry workers and shareholders is concerned? Carefully state your assumptions when making this assessment.

CASES

Case 3-1

The Globe and Mail, Toronto

Lured by recruiters, teachers head to U.S. as shortage predicted

By BEVERLY BOWEN

Canadian teachers are being recruited for jobs in the United States at a rate that some predict may eventually cause a shortage in schools here.

More than 3,600 teachers from coast to coast have responded to advertisements by their provincial teachers' associations and the San Diego Centre for Educational Management, encouraging them to go south where they are needed.

A newspaper advertisement by the Ontario Teachers Federation for a coming recruitment fair has generated so much interest that teachers' associations in Manitoba, New Brunswick, Quebec and Saskatchewan have been phoning the federation for information about the U.S. jobs.

But while some Canadian recruiters say that working in the United States may be the only option open to the growing ranks of unemployed or under-employed teachers, a Vancouver recruiter says a brain drain may be under way.

The median salary for an experienced teacher

in the United States is $23,500 U.S. ($32,400 Canadian), compared to the approximately $36,000 earned by a teacher with a large Canadian school board.

Professor Raymond Latta, director of the San Diego centre, said in a telephone interview that he expects to lure 1,400 to 2,000 teachers to California at recruitment fairs in Vancouver and Toronto at the end of April. If the pool of candidates is impressive, the same number may be hired in follow-up interviews. This would represent a significant jump from last year, when 250 teachers were hired at the first recruitment fair, held in British Columbia.

If the April fairs are successful, Prof. Latta will step up his campaign. He says the next phase will be to seek out employed teachers who want a change, and to have U.S. school boards recruit Canadian teachers as soon as they graduate from school.

"What I'm trying to do is break the border down," said Prof. Latta, a Canadian who has lived in the United States for 20 years. "We are so much like one people. I'd like us to take a look at education and say there's no border there."

The United States is experiencing a shortage of teachers because of the large number who are facing retirement or pursuing other careers, and it has been predicted that an additional million will be needed by the 1990s.

Schools in Los Angeles have already resorted to employing teachers who lack the necessary credentials, while various state agencies have been forced to look abroad for teachers — to Spain, Puerto Rico, West Germany, Belgium and now Canada.

By contrast, Canada has so many teachers that only one-third of college graduates immediately find jobs. However, educators forecast that in the next five to 10 years Canada will experience the same pressures as the United States, and that demand will sharply increase.

Mel Lehan, co-ordinator of an unemployed teachers' action centre for the British Columbia Teachers Federation, has mixed feelings about urging teachers to head south.

"I feel elated that I'm helping people," said Mr. Lehan, who estimates that there are 10,000 unemployed teachers in B.C. "But it's sad that they have to go out of the country. What is happening in the United States now is what is going to happen in Canada 10 years from now."

Nonetheless, Mr. Lehan and his association are preparing to branch out from California and establish recruitment ties with other Sun Belt states, which also have a high demand for teachers.

"They (teachers) are going down for one reason — they want to feed their families and practice their career," said Mr. Lehan.

Pierre Lalonde of the Ontario Teachers Federation says his association has no qualms about recruiting teachers for the United States because he doubts that most will remain there.

a) Looking at the statistics in the article, an economist could have predicted that (other things being equal) there would likely be a surplus of teachers in Canada and a shortage in the U.S. Why?

b) Describe diagrammatically how the process of migration discussed in the article will affect the market for teachers in Canada and in the U.S. (Use two demand-supply diagrams, one for Canada and one for the U.S.)

c) What, if any, changes in Canadian government policies (federal, provincial, local) would you recommend, and why?

Case 3-2

Forbes Magazine

Hippocrates meets Adam Smith

You've heard all about the oil glut.
Now let's talk about the doctor glut.

By ELLEN PARIS

Los Angeles cardiologist David Frisch doesn't think much of his chosen profession these days. "Medicine stinks," he says. His gripe isn't with the long hours, nor the heavy philosophical questions raised by new medical technologies. It's about the loss of control in treating patients. And it's about money. "My personal income dropped 20% in 1983 and 1984," Frisch, 39, complains. Last year was better, but only because he scrambled. "By emphasizing an office practice instead of a hospital practice," he says, "I was able to avoid the reduced income that other doctors are experiencing today."

Economics 101 says that prices rise when demand for a product exceeds the supply available at the old price. The higher price elicits additional production. Result: Either prices drop again or some production goes unsold. But does supply-and-demand economics apply to medicine?

Apparently it does. After decades of almost limitless freedom to charge what they wished for as much health care as they wished to supply, the country's doctors are suddenly finding that there is more health care available than there are customers for it.

As a result, for many doctors, income growth is beginning to slow, or stop completely. According to the American Medical Association, U.S. physicians' mean income after expenses and before taxes was $108,400 in 1984 (the 1985 figures aren't in yet) — a 2% increase over 1983, well below the rate of inflation. Some doctors — neurosurgeons and plastic surgeons, for example — fared better. But for most, the earnings trend is flat to somewhat down.

While all this hardly qualifies as an economic catastrophe for the profession, there is no question that it represents a watershed, a cresting of affluence and influence. Sighs Santa Monica surgeon Arnold Seid, "We are no longer a privileged class."

"We loved the old way," reminisces Dr. James Silverman, chief of staff at Stanford University Medical Center. "There was no shortage of work, and everyone was happy. At the beginning of the year doctors would target their income and reach it in a number of ways. You could always charge for lab tests you didn't do."

What happened? In essence, this: High medical prices induced both a greater supply of doctors and a drive by medical entrepreneurs and their customers to reorganize health care delivery so as to cut costs.

From 1950 to 1965, when Norman Rockwellesque doctors still drove Buicks, instead of Porsches and Mercedes, and made house calls, the doctors' ranks grew at less than 2% annually, while medical outlays were increasing 8% a year in the U.S. Demand and ability to pay for medical care were clearly rising much faster than the number of doctors. Doctors' incomes took off: $16,017 in 1955, $28,960 in 1965, $58,440 in 1975, over $100,000 today, according to *Medical Economics* magazine. Rising incomes elicited additional supply. In 1965 there were 277,600 doctors in the U.S., 1 for every 697 Americans. Today there are 506,000 practicing physicians, 1 doctor for every 471 Americans, with more doctors per capita every day. A recent Peat, Marwick, Mitchell study warns there will be a surplus of between 70,000 and 185,000 physicians by 1990.

The country's more money-motivated students have received the message. Medical school applications have dropped, from 42,624 for 14,579 places in 1974–75 to 32,893 for 16,268 places last year. Of particular interest, applications to Stanford, where tuition for four years of private med school now costs $65,760, fell from 5,711 in 1980 to 4,400 last year. But over the same period, applications to UCLA's public medical school, where four years costs nonresidents $25,120 ($5,920 for California residents), rose from 3,000 to 4,500. Cost consciousness is in.

How ironic. For years U.S. physicians wrapped themselves in the flag of private enterprise and lobbied hard to save themselves from socialized medicine à la Britain and Scandinavia. They forgot that free enterprise includes the freedom of newcomers to enter a business at will.

Instead of being socialized, medicine is being industrialized. Much as 19th-century France's *grands magasins* grabbed clients from the little shopkeepers, well-capitalized health care combines, such as Maxicare (Forbes, Dec. 2, 1985), Cigna Health Plan and HealthAmerica, are siphoning off the private practitioners' patients, rebundling those patients into health maintenance organizations (HMOs), preferred provider organizations (PPOs) and other forms of prepaid health care that deliver employee care to employers at lower cost. Maxicare now provides care for 745,000 workers and their dependents in several states, up from 87,000 five years ago.

Howard Fullman, for example, is a 30-year-old gastroenterologist who completed his residency in 1983. Fullman jumped at an offer to work full time in the west Los Angeles office of Kaiser-Permanente, one of the first of the country's HMOs and now the largest. Fullman earns a salary somewhat in excess of $60,000 and still owes $20,000 in med school loans. But, he says, "I am happy with the income, and the benefits are great. There is better security. I don't have to worry about what is happening in the medical marketplace."

Compare Fullman's experience with that of another young Los Angeles doctor, Michael Clements. Clements opted for a private practice. He runs a modest family practice with no nurse and a single secretary. Clements, 34, owes $10,000 in student loans. In 1981 he borrowed another $50,000 over five years to buy his practice. Clements' practice brings in around $130,000 annually. But rent, insurance, secretarial costs and whatever personal costs Clements can throw on the business ate up 70% of that gross last year, leaving him with $40,000 pretax income.

"I could have joined Maxicare for $50,000, but I don't like dancing to someone else's tune," says Clements. "My wife works as an actress

and has had some national commercials, which have helped a lot."

"We have become neighborhood doctors," says Dr. Misha Askren, who with an associate runs a family practice out of a west Los Angeles storefront. To attract patients, Askren advertises in a weekly throwaway paper put out by a local supermarket, places notices in a church bulletin, sends his patients a quarterly newsletter and gives free lectures at his office on subjects like AIDS, childbirth and aging. Askren keeps his office open evenings and, for emergencies, on weekends and even makes house calls. But just in case, Askren has also contracted with three local PPOs, agreeing to treat their patients at up to 15% off his normal rates.

There is a deeper question in all this. Will the country continue to receive an adequate level of medical care as the power of supplying and pricing the care shifts from doctors to businessmen? Part of the answer, of course, depends on what constitutes "adequate" health care. But this much is clear: Cost containment will almost surely translate to less lavish use of medical facilities.

"When an HMO doctor does expensive tests, he punishes himself economically, because there is less profit in the HMO to be distributed to the member physicians at the end of the year," warns Dr. Charles Friedman, a Santa Monica internist who recently decided against joining a local Maxicare group.

"I felt HMO health care was inconsistent with the standards I was taught in medical school," explains Friedman, adding "There is also a disincentive for HMO physicians to document complaints in a patient's chart because failure to investigate a symptom could amount to negligence. Under an HMO, a doctor may not even want to hear a complaint — much less document one — because of the fear of later being accused of malpractice or negligence." Maxicare insists it has adequate review procedures to guard against the danger of its doctors' shortchanging their patients.

When the smoke clears, medicine will still be a lucrative profession, but less open-endedly so than it was. The good news is that the spiraling medical costs that contributed so substantially to inflation in recent decades may finally be coming under control.

a) Much of the article deals with the relationship between numbers of doctors and their annual incomes. While treating the former as a Q and the latter as a P on a demand-supply diagram is not quite appropriate, it may generate useful insights. Using the demand-supply framework, illustrate the changing conditions in the U.S. "market for doctors" over the past 35 years. Do not worry about filling in all the numbers.

b) Why is it theoretically more appropriate to model the medical market with quantity of services on the horizontal axis and fee per service on the vertical axis? If you had the data, what would the diagrammatical analysis of the trends over the past 35 years look like? (in terms of shifting demand and supply curves)?

c) House calls, free lectures, quarterly newsletters and similar practices described in the article are all a sign of market disequilibrium. Explain.

d) Illustrate, in a demand-supply diagram, the proposition that "at the beginning of the year doctors would target their income and reach it. . . ."

e) What is your prediction about the future impact of the developments described in the article on the demand for health care, supply of doctors, and training at the universities?

f) In your view, should the American Medical Association insist on doctors charging no less than the fees stipulated by the Association, or should price competition be allowed? What is your opinion on the desirability of advertising by doctors?

CHAPTER 4

Consumer Demand and Product Value

LEARNING OBJECTIVES

After reading this chapter you should be able to explain:

1. The rationality of consumer behaviour.
2. The perceived value of the product and consumer demand.
3. The connection between individual demand and market demand.
4. The determinants of the elasticity of demand.
5. The special features of demand for agricultural products and government policies in agricultural markets.

4-1 INTRODUCTION AND PURPOSE

In Chapters 2 and 3, we focused on the basic market demand-supply framework for microeconomic analysis. In this chapter we analyze demand in more detail and in particular its derivation from individual consumer behaviour.

A further purpose of this chapter is to highlight the connection between market demand for a good or service and consumers' *perceived value* of that good or service. This discussion is important for an understanding of the consequences of such things as monopoly power, pollution and government involvement in the economy. Consequently, we shall rely heavily on this section for our discussions of such topics in later chapters.

In this chapter, by examining the behaviour of a single purchasing unit we take the most micro approach possible toward demand analysis. Then,

in Chapter 5 we shall probe the supply side of the market, also in the most micro fashion possible, by inquiring into the behaviour of a single producing unit — the firm — and investigating how total market supply comes about. Chapters 4 and 5 are thus designed to answer some of the "whys" and "hows" that may have cropped up in your mind during our brief outline sketch of supply and demand in Chapters 2 and 3.

4-2 DETERMINANTS OF INDIVIDUAL DEMAND

We shall now focus on a single consuming unit to see what motivates one to buy or not to buy a certain good or service at various market prices. We may consider either a household or a single individual as the consuming unit.

Rational Consumer Behaviour

If asked why we would not pay $1000 for a particular gold-trimmed, white cotton T-shirt, we would probably answer that the purchase is not worth the money. Knowing what else we could buy with $1000 — and therefore what we would have to sacrifice if we bought the T-shirt — we would probably prefer to spend our money on these other goods and services. Presumably these other things would give us more satisfaction than the T-shirt.

Most people would agree that spending income so as to get the most satisfaction from it is *normal* and *rational* consumer behaviour. Most of us would be hard pressed to identify anyone who does not behave in this fashion. Of course, consumers save some of their income each year. The ultimate purpose of saving, however, is future consumption (spending), either by the saver or by designated heirs. Therefore, we take it for granted that, in general, consumers allocate their income between present and future consumption of goods and services in a way that will *maximize their total satisfaction or happiness*.

Economic theory, in other words, views the consumer as a decision maker who has the objective of maximizing his or her satisfaction (*utility*) and goes about it in a rational manner. The word "rational" in economics has very much the same meaning as in common usage. However, economists have developed a sophisticated and formal way of representing (modelling) the rational consumer. One such approach — the **indifference curve analysis** — is presented in Appendix B to this chapter.

Consumers do not always succeed in maximizing their satisfaction. We all make expenditure mistakes. We often purchase goods and services thinking that we will derive great satisfaction from them, only to discover that the product does not deliver as promised or prematurely breaks down. Sometimes we find out that better products were available in the first place. However, we do our best and *try* to maximize our satisfaction.

Although economists, and perhaps most others, would call such consumer behaviour rational, sensible or normal, there is no moral connotation here. Most people would not go so far as to say that trying to maximize satisfaction — whether with income or with anything else — is good in a moral sense. The idea of good or bad behaviour is

a point of philosophical argument. In any case, we should try not to judge the consumer here. Instead, we might settle for the proposition that the attempt to maximize happiness, whether good or bad, is the usual motivation for consumer behaviour.

Differences in Tastes

Each of us has a unique set of tastes or preferences. With any given amount of income, we might each choose to spend it differently. From time to time, however, we all wonder why others spend their incomes the way they do. The Smiths may never save a penny, choosing instead to exhaust their income on lavish home furnishings and keeping up with the latest styles in cars and clothes. The Jones, on the other hand, always seem to be scrimping and saving every last penny.

Our possible bewilderment at the way our neighbours allocate their income might vanish if we considered differences in tastes. Even though we may not get much pleasure from being dressed in the latest styles, we should at least consider that others might. In fact, others may get considerable satisfaction from such behaviour and therefore may be quite sensible in the way they spend their income. Of course, we may argue that in the future, when their ideas and tastes change, they may wish that they had not spent their money in such a way. But this is a debatable point. In years to come, we may change our preferences and discover we made the most expenditure mistakes.

The idea of consumer rationality is a fundamental assumption of the economic theory of consumer behaviour. Even though most consumers make mistakes in deciding how to spend their income, the important point is that the vast majority of them make conscious and systematic efforts to behave rationally.

4-3 PRICE AND PERCEIVED VALUE

The individual consumer's demand for a particular good or service depends on four main factors: the consumer's tastes (or preferences), the consumer's income, the price of the good in question and the prices of other goods. To see how these elements are connected to demand and perceived product value from the consumer's standpoint, let us return to our example of athletic shoes and focus on a Toronto parent, Ms. Smith, who is deciding whether or not to buy her child a pair of fancy shoes during a particular year.

When Ms. Smith makes the expenditure decision, she is not willing to pay $400 a pair. At $4 a pair, she will probably be quite happy to make a purchase and even buy two or three pairs. However, the price is not likely to be either $400 or $4 a pair. Nevertheless, Ms. Smith knows that there is a maximum price, beyond which she will not purchase athletic shoes. Further, there is a maximum price at which she will buy only one pair per year, another at which she will buy only two pairs per year, and so on. The main influences on these maximum prices will be the strength of her preferences for these particular shoes over other shoes, the size of the family's income and the prices of inferior substitute shoes.

What might determine her preference for athletic shoes at the moment of decision? Possibly it will be pressure from the children and her belief in the quality of the shoes, both of which factors may in turn be influenced by advertising, persuasiveness of the sales clerk or experience with similar shoes.

Anyway, given Ms. Smith's present tastes, income and the prices of substitutes, suppose we ask her how many pairs of athletic shoes she would be willing to buy at various possible market prices. An important point to remember in this example is that, at any particular quoted market price, she must pay this price for each and every pair she buys. Her answers are reported in Table 4-1.

Table 4-1 Demand information concerning Ms. Smith

Q (No. of pairs per year Ms. Smith is willing to buy at the possible market prices)	P (Possible market price per pair)
0	Above $45
1	45
2	40
3	30
4	20

At various possible market prices, a consumer is willing to buy the quantities indicated in the table.

As the table indicates, she says she will not pay more than $45 per pair, and if the price is this high, she will buy only a single pair. However, if the price is $40 per pair (but not a penny more), she will buy two pairs; at $30, three pairs; and at $20, four pairs.

Value to the Consumer

We can represent the demand information of Table 4-1 in the form of a graph. See Figure 4-1. If we look carefully at the information in the figure or table we may calculate the perceived value to this particular consumer of each pair of athletic shoes. We know Ms. Smith would be willing to purchase a single pair of athletic shoes if the price is $45 but not if the price is $45.01 (we are assuming that $45 is definitely the maximum she would pay for the first pair). This information tells us that, given her income, her tastes and the prices of substitutes, she considers the *value* of a first pair of athletic shoes to be $45. Presumably, she knows what $45 will buy in terms of other goods or services. That is, Ms. Smith knows that to spend $45 on these

Fig. 4-1 The connection between perceived value and product demand

The prices an individual consumer is prepared to pay for varying quantities of a product reflect the perceived value of the product to the consumer.

athletic shoes really means sacrificing other purchases whose total value is $45. She will not pay $45.01 for the first pair, therefore, because she feels $45.01 spent on other things would yield more satisfaction (give more happiness) to the family than a pair of athletic shoes could provide.

We now wish to find out the value to Ms. Smith of a second pair of athletic shoes. We know that if the market price of the shoes is $40.01, she will buy the first pair, because it is worth $45 to her (therefore, $40.01 would be a bargain for the first pair). However, because Table 4-1 states the maximum price per pair she would be willing to pay for two pairs is $40, we know that she would only buy one pair at a price of $40.01 per pair. On the other hand, if the market price of the athletic shoes is $40 per pair, Ms. Smith will buy two pairs — as Table 4-1 points out. Therefore, a second pair must be worth at least $40 to Ms. Smith but less than $40.01. Thus (having bought one pair already) a second pair of athletic shoes is worth exactly $40 to her — at least she thinks so. It may turn out that she is overestimating the quality of these shoes and that they will fall apart after only two weeks' use. In such a case she would have mistaken their value and wish she had spent her income differently.

In a similar way, we can see that a third pair of shoes (given that she has already bought two new pairs) is worth $30 to Ms. Smith.

From the above analysis we can calculate the perceived value of each last pair and the cumulative value that this particular consumer places on various quantities purchased of these athletic shoes. We have done this in Table 4-2.[1]

An Individual's Demand Curve

If we compare the two columns of Table 4-1 with the first two of Table 4-2, we see that they are identical. The maximum price (from Table 4-1) a consumer is willing to pay for each successive unit of any good or service also indicates the perceived value (Table 4-2) of that unit to the consumer. Consequently, the height of an individual's demand curve indicates the value that the consumer assigns, mentally, to each successive unit purchased. (See Figure 4-1.)

---

1. We cannot emphasize too strongly here that these figures reflect perceived values to the particular consumer (Ms. Smith), not market values or prices.

Table 4-2 Subjective product value information concerning Ms. Smith

Q (No. of pairs per year)	Perceived value of last pair (measured in terms of dollars' worth of expenditure on other goods the consumer is willing to sacrifice)	Cumulative perceived value to consumer of all pairs bought
1	$45	$ 45
2	40	85
3	30	115
4	20	135

The perceived value to the consumer of the last unit of a product just bought declines as the quantity purchased increases (as the consumer's cumulative consumption grows).

The demand curve of an individual consumer reflects the perceived (subjective) value the consumer places on each successive unit purchased. This value declines as more of the product is purchased.

4-4 INDIVIDUAL AND MARKET DEMAND

Market demand, if related to the price of a particular good or service, represents the total quantity that would be purchased at various possible market prices. Similar to individual demand, market demand information also indicates the value the consumer market as a whole places on various quantities purchased. Both of these interpretations will be very useful in subsequent discussions.

To illustrate how market demand stems from individual demand, let us suppose that there is one other consumer, Mr. Burnett, in the athletic shoe market. The result for any number of consumers proceeds in the same fashion; we have chosen two for arithmetic simplicity.

We suppose the demand data for Mr. Burnett, who possibly has different tastes (a different num-

Table 4-3 Demand information concerning Mr. Burnett

Q (No. of pairs per year)	P ($ per pair)
1	50
2	45
3	40
4	35
5	30
6	20

At various possible market prices, a consumer is willing to buy the quantities indicated in the table. The tastes of this consumer differ from those of the consumer in Table 4-1; hence the price-quantity combinations also differ.

Table 4-4 Derivation of market demand from individual demands

Price (P)	Demand (Q)		
	Smith	Burnett	Market
Above $50	0	0	0
50	0	1	1
45	1	2	3
40	2	3	5
35	2	4	6
30	3	5	8
20	4	5	9

The market demand for a product is the sum of the quantities all consumers in the market demand at each particular price. Table 4-4 illustrates this notion for a market consisting of two consumers only.

ber of children who watch TV advertising) and income from Ms. Smith, are as shown in Table 4-3. Mr. Burnett apparently places a greater value on athletic shoes (in terms of other goods sacrificed) than does Ms. Smith.

To derive market demand data that includes both consumers we can see, for instance, that at a price of $45 per pair Ms. Smith would buy one pair and Mr. Burnett two pairs. The total market demand for athletic shoes at a price of $45 per pair would be three pairs. Total *market demand* at each possible price becomes the sum of the demands of all consumers in the market at these prices. Performing this exercise for Smith and Burnett we obtain the market demand information of Table 4-4. The market demand curve is graphed in Figure 4-2.

As stated above, market demand information relating various prices and quantities that would be purchased at these prices also reflects the value the market places on various volumes of the good in question. For example, the perceived value to the market of the first pair of shoes produced is $50 in alternative sacrificed expenditure. This is shown both by the height of the market demand curve in Figure 4-2 and the data in Table 4-4. Even though

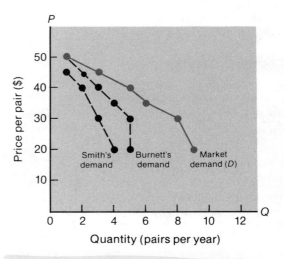

Fig. 4-2 Aggregating from individual to market demand

Graphical representation of data from Table 4-4. The height of each individual demand curve describes the perceived value to the relevant consumer of successive units bought. The height of the market demand curve describes the same for the market as a whole.

the first pair is not worth $50 to Smith, it is to Burnett. Similarly, the third pair produced is worth $45 to the market, while the fifth pair is worth $40 — and so on.[2]

The market demand curve is the horizontal summation of the individual demand curves of all consumers in the market for the particular product.

4-5 CHANGES IN VALUE AND SHIFTS IN DEMAND

If there is a change in the factors that give a consumer an idea of value concerning a particular product there will be a change in the consumer's ideas concerning the value of the product, and hence the consumer's demand. Three basic elements that induce changes in perceived product value are changes in consumer tastes, changes in income and changes in the prices of other goods. We have already encountered these factors in Chapter 3 when studying cause and effect analysis in a supply-demand framework. Here, we explore in greater depth the process of individual consumer reasoning and response to changes in circumstances affecting consumer behaviour. Let us continue our athletic shoes example.

Change in Tastes

For many reasons, consumers exhibit changes in preferences. Should an effective advertising campaign be launched for athletic shoes, our consumer might be induced to feel that the shoes are of greater use (value) than before. Therefore he or she would be willing to sacrifice greater amounts of expenditure on other products for any particular quantity of athletic shoe purchases than before. Ms. Smith might now believe that the value to her of the first pair would be $50 (instead of $45), the second pair $45, the third pair $35 and the fourth pair $30. The new maximum prices she would be willing to pay for various numbers of pairs would also be of these magnitudes. In other words, her

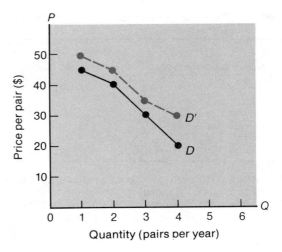

Fig. 4-3 Effect on consumer demand of a change in tastes in athletic shoes

An individual consumer's demand curve shifts to the right (or upward) as a result of a change in tastes favourable to the product.

demand curve would have shifted upward, as shown in Figure 4-3. Because the effect would be the same, it does not matter whether we refer to the shift as either "upward" or "to the right" (although "upward" is more accurate in this instance).

Change in Income

In this case assume the consumer receives a pay raise. Although some of this increase might be saved for future years' consumption, much of it would probably go toward increased current consumption. Our consumer would now have more of most goods and services he or she typically purchases. A given dollar expenditure on other goods — which would not be made if the money was spent on a pair of athletic shoes — would represent a smaller (real) sacrifice than before because the family would have more of these other goods. Consequently, Ms. Smith might be willing to spend as much as $50.00 for the first pair, $45 for a second pair and so on (the exact figures depending on how much of an increase in income the family actually experienced). As in the previous case, the

---

2. Actually, from Table 4-4, we see that both the second and third pairs are worth $45 to the market. The reason the graph does not depict this price quite accurately is that we have sketched a line through only four observed points. In markets with many consumers, there would be many observed points and this inaccuracy would not be present.

perceived value of athletic shoes to the consumer (in terms of sacrificed expenditure on other goods) would have increased, thereby increasing her demand for the product. In this instance, though, this increase was not a direct consequence of her suddenly thinking the product possessed more intrinsic usefulness or value. Rather, it was an indirect result of her placing less value on her purchases of other goods and services (because she now would have more of them).[3]

Change in Prices of Other Goods

Suppose that instead of tastes or income, the prices of competing purchases change. In particular, suppose that plain running shoes suddenly go "on special" and that their prices are reduced from $22.50 to $15 per pair. Ms. Smith now knows that each dollar spent on athletic shoes could instead have been used to buy more of a reasonably close substitute product than it would have before. For example, $45 spent on a pair of athletic shoes could have bought two pairs of plain running shoes originally, but with plain running shoes on sale, $45 could now buy three pairs. A given expenditure on athletic shoes, therefore, represents a greater sacrifice — in terms of other goods given up — when the price of other goods falls.[4] In fact, these other goods may be any other goods that the consumer usually buys, though the extra sacrifice is perhaps more readily identifiable if the goods are close substitutes for the product in question.

In the case of a price reduction for a substitute product, then, Ms. Smith would tend to reduce the maximum price she would be willing to pay for any quantity of athletic shoes. Her demand curve would thus shift downward (or to the left) as shown in Figure 4-4.[5]

Change in Population

Market demand is simply the sum total of individual demands. When individual valuation and demands are influenced, so is market demand.

---

3. Though this result is the one normally expected following an increase in income, there are exceptional cases. If an increase in income leads to a smaller quantity demanded such goods are referred to as *inferior goods* (see Appendix 4A-2 for a more detailed description).
4. Again here we really mean goods and services.
5. In Figure 4-4 we have shifted the demand curve downward by an arbitrary amount for illustrative purposes.

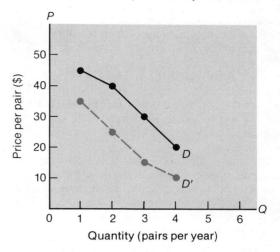

Fig. 4-4 Effect on demand of a reduction in price of a substitute

An individual consumer's demand curve shifts to the left (or downward) as a result of a reduction in price of a product which is a substitute.

Market valuation and demand are affected by taste, income, and the prices of other goods because individuals' valuations and demands are. However, there is another factor affecting market demand, and that is market population. This effect is quite straightforward. The greater the number of people in a market area, the greater will be the market quantity demanded at any given market price.

The most important factors which cause demand curves of individual consumers to shift are changes in tastes, changes in income and changes in prices of other goods. Furthermore, the market demand curve may shift as a result of changes in population.

4-6 ELASTICITY: SENSITIVITY OF DEMAND

In some instances, it is important to understand just how sensitive market demand is to such demand shocks as a change in income, a change in the price of other goods, or a change in the price of the product itself. Most economists prefer the term

elasticity to sensitivity, though the latter word may be more meaningful to noneconomists. If the quantity demanded of a particular good or service was very sensitive to changes in its price, we would say that its **price elasticity** is high. If the quantity demanded was not sensitive to changes in income, we would say the product's **income elasticity** is low — and so on. In what follows we can easily substitute the word "sensitivity" wherever "elasticity" is used.

To make demand sensitivity comparisons, analysts often compute numerical measures of elasticity. For example, the **coefficient of own price elasticity of demand** (a measure of how sensitive quantity demanded is to changes in the product's own price) is computed as follows:

$$e = \frac{\% \text{ change in quantity demanded}}{\% \text{ change in price}} \quad (4\text{-}1)$$

If $e = 2$ for example, it means that if the price rises or falls by one percent from its present level the quantity demanded will fall or rise by two percent.[6] It is perhaps easier in many instances to say this in words rather than use the shorthand symbol e.

There are three demand curves in Figure 4-5. Curve D_1 shows no sensitivity with respect to price (its coefficient of own price elasticity is zero). Curve D_2 shows an infinite amount of sensitivity with respect to price (its coefficient of own price elasticity is infinity). Finally, curve D_3 shows some sensitivity with respect to price, but not as much as curve D_2 (D_3's own price elasticity is, therefore, between zero and infinity).

Determinants of Demand Elasticity

The sensitivity of demand to changes in demand determinants depends upon a number of factors including: the urgency of our need or desire for the product's features or attributes; the availability and price of substitute products; the significance of expenditures normally made for the product in relation to the consumer's total budget; and the time over which the demand response is measured. Let us briefly consider each of these determinants in turn.

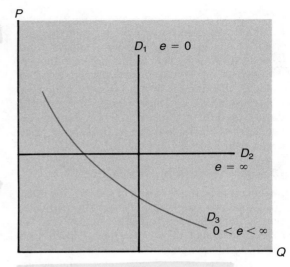

Fig. 4-5 Possible degrees of demand sensitivity with respect to price

A vertical demand curve is described as perfectly inelastic, a horizontal demand curve as perfectly (infinitely) elastic. All other demand curves have price elasticity between zero and infinity.

(i) Urgency of Need

There is no substitute for food nutrients. Regardless of how high the price of food is, there are minimum quantities that we have to buy merely to sustain a normal healthy life. Food price increases induce reductions in food consumption, but such cutbacks are limited by the urgency of product need. On the downside, food price reductions stimulate food purchases but there are natural limits to how much food we can or would wish to eat. The price elasticity of demand for food is thus rather low, as it is for other goods and services which people regard as necessities. The same reasoning process may be used to explain why we would expect the income elasticity of demand for food and other necessity items to be low.

Once basic existence needs are met, consumers then seek out those goods and services which they perceive as adding enjoyment to their lives. These goods may be called luxury items. Since the urgency of need for luxuries is somewhat less when compared with necessity goods, we expect the elasticity of demand for luxuries with respect to

---

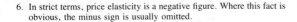

6. In strict terms, price elasticity is a negative figure. Where this fact is obvious, the minus sign is usually omitted.

both price and income to be greater than that for necessity goods.

(ii) Substitutes: Availability and Price

Two or more goods or services which fulfill similar needs are called **substitutes**. If a particular good has many substitutes at competing prices, demand for the particular good will be more price sensitive than if no substitutes are present. For instance, there is no substitute for food, and so the elasticity of demand for food is low. Within the food category, however, there are many substitutes. Margarine is a substitute for butter, poultry is a substitute for meat and a home-cooked meal is a substitute for a restaurant meal. The elasticities of demand for butter, meat and restaurant meals are therefore considerably greater than the elasticity of demand for food.

(iii) Significance of Expenditure

Expenditures for matches or toothbrushes occupy such a small proportion of the consumer's budget that the consumer is quite insensitive to price changes in these items. To contemplate changing dental habits in the face of even a significant price or income change would just not be worth the effort. As another example, since the cost of auto lightbulbs is such a small part of the purchase price of a new car, even a doubling in the price of such lightbulbs would have no material impact on auto demand or therefore on the demand for auto lightbulbs.

(iv) Elapsed time

If the price of gasoline doubles overnight, our demand for gasoline will react — but will do so differently depending on the time period under study. For example, during the very next week we probably would cut back very little on our usage of gasoline. We are used to driving to work each day, and old habits are hard to break. However, as we became more fully aware of the new costs of driving the automobile, over several months we might begin to react. We would think more about trading the old clunker in for a smaller or more efficient car. Perhaps we would try to form a car pool. Even the bus might not look so bad. Our quantity response to the price change of gasoline would, therefore, probably be somewhat greater over a longer period of time.

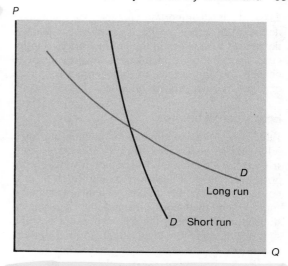

Fig. 4-6 Effect of time on demand sensitivity to price changes

When consumers have time to adjust to a price change, the price elasticity of demand increases.

It takes time for us to evaluate costs of alternatives and to change our habits. Further, it is generally more costly to change our expenditure patterns rapidly. For example, if we had only recently bought a new, large car, we might lose a great deal of money if we immediately traded it in for a compact to reduce gas consumption. In fact, we might estimate that the loss on the trade-in far outweighs the cost of two or three years of extra gasoline use with the large car. Therefore, we might rationally choose to continue to drive the large car for several more years, and thereby lower our quantity of gasoline demanded per week only by driving less. But after several years had gone by, if we finally got rid of the large car and bought the compact, the quantity of gasoline used per week would drop by a greater amount.

Because the costs of changing our expenditure patterns are higher the faster we change them, the demand for most goods and services tends to be more elastic with respect to changes in price (or changes in any other variable for that matter) the longer the time period considered relevant for analysis. That fact is illustrated in Figure 4-6.

Elasticity is an important characteristic of market demand. It refers to the sensitivity of quantity demanded to changes in the product price or to income changes or to changes in advertising or to changes in the prices of other products or to changes in other related variables.

Empirical Estimates

Table 4-5 contains estimates of income and own price elasticities derived from a data sample consisting of 13 countries. The negative signs on the price elasticities are shown explicitly. It is important in empirical studies to indicate negative signs where they apply, because as a result of statistical peculiarities the possibility of a positive sign occurs more frequently than we might otherwise expect.

Though the author regards these estimates as being subject to possibly sizeable statistical error, at least their relative magnitudes seem to fit with our prior expectations. For example, we would expect that a necessary item such as food would be income insensitive, and that durables, many of which represent luxury expenditure, would be income sensitive. For the same reasons, the relative magnitude of the price elasticity coefficients also appears to make sense.

A set of elasticity estimates related to demand for energy in Canada is reported in Table 4-6. There can be variation in the measurement of elasticities because different estimation methods can be used. Elasticities can also change over time or over price or income ranges, as shown in Appendix 4A at the end of this chapter. For these reasons, ranges of elasticities, rather than point estimates, are often given.

Table 4-5 Elasticity estimates

Consumption item	Income elasticity	Price elasticity
Food	0.5	−0.4
Clothing	0.9	−0.5
Shelter	1.7	−0.6
Durables	1.7	−1.1
Miscellaneous	1.1	−0.9

Source: H.S. Houthakker, "New Evidence on Demand Elasticities," *Econometrica* Vol. 33, No. 2 (April, 1965), pp. 277–88. Reprinted by permission of the University of Chicago Press. The author used a constant elasticity demand equation for estimation purposes.

Both income and price elasticities of demand are the lowest for food (a necessity). Durable goods (some of which may be classified as luxuries) have much higher income and price elasticities of demand.

Table 4-6 Estimates of Long-Term Price and Income Elasticities of Energy Demand in Canada

	Elasticities	
	Price	*Income**
Total energy	−0.30 to −0.59	0.96
Sectors		
Residential	−0.32 to −0.60	0.15 to 0.47
Commercial	−0.40 to −1.06	1.16
Industrial	−0.21 to −1.00	0.93
Transportation		
Road (gasoline)	−0.70	1.10
Rail	−0.10	0.30
Marine	−0.20	0.90
Air	−0.20	3.70
Energy sources		
Oil products	−0.68	0.91
Electricity	−0.57	0.80 to 1.70
Natural gas	−0.33	...

* Income refers more generally to selected indicators of economic activity for example, real domestic product, real industrial output (industry), or real disposable income (residential sector).

Source: Economic Council of Canada, *Connections: an energy strategy for the future* (Ottawa, 1985), p. 106. Reproduced with permission of the Minister of Supply and Services Canada.

In the long run, given time to adjust, consumers respond to rising energy prices. The responsiveness is especially high in the commercial sector and in road transportation. Income elasticity of demand for energy is the lowest for residential heating (a necessity) and the highest for air transportation (a luxury).

All of the elasticities in Table 4-6 are long run; that is, the various energy users had time to adjust their consumption patterns to the price or income change. Note, for example, the price elasticity of demand for energy for use in road transportation: the estimate suggests that for every one-percent rise in gasoline prices, the consumption of gasoline was reduced by 0.70 percent. The income elasticities reported in the second column of the table relate energy demand to selected indicators of economic activity. Residential demand, for example, is relatively inelastic with respect to income (since heat and light are necessities for all households). The income elasticity of demand for energy in air transport, on the other hand, is high, since air travel is greatly influenced by income levels. A more rigorous discussion of the elasticity concept and the associated algebraic formulae can be found in Appendix 4A at the end of this chapter. The information conveyed by the value of demand elasticity is obviously of great importance to marketing executives, international trade negotiators and those responsible for decisions on excise taxes, to name just a few. Some of these applications will be encountered in the chapters which follow.

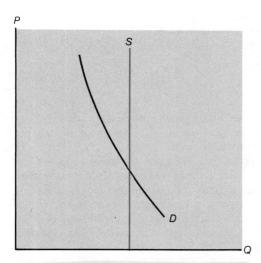

Fig. 4-7 Short-run inelastic supply and demand for agricultural products

Market price has no influence on quantity supplied in the short run, when decisions on planting have already been made.

4-7 DEMAND AND SUPPLY IN AGRICULTURAL MARKETS

In the short run — say, one production cycle (from planting till harvest time, or from the time the new calves are born until they go to market) — supply in agricultural markets is quite price insensitive (price inelastic). That is, once the decision, for example, to plant a particular acreage of wheat has been made, the market price can have little or no influence on the amount of wheat that will be produced this cycle. Diagrammatically, the short-run supply curve for most agricultural products would, therefore, be almost vertical, as shown in Figure 4-7.

Demand

Many agricultural products, such as milk, meat and wheat, are generally regarded as basic necessities of life. There are also few substitutes. For this reason, short-run demand for agricultural products is also highly price insensitive. Such a demand curve has also been represented in Figure 4-7.

Shocks to Agricultural Markets

When demand and supply are both relatively price insensitive, any shock, whether demand or supply originated, has a great effect on price. For example, suppose that Figure 4-8a represents the egg market in Canada during a particular year. With market supply relatively insensitive in the short run, if there was a sudden drop in the demand for eggs this would have a considerable downward effect on egg prices. (For comparison purposes, we have also depicted the smaller price movements that would have occurred if supply had been price sensitive.)

Now let us examine effects on the egg market of a supply shock. Suppose, for example, that on the basis of the low market prices for eggs referred to directly above, six months a year later farmers cut back on the number of egg-laying hens. Such an occurrence is depicted in Figure 4-8b. With the quantity demanded relatively insensitive to price, as the diagram shows, the price of eggs would rise significantly. (Once more we have also shown the lesser effects that would have occurred if demand had been more price sensitive.)

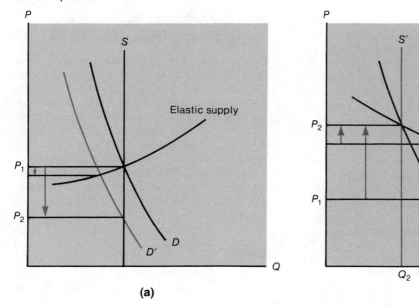

Fig. 4-8 Inelastic agricultural demand and supply in the face of market shocks

(a) A demand shock has a large impact on price when supply is inelastic (the supply curve is vertical), but a small impact when supply is elastic (supply curve is positively sloped).

(b) A supply shock has a large impact on price when demand is inelastic (demand curve is relatively steep), but a small impact when demand is elastic (demand curve is relatively flat).

Incomes and Free Market Price

We have seen above that the price insensitivity of both supply and demand conditions in agricultural markets mean that normal size shocks from both the supply and demand sides of the market can cause large effects in the prices of agricultural products. As it turns out, this fluctuation causes similarly large fluctuations in annual net farm incomes (net farm income equals farm revenue less expenses). Perhaps this aspect can be seen most clearly with respect to grain farming.

Consider, for example, the case in which the farmers have already planted their wheat acreage. Their costs for the season are pretty well fixed. They have already incurred the planting costs, and

when the wheat grows, harvesting costs too are fixed, regardless of the price farmers ultimately get for their wheat.

Suppose they get a normal wheat crop and expect normal demand conditions. In this case, they may get roughly the income that they anticipated, which may be quite adequate (or even better than adequate). On the other hand, suppose demand conditions during the year suddenly become depressed. This turn of events has no effect on the amount of crop planted, because it happens after the planting season. The costs of planting have therefore already been incurred, and harvesting costs are determined by the volume of the crop. Therefore, total costs would be unaffected. However, because of depressed demand, the price obtained for the crop will be considerably reduced. With an unchanged volume and a significantly reduced price received for each bushel sold, revenue will have declined significantly. Significantly lower revenue and unchanged costs imply a greatly reduced net farm income.

Similarly, increased demand will increase the price received for crops without affecting the volume sold. Revenue will increase sharply with no effect on costs. Consequently, an increased demand shock sharply increases farm prices and farm incomes.

Effect of Supply Shocks

The effect of supply shocks on farm incomes seems paradoxical at first glance. For example, it turns out that bumper crops may actually lower farm incomes on average, whereas poor crops may raise them. The reason for this seeming oddity lies in the insensitivity of demand for agricultural products with respect to market prices.

For example, suppose again that, with demand and supply conditions as depicted by D and S' in Figure 4-8b, normal farm incomes could be attained. Next, suppose that the weather (or some other relevant production condition) is better than originally expected so that a larger than expected crop (or volume of any particular farm commodity) is harvested. The volume put on the market then becomes Q_1 rather than Q_2. Because agricultural demand does not have a great deal of sensitivity toward price changes, the price drop will have to be significant in order to have the bumper crop sold (in this case price falls from P_2 to P_1).

In fact, it turns out that to stimulate a given percentage increase in the quantity bought (demanded) market prices will have to be reduced by an even greater percentage. (Remember the discussion of inelastic demand). For example, if a bumper crop produces an increase of 10% harvested, market prices will fall by more than 10%, and farmers' revenue receipts will fall.[7] Not only will farmers receive a lower than expected revenue, but also, to the extent that they have to harvest and market a larger crop, there will be an increase in

actual costs. Therefore, as a result of the good crop, net farm incomes on average may actually fall.

Similarly, in a year of poor harvests, crop prices may be forced upward by a greater percentage than the fall in volume (again as a result of the inelasticity of demand) and farm revenues will increase. With the increase in farm revenues and a reduction in harvesting and marketing expenses for the lower volume produced, net farm incomes will increase.

We must emphasize that though this pattern may occur on average it does not happen every time and to each farmer. For example, in a year when average Canadian farm harvests are poor, for some farmers in regions where the weather (or some other production condition) was particularly severe, harvests may be almost zero. Clearly, then, these unfortunate producers will not experience an increase in income even though, on average, the Canadian farmer may. In another situation, if the entire Canadian crop was destroyed by some blight, farm revenue would fall to zero and net farm incomes would be negative.

Generally speaking, though, high farm prices mean high farm incomes and low farm prices mean low farm incomes.

Long-Run Developments

We limited our discussion above to short-run effects of demand and supply shocks in agriculture. It is useful now to extend this analysis to the long run. One key feature in a long-run examination of an industry is whether it is growing or declining: that is, whether there is new investment in real capital; or whether the activity is occupying a greater share of overall economic activity; or whether more people are being employed in the industry. As will be discussed in Chapter 8, an industry will grow by at least one of the foregoing measures if ultimate consumers of the industry value the products sufficiently. That means they are willing to pay high enough prices to cover all nonfinancial expenses of production as well as the cost of capital funds invested in the industry (which includes giving the owners in the industry a rate of return equivalent to what they could earn elsewhere on their invested funds by taking comparable risks). If, at a given stage in an industry's

---

7. For example, if a 10% rise in output causes a 15% fall in prices, total revenue ($P \times Q$) would fall by about 5%.

development, the market price for the product is such that it will not give the owners a satisfactory rate of return, the consumers are in effect saying that they prefer to see owners' funds reinvested elsewhere and that the industry should decline. If, on the other hand, the price is such that the owners are receiving more than the rate of return they could get elsewhere, consumers are in essence providing information to present and potential producers that they are willing to provide an adequate rate of return on new investment for an expansion of the industry.

In agriculture, farm incomes have been a concern for a number of years. First, farm labour incomes have not kept pace with those of other industries. Second, there has been a rapid improvement in farm technology and farm equipment, which has increased the productivity of machinery and equipment more than that of labour. Thus, the most profitable development of agriculture has taken place by the use of more machinery and less labour. Also, the use of additional heavy equipment has generally meant that economies of scale could be reached in agriculture. Therefore, the net result has been consolidation and selling out by many farmers to large corporate farm concerns, which are generally the most efficient and profitable operators in the industry. Family farms that attempt to operate (even with new equipment) on smaller acreage and with the use of more labour incomes (and hence rates of return on invested funds) have deteriorated over the years as a result of higher cost operations.

Long-Run Demand Growth

We have already mentioned that the demand for agricultural products is relatively price insensitive. Further, as incomes increase, the demand for manufactured goods and services in general takes precedence over the demand for agricultural products. As incomes grow, we may eat more and feed our families better, but only up to a point. By and large, the volume of food bought increases little as incomes increase. In other words, the demand for agricultural products is relatively income-insensitive (see again Section 4-6). The prime reason for the growth in agricultural demand is population. If the population grows by 1% or 2% per year, so approximately will the demand for agricultural products.

The Family Farm Problem

The fact that machines have become more efficient than labour for a great many farming operations implies that the demand for farm labour has fallen over the years. The most efficient farms will expand their production facilities just up to the point where any additional long-run production would earn less than the cost of capital (and thereby provide the owners with a less-than-normal return on invested funds). However, if agricultural prices are on average such that only the most efficient farms can earn the cost of capital, this necessarily means that earnings of the less efficient family farm will be insufficient to pay all farm expenses and cover the cost of capital.

In summary, then, under a free market system farmers have in the short run tended to suffer from unstable incomes. In the long run — primarily as a result of large-scale technological advancement along a productivity front, combined with relatively slower demand growth — the small, inefficient family farm has suffered from net income deterioration.

We now discuss a number of possible solutions and policies that have been put into practice by Canadian governments.

Attempts to Alleviate Problems

(i) No Action Policy

One possible policy of the government would be to take no action. That is, the government would undertake no subsidy plans or marketing arrangements. The consequence would be that smaller, inefficient farms, earning less than a normal return on their investment, would exit from the industry. The industry would then be composed of a far fewer number of more efficient producers who, perhaps because of their diversified interests, would also be capable of handling the risks involved in agricultural price fluctuations.

At present, this policy does not appear politically feasible. In fact, it is the avowed policy of the Canadian government to maintain the existence of the small family farm. Therefore, let us examine several other methods the government has used in dealing with the farm problem.

One approach has been for the government to settle on a minimum support price, which is designed to give farmers what is considered to be a reasonable income. Within the framework of support pricing, there are two major approaches: deficiency payments from the government to farmers or government purchases of surplus produce.

(ii) Deficiency Payment Plans

Under a **deficiency payment plan**, farmers sell whatever they produce at the free market price. The government then pays the farmers a subsidy for each unit sold sufficient to bring up their per unit revenue to the support price. For example, suppose, as illustrated in Figure 4-9, the support price is $2.20 per unit, at which the farmers produce 150 million units of output per year. Given market demand conditions, the market price would

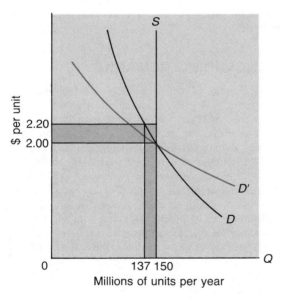

Fig. 4-9 Possible subsidy arrangements in agriculture

Under a deficiency payment plan, the government guarantees a price of $2.20 per unit. If the market price ends up being $2.00 per unit, the government pays to the farmers a subsidy equal to the horizontal shaded area. Under a purchase-price support program, the government sets the selling price at $2.20 per unit and commits itself to purchase the difference between quantity supplied and quantity demanded at that price. The cost to the government of operating this plan is equal to the vertical shaded area.

be only $2 per unit. This means that the government would provide a subsidy of $0.20 per unit, or $30 million per year, as represented by the horizontal shaded area.

A deficiency payment plan comprises part of the operations of the *Canadian Wheat Board*, a federal government agency established in 1935 as a vehicle for *orderly marketing*. The Canadian Wheat Board presently acts as the sole purchaser and seller of feed grains (wheat, oats and barley) for export.

Each year, the Wheat Board establishes a guaranteed floor price for grain. This floor price is also known as the *initial price* that farmers receive upon delivery of their grain to Wheat Board representatives at the local elevators. The Board then transports the grain to export markets. If the average price received for the grain on world markets, less the necessary marketing costs, exceeds the initial price, there is a *final payment* to producers at the end of the selling season. If the world price, less marketing costs, turns out to be less than the initial price, the deficit is borne by the federal government.

When delivering to local elevators, the farmers may choose to sell their grain to the elevators (rather than to the Wheat Board) for the Canadian market. In this instance, the farmers get a single payment upon their delivery, but this payment would, of course, be higher than the Wheat Board's initial price. Otherwise the grain would be sold to the Board instead.

(iii) Purchase-Price Support Programs

An alternative type of price-support program is one where the government tells farmers to sell their produce at a price higher than the free market price and then agrees to purchase any market surplus that results. For example, if demand and supply are as depicted in Figure 4-9 and the government-supported price is again $2.20, the farmers will sell all they can on the open market at this price, leaving unsold a surplus of 13 million units. The government then purchases this surplus at $2.20 per unit. In this case, the cost of the subsidy arrangement is $28.6 million (as represented by the vertical shaded area) plus storage costs, as compared with $30 million under the deficiency payments plan.

It would not always be the case, however, that

this latter type of arrangement would be the cheaper method of subsidy. We can see from the figure that the size of this method of subsidy relative to the deficiency payments method tends to be greater the more price sensitive is the demand for agricultural products (for example, examine the required subsidy in this case as though demand in Figure 4-9 is D'). Further, in this latter case the government also has to worry about storing and disposing of the produce it is forced to purchase. Also, in plan (2), consumers of the agricultural product are better off because they pay lower prices.

Price-support programs have been offered by the *Agricultural Products Board* and the *Agricultural Stabilization Board*. For example, the Agricultural Stabilization Board is empowered to use price support programs for slaughter cattle, hogs, sheep, corn and soybeans, among other commodities. In 1966, the *Canadian Dairy Commission* was established with powers to stabilize the market and maintain reasonable levels of dairy farm incomes by offering to purchase and dispose of major dairy products. In addition, the Commission may pay subsidies to producers of industrial milk and cream to keep market prices at reasonable levels for consumers.

(iv) Loan and Insurance Programs

Other government agricultural subsidy arrangements include low interest loans and subsidized insurance schemes under the *Western Grain Stabilization Act* (WGSA) and *The Crop Insurance Act* (CIA). The latter two plans are voluntary methods whereby farmers may purchase insurance under the WGSA against unexpected large drops in farm income (cash flow) or under the CIA against crop loss due to natural disasters, including summer drought, hail or wet weather at harvest time.

(v) Government-Sponsored Supply Limits

We have seen above that the price–insensitive nature of the demand for agricultural products ensures that greater farm revenue per year can be had with reduced industry supply. Further, annual costs will be lower because less work will be involved in production and marketing. Therefore, net farm incomes would be increased. This fact has been responsible for the proliferation of producer marketing boards in Canada operating under government auspices. Marketing boards are discussed in Chapter 7.

The Government of Canada has historically intervened in the market for many agricultural products in order to stabilize prices and farm incomes. The policies implemented over the years have included deficiency payment plans, government purchases of farm products and various loan guarantee schemes.

CONCLUDING REMARKS

Market demand when related to price may be thought of as showing either the quantities that would be bought at various market prices or, often more usefully, the maximum price consumers are willing to pay for various quantities. To analyze market demand in detail we must look to the individual consumer and discover what determines the maximum price a person will pay for any good or service. Major determinants are taste, income and the prices of other goods that compete for the consumer's dollar. Conceptually, market demand is the aggregate of individual demands. Hence population, though not an influence on individual demand, is certainly an important determinant of demand at the market level.

KEY TERMS AND CONCEPTS

indifference curve analysis
elasticity
price elasticity
income elasticity
coefficient of own
   price elasticity of demand

substitutes
deficiency payment plan
purchase-price support
   programs

PROBLEMS

Problem 1

a) What are four important factors that may affect a consumer's demand for any good or service?

b) Explain briefly how changes in each of the four demand factors could cause the market volume sold to be reduced.

c) Which of the four factors is the most difficult to directly observe, measure and predict?

d) Which demand factor does advertising affect? Since advertising costs money, how do businesses expect to make it a profitable exercise? Is heavier advertising always expected to be profitable? Explain.

Problem 2

a) What does an individual's demand curve for a particular good or service show?

b) Why might someone else have a different demand curve for the same good or service?

c) Conceptually, what is the relation between market demand for a good or service and individual consumer demand?

Problem 3

Suppose the following are two individuals' demand curves for a particular good or service.

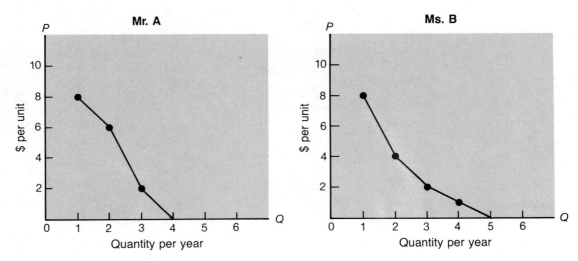

a)   Roughly what value does Mr. A place on the third unit bought per year? Ms. B?

b)   How many units per year would Mr. A buy if the price was $6 per unit? Mr. B?

c)   Sketch the demand curve for Mr. A and Ms. B combined.

d)   Sketch the market demand curve for a market that consists of 100 consumers who, on average, are like Mr. A.

e)   If Mr. A suddenly won a large amount of money in a lottery, what possible impact would this have on Mr. A's demand curve, and why? What impact would Mr. A's good fortune have on the market price?

f)   What would be the likely impact of a heavy advertising campaign on consumer demand? Depict the effect by sketching a diagram. What would happen if consumers reacted adversely to the *hard sell* approach of the campaign?

g)   Here's one to argue over. If the advertising campaign of the previous question increased demand, did it increase the true value of the product?

Problem 4

a)   Briefly, what are some of the important factors that determine just how sensitive market demand is with respect to changes in market price?

b)   Why might we expect the price elasticity of demand for nails to be less than the price elasticity of demand for housing?

c)   Why would the price elasticity of demand for beef be greater than the price elasticity of demand for food?

d)   Which would be the more price elastic and why: the demand for Toyotas or the demand for Mercedes?

e)   Explain why in the long run the demand for sugar may be more elastic with respect to price than in the short run.

Problem 5

a) Using Ms. Smith's demand data (Table 4-1 in the text), determine the numerical elasticity of demand with respect to price changes for a price drop (i) from $45 to $40 per pair, and (ii) from $40 to $30 per pair.

b) How could the price of movie tickets affect an individual's valuation of pay TV (and hence the demand for pay TV)?

c) Rank market demand as quite elastic or quite inelastic with respect to price for the following four items (two items as quite elastic and two as quite inelastic): taxi service, food, movie tickets, dental services.

d) Rank market demand as quite elastic or quite inelastic with respect to income for the preceding four items (again rank two items each way).

Problem 6

Consumer surplus is an economic term that refers to the excess of total benefits — from the consumption of a good — above the total monetary outlay (cost to the consumer) involved in its purchase.

a) If the market price in Problem 3 was $2 per unit, what would be Mr. A's consumer surplus? That of Ms. B?

b) With reference to Table 4-2, if the market price of athletic shoes was $12 per pair, what would be Ms. Smith's annual consumer surplus from the number of pairs she would buy?

c) With reference to Problem 3d, what would be the market's annual consumer surplus if the market price was $2 per unit?

d) With reference to Problem 3g, does advertising increase consumer welfare (happiness) by increasing consumer surplus?

CASES

Case 4-1

An air conditioner is in a class of products known as durable goods — durable because they provide services to the user for many years. (Other examples are cars, stereos, boats and houses). Nondurable goods, on the other hand, are used up much faster, say within a year, or less. (Examples are socks, pencils, hockey sticks and ice cream).

Another characteristic of durable goods is that they are usually expensive and may require that consumers borrow for their purchases.

The Financial Post

Air conditioners

Sales thermostat set at 'warm'

By BRIAN COUCH

If weather co-operates

In 1975, CAMA figures indicate central Canada was the prime market, Ontario accounting for 59% of the units sold and Quebec 25%.

Obviously, the weather determines the strength of air conditioner sales in any given year, but disposable income and a stable economy are also important influences. Purchases of luxury comfort products, such as air conditioners and dishwashers, have not yet reached the "necessity" stage in the minds of most consumers. While householders consider washers and dryers as being an integral part of a house, the comfort appliances are still regarded as "nice things to have, but we can get along without them until the future looks a little more secure and/or we have the extra money to spend on them."

What the industry hopes for is about seven consecutive hot days in May. The minimum consecutive number of days that are needed to plant the idea of home air conditioning in the minds of consumers is four. Any less and the heat wave is forgotten quickly as a minor inconvenience.

Obviously, seasonal or impulse buying does play a part in sales, but it is immediately reflected only in the number of room units leaving a dealership. In demand for central air conditioning for houses, a hot summer one year will tend to help sales the following spring: one summer of sweating it out leads to an insurance policy for cooling it next summer.

To be able to appreciate the benefits of air conditioning, a room temperature 12 degrees–15 degrees Fahrenheit below the outdoor temperature is the generally accepted norm. The actual temperature is not the key factor, but rather the difference between the outside and the inside.

Sam Cryer, general manager of the Heating, Refrigeration & Air Conditioning Institute (HRA) outlines some factors involved in the growth of the consumer market this way:

"The number of houses where both partners are working is increasing all the time. These people are likely purchasers of an air conditioner, since just about all their waking activity is usually done in an air conditioned environment. Their respective offices are probably air conditioned . . . they shop in air conditioned surroundings . . . their entertainment takes place in air conditioned space . . . and it's quite possible their car is air conditioned. Now are these people going to go home to a hot house or apartment? Not very likely.

"With older houses, the cost is prohibitive for installing a central system, so what you find with this sector of the market is an add-on type of growth. First, there will be a window unit for the bedroom, then maybe one for the living room, and so on throughout the house. The air flow pattern and the ducts are wrong for a central system . . . they would have to be totally redesigned, which means a lot of money.

"Another type of growth takes place in the new house market, where you may find the owner buying a room unit first. But then when the money becomes available to air condition the whole house, it is a less expensive proposition to trade in the room unit on a central system than to opt for two or three more small units. With people who are renting their homes or apartments, the sales are strictly for add-on units . . . they have to be able to take the appliance with them."

For consumers considering purchasing an air conditioner for the first time, a few tips on the sensible approach bear mentioning: deal with a reputable firm, with a known product, and pay close attention to the noise level of the unit.

As governments continue to set more rigid standards for noise emission, the location of the machine becomes more critical. A refrigeration contractor should be able to specify the correct placement to meet noise by-law requirements. It may mean a slightly higher cost for tubing, but at least you won't be told to turn it off during a heat wave.

There was one benefit to come out of the soft 1975 market. The recession allowed materials supplies to be built up, so shortages that existed during 1974 have been pretty well eliminated.

Industry spokesmen say they are finding that consumers are much more interested in knowing about the equipment than they used to be. In fact, Peter Dittmar, manager of Amana (Ontario) Sales' heating and cooling division, says market surveys indicate householders are buying good quality, luxury items for their houses since many people now feel that changing houses in a year or two is out of the question, because of escalating real estate prices.

a) Necessity and nonnecessity goods are often classified by elasticity of demand measures. For example, goods with low price elasticities of demand are classified as necessity goods. Explain the logic of this distinction.

b) Does the Canadian Appliance Manufacturers' Association (CAMA) feel that the demand for air conditioners is quite price sensitive? Explain.

c) Four major demand influences mentioned in the chapter (other than the price of the product itself) were taste, income, population and the price of other goods and services. Which two factors are primarily discussed in this article?

d) Through which factor would the hot weather and air-conditioned places of work operate and how are they expected to affect the perceived value of home air conditioners? Explain what influence you might expect air conditioned offices to have on the price and volume of air conditioners sold. Show this influence on a demand and supply diagram.

e) Current income affects consumer demand for most goods and services. One might also judge that consumer expectations of future income play a part. For example, all else being equal, would A or B be more likely to buy a central air-conditioning system if their yearly income patterns were as indicated below? Explain.

Income pattern	Current income (year 0)	Expected future income (year 1)	(year 2)	(year 3)	(year 4) ...
A	$15 000	$15 000	$15 000	$15 000	$15 000 ...
B	$20 000	0	$20 000	0	$20 000 ...

Case 4-2

The Globe and Mail, Toronto

Return of vanishing foreign students sought

By BEVERLY BOWEN

The sudden drop in enrolment of foreign students is forcing Canadian universities to look for ways to lure them back to their campuses.

A report by the Canadian Bureau for International Education, to be released later this month, reveals that between 1983 and 1985, universities experienced an 18 per cent drop in enrolment of foreign students who pay higher tuition fees.

This sharp decline represents a loss of about $9-million in tuition revenues at the universities during the two-year period, according to CBIE figures.

Because of the decrease in grants from the federal and provincial governments, universities have come to depend on tuition fees for their survival.

Some universities started setting high tuition fees for foreign students with the aim of ensuring their education will not be a drain on Canadian taxpayers and protecting places for Canadian students.

James Fox, policy director for the CBIE which represents 90 post-secondary institutions, said fees from a foreign student population of 30,000 provides about $100-million of revenue for the universities.

"Now we see the pendulum swinging to the other side," said Mr. Fox. "These students are not only a financial benefit to us, they are a cultural enrichment. We certainly are seeing some universities becoming proactive in attracting students."

One example is a recent University of Toronto task force that has recommended that "the university, as a policy, support active recruitment of highly qualified foreign students for admission" to the university.

The task force considered the differential fees for these students a discriminatory policy and called for more aid from governments so the fees could be reduced. About 7 per cent of all foreign students are enrolled at the University of Toronto.

According to the CBIE study, in 1985 foreign student enrolment declined to 29,115 from 32,610 in 1983. If present trends continue, enrolment is expected to reach about 26,000 this year compared with 36,906 in 1982.

Only Manitoba and Saskatchewan, two of the three provinces which do not impose differential fees, have experienced an increase in their foreign student population, by 29 per cent and 17 per cent respectively.

The study shows that the majority of foreign students hail from industrialized nations with the greatest number — 56.2 per cent — coming from Asian countries, followed by 19.1 per cent from the Americas and the Caribbean.

Since the students are not allowed to work in Canada, most are drawing on family allowances averaging about $15,000 a year, said Mr. Fox.

Almost half of the foreign students — 48.6 per cent — are enrolled at Ontario universities. And most have focused on certain university faculties.

"In comparison with the total student population at Canadian universities, international students continue to have high percentages of enrolment at the graduate level and higher proportions in math, physical sciences and engineering," the report states.

Mr. Fox said there is no evidence to corroborate fears that foreign students are snatching places from Canadian students in professional faculties such as medicine.

The University of Toronto task force reaches the same conclusion. "The task force concludes that any imposition of limits on admission to particular courses or programs which is based on a false perception that foreign students provide unfair competition would be ill-advised."

The task force also points out that there was

little difference in the academic performance of first-year foreign and domestic students.

However, it is still not clear whether Canadian taxpayers are subsidizing the post-secondary education of foreign students through such support programs as English-language training.

While foreign students account for 5 per cent of enrolment at Canadian universities, they make up 6 per cent of Britain's university enrolment and 10 per cent of France's student population.

A recent federal parliamentary committee, which heard submissions from concerned university groups, has concluded foreign students are "an important asset for Canada."

The committee has recommended that national goals and objectives as they relate to foreign students should be part of the discussion of the First Ministers' Conference.

a) Is the demand for university education in Canada by foreign students price elastic or inelastic?

b) Draw a demand curve for foreign student enrolment in Canada and show whether the data in the article could be consistent with the following possibilities:

  (i) between 1983 and 1985, other countries increased the fees they charge to foreign students;

  (ii) alternatively, a reduction in real income in foreign countries caused a decline in their demand for places at Canadian universities.

c) In view of the possibilities outlined in (b), how would you qualify your assessment of the price elasticity of demand made in (a)?

Case 4-3

The Globe and Mail, Toronto

Europeans advised to burn surplus food

Europe's food mountain will burn if the European Community headquarters in Brussels gets the go-ahead for a plan to destroy the huge surpluses of butter, milk powder, beef and wheat.

A confidential European Commission report recommends the wholesale destruction of what is now rotting surplus food stored throughout the community. The report — the work of market management experts in the commission's agricultural directorate — paints a gloomy picture. It says the food mountains are in some cases no longer edible; they are too expensive to store, and there are no potential buyers.

Burning food or dumping it at sea would, the experts argue, save the community much needed cash — about $300-million (U.S.) in the dairy sector alone could be recouped on storage costs. Destroying the butter would end the need to compensate exporters for the difference between the high EC price and the low world price and would bring about a $1-billion saving.

The food mountains are reckoned a dead loss in commercial terms, and some destruction has already taken place. Between 1985 and the beginning of this year, several hundred tons of long-stored wheat that had deteriorated was shipped out to sea in barges and dumped by a transport company employed by the EC Intervention Board.

The commission report calls for the destruction of at least half of the surpluses. This would probably involve burning 750,000 metric tons of butter and 500,000 tons of milk powder.

Without the embarrassing surpluses — which in the past have been sold cheaply to the Soviet Union and fed to pigs and calves, prisoners and hospital inmates — the commission thinks it might, finally, start to reform the common agricultural policy, provided an effective brake is found to stop the surpluses rising once more.

Milk quotas, the contentious measure introduced in 1984 to stem the tide of the milk lake, are proving ineffectual. The quotas, which were set too high in the first place, have been rejigged by enterprising producers so that milk and butter stocks now stand at 1.5 million tons.

This article deals with agricultural policies in the European Economic Community (EEC). The extreme nature of some of the consequences of these policies, in our opinion, justifies paying attention to this general class of problems.

a) Discuss some of the long-term economic developments which tend to cause surpluses of food in modern economies.

b) Which type of government agricultural policies explained in Section 4-7 are responsible for the developments described in the article? Illustrate with the help of diagram(s).

c) Identify, as clearly as you can, the main difficulties in handling the surplus. Can you think of a better approach?

d) Why do we not observe this type of problem in Canada?

APPENDIX 4A: MEASURING DEMAND

4A-1 Demand Measurement

Economic theory highlights factors that are expected to influence the demand for any good or service. However, for prediction and decision-making purposes, business and governments often desire *quantified estimates* of actual market demand relations. For a simplified example of how such numerical estimates of market demand may be obtained, suppose the total quantity demanded of a particular good or service is thought to be well approximated by a linear function of the market price. This demand model may be written as follows:

$$Q = a - bP \qquad (4A\text{-}1)$$

The problem now becomes one of estimating the values of a and b. To explain how this may be done, we now make a most critical assumption — namely, that *all factors affecting demand other than price have remained constant over the time period for which we have gathered data on Q and P* (Table 4A-1). This being the case, the resulting (Q, P) points, if plotted, should approximate the market demand curve. If these points are plotted on a graph such as Figure 4A-1, a line can be drawn through the middle of the observed points. The slope of this line is $\dfrac{\text{decrease in } P}{\text{increase in } Q}$ or, in this specific case, $\dfrac{-6.25}{5.00} = -1.25$. Notice, however, that the demand diagram is drawn with price on the vertical axis (as if price were the dependent variable), while in the above demand model, quantity is the dependent variable. The slope of the D curve plotted in Figure 4A-1, therefore, is an estimate of $\dfrac{1}{b}$, and the demand model above, numerically, is $Q = 5 - 0.8P$.

Table 4A-1 Price and quantity (under simplified conditions)

Months	P	Q
1	3.4	1.8
2	3.7	1
3	1	4.2
4	2.8	1.9
5	1.9	3.4
6	2.4	2.3

A possible set of prices and quantities demanded of a good or service.

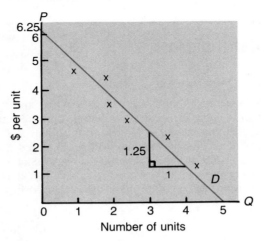

Fig. 4A-1 Estimating a demand relation

Graphical representation of data from Table 4A-1.
The *D* curve shown best represents the scatter of
plotted price-quantity combinations.

We would not expect all the sample points to lie exactly on the straight line, because very few, if any, models fit reality perfectly. The extent to which observed (Q, P) points do not lie on the line gives an indication of the approximate nature of the hypothesized model, $Q = a - bP$. Often, for example, nonlinear relations may provide a better fit with reality.

In practice, many other demand variables will probably change along with price. Suppose, for example, that income was also highly variable (along with price) over the observation period, but that other demand variables were constant. In this case a linear hypothesized demand relation would take the form:

$$Q = a - bP + cY \qquad (4A-2)$$

With this more complicated specification, statistical computation must be used to estimate a, b and c from data on quantity, price and income. Typically this is done with the aid of a computer program.

The Identification Problem

Suppose we gathered price and quantity observations on a particular good for which we were interested in estimating a numerical demand relation. Could we make use of such information alone to estimate a demand function? The answer is "probably not" since observed market prices and quantities result from the interactions of both demand and supply.

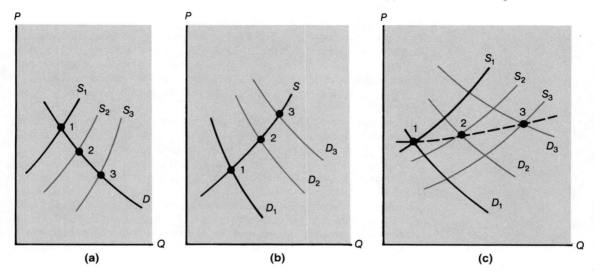

Fig. 4A-2 The identification problem

(a) When only the supply curve shifts, the resulting price-quantity combinations trace a demand curve.

(b) When only the demand curve shifts, the supply curve is traced.

(c) When both the demand and supply curves shift, neither of them can be identified from the plot above.

Suppose that over a three-month observation period the true demand and supply relations fluctuated in the fashion shown in Figure 4A-2a. In this instance the three observation points (1), (2) and (3) would correctly trace the demand relationship. Next, suppose instead that only demand conditions had changed over the three months. In such a case the observed (Q, P) plot (1), (2) and (3) would not trace the demand curve. Instead it would determine the supply curve (Figure 4A-2b). Finally, Figure 4A-2c illustrates perhaps the most common situation of all. In this instance, both demand and supply conditions have changed over the three-month period, with the result that the three observed points would identify neither a demand nor a supply relation, but rather some hybrid of the two.

An *identification problem* arises when we attempt to estimate a simple demand relation of the form $Q = f(P)$ from a series of (Q, P) data points that have arisen in all probability as a result of changing demand *and* supply conditions (Figure 4A-2c). Fortunately, economic statisticians can usually overcome these problems by careful model specification. Though such techniques are beyond the scope of this book, we might guess at this point that the solution requires a more complete and accurate specification of the various other factors (in addition to price) that affect demand.

A Similar Measurement Problem

If the price of a particular good falls by, say, 10% we expect more to be bought. This is often called the *law of demand*. But what happens if the price of a substitute good falls by 20% simultaneously with the fall in price of our particular good? In this case, less of our particular good may be bought. This is not an exceptional case. Actually, there have been two effects here, as illustrated by Figure 4A-3.

In the absence of change in the price of other goods, we would have observed after a fall in price from P_1 to P_2 an increase in quantity demanded from Q_1 to Q'_2 (sliding down the given demand curve D_1). However, the demand curve itself has been shifted to the left by the fall in the price of a substitute good. Because of this second factor, output demanded falls from Q'_2 to Q_2.

From a slightly different angle, we can see that even though the absolute price of our particular good fell (from P_1 to P_2), its price relative to that of substitute commodities did not — in fact, it rose. For this reason, economists emphasize that *relative price* rather than absolute price is the important element for demand prediction.

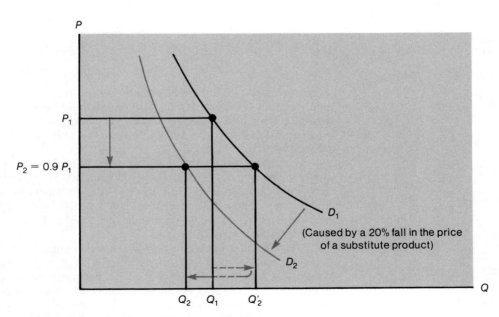

Fig. 4A-3 Importance of measuring relative price changes

When a drop in price of a good is combined with a drop in price of a substitute, the demand curve shifts to the left and quantity demanded cannot be estimated from the original demand curve.

4A-2 Elasticity Measurement

As stated in the text (4-6), demand elasticity coefficients are designed to measure the sensitivity of quantities demanded with respect to changing determinants of demand. An elasticity coefficient may be defined for each determinant of demand. For example, following are three different coefficients which could be used to measure the sensitivity of demand for product A to changing determinants of demand for product A.

(i) Income Elasticity of Demand

$$e_y := \frac{\% \text{ change in quantity of } A \text{ demanded}}{\% \text{ change in consumer income}} \qquad (4A\text{-}3)$$

This coefficient measures the sensitivity of demand for product A with respect to changing consumer income. If e_y is positive, product A is said to be a *normal good*; if negative, an *inferior good*.

This terminology makes sense. A rise in income makes all goods more affordable, and for most goods we would expect an increase in demand. However, some goods that fulfill a basic need have only a limited number of attributes relative to other goods which also fulfill the same basic need. For example, plain white canvas-topped athletic shoes may be adequate basic footwear for the average active youth, but such shoes may not convey an impression of style. Higher income, by making the more stylish high-priced athletic shoes more affordable, may therefore lower the demand for plain footwear. In this case, the plain white canvas shoes would be classified as an inferior good. As another example, a poorer cut of meat might be classified as an inferior good. As consumer income rises, the demand for such cuts would fall in favour of higher quality meat.

(ii) Coefficient of Cross-Price Elasticity of Demand

$$e_{pB} = \frac{\% \text{ change in quantity of } A \text{ demanded}}{\% \text{ change in price of } B} \qquad (4A\text{-}4)$$

This coefficient measures the sensitivity of demand for a particular item with respect to a price change in another item. If the measure is positive, goods A and B are said to be *substitutes* for one another. In very general terms, we may think of most goods and services as substitutes for most others. We achieve satisfaction in many forms. If it becomes more expensive to gain satisfaction from one form of expenditure (one type of good or service), we can generally find other goods and services that yield us satisfaction more cheaply. For example, if a California trip increases in price, we may decide not to go but instead (i) to join a golf club, (ii) take a ski vacation the following winter, (iii) buy a sailboat or (iv) save our money for future consumption. These expenditure possibilities can therefore be regarded as substitutes. However, because this sort of substitution is so indirect, estimated coefficient measures of it may not show up as significantly positive. However, in a more direct and specific sense, we might expect cross-elasticities of demand relating the quantity purchased of brand A televisions, say, to the price of brand B televisions, to be significantly positive. The more alike the goods and services are, the more likely it is that cross-elasticity measures will show up to be positive, and the goods appear to be substitutes.

Table 4A-2 Classification of demand sensitivities

Elasticity coefficient	Degree of sensitivity
$e = \infty$	Perfectly elastic
$e > 1$	Elastic
$e = 1$	Unitary elasticity
$e < 1$	Inelastic
$e = 0$	Perfectly inelastic

Degrees of price elasticity of demand according to the magnitude of the coefficient of own price elasticity of demand.

If the cross-elasticity of demand between two goods turns out to be negative, the goods are said to be *complementary* (or *complements*). Two complementary goods would be gasoline and tires. If the price of gasoline increased substantially, we would expect less driving, less tire use, and therefore, a reduction in the quantity of tires demanded.

(iii) Coefficient of Own Price Elasticity of Demand

$$e_{PA} = \frac{\% \text{ change in quantity of } A \text{ demanded}}{\% \text{ change in price of } A} \qquad (4A\text{-}5)$$

This measure is often called the *own price elasticity coefficient of demand* or, because it is by far the most common elasticity measure referred to, simply the *elasticity of demand*. We discussed this concept briefly in Section 4-6. If there are no other adjectives preceding the phrase "elasticity of demand," we may generally take it to refer to the own price elasticity of demand. As this measure is most popular, we will examine it now in greater detail.

As the price of a product rises, quantity demanded generally falls. Therefore, the (own price) elasticity of demand is normally negative.[1] Because of this fact, the convention has been to drop the negative sign. A demand elasticity of -2 is merely reported as 2.[2] We hesitantly follow the convention in this book.

Table 4A-2 categorizes the sensitivity, responsiveness or elasticity of demand with respect to any particular demand determinant. To be specific, though, let us discuss own price changes.

Unitary elasticity ($e = 1$) may be taken as a standard for comparison. If demand elasticity with respect to price is 1.0, a particular percentage change

---

1. There are possible exceptions. For example, to date we have supposed that consumers' tastes are independent of the prices of particular goods and services. However, suppose a higher price leads people to believe that the product is of better quality. Thus the higher price may actually stimulate quantity demanded. Some believe that this phenomenon occurs occasionally in the case of some expensive soaps, perfumes, prestigious automobiles, art and antiques. (A theoretically more correct interpretation of this phenomenon would be to say that the demand curve shifted to the right as perception of the good changed. Thus, the true demand curve is downward sloping while the observed plot of price-quantity combinations is upward sloping.)

2. On the other hand, a negative income inelasticity or cross-elasticity coefficient would be reported with a negative sign.

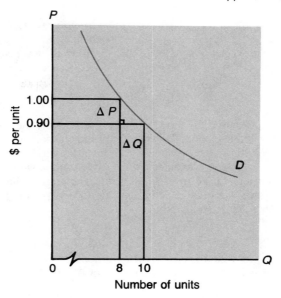

Fig. 4A-4 Arc elasticity of demand

Illustration of the magnitudes used in calculating the
arc price elasticity of demand.

in the product's price will cause demand to respond by the same percentage.
Any greater degree of sensitivity than unitary elasticity (that is, $e > 1$) means
that a particular percentage change in price would lead to a greater percentage
change in demand. Demand in this case may be thought of as *elastic* — that
is, responsive to a greater degree than the price shock itself. Ultimate sensitivity would be reflected when even a small change in price would lead to an
infinite change in quantity demanded ($e = \infty$). In this case, demand would be
said to be *perfectly* (or *completely*) *elastic*. If a given percentage change in
price causes a smaller percentage response in demand, demand is less sensitive than the unitary elasticity standard. Demand in this case is said to be *inelastic*. The extreme form of inelasticity would occur when a change in price
would have absolutely no effect upon demand. In this case, $e = 0$ and
demand is said to be *perfectly* (or *completely*) *inelastic*.

Arc Elasticity

When the elasticity coefficient is measured for finite percentage changes in *P*,
the resulting measure is termed an *arc elasticity*. In Figure 4A-4, for example,
when the price is lowered from $1 to $0.90 per unit, the quantity demanded
rises from 8 units to 10. The arc elasticity of demand defined over the price
range from $0.90 to $1.00 is roughly[3]

---

3. Strictly speaking, to convert to percentage changes we should multiply numerator and denominator by
   100%. Because this factor cancels out, we have omitted it.

$$e = \frac{\% \text{ change in } Q}{\% \text{ change in } P} = \frac{\Delta \ Q/Q}{\Delta \ P/P} \qquad (4A\text{-}6)$$

Subscripts 0 and 1 can also be used to designate original and new levels, respectively, of quantity and price. Hence,

$$e = \frac{(Q_1 - Q_0) / Q_0}{(P_1 - P_0) / P_0} = \frac{(10 - 8) / 8}{(0.90 - 1.00) / 1.00} = \frac{0.25}{-0.10} = -2.5$$

We used the term "roughly" because the method shown above leads to an arithmetic anomaly. Though the arc elasticity of demand over the price range $0.90 to $1 would be -2.5 if the price was lowered from $1 to $0.90, the arc elasticity as computed by the above method would be different if the price was instead raised from $0.90 to $1. The original and new levels of quantity and price would be exactly opposite to those of the first instance, and therefore, the arc elasticity would be

$$e = \frac{(8 - 10) / 10}{(1 - 0.90) / 0.90} = -1.82$$

To make the arc elasticity of demand over a given price range independent of whether the price is lowered or raised, the following definition of arc elasticity is generally preferred:

$$e = \frac{(Q_1 - Q_0) / \frac{1}{2} (Q_0 + Q_1)}{(P_1 - P_0) / \frac{1}{2} (P_0 + P_1)} \qquad (4A\text{-}7)$$

This is consistent with the elasticity definition as a ratio of percentage changes in Q and P, but in essence measures the change in Q and P as percentages of their average values over the range under consideration.[4] In the present case, the arc elasticity of demand measured over the price range $0.90 to $1 becomes

$$e = \frac{2 / 9}{-0.10 / 0.95} = -2.11$$

where 9 and $0.95 are the average quantities and prices over this portion of the demand curve.

Point Elasticity of Demand

If we thought of smaller and smaller price ranges over which the arc elasticity of demand is defined, we would eventually arrive at the elasticity of demand over an infinitesimal price range. In this limit the range (or arc) of the demand curve becomes a single point, and the arc elasticity of demand becomes known instead as the *point elasticity of demand*. From the definition of arc elasticity, we have

$$e = \frac{\Delta \ Q / Q}{\Delta \ P / P} = \frac{\Delta \ Q}{\Delta \ P} \cdot \frac{P}{Q} \qquad (4A\text{-}8)$$

---

4. In the above elasticity formula, elimination of the fraction ½ from numerator and denominator is valid but it somewhat obscures the fact that we are dealing with percentage changes based on average value for Q (that is, ½ $(Q_0 + Q_1)$) and P (that is, ½ $(P_0 + P_1)$) over the range.

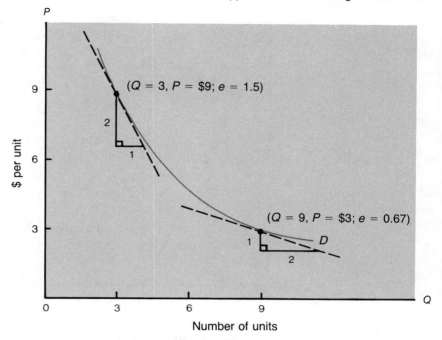

Fig. 4A-5 Calculation of point elasticities of demand

Illustration of the magnitudes used in calculating the point price elasticity of demand at two different points on the D curve.

In the limit, as ΔP approaches zero, e becomes[5]

$$\lim_{\Delta P \to 0} e = \text{point elasticity of demand} = \frac{dQ}{dP} \cdot \frac{P}{Q} \qquad (4A\text{-}9)$$

Figure 4A-5 illustrates the calculation of point elasticities. At point (3, 9) the slope of the demand curve ($\frac{dP}{dQ}$) has been estimated to be 2. Consequently, the point elasticity of demand at point (3, 9) is

$$\frac{dQ}{dP} \cdot \frac{P}{Q} = \frac{1}{2} \cdot \frac{9}{3} = 1.5$$

In a similar fashion, the elasticity of demand at point (9, 3) may be shown to equal $\frac{2}{1} \cdot \frac{3}{9} = 0.67$.

---

5. For memory purposes, the point elasticity of demand might better be written as $e = \dfrac{dQ/Q}{dP/P}$. Remember, since dQ represents a small change in Q, dQ/Q (with the "time 100%" omitted for simplicity) represents the percentage change in Q. Similarly, dP/P represents the percentage change in P. Therefore, the calculus formula for point elasticity of demand again follows directly from the definition of elasticity as a ratio of percentage changes in quantity and price.

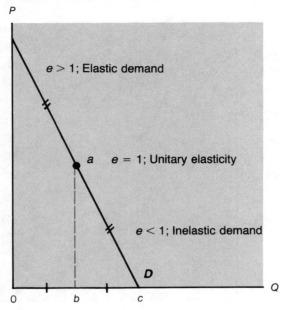

**Fig. 4A-6 Demand elasticities along a linear
demand curve**

The price elasticity of demand varies along a linear
D curve. The elasticity is unity at that quantity level
which corresponds to one-half of the distance
between the origin and the intercept of the *D* curve
with the horizontal axis. For lower quantities,
demand is elastic; for higher quantities, demand is
inelastic.

Point Elasticity along Linear Curves

Figure 4A-6 shows how demand elasticity varies along a given straight line
demand curve. To see how these results come about, let us first demonstrate
that the elasticity at a point halfway along any linear demand curve is 1.0.

The point elasticity of demand at *a* is, by definition

$$e_a = \frac{dQ}{dP} \cdot \frac{P}{Q} = \frac{bc}{ab} \cdot \frac{ab}{ob} \tag{4A-10}$$

However, from the properties of similar triangles, $ob = bc$. Therefore,

$$e_a = \frac{bc}{ab} \cdot \frac{ab}{bc} = 1 \tag{4A-11}$$

For points on the demand curve above a, $P > P_a$ and $Q < Q_a$. Thus, for such
points, $\frac{P}{Q} > \frac{P_a}{Q_a}$ applies and the point elasticities exceed 1. Also, for points on
the demand curve below a, $\frac{P}{Q} < \frac{P_a}{Q_a}$ and therefore elasticities at such points
are less than 1.

Problems for Appendix 4A

Problem 4A-1

a) Explain what is meant by the terms income elasticity of demand, cross-price elasticity of demand, own price elasticity of demand.
b) Suppose the cross-price elasticity of demand for tires with respect to a change in the price of gasoline is -0.5. What does this figure mean? Does the coefficient measure show tires and gasoline to be complementary? Or are they substitutes?

Problem 4A-2

a) Classify the income and price elasticity of demand measures for each item in Table 4-5 as either income elastic or income inelastic and as either price inelastic or price elastic.
b) What does the price elasticity for food of -0.4 mean? Why would food have a low price elasticity?

Problem 4A-3

The total money spent on a particular product within a market is the selling price multiplied by the quantity bought — that is, $P \times Q$. What happens to the total money spent in the face of a price rise in a market with (i) price inelastic demand, (ii) price elastic demand, (iii) unitary elastic demand?

Problem 4A-4

Suppose the market demand relation is $Q = 20 - 0.5 P$.
a) Compute the arc elasticity of demand over the price range $12–$14.
b) Is demand elastic over this range, or is it inelastic?
c) Compute the point elasticity of demand at $P = 12 and $P = 14.
d) What do you observe concerning the relationship between the arc elasticity and the two point elasticities at the end points of the range?

Problem 4A-5

We are given the following market demand relation for product A

$$Q_A = 4 - 0.5 P_A + 0.003 Y + 0.4 P_B$$

where Y represents average family income and B is another good.

a) Assuming the price of product B is currently $10 and the level of family income $10 000, plot the resulting demand curve on a P-Q plane.
b) Suppose income rises to $15 000 while P_B remains at $10. Plot the new demand curve for good A.
c) Suppose that, instead of a rise in income to $15 000, the price of B falls to $5. Plot the new demand curve for A.
d) Calculate the following point elasticities of demand for A when $P_A = 10, $P_B = 10 and $Y = $10 000$; own price elasticity, income elasticity, cross-price elasticity.
e) Using the information from (d), are A and B complements or substitutes? Is demand elastic with respect to price? Is demand elastic with respect to income?

Cases for Appendix 4A

Case 4A-1: Gasoline and Auto Use

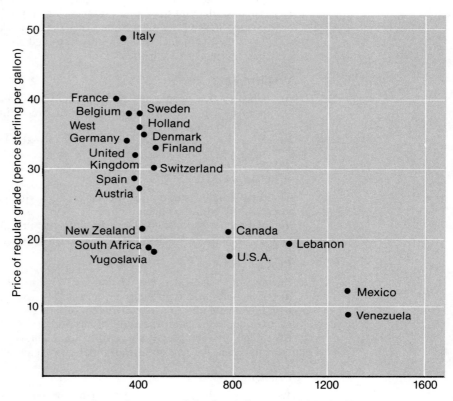

Annual consumption of gasoline per vehicle (gallons)

The data reported here appeared in a study on the role of the automobile published by Transport Canada in 1979.* Some of the information may no longer be representative since it was based on mid-1970s data. Nevertheless, it may be interesting to examine some actual elasticity estimates and their interpretation.

The graph above contains data on gasoline prices and gasoline consumption for 20 countries. Assume that we can use such information to approximate the sensitivity of gasoline consumption to changes in the price of gasoline.

---

* D.J. Reynolds, "Role of the automobile study," *Working Paper 17*, Strategic Planning Group, Transport Canada (Ottawa, January 1979).

Estimated long-term price elasticities for personal transport 1974

Mode	Area of origin	Estimated arc price elasticity
Auto	Urban areas over 100 000 population	1.5
	Urban areas 1–100 000 population	1.2
	Rural areas less than 1000 population	0.8
	Canada	1.2

Estimated potential cross-elasticities of demand for alternative types of transportation

Mode	With respect to total cost of auto use	With respect to gasoline price
Urban transit	3.0	0.6
Walking	1.0	0.2

a) Sketch a smooth curve (not a straight line) roughly through the middle of the observed scatter of points.

b) Using your curve as the approximate relation between gasoline consumption and gasoline prices, estimate the approximate gasoline consumption per vehicle at prices of (i) 50 pence per gallon and (ii) 10 pence per gallon.

c) Using your numbers from part (b), estimate the arc elasticity of demand over the price range 10 pence per gallon to 50 pence per gallon.

The study argued that "Generally speaking, the more substitutes and uses for the commodity, the more flexible margins for adjustment, and the longer the period for adjustment, the greater the price elasticity will be." The table above illustrates estimates of both the long-term price elasticities of demand for various types of personal transport and the long-term (potential) cross-elasticities of demand for alternative types of transportation to the personal auto.

d) Explain why you would expect the elasticity of demand for auto use to be less for people living in rural areas than for people living in urban areas.

e) Can you use these different elasticity measures to argue that gasoline price increases hurt those people in rural areas more than urban areas? Explain briefly.

f) How would you explain to a noneconomist what it means to say that (i) the cross-elasticity of demand for urban transit with respect to total cost of auto use is 3.0, and (ii) the cross-elasticity of demand for walking with respect to gasoline price is 0.2.

g) Explain why the cross-elasticities with respect to gasoline price are much smaller than the cross-elasticities with respect to total cost of auto use.

h) When the cross-elasticity measures were estimated, approximately what portion of the total cost of using an automobile was represented by gasoline expenditure? Suppose the proportion of total auto use cost represented by gasoline rise to ⅓, but the cross-elasticity measures with respect to total cost of auto use remained the same as reported above. What then would be the approximate percentage increase in urban transit use if the price of gasoline increased by 10%?

Finally, income elasticities for auto use are illustrated in the table below.

Income elasticities of demand for auto use by trip purpose, 1976

Main trip purpose

Commuting	1.00
Commercial	0.78
Weekend recreation	1.25
Vacation	0.67
Shopping	0.56
Average for trip purposes*	0.90

* This average is based on the trip purposes shown in the table plus others not included here.

i) Explain in words the meaning of the 0.90 measures for the income elasticity of demand for auto use as reported in the table.

j) Does it surprise you that the income elasticity measure for weekend recreation use is greater than that for commercial and shopping trips? Explain briefly.

k) Give a possible reason why the estimated income elasticity of demand for auto use for vacation purposes may be lower than the average measure of 0.90.

APPENDIX 4B: FURTHER DEMAND ANALYSIS

4B-1 Introduction and Purpose

In the text of Chapter 4, we discussed the derivation of market demand from individual consumer behaviour, along with those factors that give rise to changes in market demand. Here we wish to introduce two somewhat more technical approaches to the same phenomena: (1) *marginal utility analysis* and (ii) *indifference curve analysis*. These analytical tools are popular in more advanced treatments of demand, not only in the field of pure microeconomic theory, but also in a number of applied areas including international trade, monetary economics, public, corporate and personal finance, and marketing.

It is important to note at the outset that these more technical approaches do not bring about new theoretical developments. Instead, they are alternative techniques used to describe the same major elements of demand theory as were discussed in the chapter. Consequently, conclusions about the influence on demand of such factors as prices, tastes, income and prices of other goods are precisely the same as those we have just derived. However, these two new approaches may provide certain additional insights into consumer behaviour.

4B-2 The Marginal Utility Approach

Economists often refer to the satisfaction, happiness or well-being that an individual derives from the consumption of a good or service as *utility*. The distinction between *total* and *marginal* utility is very important. *Total utility* refers to the total satisfaction derived when an individual consumes a certain number of units of a particular good or service. *Marginal utility* refers to the extra amount of satisfaction experienced from the last unit consumed.

Hypothesis of Diminishing Marginal Utility

An important hypothesis in demand theory is that of *diminishing marginal utility*. This hypothesis assumes that as an individual consumes more of any good or service within a given time span, the marginal utility derived from successive units becomes smaller and smaller.

As an example, suppose a particular consumer experiences the following increase in units of satisfaction (marginal utility) for each additional unit of a particular good consumed (Table 4B-1). From the information contained in the first two columns we have constructed a third column indicating total utility experienced by consuming various amounts. For instance, since the first unit yields the consumer 20 units of satisfaction and the second, 12½ units of satisfaction, by consuming 2 units of the good the consumer would obtain a total of 32½ (that is, 20 + 12½) units of satisfaction. Table 4B-1 and its related graph (Figure 4B-1) reflect the hypothesis of diminishing marginal utility. As an individual consumes more and more units of the product in question he or she obtains additional utility. But this additional utility is assumed to decline as consumption grows. As a consequence, total utility increases as greater volumes are consumed — but at a slower and slower rate.

Table 4B-1 Marginal and total utility schedule

Volume (in units) Q	Marginal utility (in units of satisfaction) MU	Total utility (in units of satisfaction) TU
0	—	—
1	20	20
2	12½	32½
3	5	37½
4	2½	40

A hypothetical schedule of a relationship between quantities consumed and the utility (satisfaction) obtained by a consumer. It is assumed here, for purposes of illustration, that utility can be measured.

In some circumstances, marginal utility may even become negative at high volumes of consumption. For example, how about the marginal utility to an average individual of a twentieth box of chocolates consumed in a week.[1] This would correspondingly mean that the total utility curve would turn downward at high volumes of consumption. However, throughout the remainder of this chapter we exclude this possibility. In other words, we shall assume that more of any good or service is always preferred to less.

Notice that the "units of satisfaction" phrase for utility is rather vague to say the least. Although such units of utility are sometimes called *utils*, this renaming does not provide a unit of measurement for utility. How could we measure an individual's utility in practice? As the number of smiles per unit of time or the number of minutes per day during which his brow was not creased? Clearly, these measures would not do. Some people may smile more frequently than others even though they are no happier. Some people are most happy when their brows are creased — avid chess players, perhaps, or mathematicians or economists.

With no well defined measure for utility, *interpersonal comparisons* of utility are difficult. This is a point that economists regretfully accept. For example, with no well accepted measure for utility it is difficult to evaluate whether or not total welfare (or utility) would be increased by taxing a very wealthy individual and giving the proceeds to a much poorer person.

Even though we cannot directly measure utility, we are nevertheless able to use the concept to provide useful insights into demand behaviour.

---

1. Because to an average individual a twentieth box of chocolates consumed in one week would be negative, consumption typically would not take place at such a high level.

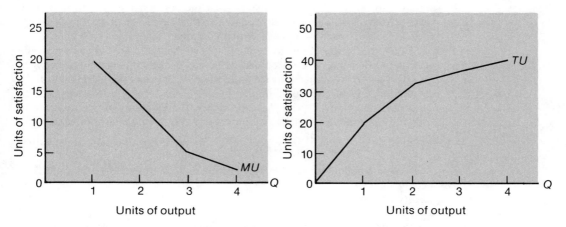

Fig. 4B-1 Marginal utility and total utility related to output consumed

Graphical representation of data from Table 4B-1. The left panel represents the second column of Table 4B-1 and the right panel represents the third column.

Consumer as Utility Maximizer

In the chapter, we argued that it was reasonable to assume a consumer would generally wish to allocate income among various goods and services so as to achieve the greatest possible amount of satisfaction. In other words, we view the consumer as a *utility maximizer*. Let us now see what sort of conditions are necessary for the consumer to maximize this utility. Even though the consumer may not in practice be able to precisely match and continually maintain these maximizing conditions, nevertheless, we might expect the individual's behaviour to at least approximate them.

Controllable and Noncontrollable Variables

The consumer is restricted somewhat in the search for the optimal (best) consumption pattern. Certain things are beyond an individual's control. For instance, although the consumer may change jobs, ask for a raise or otherwise influence personal income, as far as the short-run expenditure decision is concerned, we may suppose that the individual faces a *given monetary income*. Furthermore, the consumer is assumed to be a small buyer relative to the size of the market and, therefore, must face *given market prices*, also beyond his or her control. What the consumer can manipulate or control in order to achieve a utility maximizing consumption pattern is quantities of each good and service consumed.

Marginal Utilities per Last Dollar Spent

Given that the consumer is going to make conscious decisions concerning his or her expenditure, the problem is to decide how much of one good to buy relative to other goods. The answer — if the consumer wishes to maximize satisfaction — is to allocate expenditure so that the marginal utilities per (last) dollar spent on each good and service are equal.

As an illustration of this principle, suppose that there are only two possible goods to consume. The consumer wishes to distribute expenditure between goods A and B so as to maximize utility. Let us represent the marginal utilities of the last unit of each good bought by MU_A and MU_B. If the prices of each unit of A and B are P_A and P_B respectively, the extra amount of satisfaction derived from the last dollar spent on good A and from the last dollar spent on good B are $\dfrac{MU_A}{P_A}$ and $\dfrac{MU_B}{P_B}$ respectively.[2] To derive the maximum satisfaction, these two amounts must be equal. For example, suppose $\dfrac{MU_A}{P_A} = 5$ units of utility per dollar and $\dfrac{MU_B}{P_B} = 3$ units of utility per dollar. This means that the extra satisfaction obtained from the last dollar spent on good A ($\dfrac{MU_A}{P_A}$) is greater than the extra satisfaction obtained from the last dollar spent on good B ($\dfrac{MU_B}{P_B}$). This being the the case, if the consumer spent one dollar less on good B and instead spent it on good A, he or she would gain more utility (5 units worth) from the additional A consumed than he or she would lose (3 units worth) from the reduction in consumption of good B. For the two-good case, therefore, a necessary condition for utility maximization may be written as

$$\frac{MU_A}{P_A} = \frac{MU_B}{P_B} \qquad\qquad (4\text{B-}1)$$

4B-3 The Theory in Practice

When setting out to buy or not to buy a particular good or service, obviously the consumer does not carry out the following steps: (1) examine a notebook in which are recorded personal up-to-date MU-over-P-ratios, (2) calculate the MU-over-P-ratio for the particular good in question and compare it with the others and (3) make the necessary expenditure reallocations to equate $\dfrac{MU}{P}$ ratios. But just because consumers do not think in equation terms, or explicitly calculate marginal utilities, this does not mean that their behaviour does not approximate that which would result if they did. We shall now attempt to connect the necessary condition of Equation 4B-1 — which the consumer's behaviour must approximate in order to maximize utility through consumption — with something that may be more in line with the sort of conscious decision-making process of the average consumer.

Suppose in our two-good example that good A represents a particular product about which an expenditure decision must be made and that good B

---

2. For example, if $MU_A = 20$ units, and $P_A = \$4$, this means that the last unit of A purchased by the consumer was worth 20 units of satisfaction and cost the consumer \$4. Therefore, each of the last four dollars spent on product A added 5 units (i.e. $\dfrac{20 \text{ units}}{\$4}$) of satisfaction.

represents all other goods and services which the consumer might typically buy. To maximize utility, then, Equation 4B-1 states that the consumer should seek to make the following equality,

$$\frac{MU_A}{P_A} = \frac{MU_{\text{other goods}}}{P_{\text{other goods}}} \qquad (4B-2)'$$

We may rewrite this condition as

$$MU_A = \frac{MU_{\text{other goods}}}{P_{\text{other goods}}} \times P_A \qquad (4B-2)''$$

At this point, let us see what we have. The left-hand side of the equation (MU_A) represents the extra satisfaction from buying one more unit of good A. The first term on the right-hand side ($\frac{MU_{\text{other goods}}}{P_{\text{other goods}}}$) represents the extra amount of satisfaction per dollar of expenditure on other goods, while the second term (P_A) represents the number of dollars which would have to be spent to buy one more unit of good A.[3] Consequently, taking both terms together, the right-hand side represents the amount of satisfaction from expenditure on other goods which the consumer would have to sacrifice to buy one more unit of good A.

Nobody calculates the marginal utilities of various amounts of purchases and makes comparisons as in Equations 4B-2$'$ or 4B-2$''$. Most of us do, however, go through a thinking process which amounts to the same thing. As we ponder over a T-bone steak, feel the material of a suit on the rack or gaze at a new automobile, do we not attempt to judge whether the satisfaction we will derive from the product's use (MU_A) will be worth its price (P_A) — having, of course, a good idea as to the satisfaction we would have to sacrifice from each dollar of foregone consumption on other goods ($\frac{MU_{\text{other goods}}}{P_{\text{other goods}}}$)?

For instance, consider once more our consumer example of Section 4-3. Ms. Smith told us the maximum prices she would pay for each successive pair of athletic shoes bought during a particular year. From this information we were able to infer how much each successive pair of athletic shoes was worth to Ms. Smith. This data was summarized in Tables 4-1 and 4-2, which are combined below in Table 4B-2.

Since Ms. Smith would pay at most $45 for one pair of athletic shoes, $45 reflects the perceived value to Ms. Smith of the first pair of such shoes purchased each year. The second pair has a perceived value of $40 and so on. As we argued in the chapter, in more precise terms, the perceived value of a product to the consumer should be stated in terms of dollars' worth of expenditure on other goods than the consumer is willing to sacrifice for the product's purchase. We may now interpret the maximum price information from Ms. Smith as reflecting her marginal utility for athletic shoes. Since Ms. Smith had a good idea of how much satisfaction she and her family would get from each dollar's expenditure on other goods ($\frac{MU_{\text{other goods}}}{P_{\text{other goods}}}$), by stating the

---

3. If expenditure on A represents a small part of the budget, then we might regard "other goods" as approximately the total expenditure (income) basket of the consumer. In that case, $MU_{\text{other goods}}$ may be regarded as approximately the *marginal utility of income*.

maximum prices she would pay for each additional pair of athletic shoes (P_A), she was indirectly stating her marginal utility schedule for athletic shoes (MU_A). A market demand curve thus could be said to reflect the marginal utility to consumers of successive market quantities purchased.

Downward Sloping Demand Curve

The marginal utility condition for consumer satisfaction maximization when purchasing good *A* was summarized in Equation 4B-2' as follows.

$$\frac{MU_A}{P_A} = \frac{MU_{\text{other goods}}}{P_{\text{other goods}}} \qquad (4B-2)'$$

A drop in the price of *A* raises the marginal utility per dollar spent on good *A* ($\frac{MU_A}{P_A}$) relative to the marginal utility per dollar spent on other goods ($\frac{MU_{\text{other goods}}}{P_{\text{other goods}}}$), thereby violating condition 4B-2'. The consumer would increase total utility by spending less on other goods and more on good *A*. The conclusion from marginal utility analysis, then, is that demand is inversely related to price.

In Chapter 4 we argued in a somewhat more intuitive fashion that a fall in the price of a product would be expected to lead to more purchases, since such purchases would then represent less sacrifice in terms of alternative expenditure on other goods. That this analysis is equivalent to that of the marginal utility approach may be seen by rewriting Equation 4B-2' as 4B-2":

$$MU_A = \frac{MU_{\text{other goods}}}{P_{\text{other goods}}} \times P_A \qquad (4B-2)''$$

Table 4B-2 Subjective product value information concerning Ms. Smith (from Tables 4-1 and 4-2)

(No. of pairs per year)	Perceived value of last pair (measured in terms of dollars' worth of expenditure on other goods the consumer is willing to sacrifice)	Cumulative perceived value to consumer of all pairs bought
1	$45	$ 45
2	40	85
3	30	115
4	20	135

The perceived product value of the last unit declines as more units are consumed. (The cumulative perceived value increases at a decreasing rate.)

and then (as we did above) interpreting the right-hand side as *the amount of satisfaction from expenditure on other goods that the consumer would have to sacrifice to buy one more unit of good A*. A fall in P_A makes the right-hand side of Equation 4B-2″ less than the left-hand side. In words, the amount of satisfaction from expenditure on other goods which the consumer would have to sacrifice to buy one more unit of good A becomes less than the marginal utility (extra satisfaction) that could be derived from purchasing one more unit of good A (MU_A). Consequently, a utility maximizing consumer would buy more of good A (and fewer other goods).

4B-4 Indifference Analysis

Another form of demand analysis employs so-called *indifference curves*. Since this is yet another way of looking at the consumer as a utility maximizer we should expect the same implications for demand theory to flow from this approach as were derived from the marginal utility approach directly above.

Indifference Curves

For illustration purposes, we again assume that the consumer has to choose only between two goods (*A* and *B*). For example, suppose the consumer initially possesses quantities of the two goods as represented by point *a* on Figure 4B-2. At this point, the consumer has Q_A units of good *A* and a Q_B

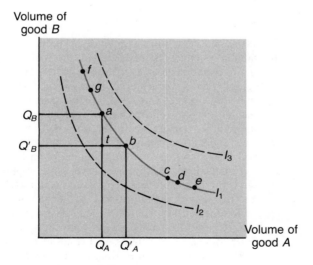

Fig. 4B-2 Indifference curves

All combinations of the quantities consumed of the two goods which lie on the same indifference curve yield identical levels of utility. Combinations on I_2 yield a lower level of utility than I_1, which in turn yields a lower level of utility than I_3.

units of good B. Also, by consuming these quantities of A and B, the consumer would experience a certain amount of utility (say, I_1 units).

Next, assume that a certain amount of product B is taken away so that the consumer winds up with only Q'_B units. As a result of this action, and our earlier assumption that more is preferred to less, the consumer will lose a certain amount of utility. Therefore, at point t, the level of utility experienced would be less than I_1 units since the consumer has the same amount of A (namely Q_A) but less of B (namely Q'_B). In order to maintain utility at its original level of I_1 a greater amount of good A would have to be consumed (say, Q'_A). Points a and b, therefore, represent different consumption combinations of goods A and B, which yield the consumer identical amounts of utility. Consequently, we say the consumer would be *indifferent* between consumption combinations represented by points a and b. An infinite number of other such indifference points could be represented in a similar manner. We have depicted but a few of these by points a, b, c, . . ., g. The entire locus or set of such points reflecting a given level of utility is called an *indifference curve*. Since for almost any possible combination of goods and its associated utility level there would be other combinations of goods that would yield the consumer an identical amount of utility, the plane of Figure 4B-2 contains an infinite number of indifference curves in addition to I_1. We have drawn but two more. Also, since more is assumed to be preferred to less, I_2 represents a set of consumption baskets yielding a lower level of utility while I_3 represents a set of consumption baskets yielding a higher level of utility.

Shape of Indifference Curves

The assumption that more of any good is preferred to less means that when an individual consumes less of one good, more of another good will be required in order to maintain a constant level of utility. This assumption implies downward sloping indifference curves. But why necessarily convex to the origin as we have drawn them? This result follows from the earlier stated hypothesis of diminishing marginal utility for any and all goods.

For instance, with regard to Figure 4B-3 and for an initial consumption point a, suppose a consumer gives up 1 unit of good B in return for, say, ¾ units of good A so that total utility remains constant. This means that a and b are two points on an indifference curve. Now, suppose another unit of good B is taken from the consumer and in return enough additional units of good A are given to maintain constant utility. If another ¾ units of A would do the trick, the indifference curves would be linear (dashed line), but if more than ¾ units of A are required to maintain a constant utility level, the indifference curve would be convex to the origin. As a result of the diminishing marginal utility assumption made earlier, the utility lost from the second unit of good B given up will be more than that lost from the first (since the consumer now has less of B), while the utility gained from another ¾ units of good A would be less than that gained from the previous ¾ units (since the consumer now has more of A). For these reasons, the consumer would require more than ¾ units of additional A to compensate in utility terms for the second unit of B given up. Consequently, the indifference curve is convex to the origin as illustrated by points a, b, c.

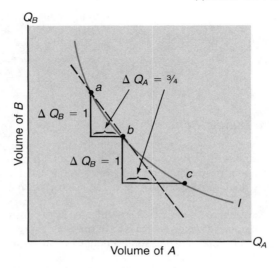

Q_B

Volume of B

$\Delta Q_B = 1$

a

$\Delta Q_A = \frac{3}{4}$

b

$\Delta Q_B = 1$

c

I

Volume of A

Q_A

Fig. 4B-3 Indifference curve convexity

Indifference curves are convex to the origin because of the diminishing marginal utility derived
from consumption of both goods.

Indifference Curves and Marginal Utility

By definition, along any indifference curve, a change in the quantity of good
A consumed (ΔQ_A) must be accompanied by a change in the quantity of good
B consumed (ΔQ_B) so that the total change in utility (ΔU) is zero.

The marginal utility of good A (MU_A) represents the extra utility experienced by an individual in the consumption of one more unit of good A.
Similarly for good B. Consequently, a change in consumption of good A by
ΔQ_A units affects the utility experienced by $MU_A \cdot \Delta Q_A$. Similarly for good
B. This means that if one's consumption of good A and good B is altered by
ΔQ_A and ΔQ_B respectively, the total change in utility experienced would be
$MU_A \cdot \Delta Q_A + MU_B \cdot \Delta Q_B$. This in turn means that along an indifference
curve, relation 4B-3 holds true.

Total change in utility experienced by a change in consumption of A by
ΔQ_A and of B by ΔQ_B can be written as follows:

$$MU_A \cdot \Delta Q_A \quad + \quad MU_B \cdot \Delta Q_B \quad = 0 \qquad (4B\text{-}3)$$

change in utility   change in utility
experienced   experienced
from a change   from a change
in consumption   in consumption
of ΔQ_A of ΔQ_B

Therefore, from Equation 4B-3, along an indifference curve we have the condition that at any point its slope ($\frac{\Delta Q_B}{\Delta Q_A}$) may be written as in Equation 4B-4.

$$\frac{\Delta Q_B}{\Delta Q_A} = -\frac{MU_A}{MU_B} \tag{4B-4}$$

The Budget Constraint

The consumer maximization problem is to achieve as high a level of utility as possible with given income. It is, in fact, limited income that restrains the consumer from achieving as high a level of satisfaction in consumption as the individual might otherwise like. Let us now examine this important consideration.

Since there are only two possible goods to consume, the consumer's *budget (or income) constraint* may be written as $P_A Q_A + P_B Q_B = Y$, where $P_A Q_A$ and $P_B Q_B$ represent the total amounts spent on good A and good B respectively.[4] For graphing purposes, the budget constraint is more conveniently written as relation 4B-5.

$$Q_B = \frac{Y}{P_B} - (\frac{P_A}{P_B}) Q_A \tag{4B-5}$$

From relation 4B-5 we can see that if plotted on a (Q_A, Q_B) plane (as in Figure 4B-4), the budget constraint is a straight line with vertical intercept ($\frac{Y}{P_B}$) and slope ($-\frac{P_A}{P_B}$). The vertical intercept represents the total amount of product B that could be purchased if the consumer's entire income was spent on B and the slope reflects the relative price of product A to that of product B. In Figure 4B-4 we have also sketched in several possible indifference curves to represent a particular consumer's tastes.

The budget line and the shaded region underneath represent the consumer's *feasible consumption set*, since any point within that area represents an expenditure in dollar terms less than or equal to total income (Y). Take point e, for example. Since it is right on the budget line, it represents an expenditure equal to the consumer's entire income. Since point a inside the region represents the same volume of consumption (and hence dollar expenditure on) good B as point e but less dollar expenditure on good A, then at point a the consumer must be spending less than the consumer's entire income. Similarly, it may be shown that all consumption points above the budget line (for example point d) represent an infeasible consumption set since they imply greater expenditure than total available income. This means that the consumer's budget constraint makes such levels of satisfaction as I_3 unattainable.

---

4. This does not mean that the consumer may not save any income. But saving now is consumption later. Therefore, in advanced treatments with more than just two types of expenditure, one of the expenditures may represent saving or expenditure on future consumption. The budget constraint may be also adapted to allow for borrowing.

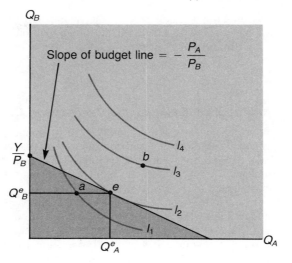

Fig. 4B-4 The consumer problem

All combinations of the two goods within the shaded area are obtainable with the given consumer budget. The objective of the consumer is to reach the highest indifference curve compatible with the budget constraint.

The Consumer Maximizing Problem

The problem for the consumer is to attain, within the limit of the budget constraint, the highest possible level of utility — that is, to achieve the highest possible indifference curve. This highest attainable indifference curve would be one that just touches (is tangential to) the budget line. In other words, the *optimal consumption bundle* for the consumer is the one at the point of tangency between the budget line and one of the indifference curves. This is represented by point e in Figure 4B-4. The highest level of utility (I_2) is attainable by consuming Q_A^e of good A and Q_B^e of good B.

Notice that to the left of point e, indifference curve I_2 is more steeply sloped than the budget line, while the opposite is true to the right of e. At e, therefore, the slope of the indifference curve I_2 is identical to that of the budget line. But with Equation 4B-4 we showed that the slope of an indifference curve at any point is represented by the ratio of the marginal utilities for the two goods at that point, that is, $-\dfrac{MU_A}{MU_B}$. Therefore, at the optimal consumption point, we have

$$-\frac{MU_A}{MU_B} \quad = \quad -\frac{P_A}{P_B}$$

(slope of indifference curve)   (slope of indifference budget line)

Dividing through both sides of this relationship by -1 and rearranging terms, we again arrive at the marginal utility condition 4B-2 derived earlier for consumer maximizing behaviour.

$$\frac{MU_A}{MU_B} = \frac{P_A}{P_B} \tag{4B-2}$$

Indifference Analysis and the Demand Curve

As we have seen above, studying how quantity demanded responds to a change in market price is equivalent to studying the slope of the demand curve in a *P-Q* plane. Again, let us suppose we are interested in examining the demand for any product (*A*) as its price changes — with everything else held constant.

Using indifference curve analysis, the approach would be to vary P_A (of the budget line) while holding P_B, *Y* and the consumer's tastes (as represented by the shape of the given indifference curves) constant, and then examine the pattern of new tangency points. For example, in Figure 4B-5a we have done just that. Budget lines 1, 2 and 3 were plotted assuming progressively lower

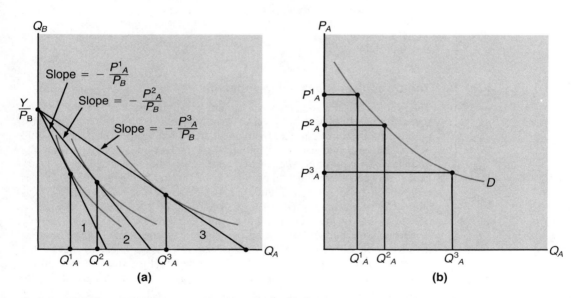

(a) **(b)**

Fig. 4B-5 The demand relation derived from indifference analysis

(a) If price P_B is kept constant and price P_A successively drops, the budget line pivots around the vertical intercept and a utility maximizing consumer increases consumption from Q^1_A to Q^2_A to Q^3_A.

(b) When the successively lower prices of good *A* are plotted against quantities from graph (a), a downward sloping individual demand curve for good *A* results.

P_A's. (Notice that the vertical intercept ($\frac{Y}{P_B}$) is unaffected by any change in P_A). The consumer is able to attain higher levels of utility as the price of A is lowered since — with product A cheaper and other products (here, product B) no more expensive — income becomes less of a constraining factor than it previously was.

As we have shown in Figure 4B-5a — and as we would normally expect to be the case — more of good A is consumed as its price is lowered. Once more, therefore, this implies an expected downward sloping demand curve as shown in Figure 4B-5b.

Problems for Appendix 4B

Problem 4B-1

a) Differentiate between total and marginal utility.

b) In Section 4-2 of the chapter we spoke of rational consumer behaviour. Using the concept of utility, how would you define rational consumer behaviour?

c) Why may two different consumers with identical monetary incomes, and facing identical prices, allocate their expenditure differently? Is it possible for one of these two consumers to reach a higher level of utility than the other? Explain.

d) Using the information on Ms. Smith provided by Tables 4-1 and 4-2, roughly graph her marginal and total utility curves for athletic shoes. (Use dollars to represent the utility measure.) Explain how we might justify the use of dollars to represent utility in such a case.

e) Does a consumer's demand for any good or service depend on marginal or total utility? Explain.

Problem 4B-2

a) Suppose we have the following information concerning a particular consumer and two products A and B: $MU_A = 6$; $MU_B = 9$; $P_A = \$5$; $P_B = \$4$. How do we know the consumer is not allocating income in an optimal manner? What should the consumer do to improve welfare?

b) In actual practice, people do not talk in marginal utility terms when making expenditures. Explain, then, the sort of thinking process that an actual consumer might go through to adjust a spending pattern if faced with the situation depicted in part (a).

Problem 4B-3

Explain, using marginal utility analysis, how the following market shocks might be expected to affect consumer demand for product A. Illustrate the effect of each shock on the market demand curve for product A. (Product B is a competitor of (substitute for) product A.)

Shocks to consider:

(i) An increase in the price of product A.

(ii) A well received advertising campaign by producers of product B.

(iii) A reduction in the price of product B.

(iv) A shift in consumer tastes toward A.

Problem 4B-4

a) Explain what is meant by the hypothesis of diminishing marginal utility.

b) What are indifference curves? What assumption leads to the conclusion that indifference curves are (i) downward sloping and (ii) convex to the origin?

c) Illustrate rational consumer behaviour (discussed in Section 4-2) with the use of an indifference curve diagram.

d) Using indifference curves, illustrate differences in tastes between two consumers with respect to different goods.

e) Using part (d), show how two consumers with identical monetary incomes and facing identical prices might allocate their incomes differently. Is one of them spending income more sensibly than the other? Explain.

CHAPTER 5

Supply and Costs: The Case of Pure Competition

LEARNING OBJECTIVES

After reading this chapter you should be able to explain:

1. The objectives of business firms.
2. The theory of the production process and the law of diminishing returns.
3. Total, average, and marginal cost of production.

4. The special features of perfectly competitive markets.
5. How business firms decide on the level of output they should supply in order to maximize profit.
6. Changes in wage rates, productivity, taxes and prices of materials and their impact on firms' costs and output.

5-1 INTRODUCTION AND PURPOSE

In Chapters 2 and 3, we sketched the basic supply-demand framework for microeconomic analysis. In Chapter 4 we investigated demand in greater detail by zeroing in on the behaviour of a single consuming unit. In this chapter we examine supply in greater detail by focusing on the behaviour of a single producing unit, the firm. Just as market demand reflects the aggregate behaviour of all individual consumers, so market supply is the combined response to all individual producers within a market.

We have argued earlier that how much a firm is willing to supply at various market prices depends upon the firm's costs. For this reason, the first part of this chapter deals with *cost structure*. As it turns out, the supply decision for a business also depends, to a considerable extent on the degree of competition within the industry, as well as on the amount of government control.

In this chapter, we investigate producer behaviour in a particular market environment called *pure competition*. In such a market, the firm has no choice but to charge the going market price. Its decisions are therefore limited to one dimension — how much to produce. In Chapters 6 and 7 we shall consider more frequently encountered market structures in which firms have to decide not only how much to produce, but also the quality of the product and the amount of advertising, as well as the price. In subsequent chapters, we analyze the effects on supply decisions of government intervention in individual markets.

5-2 BUSINESS DECISIONS AND OBJECTIVES

Most business activity is carried on by corporate business firms. Such firms typically have widely dispersed groups of shareholders, each of which may have negligible control over the management of the company. If a partial owner (*shareholder*) does not like the way corporate management is handling his investment, he may sell his shares in the stock market. Of course, this may involve a considerable financial loss. In addition, each partial owner of the corporation is able to vote for the chief policy-setting group within the corporation once a year at the company's *annual meeting*. This group is known as the *board of directors*.

One of the prime objectives of a business firm is to make the owners of the firm as wealthy as possible. This may not be the only objective, but it had better be one of the main objectives; otherwise management can expect to find their jobs in jeopardy. We shall assume that it is the only objective: the managers of the firm undertake economic decisions so as to *maximize owners' wealth*. (We examine other possible objectives in Chapter 14.) For short-run decisions this can be taken to mean **maximization of the firm's profit** (revenue less costs). The larger the profit, the greater will be the owners' wealth. For a corporation whose stock is publicly traded, the greater its annual profit per comon share, the greater will be the price of the shares on the stock market. Hence shareholders' wealth will increase or decrease in direct relation to profit.

Profit varies with the amount of output produced because both sales revenue and costs vary. An important task for management, therefore, is to understand how sales revenue and costs are related to volume produced so that the company can aim for an output level that maximizes the excess of sales revenue over costs.

In economic analysis of the firm, we assume that its objective is to maximize profits, i.e. the difference between revenues and costs.

5-3 THE PRODUCTION PROCESS

Because there are a number of different concepts to deal with, it might be helpful to illustrate each one with a specific example. For this purpose, let us consider a small fictitious company in the business of manufacturing pleasure boats. The name of the company is Boatco. Boatco is a one-plant operation with plant facilities designed for a normal work force ranging between four and eight employees. Most of the parts are prefabricated to the firm's specifications by other companies. It is appropriate, therefore, to regard the boat company as largely an assembly-type operation. Three basic processes are involved in the manufacture of each boat: (1) outside hull assembly, (2) interior fitting and (3) finishing. Finishing includes the mounting of external chrome accessories, painting, varnishing and inspection.

For purposes of analysis, we define a **production function** as a relationship which quantitatively describes how inputs (factors of production) are transformed into output. In our example, the production function would describe how the number of boats produced varies as workers are added to the plant.

The Law of Diminishing Returns

For Boatco to manufacture any boats at all requires labour. Consider the employment of a single worker. Although this may be sufficient to get production rolling, the single employee would have to perform all tasks required, from the hull assembly and interior fitting, to the finishing process, as well as activities like materials handling and sweeping the floor. It is not likely that this employee would be equally efficient at performing all processes and since a lone employee must perform each task in sequence, there is likely to be considerable time wasted. As a result, monthly output would be very small.

Next, consider adding a second worker who could split the production tasks with the first one. Each worker would now likely be more efficient handling fewer tasks. Also, more than one process could be carried out at once. While one worker is fabricating the hull, the other worker could be working on part of the interior or perhaps preparing the materials or finishing another craft. As a consequence, we would not be surprised if the addition of the second worker contributed to output (the number of boats fabricated each month) by a larger amount than the output created by the first employee working alone. In fact, such efficiency gains through the *division, specialization* and *coordination* of tasks might even grow bigger so that the increase in output caused by employment

Table 5-1 Production data for Boatco

(1) Monthly production and sales volume (no. of boats) Q	(2) Monthly labour employment (no. of hours) L	(3) Additional labour required to produce additional output (no. of hours/boat) $1/MP_L$	(4) Additional output per hour of additional labour (no. of boats/hour) MP_L
0	0	—	—
1	300	300	0.0033
2	480	180	$1/180 = 0.0056$
3	600	120	0.0083
4	780	180	0.0056
5	990	217	0.0048
6	1290	300	0.0033
7	1683	393	0.0025
8	2480	797	0.0013
9	3780	1300	0.0008

Diminishing marginal returns (bracketed for rows 4–9)

Illustration of the law of diminishing returns: As labour is added to a plant equipped with machinery, the increments in output due to each additional hour of labour in column 4 initially rise, reach a peak (at 0.0083 boats/hour) and subsequently decline as more hours of work are added.

of a third worker exceeds that created by employment of the second worker, and so on.

The increase in production volume created by an additional worker is defined as the **marginal product** of that worker. As we have just seen, there is good reason to expect that the marginal product of additional workers will increase over a low range of employment. However, within the given physical plant constraint, there is a limit to these increases in marginal product. Expanding employment beyond a certain point will lead to lower marginal product until ultimately the plant becomes so congested with workers that further labour additions will cause no increase in output at all or even reductions in total ouptut (that is to say, the marginal product of labour may become negative).

As an extreme example, suppose that 1000 workers, shoulder-to-shoulder, could be jammed into Boatco's plant. Clearly, with no space to work, the addition of a 1001st worker would not lead to any more output. Of course, neither would there have been an addition to monthly output from employment of the 1000th, 999th, 998th and so on, down to a much smaller work force. The point is that within the constraints imposed by a **fixed factor** required for the production process (here, physical plant space), the early efficiency gains in-

duced by specialization and coordination must eventually be exhausted as a **variable factor** — in this case, labour — is added. Continued additions of the variable factor yield successively lower marginal product until no further gains in output are possible (at which point the marginal product of the variable factor is zero). This economic relationship is known as the "law of eventually diminishing marginal returns to a variable factor" or more simply as the **law of diminishing returns**.

Consider now Table 5-1, which has been constructed to illustrate the law of diminishing returns. The first two columns represent Boatco's short-run production function, relating output volume to the amount of labour employed within the given fixed plant facility. As is customary, we record labour in terms of hours employed per month rather than number of workers.[1] The figures in column 3 are calculated directly from column 2 and indicate the extra labour required (per month)

1. An approximate translation may be made from hours per month to workers employed each month. For example, considering that there are approximately 158 labour-hours in each month (35 hours per week × 4½ weeks per month), 990 hours of labour required for a five boat per month production level translates into six full-time workers and one part-time worker employed for 42 hours per month.

to produce each additional boat (per month), in other words $\frac{\text{increment in } L}{\text{increment in } Q}$. The fourth column reflects the marginal product of labour (MP_L) at various employment levels. More formally, $MP_L = \frac{\text{increment in } Q}{\text{increment in } L}$. Table 5-1 is constructed in such a way that the value of each increment in Q is always 1 boat. The values of increment in L, however, vary as the level of production activity changes.

It is important to understand why the figures in column 4 are simply the reciprocals of the corresponding figures in column 3. For instance, for column 3, employment of the first 300 hours of labour increases production by one boat (from 0 per month to 1 per month). This fact implies that

each hour of the first 100 hours employed adds $\frac{1}{300}$ or 0.0033 boats to the firm's monthly production volume. Similarly, since employment of the next 180 hours of labour increases production by another boat, each of these next 180 hours of labour adds $\frac{1}{180}$ or 0.0056 boats to the monthly volume. That the data conforms to the law of diminishing returns is evident from the fact that the marginal product of labour figures decline for employment levels beyond 600 hours per month.

The data of Table 5-1 appear graphically in Figure 5-1. Since marginal product of labour refers to increments to total output resulting from additional employment, over the range $L = 0$ to $L = 600$, as marginal product is rising, total out-

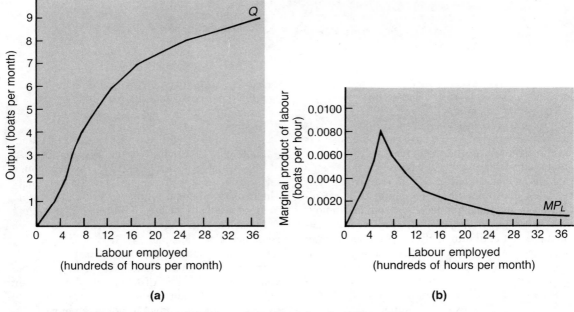

(a)   (b)

Fig. 5-1 Boatco's production function and marginal productivity pattern

(a) Total product (output) obtained from a given plant rises throughout as more labour is employed. Initially, output increases relatively fast in relation to the growth in employment of labour. As diminishing returns set in (roughly at 600 hours per month), output increases slower in relation to the growth in employment of labour.

(b) Marginal product of labour rises to the level of employment of labour at which diminishing returns set in (roughly 600 hours per month). Thereafter, as employment levels grow, marginal product of labour declines.

put increases at an increasing rate. In this example, diminishing marginal returns to labour set in at $L = 600$. Beyond $L = 600$, as marginal product falls, total output increases at a decreasing rate. As marginal product continues to decline toward zero, output approaches its maximum. We suppose here that Boatco's monthly output limit is reached somewhat beyond an employment level of $L = 3600$.

The law of diminishing returns is an important relationship between factors of production (inputs) and output. In any production process where at least one factor is fixed, the quantity of output varies with the amount of variable inputs. As the employment of variable inputs reaches a certain level, successive additions of inputs yield increasingly smaller increments to output.

5-4 COST CONCEPTS

As we have briefly argued earlier, and as we shall see in greater detail below, the quantity that any firm will willingly supply at various market prices (that is to say, the *supply decision*) depends upon the firm's **cost structure** — in other words, how the firm's costs vary with production volume.

The concept of **marginal cost** is of particular importance and is discussed first. It refers to the added cost of producing one more unit of output (in this case, one more boat) during a specified production period. Next, we investigate the behaviour of **total costs**, that is the firm's expenditures on all inputs during the production period. Finally, we turn our attention to the **per unit** (or **average**) **cost**, in this case the cost per boat produced.

Marginal Cost

If for the moment we continue to assume labour to be the sole variable input to the production process, the extra or marginal cost of producing one more boat is simply the extra labour cost required. As just shown, the additional cost of labour needed to produce one extra boat in terms of hours of labour is $\frac{\text{increment in } L}{\text{increment in } Q}$ which is simply the reciprocal of marginal product of labour (MP_L). If we wish to express the additional labour cost need-

ed to produce one extra boat in dollars, we have to multiply this term by the hourly wage rate (W), to obtain the marginal cost, that is

$$MC = W \times \frac{\text{increment in } L}{\text{increment in } Q} = W \times \frac{1}{MP_L}$$

That is to say,

$$MC = \frac{W}{MP_L} \tag{5-1}$$

To understand relation 5-1 it is necessary to interpret each expression carefully. The wage rate (W) refers to the cost of employing each additional unit (hour) of labour. The expression $\frac{1}{MP_L}$ is simply the additional amount of labour required to produce one more unit of output (one more boat). Consequently, the expression $W \times \frac{1}{MP_L}$ is nothing more than

| the cost of employing each additional hour of labour (W) | $\times$ | the number of additional hours of labour required to produce one more boat ($\frac{1}{MP_L}$) |

The product of the two expressions gives us the added labour cost of producing one more boat. If, as we have assumed above, there are no other variable costs to worry about, then the added labour cost to produce one more boat also represents the extra or marginal cost (MC) of producing one more boat.

In reality, however, labour is not usually the only variable cost and certainly is not the only variable cost for Boatco. Boatco utilizes materials in the production process. Hence, we must consider the materials input along with labour in our consideration of marginal cost. As we shall now see, the incorporation of materials as another variable input along with labour does not alter the fundamental conclusion that the marginal product of labour pattern determines the marginal cost structure.

As a general rule, the amount of material input necessary for each unit of output produced is independent of the actual volume of output. Each boat would require approximately the same amount of materials no matter how many boats are being produced. Including materials cost, the extra or marginal cost of producing another boat may therefore more properly be summarized as

$$MC = \frac{W}{MP_L} + \text{value of material necessary for the production of each unit of output} \quad (5\text{-}2)$$

| extra cost of producing one more unit of output per time period | extra labour cost of producing one more unit of output per time period | value of material necessary for the production of each unit of output |

If we suppose, for example, that $1000 of materials are required for each boat, then the expression for Boatco's marginal cost becomes

$$MC = \frac{W}{MP_L} + \$1000$$

From the marginal cost expression 5-2, we see that there is an inverse relation between the marginal product of labour and marginal cost.

Over the range of employment of labour where MP_L is rising (up to about 600 hours per month in Table 5-1 and Figure 5-1), marginal cost is falling. Likewise, at higher production levels, as the marginal product of labour falls, it requires more additional labour hours to produce each extra unit of output — hence, marginal cost rises. The impact of the constant materials cost per unit of output is simply to make the marginal cost of producing each additional boat $1000 higher than it would be otherwise. (A more detailed elaboration of this relationship is provided in Appendix 5A to this chapter.)

Table 5-2 illustrates Boatco's labour, materials and marginal cost structure. It is assumed that the wage rate is $12 per hour and the materials cost is $1000 per boat. Columns 1 and 2 are reproduced from Table 5-1. Figures in column 3 are calculated by multiplying the number of hours in column 2 by the hourly wage, i.e. by $12. The extra labour cost for each additional boat reported in column 4 is calculated from figures in column 3. For instance, the extra labour cost of producing the second boat

Table 5-2 Boatco's marginal cost structure

(1) Production and sales volume (boats per month) Q	(2) Labour employed (hours per month) L	(3) Labour cost ($ per month)	(4) Extra labour cost for each additional boat produced ($ per boat)	(5) Materials cost ($ per boat)	(6) Marginal cost ($ per boat)
0	0	0	—	—	—
1	300	3 600	3 600	1 000	4 600
2	480	5 760	2 160	1 000	3 160
3	600	7 200	1 440	1 000	2 440
4	780	9 360	2 160	1 000	3 160
5	990	11 880	2 520	1 000	3 520
6	1 290	15 480	3 600	1 000	4 600
7	1 683	20 196	4 716	1 000	5 716
8	2 480	29 760	9 564	1 000	10 564
9	3 780	45 360	15 600	1 000	16 600

Marginal costs per boat in column 4 are the sum of additional labour costs for each additional boat produced and the materials cost per boat.

is the difference between the monthly labour cost of producing two boats ($5760) and one boat ($3600), which is $2160. Adding the materials cost per boat reported in column 5 to the figures in column 4 yields the marginal cost per boat in column 6. For instance, the marginal or extra cost of producing the second boat is $2160 (extra labour cost required) + $1000 (extra materials cost), or $3160 in all.

Figure 5-2 graphically shows the inverse relation between the marginal product of labour (plotted against Q) and the labour portion of marginal cost.[2] Further, Figure 5-2 illustrates how marginal cost comprises both labour and materials cost. Note that MC is lowest when 3 boats per month are produced, which is precisely the level of output at which MP_L is the highest.

Total Cost Structure

Some of the firm's costs per production period vary with the level of output and some are constant (fixed), regardless of how much is actually produced.

Fixed Costs

Given that the company's plant facilities have already been built, there are certain costs that will be largely independent of how much the firm actually produces and sells. For example, wearing out (*depreciation*) and normal maintenance of the plant, property taxes, the manager's salary and interest expense on an outstanding company bank loan will occur month after month whether the company produces or not. Such costs are called **fixed costs**. Let us focus on a one-month production period and assume Boatco's fixed costs are $6000 per month.

Variable Costs

Variable costs are those expenses that vary directly with the volume of production. For instance, more output requires that more materials and labour be used in the production process.

2. Since the marginal product of labour is related to employment level, the MP_L relationship is usually plotted with employment rather than output on the horizontal axis. However, plotting the marginal product of labour against output (as is done here) usefully illustrates the important relation between marginal product and marginal cost.

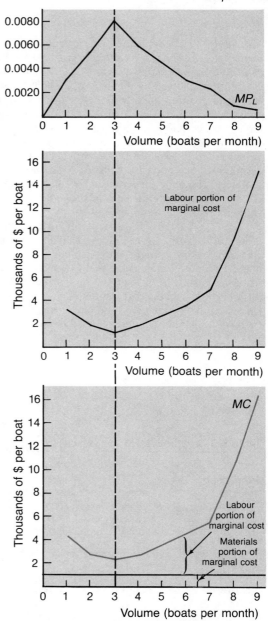

Fig. 5-2 Boatco's marginal product pattern and marginal cost structure

Graphical representation of data from Table 5-2. The marginal cost is minimized at 3 units of output per month. This is the same level of output at which marginal product of labour is maximized.

Total Cost

The *total cost* of producing any particular volume of output *per production period* is simply the sum of fixed cost plus variable cost. Boatco's total cost structure is reflected by the data of Table 5-3. The first three columns are identical with the first three columns of Table 5-2. Boatco's labour and materials cost comprise the company's variable costs. The 6th column of Table 5-3 shows Boatco's $6000 monthly fixed costs component, which, by definition, does not vary with the level of output produced. Finally, the company's total monthly costs (column 7) are the sum of the monthly variable and fixed cost components.

Figures 5-3 and 5-4 show Boatco's cost structure graphically. Notice from Figure 5-3 that materials cost appears as a straight line when plotted against output because each additional boat increases materials cost by a constant $1000. The situation is different for labour cost plotted against output since at a low production (and employment) level each additional boat requires less additional labour (since MP_L is increasing) and hence less additional labour cost. Over the higher output range, each additional boat requires a greater amount of additional labour (since MP_L is decreasing) and hence greater additional labour cost. The curvilinear shape of the variable cost curve reflects the shape of the labour cost curve.

The shape of the variable cost curve in Figure 5-3 is therefore a reflection of the law of diminishing returns — in a way, it mirrors the shape of the total product curve in Figure 5-1.

Finally, Figure 5-4 graphically shows the composition of the total cost structure as the sum of variable and fixed costs. The curvilinear shape of the total cost curve derives from the curvilinear shape of the variable cost curve, which (as explained above) arises from the marginal product pattern.

The firm's total cost per production period consists of fixed and variable costs. The shape of the variable cost curve, and hence the shape of the total cost curve, reflects the law of diminishing returns.

Table 5-3 Boatco's total cost structure

(1) Production and sales volume (boats per month) Q	(2) Labour employed (hours per month) L	(3) Labour cost ($ per month)	(4) Materials cost ($ per month)	(5) Variable cost ($ per month)	(6) Fixed cost ($ per month)	(7) Total cost ($ per month)
0	0	0	0	0	6 000	6 000
1	300	3 600	1 000	4 600	6 000	10 600
2	480	5 760	2 000	7 760	6 000	13 760
3	600	7 200	3 000	10 200	6 000	16 200
4	780	9 360	4 000	13 360	6 000	19 360
5	990	11 880	5 000	16 880	6 000	22 880
6	1 290	15 480	6 000	21 480	6 000	27 480
7	1 683	20 196	7 000	27 196	6 000	33 196
8	2 480	29 760	8 000	37 760	6 000	43 760
9	3 780	45 360	9 000	54 360	6 000	60 360

All cost figures are totals for all boats produced per month. The total cost is the sum of variable and fixed cost. Variable cost, in turn, is the sum of labour and material cost.

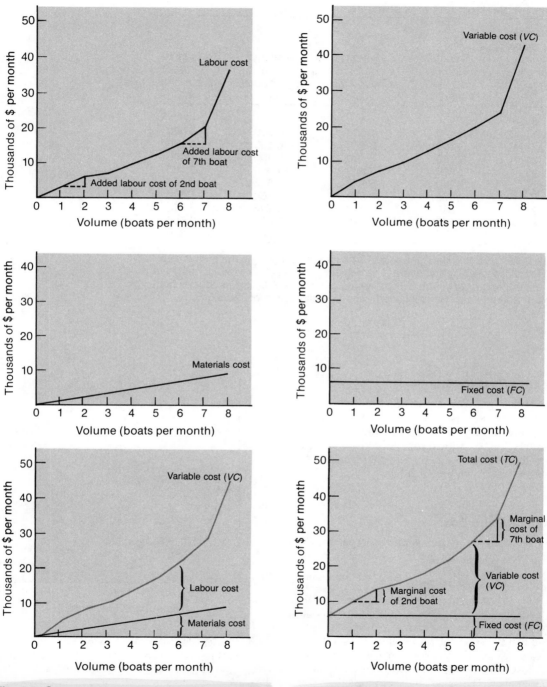

Fig. 5-3 Composition of Boatco's variable cost structure

Graphical representation of data from columns 4 and 5 of Table 5-3.

Fig. 5-4 Composition of Boatco's total cost structure

Graphical representation of data from columns 6 and 7 of Table 5-3.

Table 5-4 Boatco's unit cost structure

Production and sales volume (boats per month) Q	Average fixed cost ($ per boat) AFC	Average variable cost ($ per boat) AVC	Average cost ($ per boat) AC	Marginal cost ($ per boat) MC
0	∞	∞	∞	—
1	6 000	4 600	10 600	4 600
2	3 000	3 880	6 880	3 160
3	2 000	3 400	5 400	2 440
4	1 500	3 340	4 840	3 160
5	1 200	3 376	4 576	3 520
6	1 000	3 580	4 580	4 600
7	858	3 885	4 743	5 716
8	750	4 720	5 470	10 564
9	667	6 040	6 707	16 600

All cost figures are dollars per boat. The average cost (AC) is the sum of average fixed costs (AFC) and average variable costs (AVC). All average costs are calculated from data in Table 5-3. The marginal cost (MC) is reproduced from Table 5-2. It can also be calculated from the last column of Table 5-3.

Per Unit Cost Measures

An alternative way of depicting a firm's cost structure is in terms of per unit cost measures (in this case, cost per boat). Table 5-4 shows these cost measures, all of which can be derived directly from Table 5-3. In Figure 5-5, the average cost concepts are shown graphically.

Average Fixed Cost

Average fixed cost (AFC) is fixed cost per production period divided by the total volume of output produced ($AFC = \dfrac{FC}{Q}$). Because the numerator (FC) is independent of output, the greater the volume of output produced during each time period, the smaller the average fixed costs per unit. (Note that the AFC for zero output in Table 5-4 is indicated as infinitely large. This is because any total cost value divided by zero gives an infinitely large number. The same applies to the other average cost values in the table.)

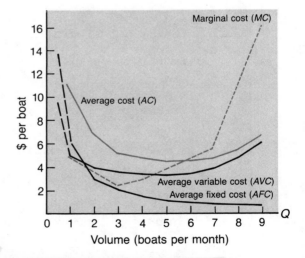

Fig. 5-5 Boatco's unit cost structure

Graphical representation of data in Table 5-4. Note that the marginal cost curve (MC) intersects both the average variable cost curve (AVC) and the average cost curve (AC) at their minimum points.

Marginal Cost

The shape of the marginal cost curve has been explained earlier. Over the range of output and employment for which the marginal product of labour is increasing, marginal costs decline. At the output level for which marginal product stops rising, marginal costs stop declining. Finally, as diminishing returns set in (that is, as the marginal product of labour begins to fall) marginal costs increase.

Average Variable Cost

Average variable cost (AVC) is variable cost per time period divided by the volume of output produced during the same time period ($AVC = \frac{VC}{Q}$).

Average Cost

Average total cost per unit of output — often called average cost per unit, average unit cost, or simply **average cost** (AC) is total cost divided by the volume of output produced. Average cost therefore equals the sum of average fixed cost and average variable cost as follows:

$$AC = \frac{TC}{Q} = \frac{FC + VC}{Q} = \frac{FC}{Q} + \frac{VC}{Q} = (AFC + AVC)$$

The average cost curve (AC) shown in Figure 5-5 must lie above the average variable cost (AVC) curve because average cost comprises average variable cost plus average fixed cost. Further, the marginal cost curve must go through the minimum point of each of the AVC and AC curves. The last two facts follow directly from the general relation between the concepts of marginal and average. Intuitively, it can be illustrated as follows.

Suppose for example that several exam papers have been marked and assigned an average grade of 70%. If the next or marginal grade is less than 70%, this will necessarily reduce the average grade of the class; if the marginal grade is higher than 70%, it will raise the average. Finally, if the marginal grade is just 70% (equal to the average grade), it will neither raise nor lower the average. Similarly, then, if the marginal cost of producing one more unit of output is less than average cost (if the marginal cost curve is above the average cost curve), marginal cost will reduce the average cost (the average cost curve will be falling). If marginal cost is above average cost (if the marginal cost curve is

above the average cost curve), marginal cost will raise average cost (the average cost curve will be rising). When marginal cost is just equal to average cost (at the point of intersection of the marginal cost and average cost curves), marginal cost will neither raise nor lower average cost (the average cost curve will be neither rising nor falling, i.e. it will be at its minimum point).[3]

In deciding how much output to supply per production period, the firm requires knowledge of per unit costs. The average cost (AC) is the sum of average fixed cost (AFC) and average variable cost (AVC). At the output level for which AC is the lowest, it must equal the marginal cost (MC). When AVC is the lowest, it also equals the MC.

5-5 THE SUPPLY DECISION

At the outset, we explained that the main purpose of this chapter was to examine the supply decision — how much a firm would be willing to produce at various possible market price levels. As we argued earlier, this question depends critically on the firm's unit costs of production. We are now ready to examine the supply decision in some detail. In this regard, we begin by considering the simplest, though least common, type of market or industrial structure — **pure competition**. Briefly, a market can be called purely competitive if each firm in it has negligible influence over the market price of the product (or service) and if there is easy (low cost) entry into and exit from the industry. For example, assume for the moment that within the boat market there are a thousand firms like Boatco, each producing a standard type of boat. Further, assume that for practical purposes boat buyers have no preference for a particular brand or make of boat. Admittedly, this is a highly unlikely set of circumstances, but we make no apologies for asking you to make these assumptions. This simplified context enables us to gain important insights that will be useful when we consider the supply decision in the context of more common market structures.

In a market with many producers and no brand preference, if Boatco attempted to sell its boats at a higher price than that of other makes, it would sell

---

3. A similar argument explains the relation between the marginal cost curve and the average variable cost curve.

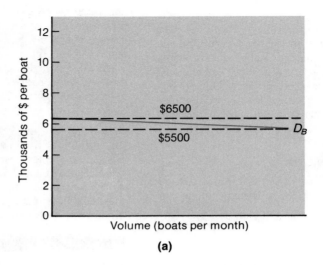

(a)

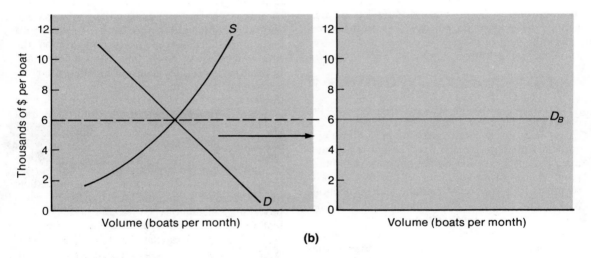

(b)

Fig. 5-6 Demand for Boatco's boats in a purely competitive market

(a)   A purely competitive firm can sell all of its output without significantly affecting the market price. Hence the demand curve facing such a firm is almost horizontal.

(b)   As an approximation, the demand curve facing a purely competitive firm is drawn as a horizontal line at the price level determined by market demand and supply.

very few boats. Only those buyers who either did no comparison shopping or who believed they saw some difference in the Boatco product would make purchases. On the other hand, consider what would happen if Boatco lowered its prices slightly. Because even a small price reduction would make its boats a bargain relative to other makes, Boatco would be able to sell a large volume.

In other words, within a market comprised of many producers who sell a similar product, each firm would perceive the demand for its product as being almost infinitely sensitive to price change. Such a situation is shown in Figure 5-6.

In the case described above and depicted in Figure 5-6a by the solid D_B curve, Boatco would have negligible control over the going market price of $6000. Offering its boats at $5500, Boatco could probably sell a great many. If Boatco wanted to charge a higher price, the most it might get is perhaps $6500, and in that case it would sell very few units.

We can see, therefore, that the demand curve facing any single firm within a purely competitive market is almost horizontal (Figure 5-6a). In fact, within a purely competitive market context, it is customary to represent the firm's demand curve as being perfectly horizontal. This representation may be extreme, but would be approximately true for a market situation such as the one described here. For all practical purposes, any single firm within a purely competitive market is so small relative to the size of the market that it can sell as much or as little as it wants without materially affecting the market price (Figure 5-6b).

The demand curve facing a firm in a purely competitive market is a horizontal line representing the going market price.

In a purely competitive market, where a single firm's actions have little or no influence on market price, the firm really has only one major decision variable, namely Q — how much to produce. Of course once it decides how much to produce, it will also have to decide on how much labour to hire, what materials to purchase and so on. But these latter choices are heavily dependent on the volume decision.

In such a market, Boatco faces the following production decision: in view of the current market price, at which the firm can sell as much as it

wants, what production volume will maximize the firm's profit? The answer depends on the particular current market price and the firm's cost structure. Boatco should, of course, continue to produce a greater and greater volume so long as the extra sales revenue generated is greater than the extra cost. Whenever this is the case, additional production will increase profit. Boatco, if it follows such a decision rule, will maximize its profit.[4]

Table 5-5 reflects the demand situation assumed to be facing Boatco together with the company's relevant cost data. As reflected in Figure 5-6b, the current market price for boats is assumed to be $6000. As a consequence, Boatco's dollar sales revenue is simply $6000 multiplied by the number of boats it produces and sells. Extra revenue per unit sold (or **marginal revenue**) in this case is simply the $6000 per unit that the firm gets from each boat produced. Total cost figures in Table 5-5 are the same as those reported earlier in Table 5-3. Marginal cost figures were reported in Table 5-4 but may again be derived by subtracting successive total cost figures. For example, the extra or marginal cost of producing the second boat is the total cost of producing two boats less the total cost of producing only one, that is to say, $13 760 − $10 600, or $3160.

From studying the Total Revenue and Total Cost columns, or more simply, merely from glancing at the Profit column, we see that the best (profit-maximizing) volume for Boatco to produce would be 7 boats per month. This volume provides the largest total monthly profit of $8804.

A profit-maximizing firm in a purely competitive market will produce and sell that level of output for which the marginal revenue generated by the last unit sold equals marginal cost of producing that unit.

Maximum Profit

We might examine why a smaller or larger volume would not earn as much profit. For instance, if Boatco produced only 6 boats each month why would this volume not yield as much profit? The

---

4. This rule would lead a firm to choose the output level associated with maximum profits. However, if it cannot operate at a profit, it may be that the firm's minimum loss is incurred by shutting down and not producing at all. This case is examined below.

Table 5-5 **Boatco's demand and cost data (competitive market price = $6000 per boat)**

Production and sales volume (boats per month) Q	Total revenue ($ per month) TR	Marginal revenue ($ per boat) MR	Total cost ($ per month) TC	Marginal cost ($ per boat) MC	Profit ($ per month) PROF
0	0	—	6 000	—	− 6 000
1	6 000	6 000	10 600	4 600	− 4 600
2	12 000	6 000	13 760	3 160	− 1 760
3	18 000	6 000	16 200	2 440	1 800
4	24 000	6 000	19 360	3 160	4 640
5	30 000	6 000	22 880	3 520	7 120
6	36 000	6 000	27 480	4 600	8 520
7	42 000	6 000	33 196	5 716	8 804
8	48 000	6 000	43 760	10 564	4 240
9	54 000	6 000	60 360	16 600	− 6 360

Profit is maximized when 7 boats are sold. At this quantity of output, marginal revenue (*MR*) equals marginal cost (*MC*). In this particular case, the equality is only approximate, since profit would actually be maximized at an output level slightly lower than 7 boats.

answer is that the 7th boat produced would increase Boatco's monthly revenue by $MR = \$6000$ and increase the company's costs by only $MC = \$5716$. Consequently, by producing 7 boats rather than 6, Boatco's monthly profit rises by $284 (the difference of $6000 − $5716). Likewise, Boatco should not produce the 8th boat (per month) since its monthly revenue would increase by less than its monthly costs ($6000 as compared with $10 564) and its monthly profit would fall by $4564.

Generalizing from our above example, whenever marginal revenue from an increase in production exceeds marginal cost (as it does in Table 5-5 up to 7 boats per month), then over this same production range it must also be true that an increase in production leads to higher total profits (as shown in Figure 5-7). Similarly, if marginal revenue from an increase in production falls short of marginal cost (as it does for output levels beyond 7 boats per month), then over this same production range, an increase in production leads to lower total profit. Finally, if after the production of one more unit the marginal revenue equals marginal cost, profit is neither increased nor decreased by the additional unit produced. At this volume (in Figure 5-7, approximately 7 boats per month) profit must be at a maximum.

An Alternative Graphical Representation

Figure 5-8 illustrates alternative ways of representing profits or losses.[5] Figure 5-8a shows a competitive firm in a profit position at Q_0, while Figure 5-8b deals with the same firm facing a much lower

---

5. Note that the curves in Figure 5-8 have the same general shape as the previous cost curves shown in this chapter, but are drawn smooth (without kinks). Economists often draw curves in this fashion for convenience. In doing so, they imply that the quantity of output can be measured in sufficiently small units that the kinks become so numerous and so close to each other that the cost and profit curves can be drawn smooth.

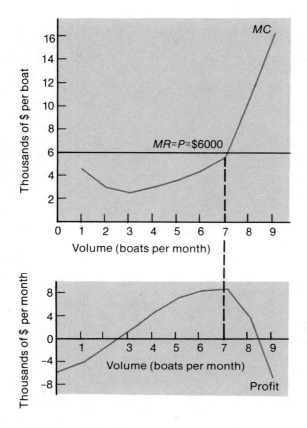

Fig. 5-7 Boatco's profit-maximizing output decisions

Graphical representation of data from Table 5-5. Given the market-determined price of $6000 per boat, a purely competitive firm will maximize profit by selling 7 boats. At this quantity of output, $MR = P = MC$ (approximately).

market price (P_1), producing at Q_1 and experiencing a loss each production period. The lower halves of each diagram depict the profit and loss figures directly as the height of the profit or loss curves at the corresponding output levels Q_0 and Q_1. This is the same method we used earlier (see again, for example, Figure 5-7). An alternative, and perhaps more popular, method of profit representation is shown in the upper halves of the two diagrams. For instance, the average profit per unit of output sold is the difference between the price

per unit sold (average revenue per unit) and average cost. Total profit per production period is, then, this difference ($P - AC$) multiplied by the number of units of output sold (Q). In Figure 5-8a, the profit per production period is thus represented by the area of the shaded rectangle, whose length is Q_0 and whose height is $P_0 - AC$. In Figure 5-8b, since the market price at Q_1 is less than the average cost of production, the firm experiences a loss on each unit sold equal to $AC - P_1$ and a total loss each production period of $(AC - P_1) \times Q_1$. This loss may be represented in Figure 5-8b by the shaded rectangle whose length is Q_1 and whose height is $AC - P_1$.

Accuracy and Errors

Once management has collected data similar to that in Table 5-5, the decision process is quite straightforward. The most difficult task of all, however, is to come up with reliable data for such a table. In the case of a highly competitive market, it would not be difficult to estimate revenue. The market price of all such boats would be known to be $6000. Estimation of costs, however, would be slightly more difficult in this case. If Boatco estimated these costs incorrectly, then the company might make a smaller profit than it could by making some other volume decision. In this respect, firms are like consumers who take action only in an *attempt* to maximize satisfaction. There are errors in decision making in both cases.

The Firm's Supply Curve

Boatco, in a large market and producing a standardized product, is essentially unable through its own actions to influence the market price, which it must accept as being determined by its environment, the market place as a whole. In this case, Boatco has only one decision instrument at its disposal — the volume of its production and sales. Realizing that the company can sell, for all practical purposes, as much as it likes at whatever the market price is, we would like to derive Boatco's *supply curve*. That is, we would like to determine how much Boatco would be willing to produce and sell at various market prices.

Presumably Boatco would like to produce, at any possible going market price, whatever volume

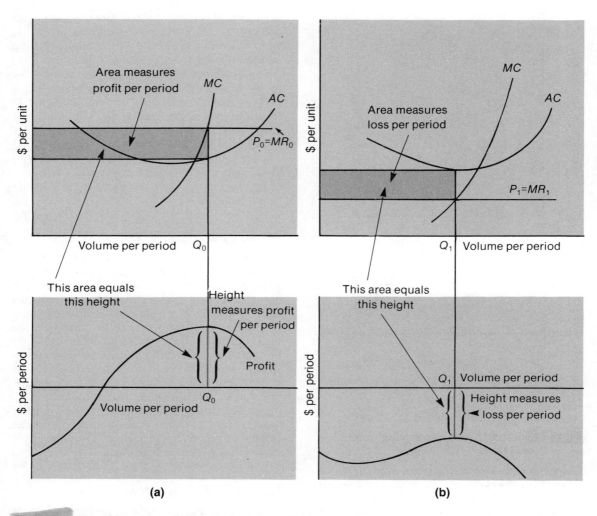

Fig. 5-8 Alternative representations of profit and loss

A generalized representation (no connection to the Boatco data) of optimum output decision by a purely competitive firm. The upper half of each diagram shows per unit costs and price as well as total profit (or loss). The lower half shows total profit (or loss) per period. The firm in diagram (a) is making a profit; the firm in diagram (b) is experiencing a loss.

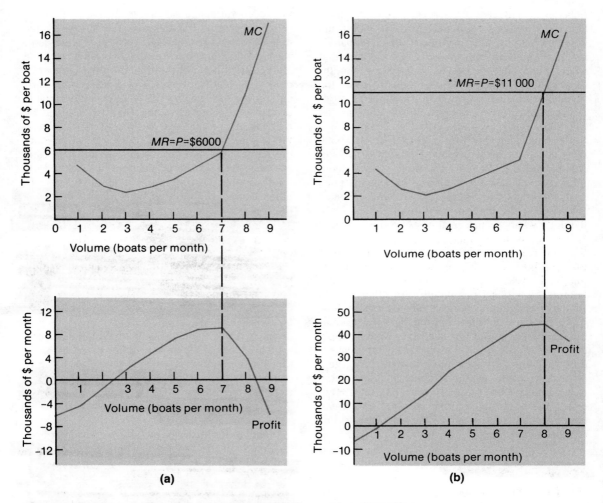

(a)

(b)

Fig. 5-9 Boatco's profit-maximizing output decision under alternative market prices

* Actually the profit-maximizing volume ($MR = MC$ point) occurs slightly beyond $Q = 8$

Given the market-determined price of $11 000 per boat, a purely competitive firm will maximize profit by selling 8 boats. At this quantity of output, $MR = P = MC$ (approximately). The cost data is taken from Table 5-5.

it believes will earn the largest profit. We have already seen that for a market price of $6000, the volume that would maximize the company's monthly profit (in other words, the volume that would make $MR = MC$) is 7 boats per month. (See Figure 5-9a.) In Figure 5-9b, we show the volume at which Boatco would maximize its profit if the market price was not $6000, but instead $11 000.

We have seen that at a market price of $6000 (and hence an extra revenue per boat of $6000) Boatco would make more and more profit by continuing to increase production as long as marginal costs were less than $6000. Consequently, Boatco would make the biggest profit by producing up to the point where its marginal costs become equal to $6000 per boat. Similarly, at a market price of $11 000 per boat, the company would maximize total profit by producing at a point where its marginal costs are $11 000 per boat (that is, at a volume of 8 boats per month). In other words, Boatco's marginal cost curve tells us exactly how much Boatco would like to produce at each possible market price. But this is exactly what a supply curve means. Hence, in a purely competitive industry, if firms are attempting to make as large a profit as possible, each firm's marginal cost curve is apparently also its supply curve. In fact, however, only a portion of the marginal cost curve comprises the supply curve. We now turn to this modification.

The Shutdown Point

By definition, regardless of how many boats Boatco decides to produce each month, the company will incur its fixed monthly costs since the fixity of such costs means that they do not depend upon how much output is produced. Fixed costs are therefore *irrelevant costs* for a firm's production (supply) decision. Variable costs are, however, very relevant since by definition they depend upon how much is produced.

If Boatco produces zero boats per month, there will be no revenue. With no revenue and $6000 worth of fixed costs to meet (see again Table 5-3), monthly profit would be − $6000; in other words, there would be a monthly $6000 loss. Hopefully, some monthly production will be better than none, in the sense that the revenue will more than cover

the added variable costs and lead to less of a loss, or even a profit. But this may not always be the case. The total revenue received from some non-zero production volume is, by definition, the market price per unit multiplied by the number of units sold, that is to say, $P \cdot Q$. Further, total variable cost of producing Q is the average variable cost of producing each unit (AVC) multiplied by the volume produced (Q), i.e. $VC = AVC \cdot Q$. For a nonzero production volume (Q) to be more profitable than no production at all, the total revenue ($P \cdot Q$) from production must exceed the total variable cost of production ($AVC \cdot Q$). In other words, *the market price* (P) *must exceed average variable cost* (AVC). For any price below minimum average variable cost even the best nonzero production volume (where $MR = MC$) would lead to a greater loss than would be incurred by shutting down production altogether and simply suffering the monthly fixed costs, because on average the revenue brought in from each boat sold would not cover the average variable cost of each boat's production.

Since at any market price below minimum average variable cost the firm would be better off shutting down and not producing at all, in a purely competitive market the firm's supply curve is not its entire marginal cost curve but only that portion of the marginal cost curve that lies above the average variable cost curve.

Figure 5-10 illustrates the above considerations. In Figure 5-10a, for all prices below P_0, not producing at all is better than producing where $MR = MC$, since at prices below P_0 variable costs would not be covered by revenue earned. For prices between P_0 and P_1, producing at the volume where $MR = MC$ would still result in losses (since the average revenue per unit — the price — would not cover average cost per unit). But average revenue per unit (P) would exceed average variable cost (AVC); hence, losses would be lower than they would be as a result of not producing at all. In this instance, we might say that the revenue being in excess of variable cost at least serves to offset in part the fixed monthly costs of production. For prices above P_1, producing where $MR = MC$ implies profits since price (P) exceeds average cost (AC).

Figure 5-10b illustrates Boatco's supply curve. Since for prices below P_0 (minimum AVC) the

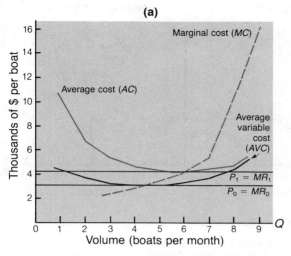

(a)

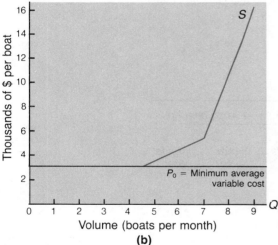

(b)

Fig. 5-10 **Derivation of a competitive firm's supply curve**

(a) When the market-determined price drops below P_1, the firm will be losing money. Nevertheless, it should keep operating (in the short run) rather than shutting down, as long as the price remains above P_0.

(b) The supply curve of a purely competitive firm is that portion of its *MC* curve which is above the *AVC* curve.

company would not produce ($Q = 0$), effectively Boatco's supply curve coincides with the vertical axis up to this price level. For prices above P_0, the company's supply curve coincides with its marginal cost curve.

It is customary to speak of a competitive firm's supply curve as that portion of its marginal cost curve that lies above its average variable cost curve.

5-6 INDIVIDUAL FIRM AND MARKET SUPPLY

Just as market demand is the sum of all individual demands at each possible price, so market supply — in a competitive situation at least — is the total quantity that would be supplied at each possible market price by all the firms in the industry. In other words, conceptually, a purely competitive market supply curve would be the horizontal sum of all the individual firms' marginal cost curves.

For example, suppose Boatco and Sunfun were two firms within the boat market. Portions of their marginal cost (supply) curves are shown in Figure 5-11. At a market price of $6000 per boat, Boatco would be willing to produce and sell 7 boats per month. Sunfun would produce and sell 5 boats per month at $6000 per boat. The total monthly volume offered (supplied) by both Boatco and Sunfun at $6000 per boat would thus be 12 boats.

The market supply curve is the horizontal sum of the supply curves of all firms in the market.

5-7 COST CHANGES AND SUPPLY SHIFTS

Earlier, in Chapter 3, we argued more or less intuitively that changes in unit production costs would lead producers to require different prices in order to produce various volumes of output. That is to say, market events which alter a firm's cost structure also affect its conditions of supply. We have now seen that the critical cost concept for the supply decision is *marginal cost*. Let us now, therefore, investigate how various events affect marginal cost structure of individual firms and thus market supply. The effects of these events are summarized in Table 5-6.

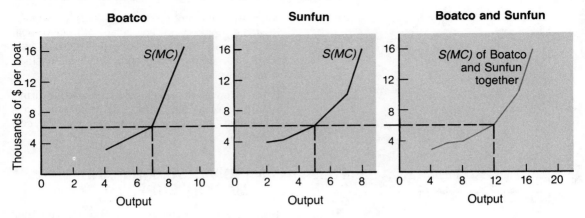

Fig. 5-11 From individual firm to market supply in pure competition

A graphical illustration of the proposition that the market supply curve is the horizontal sum of the supply curves of all firms in the market. In this case, the market consists of only two firms.

Table 5-6 Effects of changes in supply conditions

Case	Added labour required	Marginal costs for the seventh boat (in $)			
		Added labour cost	Added materials cost	Excise taxes	Marginal cost
(0) Original situation	393 hours at $12 per hour	4716	1000	—	5716
(1) Increase in wage rates from $12 to $15 per hour	393 hours at $15 per hour	5895	1000	—	6895
(2) Increase in marginal productivity (10%)	354 hours at $12 per hour	4248	1000	—	5248
(3) Imposition of 10% excise tax	393 hours at $12 per hour	4716	1000	572	6288
(4) Increase in materials cost (25%)	393 hours at $12 per hour	4716	1250	—	5966

Impact of changes in input prices, changes in productivity and the imposition of an excise tax on the marginal cost of Boatco. Original cost data is taken from Table 5-2.

Case (0) represents the original marginal cost situation that Boatco would face when producing the 7th boat each month. These data were taken from Table 5-1 and Table 5-2.

Change in Wage Rates

Suppose the wage rate that Boatco pays its workers was raised from $12 per hour (including fringe benefits) to $15 per hour. We know now that to examine the effects on supply we must focus on marginal cost impacts.

The wage rate increase raises labour's portion of the marginal cost of producing the 7th boat, and therefore also raises marginal cost accordingly. And this would be the situation not merely for an output level of 7 boats per month but for all levels of output. Now, to produce and sell 7 boats per month Boatco would require a market price of no less than $6895 instead of $5716 (and so on, over the entire production range). In other words, Boatco's supply curve would *shift upward*. If other firms within the industry were also paying higher wage rates, other individual firm's supply curves would shift upward as well — with the result that the total or market supply curve for the industry would also shift upward.

Change in Productivity

Suppose Boatco's productivity rose so that it now required 10% fewer labour hours to produce the 7th boat per month (354 hours versus 393 hours). In this case, the extra labour cost of producing the 7th boat would fall to $4248 with a corresponding reduction to $5248 in the marginal cost of producing the 7th boat. Boatco would now be willing to produce and sell a volume of 7 boats per month at a market price of only $5248 per boat rather than at a market price of $5716. If the increase in productivity was widespread throughout the industry, the market supply curve would correspondingly *fall*.

Change in Excise Taxes

As explained earlier, if part of a firm's gross receipts from customers has to be paid in excise taxes to the government, such taxes are similar to other expenses. We shall now show that an increase in excise taxes increases a firm's marginal costs at each level of production.

Suppose initially there was no excise tax on boats. The marginal cost of $5716 for the 7th boat produced per month consequently would include no excise tax expense. However, if a 10% excise tax was introduced (so that for each boat sold Boatco would now have to remit to the government part of what it collects from the consumers), Boatco would not be willing to produce the 7th boat for the final market price of $5716. In fact, marginal cost including the excise tax would increase to $6288 (which is $5710 + 10% of $5716).

In order to produce 7 boats per month, Boatco would require a final (excise tax inclusive) price of $6288. This new final price would then be sufficient to pay for Boatco's marginal costs of producing and selling the 7th boat. These costs would be $4716 for labour, $1000 for material and $572 for excise tax (Case (3), Table 5-6).

It follows that an increase in excise taxes would cause a competitive market's supply curve to *shift upward*.[6]

Change in Materials Price

If the price of materials suddenly rose by 25%, the marginal cost of the 7th boat produced per month would rise by $250 to $5966 (Case (4), Table 5-6). Marginal costs, and hence, the supply curve of Boatco would *shift upward*, as would the market supply curve for boats since other boat manufacturers would also suffer the materials price rise.

Changes in the firm's costs, or imposition of excise tax on its output cause a shift in the marginal cost curve and thus in the firm's supply curve.

5-8 MARKET SHOCKS AND THE FIRM

In a purely competitive industry, an individual firm must accept the market price as given — something that is effectively beyond the firm's control. This is shown on Figure 5-12.

The market price is determined by market demand (D_m) and supply (S_m) (Figure 5-12a). This market price effectively becomes the firm's demand curve as well as its marginal revenue curve. The only decision for the firm is to determine how

---

6. The various types of excise and general sales taxes applied in Canada are discussed in Chapter 13.

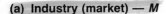

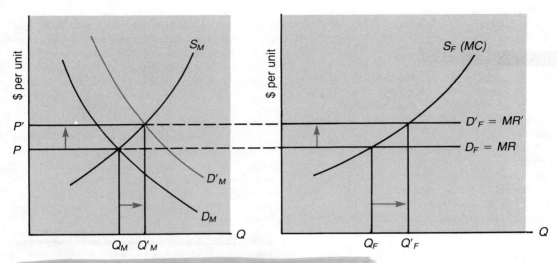

Fig. 5-12 Effect on the firm of an increase in market demand

An increase in market demand raises the market price and induces an increase in output by a purely competitive firm.

much to produce. If it wishes to maximize its profit, the firm will produce at the volume indicated by Q_F, where the extra cost of the last unit produced just equals the market price.

Market Demand Shock

If there was a sudden increase in market demand to D'_M, (Figure 5-12a), the market price would rise, as would the demand curve facing the firm (Figure 5-12b). At the former output level (Q_F), marginal revenue would now exceed marginal cost. This would indicate that the firm could increase its profit by expanding its output to Q'_F (Figure 5-12b).

Market Supply Shock

Suppose that for some reason each firm's marginal costs increase. As a consequence, the market supply curve will also rise, as shown in Figure 5-13a. This rise brings what at first may seem to be a strange result. Because the market price rises, each firm can now sell as much as it likes at a higher price (that is, the demand curve facing the firm has risen to D'_F — see Figure 5-13b). However, the firm's marginal costs are now also higher, so the firm will sell less than before, as indicated.

A purely competitive firm responds to market shocks by adjusting its level of output.

(a) Industry (market) — M   **(b) Firm — F**

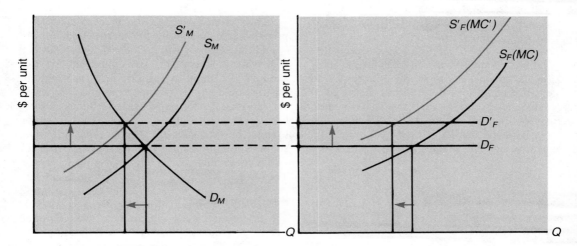

An increase in marginal costs of all firms causes an increase in the market price and also a reduction in output by each firm and in the market as a whole.

5-9 ELASTICITY OF SUPPLY

As in the case of market demand, it is sometimes useful to examine the sensitivity of market supply with respect to changes in factors that affect the quantity supplied. Such factors include the market price of the good itself, wage rates faced by producing firms, productivity within the industry and excise or sales taxes imposed on the industry. Also, as in the case of market demand, we can measure this sensitivity (or *elasticity*) to change in factors by a numerical supply elasticity coefficient. For example, we define the **elasticity of supply** with respect to changes in the price of the product itself as follows:

$$e' = \frac{\% \text{ change in quantity supplied}}{\% \text{ change in market price}}$$

Similar coefficients can be defined with respect to changing factors other than market price.

If the costs of producing one more unit of volume (marginal costs) change very slowly over a wide range of production, then for a small percentage change in market price, producers will agree to supply a large percentage increase in output. Hence, e' will be a very large number, as shown by curve S in Figure 5-14. If, on the other hand, it is difficult to produce extra units of output without rapidly increasing marginal costs, then for a particular percentage increase in market price there will be very little increased production response. In this case, e' will be very small. This case is illustrated by curve S' in Figure 5-14.

The term *elasticity of supply* refers to the sensitivity of supply toward a change in some factor. Thus, a coefficient of elasticity of supply with respect to market price equal to 1.69 indicates that a given percentage increase in the market price will cause the quantity supplied to increase by 1.69 times that percentage. If the market price increases by 10% the quantity supplied would increase by 16.9%.

Supply Shocks and Time

As in the case of market demand, the sensitivity of market supply increases with the relevant time period considered because the costs of adjusting volumes of output generally vary directly with the speed at which the adjustment takes place.

Suppose, for example, that we are studying the housing market. The sensitivity of supply for houses within a given city to increases in market prices would be close to nil if we restricted our analysis of such sensitivity to a period of a few weeks or even months. Even if there were large price increases in houses, the construction industry would find it very costly to increase the total stock of housing quickly by any perceptible amount. For example, the rapid expansion of output in the industry would require overtime premiums to workers and pressure for larger wage settlements. Less efficient tradespeople and machinery would be brought into the industry. Bottlenecks for certain supplies might result in payments being made for idle workers and equipment over limited periods. Thus, there would be a low sensitivity of market supply of houses with respect to changing house prices in the short run. However, given a period of, say, five years for our time horizon, we would see many more houses in existence if house prices were $120 000 than if they were $80 000, because this time period would allow the construction industry enough time to react to the more profitable house prices. New builders would come into the construction industry and begin to build, attracted

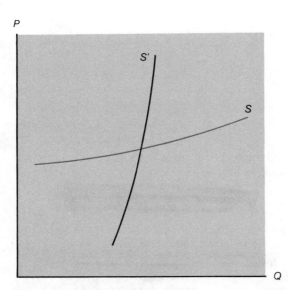

Fig. 5-14 Elastic and inelastic supply

A flatter supply curve indicates that supply is elastic with respect to price; a steeper supply curve indicates less elastic supply.

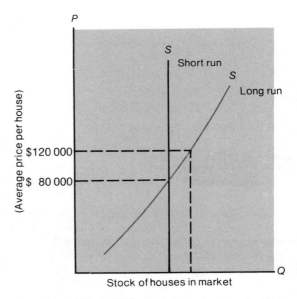

Fig. 5-15 Effect of time on supply sensitivity toward price changes

In the short run, a supply curve may be perfectly inelastic with respect to price. Over time, the same curve is likely to become more elastic as suppliers adjust their production facilities.

by the greater possible profit as a result of the higher house prices. See Figure 5-15 in this regard.

The elasticity of supply increases over time, as suppliers are given the opportunity to adjust their production facilities to the changing market prices.

CONCLUDING REMARKS

Market supply, when related to price, may be thought of as either (i) the quantities that would be produced at various market prices or, more usefully, as (ii) the minimum prices firms would accept in order to produce various quantities. *Marginal cost* is the chief determinant of the minimum prices that firms will accept in order to produce any particular quantity of output. Hence, marginal cost is the chief determinant of the market supply-price relation. In a purely competitive market, a firm's supply curve is its marginal cost curve, and the market supply curve is conceptually the horizontal summation of all the firms' marginal cost curves.

KEY TERMS AND CONCEPTS

profit maximization	per unit (average) cost
production function	fixed costs
marginal product	variable costs
fixed factor	average fixed cost
variable factor	average variable cost
law of diminishing returns	average cost
cost structure	pure competition
marginal cost	marginal revenue
total costs	elasticity of supply

PROBLEMS

Problem 1

Explain briefly how the law of diminishing returns implies that marginal costs increase as output produced per production period becomes greater. (That is to say, explain why the law of diminishing returns implies an upward sloping marginal cost curve.)

Problem 2

The following information is based on a monthly production period and concerns a particular firm employing labour and material as two variable factors. The firm's fixed costs are $2000 per month, the wage paid is $1000 per month and the materials cost are $100 per unit of output. The firm's short-run production relation between labour and output is shown below.

Workers employed per month (L)	Output produced per month (in units) (Q)
0	0
1	7.5
2	17
3	28.1
4	40.5
5	53.3
6	65.3
7	74.6
8	79.9
9	79.9

a)   Complete the table below, illustrating the company's monthly cost structure in relation to output produced.

Output volume (units per month) Q	Variable cost ($ per month) VC	Fixed cost ($ per month) FC	Total cost ($ per month) TC
0			
7.5			
17.0			
28.1			
40.5			
53.3			
65.3			
74.6			
79.9			
79.9			

b) From your completed table of part (a), complete the table below, illustrating the company's unit cost structure in relation to output produced.

Output volume (units per month) Q	Average variable cost ($ per month) AVC	Average fixed cost ($ per month) AFC	Average cost ($ per month) AC	Marginal cost ($ per unit) MC
0				
7.5				
17.0				
28.1				
40.5				
53.3				
65.3				
74.6				
79.9				
79.9				

c) From the production relation illustrated above, what would be the marginal cost for an output beyond 79.9 units per month?

Problem 3

A company had these expenses during a particular year: property taxes = $5000; depreciation of building = $15 000; bond interest = $10 000; sales taxes = $25 000; materials = $500 000; accountants' fees = $2500; assembly line workers' wages = $200 000.

a) Which of the above would generally be fixed within the short run?

b) If the above had been all of the company's expenses during the year, and the company produced 10 000 litres of a single product, what were the following cost measures for the year: Average costs? Average fixed costs? Total costs? Variable costs? Average variable costs?

Problem 4

Given the following diagram for a particular company, label the diagram with the following: average variable cost (*AVC*); average fixed cost (*AFC*); average cost (*AC*); marginal cost (*MC*).

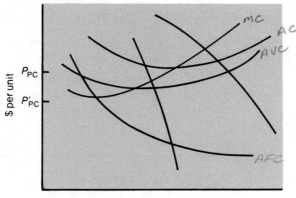

No. of units per week

Problem 5

In this chapter, we set up a somewhat restrictive market environment known as pure competition. Within that framework we examined the factors that would determine how much a profit-maximizing individual firm would produce at various market prices and the connection between an individual firm's supply and that of the whole industry (market). This problem and the next few are designed to bring out the main features of this development.

a) Assuming a particular firm is in a purely competitive industry facing a market price of $900 per unit, complete the table below concerning the firm's demand data.

Volume sold (units per week) Q	Total revenue ($ per week) TR	Marginal revenue ($ per unit) MR
0		
1		
2		
3		
4		
5		
6		
7		
8		

b) If the firm is producing and selling three units per week, and if producing the fourth unit per week would increase total weekly costs by $850, how many units (three or four) would you advise the firm to produce per week? By how much would your decision increase the firm's profit over the alternative action? What would you suggest if costs to produce the fourth unit per week increased by $950?

c) On a single diagram — with axes as shown below — draw and label: (i) the demand curve facing the firm, (ii) the firm's marginal revenue curve and (iii) the firm's average revenue per unit curve (*AR*) (where *AR* = *TR/Q*).

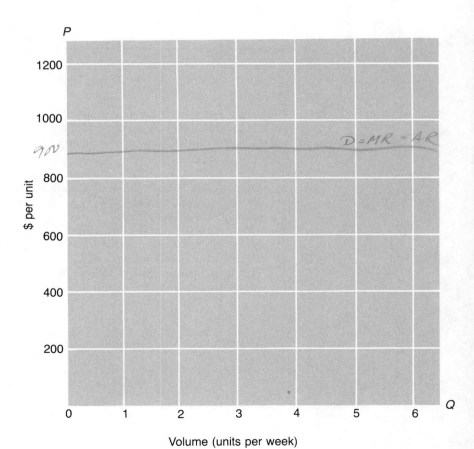

Problem 6

a) Given the following additional cost data on the above firm, complete the table and determine the best output level for management to produce.

b) Explain why maximum profit is achieved when production equals as closely as possible the output level at which marginal revenue equals marginal cost.

Volume (units per week) Q	Total revenue ($ per week) TR	Marginal revenue ($ per unit) MR	Total costs ($ per week) TC	Marginal costs ($ per unit) MC	Profit ($ per week) PROF
0			1000		
1			1399		
2			1898		
3			2497		
4			3196		
5			3995		
6			4894		
7			5893		
8			6992		

Problem 7

The object here is to graph your analysis of Problem 6. In the figure below, the first diagram shows the market determination of the going $900 price. The second and the third diagrams are designed for data concerning the individual firm.

a) On diagram (b), plot the information (from the data given in the table of Problem 6) that would enable you to determine graphically the best weekly production volume.

b) On diagram (c), plot the firm's profit pattern with respect to volume. Indicate the best weekly output levels on diagrams (b) and (c).

c) Describe the effect on diagrams (b) and (c) of a drop in the market price due to a market demand falloff. What would happen to the profit-maximizing volume for each firm?

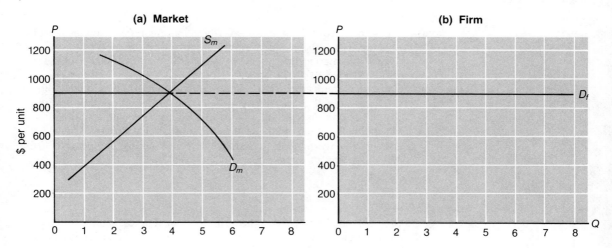

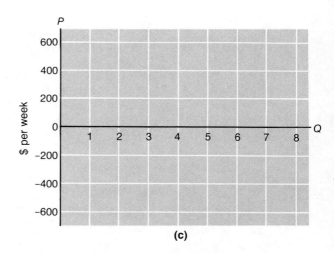

Problem 8

a)   We know profit is maximized when marginal cost equals marginal revenue. How much output would the firm in Problem 6 choose to produce if the market price per unit was $400? $500? $600? $700? $800? $900? $1000? $1100?

b)   From your results in part (a), plot how much the firm would be willing to produce and sell at various market prices from $400 per unit through to $1100 per unit (at $100 intervals). Join your points with a smooth curve. On the same graph, plot the firm's marginal cost curve. What do you conclude concerning the relation between a purely competitive firm's *MC* curve and its supply curve?

Problem 9

Suppose there are 1000 identical firms in the same market that the company of Problems 6 and 7 is in. Further suppose the market demand for the product involved is as shown below in Figures (a) and (b).

a)   Using your results from 8b, and knowing that there are 1000 identical firms in the industry, draw in the market supply curve.

b)   What would be the resulting market price?

c)   In a fashion similar to that of 7a, show on diagram b below how each firm's best production decision is related to the market price.

d)   Suppose the industry is initially producing and selling less output than the equilibrium level and at a price below the equilibrium price. What would inform the industry of this fact and what motivation would the industry have to step up its output?

e)   If one firm decided to double its size by building an identical plant, what would be the effect on market price? If instead the number of producers suddenly doubled to 2000, what would be the effect on market price, on each individual firm's production, and on profits? (Give approximate numerical answers.)

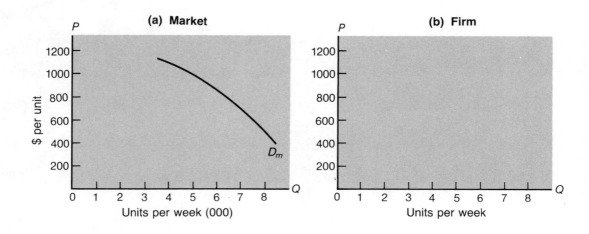

Problem 10

Suppose each of the 1000 firms of Problem 9 suddenly experienced substantial cost increase as shown below.

a)   What factors might give rise to these increased costs?

b)   Plot the old and new market supply curve on a diagram such as a of Problem 9. What would happen to (i) market price, (ii) industry and firm production volume and (iii) industry and firm profits? (Give approximate numerical answers.)

Volume (units per week) Q	Total costs ($ per week) TC
0	1000
1	1599
2	2298
3	3097
4	3996
5	4995
6	6094
7	7293
8	8592

Problem 11

Suppose that instead of the cost changes of Problem 10, there is a market demand shift, as shown below.

a)   What factors might give rise to such a demand shift?

b)   What now will be the best weekly output for each of the 1000 firms? (Use diagram b.)

c)   Calculate the new profit levels for each firm within the industry and compare them with original profits (Problem 6).

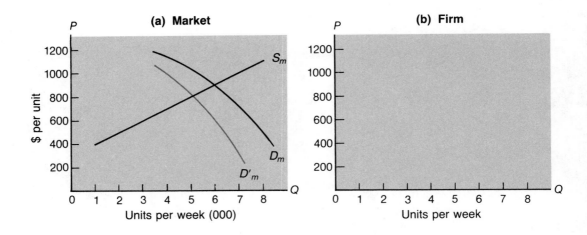

Problem 12

a)   What is the elasticity of supply of land? Why is the elasticity this measure?

b)   Compare the short-run elasticity of supply of doctors with that of bank tellers and briefly explain possible differences.

c)   Explain briefly how immigration policy might influence the short-run elasticity of supply of doctors.

d)   Why would we expect the long-run elasticity of supply of doctors to be greater than the short-run measure?

Problem 13

Explain briefly why each of the following events would or would not be expected to affect a purely competitive market price or output in the short run: (a) an increase in firms' property taxes, (ii) an increase in wage rates, (iii) an increase in excise taxes on the good in question, (iv) a new 10% customs duty (tax) on imported materials necessary for production of the good in question.

CASES

Case 5-1

The Financial Post

Price wars could bring shakeup in video stores

By JAIMIE HUBBARD

CANADA'S VIDEO movie rental business is headed for a showdown. Intense competition in an overcrowded market has seen prices slashed to as little as 99¢ per rental from an average of $3.50 in better times. While watching Sylvester Stallone at bargain-basement prices may be a boon for consumers, it spells disaster for retailers.

Canada is a nation of TV and movie addicts, with about 31% of households owning video cassette recorders (that's three million VCRs). But there are simply too many movie rental outlets — about 5,000 across the country — competing for this year's estimated $900 million worth of business.

On average, each video store serves only 600 VCR-owning homes. In the U.S., where VCRs are found in 34% of households, each outlet has an average of 1,600 customers.

Retailers pay from $80 to $100 for a new title, up from about $50 in 1983. Even if the film is rented every day, at 99¢ a crack it will take at least three months to recoup its cost, exclusive of overhead expenses. Meanwhile, demand for the film fades as the studios bring on new releases.

The cost of opening a video store is high, ranging from $100,000 for a small outlet, stocking a few hundred titles, to $750,000 for a deluxe operation. The large entry cost makes poorly financed independent retailers the most vulnerable to a shakeout. But the chains — most of which are franchise operations like Toronto-based FNC Video Inc., which has 128 National Video outlets in Eastern Canada — are feeling the pinch, too.

With larger chains beginning to bypass distributors entirely and deal directly with the studios (for estimated savings of 5%–10%), the competition at the distribution level has become as intense as that at the retail end. A fight is on between the two main national distribution companies, Vancouver-based MMC Video One Canada Ltd. and Montreal-based Bellevue Home Entertainment, a division of Astral Bellevue Pathé Inc. The companies have been offering deep discounts to retailers regardless of how much they buy.

Video One aims to put an end to that type of discounting by switching to a rebate system on Sept. 1. Every quarter, retailers will receive money back based on the volume purchased.

That system, say industry insiders, will probably be adopted as the standard. But it could further squeeze independents to the point where they cannot stay in business.

For those who can hang on, the future isn't entirely bleak. To increase revenues, retailers are pushing sales, as well as rentals, of video tapes — everything from Jane Fonda Workout tapes to classic movies appealing to collectors.

Simultaneous releases — video stores getting films at the same time they are shown at first-run theatres — are also a possibility. North American theatre box-office receipts were down about 7% in 1985, in part because of video. The studios feel they could gain back some of that business by releasing both simultaneously. That would benefit retailers, particularly when the industry scores with a box office blockbuster.

a) What features of the video rental market would suggest that it could be approximately described as "purely competitive"? Which of its features are not entirely consistent with the model?

b) Assuming the characterization of this market as purely competitive is reasonable, illustrate (without numbers) in diagrams such as those below, the effect of the following:
   (i) A decline in prices of VCRs;
   (ii) An increase in prices of new titles (such as the increase from $50 to $80–100 mentioned in the article);
   (iii) Releases of new titles by the studios.

c) The article puts the cost of entry into the video rental industry as high as $100 000–$750 000. What might be some alternative (cheaper) ways of entering the industry? How would you represent the effect of new entry in your diagrams?

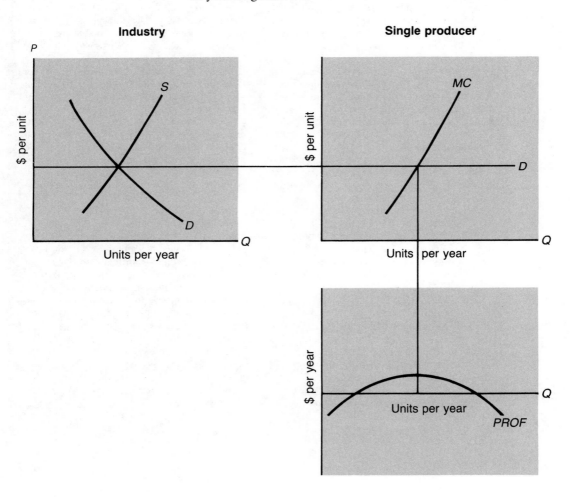

Case 5-2

The Financial Post

Market crisis deepens amid potato squabble

By JIM CLUETT

PRINCE EDWARD ISLAND'S boom-and-bust potato industry has hit an all-time low. Table potatoes, which cost nearly 6¢ a pound to produce, are selling for barely 2¢.

Industry officials estimate that Island farmers owe nearly $70 million on this year's crop and many have little or no capacity to pay it back. Indeed, after the disastrous state of the current market, many farmers will require additional credit to plant new crops.

The director of marketing for the provincial Department of Agriculture, Dave Faulkner, calls the situation "very severe," and adds that at least $50 million is required to cover the current shortfall in potato sales. "We now have a crisis," Faulkner says. "If we don't get some assistance we'll have a big crisis."

Last week provincial industry officials visited Ottawa to ask federal politicians to invoke the Agricultural Stabilization Act. Under the act, federal Minister of Agriculture John Wise could assist Island farmers by making payments to cover the difference between this year's market price and 6¢, which is the average price received over the past five years. That could cost taxpayers as much as $65 million.

Ironically, if Island farmers do receive federal assistance, they'll have another problem on their hands, one that could be just as bad. For the past several years potato farmers in Maine have been calling for countervailing duties on Canadian potatoes. The Maine growers allege that their Canadian counterparts receive unfair government assistance.

If federal stabilization payments are made, the American farmers will have the evidence they need to prove their allegations. Last year, Island growers shipped nearly $9 million worth of table potatoes to the U.S.

The president of P.E.I.'s Potato Marketing Board, Elmer MacDonald, regards the Maine threat as serious. "What do I do?" he asks.

"Do I let the industry go down the drain or take the risk? I don't have an alternative."

For years the roller-coaster potato industry in P.E.I. has veered from profit-making highs to near bankruptcy. It's a ride only the brave can endure and one that's controlled by the whims of an international market. Now things are especially bad because of an acute oversupply of potatoes throughout North America. U.S. growers increased their potato harvest by 50 million hundredweight in 1985, equivalent to total Canadian production.

"There are a lot of farmers in financial distress," Faulkner says. "They're not all going to make it, no matter what we do. Our objective is to make sure that we at least save the industry."

Roughly a third of the potato accounts with the Farm Credit Corp. are now in arrears. The corporation's regional manager in Moncton, N.B., John Van Abbema, says if it weren't for a federal moratorium on farm foreclosures, the corporation would initiate action against 20 of the accounts between now and March.

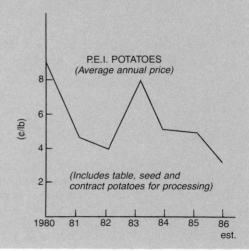

P.E.I. POTATOES
(Average annual price)

(¢/lb)

(Includes table, seed and contract potatoes for processing)

1980 81 82 83 84 85 86 est.

a) Explain, with the help of diagrams, what kind of developments in the market for potatoes led to the conditions facing a typical potato farmer.

b) The federal assistance discussed in the article is, in effect, a per-unit subsidy (exactly the opposite of an excise tax). Show its effect on the farmer and on the potato market.

c) Suppose the U.S. will impose a countervailing duty (tariff on potatoes imported from Canada calculated in such a way as to offset the effect of the Canadian government subsidy.) Show the impact of such a tariff in your diagrams. Who will benefit from the above policies? Who will suffer?

Case 5-3

The Globe and Mail, Toronto

Oil prices taking toll on U.S. rigs

The number of oil rigs in the United States is falling sharply, and industry executives say it may soon reach the lowest point since 1945.

They said the trend will continue unless oil prices rebound. They also warn that the result will be renewed heavy dependence on foreign oil supplies.

"It all depends on the price of oil. We believe this is temporary, but the question is how long is temporary," said Barney White of Zapata Corp. of Houston, an oil services company.

Since November, oil prices have fallen more than 60 percent because of ample supplies. . . .

"Earnings could be disastrous and the (oil rig) count could go to 800," said Scott Nedrow, an analyst with C.J. Lawrence. The drop in demand for rigs has been so severe that cost-cutting has become a way of life for oilfield services companies.

For instance, a semi-submersible drilling rig, used in offshore drilling, whose daily cost would have been $100,000 in the early 1980s, can be hired for about $20,000 a day now.

Some are being operated below cost to bring in much-needed cash.

"They have debt they've got to service," Mr. White said.

a) Illustrate the developments described in the article in diagrams, showing both the conditions in the market and the conditions facing a typical "oilfield service company."

b) Do you agree that the result of the trends described in the article will be "renewed heavy dependence on foreign oil supplies"? Why? Carefully state your assumptions.

c) The daily costs of a rig in the early 1980s was $100 000, but the same rig can now be hired for as low as $20 000 a day. Are the companies behaving rationally?

APPENDIX 5A: PRODUCTIVITY AND COST

5A-1 Average Productivity

The average productivity or simply the *average product* of a factor of production is defined as the ratio of total product (Q) to quantity of factor used. When "productivity" is referred to in the financial press or in everyday discussions, more than likely the reference is to the *average product of labour* $\frac{Q}{L}$. For example, if each production period a hypothetical firm was producing an output volume of 50.4 units with 9 workers and 10 units of physical capital, people would commonly refer to the firm's productivity as being (50.4 ÷ 9) — or 5.6 units of output per worker. The responsibility for rising or falling productivity should not, however, be attributed to labour just because labour input is chosen as part of the productivity measure. For example, productivity could equally well be expressed as (50.4 ÷ 10) — or 5.04 units of output per unit of physical capital employed.

5A-2 Average and Marginal Product

To demonstrate the connection between average and marginal product let us utilize the example from Chapter 5. Table 5A-1 shows the earlier assumed production function for Boatco (Table 5-1) together with marginal and aver-

Table 5A-1 Production and productivity data for Boatco

Monthly production and sales volume (no. of boats) Q	Monthly labour employment (no. of hours) L	Marginal product of labour (no. of boats/ hour) MP_L	Average product of labour (no. of boats/ hour) AP_L
0	0	—	
1	300	0.0033	0.0033
2	480	0.0056	0.0042
3	600	0.0083	0.0050
4	780	0.0056	0.0052
5	990	0.0048	0.0051
6	1290	0.0033	0.0047
7	1683	0.0025	0.0042
8	2480	0.0013	0.0032
9	3780	0.0008	0.0024

Marginal product exceeds average product up to about 900 hours per month of employment, and this causes the average product to increase. For higher levels of employment, marginal product is lower than average product, and this causes the average product to decline.

age product of labour calculations. Figure 5A-1a illustrates the relation between marginal and average product graphically.

Marginal curves always intersect average curves at *extreme points* (maxima or minima) on the average curves. We saw an illustration of this feature in the chapter in connection with marginal and average cost curves. With regard to productivities, from Figure 5A-1a, until the employment of about 900 hours per month the additional output obtained from each additional hour employed (MP_L) is greater than the average productivity of each of the hours worked (AP_L). Consequently, employment of additional labour hours up to 900 hours per month causes average product to increase. Beyond 900 hours per month, the additional output from each additional hour employed (MP_L) is less than the average productivity of the existing level of employment (AP_L) and thus pulls down average productivity. The marginal product curve thus intersects the average product curve at the latter's maximum point.

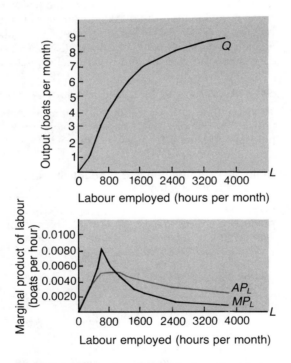

Fig. 5A-1 Boatco's production function and related marginal productivity pattern

Graphical representation of data from Table 5A-1. Total product (upper diagram) increases at an increasing rate up to the level of about 600 hours — the point of diminishing returns — and subsequently increases at a decreasing rate. The marginal product reaches maximum at the point of diminishing returns and intersects the average product curve at the maximum point of the latter.

5A-3 Productivity Measures and Unit Costs

In the chapter we showed that the marginal cost of production is related to the wage rate, the marginal product of labour and materials costs. Neglecting materials costs, the marginal cost-marginal productivity relation was summarized by Equation 5-1, which is reproduced below for convenience.

$$MC = \frac{W}{MP_L} \tag{5-1}$$

From Equation 5-1, we see that marginal cost varies inversely with marginal product. For instance, when marginal product is at a maximum value, marginal cost is at its minimum point.

A similar relation to 5-1 may be shown to exist between average variable cost and average product. Again neglecting possible materials costs, average variable costs comprise those of labour. That is to say,

$$AVC = \frac{\text{Labour costs}}{Q}$$

By dividing both numerator and denominator of the previous expression by the number of labour units employed, we arrive at Equation 5A-1:

$$AVC = \frac{\text{Labour costs} / L}{Q / L} = \frac{W}{AP_L} \tag{5A-1}$$

Expressions 5-1 and 5A-1 are parallel relations. Average variable cost varies inversely with average labour productivity and minimum average variable cost occurs at that output (and employment) level for which the average product of labour is at a maximum. Finally, just as expression (5-2) of the chapter adjusted the marginal cost expression for materials costs, so too may we adjust average variable cost for materials costs through relation 5A-2.

$$AVC = \frac{W}{AP_L} + \begin{array}{l} \text{value of material} \\ \text{necessary for the} \\ \text{production of each} \\ \text{unit of output} \end{array} \tag{5A-2}$$

The observed connections between maximum points on the productivity curves and minimum points on the corresponding unit cost curves have been discussed in the text of Chapter 5. Also, it may readily be seen by examining relations 5-1 and 5A-1 that at that employment and corresponding output level at which average and marginal productivity are equal, average and marginal cost are also equal. Finally, we may note that when the marginal product of labour is zero and output is therefore at a maximum level, the average product of labour is greater than zero. These facts imply that at that employment level for which marginal productivity is zero, marginal cost becomes infinite (from Equation 5-1), but average variable cost remains at a finite level.

Problems for Appendix 5A

Problem 5A-1

(This problem is an extension of Problem 5-2.)

The following information is all based on a monthly production period and concerns a particular firm employing labour and material as two variable factors. The firm's fixed costs are $2000 per month, the wage paid is $1000 per month, and materials costs are $100 per unit of output. The firm's short-run production relation between labour and output is shown below.

	Production Information				Cost Information		
L	Q	MP_L	AP_L	MC	AVC	AFC	AC
0	0						
1	7.5						
2	17.0						
3	28.1						
4	40.5						
5	53.3						
6	65.3						
7	74.6						
8	79.9						
9	79.9						
10	75.9						

a) Complete the above table. What are the units of measurement for MP_L and MC?

b) Explain why $MC = AVC$ when the latter is a minimum; why $MP_L = AP_L$ when AP_L is a maximum; and, finally, why these two equalities occur at the same point (that is to say, at the volume for which $MC = AVC$, the amount of labour employed is such that $MP_L = AP_L$).

c) Graph (i) MP_L and AP_L and (ii) MC, AVC, AFC and AC on two separate charts.

d) Explain why at the point where MC becomes infinite AVC and AC do not.

APPENDIX 5B: SUPPLY ELASTICITY

5B-1 Further Analytics

As in the case of demand, elasticities of supply may be defined to measure sensitivities of quantities supplied, with respect to changes in each possible supply determinant. For example, we could define an elasticity of supply coefficient with respect to changes in market price, wage rates, excise taxes and so on. However, unlike demand, elasticities of supply are almost solely restricted to price. For this reason, when the term elasticity of supply is used, it may generally be taken to mean "with respect to price." The elasticity of supply, then, is usually defined as follows:[1]

$$e = \frac{\% \text{ change in quantity supplied}}{\% \text{ change in product price}}$$

Because the short-run supply curve as a rule is positively sloped, e is generally positive as well.

5B-2 Arc and Point Elasticities of Supply

(i) Arc Elasticity. As in the case of demand, *arc elasticity of supply* is an average price sensitivity measure over a finite range. Its formula for calculation is identical to that used for demand:

$$e = \frac{\Delta Q / Q}{\Delta P / P}$$

$$e = \frac{(Q_2 - Q_1) / \frac{1}{2} (Q_1 + Q_2)}{(P_2 - P_1) / \frac{1}{2} (P_1 - P_2)}$$

(ii) Point Elasticity. In the limit, as the range over which the elasticity is measured shrinks to zero, arc elasticity becomes point elasticity. The *point elasticity of supply* has the same formula as the point elasticity of demand:

$$e = \frac{dQ}{dP} \cdot \frac{P}{Q}$$

In the remainder of this section, for convenience we shall deal with point elasticities of supply.

5B-3 Range of Elasticity of Supply Coefficient

Figure 5B-1a depicts the range of possible values e may take for any given supply curve. On the horizontal portion, the slope $(\frac{dP}{dQ})$ is zero. As a conse-

---

1. We use the same symbol (e) for supply elasticity that we used for demand elasticity. In instances where there may be some confusion as to whether supply or demand is involved we shall differentiate the two by e_S and e_D.

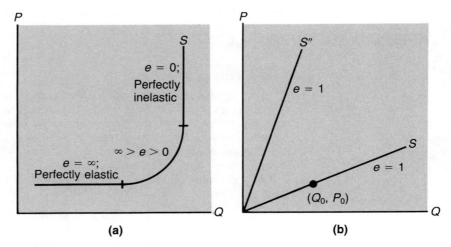

Fig. 5B-1 Elasticities of supply

(a)   Elasticity of supply varies along a curvilinear supply curve.

(b)   Elasticity of supply is constant and equal to unity along all linear supply curves emanating from the origin.

quence, $e = \frac{1}{0} \cdot \frac{P}{Q} = \infty$. On the vertical portion, the slope $(\frac{dP}{dQ})$ is infinite, with the resulting elasticity

$$e = \frac{dQ}{dP} \cdot \frac{P}{Q} = \frac{1}{\infty} \cdot \frac{P}{Q} = 0$$

In intermediate cases, because the slope $(\frac{dQ}{dQ})$ is neither zero nor infinity, the elasticity coefficient lies somewhere between infinity and zero.

It may at first seem paradoxical that the elasticity of supply is unity everywhere along any linear supply curve emanating from the origin. However, this oddity is readily explained. For example, Figure 5B-1b depicts two possible supply curves. Choosing an arbitrary point (Q_0, P_0) on any one of them, we may write the slope (dQ) at such a point as $\frac{P_0}{Q_0}$. Consequently, the elasticity coefficient is

$$e = \frac{dQ}{dP} \cdot \frac{P}{Q} = \frac{Q_0}{P_0} \cdot \frac{P_0}{Q_0} = 1$$

We leave it as an exercise to prove that a linear supply curve with positive vertical intercept has an elasticity everywhere greater than 1.0, while that with a negative vertical intercept has an elasticity everywhere less than 1.0 (see Problem 5B-2).

Problems for Appendix 5B

Problem 5B-1

Explain briefly what is meant by the following terms: arc elasticity of supply, point elasticity of supply, inelastic supply.

Problem 5B-2

Given the supply relation $Q = a + bP$, prove that supply is elastic, of unitary elasticity, or inelastic, according to whether a is greater than zero, equal to zero, or less than zero; in that order.

CHAPTER 6

Analysis within Imperfectly Competitive Markets

6-1 INTRODUCTION AND PURPOSE

In the previous chapter, we considered the supply side of the market place. We assumed an industrial structure of pure competition and no government intervention. In most instances within the Canadian economy these assumptions are blatantly false. In this chapter, we examine the opposite end of the spectrum of possible market structures, the case of monopoly. In Chapter 7, we look at intermediate positions between pure competition and monopoly.

Modifications must be made when considering managerial decisions made in the context of imperfectly competitive markets. On the other hand, most of the supply-demand analysis of market shocks and their effects on market price, volume of production and employment within the industry (as discussed in Chapters 2 and 3), remains relevant.

6-2 MONOPOLY: THE OTHER EXTREME

Strictly speaking, we define a **monopolized market** as a situation in which there is a single seller of a particular good or service for which there are no close substitutes. Just as the purely competitive case is unusual in practice, so too is the pure monopoly situation. Nevertheless, to gain a proper perspective it is important for us to examine both ends of the market spectrum, from pure competition to pure monopoly.

Demand under Monopoly

Though in some instances consumers may dislike buying, or may even refuse to buy, certain products because a particular industry is not purely competitive, this conduct does not provide a major

Table 6-1 Conglom Corporation Ltd. estimated revenue and cost data

Price ($ per boat) P	Volume demanded (000 of boats per month) Q	Total revenue (000 of $ per month) TR	Marginal revenue ($ per boat) MR	Total cost (000 of $ per month) TC	Marginal cost ($ per boat) MC	Profit of (000 of $ per month) PROF
12 000	2	24 000	—	13 760	—	10 240
10 800	3	32 400	8400	16 200	2 440	16 200
9 600	4	38 400	6000	19 360	3 160	19 040
8 400	5	42 000	3600	22 880	3 520	19 120
7 200	6	43 200	1200	27 480	4 600	15 720
6 000	7	42 000	-1200	33 196	5 716	8 804
4 800	8	38 400	-3600	43 760	10 564	-5 360
3 600	9	32 400	-6000	60 360	16 600	-27 960

Information on revenues, costs, and profits of Conglom Corporation. Profit is maximized when 5 000 boats are sold. For this volume of sales, marginal revenue equals marginal cost ($3 600 approximately equals $3 520).

influence on demand behaviour. We generally take the perceived value of a particular good or service to the consumer as being by and large unaffected by the type of market structure.

Supply under Monopoly

Even though market demand is largely uninfluenced by market structure, business decision making is materially affected. Managers of a monopolized industry, in attempting to maximize profit for their shareholders, will make significantly different decisions than managers of purely competitive firms. The following example illustrates the effect that monopolization of an industry has on market prices, output, employment and profits.

Remember from Chapter 5 that Boatco was assumed to be one of a thousand similar firms producing identical boats for the Canadian market. These conditions formed the basis for our purely competitive industrial structure. We now suppose that Boatco and the other 999 firms are suddenly bought out by a large conglomerate, Conglom Corporation Ltd. Conglom will now operate the industry as a monopoly consisting of 1000 branch plants.

Here are some questions that will emerge. Will Conglom change the volume of production in total

or raise prices? What will happen to employment and profits within the industry? Will consumers be better or worse off as a result?

Conglom naturally wishes to make as much profit as possible from its takeover. Consequently, the first thing it might do is summarize all available cost information on its 1000 separate plants and then analyze the market demand.

At this point, we make a rather important assumption, which we shall scrutinize later. We assume that Conglom's resulting cost structure is the same as that of the original purely competitive industry as a whole. This simply means that Conglom keeps operating with all of the 1000 plants it owns. Consequently, in Table 6-1, the volume and total cost figures are 1000 times those that appeared earlier in Table 5-3, which reflected Boatco's cost structure. From Table 5-3 we saw, for instance, that Boatco could produce 4 boats per month at a total cost of $19 360, and so could each of the other original manufacturers. We assume, therefore, that Conglom, which owns all 1000 original firms, is able to produce 4000 boats (1000 × 4) per month at a total cost of $19.36 million (1000 × $19 360).

Demand analysis is something the purely competitive firms did not have to worry about, because each knew that being small relative to the total market, it could sell all it wished at the going market price. However, what is true for each pure competitor is not true of the industry as a whole. Conglom realizes that given demand, the amount it decides to produce certainly will affect the market price.

monopol

The most significant difference, insofar as the demand data of Table 6-1 is concerned, is that from Conglom's standpoint marginal revenue is not identical with market price (as it was for Boatco Ltd.). Neither is the marginal revenue a constant figure as it was for Boatco. Instead, marginal revenue falls as Conglom produces and sells more to the market — and falls more rapidly than the market price. Let us now investigate the reason for this.

In the purely competitive situation Boatco was so small relative to the entire industry that it could not affect the market price by varying its own production volume. Conglom, however, is now the only producer in the market. It faces the entire market demand curve for boats. If Conglom is to sell significantly more or less output it will certainly have an impact on the market price.

For example, suppose Conglom wishes to sell 5000 rather than 4000 boats per month. Consumers will buy 5000 boats if the price per boat is reduced from $9600 to $8400 (Table 6-1). Therefore, to sell 5000 boats per month, Conglom will have to make the price of each boat $8400.[1] For the extra one thousand boats sold monthly, the company will receive $8400 per boat — which it would not have got if the price had not been reduced. This amount alone represents an addition of $8 400 000 to total revenue. On the other hand, the company will now get less revenue from selling each of the first four thousand boats than it would have received if it had left the price at $9600 per boat — in fact, $4 800 000 less revenue (the $1200 price reduction per boat ($9600 − $8400) × 4000 boats). The net effect on total revenue is an increase of only $3 600 000 (the difference between the gain in revenue of $8 400 000 and loss in

revenue of $4 800 000). Therefore, the extra revenue per boat obtained from selling the additional one thousand boats is $3 600 000 ÷ 1000 boats, or $3600. This marginal revenue figure is less than the new price of $8400, because for each additional boat sold at $8400 Conglom must give up $1200 revenue, which would have been earned from each of the first 4000 boats that it could have sold at $9600 per boat. If a firm has to reduce its price on all sales in order to sell a greater volume, its marginal revenue (extra revenue on each extra unit sold) will always be less than the new price.

As Figure 6-1a illustrates, the marginal revenue curve for Conglom lies below the demand curve. If Conglom's management wishes to maximize profit, it will produce up to, but not beyond, the point where marginal revenue equals marginal cost. As can be seen from Figure 6-1a (and from Table 6-1), for a total production volume of less than 5000 boats per month the marginal cost of producing each extra boat is less than $3520. Also, from the demand information depicted in Figure 6-1a, we see that the marginal revenue from selling each extra boat at volumes below 5000 is greater than $3520. Therefore, at volumes below 5000 it would yield Conglom more profit to increase production. Similarly we can see that to produce and sell more than 5000 boats, the extra revenue would be less than the extra cost. Therefore, it would not pay Conglom to produce and sell beyond five thousand boats per month. This action would reduce Conglom's total profit. Of course, this calculation is based on demand and cost *estimates*. However, Conglom would expect to earn the greatest profit by producing 5000 boats per month in 19X1.

If it wished to maximize its expected profit, Conglom would attempt to produce and sell 5000 boats at a price of $8400 per boat. As can be seen from Table 6-1, this is the highest price the market is prepared to pay when 5000 boats are offered for sale.

As a consequence, the monopolist would produce a lower total industrial output than the purely competitive industry. Market output would be reduced from 7000 to 5000 boats a month. This reduction would entail lower employment. Further, the market price would be higher than in the purely competitive industry. The reason for both of these results is that the monopolist maximizes profit by

---

1. An important point here is that we assume that all 5000 boats Conglom sells carry the same price tag, namely, $8400. Conglom cannot sell the first 4000 at $9600 and then the next 1000 at $8400. This action would be an entirely different consideration.

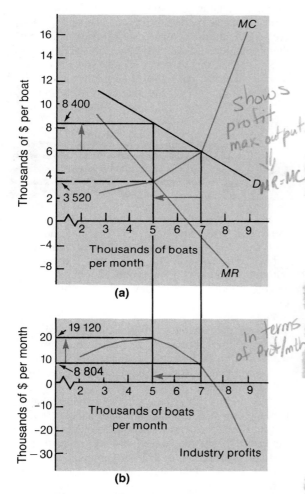

(a)

(b)

Fig. 6-1 Profit-maximizing price and volume decisions

Graphical representation of data from Table 6-1. Part (a) is in dollars per unit and shows the profit-maximizing level of output as one for which $MR = MC$. Part (b) shows the same outcome in terms of total profits per month.

acting in such a fashion. The new monthly profit of the industry after the restriction of output and the higher prices is $19.12 million, as compared with a monthly industry profit in pure competition of $8.804 million. (These figures may be found in Figure 6-1b or from Table 6-1.)

A monopoly firm faces a downward sloping demand curve. Consequently, marginal revenue is less than price. The profit-maximizing output for a monopoly is determined by equating MR and MC. The output level chosen by a monopolist is lower than would be the case if the industry was purely competitive.

Industry Profits

In Chapter 5 we showed that in a purely competitive industry, with each firm attempting to maximize its profit, the industry supply curve and industry marginal cost curve are one and the same. Consequently, the purely competitive market price and production volume (according to the market demand and marginal cost data of Chapter 5, which is reflected in Figure 6-1) would be $6000 per boat and 7000 boats produced per month. Although each firm may individually be attempting to maximize its profit, a purely competitive industry as a whole is not maximizing profit. The total industry profits can be increased by industry-wide management action such as would be forthcoming if a single entrepreneur took over all the original purely competitive firms as in our above example. (Alternatively, all firms could remain independent, but could agree, or "collude" to restrict output and raise price so that their joint profits would be maximized. This type of industry behaviour is discussed in Chapter 7.)

Conglom is able to increase industry-wide profit by cutting back production from 7000 boats per month to 5000. For each boat *not produced* over this output range the marginal cost saved by not producing exceeds the marginal revenue lost by not producing (see again Figure 6-1).

6-3 WELFARE CONSIDERATIONS

It is important to investigate whether monopoly is good or bad. To a considerable extent the answer depends on where we stand. As far as consumers are concerned, they are worse off facing a monopolistic market. They are now sacrificing more alternative expenditure for each boat. On the other hand, shareholders within the industry will earn higher profits under monopoly conditions than under purely competitive ones.

As far as workers are concerned, there will be less employment within the industry. It is not clear, however, to what extent workers will be hurt by this reduction. This will depend on how fast Conglom decides to adjust to a lower level of production. One possibility is that the process will be gradual, so that as employees retire or leave voluntarily they are not replaced. On the other hand, adjustment may be more rapid, so that some employees are forced to leave. These employees typically will get other jobs, but may suffer hardships in the interim.

In the discussion that follows, we neglect the adjustment costs that occur during a transformation of a purely competitive industry into a monopoly. We consider welfare differences between the two once the transformation is completed. We also abstract from comparing shareholders' gains from monopoly with consumers' and workers' losses. For example, we might pretend the consumers, workers and shareholders are the same group of people. Given these strict conditions, we examine whether there are any further welfare differences between monopolistic and competitive markets.

Social Evaluation of a Market Performance

A market's contribution to the material welfare (or happiness) of society may be assessed by comparing the value of its output, as perceived by society, with the cost of resources used up in production of that output. With reference to Figure 6-1, the height of the market demand curve reflects the value that consumers place on different volumes of the particular good or service (pleasure boats in this case). Similarly, marginal cost represents the extra cost of each unit of output (each boat). For instance, the five thousandth boat costs an additional $3520 (marginal cost) to produce. However, from the demand information, the five thousandth boat is worth $8400 to society. (Some consumer is willing to pay as much as $8400 to get the five thousandth boat).

As a consequence it would be worthwhile for society (everything else being equal) that the five thousandth boat be produced. Because consumers place $4480 more value ($8400 − $3520) on the finished product (boat) than on the resources (for

example, labour and materials) used up in its production, the market process can be said to have created an additional $4480 net value to society by the production and sale of the five thousandth boat.

So long as the value to society (*height of the market demand curve*) of one more unit of a finished product exceeds the cost of resources (*height of MC curve*) required for that extra unit's production, it is worthwhile to society (everything else being equal) to have that unit produced. This means that the **net contribution (value) to society of a market activity** is maximized when production takes place at the point where the value of the last unit produced is just equal to the cost of resources used to produce it. If this is the case within all markets in the economy, then (everything else being equal) input resources (land, labour and capital) are said to be *efficiently allocated across industries*, in the sense that the "right" amount of output is being produced and hence the "right" amount of inputs devoted to production in every industry.

Notice also that if output is pushed to the point where the demand curve crosses the marginal cost curve, the market price (*P*) will equal the marginal cost (*MC*) of the last unit produced (see Figure 6-1). Economists use this principle as one test for **allocative efficiency**. Since we always know the market price in any given industry, the problem becomes one of estimating the marginal cost of the last unit produced (from accounting and engineering data). If we discovered, for example, that a particular market price exceeded marginal cost, the conclusion would be that the given market was not benefitting society as much as it could. In fact, we would realize that entry of more input resources into the market should be encouraged so that output could be expanded.[2]

In making judgements about the desirability of pure competition, monopoly and other market structures, economists frequently employ the concept of allocative efficiency. Resources are said to be allocated efficiently if the market price equals the marginal cost of the last unit just sold.

---

2. The $P = MC$ test is only one of two basic tests for allocative efficiency. The other is to see whether economic profits are being earned. This aspect is discussed in detail in Chapters 8 and 10.

Everything Else Being Equal

The phrase "everything else being equal" was emphasized in the above discussion for good reason. There are instances in which the $P = MC$ rule does not indicate that a market is producing at the level that maximizes its welfare contribution to society. We mention a few of these instances below, but defer detailed discussion of most of them until Chapter 12 and beyond.

(1) In the preceding argument, we assumed that the firm was operating as efficiently as possible, that its marginal cost curve was as low as possible. Clearly, even with $P = MC$, the given market would not be providing the maximum benefit to society if the producers could lower their marginal costs by acting in a more efficient manner. It is also possible that monopolization of the industry may lead to lower production costs and, conceivably, also lower prices than those under pure competition. Yet allocative efficiency would not be achieved as long as $P > MC$.

(2) We also assumed that the perceived value of a good or service to consumers (which is reflected by the market demand curve) approximates the actual value to consumers when the use of the good or service is experienced. If, for instance, misleading advertising boosts consumers' perceptions concerning the product's worth above the actual value experienced after the product is purchased, the $P = MC$ rule will not indicate the production point at which a market's contribution to society is maximized.

(3) External costs or benefits connected with a particular item's production or use also destroy the validity of the $P = MC$ rule. In this case, cost figures reflected by individual producers' financial statements may not reflect full costs to society of the item's production, nor may market price accurately reflect social value (see Chapter 12).

(4) The market demand curve reflects not only people's desire to purchase, but also their ability to pay. One cannot buy (demand) a product without the income or wealth required to make payment. If we regard the present distribution of income and wealth in society as being in some sense inappropriate (unfair), we might be equally reluctant to regard the contribution to society at large as being reflected by a current market demand, which depends on this inappropriate income distribution. More will be said about this in later chapters.

(5) These welfare comparisons are sometimes labelled *static*, because they are concerned with the present level of price, output, and the relationship between P and MC. Welfare considerations in a *dynamic* context would also inquire whether invention and innovation (and thus future prosperity) are better stimulated under monopoly or under competition.

As we have seen, a purely competitive market will tend to produce a level of output at which $P = MC$, whereas a monopolistic market will tend to restrict output to a lower level, where $P > MC$ is the case. Everything else being equal, a purely competitive market tends to maximize the net economic contribution to society whereas a monopolistic market does not. This tendency provides the basic rationale for economists who consider a purely competitive economy as an ideal model. However, economists realize that in many instances everything else is not equal, and that, consequently, there may be justification for advocating a market structure that is less than purely competitive. Yet the appeal of competitive allocative efficiency should motivate us to require substantial evidence to the contrary before we advocate a noncompetitive market structure.[3]

6-4 A MARKET SUPPLY CURVE?

In a purely competitive market the market supply curve is the horizontal sum of the individual firms' supply curves (marginal cost curves). An adding-up process is not necessary in a monopoly market, because there is only one producer. Unlike in pure competition, the marginal cost curve of a monopolist is not the supply curve. Whereas a purely competitive firm is willing to accept a market price equal to the extra cost of producing the last unit (its marginal cost), a monopolist charges a higher price than this. In fact, the monopolist does not have a supply curve as such. If we asked the management of a monopoly how much it would be willing to produce (in order to maximize profits) at various market prices, it would be able to identify (for a given market demand and cost estimate) only one price at which a profit-maximizing monopolist

---

3. It may be shown, though it is not done here, that the $P = MC$ rule for allocative inefficiency in any given market breaks down if the condition does not hold in all other markets.

would be willing to produce. For example, in Figure 6-1 (with the given demand curve) there is only one possible profit-maximizing price for Conglom, namely, $8400 per boat. Therefore, if you happened to ask Conglom how much it would be willing to produce at a price different from this, there would be no answer. Conglom would not voluntarily produce at any price different from $8400.

What is true for a monopolist in this regard is true for any imperfect competitor. If ever price is a control variable (that is, if ever a firm faces a downward sloping demand curve) the firm will attempt to choose the single price that maximizes profit.

Since a monopolist would not voluntarily produce at other than profit maximizing price, a series of price-quantity combinations supplied by a monopolist cannot be traced. Hence, the concept of market supply curve is not well defined for industries which are not purely competitive.

6-5 CAUSE AND EFFECT ANALYSIS

For some purposes, it is important to establish whether the market resembles pure competition, pure monopoly or something between the two. However, the broad qualitative effects of most shocks on microeconomic markets tend to be the same, regardless of market structure.

Let us consider the qualitative impact of demand and supply shocks on market price and quantity produced, first within the context of a purely competitive industry, and then for a monopoly situation.

Demand Shocks

We do not have to examine every possible demand shock, because the analysis is identical in each case once we know whether demand has increased or decreased. Therefore, let us consider a decrease in consumer income, which leads to a decrease in quantity demanded at every price.

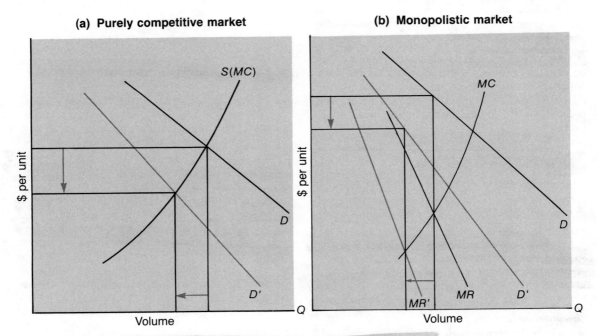

(a) Purely competitive market　　　　**(b) Monopolistic market**

Fig. 6-2 Demand shocks and their effects on market prices and volume

A downward shift in demand leads to a reduction in price and quantity sold, both in a purely competitive market (part (a)) and in a monopolistic market (part (b)).

Suppose that the original and new market demand information is as shown in Figure 6-2. A comparison of the old and new demand curves (*D* and *D'* respectively) indicates by how much the quantity demanded has fallen at each and every price level. The corresponding marginal revenue curves are designated by *MR* and *MR'*. As we see from Figure 6-2, regardless of whether an industry is purely competitive (Figure 6-2a) or monopolistic (Figure 6-2b), a reduction in demand tends to lead to a decrease in market price in industry sales volume and hence also in industry employment.

Supply Shocks

Here, again, we examine the effect of only one particular type of supply shock on the market, because others would have similar impact. Since demand conditions are assumed to remain constant, any impact on market price or volume must come through the influence of the supply shock on marginal costs.

For an example, consider an increase in material input prices, which affects both total and marginal production costs. The net result on both the purely competitive and monopolistic industries is shown in Figure 6-3. In both markets producers will raise prices as a result of higher costs (higher marginal costs, that is). The demand response to the higher prices will necessitate a reduction in sales volume and, consequently, industry employment.

Shorthand Analysis

Analysts often use a diagram with market demand and supply curves to demonstrate the effect of a particular shock on market price and production volume — even though the actual market structure may resemble a quasi-monopolistic situation. There is no formal market supply curve for a market structure in which firms have some degree of monopoly power. Nevertheless, an artificial supply-demand descriptive approach is often a convenient visual aid in analyzing the situation. If

(a) Purely competitive market
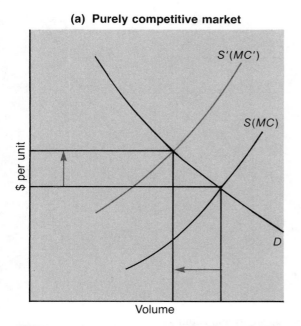

(b) Monopolistic market
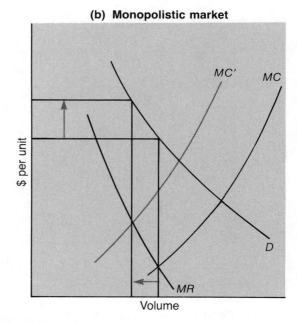

Fig. 6-3 Supply shocks and their effects on market price and volume

An upward shift in the marginal cost curve leads to an increase in price and a reduction in quantity sold, both in a purely competitive market (part (a)) and in a monopolistic market (part (b)).

we do use such shorthand in our analysis of an imperfect market, however, we should emphasize that we are not assuming the market to be purely competitive.

To give an example of what is meant here, suppose we are analyzing the effect of an increase in federal excise taxes on automobiles. The correct form of graphical analysis is shown in Figure 6-4b. On the other hand, a verbal explanation, such as that which follows, may be more useful, perhaps supplemented by Figure 6-4a. The correspondence between the formally correct graphical analysis of Figure 6-4b and the perhaps more intuitively appealing diagram in Figure 6-4a is shown also.

The increase in federal excise taxes entails, out of each dollar received from automobile buyers, a greater amount to be remitted to the federal treasury. This increase in effect raises the cost of producing and selling each car, just as would an increase in the cost of steel or the wages of automobile workers. As a result of these increased unit costs, higher prices will be asked for each possible volume of production. Faced with higher prices, the consumer will respond by reducing the number of cars purchased. Estimates of this effect see automobile volume reduced to 188 000 cars — from a projected 200 000 for this year — and the final price to the consumer on the average car raised from a projected $9700 to $10 500. (See Figure 6-4a.) The effect on employment within the industry has been estimated. . . .

At this point we have come full circle from the simplified demand-supply analysis presented in Chapter 2, through a detailed examination of demand and supply, and now back to a shorthand representation of the more complex market structures by simple market demand-supply analysis. With respect to supply, we find that the structure of the market may affect the details of the analysis, though not the broad qualitative conclusions concerning the market effects of economic shocks.

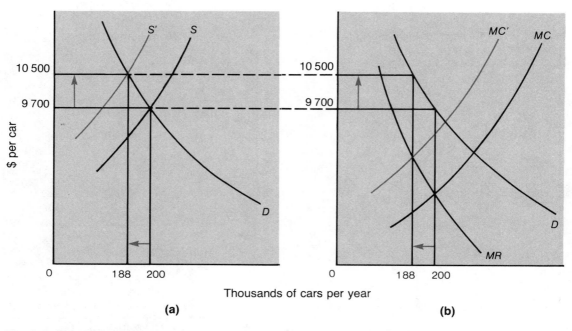

(a)   Thousands of cars per year   **(b)**

Fig. 6-4 Simplified representation of a supply shock upon an imperfectly competitive industry.

The effect of an increase in federal excise tax on cars may be illustrated either with a simple demand-supply diagram (part (a)) or with the marginal revenue–marginal cost curves of monopoly theory (part (b)).

Therefore, it is often sufficient (unless greater detail is deemed important) to carry out the same sort of cause and effect analysis and the same sort of diagrammatic representation that were presented in Chapter 2.

Although supply curve of a monopoly is not well defined, the analytical device of shifts in demand and supply curves provides useful insights into the consequences of changes in economic variables.

A Word of Caution

Though broad qualitative conclusions may be acceptable for many purposes, they are not suitable for detailed study. In the behaviour of monopolistic competitors and oligopolists, there are significant differences that we have neglected here that may become important in advanced analysis. We therefore give the subject a more thorough study in the following chapter.

6-6 DECISION MAKING IN PRACTICE

If we asked business firms how they formulate their prices, most would say they had never estimated demand or marginal revenue for their products, or attempted to choose a price that equated marginal revenue with marginal cost (as was done via Figure 6-1). Many firms estimate their costs per unit of output and add an appropriate markup on cost. For example, a food supermarket may operate on an average markup of 5%, or less on cost, whereas a clothing or sporting goods store may have markups in the order of 100%.

Does this mean that the concepts of marginal cost and marginal revenue are irrelevant to practice? The answer is no. If firms wish to maximize profit they must set a price at which marginal revenue equals marginal cost — whether they realize it or not. If we asked a particular firm why it chose a 25% markup on cost rather than some other percentage, the company would no doubt argue that 25% is best for the firm in the sense that it provides a larger profit than some other markup. If this is the case (management could, of course, be wrong), then in fact the firm must be choosing a price at which $MR = MC$.

Because all firms within a purely competitive market must sell at the going price, a firm that is at liberty to choose various possible markups must be an imperfect competitor. If Conglom Ltd. wishes to make as much profit as possible and does not have prior information concerning demand, it may experiment by changing its markup from time to time and observing the change in profit that results. If it experiments with enough different markups, the firm might eventually arrive at the one that would give the largest profit. (It can be shown that the size of such markup is a function of price elasticity of demand.)

With the cost and revenue figures of Table 6-1, the profit-maximizing price and volume for Conglom is $8400 and 5000 boats per month. There would be total costs of $22.88 million — that is, average costs of $4576 per boat. Hence, the best markup for Conglom to charge on average cost is $3824 (the difference between $8400 and $4576) — or 83.6% of average cost of $4576 (that is, $\frac{\$3824}{\$4576} \times 100\%$).

If Conglom attempts to set a price on a cost markup basis, perhaps experimenting with the size of the markup, it would probably not be able to experiment enough to hit the profit-maximizing markup precisely. In fact, it may stop with a lower or higher markup, believing that this was about as well as it could do. However, this sort of mistake is no different from the type made by a firm which, through surveys or some other such statistical method, estimates incorrect demand and marginal revenue data. For in the latter case, attempting to choose a price that equates expected MR with MC would also be in error and cause lost profits.

In a purely competitive market, each firm can sell all it wishes at the known prevailing market price. Therefore, in such a market there is little uncertainty concerning current demand or marginal revenue. In such a situation, each firm can likely approximate profit maximization more closely than in other types of market structures. The chief source of short-run decision errors is in the estimation of costs. Purely competitive firms do not have to worry about optimal pricing, because the market price is beyond their individual control.

The business practice of charging a price equal to cost plus markup is equivalent to setting $MR = MC$, provided the markup is determined in such a way as to take account of price elasticity of the market demand curve.

The Drive for Monopoly Power

Until now we have supposed that firms accept their product demand conditions as given and within such conditions attempt to maximize profit by choosing either the appropriate price or volume of output. Such a narrow viewpoint is incorrect and assigns far too limited a scope to the role of **marketing**, which comprises product development, packaging, advertising and distribution. Marketing on average absorbs approximately one half of all production costs. A considerable amount of marketing effort is geared toward **product differentiation** — the process of making the product different (at least in the minds of consumers) and in some sense better than the competing brands. Through successful product differentiation comes monopoly power and through monopoly power comes the potential for greater profitability.

Consider once again the athletic shoe market of earlier chapters. Over the last decade or so, athletic shoes have been a perfect example of marketing in action, and specifically of product differentiation. Let us focus for the moment on Stripes Ltd., which we assume to be one company among many producing a plain white canvas-topped rubber-soled athletic shoe. In other words, suppose Stripes is operating in a purely competitive market. A reasonable course of action for Stripes might be to attempt to differentiate its shoes from those of other brands with the hope of increasing profit. In taking this course, Stripes may, for example, consider heavy increases in advertising expenditure to convince some consumers that its brand is better in certain respects than others. To aid in this brand identification, and also to allow consumers to show off their discriminating tastes, Stripes might even add a range of coloured shoes or perhaps a distinguishing design on the sides of each shoe. To the extent that these differentiation efforts are successful, they will reduce consumer sensitivity toward changes in the price of Stripes shoes because the plain white shoes of other manufacturers will, to some consumers, now appear as inferior substitutes. That is, Stripes' demand curve will now become downward sloping rather than be horizontal, as shown in Figure 6-5.

If successful in affecting demand, the product differentiation techniques, though not making Stripes a monopolist (there are still reasonably

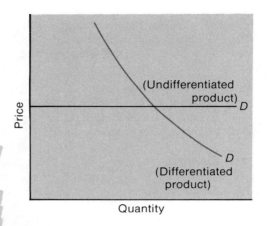

Fig. 6-5 Effect of product differentiation on demand

A successful product differentiation makes the demand curve downward sloping (less elastic).

close substitute brands on the market), would make price a controllable variable from the firm's standpoint. In a purely competitive market without product differentiation, Stripes was forced to accept the market price as something beyond its control. Now that the consumer is less sensitive to Stripes' price changes, the company can manipulate the price in an attempt to achieve a higher profit. Such price action is not feasible for a firm selling an undifferentiated good or service in a purely competitive environment.

Although product differentiation creates monopoly power and allows price to become a controllable variable, such action is not always profitable. For example, suppose Figure 6-6a reflects Stripes' situation within a purely competitive market environment, facing a price of $35 per pair. Given Stripes' marginal cost situation as illustrated, maximum profit occurs at an output volume of Q_1. Next, suppose the company undertakes a $100 000 a year advertising campaign designed to differentiate its product in the minds of the consumer. Whether or not the advertising campaign is profitable depends on the strength of the

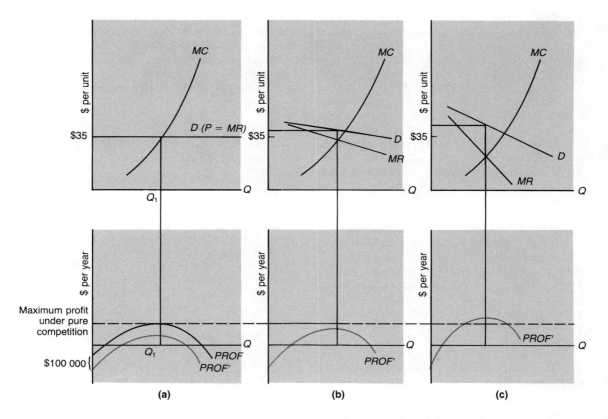

Fig. 6-6 Profit effect of successful and unsuccessful product differentiation through advertising

(a) Advertising campaign costing $100 000 did not succeed in changing the slope of the demand curve. It did, however, raise the firm's total cost. Hence profits are reduced by $100 000.

(b) Advertising campaign succeeded in changing the slope of the demand curve, and the firm can raise its price above the purely competitive level of $35. However, the revenue increase is less than the cost increase, and profits drop.

(c) Advertising campaign was more effective than in (b), and the firm can raise its price more than in (b). Hence profits increase above the purely competitive level.

advertising effect on demand. Figure 6-6 illustrates three possibilities. The limiting case shown in Figure 6-6a assumes that the advertising campaign is so ineffective that it has no influence whatever on the demand for Stripes' shoes. It does, of course, raise the firm's total cost by $100 000. In this instance, the profit-maximizing price remains at $35 per pair. The effect of the advertising expenditure is simply to reduce all possible profit levels, including the maximum profit level by $100 000 per year.

Figure 6-6b illustrates partly effective advertising that has some impact (although still very little) on demand for Stripes' shoes. Fixed costs increase once more by the amount of the $100 000 annual advertising expenditure. There is some demand effect but not enough to prevent maximum profit from falling below that available without advertising.

Finally, Figure 6-6c shows what management would regard as a successful advertising campaign in that it creates sufficient monopoly power (as evidenced by the reduced price sensitivity of demand) to enable Stripes to achieve a greater profit potential.

As we saw earlier in the chapter, industrial profits can always be increased by monopolization of a purely competitive industry. Here we see that the drive for product differentiation may not always be a profitable one. For product differentiation to be successful, the product differentiation costs must be more than met by the effect on demand and revenue. Nevertheless, there is considerable evidence around us to indicate that product differentiation is often a profitable venture.

Once again, it becomes clear that demand-and-cost estimates are critical to a company's ability to make profit-maximizing decisions. Also, because no firm can forecast the future with great precision, no firm escapes making incorrect decisions. Firms that are able to estimate costs and future demand more accurately than others (everything else being equal) will be more profitable and more successful than firms who cannot. Those that make fewer mistakes than average will make above average profits. From here on in our discussions, for convenience sake, we shall often neglect to mention that we are working only with forecasted estimates of demand and cost figures. But this is something we should not forget. If accurate numbers were easily obtainable, best decisions could be made without much difficulty. Unfortunately, such data are often quite costly and difficult to obtain.

Successful product differentiation, by means of advertising, for example, makes the demand curve for the product less elastic. The firm can therefore raise its price and increase revenues. Profits will increase only if the increase in revenues outweighs the cost of the product differentiation activity.

6-7 COST-VOLUME-PROFIT ANALYSIS

Decisions that equate marginal revenue with marginal cost are profit maximizing. The trick is to get reliable information on marginal revenue and costs. To estimate marginal revenue requires a firm in an imperfectly competitive market (which is the typical situation in the economy) to estimate the sensitivity of demand for its product in view of price changes. For example, Conglom would be required to estimate data such as those of the first two columns in Table 6-1. Some larger firms estimate such demand information by means of surveys or by using statistical techniques and historical data. Other firms, however, believe that the cost of doing this would outweigh the benefits.

Though demand information is difficult to get, reasonably reliable cost information can usually be obtained by the firm's accountants and engineers at relatively low cost. This fact has led to the development of a form of analysis that often takes the place of marginal revenue-marginal cost methods for business firms. This type of analysis is referred to as **cost-volume-profit analysis**. In what follows, we describe this method and possible sources of error.

We proceed by plotting in Figure 6-7 the total cost structure of Conglom during 19X1. (This information comes from Table 6-1.) Note that in all cases we are plotting totals, not per unit costs. So far, we have what one might describe as a *cost-volume analysis*; the diagram shows what happens to fixed, variable and total costs as volume changes.

Total Revenue-Volume Relations

Remember, in a purely competitive market each firm is so small relative to the industry that it can produce and sell any volume it wishes without affecting the market price. For example, when we assumed in Chapter 5 that Boatco was in such an

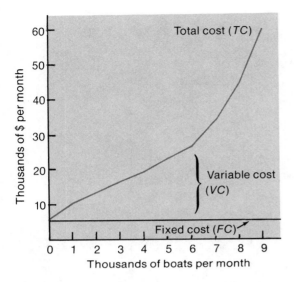

Fig. 6-7 Cost-volume chart for Conglom Ltd.

Diagrammatical representation of cost data from Table 6-1. All figures are totals per production period.

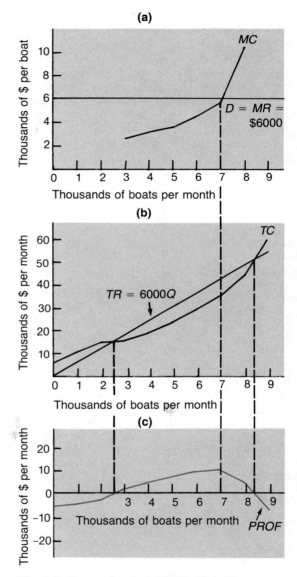

Fig. 6-8 Cost-volume-profit analysis for Conglom during 19X1 under pure competition

Diagrammatical representation of cost data from Table 6-1 together with revenue data based on price of $6000 per unit. Part (a) is in per unit terms and shows the profit-maximizing level of output. Part (b) is in totals per production period and shows the two break-even points. Part (c) shows the total profits or losses the firm would make at various levels of output.

environment we saw that it could not alter the going market price of $6000 per boat. If it sold one boat, its revenue would be $6000; two boats, twice that amount; three boats, three times, and so on. In other words, in a purely competitive environment the relation between total revenue (TR) and volume of output (Q) is, as always, $TR = P \cdot Q$ — but in addition the price is constant (not constant over time, but unaffected by the volume sold by any single firm during any given year).

Diagrammatically, then, if Conglom is a pure competitor (which in actuality it is not), the total revenue-volume relation would be as shown in Figure 6-8b. Also shown is the total cost-volume relation for the firm. In Figure 6-8c, the difference between total revenue and total cost (in other words, profit) has been plotted. The bottom two diagrams together make up the cost-volume-profit analysis. Zero profit volumes are called *break-even points*. In this case, the company would break even by producing either 2500 or 8400 boats per month. The profit-maximizing volume is 7000 boats per month.

Because Figures 6-8b and 6-8c each indicate the best volume to produce, only one is necessary. Though it might seem to make more sense to use only the bottom diagram (total profits can more easily be read off it), often only a diagram such as Figure 6-8b is used.

Notice also that the graphical analysis of Figure 6-8b and 6-8c corresponds directly with the earlier marginal analysis of Chapter 5 (see, for example, Figure 6-8a.) Both methods of analysis give us the same information; namely, the best volume of output to produce. When all the data are available, it is purely a matter of taste as to which type of analysis to use.

An Imperfectly Competitive Market

In markets where a particular firm has a degree of monopoly power (which is certainly the case with Conglom), the firm may vary product quality and its advertising budget to further differentiate its brand and increase profitability. As stated earlier, the emphasis in these chapters is on the relation between price, volume and profitability. Therefore, let us suppose that Conglom has already established what it believes to be the best (profit-maximizing) advertising budget and product quality mix and that the product price decision can be made independently of these other two elements. The demand that faces Conglom (the position of the demand curve) — including its sensitivity toward changes in price — has therefore been established by Conglom's prior decisions. Of course, other microeconomic as well as macroeconomic events will also play a part here. For instance, incomes and the prices of other goods will partly determine the demand conditions a firm faces.

Suppose, therefore, that the demand information facing Conglom in 19X1 is as depicted in Table 6-1 and Figure 6-9a. If Conglom lowers its price, it will sell more boats. Its revenue at first increases as the increase in volume outweighs the reduction in price. As Conglom continues to lower its price, though the sales volume (number of units) continues to increase, this effect eventually becomes outweighed by the decrease in price, and total dollar revenue declines. The relation between

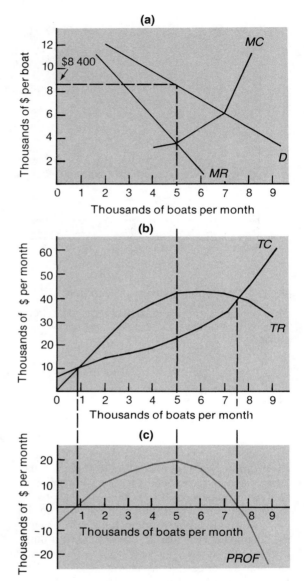

Fig. 6-9 Cost-volume-profit analysis for Conglom during 19X1

Diagrammatical representation of cost and revenue data from Table 6-1. Part (a) is in per unit terms and shows the determination of profit-maximizing level of output. Part (b) is in totals per production period and shows the two break-even points. Part (c) shows the total profits or losses the firm would make at various levels of output.

volume sold and total revenue is plotted in Figure 6-9b as the *TR* curve. The difference between total revenue and total cost represents profit. The *best* annual output for Conglom to produce and sell appears to be 5000 boats per month, an amount it could achieve if it priced its product at $8400 per boat. Again we see that this graphical analysis leads to precisely the same answer for the best volume and price decision as that done on a marginal basis (see Figure 6-9a). (Note, again, there are two break-even points. The only difference between this and the analysis within a purely competitive market is the shape of the total revenue curve.)

The cost-volume-profit analysis is a practical approach to the determination of the optimal level of production by a firm. It yields results which are identical to those generated by the marginal revenue-marginal cost method.

A Loss Operation

Even though the demand for a company's products and its cost structure may be such that its maximum profit is actually a loss, it may still be worthwhile for the company to produce rather than to shut down. Figure 6-10a illustrates this case. The company is forced to operate at a loss, but it can minimize this loss in the short run by continuing production at Q_1 and charging a price P_1. Because total revenue at least exceeds variable costs at Q_1, the difference offsets some of the fixed costs. However, if these losses are permanent, the firm will eventually go bankrupt.

The Shutdown Point

In the short run, even if the firm cannot earn profits, as long as total revenue from producing exceeds variable production costs the firm can reduce its losses to a level below the fixed cost figure (which would be the amount of its losses if it produced nothing). However, if demand and the firm's cost structure are such that the total revenue from production will not exceed even variable costs, the maximum profit (or minimum loss) decision will be to shut down the plant and produce nothing at all. Figure 6-10b illustrates this case. If this condition is expected to be permanent, the firm will be liquidated.

Assumed Independence

The cost structure of the firm has been assumed to have nothing to do with the particular market structure. Conglom is assumed to have this cost structure whether the firm is in a purely competitive market, an oligopoly or even a monopoly situation. In practice, this may or may not be the case. For example, in a regulated monopoly, whereby a government body forces the company to charge prices that do not yield more than a normal or fair rate of return, there may be little incentive for management to maintain the most efficient production techniques. Such profit-maximizing effort only encourages the regulatory board to restrict the firm's prices and puts its profit situation in the same position it was in before the efficiencies were undertaken. Therefore, some argue, government regulation of this sort reduces the efficiency of such firms and brings about higher cost structures than otherwise.

Some also argue that a great deal of competition within an industry tends to force management to operate as efficiently as possible, thereby causing lower cost (lower fixed costs, variable costs, marginal costs and so on). Others argue, though, that in a market with monopoly power and barriers to entry, firms have additional incentives to carry out research and development and institute cost-cutting programs, because they realize they will be able to benefit from the higher profits without fear of increased competition from new entrants attracted by the higher profitability.

Theory versus Practice

If the required cost and demand information was known, correctly drawn cost-volume-profit charts would, in general, roughly have the curvilinear shapes indicated on the figures above. However, in practice, there is sometimes considerable difficulty in estimating demand and the precise cost structure of the firm. For these reasons, business firms often construct approximate *linear* versions of cost-volume-profit charts. It is important to examine such charts and relate them to the ones discussed above so that we may understand exactly the sort of simplification introduced in their construction. Though these charts can be a useful management tool for profit planning, their simplifying assumptions explain in large part the inaccuracies they contain.

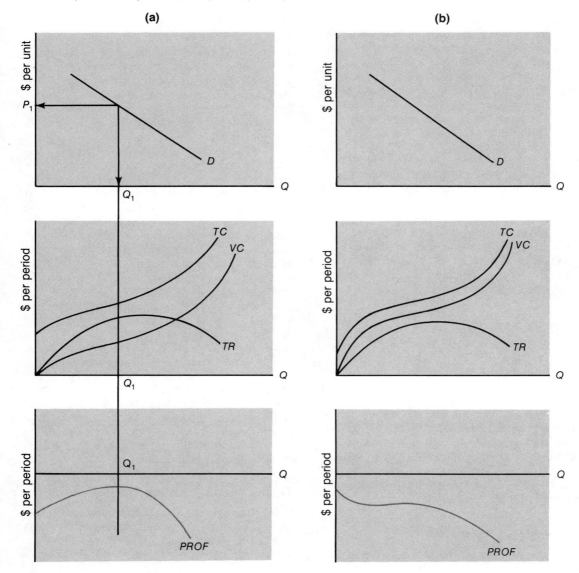

Fig. 6-10 Loss operations and shutdown points

(a) The optimal level of output and price charged by the firm generates revenue which is insufficient to cover total cost. However, it is preferable for the firm to keep operating in the short run rather than shut down, since total revenue exceeds total variable cost.

(b) Demand conditions are such that there exists no price and output level which would generate enough revenues to cover variable cost. The firm should shut down.

Pure Competition

With reference to our earlier example, Boatco operating in a purely competitive market and observing a \$6000 price will know that its total revenue relation is simply $TR = \$6000 \cdot Q$. Boatco may not be aware of its entire cost structure as reflected earlier in Table 5-3, but supposing that the company produced 7 boats per month during a particular year it would at least be aware of its total monthly costs of producing at this volume — namely \$33 196. The next step is to have the company's accountants break the actual observed costs of \$33 196 into fixed and variable components. We suppose this analysis yields the correct fixed-variable cost breakdown (as per Table 5-3) of \$6000 and \$27 196 respectively. Variable cost on a per boat basis is thus \$27 196: 7 = \$3885. If the analyst takes this variable cost per boat figure to be representative for the entire production range, the estimated total cost relation becomes $TC^{est} = \$6000 + 3885 \cdot Q$.

Figure 6-11 plots the total revenue and estimated linear total cost relation. Such charts are typically called **break-even charts** since they are often constructed to estimate the minimum output volume that the firm must produce and sell in order to earn just a zero profit, that is to say, *break even*. If the price is known, then within a purely competitive market the total revenue relation is accurate. However, by assuming average variable cost to be a constant figure, as Figure 6-11 shows, this is equivalent to approximating the actual curvilinear total cost relation by a straight line. We have plotted the actual total cost structure from Table 6-1. In general we see that a linear approximation leads to an underestimation of cost and hence an overestimation of profit at high output volumes. Also, whereas in reality there are two break-even points — one at a low volume (Q_{BE1}) and one at a high volume (Q_{BE2}), linear break-even charts indicate only one break-even point (Q^{est}_{BE}), which is an estimate of the low volume break-even point.

Another weakness introduced into the analysis by the linear total cost approximation (constant unit variable cost assumption) is that no maximum profit volume is indicated. In fact, the implication of the approximate chart is that there is no profit-maximizing volume; the greater the volume, the higher the profit. Since this implication is known

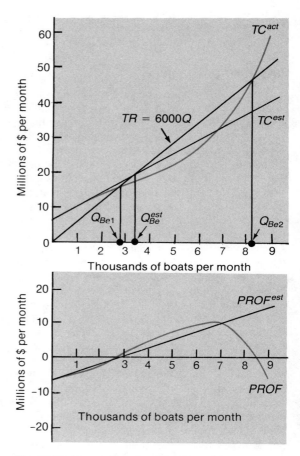

Fig. 6-11 Linear break-even chart for a pure competitor

For purposes of quick business calculations, the correct nonlinear cost curve is approximated by a straight line. This underestimates the total costs at high output levels.

to be wrong, the primary focus of analysts using such charts is on the break-even point.

Imperfect Competition

The use of linear break-even charts by imperfectly competitive firms introduces another source of error, since total revenue relations are curvilinear along with total costs. For our example here, we have chosen the cost and revenue data for Conglom Ltd. as reported earlier in Table 6-1. Assuming that Conglom produced 5000 boats during the year and sold them at a price of $8400 per boat, the accountant may estimate the total revenue relation as $TR = \$8400 \cdot Q$. This is only an approximation since it assumes incorrectly that Conglom can sell as many boats as it wishes without having to change its price of $8400. The actual reported total cost figure of $22 880 000 (see again Table 6-1) is broken down into its approximate fixed and variable components of $6 000 000 (fixed) and $16 880 000 (variable). Again, if it is assumed that average variable costs are relatively constant over the production range, the estimated total cost relation becomes $TR = 6000 + 3376 \cdot Q$.

Figure 6-12 illustrates the estimated linear cost-volume-profit chart for Conglom Ltd. In general, we can see that such approximations will underestimate total revenue at low volumes and overestimate total revenue at high volumes. As in the purely competitive case, total cost will be underestimated and total profit overestimated at high output levels.

In managerial practice, the marginal revenue–marginal cost method is frequently replaced with cost-volume-profit analysis and break-even analysis. Both revenue and cost curves are often drawn linear, to simplify calculations. The profit-maximizing output and price may therefore be established with varying degrees of error.

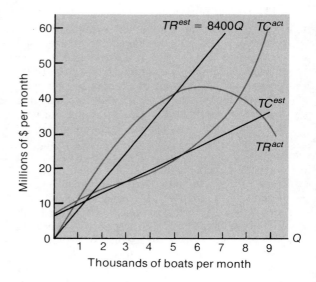

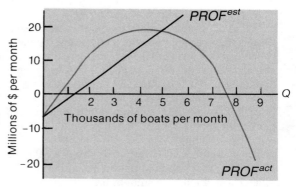

Fig. 6-12 Linear break-even chart for an imperfect competitor

For purposes of quick business calculations, both the nonlinear cost curve and nonlinear total revenue curve are approximated by straight lines. As a result, total cost is underestimated and total profit overestimated at high output levels.

CONCLUDING REMARKS

In a market with monopoly power, each firm sells a product that is somewhat different from other products. Each firm, therefore, has at least some control over its price, in that it may raise the price without losing all its customers or lower the price without increasing sales volume beyond limit. A profit-maximizing firm with monopoly power will attempt to choose the particular price at which marginal revenue equals marginal production cost (from the last unit sold each operating period). This practice generally leads to a market price that exceeds marginal cost, and thus the extra benefit to society of one more unit produced (as approximated by the market price) exceeds the extra cost to society of one more unit produced (as approximated by the marginal price). Since the firm with monopoly power will not willingly produce this next and other such units, in this sense monopoly power tends to restrict output and create less economic welfare than does a purely competitive market.

In practice, managerial activity is not restricted to price and output decisions. Product differentiation is an important marketing tool designed to influence product demand and thereby profitability. Information, or the lack of it, is a key problem for the firm. Much day-to-day analysis and decision making must take place within the context of insufficient information.

KEY TERMS AND CONCEPTS

monopolized market
net contribution (value) to society
   of a market activity
allocative efficiency

marketing
product differentiation
cost-volume-profit analysis
break-even chart

PROBLEMS

Problem 1

a) Does there appear to have been a trend in the amount of monopoly power throughout the Canadian manufacturing industry over time? What is your evidence?

b) Some people argue that firms with monopoly power can charge whatever they like for their goods and services. Discuss briefly.

Problem 2

a) Depict on the industry (market) diagram below the resulting market price and volume, assuming the industry to be (i) purely competitive, (ii) monopolistic.

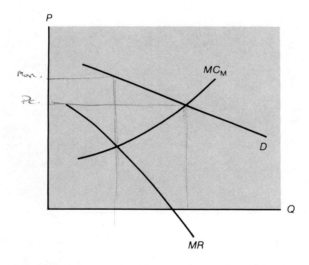

MC_M = horizontal sum of all individual producers' marginal cost curves in the purely competitive case = the monopolist's marginal cost curve in the case of monopoly.

b) Is the marginal revenue curve shown that for a purely competitive firm or for a monopolist? Draw on a separate diagram the demand curve and the marginal revenue curve that would face any particular firm if the industry was purely competitive.

Problem 3

a) With reference to the diagram in Problem 2, explain why greater industry profits are available through a restriction of output below the purely competitive level where *P* equals *MC*.

b) Explain why, though greater industry profits are available through a restriction of output below the purely competitive level, it would not make sense for a single pure competitor to restrict his output to a position where *P* is greater than *MC*.

c) With the lure of monopoly profits in mind, suggest possible strategies producers could take if they found themselves in a highly competitive industry.

Problem 4

a) Explain why (everything else being equal) purely competitive markets would tend to maximize social welfare from production and consumption.

b) What factors may lead to a particular purely competitive market's not being desirable from a maximum social welfare standpoint?

c) Everything else being equal, who loses and who benefits from monopolization of an originally competitive market?

Problem 5

In a particular market there are 100 identical firms with market demand and cost information given in the following table.

Market demand data		Individual firm costs	
(000s of units per year) *Q*	($ per unit) *P*	(000s of units per year) *Q*	(000s of $ per year) *TC*
0	1400	0	700
100	950	1	1099
200	775	2	1499
300	660	3	1904
400	600	4	2323
500	475	5	2798
600	300	6	3418
700	100	7	4318

a) Determine market price, firm and industry volume, and firm and industry profits.

b) Why would each firm experience some yearly costs ($700) even if it produced nothing?

c) Using graphs similar to those of Chapter 5, Problems 7(a) and (b), plot the marginal revenue curve each firm within the industry would face if the market was purely competitive.

d) Plot the marginal revenue curve for a single monopolized firm that controls the entire industry.

e) Explain why the marginal revenue curve is horizontal for the pure competitor but falling for the monopolist.

Problem 6

Using the data of Problem 5, answer the following questions.

a)   If the industry was purely competitive, how much would it (all the firms together) be willing to produce at the following prices per unit: $399? $400? $405? $419? $475? $620? $900? Plot the resulting information. What is the name of this curve?

b)   Approximate the market price and output level, assuming that the industry is monopolistic.

c)   If the industry is monopolistic, how much would the monopoly be willing to produce at the following prices per unit: $399? $400? $405? $419? $465? $620? $900?

Problem 7

Using diagrams, chart the effects of the following market shocks on industry output and market price. Assume first that the market is purely competitive and then that it is monopolistic.

(i)   An increase in excise taxes
(ii) An increase in the price of a substitute commodity
(iii) An improvement in productivity
(iv) A change in tastes away from the particular good in question

Problem 8

a)   If a particular firm's management prices its products by assigning a markup to per unit costs, is this fact evidence that the market is purely competitive? Explain.

b)   Would this firm be maximizing its profit? Explain.

Problem 9

A particular firm wishes to choose its best advertising budget, packaging and price. It has done a pilot survey and, based on the results, the demand-and-cost estimates presented below were made.

Decision Set 1
  $5 000 advertising and plain packaging

Price ($ per unit) P	Volume demanded (000s of units per year) Q	Total cost (000s of $ per year) TC
10	4	35.0
9	5	36.9
8	6	39.8
7	7	43.7
6	8	49.6
5	9	58.5
4	10	72.4

Decision Set 2
  $10 000 advertising budget and fancy packaging

Price ($ per unit) P	Volume demanded (000s of units per year) Q	Total cost (000s of $ per year) TC
10	5	47.0
9	6	48.9
8	7	51.8
7	8	55.7
6	9	61.6
5	10	71.5
4	11	85.4

a) What evidence is there from the survey that the firm has some monopoly power — that is, that the firm's product is differentiated from competitive brands (substitutes) in the mind of the consumer?

b) On the basis of the preceding answer, determine which would be the best price-advertising-packaging decision.

c) Does the fancy packaging and the extra $5000 advertising further differentiate the product in the minds of consumers? Explain. In what sense, given the preceding data, would the heavier advertising budget and fancy packaging be considered "unsuccessful"?

d) What are the sources of possible error for this decision?

Problem 10

a) Using the information in the 19X1 statement below, construct a cost-volume-profit chart for 19X2. You will see that you have to make your own assumptions about which expenses are fixed and which are variable. The company's 19X1 selling price of $5 per unit is expected to remain constant in 19X2.

b) What is the company's approximate break-even volume for 19X2 in terms of both number of units and dollar sales?

c) What dollar sales volume would generate the firm a $50 000 accounting profit in 19X2?

d) What could make your forecasts in (b) and (c) parts go wrong?

Co. A. Ltd.
Income Statement
for 19X1

Sales			$500 000
Less:	Manufacturing expenses		
	Cost of materials used	$100 000	
	Factory labour	200 000	
	Heat, light, power	5 000	
	Depreciation:		
	Factory building	80 000	
	Machinery	20 000	
Less:	Selling and administration expenses		
	Sales commissions	60 000	
	Delivery expenses	15 000	
	Packaging materials	7 000	
	Accounting, clerical & admin.	100 000	
	Miscellaneous	1 000	588 000
	Net loss for year		$(88 000)

CASES

Case 6-1

Financial Post

THE COLA WARS

Coke, Pepsi keep the fizz in their feud

By JAIMIE HUBBARD

THE JURY is still out on whether the introduction of New Coke was the marketing blunder or coup of the century. More than a year later, Coca-Cola is hitting its stride again after having taken a beating from Pepsi in the endless battle for supremacy in the cola wars.

As some see it, the venerable cola giant stumbled badly when it introduced New Coke and alienated an entire generation of Cokeholics. Others point to the free publicity created by the affair, and the salutary effect it all had on the bottom line. These days, the company has defined a niche for its three main soft drinks and is spending millions of dollars on advertising in an attempt to dominate those markets.

But competitor Pepsi is determined that won't happen. For its part, it continues to fire advertising broadsides, keeping the cola wars — or at least the skirmishes — alive.

The conflict between the battling cola Goliaths escalated in the summer of 1985, when Atlanta-based Coca-Cola Co. altered its 100-year-old winning formula under pressure from Pepsi's aggressive marketing.

Pepsi's tactics included the Pepsi Challenge, a taste test which Pepsi — naturally — won, and its New Generation campaign featuring some of the hottest names in entertainment. The hoopla surrounding the signing of superstar Michael Jackson, whose moonwalk and glittering glove launched the series, won Pepsi lots of free press and the wrath of Coca-Cola executives.

They responded to Pepsi's blow-'em-out-of-the-water strategy by introducing New Coke and yanking old Coke off retailers' shelves. That move produced howls of protest from loyal Coke drinkers. In what was perhaps the quickest turnaround in business history, Coke reintroduced its old drink as Coca-Cola Classic, less than three months after the ballyhooed launch of New Coke.

'Colossal blunder'

But the battle continues on all fronts and this fall it moved into bookstores. Roger Enrico, president of Pepsico Worldwide Beverages, has written *The Other Guy Blinked* (Random House, 195 pp, $27.25), his version of the New Coke/old Coke tale. Enrico takes full credit for Coke's mistakes.

"I really believe that if it weren't for those Michael Jackson commercials, the Coca-Cola Ltd. wouldn't have made the colossal blunder that was New Coke," he writes.

Coke's side has been pulled together in *The Real Coke, The Real Story*, by Atlanta journalist Thomas Oliver (Bantam, 280 pp, $22.95). Oliver describes the reasoning behind Coke's decision to reformulate its product, and details the swiftness with which management put old Coke back on the shelves again.

So far, there's no word on which book is selling better.

The struggle between the giants isn't confined to colas, either. The market for soft drinks in Canada is growing at a rate of only 3% annually. That means any significant sales increase must come by enticing away the other company's customers.

Both cola producers have lemon-lime drinks, for example, a small but growing segment of the soft-drink market — about 16%, vs cola's dominant 60%. Pepsi is currently the leader, having purchased Seven-Up's international operations this summer, while Coke trails with Sprite. Industry observers aren't being particularly clairvoyant when they predict a fight.

New juice-added products, a category Pepsi virtually invented when it added 10% real juice to an orange drink, also present opportunities for a donnybrook. Coke's Minute Maid Orange Soda is the only entrant in the Canadian market so far, but Pepsi's Slice has already drummed up $1 billion in sales in the U.S. since it was launched in 1984. It's a safe bet that introduction to Canada and a full-scale advertising war are only a matter of time.

The main battle continues to be fought on the cola field, and here the advantage swings back and forth between the combatants. Bringing back old Coke has been touted as a marketing masterstroke for Coca-Cola. It certainly has paid dividends for the company.

John Brennan, senior vice-president of Coca-Cola Ltd., Toronto, says Coca-Cola Classic has grabbed 53% of the company's "sugar-cola" (as opposed to diet) business, while New Coke hangs in with 47%. Some U.S. reports have Classic outselling New Coke by as much as four to one.

The stakes are high. The Canadian soft-drink market is worth about $2.5 billion at the wholesale level (in the U.S., it's an even more impressive $25 billion). Until this summer, Coke had a commanding lead in Canada, with about 45% of the market. However, Pepsi's purchase of Seven-Up changed all that and pushed its share up to 41% from 30%.

To keep its edge on Pepsi, Coke has segmented its marketing. It spends its $25-million Canadian advertising budget linking each of its three major colas to a different group. About 70% of the ad material comes from the U.S. parent but is adapted for Canadians.

One upbeat television campaign, aimed at the under-20s, features video star Max Headroom, a half-human, half-computer-generated graphic. Tagged with the surfer phrase,

"Catch the Wave" (referring to the stylized wave on coke cans), the ads promote New Coke — which, by the way, is no longer called New Coke, but is just plain Coke.

Diet Coke's appeal to the calorie-conscious but fun-loving consumer is emphasized in a finger-snapping TV commercial featuring this year's singing mega-star, Whitney Houston.

If Coke is intended for those under 20, Coca-Cola Classic is being marketed to everyone else in a campaign called "Red, White & You." In a return to coke's apple-pie image, the commercials show a series of vignettes designed to appeal to Middle America. The same commercial is used in Canada, with heartwarming Canadian scenes being substituted for the U.S. ones.

The Red, White & You campaign is a smart move by Coke, says Ian Mirlin, senior vice-president at Toronto ad agency Miller Myers Bruce DallaCosta Harrod Mirlin.

He maintains Pepsi forced Coke into "perpetual launch advertising" in 1985. Before that, Coke had been able to capture what he calls "share of heart." It became a modern icon, as much a symbol of the U.S. as the Statue of Liberty. This image was fixed in the mid-1970s radio and TV campaign centering on the song I'd Like to Buy the World a Coke, performed by a multinational group of children. The song coincided so strongly with the feeling of the time, it became a hit in the U.S.

However, Mirlin says that association was lost with the introduction of New Coke.

"Consumers came to view Coke as something brand new. But with the Red, White & You campaign, the company's come back to what they consider to be their strength: Coke's rightful place in America's heart."

While advertising industry executives applaud Coke's response to the pressures from Pepsi, they suggest consumers are confused by the variety of messages and brands. As well as the three main colas, Coke has caffeine-free, diet caffeine-free and cherry versions. The result is bewildered consumers.

That's not a problem for Pepsi-Cola. Though it also has cherry and caffeine-free colas, along with main brands Pepsi and Diet Pepsi, its advertising delivers one strong message: Pepsi is the choice of a new generation. The company has aggressively tried to corner the youth market — anyone from age 12 to 34.

"Soft drinks are fun and we get that message across with the up-tempo, rock-and-roll image we've created," says Colin Moore, director of marketing for Pepsi-Cola Canada Ltd. in Toronto. Because the Canadian and U.S. strategies are similar, the Canadian subsidiary can use much of the material produced in the U.S.

Pool of talent

That gives the company access to a remarkable pool of talent, such as gravel-voiced rock singer Tina Turner; actor Michael J. Fox, who is Hollywood's hot property this year; super-cool Don Johnson, of the hit TV show *Miami Vice*, and of course, Michael Jackson, who will perform in two new Pepsi commercials to be unveiled during the music industry's Grammy Awards in February.

Pepsi has committed US$50 million to this project. This time around, Jackson will be paid more than the US$5 million he received for the last commercials, but less than the US$15 million that's been reported, says the company. It's betting the singer's much-anticipated new album, due out next year, will equal the success of *Thriller*, which sold 60 million copies and became the best-selling record album ever. Pepsi Canada gets all this on an advertising budget of less than $10 million.

Certainly, celebrity advertising seems to be paying off. Moore says the company has already sold more than 125 million more glasses of Pepsi this year than last. "That is equal to another $30 million in sales at the wholesale level."

But Pepsi has been taken to task by both consumers and the ad industry over some of its ploys. This summer, Coke and Pepsi became embroiled in a tussle over Diet Pepsi's "Taste Above All" television campaign, which showed Diet Coke drinkers madly switching to Diet Pepsi.

Coke had the commercials reviewed by Ottawa's Department of Consumer & Corporate Affairs, which deemed them unfair. Pepsi was forced to withdraw them.

But in the battle to be king of the colas, you can't keep a good fighter down. Pepsi returned with altered versions of the commercial, featuring *Monty Python* alumnus Graham Chapman, poking fun at Coke. "Unfortunately, the Diet Pepsi ads presume the viewer is aware of the commercial's history, and that's not necessarily the wisest approach," says MMB's Mirlin.

Even Pepsi admits one of the four spots required background knowledge consumers don't usually need to understand soft-drink commercials.

The companies went head to head again last month when Coke announced it was increasing its bottle deposits; for example, the deposit on a 750-millilitre bottle went to 40¢ from 30¢. Pepsi, which has not yet raised its deposit, responded with a full-page newspaper ad captioned, "Hey Buddy, can you spare a dime?" That's what Pepsi accused Coke of asking its customers.

So far, Coke has remained silent.

Moore defended the potshots, saying the public enjoys Pepsi's behaviour as the scrappy underdog. "The distinction is to make consumers say 'Oh look, they're at it again,' which is an upbeat approach, not 'Oh dear, they're doing it again,' which isn't."

Both companies admit the corporate sniping is often carried out more for the benefit of their own organizations than for the consumer. The idea, they say, is to boost morale among employees and bottlers.

And Pepsi's Enrico says it works. There's been a groundswell of excitement among Pepsi employees, he says, because of the company's marketing direction and its ability to make the news.

Indeed, the cola wars may be just as notable for providing free publicity — which one observer estimates is worth hundreds of millions of dollars to the companies — as for generating sales.

Certainly, Enrico doubts there will ever be a clear winner in the cola battle. In fact, he believes it would be tragic if one company dominated. He writes, "By now, both of us know that neither Pepsi nor Coke wins decisively in this game. As I see it, the important thing in all this is that we keep demonstrating that we have the capacity to surprise you."

a) An economist would likely characterize the Canadian cola market as lacking in competitiveness and the actions described in the article as anticompetitive behaviour. For most businessmen, however, this would be an example of "highly competitive industry." Which characterization is correct? Explain.

b) Based on the information provided in the article, which panel in Figure 6-6 in Chapter 6 seems to describe best the impact of the introduction of New Coke?

c) How have consumers benefited from the rivalry between the two cola companies? Can you think of potential negative effects of the rivalry on consumers or on society at large?

d) Identify the various methods of product differentiation discussed in the article. Are they are equally beneficial to the consumer?

e) How would you interpret the next to last paragraph, dealing with "free publicity"?

APPENDIX 6A: PRICE, REVENUE AND PROFITS

6A-1 Price Elasticity of Demand, Total Revenue and Profits

The price elasticity of demand is defined as $e = \dfrac{\Delta Q/Q}{\Delta P/P}$. Further, total revenue is defined as price times quantity sold — that is, $TR = P \cdot Q$. There is a connection between the elasticity of demand, changes in price, and changes in total revenue. In addition, *there is in the case of inelastic demand ($e < 1$) an unambiguous connection between changes in price and changes in profit.* We now investigate these connections.

If the elasticity of demand is greater than one, quantity sold responds by a greater percentage amount than the magnitude of the price change. For example, if the price is reduced by ten percent, quantity sold will rise by more than ten percent. Because total revenue equals price times quantity sold, total revenue responds in an opposite direction to any price change when the elasticity of demand is greater than one. In the present instance, a ten-percent *reduction in price* leads to an increase in quantity sold in excess of ten percent, and therefore leads to an *increase in total revenue*. It may similarly be shown that when the elasticity of demand is less than one, total revenue will respond in the same direction as that of a price change. Finally, for the borderline case of unitary elasticity, a price change leaves total revenue unchanged.

The three possible cases are summarized in Table 6A-1. Case (iii) has an interesting implication. If demand for a firm's product at the present price level is inelastic, the firm can always increase profits by raising its price. This must be so because, for inelastic demand, raising the price causes an increase in total revenue along with a reduction in volume sold. The reduction in volume sold will mean less total production costs, and combined with the increased revenue entails a greater profit.

Table 6A-1 Elasticity, price changes, and changes in total revenue

(i) $e > 1$	total revenue changes in opposite direction to price change
(ii) $e = 1$	total revenue is unchanged in face of a price change
(iii) $e < 1$	total revenue changes in same direction as price change

If demand is elastic, total revenue increases as a result of a price cut; if demand is inelastic, total revenue declines as a result of a price cut; if the demand curve has unitary elasticity, total revenue remains constant as the price changes.

Problems for Appendix 6A

Problem 6A-1

Explain why a firm with monopoly power would not be expected to price its product willingly on the inelastic portion of its demand curve.

Monopolistic Competition and Oligopoly

7-1 INTRODUCTION AND PURPOSE

In Chapters 5 and 6, we examined two extreme forms of industrial organization — pure competition and monopoly. Most industries in Canada operate somewhere in between these extremes. This chapter examines the more typical sorts of market structure found in Canada today — *monopolistic competition* and *oligopoly*.

We investigate the effect of market shocks on price and output and find that, apart from some stickiness (or inertia), the general tendencies are the same under the market structures as under pure competition and monopoly.

Among the most striking characteristics of monopolistic competition and oligopoly are the attempts at product differentiation and other forms of *nonprice competition*. In the case of oligopoly, we investigate managerial strategies and the incentive to engage in collusive behaviour in pursuit of *joint profit maximization*.

7-2 MARKET STRUCTURES IN CANADA

The structure of most markets in Canada lies somewhere between the two extremes of pure competition and pure monopoly. Though most firms have some influence over their product price, they are usually subject to competitive pressure from other companies selling a similar product.

Economists distinguish two types of market structure within the spectrum between pure competition and pure monopoly. These two intermediate market structures are referred to as **monopolistic competition** and **oligopoly**.

A monopolistically competitive market structure is characterized by many small competitors who sell a product that is similar, but somewhat differentiated in the minds of the consumer. Often there are various identifiable *brands*. The important thing is not whether there is a significant difference between brands, but rather that the consumer thinks there is. Therefore, in such a market there may be many different sizes, packages and advertising, designed to convince consumers that important differences exist between brands.

If the consumer thinks there are real differences between brands, there will be *brand allegiance* (loyalty) even when the price is increased. That means that some consumers keep buying the brand even after its price goes up. However, there will be some brand switching. If a firm raises its price, sales will not drop off to zero as in the case of pure competition, but there will be greater reduction in sales than in the case of pure monopoly. The firm's demand curve will have a downward slope, unlike the demand curve facing a purely competitive firm. However, it will not be as steep as the demand curve facing a monopolist.

One further feature of a monopolistically competitive market is that each firm is small enough so that its actions on pricing, advertising, packaging and the like will not have any significant short-term impact on the behaviour of its competitors (being small relative to total market, its actions are likely to go unnoticed).

Oligopoly

In an oligopolistic market there are a few large sellers of a particular good or service. They are sometimes surrounded by a number of smaller sellers. Because there are only a few major sellers, any action on price, advertising or new product development will cause a significant reaction by the other sellers in the market. These reactions have to be taken into account in the firm's decision making.

An interesting source of confusion in language between economists and noneconomists often occurs concerning reaction by competitors within oligopolistic and monopolistically competitive markets. Economists often advocate increasing the degree of competitiveness in such markets (in the sense of increasing the number of competitors and making the market more closely approximate pure competition). Business people often argue, on the other hand, that in such markets competition is already intense. What the business people really mean, however, is that there is much rivalry and competitive moves and countermoves within the industry, as each producer attempts to build up

consumer brand loyalty in order to increase profits. In a purely competitive market, there can be no such behaviour because each product is identical in the mind of the consumer.

Tables 7-1 and 7-2 give some insight into the structure of the Canadian microeconomy. Table 7-1 indicates the total number of firms within various manufacturing industries, together with the approximate percentage of total business activity carried on by the four largest firms in each case. As might be expected, industries with a lower number of firms are more heavily concentrated in terms of the percentage of business carried on by the largest four.

Table 7-1 is by no means all-inclusive. For one thing, the data refer only to manufacturing industries. However, there are no pure monopolies in the sense of a single-firm industry. There are also no purely competitive industries. The least concentrated manufacturing industry in 1982 was, perhaps, women's clothing, with 889 firms and the largest 4 accounting for only 8.9% of the market. However, we know that even within this industry there are a number of readily identifiable brands, for which other brands are not deemed to be perfect substitutes, and for which shoppers are willing to pay higher prices.

Table 7-2 attempts to classify various industries (not only manufactured goods, but also services and products of natural resource industries) along the spectrum from pure competition to monopoly. This classification is not rigid and certain. Some will disagree with the slotting of various industries.

No purely competitive industries or pure monopolies are found in Canada. Most Canadian industries are quite highly concentrated and are best described either as oligopolies or as monopolistically competitive.

7-3 MONOPOLISTIC COMPETITION

This form of market structure is characterized by a reasonably large number of sellers, each of them small as compared with the size of the market and each producing a similar yet somewhat differentiated product. Further, there is reasonably easy (low cost) entry into and exit from the industry. Because

Table 7-1 Market share concentration in selected Canadian manufacturing industries

Industry	Market share (by value of shipments) held by four largest firms (%)		Total number of firms in the industry		Industry	Market share (by value of shipments) held by four largest firms (%)		Total number of firms in the industry	
	1965	1982	1965	1982		1965	1982	1965	1982
Beer	94.5	98.8	12	8	Brooms, brushes, and				
Motor vehicles	93.3	94.7	20	14	mops	48.4	X	85	62
Cane and beet sugar					Paper and plastic bags	47.6	28.2	55	102
1968	(92.4)	X	8	7	Fabric gloves	46.3	X	18	9
Aluminum rolling,					Paint and varnish	46.0	30.8	130	114
casting, etc.	88.1	83.9	43	56	Soft drinks	40.8	51.6	409	165
Refined petroleum	84.8	61.4	12	16	Canvas products	33.0	25.2	143	172
Fibre and filament yarn					Publishing	31.5	40.0	424	757
1970	(82.7)	89.2	8	14	Heating equipment	29.8	26.5	105	151
Smelting and refining					Toys and games	27.1	56.0	81	71
products	80.6	75.7	13	14	Pharmaceuticals and				
Steel pipes and tubes	78.2	77.2	14	32	medicines	26.1	28.9	152	114
Soap and cleaning					Truck bodies	—	45.0	—	126
compounds	79.0	63.5	124	110	Signs and displays	21.6	17.9	391	474
Aircraft and parts	76.8	68.4	76	143	New and repaired boats	21.5	22.9	242	287
Cement	76.7	84.3	10	9	Shoes	20.2	21.8	205	146
Clocks and watches					Hosiery	18.1	X	130	60
1986	(75.5)	X	20	27	Sawn and planed				
Agricultural					lumber	16.8	18.1	2464	1081
implements	71.6	57.4	94	187	Dental products	15.7	13.0	558	579
Slaughtered and					Commercial printing	13.5	17.9	1956	2574
processed meat	61.8	39.8	365	426	Women's clothing	6.4	8.9	623	889
Carpets, rugs, and mats	57.0	43.8	24	30					
Household radio									
and TV	53.4	87.9	25	16					
Commercial refrigeration and air conditioning equipment	51.5	46.9	36	49					

Source: Statistics Canada. 31-514 and 31-402. The symbol X indicates that data is not reported for reasons of confidentiality.

Selected Canadian manufacturing industries ranked by their degree of concentration. Over the period shown, there has been a small increase in average concentration.

each firm accounts for only a small proportion of the market, any change in output volume by a single producer will have a negligible effect on the market share enjoyed by other firms. A single firm's actions are therefore not likely to draw serious reactions from these other producers in the short run. The single firm within a monopolistically competitive setting may make decisions concerning such things as price, output and advertising without fear of immediate repercussions from other firms. This is an important feature, differentiating this form of market structure from that of oligopoly (which we shall consider later).

Because each firm produces a similar yet "somewhat differentiated" product, it faces a slightly downward sloping demand curve. In other words,

Table 7-2 Industrial organization involving production of various goods and services

Pure competition	Monopolistic competition	Oligopoly	Pure monopoly
(Manufactured goods)			
Dental products	Canvas products	Refined sugar	
Women's clothing	Electric lamps & shades	Beer	
Sawn & planed lumber	Publishing	Automobiles	
Household furniture	Heating equipment	Explosives & ammunition	
Commercial printing	Pharmaceuticals & medicines	Cement	
(Services)			
Men's & women's hairstyling	Trucking	Airlines, Railroads	
Some retailing	Some retailing	Ad agencies	
		Professional groups (e.g., doctors, lawyers)	
		Unions	
		Pipelines	
		Hospitals	
		Public utilities	
		Police	
(Resource industries)			
Some agriculture	Gold & copper mining	Some agriculture	
Logging	Iron mining	Uranium mining	
	Oil extraction		

A tentative categorization of selected Canadian industries, based on their degree of concentration.

with regard to Figure 7-1, the firm is able to raise its price from the current one (P_0) without pricing itself completely out of the market — as it would, for example, if it was within a purely competitive market. Though, for instance, it would lose some sales volume $(Q_0 - Q_1)$ if it raised its price from P_0 to P_1 (through customers switching to similar products of competitors), it would not lose its entire market share.

Examples of monopolistic competition may normally be found within the retail and service sectors in medium or large cities. These examples might include nonsupermarket grocery stores, florists, second-hand car dealers, electrical contractors, TV repair shops, printers, motels, restaurants, accounting and law firms (for standard accounting and legal services). In certain cases, however, some of the above businesses may be monopolistic. For instance, in smaller towns there may be only a single florist or one motel or hotel.

Product Differentiation

Product differentiation is one feature of a monopolistically competitive market which distinguishes it from pure competition. Product differentiation may take many forms. First of all, actual physical characteristics may be different, causing the product to perform in a somewhat different manner; or at least leading the consumer to think that the product will perform in a somewhat different manner — and what the consumer *thinks* is the im-

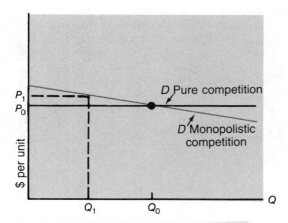

Fig. 7-1 Demand conditions facing a monopolistically competitive firm

Monopolistic competition is characterized by product differentiation, and thus, a monopolistically competitive firm faces a downward sloping demand curve.

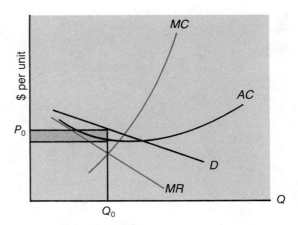

Fig. 7-2 Market position for a monopolistic competitor

Monopolistically competitive firms may temporarily make economic profits which are likely to be competed away in the long run.

portant thing. Perhaps the services performed by the seller in connection with the product are of a different quality from those performed by other sellers — or at least the consumer thinks they are. "Our service department is the best in town" is a common claim of most second-hand car dealers, for example. If a consumer believes this to be true of one particular dealer, this factor differentiates in a favourable manner the product of this competitor from the others. There are other ways of differentiating the total product (product plus connected services): better and easier credit, attractive stores, free coffee and doughnuts, courteous sales assistance. In the minds of many consumers, these factors are important in the choice of the basic product itself, and so differences in these extras differentiate the whole product.

Price and Output Determination

The profit-maximizing output and price combinations (Q_0, P_0) as shown in Figure 7-2 are determined as always where marginal revenue equals marginal cost. As we have depicted the situation in Figure 7-2, the monopolistic competitor is current-

ly earning a profit as represented by the shaded area. These profits may not last long, however, since their existence may attract new firms into the industry. This process is discussed in Chapter 9.

The main distinguishing feature of monopolistically competitive markets is a large number of firms selling differentiated products. Because of the large number of firms operating in such industries, competitive reactions are likely to be slow.

7-4 OLIGOPOLY

A little further up the industrial organization spectrum toward monopoly is the market structure referred to as oligopoly. Typically, oligopoly will have fewer sellers than monopolistic competition — perhaps 4 to 50. The smaller number of sellers, however, is not the main feature distinguishing oligopoly from monopolistic competition. The important factor is that firms that account for the bulk of the output within a particular market are few in number, so few in fact that each has a significant market share. This being the case, any attempt by one of these major producers to enlarge its share of the market would have a significant effect on the demand facing other major producers and cause them to react.

Any one firm's desire to gain monopoly power, and hence monopoly profits, is a strong reason for wanting few competitors within a particular industry. One way of eliminating competitors is to be more innovative in developing and advertising new products for which others become inferior substitutes. Another way is the merger. A **merger** or **takeover** occurs when one firm buys the control of another and then continues to operate as one consolidated enterprise. Typically, a large firm buys out smaller ones. The means of payment may be cash to the owners of the smaller firms or, if corporations are involved — as they usually are — by the buying firm's giving its own shares to the owners of the smaller firm in exchange for shares in the smaller firm.

Because it is in the best interests of a firm with monopoly power to restrict output, we may find that merged firms provide less total output than the two firms did separately. This means that the purchasing firm may sell off some assets of the consolidated enterprise and operate with an overall smaller physical base. On the other hand, it is possible — if overhead efficiencies are present — that the merged firm's unit costs may be reduced to such an extent that even greater output is produced by the merged enterprise than was produced in total by both firms operating alone.

Desire for increased profits, either from increased monopoly power or from cost economies, is an important incentive leading toward oligopolized industrial structures. Much of Canadian industry may be characterized as oligopoly, including oil, new automobiles, designer clothing, athletic shoes, hockey skates, cameras, golf and tennis equipment, soft drinks, cereals, soaps, grocery supermarkets, computers, photocopying equipment, financial auditing services for national companies, banking, insurance, broadcasting and air transport. (See again Tables 7-1 and 7-2.)

Price and Output Determination

Though the treatment of the determination of market price and output volume is fairly straight-forward in pure competition, monopoly and monopolistic competition, the same cannot be said of oligopoly. Unlike the other market structures discussed so far, oligopoly decisions require a great deal of strategy. Decision makers must not only evaluate costs of production and consumer demand sensitivity toward price in arriving at profit-maximizing decisions, but as well must take into account the sensitivity of competitors' prices in response to their own and the sensitivity of demand with respect to competitors' prices. The following discussion illustrates the problem.

Manager 1: "Suppose we lower our prices by 10%. If our competitors don't react, my staff thinks on the basis of our analysis of consumer price sensitivity, that we will sell roughly 20% greater volume."

Manager 2: "Just a minute — your estimates are based on the assumption that our competitors aren't going to fight back and also lower their prices. I don't question your cost data, or even your estimate of consumer response to our price cuts, but this is not going to be the end of the story. From experience, I would judge that our competitors aren't going to sit by and let us reduce their market share and profitability. My guess is that they are likely to follow suit with 10% price reductions of their own — possibly greater."

Manager 1: "You're suggesting, then, that we shouldn't change our price?"

Manager 2: "No. I'm not sure. It certainly reduces the likelihood of a price reduction being a profitable decision, but doesn't eliminate the possibility. For example, my guess is that a 10% reduction by us, followed by a similar price reduction by our competitors would more likely lead to a 15% volume increase rather than 20%. This still means a revenue increase of about 5%, but then I'm not sure how much a 20% volume increase would affect our total costs."

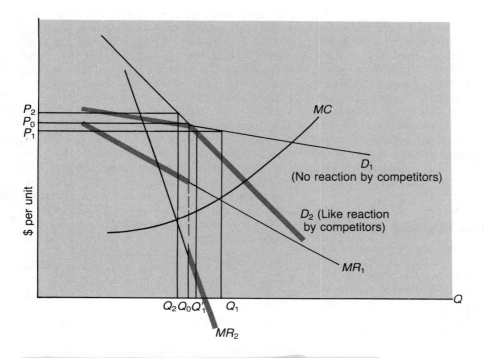

Fig. 7-3 The kinked demand curve case in oligopoly markets

With the current price at P_0, a typical oligopoly firm is reluctant to raise its price, since competitors would not follow and the firm would lose sales (move along the heavily shaded flatter portion of the demand curve). A price cut, on the other hand, would be followed immediately, and only a small gain in sales would materialize (move along the heavily shaded steeper portion of the demand curve). Consequently, prices tend to remain rigid at P_0.

Manager 1: "All right, I'll have my staff rework their figures on your assumption of full competitor reaction."

Manager 2: "Good idea. Try some intermediate possibilities too. They may meet only half of our price cut. See what they've done in the past."

Each firm in an oligopolistic market realizes that its competitors will probably react if it lowers its prices. This knowledge removes some of the anticipated advantages of a price reduction in the first place, but does not mean that oligopolists

never lower prices. **Oligopolistic price inertia** is considered more explicitly below with reference to Figure 7-3, where we examine the possibility of price increases as well as price reductions.

(i) No Competitive Response

Figure 7-3 illustrates two possible demand and corresponding marginal revenue curves. Demand curve D_1 is designed to show the price-quantity combinations that would face the firm if its major competitors did not react either to price increases or reductions the firm might make. Each oligopolist produces similar products. Therefore, if the particular firm in question lowered its price and the other firms did not, it would attract a large number of customers away from its competitors. On the other hand, if the oligopolist raised its prices and its competitors did not, it would lose many customers to its competition. Consequently, under the "no competitive response" assumption, the firm's demand would be very price sensitive as shown by D_1. Under these conditions, if the present price is P_0, (determined, perhaps, by some markup pricing procedure) the firm should lower its price to P_1 and sell Q_1 (because at Q_1, $MR_1 = MC$).

(ii) Full Competitive Response

Another possibility is that the oligopolist's behaviour will bring forth a like response from competitors. In this instance, if the firm lowered its price to, say, P_1, its competitors, not wanting to lose a significant share of the market, would lower their prices accordingly. This would mean that the firm in question would not experience as large an increase in demand as would be the case under conditions of no competitive response. For example, by lowering the price to P_1 the quantity demanded might only increase to Q'_1, as we have shown it (on D_2), instead of Q_1 (on D_1). Similarly, it is possible that in the face of a price increase by our firm, its competitors would also raise their prices. Our firm would not lose as many customers as in the no competitive response case. All in all, then, if the firm expected imitative behaviour on the part of its competitors in response to either price reductions or increases, demand would be less price sensitive than in the no competitive response case. We have illustrated the full competitive response demand curve by D_2 (with corresponding marginal revenue curve, MR_2). In this instance, to earn the most profit the firm should raise its price to P_2 and sell Q_2 (because at Q_2, $MR_2 = MC$).

(iii) The Kinked Demand Curve

A third, and possibly more likely, alternative exists to both the no competitive response and full competitive response cases. Suppose that an oligopolist's competitors, for fear of losing their market shares and suffering consequent profit reductions, lower their prices in response to similar action by the initiating firm, but do not follow the initiating firm in the case of price increases. After all, if one oligopolist raises its price, this will increase the market share and profits enjoyed by other firms.

Diagrammatically this intermediate possibility shows up on Figure 7-3 in such a way that D_2 (and MR_2) would reflect the demand relation with respect to a price reduction from P_0, and that D_1 (and MR_1) would reflect the demand relation with respect to a price increase. In other words, the relevant demand and marginal revenue curves are those indicated by heavy lines. This leads to the conclusion that, at P_0, any price change would involve a reduction in profits. Marginal revenue lost would exceed marginal costs saved for all output levels below Q_0, which would result from a price increase, and marginal revenue gained would be less than marginal costs incurred for all ouput levels above Q_0, which would result from price reductions.

This intermediate **kinked demand curve** case has often been put forth as an explanation of certain **price rigidities** that have been observed to exist in oligopoly markets. However, as we will show below even in oligopolistic industries prices are changed as a result of sizable market shocks and as a result of an action by a price-leader firm.

We have now investigated the nature of monopolistically competitive and oligopolistic market structures. By definition, each monopolistic competitor is small relative to the size of the market. Actions by any one firm have negligible influence on the market as a whole. Because of this, decisions by the individual firm may be taken without fear of competitor reaction. This is not the case for oligopolies. Each firm is large enough to have a significant market share. Any action it may take will, therefore, be felt by the other firms. We have already investigated how oligopolists might react to each other's behaviour changes. Of further interest is how monopolistic competitors and oligopolists react to external economic shocks of both a demand and supply nature.

The key feature of an oligopolistic market structure is a small number of large firms. Given the strong interdependence among them, competitive reactions are immediate. Consequently, price competition in oligopoly is rare.

7-5 MARKET REACTION TO ECONOMIC SHOCKS

In the case of monopolistic competition and in the case where oligopolists either always or never follow suit with respect to each other's actions, the analysis of demand and supply shocks is exactly as in monopoly. We may treat each firm as having a certain degree of monopoly power over the market, and proceed accordingly. A different sort of analysis is necessary, however, in the oligopoly case, under the likely possibility of asymmetrical competitor response to price changes. We will now, therefore, consider this case and compare it with that of monopolistic competition.

Demand Shocks

We are by now familiar with the various possible demand shocks that may occur, for example, a change in the price of other brands, a change in consumer income, a change in consumer tastes or a change in population. Here, we wish to analyze how an oligopolist might change the price of its product, taking into consideration a likely asymmetrical price response by other brand competitors. It is therefore unimportant which possible demand shock we treat. For simplicity we will consider only increases in demand.

Figure 7-4a illustrates the case of a monopolistic competitor faced with a demand increase (that is, more output is demanded at every price, perhaps as a result of an increase in consumer income). In response, it would raise the price of its product to P_1 and increase production and sales to Q_1. Contrasted with this is the case of an oligopolist (Figure 7-4b) that also experiences an increase in demand for its brand at each and every price. In fact, we have supposed for comparison purposes that the demand increase facing the oligopolist is of precisely the same magnitude as that which the monopolistic competitor experiences. In this situation, the oligopolist would find it most profitable to increase production to Q_1 (because now $MR = MC$ at this new production point), but leave the price unchanged at P_0.

This pattern of response is consistent with profit maximization, because of the peculiar shape of the MR curve in the kinked demand curve model. As shown in Figure 7-4b, price P_0 remains the profit-maximizing outcome for a whole range of shifts in the MR curve. This does not mean that an oligopolist would never raise its price in response to a demand shock. If the demand increase was sizable, the oligopolist might think that the market share loss from raising its prices while others do not would be more than compensated by the higher prices. This possibility is depicted in Figure 7-4c, where to maximize profits, even in the face of expected asymmetrical competitor reaction, the oligopolist would raise its price to P'_1 and produce at Q'_1.

The main point to note here, though, is that the feared asymmetrical response by competitors within an oligopolistic market tends to lead to *price rigidity*. In situations where economic shocks within other market structures, ranging from pure competition through monopolistic competition to monopoly, would tend to cause price changes, oligopolists may be unwilling to alter their prices. Though we illustrated an example of upward price rigidity, downward price rigidity in the face of a demand reduction follows the same logic.

Supply Shocks

Let us also choose for illustration purposes a supply shock in only one direction, one that raises marginal costs of production. Figure 7-5a shows the case of a monopolistically competitive market in which such cost increases would tend to lead to price increases and reductions in sales volume. On the other hand, in the oligopolist's case depicted by Figure 7-5b, cost increases of an equal size may have no influence either on the price of the oligopolist's brand or the volume produced and sold. Once again, then, price rigidity is seen to be characteristic of oligopoly markets. However, as Figure 7-5c shows, if the cost increases are significant enough they will lead to increases in price and a reduction in volume sold.

Oligopoly firms respond to demand and supply shifts in much the same way as firms in other types of markets. However, because of built-in price rigidity, the oligopoly price may not be responsive to shifts of smaller magnitudes.

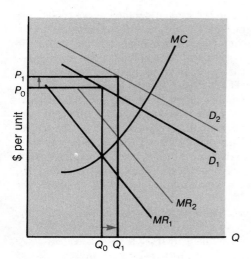

(a) Monopolistic competitor

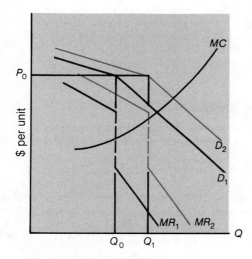

(b) An oligopolist:
small increase in demand

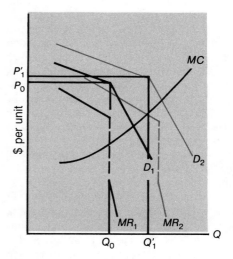

(c) An oligopolist:
large increase in demand

Fig. 7-4 Demand shocks in monopolistically competitive and oligopolistic markets

(a) A monopolistically competitive firm increases output and raises price in response to an increase in demand, however small.

(b) An oligopoly firm may not change price in response to a small increase in demand.

(c) An oligopoly firm raises its price in response to an increase in demand sufficiently large to require an adjustment to a new intersection of *MR* and *MC* curves.

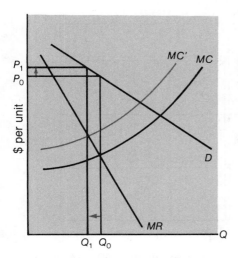

(a) **Monopolistic competitor**

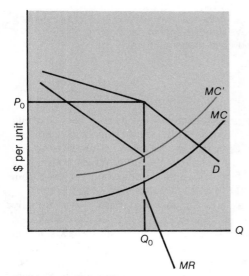

(b) **An oligopolist:**
    small increase in marginal costs

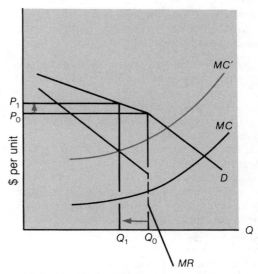

(c) **An oligopolist:**
    large increase in marginal costs

Fig. 7-5 A supply shock in monopolistically competitive and oligopolistic markets

(a) A monopolistically competitive firm reduces output and raises price in response to an increase in marginal cost, however small.

(b) An oligopoly firm may not change price or output in response to a small increase in marginal cost.

(c) An oligopoly firm raises price and reduces output in response to an increase in marginal cost sufficiently large to require an adjustment to a new intersection of MR and MC curves.

7-6 OLIGOPOLY AND THE THEORY OF GAMES

Because oligopoly markets characterize a large segment of economic activity, it is important to get a good feel for the type of considerations involved in managerial decision making within such an environment. As we said earlier, a chief characteristic of oligopoly from the standpoint of management is the knowledge that its decisions will, if they are at all significant, not go unnoticed by its competitors. The management may therefore be constantly strategizing.

If our firm raises its advertising and lowers its price our competitors will react. How will they react? They may increase their advertising and lower their prices, which will partly counteract our moves. Maybe they will completely counteract our moves, in which case we should perhaps not have acted in the first place. Perhaps we should instead repackage our product in a fancier way and leave its price intact. But our competitors may still react to this by lowering their prices. . . .

Strategy — that is, contemplation of competitor moves in planning one's own — is also common in such games as chess or poker. In fact, economists have developed a **theory of games** that may usefully be employed to examine the very nature of oligopoly behaviour.

As an example, consider Table 7-3, which is designed to reflect the joint profit positions of two oligopoly firms (X and Y) for different possible prices. The table is drawn up on the assumption that all other major decision variables of each firm remain constant — that is, things such as advertising, packaging and product development. Firm X's prices are along the top row; those of Firm Y are down the side. Each cell within the main body of the table indicates the profit of X and Y at various prices that each may charge for its own brand. For example, cell 6 indicates that if X charges $4 a unit, while Y charges $4.50, X and Y's annual profit will be $153 000 and $80 000 respectively.

Given that a competitor maintains a constant price, the table assumes that each firm's profit will increase as it lowers its price. (Of course, this would not be true over the entire range of possible prices, because at some point the revenue increase

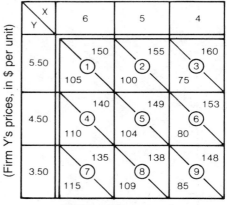

(Firm X's prices, in $ per unit)

(000s of $ per year)

Table 7-3 Profits payoff table for a two-firm oligopoly

A set of possible profit payoffs for different combinations of prices of two rival firms. Profits of firm X are above the diagonal in each cell; profits of firm Y are below the diagonal in each cell.

from a price reduction — if there is one — would be outweighed by the increase in costs.) For example, as Firm X lowers its price from $6 to $5 and then to $4, if Firm Y left its prices constant at $4.50, Firm X's annual profit would increase from $140 000 to $149 000 and then to $153 000.

Let us now suppose that Firm X was initially charging $5 while Firm Y's price was $4.50. In other words, we are in cell 5 with Firm X's annual profit $149 000 and Firm Y's, $104 000. We might ask whether Firm X should increase its price to $6. If Firm Y did not react, Firm X's annual profit would fall to $140 000 as a result of its loss in customers. In fact, Y would not be likely to react, because by keeping its price at $4.50 (cell 4) it would now earn a higher annual profit ($110 000) than would be the case if it too raised its price by $1 to $5.50 (cell 1). Therefore, by raising its price from $5 to $6, Firm X would likely become worse off.

Let us now examine the possibility of Firm X's

lowering its price from $5 to $4. Such a price reduction, if not accompanied by a similar response from Y, would enable X to raise its annual profit from $149 000 to $153 000 (moving from cell 5 to 6). It is likely, however, that Y would respond in this instance by also lowering its price by $1 to $3.50, because by doing so its profit would increase from $80 000 (cell 6) to $85 000 (cell 9). This reaction by Firm Y would finally result in Firm X's earning a lower profit than it did in its original position (cell 5).

Because by either raising or lowering prices Firm X would be in a worse profit position, it would find it best to sit where it is with its price at $5 per unit. By similar reasoning we could likewise show that Firm Y would find it best to maintain its present price of $4.50 per unit.

The game theory is a modern and possibly fruitful approach to analyzing competitive reactions in oligopolies. A simple payoff matrix illustrates the type of considerations inherent in oligopolistic strategies.

7-7 COLLUSIVE BEHAVIOUR

Because oligopolies are characterized by a relatively small number of major producers, there is at least the opportunity, either explicitly or implicitly (tacitly), to agree on policies that would be of mutual advantage to all participants. We have seen that independent rivalrous behaviour is largely self-defeating and wasteful, and may be harmful to all producers. We have also seen that the most profitable form of market structure for producers as a whole is that of monopoly. One way for oligopolists to increase their joint profits is, therefore, to merge together into a single firm and reap monopoly profits. Another possibility is to collude openly or secretly and agree on *mutually profitable behaviour*.

Table 7-3 illustrates this possibility with respect to an agreement between two firms to raise prices simultaneously. Suppose again that the firms are currently in cell 5 — with Firm X's price $5 and that of Firm Y, $4.50. For these prices we have the profits of Firm X and Y at $149 000 and $104 000 respectively. We have also seen above that it does not appear profitable for either firm independently

to raise or lower its prices. However, it would be possible for both firms to earn higher profits if they both agreed to raise their prices by $1: Firm X to $6 and Firm Y to $5.50 (that is, move into cell 1).

We might imagine a phone call or a meeting between the president of company X and the president of company Y during which the following sort of conversation takes place.

President of X: "You know, we've been batting our heads against the wall for years now, getting nowhere fast. Why should we fight each other? There's plenty of room in this market for both of us. I propose a deal. If we raise our prices by $1, will you agree to do the same?" (That is, move to cell 1.)

President of Y: (Not yet convinced of the advantage of this arrangement) "Why would I? Our company would earn more by letting you raise your price to $6 and keeping ours at $4.50." (In cell 4 company Y's annual profit is $5000 more than in cell 1.)

President of X: "But if you follow that policy — as you have in the past — you know that we will retaliate by lowering our price back to $5 (to cell 5) and limit your profit to its original level."

President of Y: (Becoming convinced) "That's true, I suppose."

President of X: "Well, then, agree with me now that we will both raise our prices, and as a result we will both be better off profit-wise (cell 1) than by leaving our prices at their present levels (cell 5)."

President of Y: "Agreed. But we will still watch your advertising and packaging policy very carefully to see that you do not attempt to gain a competitive edge along these lines."

President of X: "Fine. And we will also watch you in these areas."

The above is an example of blatant price fixing, which, of course, is illegal in Canada (see Appendix 9B). However, there are more subtle ways of achieving the aims of joint monpolization by means of implicit collusion. After years of experience in an oligopoly market, there is no real need of formal discussions among the participants to convince the parties that in many instances joint price increases may be profitable for all, and that price wars will almost certainly cause losses for all concerned. As a result, in an oligopolistic market there may develop *implicit rules of behaviour*.

Price Leaders

The most common of these unwritten agreements is price leadership. Under such a scheme, the dominant (perhaps the largest) firm within the market acts as a recognized **price leader**, with the other firms falling in step. The price leader raises (typically) or lowers (less frequently) prices whenever cost or demand conditions within the industry change and warrant such price action. In effect, an acknowledged price leader performs the function of pricing so that *quasi-monopoly profits* may be earned by the industry.

For example, in attempting to explain the function of a price leader, we may make use of a monopoly-type diagram such as Figure 7-6. The figure is designed to represent the volume of all brands produced within the market, neglecting product differences between brands. Similarly, the price is designed to reflect an average price of the various brands. For example, if an adverse shock hits this industry and pushes up unit costs, the price leader is supposed to recognize that it would be in the industry's best interest if prices were raised (for example, from P_0 to P_1). As a result, it would act accordingly. Because it knows it is the leader in the market, and because it knows all its competitors also know this, it may assume that the other firms will follow its lead in raising their prices. With little fear of loss of market share from a no-action policy by its competitors, it raises its own prices. The others follow suit shortly thereafter and greater profits are achieved by all concerned than might otherwise result from more independent action under conditions of rivalry.

Incentive to Undercut Prices

Even in an oligopoly market where price leadership is effective, each participant has an incentive to attempt to undercut the established price in some manner or other if the other oligopolists do not notice the tactic. To see this clearly, examine Figure 7-7.

Figure 7-7a disregards possible differences between brands and lumps the sales of all brands together as Q. We suppose for simplicity that there are four firms in the market with identical cost structures. For example, when each firm produces 50 000 units, its marginal costs are $2.50. In other words, the extra cost to each firm of producing the 50 000th unit of output is $2.50. Therefore, the extra cost of the 200 000th unit produced (50 000 from each firm), as far as the market is concerned, is also $2.50.

Now let us suppose that the implicit price arrangement carried out by this four-firm oligopoly is perfect in the sense that joint profits are maximized. This would be the case in our diagram if each firm agreed to charge $5.25 for its brand. Together the firms could do no better, as Figure 7-7a shows, because at a price of $5.25 and a volume of 200 000 (50 000 units each) they would be extracting maximum monopoly profits (where industry $MR = MC$).

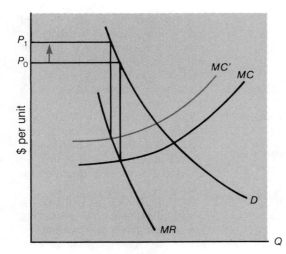

Fig. 7-6 Joint monopoly behaviour

The optimal response to an increase in marginal cost from *MC* to *MC'* is to raise price from P_0 to P_1. In an oligopoly, all firms will make this adjustment, if it is initiated by a recognized price leader.

With reference to Figure 7-7b, at $5.25 each oligopolist can sell as much as desired up to 50 000 units. This assumes its competitors are also selling the full 50 000 units at $5.25. The horizontal broken line on Figure 7-7b indicates that no one firm can produce or sell more than 50 000 units at $5.25, assuming the others are also selling all they can at $5.25. And, at an implicitly agreed price of $5.25, each competitor certainly will want to sell as much as possible. Every unit sold brings in $5.25 additional revenue (*MR*), which well exceeds the additional production costs (*MC*). Therefore, under an agreed price of $5.25 (which maximizes joint profits), each firm sees the marginal revenue from additional production exceeding its marginal cost and, therefore, will be led to produce and sell the maximum amount the market can absorb at that price (50 000 units each, or 200 000 units in total).

With marginal revenue exceeding marginal cost, there is always the urge to expand output. However, when an agreement such as this one is in place, expanding output amounts to cheating on one's rivals.

An executive of one oligopoly might mutter to himself, "We are currently bringing in $5.25 for each extra unit we sell, and this well exceeds our added production costs of $2.50. But we are restricting our sales at this $5.25 price. We could sell much more by lowering our price just a bit. Of course, since we would have to lower the prices on each and every unit of the 50 000 we are currently selling, this would tend to lower our extra revenue (*MR*) we bring in on each extra unit sold, but I think our volume would expand enough to more than compensate for this."

The executive may think that he or she can disguise the price reduction from his or her rivals by offering coupon discounts or perhaps gifts. If he or she is wrong, though, and the rivals interpret the action as a price reduction and follow suit, the oligopolists as a group will definitely be worse off as a result — because the present situation maximizes joint profits.

In practice, one is never quite sure whether existing prices in fact maximize joint profits, and there is always the possibility that with clever pricing strategy one will get the jump on one's rivals.

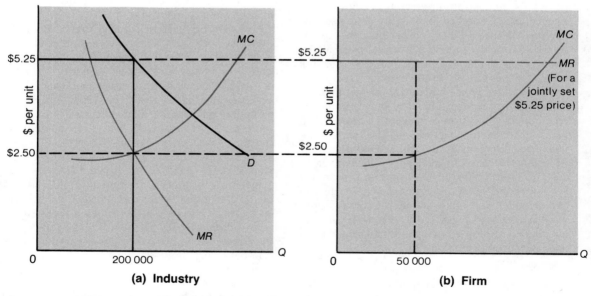

(a) Industry **(b) Firm**

Fig. 7-7 Incentive to undercut joint monopoly prices

The levels of output and price which maximize total industry profits (part (a)) require that each firm in the industry produce output for which *P* > *MC*. Therefore, each firm is tempted to expand output beyond that level.

Oligopoly Wars

Even in the case of a well-established price leadership, or in the presence of tacit agreement not to compete on a price basis, oligopoly discontent may arise. The temptation of monopoly profits is strong. Even though an oligopolist may have played by the rules of the game in the past and perhaps followed the leader in price changes, it may suddenly come to believe that it is getting the short end of the stick. It may really believe that it has a superior product or greater brand allegiance among its customers than the other producers have. In other words, it may think that it has differentiated its product to such an extent that it is able to escape the restrictive bounds of oligopoly and become an effective monopolist.

In such an instance, the rebellious firm may seek to break away from the established rules of pricing and price its product independently. Several outcomes are possible. First, the firm may be correct in its strategy. It may really have a product which its customers regard as much superior to competing brands. Therefore, sizable competitive price cuts may not be significant enough to erode the profit position of the initiating firm. On the other hand, the firm may be wrong. Customers may not regard its product as different from those of its competitors. Another possibility is that its competitors may be bent on bringing the upstart firm back into the fold by substantial price reductions, even in the face of significant short-run losses for themselves. In the extreme case, if the competitors are financially much stronger than the particular firm in question, they may become set on eliminating this firm permanently from the market as a warning to others who may be tempted into independent action. To do this, competitors must be willing to charge market prices below average costs in order to force losses on the firm until it becomes bankrupt or agrees to a merger. At the end of the conflict, prices may once more be brought up to more normal and profitable levels, with each remaining competitor enjoying a somewhat enlarged market share after the shakeup.

Various forms of collusive behaviour have developed in oligopolistic industries in an attempt to maximize the joint industry profits and avoid damaging price wars. However, most such efforts are successful only temporarily. Individual oligopolistic firms have a strong incentive to undercut the price that maximizes the joint industry profits.

7-8 CARTELS

A formal association of producers designed to act in a monopolistic fashion is known as a **cartel**. International cartels have operated generally in the agricultural and natural resource industries including sugar, copper, uranium and oil, but also in international air transportation and in shipping. An example of a form of cartel pervasive in one sector of the Canadian economy are the agricultural marketing boards (discussed below). From an economic point of view, professional organizations (of doctors, lawyers, dentists, engineers, accountants and others) are also a form of cartel.

Perhaps the most famous (or infamous) cartel of recent years has been the **Organization of Petroleum Exporting Countries** (OPEC). Two-thirds of OPEC's production comes from the Middle East, of which the largest producer is Saudi Arabia. In 1973, following the Arab-Israeli war, OPEC temporarily placed an embargo on Middle East oil exports. Shortly following this action, the price of OPEC oil was raised from about $3 per barrel to $12 per barrel. In order to maintain this much higher monopoly price, production and exports were reinstituted at much reduced volumes relative to the pre-embargo era and strict production limits or quotas were imposed on OPEC members.

With the marginal cost of each barrel of oil much less than even $3 per barrel, many people predicted in the early 1970s that the various individual countries of OPEC would have such an economic incentive to go beyond their output quotas at the $12 per barrel price that the necessary overall restrictions to supply could not be maintained and the cartel would soon disintegrate. In fact, these predictions were highly inaccurate, and by 1981 OPEC had forced the world price to $39 per barrel and the cartel remained intact. However, in late 1982, various members of the cartel were beginning to undercut the official OPEC price, which had already fallen to $34 per barrel in the face of a worldwide recession-induced drop in the demand for oil. In the following years, OPEC seemed to have lost its grip on the world oil prices, which dropped to the $10 per barrel range by mid 1986. They rose again, to the $15 per barrel range, by the end of 1986 as OPEC managed (temporarily?) to bring member countries into line and to agree upon production cutbacks.

The success of OPEC demonstrated to other producer groups that tremendous economic gains were possible through cooperative action. This is unfortunate, since the economic gains of artificial output restriction come at the expense of consumers.

Marketing Boards

A major part of Canadian agricultural production is carried on under government-authorized — but producer-controlled and managed — provincial and national marketing agencies. There are over 120 federal and provincial marketing boards in Canada. In 1983, they controlled 55 percent of farm cash receipts (up from 14 percent in 1962).[1] Among the farm products under the control of marketing boards are sheep, wool, hogs, milk, eggs, broiler chickens, turkeys, fruit, vegetables, tobacco, and honey.

Some marketing boards merely facilitate the common marketing of farm products (for example hogs, fruits and vegetables). Others, however, control the quantity of agricultural output and entry into the industry (for example eggs, chickens, turkeys, milk). In what follows, we deal mainly with the economic effects of the latter type of marketing boards (those with *supply management* powers).

The history of producer marketing boards in Canada dates back to the 1920s. Early voluntary farm cooperatives were formed as an attempt to offset what was regarded as exploitative practices of processors, packers and grain merchants aimed at keeping farmers' prices lower than they otherwise might be. These initial attempts failed because their actions were voluntary. Any temporary co-op success in driving up prices by holding product off the market was quickly erased by outside producers taking advantage of the higher prices and increasing their supply. In the 1930s, legislation was passed to permit province-wide marketing boards to be established with compulsory membership, should a majority of provincial producers so desire. In 1949, the *Agricultural Products Marketing Act* permitted provincial boards to restrict interprovincial movements of farm products. Finally in 1972, the *Farm Products Marketing Agencies Act* was passed, permitting active cooperation among the provinces regarding the national production and distribution of agricultural commodities.

1. *Report of the Royal Commission of the Economic Union and Economic Prospects for Canada*, Vol. II (Ottawa: Supply and Services Canada, 1985), p. 212.

National coordination and production control under the 1972 Act is most effectively carried out through national supply management marketing boards. The *Canadian Egg Marketing Agency* (CEMA) was established in 1973, the *Canadian Turkey Marketing Agency* in 1974 and a broiler chicken agency in 1978. There were also discussions concerning a national beef marketing agency, but as of 1986 it appeared unlikely that one would be formed.

As an example of how such boards operate, it may be useful to discuss one particular case — egg marketing. The production and marketing of eggs is controlled by the Canadian Egg Marketing Agency (a national marketing board known as CEMA) in conjunction with the provincial marketing boards. Neither CEMA nor the provincial marketing boards are government bodies in any sense. Members of these boards at both the national and provincial levels are chosen from among producers and have primarily producer interests in mind.

Production Controls

(i) Volume

National production volume is controlled at two levels. First, each producer has an egg production quota, which was established when the provincial marketing board was first set up and related to each farmer's production volume at that time. Second, the total *national* quota (production target) is set by CEMA. It depends on the anticipated demand for eggs at the time and is designed chiefly to provide a satisfactory income for producers. This national production target is then allocated among the provincial boards according to prior agreed upon shares. For example, the 1973 National Egg Production Base and the 1973, 1979 and 1986 Provincial Shares were as shown in Table 7-4.

Provincial boards allocate their production target for the year among individual producers, on the basis of their quota. For example, if in 1973 total quotas in farmers' hands in British Columbia were, say, 65 000 000 dozen, while only 57 250 000 dozen were needed, each farmer would have been asked to produce and market to the provincial boards in 1973 only 88% (that is 57 250/65 000 × 100%) of the assigned quota. It is not hard to imagine the frictions that may develop in years when farmers are asked to fill considerably smaller amounts of production than their full quotas would otherwise allow.

Table 7-4 **Allocation of national egg quota**

	1973		1979		1986	
	000s of doz.	% of total	000s of laying hens*	% of total	000s of laying hens*	% of total
B.C.	57 250	12.1	2 356	12.5	2 435	12.5
Alberta	41 344	8.7	1 470	7.8	1 504	7.7
Saskatchewan	22 611	4.8	677	3.6	701	3.6
Manitoba	54 189	11.4	2 218	11.8	2 325	11.9
Ontario	181 264	38.2	7 321	38.7	7 449	38.2
Quebec	78 647	16.5	3 119	16.5	3 229	16.5
New Brunswick	8 683	1.8	374	2.0	418	2.1
Nova Scotia	19 504	4.1	811	4.3	853	4.4
P.E.I.	3 028	0.6	130	0.7	143	0.7
Newfoundland	8 477	1.8	397	2.1	442	2.3
Canada	474 997	100.0	18 873	100.0	19 499	100.0

* In 1975, CEMA began to allocate and control quota on the basis of "number of hens" rather than "dozens of eggs," because it is easier to inspect farmer hen flocks than keep track of the number of eggs each farmer produces. Since it is relatively easy to estimate how many eggs the average hen lays, this policy is still consistent with CEMA's primary objective — controlling the number of eggs produced.

Source: Food Prices Review Board and Canadian Egg Marketing Agency Annual Reports. Reproduced by permission of the Minister of Supply and Services Canada.

National quota is first allocated to provinces and then to individual farmers within each province.

(ii) Price

The price a producer receives for eggs produced and sold in the same province is set by the provincial producer boards, and is based on the price the board expects to receive on the sale of the eggs to egg wholesalers.

In addition to production and price controls, advertising campaigns to encourage egg consumption are carried on by the boards.

(iii) Industry Entry and Exit

As total demand for eggs increases, the provincial boards may decide to expand the total quota for production within the province. At this point, they have to decide whether to distribute the extra quota among existing producers or allow new producers into the industry. The board may also allow existing producers to sell their quota to other existing or new producers.[2]

---

2. Some marketing boards have more powers than others. Not all marketing boards, for instance, have quota systems or power to fix prices.

Producer Incentives and Marketing Boards

Though the establishment of an orderly market is one objective of producer marketing boards, the primary incentive of supply management boards is to raise total profits of the industry through production. For example, if a particular agricultural submarket (say, for eggs) is purely competitive, we know (from Chapter 6) that industry profits over any period of time will be less than if the industry is a monopoly.

In Figure 7-8 the purely competitive price and output would be at P_1 and Q_1 respectively. These levels would yield a total industry profit of $PROF_1$, and this profit will necessarily be less than the total industry profit that would emerge if producers acted in concert — as a monopoly charging P_2 and producing at Q_2. There are larger potential producer incomes to be made if output can be restricted and the price raised. That can be done by either attempting to have prices raised beyond P_1 (ideally to P_2), in which case the output sold would be Q_2, or by restricting output (ideally to Q_2), in which case the market price would become P_2. In both instances, total industry profits would be maximized.

Efficiency Considerations

The defenders of marketing boards argue that they guarantee stability of farm incomes and thus a stable supply of agricultural products of high quality and stable prices to consumers. The critics note that those marketing boards which have supply management powers negatively affect efficiency. In addition to restricting output and raising prices, marketing boards insulate domestic producers from foreign competition and reduce interprovincial trade in agricultural commodities. As a result, consumers are not necessarily supplied from the province which can produce these commodities at the lowest cost.

Since prices are raised, incomes of farmers increase, but consumption of agricultural products is reduced. Consumers are therefore deprived of that amount of perceived value of agricultural products which corresponds to the volume of sales cut back by the marketing boards. Furthermore, efficient foreign suppliers are sometimes replaced by inefficient Canadian suppliers — members of marketing boards. These aspects of the operation of marketing boards constitute waste of resources. Some economists estimate that for every one dollar transferred from consumers to farmers, approximately 25 cents is wasted. Other studies estimate that the allocative inefficiencies created by marketing boards are such that it may cost as much as $3 to transfer one dollar from consumers to farmers.[3]

Quota Values

Marketing boards, by making possible the joint maximization of industry profits, raise farmers' incomes over and above the purely competitive level. This extra income cannot be competed away as is the case in many other industries (see Chapter 9), since any new farmer wishing to share in the extra profits has to have a quota.

A quota can, of course, be bought from an existing farmer, but at a price. The possession of a

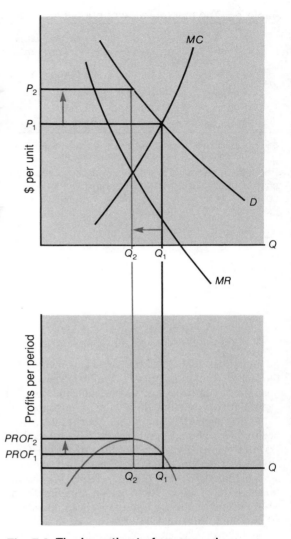

Fig. 7-8 The incentive to form a producer marketing board

The restriction of output (to Q_2) and increase in price (to P_2) accomplished by the marketing board raises industry profits above the purely competitive level (at output Q_1).

3. *Report of the Royal Commission on the Economic Union and Economic Prospects for Canada*, Vol. II (Ottawa: Supply and Services Canada, 1985), p. 431.

Table 7-5 **The market value of quotas in Ontario, 1984**

Product	Unit price	×	Size of family farm unit	=	Quota cost to acquire farm
Eggs	$23 a hen		25 000 birds		$580 000
Milk	$3 500 a cow		40 cows		$140 000
Tobacco	$1.50 a pound		40 acres		$310 000
Turkeys	54¢ a pound		25 000 birds a year		$270 000

Source: World Bank, *World Development Report 1986* (New York: Oxford University Press), p. 118. Reprinted with permission of the World Bank.

For selected types of marketing boards in Ontario, the quota values for a typical size of family farm unit (defined in the third column) are reported in the last column.

quota entitles its holder to a stream of income in the future. The quota price, therefore, depends on the size of the stream of income and the cost of capital funds (see the discussion of net present value in Chapter 9). The recent quota prices have been quite high and the initial investment needed just to obtain the right to produce (that is *before* any land, farm buildings, equipment and animals are purchased) is considerable. Table 7-5 shows selected quota costs for Ontario, ranging from $140 000 needed to acquire the right to operate a 40-cow milk farm to $580 000 needed to acquire the right to operate an egg farm with 25 thousand laying hens.

Farming is not unique in this regard. Entry restrictions will create an asset value similar to the price of a quota in other markets as well. An example are the prices of taxi licence plates in cities where entry into the taxi business is restricted. As a case in point, a taxi licence for Metro Toronto was advertised in October 1986 for $100 000.[4]

And in New York City, where the total number of taxi licences has remained frozen at 11 787 since 1937 despite a sizable growth of population, the price of a licence in early 1986 was $135 000 (in Canadian funds).[5]

A final comment — to deter a mass exit from your economics class into the farming or taxi business: While cartel restrictions on entry raise incomes in such industries, every new entrant has to make a large initial outlay on purchasing a quota or a licence. The return on his or her total investment (including the purchase of a quota or a licence) is therefore likely to be no higher than in other lines of business with similar risk.

Marketing boards as a means of stabilizing farmers' incomes are not without drawbacks. They shelter their members from competition and thus encourage inefficiency. The high quota values characteristic of some marketing boards represent a significant and growing barrier to entry.

---

4. *Toronto Star*, October 27, 1986, Classified Ads.

5. *The Financial Post*, April 5, 1986.

THIS MORNING WE'RE GOING TO DISCUSS PRODUCTION CONTROLS

CHICKEN FEED

By Trevor Hutchings. Reprinted by permission.

7-9 NONPRICE COMPETITION

The self-defeating effects of open price competition and ruinous consequences of price wars among competing oligopolists tend to discourage the use of price as a strategic decision variable in oligopoly markets. As a result, attention is often directed toward various forms of nonprice competition, such as *product development* and *advertising*. If a firm can create stronger brand allegiance by developing a more differentiated product, it may be able to earn a greater degree of monopoly power by reducing demand sensitivity to its price changes. If successful in this regard, the firm may have a product so differentiated from those of its competitors that competitive brands become very poor substitutes indeed. In such an instance, the firm will become insulated from competitor reactions to its own price changes.

Product development, therefore, can become an important tool in the task of insulating oneself from competitor reactions and carving out one's own monopoly niche in the market place. Many critics argue that oligopolists' claims to product differentiation from competitive brands are typically exaggerated. Some would say, for instance, that a so-called "new improved" ingredient does not materially influence the performance of the

product; all that is changed is the package. Whether a brand in some way is truly different from another may be quite academic to the producer, however. The important thing from the producer's standpoint is that consumers *think* it is different — better than it was before or perhaps better than some other product. Demand is determined by consumer beliefs and perceptions concerning the ability of a product to fill certain needs. If such demand may be influenced by the producer's putting the same old product in a new package or adding a useless ingredient (say, chlortripolite 45 +) then this may be a more profitable strategy than materially changing the product.

Advertising

The stated purpose of advertising is to inform consumers about the particular qualities of a product so that consumers, in light of their tastes and income, may be able to make an *informed purchasing choice*. Many critics argue, however, that advertising emphasizes minor or even nonexistent attributes of a product in persuading consumers to purchase. Extreme critics of advertising even say that advertising is an insidious tool of producers, designed to remove all free choice and manipulate consumers into purchasing whatever new gimmick is thrown on the market. These people see consumers as persons whose tastes are not developed individually, from within, but rather are created and twisted by clever ad agencies.

Advertising certainly provides information *and* persuasion — some advertising more of one, and some more of the other. For an example of **informational advertising** consider store catalogues and flyers that are received at the door or in the newspapers. These advertisements provide valuable information for consumers and enable them to carry out an uncomplicated, low-cost preliminary search process when engaged in comparative shopping. Contemplating a purchase of a pair of skates, the average consumer will probably have on hand at least two or three catalogues that show prices, together with pictures of various brands. Very often the same brand will be found to be cheaper in one store than in another. However, not even catalogue advertising is purely informational. Products are presented in their best light, and attractive models in just the right poses appear on the fashion pages. A well-known hockey star may be pictured holding up a particular brand of skates.

For examples of **persuasive advertising**, some might point to beer commercials on television. How much informational content concerning either the price or quality of a particular beer is contained in a message that depicts sky divers, ex-football or hockey players, truck drivers or friendly neighbours having a glass of brand X?

Also, by its very nature, some advertising within an oligopoly market is self-defeating from the firm's standpoint and wasteful from society's standpoint. Suppose, for instance, one oligopolist undertakes a successful competitive advertising campaign which threatens the market share of its competitors. The competitors may react by increasing their advertising. This advertising increase will erode some of the sales gain made by the original oligopolist's advertising campaign. In the limit, we could envisage all firms ending up with precisely the same sales volume as before but, now that each firm has increased advertising expenditure, costs will be higher and profits lower. This limiting possibility is not likely to occur, but certainly some of the advertising expenditures will merely counteract the competitors' advertising instead of increasing the total market for the particular product in question.

Suppose, for example, that within a given industry and a given year, $1 million of the total advertising done by all firms was of this self-defeating nature. If no part of this expenditure had been made, total industry sales volume would have remained intact but total costs would have been $1 million less, and the resources (labour and capital equipment used to produce this advertising) could have been used by society to increase the production of other goods and services, including leisure.

Obviously, not all advertising expenditure is wasteful. The public must be informed of the availability of a firm's products one way or another, or else no sales will be made at all. Clearly, therefore, a certain amount of advertising by all firms is desirable and profitable, even if this just involves painting a sign on a store front or acquiring space in the yellow pages of the telephone directory. Also, well advertised information concerning product price, availability and performance is valuable to consumers, enabling a better allocation of consumer incomes and a higher level of satisfaction.

Price competition in oligopolistic industries has a tendency to degenerate into price wars. Oligopolist firms, therefore, try to avoid price competition and replace it with nonprice competition, based on product differentiation and especially advertising.

7-10 BARRIERS TO ENTRY

Oligopoly markets, as well as monopolies, tend to be protected by certain **barriers to entry**. These barriers may not be insurmountable, but they can act as a significant deterrent to a prospective new firm. Some barriers are created by the incumbent firms, some arise from technical features of the market, and some are erected by governments.

Brand Loyalty or Habit Persistence

Suppose a new firm attempting to break into an oligopoly market comes in with a similar but differentiated product. Consumers are familiar with existing brands but completely unfamiliar with the product of the new entrant. For consumers to turn away from their usual brand and buy that of the new competitor presents a risk — namely, that the new product might be inferior to the known brands. As a result, consumers have a natural inclination (everything else being equal) to stick with their present brand. This is known as **habit persistence** or **brand loyalty**. A new firm must, therefore, break this barrier and induce consumers to take the risk and switch brands on an experimental basis. In order to do this, consumers must either be convinced through an aggressive advertising campaign that the new product is superior to existing brands, be given free samples or be persuaded in some other way. These inducements may impose a significant initial cost on the new entrant and hence be a barrier to entry.

Fighting Brands

One method of reducing the possibility of market erosion by present competitors or new entrants is for existing oligopolists to use **fighting brands**. Let us explain this strategic marketing tool by means of a numerical example.

Suppose a cigarette market consists of 1 000 000 consumers split equally between four firms. Some consumers will have a high degree of brand loyalty and would rather "fight than switch," whereas others will switch brands under the slightest persuasion. To simplify matters, let us suppose that 80% of consumers (800 000) will not switch brands without great inducement, while 20% of them (200 000) purchase on a purely random basis — one brand one day, another brand, the next. Each brand (suppose each firm has one brand) then has 250 000 customers, of whom 200 000 are loyal and 50 000 attracted purely by chance.

In this instance, a new brand should be able to pick up one-fifth of the random market (or 40 000 customers because there will then be five brands available). Of course, it would be much harder to break into the main part of the market, where brand loyalty is strong. Nevertheless, each of the original four brands would stand to lose 10 000 of its random customer market to the new brand.

To combat this possibility, however, each of the oligopolists might introduce a second brand. Supposing that these seconds fight only for the random customer group, each firm will still have 250 000 customers. Each of the old brands will still have its 200 000 faithful customers plus one-eighth of the random customer group (since there are now eight brands fighting for this market segment) — or 225 000 customers in all. Each of the new brands will also have an eighth of the random customers group — or 25 000. As a result, each oligopolist's market share remains intact. The advantage of the fighting brands is evident, however, if we again suppose that a new brand enters the market. Vying for random customers, it will now pick up only one ninth of this market segment ($\frac{1}{9} \times 200\ 000$) — or 22 222 customers in all. This customer gain by the new competitor represents a loss to each original oligopolist of only $\frac{22\ 224}{4} = 5\ 555$ customers (as compared with 10 000 before). The introduction of fighting brands, therefore, tends to protect existing market shares and makes it more difficult for new entrants — or for that matter new brands of existing firms. This tactic explains in part the tendency for *brand proliferation* among oligopoly markets.

Cost Advantage

Existing oligopolists may have been in the industry for many years and have built up a relatively large annual volume of sales. This experience and high volume of output may mean that existing prod-

ucers have a significant cost advantage over a new firm just starting production at a low volume.

The *learning by doing* experience that has been gained over the years by the established firms' engineers, managerial staff and other workers may have resulted in cost savings. A new firm will likely have to go through various teething problems before it can hope to acquire these cost advantages.

Also, it is often the case that high volume production techniques are more efficient than low volume production techniques. If a new company has to gear its physical plant and machinery for low volumes in its early years, it may not be able to employ the same low cost production methods which are currently used by the existing producers. This low volume source of inefficiency may also put a new company at a cost disadvantage when seeking to enter an established oligopoly industry.[6]

Patents

A **patent** is the grant of an exclusive right, usually for a period of 17 years, to an inventor (a person or a firm) to exploit the benefits of an invention. By definition, it excludes others from producing and selling the patented product and makes it possible for the patent holder to make higher profits. The rationale for this type of barrier to entry is the desire to encourage and reward research, invention and innovation.

There are, however, obvious welfare tradeoffs. The case of the Canadian patent protection of prescription drugs is an excellent illustration. In 1969, Parliament was persuaded by statistical evidence that Canadian prices of prescription drugs were among the highest in the world. It enacted a law making it possible for qualified drug manufacturers to apply for and obtain a licence to produce and sell a drug patented by another firm (for a minimal royalty fee paid to the patent holder). These drugs produced under licence (generic drugs) frequently sold at a fraction of the price of the original product. According to a 1985 estimate, the resulting competition saved the Canadian consumers about $200 million annually. However, the research-based multinational pharmaceutical com-

---

6. The connection between volume, long-run production methods and unit costs is explored below, in Chapter 9, Section 9-3.

panies vigorously protested this "theft of intellectual property" and curtailed their research activities in Canada. In 1986, therefore, the government introduced a bill strengthening patent protection of prescription drugs in Canada and reducing the opportunities for licensing of patents. The bill was enacted in November 1987.

Government Regulation

These are probably the most effective and most durable barriers to entry, since they are sanctioned and enforced by the coercive power of governments. Examples of barriers to entry in the form of government regulations are many. *Marketing boards*, discussed above, represent a regulatory barrier to entry. *Occupational licensing regulations*, which restrict the right to practise certain occupations only to those persons certified by a government body, are another example. Next, there is a whole gamut of *product safety regulations* which, in effect, keep certain products from entering the market or allow them to enter only after certain onerous and costly requirements are satisfied. In order to approve a new prescription drug (Tagamet, for treatment of stomach ulcers) for the U.S. market, for example, the originating company was required to submit to the government 45 000 pages of evidence in 160 volumes, including reports on 42 000 patients.[7] Another type of entry barriers are *import restrictions*, such as import quotas on shoes and textiles, which allow only certain limited quantities of foreign-made products on the Canadian market. Finally, the government of Canada screens proposed foreign takeovers of Canadian companies. In some cases, disallowing such a takeover amounts to preventing entry by a vigorous competitor.

All of these regulations have been implemented and justified on the grounds of protecting the public or the "national interest" or some "vital" sector of the Canadian economy. Their adverse impact on competition, however, may in some cases outweigh their benefits.

Barriers to entry are one of the most important determinants of the degree of competitiveness within a market. It is a vital task of public policy to assess the welfare implications of those barriers that may be amenable to government action.

7-11 WELFARE CONSIDERATIONS

Monopolistic competition, oligopoly and monopoly are the three examples that we generally classify under the heading *imperfect competition* (that is, not pure competition). Oligopoly is perhaps the most common form of imperfect competition in Canada, but all three forms have one common strike against them as far as allocative efficiency considerations are concerned. Profit maximization implies that firms within these market structures will produce at output volumes where *price exceeds marginal cost*. This means that the last unit of ouput produced is worth more to society than the cost of resources used up in producing it. Everything else being equal, this suggests that any market structure with monopoly power creates a welfare loss in comparison to the benefit that would be provided if the market was purely competitive. But is everything else equal?

Many economists have criticized the above sort of welfare analysis as being too *static* in scope. *Dynamic analysis* would try to account for different unit cost and product development trends which might occur over time under alternative market structure. Those who challenge whether pure competition is the ideal form of market structure often argue that firms with protectable profits (oligopolies and monopolies) have a greater incentive to search for more efficient (cost reducing) production techniques and new products, which results in benefits to consumers as well as producers.

This is the case for two reasons: First, oligopolies and monopolies are typically large firms with sufficient cash flow and other resources to be able to support a research laboratory. Second, firms in such markets are faced with less vigorous competition and are therefore relatively free to engage in high-risk activity such as research and development. Others reply that the greater the degree of competition, the greater the incentive to cut costs and innovate just to survive in the industry. These people contend that within the more protected industrial structures of oligopoly and monopoly, managers can afford to relax their efforts toward efficiency and innovation. A great deal of effort has been spent on empirical testing of these competing hypotheses. The problem is, however, complex and no clear consensus has emerged as yet.

---

7. *The Economist*, October 18, 1986.

Like monopoly, the monopolistically competitive and oligopolistic markets exhibit static allocative inefficiency ($P > MC$). However, when dynamic considerations are taken into account, the case against these market structures is less strong.

CONCLUDING REMARKS

Most markets are not as simple as either the pure competition or pure monopoly cases considered earlier. Most firms possess at least somewhat differentiated products relative to those of their competitors and therefore have some degree of monopoly power. Price, advertising, packaging and product quality are all decision variables for these firms. In oligopoly markets, major producrs are very aware that whatever they do to their price will initiate a response from their competitors. The nature of this response is always to reduce the likelihood of the original action's being profitable. Realization of this leads to sticky price behaviour and more emphasis being placed on the other decision variables of the firm, especially product differentiation. Product differentiation is generally difficult to duplicate quickly (relative to price changes). If the product differentiation is very successful competitors may be unable to duplicate it for a long time. This fact carries with it the possibility of increased monopoly power and nonerodible profits.

KEY TERMS AND CONCEPTS

monopolistic competition	Organization of Petroleum
oligopoly	Exporting Countries (OPEC)
merger	informational advertising
takeover	persuasive advertising
oligopolistic price inertia	barriers to entry
kinked demand curve	habit persistence
price rigidities	brand loyalty
theory of games	fighting brand
price leader	patent
cartel	

PROBLEMS

Problem 1

Differentiate between the market structure of monopolistic competition and oligopoly.

Problem 2

a) What chief characteristic of an oligopolistic market may lead to a degree of price rigidity?

b) The diagram below depicts the market situation facing a monopolistic competitor. The current price is P_0 and the quantity produced and sold is Q_0. The demand curve, D_1, is drawn under the assumption that there would be similar competitive response to both price increases and price reductions by this particular firm. Under this assumption what would be the best price action for the firm to take?

c) Draw another demand curve, D_2, under the assumption that there would be no competitive response to either price increases or price reductions by this particular firm.

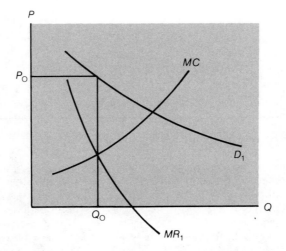

d) Now, under the assumption that competitors would react to price decreases by our firm but not react to price increases, sketch three separate diagrams depicting each of the following possibilities: (i) the case where a price increase would be in order, (ii) the case where a price decrease would be in order and (iii) the case where the price should be left at P_0. (In each case disregard the diagram shown above in part (b), but instead draw your own, placing the various curves in such positions as to obtain the desired results.)

Problem 3

a) Consider the oligopolist of Problem 2d. Show the effects on price and volume produced by the following market shocks (in each case illustrate the rigid price possibility, that is, where there would be no price change following the shock): (i) an increase in materials prices, (ii) a reduction in the price of a foreign-produced substitute product.

b) For each shock of part (a), illustrate the possibility that price may be affected.

c) Illustrate the effects of each shock given in part (a), assuming the market is (i) purely competitive, (ii) monopolistic, (iii) monopolistically competitive.

Problem 4

a) Explain why it may be attractive for firms in a few firm industry to collude and utilize a price leader-follower pattern.

b) What is the incentive for firms in a leader-follower price relationship to try secretly to undercut prices by offering discounts, "cents-off" coupons, free giveaways and the like?

Problem 5

Explain the concept of industrial "barriers to entry" and list three common barriers to entry into oligopoly industries.

Problem 6

a) Discuss the often heard remark that "advertising pays for TV programs."

b) There is clearly a need for information concerning goods and services available, so that consumers may make wise purchasing decisions. Some people would refer to such advertising as "informational advertising" and distinguish it from advertising of the persuasive or promotional type. Some also advocate control of promotional advertising. Would you advocate control of advertising? Why or why not?

CASES

Case 7-1

The Globe and Mail, Toronto

Car rental war means prices cut to 1¢ a day

By ROBERT WILLIAMSON

VANCOUVER — A man drove away from Vancouver International Airport this week in a Tilden Chevrolet Chevette rental car that will cost him seven cents — one cent a day — plus gasoline, for a week of driving.

Consumers have been scrambling for bargains across Canada as a three-month price war between Tilden and Budget hit peaks of absurdity in recent days.

The two large companies are lockstepped in a low-season poker game for slices of the lucrative airport car rental business. It's a deadly serious competition of move and matching move that has spread to all major airports across Canada.

"We plan to hang in there," Tilden chairman Walter Tilden said yesterday. "We could afford to go on for a long time."

"It took me 17 years to build up my market share," said Sydney Belzberg, Budget franchise owner-operator for British Columbia. "I am not about to relinquish it to Mr. Tilden."

When prices began plummeting last November from the summer season high of about $17 a day for a sub-compact, Mr. Belzberg actually advertised at one point that his cars were free.

The provincial consumer protection branch drew the line at that because there were, in fact, conditions such as time, limits and gasoline charges.

So the price went up to one cent a day and since then, Budget and Tilden have played sometimes minute-by-minute variations on the penny-a-day rate. Even luxury Cadillacs and sport Camaros are part of the penny-a-day parade.

Keith Nash, Toronto district manager for Tilden, said prices were being changed three times a day earlier this week.

"For the past two years, Budget's been about five cents a day below us," he said. "Then they decided to drop $1 below us.

"We said we could live with five cents, but not with a dollar. So it became our policy to stay equal to or below them."

Sam Bresler, who has the Budget franchise in Toronto and has a fleet of 300 cars at the airport, blamed Tilden for the price war which, he said, has cost his company tens of thousands of dollars.

"We have always been the innovators, the Honest Eds of the car rental business," he said.

"It's the public that's the winner in all this. In Montreal one day this week, the rate went to 1 cent for the second day, too."

And the result of the war? "We're renting more cars than we were before."

Yesterday, the Vancouver war opened at one cent for the first and 95 cents for the second day, with a minimum rental of two days, for a Chevette or a Datsun 510. A Chevrolet Nova compact was $10.95 for the second day and an Impala was $21.95 for the second day.

On Wednesday, second-day prices posted at the companies' rental booths at the airport changed about every 10 minutes in a frenzied bidding for business. It worked all the way down to a penny for any day, where it stood for about two hours before working back up to $11.95 for the second day.

The Budget franchise estimates it is losing $40 000 to $50 000 a month on the penny-a-day prices.

While both companies blame each other for firing the first shot, the land office business they are generating means the overflow is going to spectators such as Avis and Hertz, who have not lowered their prices.

Tilden executives, who have always traded on the company's all-Canadian ownership, are saying that their competitor's price cutting is being directed from Budget's head office in Chicago.

Mr. Belzberg said Tilden started the price cutting in Vancouver with a low $11.95 weekend package last fall.

a) Suppose P_1 in the accompanying diagram represents Budget's car rental price before the price war. What do you think D_1 and MR_1 are designed to represent?

b) If D_1 and MR_1 are relevant, what was the appropriate course of action for Budget?

c) The article shows clearly that Budget's decision was a bad one. Which demand and marginal revenue curves on the above diagram reflect the real situation at Budget's initial price?

d) Explain how it is possible that Avis and Hertz, who have not lowered their prices, are nevertheless benefiting from the Budget-Tilden price war.

e) Sam Bresler from Budget says, "It's the public that's the winner in all this." Explain a situation that could emerge from this price war that would put the consumer in a worse position than ever.

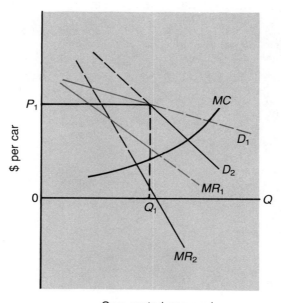

Cars rented per week

Case 7-2

The Globe and Mail, Toronto

Petrocan triggers 2-cent cut in gas price

By VICTOR MALAREK

Petro-Canada triggered another round of price cuts in the oil industry yesterday by announcing it would lower the price of gasoline at the pump by at least two cents a litre.

Shortly after the announcement, spokesmen for several other oil companies said they would match the price cut.

Greg MacDonald, spokesman for Imperial Oil Ltd. said tersely: "We'll stay competitive." Jim Tannian, manager of public relations for Texaco Canada Inc., said the company "will match (the cut) and remain competitive."

The latest cut and two earlier ones, on Feb. 20 and March 12, add up to reductions of six cents a litre by Petro-Canada and the other major companies in less than five weeks — the equivalent of more than 27 cents a gallon.

The effect on retail prices will vary according to local market forces, Petrocan said. Prices at the Crown-owned company's service stations across the country range from a low of 40 cents a litre of regular leaded gasoline, in areas where there are price wars, to a high of 53 cents.

Petro-Canada, the country's biggest oil company, also announced it will absorb the one-percentage-point increase in federal sales tax that goes into effect on Tuesday — a move that will prevent an increase of 2.4 cents a litre.

Mr. Tannian of Texaco said his company will also withdraw its application before the Nova Scotia Utilities Board for an increase of 0.8 cents a litre to cover the new federal tax.

Bob Mayo, president of Petro-Canada Products, said in a statement that the price cut is the result of general market conditions, in particular the continuing "drop in crude oil prices." Since December, the price Petro-Canada pays for foreign crude oil has fallen by more than 50 per cent.

Analysts predict further drops in the price of crude in the wake of the failure on Monday of the Organization of Petroleum Exporting Countries to agree on production cuts. One trader predicted oil could hit $10 U.S. a barrel by the end of the week. Prices have been hovering at around $14.

The OPEC oil ministers had hoped to reach agreement on a production ceiling of 14.5 million barrels a day, compared to the current 17 million barrels.

The Globe and Mail, Toronto

Petrocan leads way as gasoline prices climb

By THOMAS CLARIDGE

Petro-Canada stations led the way as gasoline outlets in the competitive Southern Ontario market suddenly reversed more than two months of price declines yesterday.

With industry profits apparently near the vanishing point, prices at Petro-Canada and Petrocan-owned Gulf stations were increased to 39.9 cents a litre at full-serve outlets and 39.5 at self-serve stations.

By late yesterday Imperial oil had decided to follow suit and an Imperial spokesman said he understood other companies were moving, too.

Greg MacDonald of Imperial's Esso Petroleum Canada subsidiary said the new prices will still leave gasoline cheaper in the Toronto area than in other parts of Canada with provincial gasoline taxes.

Mr. MacDonald said a retail price survey for Esso showed that earlier this week motorists were paying 52.4 cents a litre for leaded gasoline in Saint John and 50.1 cents in Halifax.

The increases came in the wake of price wars that led to gasoline selling for as little as 34.5 cents a litre in the Barrie area and between 36 and 38 cents in most parts of Southern Ontario.

Mr. MacDonald said the low prices were largely a result of cheap imports from the United States, which may start to disappear following a sharp increase in wholesale gasoline prices at New York Wednesday. There, leaded gasoline which a few weeks ago could be had for 40 cents a gallon (about 10.5 U.S. cents or 14.7 Canadian cents a litre) was

commanding 52.25 cents a gallon (13.75 U.S. cents or about 19.25 Canadian cents a litre).

The Esso official said the imports helped push his company's Toronto "rack" price for leaded gasoline down to 19.1 cents. In comparison, Esso's rack price in the less-competitive Quebec City area was 22.5 cents.

Mr. MacDonald said addition of 15.78 cents a litre in federal and Ontario gasoline taxes makes the after-tax cost of a Toronto rack-price purchase (by one of Esso's major independent customers) about 34.8 cents a litre, leaving little room for retailers' profits with pump prices at 36 or 37 cents.

He said that if the higher prices stick — "and that's a $64-million question" — Toronto-area prices will be beaten only in Alberta and Saskatchewan, where there is no provincial gasoline tax.

The Esso survey showed Regina motorists enjoying the best bargain at the pumps, with self-serve outlets selling leaded gasoline for 30.9 cents a litre. The price was nearly 5 cents higher in Edmonton, and other large cities had prices close to the 45-cent mark: Victoria 44.5, Vancouver 44.8, Winnipeg 45.4, Ottawa 44.6. Montrealers were paying 49.9, the higher price reflecting a higher provincial tax in Quebec.

The price decline, following a collapse in world crude oil prices, began Feb. 20 when Imperial and Petro-Canada lowered pump prices 2 cents a litre. A Globe and Mail survey at the time showed prices before the cut ranging from 44.3 cents in Regina to 61.8 cents in Saint John.

a) Oligopoly theory predicts that a price cut will be followed, exactly as reported in the first article. The second article, however, shows that this time competitors also followed a price increase. Is this consistent with the kinked demand curve model? What special factors were relevant here? Illustrate their impact in a kinked demand curve diagram.

b) Would the response of competitors have been different if the firm initiating the price increase was not Petrocan? What are the pertinent characteristics of firms in such a position?

c) Discuss some of the reasons for the wide range of retail gasoline prices observed across the country. What is the relevance of the oligopolistic structure of the industry in this regard?

Case 7-3

The Globe and Mail, Toronto

Farmer scrambles to beat egg quotas

By RUDY PLATIEL

SEELEYS BAY — "What has become of free enterprise in this country?" the hand-written note asks.

It is one of 11 testimonials from people who regularly buy eggs from farmer Ronald Fitzgerald and his wife, Carmel.

These are loyal, long-standing customers who have no hesitation in writing letters "to whom it may concern" expressing both their satisfaction with the quality of Fitzgerald eggs and their concern that they might not be able to get any more because of quota reductions by the Ontario Egg Producers Marketing Board.

It seems so simple to them: They want to buy eggs from the Fitzgeralds and the Fitzgeralds want to sell eggs. What's the problem?

The problem is that while Canada is annually importing millions of eggs, Mr. Fitzgerald says he is being forced by quotas to cut production to the point at which he cannot meet the demands of customers he has served for years.

His customers ask him what is wrong with the good old free-enterprise rule that business goes to the person who works hard to please customers and provide a better product.

When it comes to producer quotas, Mr. Fitzgerald is a bit of a rebel. For several years he has had a running battle with the Ontario Egg Producers Marketing Board. He has been convicted and fined $50 for refusing to allow board officials to count his flock (he still disputes the facts of the case) and recently he was acquitted on a charge of having too many laying hens.

He is also being sued, along with a number of other egg producers, by both the Ontario board and the Canadian Egg Marketing Agency for refusing to pay thousands of dollars in back egg levies. He and the other producers are opposing the levies on the grounds that they are unlawful and improper.

Mr. Fitzgerald says he is being squeezed out of business by a gradual reduction in his quota by the provincial egg board. That means, Mrs. Fitzgerald says, that some long-standing customers are going to have to be told "that we can't supply them any more."

The couple's customers include rural grocery stores, restaurants, hotels and the caterer for the student cafeteria at Queen's University. Their market area between Kingston and Gananoque is a relatively small one within the greater Eastern Ontario market region, largely dominated by one large egg producer.

The Fitzgeralds say they are angry because while they are being cut back, CEMA is allowing in millions of U.S. eggs in excess of the import quota that already allows about three million dozen into Canada annually. To top it off, the Ontario board, financed by levies on producers, is spending $450 000 on advertising to encourage Ontario consumers to buy more eggs at a time when the Fitzgeralds are not being allowed to meet even their present demand.

What Mr. Fitzgerald is bucking is a basic philosophy that by now is well entrenched at both the provincial and federal levels of government — the concept of having marketing boards divide a market among producers through quotas.

The idea is to stabilize prices by controlling production, eliminating the periodic market gluts that drive down prices. (Such overproduction gives consumers a bargain, but the low prices can drive producers to the economic wall.)

The egg boards also guarantee they will buy, store and market any unsold eggs produced in compliance with the quotas they set. To finance this, they charge all producers a levy (it has been as high as nine cents a dozen) on each dozen eggs the producer sells.

Money from the levies pays the difference

between the "table egg price" and the actual price that surplus eggs bring when sold in bulk to processed-food manufacturers.

James Johnstone, chairman of the seven-year-old Ontario board, says "everybody is in the same boat as Mr. Fitzgerald.

"Virtually every (agricultural) producer in Ontario could find a market for more product if he was allowed to produce it. . . . But every time someone increases their share of the market for their product, they take it away from somebody else. The idea of the quotas is to divide the existing market up equitably among those people engaged in the business."

Six years ago Mr. Fitzgerald moved off the farm he had been renting and bought the farm and egg business of William Stolicker, who had a quota permitting him to keep 8,000 hens.

But since then, because of market conditions, the board has cut quotas to the point that it now allows producers to keep only about 61 per cent of their previous flocks. Mr. Fitzgerald says the 4,802 hens to which the board wants to restrict him are not enough to meet his customers' demands. The way he sees it, they are his customers and he is not taking away anyone else's market.

But to Mr. Johnstone and the egg board, Mr. Fitzgerald is "an outsider" who has never paid any fees, "doesn't accept marketing board philosophy and has never gone along with the majority of producers."

Mr. Johnstone says the Fitzgeralds could have expanded by purchasing more quotas two years ago, when the board went through a process of acquiring unused quotas and selling them to other producers.

Mr. Fitzgerald could have, except for the fact that at the time he was fighting the board and refusing to pay the egg levies. He says he paid the levies for the first few years until they went up to nine cents for each dozen sold. "At that time I couldn't make nine cents (profit) on a dozen eggs. It seemed ridiculous that I was doing all the work and they were getting more than me."

Mr. Johnstone says the quota system eventually works to the advantage of all producers because it guarantees a market, allowing them to work out in advance what income they can expect and what business debt they can handle.

Importing U.S. eggs is necessary, he says, because it is the only way to cope with the sharp jump in the market for eggs at Christmas and Easter. The alternative, increasing Ontario production over-all, would simply mean large surpluses at other times.

It is the federal egg agency that sets total quotas for each province, and the Ontario board disagrees with Ottawa on the correct level, Mr. Johnstone says. The federal philosophy "seems to be what we should produce just slightly under what we think the market will be, and import the balance. The philosophy of the Ontario egg producers is that we should produce slightly more and promote and try to sell this product. We are at loggerheads over that one."

a) Suppose you are an economist for the Ontario Egg Producers Marketing Board. Explain why the marketing board quota system is in the best interest of all producers, including Mr. Fitzgerald even though Mr. Fitzgerald sees it as restricting his sales and profits.

b) How does it make sense to spend $450 000 on advertising to increase demand for eggs and at the same time restrict Mr. Fitzgerald from selling to ready customers?

c) Explain how the consumer is hurt by marketing boards.

d) The farmer is allowed to sell all eggs within an agreed-upon quota to the marketing board at a previously agreed-upon price (P_0), which is estimated by the marketing board to be the market price that would see all the quota-produced eggs sold. Actual demand, however, may be less than that estimated by the board, in which case there may arise a surplus of eggs at the agreed-upon price. These eggs are then sold to processed food manufacturers or abroad at lower prices, so that in essence the average price received for eggs may turn out to be less than P_0. Explain the conflicts that can arise (i) between producers and their marketing board and (ii) between Canadian consumers and producers, the marketing board or the government (which has passed legislation allowing marketing boards to be set up in the first place) when a surplus arises.

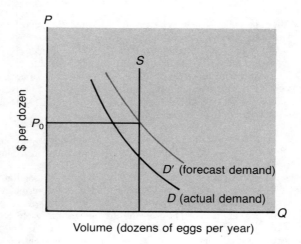

Volume (dozens of eggs per year)

e)   On the accompanying diagram, indicate at the Canadian price (P_0) the surplus of eggs that would emerge. Explain why, if demand is inelastic, it may be more profitable for the producers as a whole to have the marketing board keep the Canadian price at P_0 and sell the surplus eggs in a foreign market for, say, 50% or 60% of P_0 (or for that matter just give them away), rather than sell all the eggs produced under the quota system in the Canadian market for whatever price they would bring.

f)   Explain why it is in the interests of producers as a group to be restricted in the number of egg laying hens even if it means that at Christmas and Easter foreign eggs have to be imported to meet seasonal shortages.

Business Organization
and Profits

8-1 INTRODUCTION AND PURPOSE

In the previous chapters, we considered the interplay between product demand and costs in the determination of market prices and output. Firm profitability is determined by demand and cost conditions as well as by management's ability to favourably alter such demand and cost conditions through product differentiation and technological development. The value of a firm depends crucially on profitability and indirectly, therefore, on managerial decisions with respect to demand and cost. This chapter considers the determination of the value of a business enterprise. In a private enterprise economy, this concern is of utmost importance for efficiency of resource allocation.

Although the principles dealt with in this chapter apply to all forms of business organizations, we shall concentrate on the corporate form of enterprise, since it is by far the most common type. The ownership of large corporations is generally dispersed among thousands or even millions of different owners. Ownership is evidenced by certificates known as **common stocks**, which may be transferred from one investor to another through the *stock market*. This chapter focuses attention on how the participants within the stock market determine the value of the firm and the important role of such valuation in the *economic allocation of resources*.

8-2 TYPES OF BUSINESS OWNERSHIP

In a private enterprise economy, individuals are allowed to own businesses, unlike economies with complete government ownership. The three main types of private enterprise ownership are: *individual proprietorship, partnership* and the *corporation*. Most economic activity is carried out by the corporate form of business. For example, about 80 percent of all manufacturing firms in Canada are corporations, and their sales represent some 97 percent of total sales of all manufacturing firms.

Sole Proprietorship

Sole proprietorship means that a business firm is owned by a single individual, who typically also makes all management decisions. The corner grocery store is an example. Other examples may be found in retail merchandising, plumbing, carpentry and other service trades, and in agriculture, as well as in manufacturing. However, in almost all industries sole proprietorships account for only a small amount of total economic activity.

The prime advantage of the sole proprietorship is *control*. The owner makes the management decisions and carries them out. There can be no conflict of interest between management and owner. The main disadvantages are that the owner may not be able to raise enough capital funds at reasonable cost, and that the owner is personally liable for all business debts.

Partnership

This type of organization has two or more joint owners, who share in the management of the firm and division of profits. The division of management responsibilities and the proportionate share of any profits is generally written down in a legally binding partnership agreement.

The advantages of this type of organization are that it allows for division and specialization of management responsibilities, thus lighter workloads for each partner, and a sharing of the financial responsibilities of the firm.

Corporation

The most popular form of business ownership in Canada is the corporation. Ownership is evidenced by the holding of common stock (common shares), which is issued (sold) by the corporation to raise investment funds. The degree of ownership depends on the proportion of common shares held. For example, if 100 000 shares of a particular company were issued and outstanding, and an individual owned 1 000 of these, the individual would own one percent of the corporation.

The main advantage of the corporate form of ownership is *limited liability*. If the corporation goes bankrupt the value of the common shares may fall to zero. However, if the corporation cannot pay all its debts after selling off its assets, the shareholders do not have to make good the difference out of other personal assets, as is the case for a sole proprietorship or partnership form of ownership.

A **private corporation** is one in which the number of common shares issued is less than 50 (20 in Quebec). There are also restrictions on transfer of these shares. A **public corporation** does not have these restrictions; its shares are held by the public, and typically the number of shares outstanding is many more than 50.[1]

Public corporations may have their shares listed on one or more **stock exchanges** across Canada or internationally. In this case, trading in the stock takes place at these exchanges with the help of **stockbrokers**. On the other hand, the stocks may be **unlisted**, in which case potential buyers approach stockbrokers, who in turn attempt to contact potential sellers.

As a result of the predominance of corporate ownership and, therefore, the central position of the stock market in the evaluation of business enterprise, we will now discuss the important connection between the stock market and the allocation of economic resources.

Corporation is the dominant form of business organization in Canada. Corporations are owned by shareholders, and the shares of most corporations are traded on the stock market.

---

1. Sometimes the adjectives "public" and "private" are used with reference to government versus nongovernment ownership, respectively, of enterprises. However, confusion may usually be avoided by an examination of context.

8-3 THE STOCK MARKET

The degree of business success in the product market place is reflected by the value placed upon the enterprise by existing and potential owners. If we restrict our attention to corporate businesses (which account for most business activity), the market value of shareholders' investment is reflected by the price that investors in the stock market are willing to pay for a share of the company's common stock. These prices are reported minute by minute by brokerage firms and various cable TV news networks and appear daily in most local newspapers. For example, Figure 8-1 contains an excerpt from *The Globe and Mail*'s "Report on Business" section, reporting stock movements of the previous day.

We can see that the market value of Abitibi Price common shares on the Toronto Stock Exchange (TSE), February 6, 1987, was $37¾ per share, though they traded as high as $38¼ per share on that day. A total of 41 074 Abitibi Price shares was bought and sold that day on the TSE. This may not, however, have been the total number traded, because Abitibi Price also had their shares listed on other stock exchanges. If a stock does not trade on a given day, it is because those who already own the stock are asking a price that is considered too high (higher than the price they are bidding) by those who might like to own the stock. The bid and ask prices for some shares that did not trade on February 6 (on the Toronto Stock Exchange) are also shown. In such cases as these, the market value of the stock is taken to be the bid price, because this indicates how much someone is willing to pay for the stock.

Current and potential owners evaluate the performance of business firms daily. Information flowing to shareholders concerning managerial decisions is very quickly translated by investors in the stock market into anticipated effects on the future profitability of the company in question. We can distinguish two cases. If a particular decision raises the market's *expectations* concerning the future profitability of a business, demand for that stock will increase, pushing up its price. If, on the other hand, a decision lowers the market's expectations concerning the company's future profitability, demand for the stock, and consequently the price, will fall.

The Value of a Corporation

To understand how participants in the stock market determine the per share value of a company's common stock, we must first of all consider what they are buying. Each potential shareholder has a certain amount of financial information with which to make an appraisal of value. An integral part of this information is usually the particular company's most recent **annual report**. These reports contain information concerning the company's operations for the past year and why the company performed the way that it did. They may also contain profitability forecasts of certain important managerial decisions either made or about to be made.

Included in all annual reports is a set of *financial statements* concerning the company's progress during the past year and its financial position as of the end of the year in question. The two most important statements of this type are the income statement and the balance sheet. The **income statement** is a flow or period statement that reports the company's most recent year's dollar sales, expense and profit figures. The **balance sheet** reports the company's financial position at a particular point in time. Let us now examine briefly the sort of information conveyed to shareholders by these two financial statements.

For purposes of illustration, suppose the financial statements of Table 8-1 are those of Acme Ltd., a small sportswear manufacturer. The figures contained therein reflect Acme's revenue = cost-profit experience during 19X1 and the company's financial position as of the end of that year.

The Income Statement

As we can see, Acme had a dollar sales revenue for 19X1 of $1 500 000. This, of course, resulted from a year's production and sales. Out of this revenue, the company had to pay operating expenses and interest expenses incurred on its debts. Operating expenses include everything from sales taxes and cost of goods sold to selling and administrative expenses. It should be noted, however, that methods of presentation of financial statements are not entirely uniform. In particular, many accountants would compute, directly after sales taxes, a subtotal for net sales (sales revenue less sales

Fig. 8-1 Toronto Stock Exchange quotations, February 6, 1987

Toronto quotations

52-week High	52-week Low	Stock	Div	High	Low	Close	Ch'ge	Vol
17	$5\frac{7}{8}$	A.G.F.M.	.32	$\$16\frac{3}{4}$	$16\frac{1}{4}$	$16\frac{1}{2}$	$-\frac{1}{8}$	13030
$10\frac{1}{8}$	$5\frac{1}{2}$	AHA Auto o		$\$6\frac{3}{8}$	$6\frac{3}{8}$	$6\frac{3}{8}$		1800
20	9	AMCA Int	a .25	$\$10\frac{7}{8}$	$10\frac{3}{8}$	$10\frac{7}{8}$	$+\frac{5}{8}$	29729
$28\frac{1}{4}$	$23\frac{1}{4}$	AMCA p	2.21	$\$23\frac{5}{8}$	$23\frac{1}{2}$	$23\frac{1}{2}$		1300
$29\frac{3}{8}$	19	AMCA 2 p	2.37	$\$21\frac{3}{8}$	$20\frac{7}{8}$	$21\frac{3}{8}$	$+\frac{1}{2}$	5400
$25\frac{1}{2}$	$23\frac{1}{4}$	AMCA 3 p	2.31	$\$23\frac{1}{2}$	$23\frac{1}{2}$	$23\frac{1}{2}$		2550
$5\frac{1}{2}$	425	ARC Int		$\$5\frac{1}{8}$	490	$5\frac{1}{8}$		6500
52	10	Abatera o		20	18	19	−1	47000
270	106	Abermin o		194	185	194	−1	16000
$38\frac{1}{4}$	20	Abti Prce	.60	$\$38\frac{1}{4}$	$37\frac{3}{8}$	$37\frac{3}{4}$	$+\frac{1}{2}$	41074
$48\frac{1}{4}$	44	Abitibi $7\frac{1}{2}$p	3.75	$\$47\frac{1}{4}$	$47\frac{1}{4}$	$47\frac{1}{4}$	$-\frac{1}{2}$	150
$10\frac{1}{2}$	350	Abitibi w		$\$10\frac{3}{8}$	$10\frac{1}{8}$	$10\frac{1}{4}$	$+\frac{1}{8}$	27750
295	125	Acadia M o		295	265	295	+25	81350
490	50	Aces ATM o		60	60	60		7500
7	225	Acugrph A o		$\$6\frac{3}{8}$	6	$6\frac{3}{8}$	$+\frac{1}{8}$	15600
240	35	Acugraph w		180	150	170	+25	14800
21	16	Acklands	.60	$\$17\frac{1}{2}$	$17\frac{1}{2}$	$17\frac{1}{2}$		400
425	250	Agassiz		400	390	400	+10	2000
$34\frac{3}{4}$	$19\frac{7}{8}$	Agnico E	a .20	$\$29$	$28\frac{3}{4}$	$28\frac{7}{8}$	$-\frac{1}{8}$	27200
$17\frac{3}{4}$	$10\frac{3}{4}$	Agra B f	.24	$\$12\frac{3}{4}$	$12\frac{1}{2}$	$12\frac{3}{4}$	$+\frac{1}{4}$	223500
34	17	Ahed C		440	430	430	+5	5800
400	81	Aiguebel o		90	90	90	−3	3500
$17\frac{1}{2}$	$9\frac{3}{4}$	Alt Energy	.30	$\$17\frac{1}{2}$	$17\frac{1}{2}$	$17\frac{1}{8}$	$-\frac{1}{8}$	141540
$35\frac{1}{2}$	27	Al Enr 1125	2.81	$\$33\frac{1}{4}$	$33\frac{1}{4}$	$33\frac{1}{4}$	$+\frac{5}{8}$	400
$27\frac{3}{8}$	$21\frac{5}{8}$	Al Enr 775	1.93	$\$27\frac{1}{8}$	$26\frac{3}{4}$	$27\frac{1}{8}$	$+\frac{1}{4}$	4200
$15\frac{7}{8}$	11	Alta Nat	.64	$\$14\frac{3}{4}$	$14\frac{3}{8}$	$14\frac{3}{8}$	$+\frac{1}{8}$	4400
$48\frac{3}{8}$	$38\frac{1}{8}$	Alcan	a .80	$\$48\frac{1}{8}$	$47\frac{5}{8}$	$47\frac{5}{8}$	$-\frac{3}{8}$	197942
$26\frac{3}{8}$	25	Alexis N 1	1.85	$\$26$	26	26	$+\frac{1}{4}$	1000
$8\frac{3}{4}$	$7\frac{1}{4}$	ALGO Gr u		$\$8\frac{1}{2}$	$8\frac{3}{8}$	$8\frac{3}{8}$		800
24	19	Algo Cent	.40	$\$20\frac{1}{2}$	20	$20\frac{1}{2}$	$+\frac{1}{2}$	800
20	$10\frac{1}{4}$	Algoma St	y .30	$\$10\frac{1}{4}$	$10\frac{1}{4}$	$10\frac{1}{4}$	$-\frac{1}{4}$	631528
$25\frac{1}{2}$	13	Algoma St p	2.00	$\$13\frac{1}{2}$	13	$13\frac{1}{4}$	$-\frac{1}{4}$	5850
$24\frac{1}{2}$	$13\frac{1}{2}$	Algoma St B	2.00	$\$14\frac{3}{8}$	$13\frac{3}{4}$	14	$-\frac{3}{8}$	6030
112	48	Altex		105	101	105	+5	3000
$27\frac{1}{4}$	$25\frac{1}{2}$	Alum A	2.31	$\$26\frac{3}{8}$	$26\frac{3}{8}$	$26\frac{3}{8}$		23100
$27\frac{1}{4}$	$25\frac{1}{4}$	Alum 1st p	2.00	$\$25\frac{3}{8}$	$25\frac{3}{8}$	$25\frac{3}{8}$		280
		Alum B	see US funds					
$25\frac{3}{8}$	$22\frac{5}{8}$	Alum c p	v.189	$\$24\frac{7}{8}$	$24\frac{3}{8}$	$24\frac{7}{8}$	$+\frac{1}{8}$	7050
$26\frac{3}{8}$	$25\frac{5}{8}$	Alum E p	2.16	$\$25\frac{3}{4}$	$25\frac{3}{4}$	$25\frac{3}{4}$		4700
		Alum d pr	see US funds					

52-week High	52-week Low	Stock	Div	High	Low	Close	Ch'ge	Vol
30	$9\frac{1}{8}$	A Barick		$\$30$	$28\frac{5}{8}$	$29\frac{5}{8}$	$+1\frac{1}{8}$	138835
440	55	A Barik w		440	400	420	+20	303500
230	160	ABarik A w		198	195	198	+3	9200
145	100	Am Eag o		115	112	112	−7	6398
$26\frac{1}{2}$	14	Andrs WA f	$.59\frac{3}{4}$	$\$20\frac{5}{8}$	$20\frac{5}{8}$	$20\frac{5}{8}$	$+\frac{1}{8}$	200
26	15	Andres W B	.52	$\$21$	21	21	+1	200
80	18	Ang CdnM o		30	30	30	+2	24000
$29\frac{1}{2}$	25	Ang CT $4\frac{1}{2}$	2.25	$\$29\frac{1}{2}$	$29\frac{1}{2}$	$29\frac{1}{2}$	$+\frac{1}{2}$	100
$39\frac{1}{4}$	36	Ang CT 315	3.15	$\$39\frac{1}{4}$	$39\frac{1}{4}$	$39\frac{1}{4}$		225
120	50	Anthes		95	90	91	−4	71500
$18\frac{1}{2}$	11	Arbor A	.07	$\$16\frac{1}{2}$	$16\frac{1}{2}$	$16\frac{1}{2}$	$+\frac{1}{2}$	100
$16\frac{7}{8}$	11	Arbor B f	.07	$\$16$	16	16		500
49	$30\frac{1}{2}$	Argus 250 p	2.50	$\$41\frac{1}{4}$	$41\frac{1}{4}$	$41\frac{1}{4}$		z50
$36\frac{3}{8}$	29	Args 260 p	2.60	$\$36\frac{3}{4}$	$36\frac{3}{4}$	$36\frac{3}{4}$		z50
160	45	Argyll A f		77	68	74	+1	24500
$13\frac{3}{8}$	$7\frac{1}{8}$	Asamera	.20	$\$13\frac{3}{8}$	$12\frac{7}{8}$	13	$+\frac{1}{4}$	252350
28	$20\frac{3}{8}$	Asamera 8	2.00	$\$28$	$26\frac{3}{4}$	$27\frac{1}{4}$	$+\frac{5}{8}$	11600
$13\frac{3}{4}$	$9\frac{1}{2}$	Asamera 7	1.05	$\$13\frac{3}{4}$	$13\frac{1}{4}$	$13\frac{5}{8}$	$+\frac{1}{4}$	15018
270	80	Asamera w		270	220	230	+11	141506
340	130	Asac Porc o		250	245	245	−15	2600
$15\frac{7}{8}$	$10\frac{7}{8}$	Astral A f	.15	$\$11\frac{5}{8}$	$11\frac{5}{8}$	$11\frac{5}{8}$	$-\frac{1}{8}$	626
16	11	Astral B f	.15	$\$11\frac{5}{8}$	$11\frac{5}{8}$	$11\frac{5}{8}$	$-\frac{3}{8}$	4750
11	$7\frac{1}{2}$	Atco I f	.20	$\$9$	$8\frac{3}{4}$	9	$+\frac{1}{8}$	59308
11	$7\frac{1}{2}$	Atco II	.20	$\$9$	9	9		2614
258	6	Atco w		38	34	38	+3	71950
185	110	Atl C Cop		145	145	145	−20	100
$11\frac{7}{8}$	10	Atl Shop A f	.12	$\$11$	11	11		200
110	45	Atlantis o		85	75	85		15180
27	14	Atlas Yk o		17	16	17		11000
150	80	Augmitto o		135	125	126	+4	79412
6	230	Aur Res o		$\$5\frac{1}{2}$	$5\frac{1}{4}$	$5\frac{1}{2}$	$+\frac{1}{8}$	46775
75	21	Avinda o		40	38	38	−2	13250
6	266	BCED		335	325	325	−10	61175
$7\frac{1}{2}$	415	BCED A	.75	$\$6\frac{5}{8}$	$6\frac{5}{8}$	$6\frac{5}{8}$		2700
$9\frac{3}{4}$	$5\frac{7}{8}$	BCED $8\frac{5}{8}$	$86\frac{1}{4}$	$\$9\frac{5}{8}$	$9\frac{1}{2}$	$9\frac{1}{2}$		3600
$10\frac{1}{8}$	$6\frac{3}{4}$	BCED $9\frac{1}{2}$	.95	$\$10\frac{1}{8}$	10	10		3700
165	55	BCED w		115	107	110	−5	26750
$27\frac{3}{4}$	$25\frac{3}{4}$	BC Rail p	2.31	$\$27\frac{1}{8}$	27	27		4350
$24\frac{1}{4}$	19	BC Sugar A	1.20	$\$23$	$22\frac{3}{8}$	$22\frac{3}{4}$	$+\frac{1}{2}$	7262
340	115	BC Sugar w		245	220	245	+10	6200

TSE bid and asked (stocks not traded)

	Bid	Ask
Abford	460	470
Abfor w		1
Adanc	40	47
Agra A	$\$13\frac{5}{8}$	14
Akaitc	95	100
Albany	19	22
Algon	$\$47$	55
Algn pr	$\$40\frac{1}{2}$	48
A Expr	$\$88$	91
A Led	35	36
ACT 265	$\$33$	34
ACT 290	$\$35\frac{1}{2}$	$36\frac{1}{2}$
Ang DG	205	215
Arg B p	$\$32\frac{1}{8}$	33
Argl E B	150	175
Asbsts C	495	$\$5\frac{3}{4}$
At Shp p	$\$27\frac{3}{8}$	$27\frac{5}{8}$
A Yk w	$2\frac{1}{2}$	4
Aug w	9	15
Atrx A	195	220
Atrx B	195	200
BC Su p	$\$13\frac{1}{2}$	14
BGR w	175	180
Bkrtic	58	62
Barin f	$\$7$	$7\frac{1}{4}$
Barin w	90	100
Bath p	$\$13$	$13\frac{1}{2}$
Bcoup	55	57
Bce 196	$\$49$	$49\frac{1}{2}$
Biltrite	$\$7\frac{1}{8}$	$7\frac{3}{8}$
Biltrit w	70	80
Bral w		1

	Bid	Ask
McDl	$\$94\frac{1}{4}$	$94\frac{3}{4}$
Melcor	$\$6\frac{1}{2}$	7
MCIL p	$\$25\frac{1}{8}$	$25\frac{1}{4}$
MLP	30	
MLP p	250	
Midcon	305	310
Mrt B w	42	47
M Inv	$\$29\frac{3}{4}$	
MCty B	$\$16\frac{3}{4}$	
M Cty p	$\$28$	$28\frac{1}{2}$
Mun F	$\$10\frac{3}{8}$	
MFC A f	$\$9$	$9\frac{1}{4}$
Mun F p	$\$10\frac{3}{8}$	
Mun w	$\$10\frac{1}{4}$	$10\frac{3}{4}$
MF A w	190	220
MSL p	$\$10\frac{1}{8}$	$10\frac{3}{4}$
Muph	$\$23\frac{3}{4}$	$24\frac{1}{4}$
NB Cook	23	26
Nahani	21	25
N Pete	19	23
Nat Res	41	50
N Trst p	$\$30$	39
Nelsn p	$\$5$	$5\frac{1}{8}$
Nemar	31	35
NB 1.37	$\$17\frac{1}{4}$	$17\frac{3}{4}$
NB 1.85	$\$22$	$22\frac{1}{2}$
NPro D	26	29
N QRagl	165	190
NYrk O	23	80
N Cap B	$\$\ 9\frac{1}{2}$	$10\frac{7}{8}$
Nf LP B	$\$20$	$20\frac{3}{4}$
N Tel 975	$\$21\frac{1}{2}$	$22\frac{1}{2}$

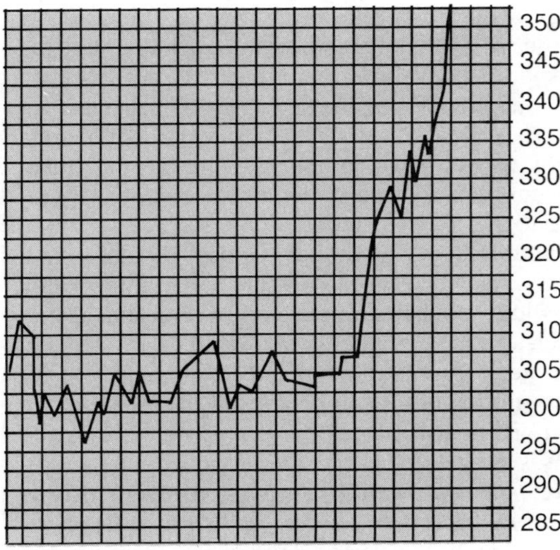

TSE 300 Composite

Source: *The Globe and Mail, Toronto*

Randomly selected parts of the stock market report pages from a daily newspaper.

Table 8-1 **Financial statements of Acme Ltd.**

(a) Acme Co. Ltd.
Income Statement for the year ended Dec. 31, 19X1

Sales revenue			$1 500 000
Deduct:			
Sales taxes		$ 95 000	
Cost of goods sold:			
Raw materials	$100 000		
Labour	700 000		
Other variable expenses	50 000		
Factory overhead	45 000	895 000	
Selling expenses		110 000	
Administrative expenses		85 000	1 185 000
Net Operating Income			$ 315 000
Less: Interest expense			65 000
Net Profit for the year			$ 250 000

(b) Acme Co. Ltd.
Balance Sheet as of Dec. 31, 19X1

Assets			*Liabilities*		
Cash		$100 000	Bank loan		$500 000
Accounts receivable		250 000	Accounts payable		100 000
Inventory		350 000			
		$700 000			$600 000
Land and buildings (cost)	$630 000		Bonds		200 000
Less:					
Accumulated depreciation	30 000	600 000	Shareholders' equity:		
Machinery and equipment	$550 000		Common stock		
Less:			(50 000 shares)		1 000 000
Accumulated depreciation	50 000	500 000			
		$1 800 000			$1 800 000

Simplified financial statements of a fictitious sportswear manufacturer, Acme Ltd. Part (a) is the income statement, reporting flows of revenues, costs and profits for a particular period. Part (b) is the balance sheet, reporting the levels of assets and liabilities at a particular point in time.

taxes). Others might begin the income statement with the net sales figure, without showing the detailed breakdown.

As we can see, the cost of goods sold item refers not to the total cost of producing and selling the sportswear, but only to the factory costs associated with the goods. This is merely an accounting convention in terms of itemizing the expense breakdown. Acme's total 19X1 accounting costs of producing and selling sportswear were $1 250 000 which, out of a sales revenue of $1 500 000, left an accounting profit of $250 000 for the shareholders.

The Balance Sheet

The balance sheet indicates the things of value (**assets**) owned by Acme and the sources of funds that are providing the financing of these assets (**liabilities** and **shareholders' equity**). All the items above the shareholders' equity section are liabilities or debts of the firm. The shareholders' equity figure of $1 000 000 is an accounting estimate of the value of the shareholder group's investment in the firm as of December 31, 19X1. Because the shareholders have a *residual claim* on the assets of the corporation, the $1 000 000 figure must by necessity equal the total estimated value of assets less what is owned by the firm (liabilities).

The word "estimate" is emphasized in the above description; accounting figures are not exact measures of market value by any means. Barring fraud, the liabilities figures are precise, as is the asset figure for cash. However, all other asset figures are estimates. As a result, the shareholders' claim upon the enterprise is also an estimate. We shall discuss this in further detail below.

There may be several other unfamiliar terms within the balance sheet. The term **accounts receivable** refers to amounts owing to Acme as a result of some customers buying sportswear on credit. **Accounts payable** refers to amounts that Acme owes its suppliers of materials for purchases Acme has made on credit.

When Acme began operations a year ago, it sold 50 000 shares of common stock (common shares) for $20 per share to provide the initial financing. By doing so, the company acquired $1 000 000 that it used to buy assets and begin its operations. This amount was recorded as *common stock*. (Incidentally, if at any time one of the original Acme

shareholders wishes to liquidate shares, Acme is not obliged to repurchase them. Instead, the shareholder must sell them with the aid of a stockbroker on the stock market, through a stock exchange, if the shares are listed). For simplicity, suppose that Acme pays out to its shareholders all its accounting profits as they are earned. Such distributions of profits to shareholders are known as **dividends**.

Now that we have discussed the chief source of financial information on a corporation, the next question is how to use such data to arrive at a valuation estimate of the company's common stock.

Acme Ltd.: A Going Concern

If a company is expected to continue operations into the indefinite future, it is referred to as a **going concern**. In such a case, potential shareholders do not consider that they are buying the assets of the firm (because there is no intention to sell these assets) but, rather, the future profits (earnings) that these assets and management may generate. Therefore, any prospective shareholder of a going concern is actually bidding for the right to a per share portion of the company's future profits.

Suppose (as we did above) that Acme Ltd. has 50 000 common shares currently issued and outstanding. Suppose also, for simplicity, that the current year's profit of $250 000 or $5 per share ($250 000/50 000) is expected to continue indefinitely.

Naturally, these expectations could be wrong. The economy could experience an exceptional boom or slump. New competitors could enter the sportswear industry. Consumer tastes could either turn away from or move toward Acme's products. There is a multitude of events that could happen in the future to affect these forecast earnings per share. With this sort of uncertainty concerning Acme's future prospects, the shareholders are never quite sure of what they will get back from their investment.

This is very much different from depositing money in the bank, which pays an annual interest rate of, say, 8%. In this case, there is almost complete certainty that the depositor will receive a return of $8 each year for each $100 invested.

Participants in the stock market would not accept an expected return from Acme's stock as low as bank interest rates. In fact, because of the extra risk that shareholders are taking by buying

Acme stock rather than putting their money in the bank, they will demand a higher expected rate of return in order to buy the stock. If we suppose the extra compensation expected for the extra risk to be, say, 2% per annum, potential Acme shareholders would require a 10% expected annual return. Given the annual profit expectations of $5 per share, the market price of Acme stock would be bid toward $50 since this is the price at which the stock would yield the investor a required 10% annual rate of return.

The determination of the price of Acme shares in the stock market can be viewed diagrammatically. Figure 8-2 shows the demand and supply for Acme stock as of December 31, 19X1. Notice that the supply of Acme common stock as of this date is a fixed quantity of 50 000 shares. This amount is not going to change on that day regardless of the share price, because it represents the number of shares that the company has issued in the past. Therefore, the supply curve is vertical at 50 000 shares.

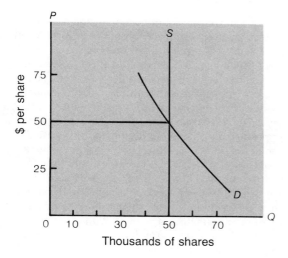

Fig. 8-2 Market price of Acme common stock, 19X1

At any given time, the number of shares outstanding is fixed. The share price is therefore demand-determined.

The demand curve, given the above information, would intersect the supply curve at $50 per share. At this price, the estimated annual rate of return is just 10%.

We do not know the precise shape of the demand curve, but if Acme's stock temporarily sold below $50 per share — say, at $40 per share — there would certainly be a shortage (demand would be greater than supply). This is because at $40 per share, the estimated annual rate of return to the average prospective shareholder becomes 12.5% (i.e. $\frac{\$5}{\$40} \times 100\%$). However, the average investor requires only 10% to make the prospect of investing in Acme a reasonable one compared with investing funds elsewhere at a similar risk — or safely depositing funds in a bank at 8%. As a result of the shortage, the price of Acme's stock would be pushed up toward $50.

On the other hand, if Acme's stock temporarily sold above $50 — say, at $60 per share — there would be a surplus on the market (supply would be greater than demand), which would drive the price down toward $50. The reason is that at $60 per share the estimated annual rate of return from buying its stock would be only 8.3% (that is, $\frac{\$5}{\$60} \times 100\%$). This is less than could be earned elsewhere for a similar risk. Further, the 8.3% is not judged sufficient compensation when compared with a risk-free bank deposit earning 8%.

Acme Ltd.: The Liquidating Firm

A less frequent possibility the stock market faces when bidding for a corporation's shares is that the company is no longer a going concern but instead is about to cease operations and *liquidate* (sell) its assets. In such circumstances, the proceeds from sale of the assets must first be used to pay off the company's debts, which in Acme's case, as of December 31, 19X1, amount to $800 000. Any residual proceeds are then distributed equally on a per share basis among the common shareholders.

In this instance, there are no future earnings. It now becomes important for the stock market to consider the firm's **realizable net asset value** (assets minus liabilities) on a per share basis. Expectations in this regard will determine the price of the company's stock.

In such a situation, investors know that though the balance sheet figures representing the firm's liabilities are accurate, those representing assets may be poor measures of the *liquidation, breakup* or *replacement value* of such assets. In our example, we take these three expressions of value to be equivalent. The first two are synonymous. Further, the cost to a company of replacing certain assets with equivalent ones (replacement costs) may not differ greatly from the proceeds the company could get by selling these assets.

Accounting figures for the most part are based on *original cost*, which may differ significantly from *current value*. For example, land and buildings are on the balance sheet at $630 000, less an estimate for the depreciation of the buildings of $30 000 — or $600 000 on a net basis. The $630 000 figure represents the original cost of the land and building. However, because of inflation — even though there has been some depreciation of the building during the year — the land and buildings may now be worth more than the net accounting figure.

On the other hand, other assets could be worth much less than recorded cost if Acme sold them. For example, to sell off inventory may require selling below cost. Further, there are considerable expenses involved in liquidating a business. There may be salary settlements to be paid for termination of employees' contracts, legal expenses and payments for wages and other expenses connected with the selling-off process.

As a result, when a business is liquidated the breakup value of the assets less the liabilities owed may be different from the accounting value of shareholders' equity. However, in this instance suppose the expected breakup value of Acme's assets is deemed by stock market participants on average to be roughly in line with the *book figure* (accounting figure) after all liquidation expenses are paid. In this case, after paying off $800 000 in liabilities, the shareholders expect to split $1 000 000. This, on a per share basis, would be $20. In the event of an impending liquidation, the market price of Acme's common stock would gravitate to this figure.

Notice that in this example the company is worth far more to the shareholders as a going concern than in liquidation ($50 per share as compared with $20). In other circumstances, though, a firm could be worth more to the shareholders if it was liquidated. In such a case, the shareholders would, in fact, vote to cease operations of the company and sell off the company's assets.

Mergers and Sellouts

One alternative to liquidation is to *merge* with (or sell out to) another company. Such a buying company may think that it can increase the profitability of a sluggish concern, perhaps by replacing the existing managers. The buying company usually offers cash and/or its own shares in a trade for all the outstanding common stock of the company selling out. The shareholders may then sell the shares of the larger company. Conversely, they may continue to hold them if they think the rate of return will be satisfactory.

The value of shares of a corporation is determined by the future profits (earnings) the corporation is expected to generate. The market value of a corporation usually differs from the value recorded on the balance sheet and from the liquidation or replacement value of its assets.

8-4 DIFFERENT TYPES OF PROFIT

One of the more controversial public issues involves the notion of *profits*. Are the profits earned by a particular firm in some sense *excessive* or unfair? Much heated discussion of this type of question takes place among consumers, workers, shareholders and government officials. Unfortunately, there is often considerable confusion with regard to what "profit" means in the first place. Frequently, opposing sides in the discussion on profits use different definitions as bases for their arguments that profits are, for example, too high or too low.

It seems appropriate, then, to spend some time sorting out the various notions concerning profits. In what follows, we investigate three basic profit concepts and their connections with one another: *accounting profit, normal profit* and *economic profit*. We hope that this discussion will shed some light on various less well-defined profit notions, such as "fair profit" and "unfair profit."

Accounting profit refers to the figure reported in a company's financial statements (the so-called *bottom line* of the income statement). For Acme, during 19X1, this figure was $250 000. **Normal profit** refers to the minimum amount of accounting profit required to prevent the shareholders as a group from voting to cease the company's operations and liquidate all assets. This figure (otherwise known as **required profit** for the reason just stated) is the product of two things: (1) how much the shareholders could get if they liquidated the company and (2) the rate of return obtainable if the shareholders invested their funds *elsewhere for a similar risk*. In our example, we have supposed the liquidation or breakup value of the shareholder group's investment in Acme to be $1 000 000. Further, we assumed that these shareholders could earn 10% elsewhere on their money by taking a similar risk. Consequently, the Acme shareholders as a group have the opportunity to earn $100 000 annually ($1 000 000 × 10%) by liquidating Acme and investing elsewhere. For Acme, the normal annual profit figure is, therefore, $100 000.

Any accounting profit above the normal profit figure is *excess* in the sense that it is above that required to prevent the company from being liquidated. Such excess accounting profit is called **economic profit** (or **pure profit**). For Acme, the annual economic profit figure is $250 000 minus $100 000, or $150 000. Economic profit is generally what an economist refers to when using the term "profit," and accounting profit is typically what the public is referring to when they speak of profit. In this book, we shall not hesitate to use profit in either sense as long as the meaning is clear from the context.[2]

---

2. The terminology used in this area can be quite confusing. Three other popularly used economic expressions are: *explicit cost, implicit cost* and *economic rent*. Accounting expenses such as those in Acme's income statement of Table 8-1 are sometimes referred to as *recorded* or *explicit costs*. In contrast, nonrecorded or hidden expenses, which must nevertheless also be accounted for in arriving at economic profit, are called *implicit costs*. For example, Acme's normal annual accounting profit of $100 000 is an implicit cost that Acme must cover out of revenue each year if it is to remain in business.

Economic rent may be used synonymously with economic profit. Typically, though, economic profit is the term used to refer to income earned on capital funds in excess of that which could be earned elsewhere. Economic rent is more generally used to refer to income earned by any input or factor of production in excess of what the factor could earn elsewhere. For example, if my labour income working for myself is $10 000 higher than I could earn as a salary working for someone else, the annual economic rent on my labour when working for myself is $10 000. The principles involved here are illustrated in Problem 4.

Who Gets the Economic Profits?

This is an interesting question. The most important point to recognize is that once information concerning any profit is communicated to stock market participants, the market value of the company's shares adjusts very quickly to reflect this information. A year ago when the company began operations, the market price of the company's stock was only $20, in which case stock market participants on average must have been expecting the company to earn an annual accounting profit of only $2 per share, since $\frac{\$2}{\$20} = 10\%$.[3] As we pointed out above, once information concerning Acme's $250 000 annual accounting profit ($5 per share) either leaks out or is published, the price of Acme's stock will be bid to $50 (with the assumption that the $5 per share figure is thought to reflect correctly the company's future average performance). In essence, the stock market is saying that it now thinks the company's accounting profit is going to average $3 per share more than originally thought ($5 instead of $2), and for the right to receive this extra annual $3 per share, it is willing to pay an extra $30 (i.e. $50 instead of $20) in purchasing a share of Acme Ltd.

We can now see that the shareholder who owns the shares when the excess profits are first noticed gets all the benefit from such excess profits. Once the company's stock price is bid up to reflect the true profit picture, each subsequent stock purchase can expect to receive only a normal rate of return on invested funds ($5 on $50 invested, or 10%). Whether or not an original shareholder chooses to sell his or her shares in Acme at the end of year 19X1, those shares are now worth $50 instead of $20. The shareholder's wealth has increased, therefore, by the amount the stock market is willing to pay for all foreseeable annual $3 per share excess profits the company is now expected to earn. If the shareholder chooses not to sell the stock, then during the next and subsequent years the shareholder can expect once more to earn 10% (that is, $\frac{\$5}{\$50} \times 100\%$) annually on the present investment.

---

3. This calculation assumes that the required rate of return one year ago was 10% as it is now.

However, the $30 capital gain ($50 − $20), obtained in 19X1 when the value of the stock rose, means that over the entire life of the investment the shareholder will have earned an annual rate of 25% on the originally invested funds ($5 on $20) as compared with the 10% that could have been expected elsewhere for a similar risk.

This latter point warrants further emphasis. As soon as stock market participants recognize the presence of economic profit, the price of the company's stock is bid up to such a level that new shareholders do not have an opportunity to capture any of it. This does not mean that the economic profits themselves disappear. They remain, but all the benefits of them are captured by those who owned the stock before the economic profits became known. To understand that the economic profits do not disappear by the increase in the company's stock price, we must remember that economic profit refers to accounting profit in excess of that which the shareholder group could earn elsewhere if it liquidated the firm. This latter amount in our example remains at $1 000 000 × 10% = $100 000 annually, and so the expected annual economic profits of Acme remain at $250 000 − $100 000 = $150 000 annually in spite of the increase in the value of the company's common stock.

This does not mean, though, that economic profit can never be eroded. On the contrary, with easy (low cost) entry into Acme's industry, other investors may be encouraged (by the ability of Acme to earn an above normal rate of return) to form their own companies and compete with Acme. This would in the long run tend to reduce the market price of sportswear and correspondingly reduce Acme's profit. In practice, therefore, stock market participants must attempt to evaluate the effect of possible new competition on a company's future earnings when bidding for its stock.

The distinction between normal profit and economic profit is crucial for understanding much of the theory of competition and efficiency of resource allocation. Economic profit is the excess of accounting profit above normal profit, that is, above that level of profit which is needed to insure that shareholders do not invest their funds elsewhere, given comparable risk.

Mind you, there isn't the sporting feeling you get at the track . . .

8-5 CORPORATE PROFITABILITY

There are a number of ways of measuring corporate performance. Does the company produce quality products? Does the company use ethical advertising techniques? Is the company a good corporate citizen? Does the company earn an adequate profit? Depending upon our viewpoint, any of these questions might be important in judging overall corporate performance. However, as far as the shareholders and the stock market are concerned, one of these questions is more important than the rest. This is the criterion of *adequate profit*.

Measuring Profitability

Is a million dollars a year a lot of profit? The answer is "maybe and maybe not." If a company has only $500 000 invested, it represents a 200% annual rate of return (yield) on invested funds $(\frac{\$1\ 000\ 000}{\$\ 500\ 000} \times 100\%)$. On the other hand, if the amount tied up in the enterprise is $50 million, this profit represents only a 2% annual rate of return on invested funds, and if the current interest rate offered at banks is 8% per year, the profit is very low. The $50 million placed in the bank for one year would have earned 8% × $50 million, or $4 000 000.

Clearly, then, in judging the adequacy of a particular firm's annual profit, what matters is not the absolute dollar amount but instead the rate of return earned by investors compared to what they could have earned if they had invested their capital funds elsewhere at similar risk. As stated above, this latter rate is sometimes referred to as a *normal rate of return*.

Normal Rate of Return

Suppose Acme undertakes an expansion program, believing that this will result in increased profitability. To be specific, suppose the expansion involves construction of a factory addition costing $1 000 000. The project is financed by a new $600 000 bond issue, carrying an 8% interest rate, and a new issue of common stock for the balance. Because the current market price of the common stock is $50 per share, this will require a sale by the company of 8000 new shares ($400 000 ÷ $50 per share = 8000), bringing the total number of common shares issued and outstanding to 58 000.

Next, let us suppose the expansion program generates yearly additional sales revenue in excess of additional nonfinancial operating expenses by $52 000. Out of this amount, however, the company would also have to meet additional financial expenses in the form of $48 000 new annual bond interest (8% × $600 000). This means that the expansion program has added $4000 (i.e. $52 000 − $48 000) additional annual accounting profit to Acme. At this point, we might be tempted to conclude that the expansion program was a wise economic decision. But was it?

If it is assumed that this increased annual accounting profit of $4000 is not expected to grow, it represents only a 1% annual rate of return on the additional shareholder funds invested $\left(\frac{\$\ 4000}{\$400\ 000} \times 100\%\right)$. Because this is less than the 10% rate of return we earlier assumed Acme shareholders required as normal compensation, the demand for Acme shares would fall and, consequently, so would the price of Acme stock. Not only would the new Acme shareholders suffer but the old ones would as well. When the share price falls, all shareholders suffer a capital loss.

We may in fact calculate the approximate amount by which Acme's shares would fall, given that average investor expectations become geared to the increase of $4000 in Acme's yearly profit.

Acme's total annual profit would become $254 000 (or $250 000 + $4000), which is $4.38 per share. Therefore, the expansion project has reduced Acme's earnings per share by $0.62. Because this new level is expected to remain indefinitely, and investors require a 10% return on their invested funds, the shares would be bid down in price to $43.80 (since $4.38/$43.80 = 10%). Therefore, each shareholder — old and new — would incur a capital loss of $6.20 per share ($50 − $43.80). From then on, of course, their return is expected to be 10% each year on their investment ($4.38 on $43.80 invested), but the initial $6.20 capital loss on each share, in effect, has reduced their average annual rate of return over the life of their investment below 10%.

The additional annual accounting profit of $4000 was not adequate to maintain a balance between shareholders' expected rate of return and that which they thought they could earn elsewhere for a similar risk. We could easily compute how much extra annual accounting profit would in fact be necessary from the expansion to maintain shareholders' expected rate of return intact and, therefore, to prevent a fall in Acme's stock prices (or, in other words, to prevent a reduction in the wealth position of Acme shareholders). This amount would be 10% of the additional equity funds, that is, $40 000.

The dollar volume of corporate profits does not provide sufficient information. A more meaningful measure of profitability is the rate of return on investment which relates profit to the invested funds.

8-6 THE COST OF CAPITAL

Economic profit is accounting profit above that required to provide the shareholder with a normal rate of return on investment — in this case, 10%. In our example, $40 000 was the break-even accounting profit on the factory expansion project; that is, the increase in accounting profit necessary to provide a 10% return on the $400 000 of additional shareholder funds. If the annual accounting profit was increased by only $35 000, we could say that the firm incurred an annual economic loss of $5000 on the expansion., If the accounting profit was increased by $47 500, we could say that the expansion earned the firm an annual economic profit of $7500.

When a firm raises funds to finance investment projects, it can either borrow or use equity funds. As shown above, for a project to be economically viable it must earn enough additional sales revenue to cover additional nonfinancial operating expenses, and over and above this, pay the interest cost of the debt incurred as well as provide enough additional (accounting) profit to earn the shareholder a normal rate of return. In our example, because $600 000 was borrowed at 8% and $400 000 equity funds were raised (which have to earn 10%), then on the total $1 000 000 of funds required to finance the new project the company has to earn ($600 000 × 8%) + ($400 000 × 10%) — or a total additional amount of $88 000 per year over and above nonfinancial operating expenses. That is, the company has to earn 8.8% annually (after paying nonfinancial operating expenses) on any new funds invested to be able to pay the interest costs and still have sufficient accounting profit to give the shareholders a 10% rate of return.

On all additional funds invested, the required return (after nonfinancial operating expenses) to maintain shareholder yield intact is a weighted average of individual percentage costs of the funds raised. In our case it is (0.60 × 8%) + (0.40 × 10%) = 8.8%, where the weights 0.60 and 0.40 are the proportions of total new funds raised by debt and equity respectively, and the 8% and 10% are their respective annual percentage costs.

This required annual percentage yield, which the company must earn (after paying nonfinancial operating expenses) to cover any interest expense and provide shareholders with a normal rate of return, is called by financial economists the **cost of capital funds**, or, more simply, the **cost of capital**. We often read, for example, that a particular investment proposal is not expected to provide sufficient funds to cover the cost of capital. This means that even though the new project may be expected to generate a healthy additional sales revenue (perhaps well above additional nonfinancial operating expenses such as cost of goods sold, administrative and selling expenses) it is not expected to be profitable enough to provide for all additional interest costs and still leave sufficient residual accounting profits to yield an adequate rate of return for the shareholder.

Though for simplicity we omitted them in our Acme example, corporate income taxes have to be paid on accounting profits. Hence, the shareholder's rate of return on invested funds is affected by this important consideration as well.

It seems wise at this point to summarize the preceding developments. First of all, accountants refer to "profit" (for financial reporting purposes) as the difference between revenues and expenses, which include any interest expenses on debt. However, accountants as well as economists do not regard any accounting profit as true or economic profit unless it is at least as large as could be earned elsewhere by the firm's owners for a similar risk. It would be silly to refer to a firm as being profitable if its common shares were declining in value on the stock market and thereby continually reducing its shareholders' wealth — and this reduction would be the case if the accounting profit was lower than that which could be earned elsewhere at similar risk. For this reason, accountants and economists regard as *true* or *economic profit* only that portion of accounting profit which is in excess of what could be earned elsewhere at similar risk. Finally, the cost of capital reflects the annual (percentage) rate of return that must be earned (after all nonfinancial expenses) on business investment to provide a normal accounting profit. If a firm can earn a higher rate of return than the cost of capital, the firm is earning above normal (that is, economic) profits.

Industrial Expansion and Contraction

The relation between industrial growth and decline and industrial rate of return available to investors is as follows. If an industry cannot find new investment projects that are expected to provide sufficient earnings to cover at least the cost of capital funds, it cannot expand. In fact, companies within the industry may not successfully manage their existing assets so as to create enough profitability to meet the cost of capital. That is, some cannot earn enough revenue to pay their normal operating and interest expenses, and still leave an accounting profit large enough to give the shareholders a rate of return comparable to that earned by investing in other industries of similar risk. Thus, these companies will not only cease to expand their asset bases, but will also allow normal depreciation to take place and wear down their plant, machinery and other operating assets. In short, the industry will begin to *shrink* and *decline*.

To demonstrate that this is necessarily the case, suppose that a management chose to disregard its company's cost of capital and continually invested in projects yielding less than this figure. As was the case with Acme, its common share prices would fall and continue to fall as long as the company pursued this policy. Eventually, after many projects had been undertaken that yielded less than the cost of capital, the market value of shareholders' stock would drop below the breakup or liquidation value of the firm. This means that it would become profitable for some group to buy up all the common stock of the company, fire all the employees — including management, who chose to follow this self-destructive policy — and liquidate the firm.

If, on the other hand, firms within a particular industry are able to foresee profitability on new asset investment that would more than cover the cost of capital funds, such investment will be undertaken. In doing so, management will increase profits per share for the shareholders and consequently cause the price of common shares to be bid up, thereby increasing shareholders' wealth. Companies in such industries which are able to foresee a rate of return in excess of the cost of capital will be eager to expand their asset bases by adding to physical plant, machinery, offices, inventory and other investments to provide for increased sales. These are known as **growth companies** (and **growth industries**).

The viability of capital projects of a firm (or an industry) depends on the comparison of earnings these projects are expected to generate with the cost of capital funds. The expected earnings, in turn, depend on the future consumer demand for the firm's (or industry's) products. Consumer demand therefore ultimately determines the growth or decline of firms and industries.

8-7 RESOURCE ALLOCATION EFFICIENCY

The allocation of an economy's scarce resources (land, labour and capital) for the production of those goods and services that provide the most benefit to society is an important problem. In fact, earlier we gave as a common definition of economics "a study of the allocation of scarce resources among competing ends."

Certainly it would not be beneficial to society to have a considerable amount of resources devoted to the production of goods or services that nobody wanted — say, buggy whips and oil lanterns. In fact, as we have seen earlier, the value of a good or service to society (as a first approximation) is reflected by its market price. If people are willing to pay $45 for a pair of athletic shoes, that is how much we say they are worth. We may not be willing to pay that much, of course, but as long as the market is willing we say they are worth $45.

Suppose that the market demand for athletic shoes increases as a result of a change in tastes toward the product. This trend will increase the current annual profit earned by each firm within the industry and increase the expected profitability of expansion projects — if the increase in demand is thought to be permanent. That is, if the increased demand is expected to continue or perhaps even become larger in the future, it might be expected to be sufficient for plant expansion programs to generate enough new revenues to meet additional nonfinancial expenses and also cover the cost of new capital funds required to finance the expansion. In fact, this kind of expectation is what causes most industrial expansion. As demand for the product increases (it becomes worth more to society than before), it is bought in greater amounts at prevailing prices. Initially, the firms may meet the demand increase in the short run by running down inventories or by overtime shifts and stepped-up production within existing plant facilities. Even these actions may not be enough, however, to prevent shortages from arising. In the longer run, the increased demand causes firms to raise new capital funds and use the proceeds to acquire new land, capital goods (factories, machines and tools) and labour to increase production.

In another industry, product demand may be falling, thereby reducing profitability and hence shareholder rates of return. This second industry's stock prices would be bid down as shareholders begin to sell their stock to purchase a new stock in the expanding industry (which is expected to provide an adequate rate of return by reason of the increased demand for its product).

The distribution of society's demands and corresponding valuation of goods and services in free markets thereby dictates whether or not it will be

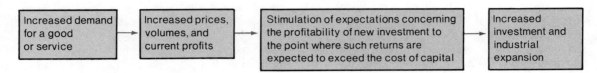

Fig. 8-3 Demand-induced industrial expansion

A stylized representation of the mechanism through which a change in consumer demand favourable to a good or a service affects a resource shift toward its production.

economically feasible for particular industries to expand or contract. Therefore, the allocation of resources (land, capital goods and labour) is also determined by society's valuation of the products and services that these various industries produce. This dynamic process for allocating resources is represented schematically in Figure 8-3.

Other reasons for industrial expansion or contraction may lie in changes in the cost side of production or the introduction of new products. If costs within an industry rise significantly faster than those of other industries, the prices of the former industry's products correspondingly will be forced up faster than the prices of the other industry's products. In the absence of a coincidental shift in demand favourable to the product, these price increases will cause a natural substitution of other, now cheaper, goods, satisfying similar needs. The industry profits will therefore shrink, reducing the shareholders' return on investment below that which could be obtained elsewhere. The stock market's response will be a reduction in demand for the companies' stocks, resulting in lower share prices and a wealth loss for the shareholder group. Further, the likelihood is reduced that future investment will bring in a high enough return to pay for the cost of capital. Therefore, the industry will not replace its old factories and equipment as they wear out and will consequently shrink — as evidenced by both a sales reduction and a decline in physical assets. This process is represented schematically in Figure 8-4.

The introduction of new products, which is another reason for industrial growth, involves an increase in demand and is therefore part of the first

reason for industrial growth. If a new product is deemed to have a sufficient value by consumers (as evidenced by the price they are willing to pay for the good), the revenue so generated, above non-financial operating expenses, will be enough to pay the cost of capital funds required to finance any new investment in physical facilities for the product's production. In such a case, investment will be made and industrial growth in capital stock, employment and sales volume will take place.

The point is that in a market economy, capital funds flow to finance those industries for which the goods and services are valued sufficiently to enable recovery of the annual percentage cost of invested capital funds. Capital funds flow away from industries whose products society does not value enough to pay a price that would cover the cost of capital funds. Such a resulting allocation of capital funds, and the capital stock which they finance, are usually thought of as being economically efficient. The capital stock is the real resource, of course, because the capital funds are merely pieces of paper evidencing debt or equity claims on the capital stock.

If it is not clear why such a distribution is referred to as efficient, think of an alternative distribution of capital funds. For instance, suppose some industries are kept from expanding even though demand for their products would warrant growth. At the same time, suppose other industries are being supported (perhaps by government financial aid) so that they do not contract, even though the demand for their products is insufficient to allow the products to sell at high enough volumes and prices so that the annual percentage cost of

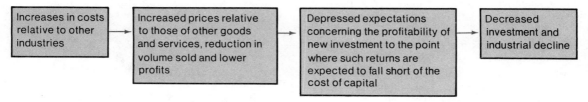

Fig. 8-4 Cost-induced industrial contraction

A stylized representation of the mechanism through which a deterioration in an industry's relative cost position causes a shift of resources away from the industry.

capital funds in the industry can be recovered. Certainly, we would need fairly strong reasons for advocating this kind of distribution of capital goods and capital funds. In the absence of such reasons, however, it would be an economically inefficient allocation. In later chapters, we discuss possible reasons for government policies leading to what may appear on the surface to be inefficient distribution of capital investment.

In a market economy, where capital funds flow out of declining industries into growing industries, resources tend to be allocated efficiently among the various sectors of the economy. This is because the growth or decline of industries reflects the changing consumer valuation of their respective products.

8-8 UNFAIR PROFITS

As we have shown above, some accounting profit is necessary for all industries to meet the total cost of capital funds invested in the industry. Specifically, enough accounting profit must be earned to yield shareholders at least their normal rate of return, given the element of risk within the industry. Other things being equal, if an industry does not accomplish this, consumers will indicate that the industry should contract and reduce its command over the economy's scarce resources.

What, then, do people mean when they talk of companies or industries earning exorbitant or *unfair profits*? Clearly, such critics must be referring to the fact that some companies or industries have, through the market place, been able to earn large profits which yield the shareholder rates of return well in excess of normal, relative to the risks undertaken. Many would argue that in such cases these economic or excess profits should be taxed away.

If the accounting profits are in excess of normal — that is, if the company or industry is earning economic profits — most of these may be taxed away with no effect on industrial investment, because as long as an investment earns the cost of capital, it will be undertaken. However, if government taxation causes the expected rate of return on certain investment projects to fall below the cost of capital, then such taxation will cause the abandonment of these projects, and lower investment will result.

Taxing away economic profits will also reduce net earnings per share, thereby causing a lower demand for individual companies' common stock and, therefore, reduced prices for these shares. As a result, the shareholders of such companies will be less wealthy than they otherwise would be. On the other hand, the extra tax revenue from this source may mean lower taxes of other kinds. Therefore, other groups will benefit through lower taxes (or additional government services if the government does not lower taxes elsewhere).

Well, then, what is the answer? Are economic profits excess or unfair? Should they be taxed away? This is a value judgement. To come to a decision we must weigh the gains to those who would benefit from the profits tax against the losses to the shareholders. Such estimates are difficult to make. Discussions of this sort in any group of people produce all sorts of disagreements. "Many of the shareholders are pensioners and widows," someone may contend. "Doctors, lawyers and professional athletes are really the ones who receive unfair incomes. Let's tax them more heavily." And so the argument continues.

Some point out that any rate of return is fair if we all have an equal opportunity to earn it. Pick any stock whose company's profit per share grew by, say, 100% in the past year. The stock price will also have increased significantly (barring any overall stock market slump as a result of macroeconomic factors in the meantime), and the shareholders will probably have earned an above-normal rate of return (at least for one year). The shareholders are fortunate to have earned such a healthy rate of return — as are winners of lottery tickets. But are the winnings of lottery tickets unfair? We each could have bought the shares of the company whose earnings doubled and, therefore, have been equally fortunate — just as we might have had the winning lottery ticket. However, we may have chosen instead to buy a new car, take a trip to Hawaii or put our money in the bank. In such a case, it may not be reasonable for us to cry "foul" as a result of someone else's good fortune.

Insider Trading

On the other hand, there are many instances of unequally distributed opportunities for taking advantage of abnormally profitable ventures. For example, certain people within corporations or government may become aware, well before the public, of events that are likely to materially affect a particular company's future profitability and consequently the company's stock prices. Such **insiders** are not supposed to use this information for their own gain, but they have done so in the past and may continue to do so in the future, in spite of closer control by the authorities. In this case, most would acknowledge that such profits end up being unfairly distributed to those who had *privileged advance information.*

If an unequal distribution of information yields an unfair distribution of profits among the public, the solution may lie in attempting to disseminate information to the general public as quickly and as efficiently as possible. Then we could each make a

free choice, on an equal footing with others, as to whether or not to buy a given share of stock, with the hope of earning an attractive rate of return on our funds.

Distribution of Wealth

Another possible reason for believing that there are unfair profits made by some investors may be that we realize that some people, through none of their own doing, are born into positions of wealth and power or with abilities that enable them to command large incomes with little or no effort. The incomes so obtained may then be invested in profitable ventures not open to those of us with lesser wealth. These cases exist. However, the remedy may lie, not in disallowing profits, which perform a beneficial resource allocation function for consumers, but instead in redistributing income or wealth by some other means. If achieving this is impossible, however, one may decide to tax profits more heavily and accept some inefficient allocation of economic resources as a *price* for a fairer distribution of wealth.

The concepts of normal and economic profits are useful in analyzing the efficiency of resource allocation. However, it does not necessarily follow that economic profits are unfair and should be taxed away. Economic analysis in this area, more than in many others, is influenced by value judgements.

CONCLUDING REMARKS

The stock market reflects investor expectations concerning the economic viability of business firms in the market place. Firms that are able to produce desired products and sell them at a price above production costs (including a normal rate of return on shareholder funds) will find their share values rising as financial investors bid for the right to these economic profits. Firms that are not able to produce products that have a perceived value in excess of the cost of the resources incur economic losses and, if the process continues, will find the value of their shares eventually falling to a level below the realizable net value of the firm's assets less creditor claims. When this happens, the firm is in danger of liquidation or takeover and has ceased to be a viable economic entity.

KEY TERMS AND CONCEPTS

common stocks	dividends
private corporation	going concern
public corporation	realizable net asset value
stock exchange	replacement value
stockbrokers	accounting profit
unlisted stocks	normal profit
annual report	required profit
income statement	economic profit
balance sheet	pure profit
assets	cost of capital (funds)
liabilities	growth companies
shareholders' equity	growth industries
accounts receivable	insiders
accounts payable	

PROBLEMS

Problem 1

What are the major differences between the sole proprietorship, partnership and corporate forms of business organization with respect to the sharing of profits and risk?

Problem 2

a) What two factors determine the market price of any given company's common stock? What determines the accounting value?

b) The value or worth of a company is typically related to the market value of the comon shareholder group's investment in the company. Is the value of a company better reflected by its book (accounting) figures or is the stock market a better indicator? Why?

Problem 3

An investor is attempting to judge which of two common stocks to purchase for a portfolio. Suppose the investor estimates the following information.

	Current annual earnings per share $	Forecast average annual earnings per share $	Required compensation for risk (over and above compensation for a riskless investment) %	Current stock market price per share $
Co. A	1.50	2	3	18
Co. B	3	3	2	36

The current risk-free rate of return is 7%.

a) Define what is meant by opportunity or normal rate of return in the face of a given investment prospect.

b) Which stock would the investor consider the better buy, and why?

c) How do we know that the average investor's expectations do not agree with our investor's expectation? What are possible sources of disagreement?

Problem 4

Suppose you are going into business for yourself and expect to have to invest $30 000. You forecast the following average annual revenue and expense items. You also have the following information.

Revenue		$100 000
Expenses:		
Materials	40 000	
Wages*	30 000	
Heat, Light, Rent, Misc.	9 000	79 000
Owner's Income		$21 000

* There is no allowance here for an owner's salary.

    (i) you have been offered a job elsewhere at $20 000 a year

    (ii) you could earn 8% interest if you put your money into Canada Savings Bonds

    (iii) you estimate that the risk taken by investing your own money in the business requires an annual compensation of 5% above that for a riskless investment

a) What is the forecast rate of return on your $30 000 of invested funds?
b) What is the forecast annual economic profit and what does the resulting figure mean?
c) Suppose the nonmonetary benefits of being one's own boss are anticipated to be worth $5000 a year. What now would be the economic profit and what does the resulting figure mean?
d) "There are some aspects of one's job that cannot be assigned a monetary value." Discuss this statement.

Problem 5

A company is contemplating a $100 000 investment project to be financed by $50 000 of 8% bonds and $50 000 of common stock. Suppose companies in a comparable risk class usually earn their investors a 10% annual return. With tax considerations neglected:

a) What annual dollar income (after all nonfinancial operating expenses) would the company have to earn to make this a worthwhile investment from the shareholder's standpoint?
b) Bond interest expense is usually deducted along with nonfinancial expenses from sales revenue to arrive at a profit figure (in an accounting sense). This being the case, what accounting profit would have to be earned to make the investment worthwhile from the shareholders' standpoint? What economic profit?
c) Given the above information, what is the cost of capital in annual percentage terms and what does the cost of capital figure mean to management?

Problem 6

a) In which of the industries listed below do you detect a poor allocation of resources, and why?
b) In industry (3) what is the annual economic profit? What is the excess rate of return earned by the shareholders?

Industry #	Price $ per unit	Marginal cost $ per unit	Cost of capital %	Economic profit $ per year	Accounting profit $ per year	Shareholders' investment $	Shareholders' normal annual rate of return elsewhere %
1	10	8	12	—	9 000	65 000	—
2	6	6	—	4 000	10 000	100 000	—
3	50	—	13	—	1 000	4 000	15
4	10	10	8	—	900	10 000	9
5	5	5	10	—	10 000	100 000	12
6	4	4	8	− 500	90 000	—	—
7	7	7	—	—	5 000	20 000	16

Problem 7

The following two retail companies operate in different industries. Data shown below describe various financial operations of the companies.

	Co. A Ltd.	Co. B Ltd.
Market price	$4 per litre	$0.10 per unit
Wholesale cost to company	$3.60 per litre	$0.04 per unit

Co. A Ltd.
Income statement for the year

Sales revenue		$6 000 000
Less expenses:		
Wholesale cost of goods sold	$5 400 000	
Labour costs	400 000	
Heat, light, rent, advertising	100 000	5 900 000
Profit before tax		100 000
Less: Income tax		50 000
Profit after tax		$ 50 000

Co. B Ltd.
Income statement for the year

Sales revenue		$ 500 000
Less expenses:		
Wholesale cost of goods sold	$200 000	
Labour costs	125 000	
Heat, light, rent, advertising	125 000	450 000
Profit before tax		$ 50 000
Less: Income tax		25 000
Profit after tax		$ 25 000

Both companies are financed solely by $500 000 shareholders' funds (common stock plus retained earnings).

a)   Assuming the companies attempt to maximize profits for their shareholders, how might they have arrived at the prices they are charging for their products?

b)   A consumer group has made a recent study of these firms' activities and reported the percentage markup involved on wholesale prices (that is, the difference between retail and wholesale price expressed as a percentage of the wholesale price). What are these markups?

c)   The consumer group reported that there appeared to be a "corporate ripoff" for one or more of the products. Do you agree? Which ones and why? Do you think an examination of their entire operations (their income statement figures) is relevant? Why or why not? Would the fact that investors in these particular industries require a 12% annual return on their funds (given what they can earn elsewhere for a comparable risk) play any part in the analysis? Explain.

CASES

Case 8-1

The following are excerpts from two newspaper articles concerning profit. The first clipping deals with the definition of profit and the concept of fair or appropriate profit. The second shows the results of a cross-Canada survey of people's notions with regard to manufacturers' profits as a percentage of sales revenue. Although the articles are more than a decade old, the issues discussed remain very relevant today. The Anti-Inflation Board (AIB) referred to in the article was a government body in existence from 1975 to 1978, whose objectives were to limit wage and price increases as part of a fight against inflation.

The Globe and Mail, Toronto

What has made profit into a dirty word?

By TIMOTHY PRITCHARD

Thanks to the Anti-Inflation Board, profit is a dirtier word than ever, despite the continuing efforts of some to clean it up.

Under the controls program, profits above certain levels are illegal, so some assume any profit must be — at least — immoral. It does not matter that the AIB talks about excess revenue; the man on the street knows excess revenue leads to excess profit.

Clearly, there is a lot of confusion over what profit is and who benefits from it. Many people apparently believe it is a surplus from doing business that goes entirely into the pockets of management and the owners of a company.

Others — generally those in management — argue that profit is just another cost of doing business. It represents the return on capital that is required to keep money in the business or to raise additional capital to help it grow.

Many in business believe the confusion over profit can be corrected with some basic business education in secondary schools. Material is available to teachers through the Canadian Foundation for Economic Education in Toronto but use is strictly voluntary.

One of the booklets teachers have access to, for example, is one prepared a few months ago by the Canadian Manufacturers Association. It is called *Profits — and Losses* and offers this description of a profit:

"Profit — the difference between income and expenses — can be used in a number of ways: to expand or modernize the business by way of buildings or new equipment, to hire additional people, to pay a return on the owner's or shareholder's investment, or to hold in the business as cash reserves.

"It is a totally mistaken idea to suppose that corporate profits go to shareholders; only dividends go to shareholders. Profits go in roughly equal proportions to governments (through taxation), to shareholders, and to investment in the business (thereby providing jobs, new machines and equipment and general improvements)."

The foundation also has material on profits from the Canadian Chamber of Commerce and others to distribute. The chamber is currently working on a new booklet to replace the decade-old folder it now provides.

Not surprisingly, the CMA is concerned that many Canadians (according to opinion polls) believe industry's profits run to 30 per cent of sales. In fact, says the CMA, profits have averaged less than 5 per cent of sales over the past 20 years.

"In 1975, the average profit on every dollar received by manufacturers from the sale of their products was under 5 cents. Of this, just over 3 cents were retained for the future development of the business and just over 1 cent was issued to investors in the form of dividends."

(The big chunk of the sales dollar was spent on materials — 56 cents — and salaries and wages — 20 cents.)

The booklet goes on to say that different levels of profit in terms of sales are required for different types of businesses. It does not get into the thorny area of return on investment — or what is a fair return on investment.

The central theme is that the competitive enterprise economy is "the most efficient and progressive economic system ever evolved. Without investors this system could not survive. Without the profit urge there would be no investors."

Profit supports the output of goods and services to raise Canada's standard of living, it provides for good wages and benefit programs for employees, taxes to support government services and so on.

That reasoning may be accepted by those who bother to read the CMA's booklet, but the controls program has undoubtedly started many thinking that if profit regulation is good for the short term (to fight inflation), why not some more permanent arrangement.

That again opens up the question of what is a fair profit — and how it should be arrived at.

The answer in the competitive enterprise system is provided by the marketplace. If the return in an industry is high, new capital should be attracted into new businesses. The ensuing competition could force down prices and profits — although those continuing in business would reap for them a "worth-while" return.

Without doubt, Bell Canada of Montreal is a big profit-maker. In 1975 the telephone utility had a profit of $317.4 million — more than twice as much as was earned in 1971.

Was last year's profit excessive? Bell's management and shareholders do not think so. That huge profit (in dollar figures) represented a modest 8.5 per cent return on all the debt and equity capital in the business. Canada Savings Bonds provided a better return.

And despite regular increases in Bell's dividend to common shareholders, last year they received a lower percentage of profit than five years ago — 56 per cent compared with 68 per cent. Higher retained earnings are for capital spending that has jumped to $1-billion a year from $555-million over the five-year period.

Profit is what's left out of money collected from sales revenues after all expenses have been paid, including all kinds of taxes that for manufacturing companies probably amount to 20 or 25 per cent of revenues. Out of profit you have to set aside some money to replace buildings and equipment. If you don't replace them you're going to be out of business. This has happened in a number of countries. Profit is also a scoresheet of how well you're doing. If you're doing a good job of serving your customers, they'll reward you for doing it.

Profit has to be looked at in terms of risk. A minimum return is determined by a no-risk type of return. Right now you can get about 9.5 per cent pretty readily on a no-risk, high-security government bond. If you're asking somebody to invest in something that involves a risk, they've got to see a better return than that. You can see situations where the risk is such that even with the potential of a 25 per cent return people wouldn't be prepared to take a chance on it. But even that would be a lower return than many people think manufacturing profits to be. The actual return on investment is about 10 per cent. — **Roy Phillips, executive Director, Canadian Manufacturers Association.**

Profits are rewards for taking risks in the marketplace. They are a residual — the amount left over when all the costs of doing business have been met. Profit acts as a carrot, attracting new investment, and as a stick, punishing those who do not produce efficiently.

There is no reasonable level of profit for all industries. Profit in a healthy market economy should vary over a wide range to reflect dif-

ferences in market conditions and in the efficiency of firms. High profits are normal and necessary in some cases as an incentive for people to take more risks. Low profits are quite normal in cases where it is necessary to encourage producers to withdraw from the market. — **Judith Maxwell, senior economist, C.D. Howe Research Institute.**

In simplest terms, profits are the difference between revenues and costs in a business activity (with costs including taxes and royalty payments to government). In more philosophical terms, profits are a reward to the owner of the business and a signal to the market as to where to allocate resources. Profits are a reward for producing a product desired by the public in an efficient manner and for supplying the capital needed to produce the good or service. Profits are the incentive provided to the businessman to keep costs of production as low as possible, thereby making the gap between revenue and costs as high as possible. As a reward for supplying capital, profits are in effect a payment to the owner for waiting — for giving up the chance to obtain immediate satisfaction from his funds by forgoing some current consumption.

Profits can be measured in a number of ways. One way is the absolute dollar amount; another is the rate of return on capital invested in the business. The most reasonable measure is the rate of return. Investing funds in a business is, except for the risk factor, the same as putting money in a savings account — but that kind of return should not be considered a fair rate of profit. The fairness of profit is bounded by three things: the riskiness of the activity; the relative efficiency of the activity; the degree of freedom of entry into the business activity by competitors. A return on investment or the cost of capital, therefore, becomes the measure of a fair profit. It can vary from 5 per cent on a completely risk-free venture to 20 per cent or more on highly speculative activities. — **Donald McIvor, executive vice-president, Imperial Oil Ltd.**

Profit or net income is the excess of revenue less expenses, including corporate income taxes, measured over a period of time. This return to shareholders can be paid out in dividends or retained in the business.

A reasonable profit should be measured in the context of the return on equity capital. The size of the return depends on the risk element in the particular business. At the minimum, the return should be greater than from low-risk situations, such as government bonds — **Robert Schultz, vice-president, finance, Merrill Lynch, Royal Securities Ltd.**

A profit results when an amount is received over and above the cost of producing a good or service and after all taxes have been paid. The problem lies in defining "cost". It must include not only the visible amount expended, but, in addition, the cost of replacing the assets used in production or which become obsolete through technology. A profit, although regarded as such, may also be illusory, as in the case of an inventory profit, where the inventory must be replaced at higher prices.

"The question of what constitutes a "suitable" profit can also be debated. Obviously, it must be related to the capital employed and the risk involved. In the final analysis, it must be an amount sufficient to induce investment and encourage production. Anything else will eventually lead to the abandonment of the activity." — **Ward Pitfield, president, Pitfield, Mackay, Ross and Co. Ltd. and chairman, Investment Dealers Association of Canada.**

We acknowledge the need for profits. It would be absurd to do otherwise. . . . But if there was going to be any fairness in this program, the Anti-Inflation Board would have established absolute profit limits. Instead, profits can increase by $3-million, $4-million, $10-million, $20-million or more, while working men and women are restricted to an annual increase of $2,400. — **Edward Broadbent, New Democratic Party leader.**

The Globe and Mail, Toronto

Survey finds public believes profits are excessive

By LAWRENCE LEDUC AND J. ALEX MURRAY

**Perceptions by Canadians of excess business profit
by region**

Is there excess profit?		Canada %	Atlantic %	Quebec %	Ont. %	Prairies %	B.C. %
Yes	1975–76	56	60	66	47	58	50
	1974–75	63	64	63	64	65	56
No	1975–76	18	11	17	19	18	25
	1974–75	15	15	14	15	16	16
No opinion	1975–65	26	29	17	33	24	25
	1974–75	22	21	23	22	19	29
Average excess profit, cents/dollar	1975–76	15.5¢	18.9¢	15.8¢	15.2¢	14.6¢	13.8¢
	1974–75	18.6	17.8	20.9	18.4	17.0	16.2

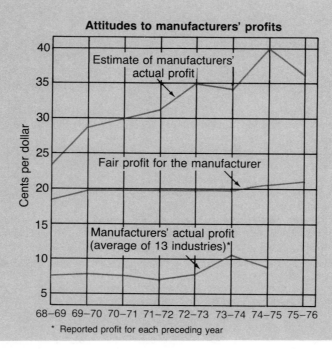

Attitudes to manufacturers' profits

Estimate of manufacturers' actual profit

Fair profit for the manufacturer

Manufacturers' actual profit (average of 13 industries)*

Cents per dollar

68–69 69–70 70–71 71–72 72–73 73–74 74–75 75–76

* Reported profit for each preceding year

a)   Are these two articles referring to accounting profit or to economic profit? Explain.

b)   Read the six definitions of profit and fair profit given toward the end of the first article. Rank these from 1 to 6 (with 1 being the highest ranking and 6 the lowest) in terms of clarity and precision. Explain the reasons for your first and sixth rankings.

c)   The first article quotes a CMA booklet as saying, "It is a totally mistaken idea to suppose that corporate profits go to shareholders." The CMA booklet goes on to say that only a fraction of after-tax profits winds up as dividends in the hands of shareholders. The implication seems to be that shareholders do not benefit from the portion of profits reinvested in the company. Is this the way you interpret such statements? If so, discuss the accuracy of this implication.

d)   The CMA booklet seems to relate fairness of profit to some low percentage of sales revenue. The opinion survey of the second article also takes this approach. On the other hand, five of the six people asked to explain the notion of fair profits related it to a percentage of funds invested. Which do you think is the more appropriate approach? Explain.

e)   Either support or attack Ed Broadbent's statement.

f)   Was Bell Canada's profit in 1975 excessive in your opinion? Explain.

Case 8-2

The Financial Post

OSC to review Grandma's reporting

By PATRICK BLOOMFIELD

"Grandma is over 100 and going strong," proclaim the quarterly reports of Grandma Lee's Inc. From now on, however, Grandma is going to have to pick up her skirts and start running pretty hard just to stay in the same place in investors' affections.

Last year, the stock of this company, which develops, licenses, franchises and services a chain of food and bakery products outlets, put on the biggest gain of any industrial stock in Canada (climbing to $15.50 from $3.50). In the fall, Grandma Lee's management reported — amid the general clatter of tumbling corporate earnings — that net income had all but tripled to $4.8 million from $1.7 million.

The net effect of an Ontario Securities Commission order last Friday to 10 insiders to

cease trading in the company's stock pending a hearing, Tuesday, April 13, can only be to cast some shadows on what analysts call "the quality" of these earnings. (The insiders named included chairman Allan R. Biggs, president William W. Hood, and the investment company of which Maurice Strong is a principal.)

Make no mistake about it. There is no allegation that the company's financial affairs lack order or that it is anything but a thriving enterprise. The prime issue to be hammered out at 10 Wellesley St., Toronto, on Tuesday will be whether sufficient information was given in that annual report to present the fiscal 1981 results fairly.

The issue is crucial to the company and to

the marketplace because professional investors and security analysts assess their buying and selling prices on the basis of the present value of a future stream of earnings. The most important single piece of information they need is some indication of the composition and staying power of earnings in the past.

What has been bothering the OSC staff is that Grandma Lee's earnings for fiscal 1981 were based on $12.6 million in revenues that included the sale of area franchises, though (in the words of the notice of hearing) "there exists no assurance of collectability of payments" in respect of such franchises and the major portion of these sales is being satisfied by long-term debt at "significantly" below-market interest rates.

• • •

Sprott Securities Ltd., a young brokerage firm that keeps its eyes open for potentially overvalued situations, put Grandma Lee's in the category in a letter to clients in mid-March, citing, among other reasons, "a lack of disclosure by the company which precludes an ability to value the true earnings power of the restaurants."

• • •

However, more than the market value of the stock (still subject to a trading halt when The Post went to press) hangs on the OSC hearing.

Recent OSC insider trading records list the sale of about 100,000 common shares. Should the OSC decide that outsiders buying the stock knew less about the company's sales mix than insiders, because of lack of disclosure, then the whole area of liability under the 1978 Ontario Securities Act could come under consideration.

• • •

The information the stock market wants above all else is some indication of the degree of profitability of the nuts and bolts of the business, the outlets themselves. Pending the further disclosure planned by Grandma Lee's, this could only be a matter for speculation as The Post went to press.

Grandma Lee's

The above article illustrates how important accurate accounting information is to stock market participants. It is part of the economic function of provincial securities commissions such as the OSC to make sure that "outside" investors have up-to-date accurate information and that "insiders" (people within the firm) do not profit from stock transactions to the detriment of outsiders.

a) What was the reason in 1981 for Grandma Lee's stock climbing from $3.50 to $15.50 per share?

b) Explain how each of the following two events would affect the price of Grandma Lee's stock: (i) an increase in potential rates of return available in other companies' stock, (ii) an expected reduction in Grandma Lee's future profits. Show each of the effects (i) and (ii) on demand and supply diagrams.

c) Every investor knows that firms do nct ultimately collect on all their credit sales because some customers go bankrupt, some customers are dishonest and others refuse to pay for a variety of reasons. Why, then, did the stock price fall significantly in April 1982, and why is the OSC concerned about the recent sales of 100 000 common shares by Grandma Lee insiders?

Case 8-3

On October 19, 1987 (known as "Black Monday"), the Dow Jones Industrial Average Index lost a record 508 points (it dropped from 2 246 points to 1 738 points). The Toronto Stock Exchange 300 Composite Index lost 407 points (it dropped from 3 598 to 3 191 points) on the same day and another 221 points the next day. The Dow Jones Index staged a rally the next day and the TSE Index rallied later as well, but further declines occurred on the days to follow. Similar tumbles in share prices occurred on stock exchanges around the world. The following article considers some implications of the stock market crash.

The Financial Post

The big chill
Financial quake will shake up a generation
By JENNIFER WELLS

THE TRAUMA sweeping world financial markets will reach far beyond stock prices.

In business boardrooms, living rooms and even along assembly lines, change is on the way. The heyday of excess, when fresh, young brokers ordered hot, fast cars in the belief that the boom would never end, may be over. The cocksure style of the five-year bull run, typified by bought deals, high-flying new issues and leveraged buyouts, is about to be tempered. The risk of an economic slowdown — and a consequent fall in living standards — has grown.

Some of the changes will be short-term, possibly temporary. Others will not make themselves felt for another month, or perhaps another year.

Those affected are not just floor traders, brokers and dealmakers. The distemper of the market will touch small-business owners, home renovators, car salespeople and many others.

The malaise has already hit new equity issues and those involved with them. While mergers and acquisitions are still going gangbusters, leveraged buyouts and bought deals are in for a beating.

Mutual funds, the investment that brought

some sizzle to fledgling investors, are starting to lose their shine.

While trend watchers are wary of over-dramatizing — and ending up with egg on their faces — they are beginning to assess the ways our lives will be transformed.

Lorie Waisberg, a partner specializing in mergers and acquisitions with the Toronto law firm Goodman & Goodman, has a simple summation: "Monday changed the world."

Lloyd Atkinson, senior vice-president and chief economist at Bank of Montreal, says regardless of what happens to the stock market, the confidence of consumers and business people has been shaken.

"Business plans that can be shelved will be; consumer purchases that can be shelved will be," says Atkinson.

Shrinking outlays mean slower growth. But Atkinson does not consider himself an alarmist. "This is not 1929," he says. "To build a scenario of disaster is easy to do, but I don't know that it has any credibility."

Opportunities narrowed

On the other hand, "there's no mistaking we've seen one hell of a shove to the system."

A crippled stock market inevitably narrows opportunities. Many businesses forced to cancel or postpone share issues will have to curtail expansion plans. Less expansion equals slower growth, which equals fewer new jobs. Workers, surveying a stagnant labor market, concentrate on job security rather than wage hikes. Spending is cut back.

Steve Tanny, economist at management consultant Woods Gordon, says conspicuous consumption — the BMWs, the $20,000 dining room suites — will likely to be the first to suffer.

According to a downtown Toronto car dealer, upscale buyers weren't yet pulling their names off Porsches at the end of last week. But Earl Berger, vice-president of Environics Research Group Ltd., expects to see a lot of second-hand Audi Quattros come up for sale soon.

An executive with one of the Big Three carmakers fears that consumers wary of recession may delay planned purchases. "We're just hoping now that low interest rates will keep buyers coming," he says.

Berger predicts the low interest rates will help insulate much of the housing market. But high-priced homes will suffer.

What Berger calls the wheelers and dealers — the heavy market players caught when their brokers issued margin calls — may have little choice but to throw their houses onto the market.

Tanny says there will be a second wave of spending cuts. New York hoteliers can expect fewer Toronto visitors heading down for an afternoon at Bloomingdale's.

Those, of course, are not average Canadians. Tanny says the Crash won't have much direct impact for the man on the street. But the prospect of businesses scuppering expansion plans is real, and that will cut a far wider swath.

The fallout began when numerous new issues came screeching to a halt last week. Almost $1.2 billion of new equity issues have already been deferred. That's 10% of the total equity raised last year.

Douglas Mackay, vice-chairman at Dominion Securities Inc., predicts it may be two–three months, possibly longer, before the new-issues market reopens. When it does, well-established companies will hold the most appeal for underwriters. Many small companies and initial public offerings may go begging.

"At the top of the market you see a lot of junk," says Tom Tutsch, director of corporate services at Burns Fry Ltd. "I think that will go away."

The drying up of new issues, and the prospect of lower trading volumes, translates into reduced revenues for investment houses. That would lead to reduced staffing.

A more conservative posture across the investment community is in the cards. The popularity of bought deals — in which the underwriter takes up an entire issue and thereby bears any losses — is likely to wane, at least for now.

It was the bull market that made the bought deal so compelling. Says one investment house executive dejectedly: "I can't say they're dead, but in the short term they're certainly dying."

The outlook on the mergers and acquisitions front is different. Waisberg, at Goodman & Goodman, says the firm has been retained on a number of transactions since Black Monday, some involving hundreds of millions of dollars.

He suspects, though, that management-led leveraged buyouts, which finance takeovers with little equity, may be in difficulty. Creditors' confidence in management expertise, or lack of it, could turn the screw.

Some businesses whose share prices collapsed started buying up their own shares last week. They may want to fend off potential acquisitors. On the other hand, they may be trying to set a floor price for their stock.

Such tactics draw a cynical response from Charles Kindleberger, respected professor emeritus of economics at Massachusetts Institute of Technology, who snaps, "It's too bad they're not investing in capital equipment for real output instead."

Does all this mean another recession is in the offing? Tanny believes not. He hopes policy moves in the U.S., prompted by the upcoming election, will offset that possibility.

To some extent, economic theory may not be relevant. Bank of Montreal's Atkinson notes that, on a trip to the drug store, he runs into people who've never invested in the market but want to talk about it. Those people could fly into safety by saving more and spending less.

Some market insiders are already feeling the pinch. One Toronto broker who planned a $100,000 extension on his house canned his plans after losing $25,000 in paper on Black Monday.

Lawyers will survive nicely. Says Waisberg: "We may stop doing real estate but maybe we'll do more bankruptcies and workouts. People litigate when they're in trouble, and that's good for lawyers."

a) Is the "risk of an economic slowdown" (or recession) referred to in the article the cause of the stock market crash or its consequence?

b) Why have the new equity issues been negatively affected?

c) Why are "conspicuous consumption" and "high-priced homes" likely to be among the first to suffer?

d) The stock market crash seems both to encourage and discourage mergers and takeovers. Explain.

APPENDIX 8A: THE STOCK MARKET

8A-1 Reasons for Yield Differences among Stocks

If we examine the financial pages, we may see beside the stock quotations the *current earnings yield* on particular stocks. The current earnings yield is defined as the ratio of the most recently reported annual earnings (net accounting profit after tax) per share to the current market price of the stock. Actually, it is more common to find the *current dividend yield* reported. This is defined as the ratio of the most recently reported annual dividend per share to the current price of the stock. Here, we discuss earnings yields because all corporate earnings accrue to shareholders whether they are currently receiving them as dividends or not. This section could be discussed equally well, though, with dividends yields replacing earnings yields.

(i) Perceived Risk Differences

If we see two stocks showing different current earnings yields, it may mean that investors perceive a *risk difference* between them.

As an example, suppose two stocks have the same annual earnings per share. People's best estimates are also that both stocks will maintain these earnings per share for some time in the future. However, suppose the market is more confident about company A's maintaining its earnings per share at the current level than they are about company B. Company B's future annual earnings per share may be higher or lower than they are now, but the market is undecided as to which likelihood is the greater. Disliking risk and uncertainty, the market would require a higher expected rate of return from company B's stock than from company A's.

Suppose the current earnings per share for each of company A and B are $2. In this case, the prices of A and B's stock may be bid to, say, $20 and $16.67 respectively. These prices would reflect a desired 10% annual yield by investors buying the right to the more certain future earnings stream of company A and a desired 12% annual yield ($\frac{\$2}{\$16.67} \times 100\%$) by investors taking a greater risk in buying the right to the less certain future earnings of company B.

(ii) Potential Earnings Growth

Another reason for different current earnings yields of two companies' stocks could be that the stock market expects one company's annual earnings per share to grow faster than the other's, even though the degree of uncertainty connected with these expected earnings is the same in each case.

This explanation may seem confusing and even contradictory at first, so let us examine some numbers. Suppose, for example, company A and B are currently earning $2 annually per share. The predictions on average may be that company A's annual earnings per share will grow within the near future to $2.50 per share, plus or minus 10¢. On the other hand, the prediction for B's stock may be that annual earnings per share will grow within the same period of time to $2.30 per share, plus or minus 10¢. Roughly speaking, the degree of uncertainty of each prediction (as indicated by the plus or minus 10¢) is the same in both cases. However, the general feeling is that company *A*'s annual earnings per share will grow faster than company *B*'s.

Therefore, over this future time period expectations are that company *A*'s earnings per share will average more than those of company *B*, even though at present they are equal. As a result, the market may price company *A*'s stock at, say $33.33, indicating a current earnings yield of 6% (that is, $2/$33 × 100%) and company *B*'s stock at, say $25, indicating a current earnings yield of 8% (that is, $2/$25 × 100%).

Incidentally, the preceding also explains why we often observe current earnings (or dividend) yields for stocks lower than those for bonds even though bonds are less risky financial instruments. Though the dollar interest to be received each year per bond is fixed, most earnings per share for common stocks experience positive growth over time.

Long-Run Supply Decisions

9-1 INTRODUCTION AND PURPOSE

This chapter analyzes the supply decision from a long-run perspective. For profitable production decisions, those cost elements which are important in the long run are different from those which are important in the short run. In the short run, fixed costs are independent of the volume of output produced and sold and are therefore irrelevant for the output decision. In the longer run, all costs are affected by the scale of operations and level of output which the firm decides to produce. In the long run, therefore, all costs are relevant for the output decision.

Of course, the basic principle in examining the influence of costs on decision making is always the same. Assuming profit maximization is the objective, additional sales should be undertaken as long as their effect on costs and revenue is such that revenues increase by more than costs, or costs decrease by more than revenues — and so on. However, in this chapter we go beyond a restatement of this basic principle to a description of the type of cost information (and revenue information, where pertinent) that management ideally should seek and refer to if it wishes to maximize profit in the long run.

Another important concern of this chapter is the integration of short- and long-run analysis of market demand and supply shocks within purely competitive and monopoly market structures.

Let us begin with a brief review of the distinction between fixed and variable costs.

9-2 THE NATURE OF COSTS

Short-Run Fixed Costs

In the short run, regardless of the level of output produced, the amount of certain inputs to the production process is fixed. Likewise, the costs or expenses connected with these inputs are fixed and, consequently, independent of the volume of production. For example, the amount of property the company has will not change in the short run (say within a week, month or even a year), nor probably will the level of administrative staff, maintenance or clerical personnel. Therefore, regardless of the volume of output the firm produces within the short run, property taxes, administrative, maintenance and clerical salaries will remain at a certain fixed amount. Some companies are more flexible than others, though, because of the technological considerations of their industry. Therefore the relevant time period over which certain costs are fixed is much shorter for some firms than it is for others.

One of the first decisions a firm has to make before it begins production is the *scale* on which it will operate. That question concerns the planned size of the firm's capital stock — how large it should make its offices or factory, how many factories and machines there should be, and so on. These considerations all depend on the average yearly volume the firm expects to be able to produce and sell. Coincident with this decision is the amount and type of financing (or capital funds) required for the asset investment.

When the physical facilities have been built, the company is then constrained to operate within certain bounds. For one thing, the firm cannot produce output volume much in excess of that for which the physical facilities were designed. Further, the company must pay the entire annual financing costs each year, regardless of the portion of physical facilities actually utilized. As a result, one particular fixed short-run cost is the cost of capital. The portion of financing costs which takes the form of owners' (shareholders') *normal profit* is often overlooked. Nevertheless, inasmuch as this amount of accounting profit must be earned on average in the long run to prevent the company from being liquidated and investment funds placed elsewhere, normal profit is an economic cost no different from payments for materials, electricity or labour.

Short-Run Variable Costs

Some inputs in the short run vary directly with the volume of production. The costs associated with variable inputs are called variable costs. Payments for material and wages of factory workers would be examples of two such variable expenses. As production is increased, more material must be used and the number of paid hours of factory labour increases. If, on the other hand, less output is required during the year, though there could be no saving from property taxes and the dollar cost of capital funds, and probably little reduction in administrative or clerical expenses, the materials expense is reduced proportionately and selected layoffs would save some labour costs.

Another short-run variable cost is the interest expense of financing short-term assets. The need for accounts receivable, cash, inventory and the like varies directly with the volume of business carried on within each month or year. As a result, the cost of financing these short-term (or current) assets is a variable cost of production. Remember, production costs are all costs associated with producing and marketing goods and services.

Relevant and Irrelevant Costs

Because extra (marginal) cost is the increase in cost that results from an extra unit of production, and we know marginal cost is the cost to focus on for decision making (that is, produce where $MR = MC$), we also know that fixed costs are completely irrelevant for managerial decision making. Regardless of the level of production during a month or a year, a firm will experience the same level of fixed cost. Variable costs depend, however, on the particular volume produced during the production period. Management decisions about the volume of production will determine the quantity of materials to be used, the amount of labour that will be employed, and to some extent the amount of heating, lighting and selling expenses incurred. Therefore, a company has control over its total costs via its control over variable costs.

To maximize profit, a firm must continue to produce more output as long as the marginal revenue exceeds the marginal cost. Marginal cost is the extra cost which results when one more unit of output is produced. The only extra costs that result are variable costs. Therefore, the marginal cost of producing one more unit equals the increase in variable cost.

To this point, we have shown that the only relevant costs for the production decision are marginal costs, or in other words, changes in variable costs that occur when production volumes change. But we must not lose sight of the fact that costs are only half of the influence in any decision. Revenue information from demand analysis provides the other half.

As discussed in Chapter 6, business managers often form their pricing policies by attempting to choose an appropriate (*best profit*) percentage markup on some (per) unit cost measure other than marginal cost. However, as we also argued earlier, this attempt to search for the best profit markup on, say, average unit cost is necessarily equivalent to attempting to equate marginal revenue with marginal cost. For instance, if one person actually found the best profit markup on average cost whereas another person priced the product so that marginal revenue equalled marginal cost, both would end up with the same price, the same volume of output produced and sold and the same profit.

In the short run, some costs of production are fixed and some are variable. Only the variable costs, and associated marginal costs, are relevant in determining the profit-maximizing level of output.

9-3 ECONOMICS OF THE LONG RUN

The feature that distinguishes the short run from the long run in economics is that in the short run certain costs are fixed. In the long run, though, no costs are fixed. In addition to the amount of labour employed, the amount of capital equipment and the size and number of plants within the firm may be altered. Therefore, *in the long run all the firm's costs are variable.*

The principle for decision making over a long period of time is essentially the same as that of the short run. Assuming the firm wishes to make its owners as well off as possible, it will attempt to maximize long-run profit.

The Scale of Operations

When a firm changes the size of its physical plant in some way, or perhaps increases the number of plants (or stores), it is said to be changing the scale of its operations. An important long-run management decision concerns the best size or number of factories, machines, trucks or amount of office furniture to invest in. In other words, what type and quantity of physical capital will maximize average annual expected profit for the shareholders?

The factors that affect this decision are such things as the pattern of expected demand for the company's products in the foreseeable future; the cost of labour; the cost of equipment, land and plant buildings; and the relative productivity of workers versus machines. Consider the following example.

Efficient Labour-Capital Choice

Suppose that to produce an expected volume of 1000 units of a particular product per week (52 000 per year), a plant building costing $800 000 is required regardless of how much labour or machinery may be included in the process. (This may be an unrealistic assumption, but it is only hypothetical and used to simplify the problem). The firm must decide how much machinery to purchase and how many workers to employ. There are two choices: (i) a highly mechanized process requiring $1 000 000 worth of machinery and 5 workers, or (ii) a process requiring 20 workers but no machinery (except for $1000 worth of hand tools).

Since the mechanized process involves a large amount of physical capital per worker it could be characterized as a **capital intensive** process while the manual process is **labour intensive**. Suppose the annual costs are as shown in Table 9-1. Important costs associated with the machinery and building would be the annual depreciation (wearing out) expense and the annual cost of financing the investment. Labour costs take the form of wages. It is assumed that material costs would be the same under either process.

In this instance, it would be more efficient to use the capital intensive approach, since the total cost of producing with the mechanized process (last column of Table 9-1) is lower than the total cost of producing with the manual process. In practice, there may be intermediate choices of capital and labour intensiveness. It seems clear, for example, that an increase in labour efficiency or a reduction in labour wage rates would tend to swing firms to-

Table 9-1 Annual cost of producing 52 000 units per year

	Depreciation and financing cost of building ($)	Depreciation and financing cost of machinery and tools ($)	Labour cost ($)	Materials cost ($)	Total cost ($)
Merchanized process	200 000	200 000	100 000	500 000	1 000 000
Manual process	200 000	250	400 000	500 000	1 100 250

Two different production processes are illustrated. Both have identical building and materials costs, but very different machinery cost and labour cost. The choice between the two depends upon the total costs indicated in the last column.

ward a more labour intensive approach. On the other hand, increases in the productivity of capital equipment, a reduction in the price of capital equipment or a lowering of the cost of capital funds necessary to finance capital equipment would lead firms toward a more capital intensive approach, with more mechanized factories.

One choice every firm has to make in the long run has to do with the most efficient combination of labour and capital needed in order to undertake any given volume of production. In some instances the choice may be fairly uncomplicated. For example, a taxi company normally employs one person for each shift in every car but still has to make some choices. For example, should the company purchase standard-sized cars or subcompacts (minicabs), or perhaps limousines or small buses?

Another choice the firm has in the long run is the scale of operations deemed appropriate. The answer depends on anticipated demand. Suppose, as was the case above, that the most efficient (cheapest) combination of workers and capital goods for a particular industry is $1 000 000 worth of plant and equipment and 5 workers for each 1000 units of anticipated production per week. The next question is, how many such bundles of labour and capital is it best for the firm to have? The answer depends, of course, on whether the firm expects demand to be such that it will be producing 1000 units or 10 000 units a week.

Operation Scale and Costs

As the scale of the plant or firm increases, the firm may experience lower average costs of production — or **economies of scale**. Economies of scale may arise for a number of reasons. At the plant level, larger volumes may allow for much greater specialization of tasks and division of labour. The application of certain types of specialized machinery may only become feasible at high volumes. At the firm level, a doubling of output and sales volume may require a doubling of salesmen but not necessarily a doubling of marketing managers, accountants or other administrative personnel, thus leading to reduced per unit costs.

At the other extreme, plants or firms can be too large for efficiency purposes. For example, if a firm produces and sells for the entire national market, transportation costs may make it cheaper to produce in two or three plants across the country rather than in one large plant. Companies may become so large and bureaucratic that top management loses control over operating costs. In such instances, firms may split into smaller self-contained divisions or subsidiaries for the purposes of cost control and decision making. If average costs increase as plant scale or size of firms becomes larger, **diseconomies of scale** are said to have set in. In between economies and diseconomies of scale is the situation of *constant (average) costs*. Let us now investigate the relationship between scale and costs within a more general framework.

Suppose a company has the opportunity to build three possible scales of operation as characterized by the size of its physical plant base. For instance, let us think of the company being able to build a small physical plant (scale 1), a medium-sized plant (scale 2) or a large plant (scale 3). For any output volume, since scale 3 works with more physical capital per unit of labour, it is the most capital intensive possibility. Likewise, scale 1 involves the most labour intensive production arrangement. The fixed costs involving plant and machinery maintenance, depreciation, property taxes and the cost of capital funds used to finance the physical investment will be highest for plant 3 and lowest for plant 1. The question we seek to solve is "What size plant should the company build?" As always, both cost and demand considerations play a part in this decision. First of all, let us focus our attention on cost aspects and then turn toward demand.

Figure 9-1 illustrates the nature of the choices faced by management. First, an estimate (forecast) of the expected volume of output is made. Suppose, for example, that management considers three alternative scenarios: output level less than Q_1, output level larger than Q_1, but smaller than Q_2, and output level larger than Q_2. The next step is to identify what kind of per unit cost patterns would result if the firm built plants of different sizes capable of producing these ranges of output. Suppose that the best available technology allows the construction of three alternative plants, with cost structures represented by short-run average cost curves SAC_1, SAC_2, and SAC_3.

What we can say without even knowing demand is that the company will prefer the *least cost scale of producing any possible volume*. For instance, to produce volumes of output below Q_1, the company would not even consider plant scales 2 or 3 but instead built plant scale 1 and operate with cost structure, SAC_1. Similarly, for anticipated output volumes between Q_1 and Q_2, the company would choose plant scale 2 and cost structure SAC_2. For volumes beyond Q_2, the company would build plant scale 3 and operate with cost structure SAC_3.

Figure 9-2 is designed to show the cost structures of the three scale possibilities in more detail,

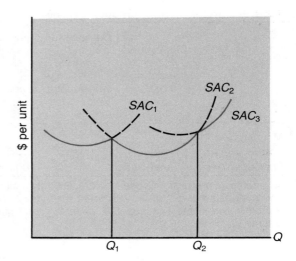

Fig. 9-1 Choice of plant scale

The choice of least cost plant scale. If output Q_1 or less is desired, plant SAC_1 should be chosen, since it is capable of producing that output with lower cost than SAC_2 or SAC_3. For output between Q_1 and Q_2, plant SAC_2 is the least cost option. For output Q_3 or somewhat larger, plant SAC_3 should be built.

including their total and marginal cost curves. Naturally, a smaller plant is cheaper than a larger plant for producing relatively small volumes of output, since the smaller plant has a lower level of fixed cost. Below volume Q_1, plant 1 has the lowest total and average production cost, whereas beyond Q_1, plant 2 is more efficient on both a total and average cost per unit basis.[1] Similarly, plant 3 is more efficient than the other two plants on both a total and average cost basis for output volumes beyond Q_2.

Depending on the desired volume of output, the company would choose either plant scale 1, 2 or 3 and correspondingly, therefore, either cost structure (SMC_1, SAC_1), (SMC_2, SAC_2) or (SMC_3, SAC_3).

---

1. Note that if the total cost (TC) of producing a particular volume of output (say Q_1) is lower with plant size 1 than with another plant size then so too must average cost (AC) be lower since $(AC) = \dfrac{TC}{Q_1}$.

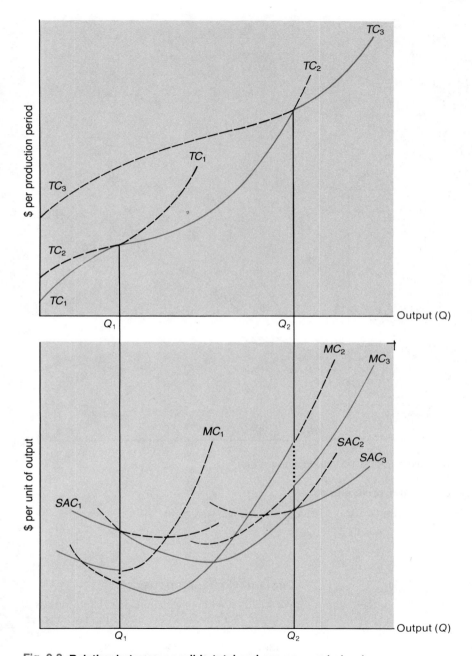

Fig. 9-2 Relation between possible total and average cost structures

The cost structures for three possible plant sizes. The upper diagram shows total cost curves and the lower diagram the average and marginal cost curves. The curves are drawn with solid lines over those ranges of output for which the relevant plant size represents the least cost choice.

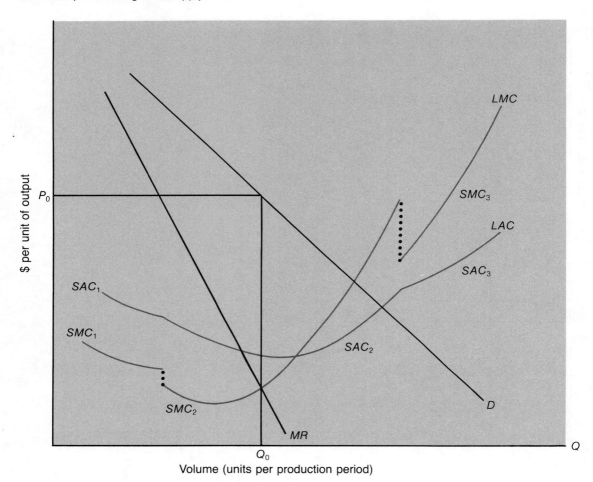

Fig. 9-3 Long-run price, output and scale choice

Profit-maximizing choice of output. The firm should produce output Q_0 with plant
size SAC_2 and charge price P_0.

In Figure 9-3, we show the least cost portions of
average and marginal cost curves from the bottom
half of Figure 9-2. In other words, Figure 9-3
shows the unit costs that the firm would effectively
face for various possible volumes of output *if it
had enough time to adjust its plant base*. In other
words, the *LMC* and *LAC* curves in Figure 9-3 indicate the firm's **long-run average cost** structure
and **long-run marginal cost** structure respectively.

Demand Considerations

We still do not know which plant size the company
would in fact choose in the long run. This answer
depends upon the firm's expected long-run demand
conditions. Once demand is estimated, the long-
run scale and production choice will, as usual, be
chosen by maximum expected profit considerations. For example, let us suppose our particular
firm has monopoly power and that its expected
long-run demand and marginal revenue conditions

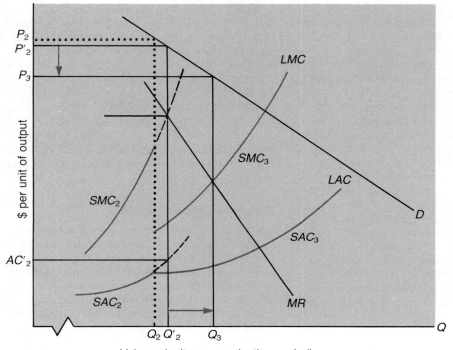

Fig. 9-4 Plant scale error

The firm's forecast called for output level Q_2, plant size SAC_2 and price P_2. Actual demand conditions, described by the D and MR curves, call for higher output. Since only plant SAC_2 is available, the firm's optimal behaviour is to produce output Q'_2, with per unit costs of AC'_2 and charge price P'_2. The long-run optimum is plant SAC_3, output Q_3 and price P_3.

are as reflected in Figure 9-3. Long-run profit would be maximized by producing with that scale of plant and at that output level for which marginal revenue equals marginal cost. In our example, this can be seen to occur within plant scale 2 at a production level Q_0. Plant scale 2 contributes most to long-run profit maximization since it is the least cost plant at volume Q_0. Second, the volume choice is correct since to produce less than Q_0 means more revenue lost than cost saved (at volumes below Q_0, $MC < MR$) and to produce more than Q_0 means more added costs than revenue gained (at volumes above Q_0, $MC > MR$).

The long run is a decision situation where the firm must determine the optimal quantities for all outputs, including the plant size. Profits are maximized by the choice of that scale of plant and that level of output for which marginal revenue equals marginal cost.

Short-Run Constraints

Decisions on the appropriate fixed asset base are long-run commitments based on long-run demand and cost forecasts. If, after the fact, due to poor forecasting, the plant scale actually set up is found to be inappropriate, the firm will seek to adjust by either expanding or diminishing its base of operations. But such adjustment may take as long as several years. In the meantime, long-run profitability is best served by seeking to equate marginal revenue with marginal cost within the given short-run fixed scale constraints.

For instance, considering the above example once more, suppose that after having built plant 2, actual demand conditions in a particular year turn out to be as indicated in Figure 9-4. (Figure 9-4 is a magnified version of the high-volume half of Figure 9-3.) If this high level of demand was thought to be permanent, the company would wish that it had constructed plant scale 3. Its long-run profit-maximizing price, volume and plant scale would be P_3, Q_3 and scale 3 respectively. However, in the short run, the company is stuck with plant scale 2, which it built based on more pessimistic demand expectations. In the short run, therefore, the maximum contribution toward long-run profitability must be attained within the company's actual short-run cost structure (SMC_2, SAC_2). The company would therefore seek to charge a price of P'_2 and produce a volume Q'_2 while at the same time undertaking an investment program of plant expansion.

Capacity

The word **capacity** can cause confusion. There are at least three possible meanings, as follows:

(i) Some people regard the capacity of a plant or business firm as a maximum output level, beyond which the firm (for all practical purposes) cannot produce. This output volume would occur at an employment level for which the marginal product of labour is zero.

(ii) Another definition for capacity is the level of output at which short-run average unit costs are at a minimum.

(iii) Finally, a third definition regards capacity as the output level beyond which a larger scale would offer lower average costs. Using this definition, the capacities of plants 1 and 2 of Figure 9-1 are Q_1 and Q_2 respectively.

Unless stated otherwise, in this book we will employ the third definition. For instance, we might say in the context of our example directly above

(see again Figure 9-4) that the unexpected high level of demand has induced the company in the short run to produce beyond its *normal operating capacity* ($Q'_2 > Q_2$). This fact caused abnormally high unit costs of production (both average and marginal) and higher prices than would have occurred if the company had enjoyed larger physical facilities. Further, the higher prices caused by the capacity limitations yielded a lower production and sales volume (Q) than would otherwise have occurred. Such effects are typical of situations where temporary demand-increase induced volumes are produced in excess of normal operating capacity.

Minimum Efficient Scale

Above we supposed for simplicity that there were only three possible sizes or scales of plant that could be built. In practice, there are typically many more possible plant sizes than just three. Figure 9-5 illustrates this situation. In addition, cost studies have shown that in many industries there may be a number of efficient plant sizes rather than just one.

For the example of Figure 9-5a, plant scales 7, 8, 9, 10, 11 and 12 all offer about the same average production costs in the neighbourhood of capacity. Therefore, plant scales 7, 8, 9, 10, 11 and 12 are equally efficient in terms of average cost. Plant scale 7 would be the smallest plant to take advantage of the available economies of scale and be efficient in this sense. Plant scale 7 would therefore typically be called a **minimum efficient scale** (*MES*) plant size, in the sense that any smaller plant would have higher average costs and not take advantage of all possible economies of scale efficiencies.

Economists often draw the long-run average cost curve (*LAC*) representing the many possible plant sizes as a smooth line such as that in Figure 9-5b. Strictly speaking, this implies that a continuum of plant sizes can be designed, with very small differences among them. Both *LAC* curves in Figure 9-5 are drawn "L-shaped." This is the case as long as the plant expansion does not run into diseconomies of scale. This shape of the *LAC* curve does not mean diseconomies of scale will never occur; it simply indicates that the plants presently operating have not yet reached the size at which they would be "too large."

A number of studies have shown that many

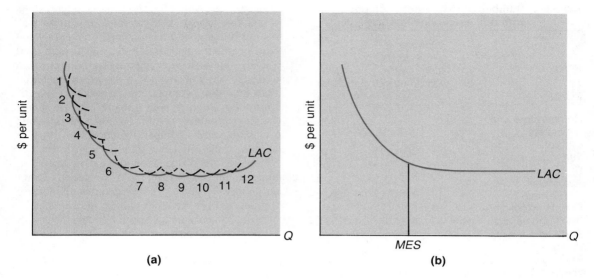

Fig. 9-5 Cost patterns and minimum efficient scale

(a) Diagrammatical representation of cost structures for 12 plant sizes. Available economies of scale are exhausted with the plant size described by cost curve number 7 (the minimum efficient plant size, or *MES*).

(b) A stylized representation of the long-run average cost curve (*LAC*) generated by the 12 plants in graph (a).

Canadian industries operate within plants that do not take full advantage of economies of scale (i.e. the plants are smaller than the *MES* size for the industry). Table 9-2 shows one estimate of the number of *MES* plants in various industries that the Canadian market could support in comparison with the actual number of plants that were in existence in 1968. For example, the domestic petroleum products market could support about 6 efficient (*MES*) refinery plants. In fact, there were 41 refineries, indicating that average unit costs were higher than they could have been if there had been fewer refineries.

The fact that so many small (and inefficient) plants have been able to operate and survive can be explained in part by tariff protection against import competition, by various government subsidies and support measures, and by oligopolistic collusive behaviour in the industries concerned.

One indication of the oligopolistic nature of much of Canadian industry is the degree of business or corporate concentration as measured by the percentage of an industry's sales, which are accounted for by the four largest firms. This information for Canadian manufacturing industries was reported earlier in Table 7-1 where we saw that in

Table 9-2 Number of MES plants compatible with domestic consumption, 1968

Industry	Number of MES plants compatible with domestic consumption	Actual number of plants
Refrigerators and freezers	0.7	33
Cigarettes	1.3	21
Integrated steel	2.6	44
Breweries	2.9	48
Automobile storage batteries	4.6	24
Petroleum refining	6.0	41
Paint and varnish	6.3	159
Portland cement	6.6	24
Bricks	32.0	78
Bakeries	40.8	2275
Nonrubber shoes	59.2	206

Source: *Report of the Royal Commission on Corporate Concentration* (Ottawa: Minister of Supply and Services Canada, 1978). Reproduced with permission.

Technology in some industries exhibits substantial economies of scale. Minimum efficient size of plant may be such that only a few plants are needed to satisfy the whole Canadian market for the product.

numerous markets the four largest firms accounted for more than 50% of total sales volume. In some cases the four largest firms dominated over 90% of the market. The 1978 Royal Commission on Corporate Concentration concluded that such concentration of production activity was not restricted to the manufacturing sector but in fact was widespread throughout the Canadian economy. Even so, the Commission commented upon the small scale of firms in Canada relative to *MES* and relative to similar operations in the U.S. and other industrialized countries. The Commission concluded that to take greater advantage of economies of scale it may be required to allow Canadian industries to become even more highly concentrated than at present by permitting mergers and growth of larger firms. Larger lower cost firms means greater efficiency and possible benefits for consumers. On the other hand, greater economic concentration implies greater potential oligopoly

power and possible allocative inefficiencies from the exploitation of such power. The Commission concluded that government competition policy and possibly government regulation could be employed to avert abuses in this regard. The Commission advocated an objective of *workable competition* rather than price competition. Workable competition implies large enough firms to take advantage of scale opportunities within a framework designed to make the firms competitive enough to pass on the bulk of the efficiency gains to consumers.

Similarly the Royal Commission on the Economic Union and Development Prospects for Canada, in its 1985 Report, concluded that an increase in producers' concentration in a market can be harmful, but only under special circumstances. It will not have adverse consequences if the industry is exposed to international competition or if there are only minimal barriers to entry. A major thrust of the Commission's policy recommendations in this regard is liberalization of international trade, especially a move toward a freer trade between Canada and the United States. This matter will be explored in greater detail in Chapter 11.

Most production processes are characterized by economies of scale, that is, a decline in the per unit costs as the size of a plant or a firm increases. The plant size at which economies of scale become largely exhausted is called Minimum Efficient Size (*MES*). In many Canadian industries, a sizeable share of production takes place in plants smaller than *MES*.

Learning by Doing

Economies of scale are cost efficiencies that may be had by a firm or plant producing a reasonably high volume per production period (day, month or year). Another source of efficiency may be attainable by gradually learning about the production process, ironing out production snags, making adaptations to improve worker productivity. Such efficiencies as these result from **learning by doing** the production activity time and time again, and are likely to be greater, the greater the total length of time production has been taking place. In other words, such efficiencies are likely to depend on the cumulative volume that the firm has produced (and not just the rate of production or volume per year).

Learning by doing economies are not restricted to manufacturing operations. Efficiencies of transport, marketing and transacting of financial arrangements generally improve as producers gain more experience in handling their particular good or service.

Economies of Scope

A conceptually different type of efficiency originates in situations where two or more products or services interact. **Economies of scope** exist whenever it is cheaper to produce two or more products in one firm rather than separately by different (specialized) firms. There are two main sources of economies of scope: first, employment of a common fixed factor and spreading of fixed costs among the two or more products; second, existence of complementarities in production among the two or more products. For example, commercial airlines take advantage of economies of scope when a passenger airplane also carries freight. Or a financial institution may gain economies of scope if it adds, for example, personal savings accounts operations to its mortgage business (or vice versa).

Mergers and Specialization Agreements

The desirability of preserving the benefits of economies of scale while safeguarding competition has been recognized in the new Canadian competition legislation. (For a comprehensive review of the legislation, see Appendix 9B.) The *Competition Act*, passed by Parliament in June 1986, created a new expert body, the *Competition Tribunal*. Among its responsibilities is to decide whether specific mergers are in the public interest and to register and approve specialization agreements among competing firms.

Specialization agreement allows two or more firms to agree that each of them would produce only a part of a product range, instead of both (all) firms competing in the whole range of products. Such agreements make it possible for each participating firm to handle a smaller number of product lines, thereby achieving longer product runs. This reduces the time (and cost) required for retooling and other adjustments associated with product changeovers.

The new approach to **merger policy** may be illustrated by the following example. Suppose the pattern of economies of scale in a particular industry is characterized by the *LAC* curve in Figure 9-6. Let us suppose further that the Competition Tribunal receives notification of two proposed mergers: the first merger between Firm 1 and Firm 2, and the second merger between Firm 3 and Firm 4. Assume that each firm operates with a single plant.

From Figure 9-6, it is evident that Firms 1 and 2 operate with plants of smaller size than *MES*. Since economies of scale have not yet been exploited, a merger is likely to improve efficiency. Firms 3 and 4, on the other hand, operate with plants which are already of efficient size. A merger between them would thus not lead to a further reduction in unit costs and may not be in the public interest. (However, factors other than economies of scale are also considered by the Competition Tribunal. For details, see Appendix 9B.)

9-4 LONG-RUN INVESTMENT DECISIONS

The decision concerning the appropriate scale of plant is an investment decision of the firm. The first thing to emphasize is that in practice future long-run demand and costs are not known with certainty. Therefore, the firm must attempt to make rough estimates of such information when deciding whether or not to undertake physical expansion or contraction. Second, rather than attempting to directly equate *LMR* and *LMC*, management more commonly uses a technique known as **net present value analysis**. It is important, however, to understand that the net present value approach and that of equating *LMR* and *LMC* are equivalent. Although in many respects the net present value technique is more useful for management decisions concerning investment, the *LMR-LMC* framework is most useful for analysis of the effect of market supply and demand shocks as well as for questions involving the efficient allocation of resources.

In practice, a handful of management personnel may sit down around a table and discuss an investment proposal, without putting pen to paper. In the discussion, some managers may ask for a rough projection of demand that the firm might expect over the next few years. The answer may even

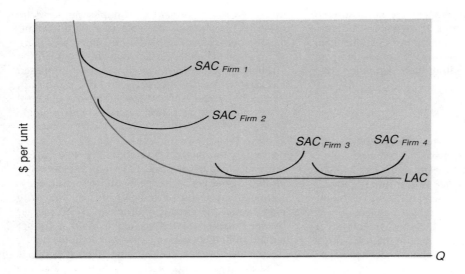

Fig. 9-6 Evaluation of benefits from merger

A merger between Firm 1 and Firm 2 would have potential social benefits, since economies of scale would result. A merger between Firm 3 and Firm 4, on the other hand, would not contribute to lower per-unit costs.

come back in dollar sales rather than in number of units. From this information they would estimate the expenditure on plant required to provide such a dollar volume. Finally, they might attempt to guess at the annual operating profit (excluding financial expenses) that could be expected from the sales forecast and compare it with the estimated annual dollar cost of capital funds required to finance the new plant. If the former is expected to be considerably larger than the latter they might decide to go ahead.

The above could certainly be termed a "guess-and-by-golly" method of investment analysis. Do not think, though, that such discussions do not happen, or that a considerable amount of business investment is not undertaken on the basis of just that sort of analysis. Of course, most companies have engineering staffs, which are continually advising management on the most efficient combinations of labour and capital.

There are also many instances — and a growing number of them — of business firms carrying on more sophisticated analysis for investment proposals, including the most appropriate scale of plant. The type of analysis often done is equivalent to that presented above but more general in certain respects. In the following example, simplifying assumptions will be made initially so that the parallel may be seen between this type of analysis and the type presented above.

Net Present Value Analysis

A popular technique for analyzing the profitability of investment proposals is known as the net present value method. Unfortunately, the concepts involved in a full discussion of net present value calculations require more space than can be allotted in this book. Usually this topic is discussed in the subject of finance. The relevant calculations are sketched below to show what is done in practice as well as the connection between this type of analysis and the standard economic *LMR* = *LMC* approach.

Suppose a firm has the opportunity to undertake a plant expansion at a cost of $50 000, which will permanently increase its annual net operating income (before the cost of capital funds is considered) by $8000. If the cost of capital funds is 10% per annum the firm would have been willing to pay up to $80 000 for the plant expansion — because to invest $80 000 would require $8000 annual financing costs (10% × $80 000), which would just eat up the entire expected increase in net operating income.

Because the firm is willing to pay a maximum of $80 000 for the plant expansion, that is what the investment is worth to the firm. However, the firm can acquire the plant expansion for only $50 000. Therefore, it is customary to refer to such an investment proposal as having a net present value (*NPV*) to the firm of $30 000 (i.e. $80 000 − $50 000).

Noting that the maximum amount that a firm would be willing to pay for an investment ($80 000 in this case) can be calculated by dividing the annual operating profit of the investment by the cost of capital ($8000 ÷ 10%), we can write the expression for the net present value of an investment as[2]

$$NPV = \frac{\text{annual operating profit from the investment}}{\text{cost of capital (\%)}} - \text{initial investment (\$)}$$

which may be rewritten as

$$NPV = \frac{\text{annual operating profit from the investment} - \text{cost of capital (\%)} \times \text{initial investment}}{\text{cost of capital (\%)}}$$

The numerator is the expression for annual economic profit. Therefore

$$NPV = \frac{\text{annual economic profit from the investment}}{\text{cost of capital (\%)}}$$

From this development, it may be seen that a proposal with an annual (economic) profit will also have a positive net present value. Also, the popular management technique of choosing investments that have the largest positive net present values is consequently equivalent to maximizing (economic) profit, which is what would be done by attempting to equate long-run marginal revenue with long-run marginal cost. If net present value is really maximized, then the scale of plant and level of output produced is that for which *LMR* = *LMC*.

The net present value technique is very flexible and can handle cases in which profit flows are not expected to be of exactly the same value each year, cases in which the firm does not intend to replace plant and equipment each year as they depreciate, and also cases in which the profit flows are not expected to continue indefinitely. Today, present value analysis is possibly one of the most widely used economic tools of business.

In making their investment decisions, business firms frequently employ the net present value analysis. If applied correctly, this method results in the choice of plant scale and level of output which equate long-run marginal revenue and long-run marginal costs and thus maximize the firm's profit.

9-5 LONG-RUN PROFITS AND EFFICIENCY

Earlier in this chapter we considered the long-run determination of firm size and output volume. Although our illustration was within a monopoly context, the basic approach is independent of market structure. To maximize profit over the long haul, a firm must attempt to produce with the most efficient (least cost) labour-capital production technique, at that output level where long-run marginal revenue equals long-run marginal cost. However, depending on market structure, the long-run position of the average firm may or may not tend toward minimum average cost and zero profit. To examine this question, let us consider the **long-run equilibrium** profit and cost characteristics of firms within both *purely competitive* and *monopoly* markets.

As we saw in Chapter 8, profitability or lack thereof is the key determinant of long-run industrial growth or decline. If one industry is more

---

2. An implicit assumption here is that annual expenditures are made for replacement of the machinery and plant as they wear out (depreciate) each year.

profitable relative to other industries, existing firm owners will want to invest their funds in physical additions to their companies in the form of new land, buildings and equipment while outside investors will be encouraged to create new firms within the industry. Economic profits provide the *market signal* to attract economic resources from less profitable industries toward more profitable industries. Such resource transfer is necessary to provide an efficient allocation of scarce resources (land, labour and capital) throughout the economy.

If there are no barriers preventing industrial expansion, whenever abnormally high rates of return are earned in an existing industry the entry of new investors will lead to an overall increase in supply and have the effect of driving the market price down, eventually to such a level that economic profits disappear and only a normal rate of return is earned on invested funds. At this point, there will be no further incentive for the industry to expand, and the industry may be said to be in a state of long-run equilibrium. This process is what we

would expect to take place in a purely competitive industry where, by definition, there is a standard product, many producers and easy entry to and exit from the industry. In a monopoly situation, however, since by definition the firm is the sole producer of the particular product, we might expect that there would exist various barriers preventing new firms from entering the market. As explained in Chapter 7, among the most important barriers to entry are brand loyalty, cost advantage for existing producers, patents and government regulations.

Long-Run Equilibrium: Pure Competition

Figure 9-7 illustrates a purely competitive market structure and a typical firm with the relevant portions of its unit cost curves which comprise the firm's long-run cost structure. The firm is currently operating at scale 2 (with cost structure SMC_2, SAC_2). The firm's profit-maximizing output level is shown to be Q_1, at which economic profits are

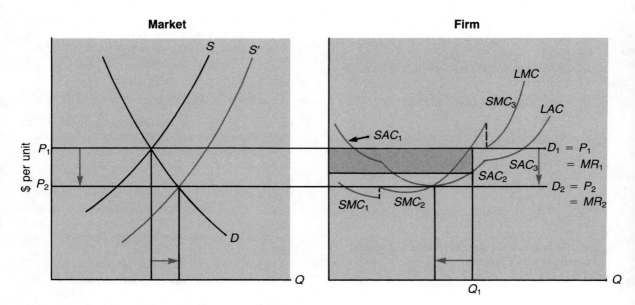

Fig. 9-7 Long-run purely competitive equilibrium

The original market demand and supply curves *D* and *S* in the left-hand diagram determine price P_1 at which a typical firm makes economic profit. The existence of economic profit attracts entry, shifting the market supply curve to *S'*, driving the price down to P_2 and establishing a long-run equilibrium with zero economic profit and production at minimum of *LAC*.

earned (represented by the shaded area). The economic profit implies that the owners of the firm are earning a rate of return on their invested funds which exceeds the rate of return that could be earned elsewhere with a comparable risk. Outside investors, seeing this profit situation, will thus be attracted to start new business firms within this industry. This action in the long run increases the market volume supplied at each price level (the *S* curve shifts toward *S'*) and reduces the market price. Although the entry of new firms causes an overall increase in market volume, the market price reduction induces each original firm in the long run to reduce its output level and scale of operations since there are now more firms in the industry. As long as economic profits remain, this process will continue. The erosion of all economic profit will finally halt the entry of new firms. In Figure 9-7, the zero economic profit situation occurs when the market price is such that the demand curve facing the typical firm is just tangent to (just touches) the long-run average cost curve.

Long-run equilibrium within a purely competitive industry is characterized by zero economic profits. Each firm produces at a volume that takes full advantage of all economies of scale and yields minimum average costs.

Long-Run Equilibrium: Imperfect Competition

Within an oligopoly or a monopoly industry, with barriers preventing entry by new firms, there is no comparable mechanism to eliminate economic profits and force the industry to operate at minimum average cost. For example, Figure 9-8 illustrates two feasible long-run positions for an imperfectly competitive firm. In the first instance (Figure 9-8a), the firm operates at a scale that does not exhaust all economies of scale opportunities (since $Q_1 < Q_0$) while in the second case (Figure 9-8b), the firm operates at a scale beyond the minimum average cost volume (since $Q_3 > Q_2$). Since the firm is presently maximizing profit, and

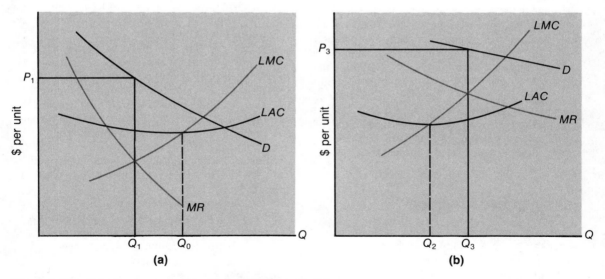

(a)   **(b)**

Fig. 9-8 Possible long-run monopoly equilibrium positions

(a) A monopoly firm in long-run equilibrium, in this case, maximizes profits by producing output (Q_1) smaller than that which corresponds to minimum *LAC* (output Q_0).

(b) A monopoly firm in a long-run equilibrium, in this case, maximizes profits by producing output (Q_3) larger than that which corresponds to minimum *LAC* (output Q_2).

there are barriers preventing entry into the industry by other firms, either case represents a possible long-run equilibrium situation.

Contestable Markets

A rather new development in microeconomic theory of market structures is based on the observation that some markets may be competitive, even though they are highly concentrated, and significant economies of scale are available. Such markets are **contestable**, in the sense that the possibility of "hit-and-run entry" forces firms in the market to operate in a cost-efficient manner and earn zero economic profits in long-run equilibrium. This outcome is only possible if both entry and exit are free, that is, entry into the market does not require any investment outlays or other entry costs (such as, for example, substantial licensing fees) which could not be recovered at the time of exit from the industry. One example of virtually costless entry and exit is the airline business, where a firm established in one market can enter and exit another market (airline route) without significant entry costs. Another example is the financial services sector, where banks have entered the mortgage lending business, trust companies entered the business of deposit operations (savings accounts for general public) and several types of financial institutions may be able to enter the stockbrokering business — all without significant entry costs. The contestable market theory therefore suggests that criteria such as concentration and existence of economies of scale are not sufficient in categorizing markets into purely competitive and imperfectly competitive.

9-6 MARKET SHOCKS

Until now our analysis of the effects of market shocks on price and output has been restricted to the short run. That is, we have assumed that the scale of operations within the industry remains fixed. We now wish to extend our analysis by considering not only the short-run market impact of supply and demand oriented events but also the long-run implication involving industrial growth or decline.

The analysis of longer-run effects of market

shocks depends critically upon whether or not there exist barriers preventing entry into the particular industry in question. We will consider the two extreme cases of pure competition and monopoly. In the first instance, there are no barriers to entry, and in the second instance such barriers exist.

Demand Shock

(i) Pure Competition

Let us suppose for convenience sake that a purely competitive industry is in long-run equilibrium with each firm earning a zero economic profit, when there occurs a sudden and permanent increase in product demand at each and every price level. The increase in demand might first be noticed through unplanned inventory rundowns by existing firms, which will thereby be induced to expand production. The increase in output will necessitate an increase in employment that, within the constraints imposed by a fixed plant base, will induce a drop in the marginal product of labour and thus higher marginal production costs. Even though it means asking for higher prices to meet the higher marginal costs, it will be profitable to expand output, since the demand expansion means consumers are willing to pay higher prices. A new *short-run equilibrium* will be attained when production has expanded to such a level that the higher marginal costs just match the new higher price level. The situation is shown in Figure 9-9. Market demand increases from D to D' causing the market price to rise from P_0 to P_1 and the demand facing each firm to rise correspondingly. In the short run, the firm expands output from Q_0 to Q_1 within its particular scale of operations (as reflected by the unit cost structure SMC_1, SAC_1 in Figure 9-9b).

The short-run increase in profitability means that firms are now earning positive economic profits (shaded area in Figure 9-9b). In other words, the firms' owners are earning a rate of return on their invested funds that exceeds that which can be earned elsewhere. These economic profits will encourage new investors to create their own firms and enter the industry. Entry of new suppliers means that a greater volume of output will be produced at each and every price level. (The market supply curve shifts to the right. This *long-run market supply shift* is shown explicitly in

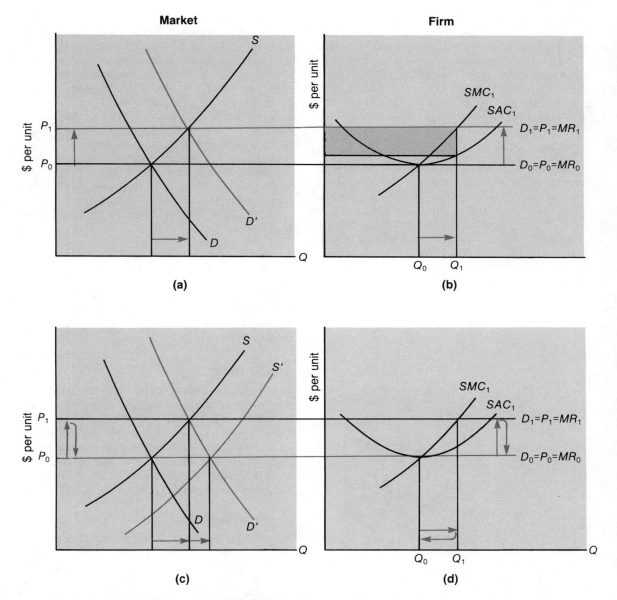

Fig. 9-9 **Short-run and long-run effects of demand expansion under pure competition**

A shift in demand curve raises the market price (part (a)), and a typical firm temporarily makes economic profit (part (b)). In the long run, as new firms enter the industry in response to economic profit, supply curve shifts to the right (part (c)), driving down the price and eliminating economic profit (part (d)).

Figure 9-9c.) The increased competition thus lowers the market price eventually to a level consistent once again with zero economic profits (Figure 9-9d). In the long run, therefore, each firm is producing the same volume as originally and earning just a normal return on invested funds. The long-run increase in market production in this case is provided entirely by the new firms.

(ii) Monopoly

As we saw in Chapter 6, we expect the increase in market demand to make it profitable in the short run for a monopolist to expand output and raise the market price (see Figure 9-10). In the longer run, if the higher volume of output could be more cheaply produced by having a larger fixed asset base (larger scale), then the monopolist would expand its physical facilities. This action would mean a dampen-

ing in the price rise or even lower prices if sizeable economies of scale are realized. It is also possible that, as output expands, the firm can obtain its inputs at lower prices (volume discounts from suppliers). For both of these reasons, the *long-run supply curve may be downward sloping*, that is, price drops as more is supplied.

An important difference between the purely competitive and monopoly cases concerns economic profit. The increased short-run profit that the monopolist would experience from the demand expansion is not eroded in the long run by new entrants if significant entry barriers exist. In fact, the longer-run adjustment by the monopolist to a larger, more efficient physical base will even enhance profits.

An increase in demand leads to an increase in profits above the normal level. In a purely competitive industry, economic profits will be competed away in the long run, because of new entry. In a monopolistic industry with barriers to entry, economic profits may persist even in the long-run equilibrium.

Supply Shock

The analysis of supply shock depends to a somewhat greater extent on the nature of the shock than does the analysis of demand shock. We consider the following two possible supply events: an increase in industry wage rates and an increase in interest rates. For simplicity we will restrict our analysis here to the purely competitive situation and leave the monopoly case for the problem set.

(i) Wage Rate Increases

An increase in industry wage rates in a purely competitive situation raises marginal and average production costs at every output level. Higher marginal production costs throughout the industry will cause an increase in market prices and a reduced volume of output produced and sold (see Figures 9-11a and 9-11b). In the short run, the extent of the increase in market price will depend upon the elasticity of demand, but unless market demand is quite price insensitive, the market price will rise by less than average cost. This means (as we would have expected from the outset) that a wage increase causes the average firm within the

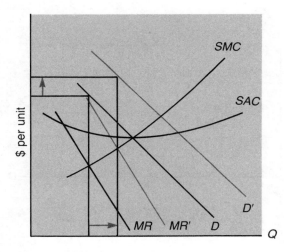

Fig. 9-10 Effects of demand expansion under monopoly

As the monopolist's demand curve and the associated marginal revenue curve shift to the right, profit maximization requires that both price and output be raised.

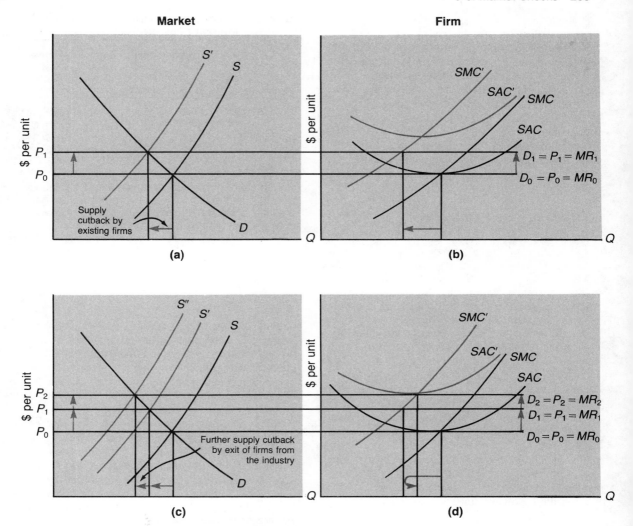

**Fig. 9-11 Short-run and long-run effects of a wage increase under
pure competition**

An industry-wide increase in wage rates raises the market price and reduces
output (part (a)), because the production costs of all firms in the industry increase
and the firms' marginal and average cost curves shift upwards (part (b)). Some
firms suffer economic losses and in the long run exit from the industry, shifting the
supply curve further to the left (part (c)). Exits continue until market price rises sufficiently so that the remaining firms experience no economic losses in long-run
equilibrium (part (d)).

industry to experience short-run economic losses $(P_1 < SAC')$.[3]

In the longer run, the short-run losses will mean an exit from the industry by some firms whose owners will invest their funds elsewhere.

Fewer suppliers in the longer run mean even less market output and higher market prices (Figure 9-11c). The new long-run equilibrium would be characterized by a situation in which exit of firms has caused the market price eventually to rise by the full amount of the average unit cost increase. Such a price rise is necessary to remove economic losses in the long run (see Figure 9-11d).[4]

(ii) Interest Rate Increases

Suppose there is a general increase in interest rates. This means that firms have to pay a greater fixed annual cost to borrow funds for the purpose of financing their physical asset base (plant, machinery and equipment). Since the owners of the firms would now be able to earn a higher rate of return by depositing their funds in savings accounts or by purchasing bonds, the annual accounting profit required to provide a normal return on investment will also have increased. In short, each firm's annual fixed financing costs (cost of capital in annual dollar terms) will have increased. Although these aspects will increase the firm's average short-run cost of producing any volume of output, they do not influence short-run marginal cost. The largest components of short-run marginal cost include labour and materials, neither of which are influenced in the short run by higher interest rates. Because this point is important, it is illustrated in the following numerical example.

Table 9-3 shows the major impact that rising interest rates have on short-run cost structure. For simplicity, costs for only two possible annual

Table 9-3 Effect on cost structure of a rise in interest rates

Q (units per period)	Fixed cost ($ per period)	Variable cost ($ per period)	Total cost ($ per period)	Average cost ($ per unit)	Marginal cost ($ per unit)
100	1000 (1400)*	500 (500)	1500 (1900)	15 (19)	— —
101	1000 (1400)	505 (505)	1505 (1905)	15.05 (19.05)	5 5

* Bracketed numbers reflect cost figures after interest rates rise

An increase in interest rates is assumed to affect only the plant financing costs. In other words, only the fixed costs and the total costs increase, but variable and marginal costs are unaffected.

output volumes of 100 and 101 units are shown. Momentarily focusing on the original cost figures (unbracketed), notice that the fixed costs including plant financing do not vary with short-run volume but remain constant at $1000 per year. Variable labour and materials costs increase from $500 at $Q = 100$ units per year to $505 at $Q = 105$ units per year. The original marginal cost of producing the 101st unit each year thus equals $5. Next, consider a rise in interest rates, which increases the fixed annual plant financing costs to $1400 per year but which has no impact on materials or labour costs. Total and average costs of producing at either volume increase because of the rise in fixed cost, but since variable costs are uninfluenced, so too is marginal cost, which remains at $5 for production of the 101st unit.

Since the impact of an interest rate rise on fixed annual financing costs of the firm's physical capital has no influence on the firm's short-run marginal cost structure, there is no effect on market supply or therefore on market price. The rise in average cost combined with unchanged market price implies that the increased plant financing costs are not passed on to consumers in the short run, but that instead firms absorb them all and incur economic losses. The market and firm situations are depicted in Figures 9-12a and 9-12b.

---

3. If demand is completely price insensitive it may be shown that an increase in wage rates can lead to an increase in short-run profitability within a purely competitive market. This counter-intuitive case does not occur if demand is relatively price sensitive or if the market exhibits some degree of monopoly power. Practically speaking, then, we may disregard this unusual possibility.

4. This conclusion should be modified slightly. In the long run, the market price would not rise by the full amount of the initial increase in average cost since, faced with an increase in the price of labour, each firm would in the long run turn toward mechanization and labour-saving production techniques.

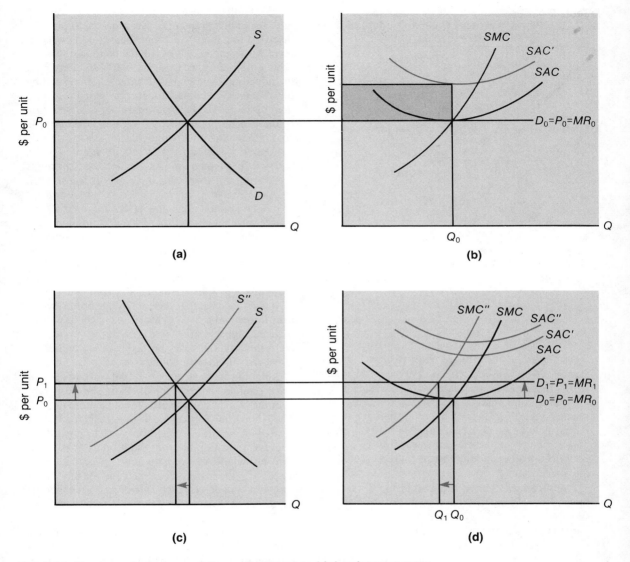

Fig. 9-12 Short-run industry and firm adjustment to higher interest rates

(a) Assuming that an increase in interest rates affects only the plant financing costs, the market price and quantity remain unchanged.

(b) At the level of the firm, marginal cost is not affected, but fixed cost rises and the average cost curve shifts upwards, causing firms to suffer economic losses.

(c) If, however, the increase in interest rates also raises the cost of carrying inventories and accounts receivable, the marginal cost also rises and the industry supply curve shifts to the left.

(d) At the level of the firm, both the marginal and the average cost curves shift upwards.

Table 9-4 Effect on accounts receivable and inventory financing costs of a rise in interest rates

Interest rate (% per annum)	Q (units per period)	Accounts receivable and inventory balances ($)	Interest cost of accounts receivable and inventory balances ($ per period)	Marginal interest costs ($ per unit)
10 (20)	100	1000	100 (200)	—
10 (20)	101	1100	110 (220)	10 (20)

An increase in interest rates is assumed to raise the carrying costs of inventories and accounts receivable. As a result, the firm's marginal costs increase.

In a purely competitive market, the industry supply curve is determined by the component firms' marginal cost structures, which so far are unaltered. The market price, therefore, remains unchanged (at P_0) as does the representative firm's output volume (at Q_0). Since the short-run average cost structure has shifted upward to SAC', there now occurs an economic loss at Q_0 represented by the shaded area.

Our treatment above is incomplete. So far we have neglected the fact that the level of some assets (notably accounts receivable and inventory) do vary, even in the short run, directly with output. For example, if a firm increases its production and sales, although it will not increase its plant base in the short run, it will carry a higher inventory and accounts receivable level, both of which must be financed. Consequently, interest costs on these two assets are properly treated as part of marginal production cost. For a numerical illustration, consider Table 9-4.

A volume of 100 units per year is assumed to require the financing of $1000 worth of accounts receivable and inventory, whereas a volume of 101 units per year is assumed to require financing of

$1100 worth of these two assets. At a 10% interest rate, the added financing costs required to produce the 101st unit is $10 and contributes, along with labour and materials, toward the marginal cost of producing the 101st unit. At a 20% interest rate, the added financing costs of producing and selling the 101st unit become $20. Increased interest rates thereby raise the short-run marginal cost structure of the firm's operations by increasing the carrying cost of accounts receivable and inventory.

Figures 9-12c and 9-12d modify Figures 9-12a and 9-12b to take into account added accounts receivable and inventory financing charges. Such charges raise short-run average costs of the firm by a greater amount than the effect of interest rate charge on financing costs of fixed plant alone (for example to SAC'' instead of to SAC' as Figure 9-12b assumed). Also, since these charges raise marginal production costs for each firm (to SMC''), industry supply will be affected as shown. Taking these aspects into account, although we expect higher interest rates to be mostly absorbed by the firm in the short run, to some extent there will be induced higher market prices, reduced production and sales.[5] In any case, in the short run higher interest rates imply economic losses for the firm.

Although interest rates may put only minor upward pressure on industry prices in the short run, over the longer haul the effect will be more drastic. The short-run economic losses analyzed above imply that the firm's owners are not earning as high a rate of return on their invested funds as is available elsewhere in the economy. In reaction, the assets of some firms will be sold and the number of suppliers will decline, which will mean less market supply at each and every possible price level and therefore a higher resulting market price. Ultimately, the price will rise enough to eliminate the economic losses and thereby establish a new long-run equilibrium. In this new long-run equilibrium, the higher market price will mean a reduced overall volume of industry output.

---

5. There may also be a temporary *inventory unloading effect*, which we have neglected. In the short run, firms may attempt to escape some of their increased inventory financing costs by reducing their inventory levels. To get rid of this unwanted stock quickly may require firms to initiate temporary "sales" prices. Once the more appropriate inventory levels are reached, such sales prices would be removed and the above-mentioned effects would dominate.

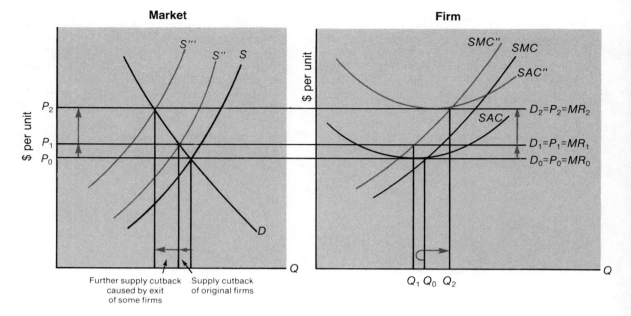

Fig. 9-13 Long-run industry and firm adjustment to higher interest rates under pure competition

An increase in interest rates raises the cost of carrying inventory and accounts receivable of all firms. In the short run, the industry supply curve shifts to S'', price rises to P_1 and the firms' cost curves shift to SAC'' and SMC''. Firms are suffering economic losses, some of them exit in the long run, and market supply curve shifts to S''', driving the price to its long-run equilibrium level, P_2.

Comparison of the short- and long-run equilibrium situations within the industry and representative firm is shown in Figure 9-13. In the short run, the market price rises from P_0 to P_1 as interest rate increases force up marginal costs of financing receivables and inventory. The firms experience losses (since $P_1 < SAC''$) and begin to leave the industry. Exit of the financially weaker firms further reduces market supply (to S''') and forces prices even higher (to P_2).[6]

An industry-wide increase in wage rates causes an upward shift in the market supply curve, a reduction in quantity supplied, and an increase in price, both in the short run and in the long run. An increase in interest rates has no short-run effect on market price and quantity if it merely raises the plant financing costs. If the increase in interest rates also affects the cost of inventories and accounts receivable, it will have both a short-run and a long-run effect on market price and quantity.

6. We are assuming that demand within the industry is not directly affected by higher interest rates. This would be roughly the case for most industries where the consumer does not have to borrow to finance a purchase. On the other hand, the demand for some products is highly interest sensitive. Consider the housing and automobile industries, for instance. Any increase in the general level of interest rates has a significant direct dampening effect on the demand for houses and cars.

As a result, within those industries for which the cost of financing a purchase plays a major role for the average purchaser, an interest rate increase will reduce product demand at each and every market price, thereby tending to cause lower market prices and output volume. In the longer run, the supply effects will work to reduce output even further, as explained above, and tend to offset partly or completely reverse the short-run demand-induced price drop.

CONCLUDING REMARKS

The firm presumably wishes to maximize its profit over the long term — that is, its long-run profit. In effect, it may approach the problem in a very rough fashion, relying on rules of thumb and hunches for decision making. Conversely, it may use sophisticated tools such as net present value analysis, as larger concerns do. Most likely, though, the firm does not draw the sorts of *MR-MC* diagrams that we drew in this chapter. Nevertheless, if it is attempting to maximize its profit, either via "cost-volume-profit" or "net present value" analyses, the firm is acting as though it has drawn such diagrams in its attempt to search out the $MR = MC$ point.

Further, for analysis of the effects of many external events (for example, when considering the effect of market demand and supply shocks) a diagrammatic approach is useful.

KEY TERMS AND CONCEPTS

capital intensive
labour intensive
economies of scale
diseconomies of scale
long-run average cost
long-run marginal cost
capacity
minimum efficient scale

learning by doing
economies of scope
specialization agreement
merger policy
net present value analysis
long-run equilibrium
contestable markets

PROBLEMS

Problem 1

a) Assume that accurate cost and demand data are available and that you have already chosen the best advertising budget, quality of product, packaging, and so on, with only the volume of output and pricing decisions left to make. How would you attempt to maximize profit by these decisions? What difficulties are you likely to face in making the appropriate decision?

b) Explain why the pricing and volume choice is typically a single decision.

c) In what situation would the firm be unable to choose its price?

Problem 2

A company had the following expenses during a particular year: property taxes = $5000; depreciation of building = $15 000; bond interest = $10 000; sales taxes = $25 000; materials = $500 000; accountants' fees = $2500; assembly line workers' wages = $200 000.

a) Which of the above would generally be fixed within the (i) short run? (ii) long run?

b) If property taxes rose substantially, how would this event affect the company's profit-maximizing price or output level in the (i) short run? (ii) long run?

Problem 3

The following diagram is for a particular company.

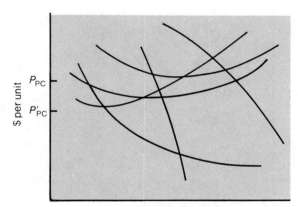

No. of units per week

a) Label the diagram with the following: average variable cost (*AVC*), average fixed cost (*AFC*), demand (*D*), average cost (*AC*), marginal revenue (*MR*), marginal cost (*MC*). Is this a picture of the firm's short-run or long-run cost structure, and how do you know?

b) Indicate on the diagram the maximum profit choice of output and price. Does the firm have any monopoly power? Explain. Label the firm's average revenue per unit of output curve.

c) Assuming the firm is instead a pure competitor and the market price is P_{PC}, indicate on the diagram how much the firm would choose to produce. Why would it want to produce at this level? Would the firm be earning an economic profit or loss? How much would the firm produce as a pure competitor if the price was instead P'_{PC}?

d) Might the firm in either case of part (c) (that is, for $P = P_{PC}$ or $P = P'_{PC}$) be earning an accounting profit? Explain.

Problem 4

Suppose the figure below represents the cost and demand situation facing a particular firm. It may effectively choose from among three possible physical scales as indicated by the numbers 1, 2 and 3 on the figure.

a) Indicate, either directly or on the graph or on one of your own making, the firm's long-run cost structure (long-run average and long-run marginal costs).

b) If the demand facing the firm is regarded as long term, what would be the profit-maximizing (i) scale of operations, (ii) price and (iii) output?

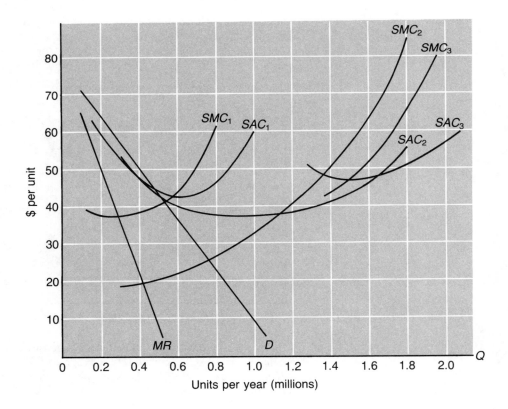

c) If the firm had already built scale 2 when faced with the indicated level of demand, what would be the best short-run price and output level for the firm? In this instance, what would be the longer run investment strategy of the firm?

d) Given long-run demand and cost conditions, would the firm in the long run operate at a minimum efficent scale? Suppose there was another firm in a similar demand and cost position within the industry. Briefly show how a merger between the two firms could lead to greater efficiencies and possibly lower prices for the consumer.

Problem 5

a) Explain what is meant by the following terms: economies of scale, diseconomies of scale and increasing returns to scale.

b) Explain why increasing returns to scale lead to economies of scale.

c) Explain the difference between economy of scale efficiencies and learning by doing efficiencies.

Problem 6

A new manufacturing technique is expected to require $100 000 of investment in new equipment. Maintenance expenditures of $5000 per year will keep it in good running order indefinitely. Production cost savings (excluding equipment maintenance considerations) are expected to be $13 000 per year. The firm has a cost of capital of 10%.

a) What is the annual economic profit from the investment in new equipment?

b) What is the net present value to the investment in new equipment?

c) Should the investment be undertaken?

d) At what cost of capital (%) would the investment be just a break-even proposition?

Problem 7

a) Explain briefly what circumstances could arise to allow firms within a purely competitive market to earn above normal rates of return on investment (economic profits) in a particular year.

b) Given part (a), explain briefly why it might nevertheless be more attractive from a firm's standpoint to be part of a tightly controlled oligopoly industry than to operate within a purely competitive market.

Problem 8

Suppose a particular industry is influenced by the following economic events:

  (i) an increase in wage rates
 (ii) an increase in excise taxes
(iii) an increase in import duties on an important necessary material input
 (iv) a reduction in interest rates

Explain briefly how each of the above events would be expected to influence the following variables in both the short and longer run: price, output, employment and profits (not necessarily in that order). Assume that the industry in question is imperfectly competitive.

CASES

Case 9-1

The article below discusses the economic viability of the Blue Jays baseball club in its early years of operation. The viability of the club as a pennant contender is not discussed.

The Financial Post

Blue Jays fly with financial firepower

By JAMIE WAYNE

DON'T TELL Peter Bavasi, executive vice-president and general manager of the Toronto Blue Jays Baseball Club, that you can't make something from nothing.

When he was hired last June by the team's trio of owners — John Labatt Ltd., businessman Howard Webster, Canadian Imperial Bank of Commerce — the Blue Jays "as yet were unnamed, there was no front office, no players, or any bats and balls," Bavasi says. "There wasn't even a pencil or paper clip belonging to the organization. We had, if you'll pardon the expression, no nuthin'."

Now, just 10 months later, the Blue Jays are officially into their first season (Opening day: April 7) in the American League. In that time Bavasi arranged and assembled:

- A 25-man player roster.
- A manager and nine coaching assistants.
- A five-man scouting staff.
- A farm system (Class A — Utica Blue Jays).
- Spring training, including a 25-game exhibition schedule.
- A leasing arrangement with the Canadian National Exhibition Stadium for 77 home dates.
- A grounds and maintenance crew to service the stadium.
- A concession contract with VS Services for refreshments.
- A radio contract with station CKFH and 17 affiliates throughout Ontario.
- A television contract with CBC (not yet completed) for 11 nationally televised games and five regional telecasts.

- A licensing contract with Irwin Toy Co.
- Advertising and promotional arrangements.
- A front office of 40.
- A part-time staff of 250.
- Playing equipment — baseballs, bats, uniforms.

Bavasi has been through league expansion once before, having helped start the San Diego (California) Padres franchise in 1969, and serving as that team's vice-president and general manager from 1973. His father, Buzzie Bavasi, was associated with the Brooklyn Dodgers organization for 17 years (for three of them general manager of the Montreal Royals of the International League), and Peter served as general manager of two Los Angeles Dodgers farm clubs after graduating from college.

That experience of course helped Bavasi set up the Blue Jays in such short time. But the job was also eased by what Bavasi calls "the financial firepower of our owners." Labatt, Webster and the Commerce have pumped in at least $10 million to get Blue Jays off the ground.

What's it cost to operate a major league baseball team? According to Bavasi, during the 1977–78 season about $4.5 million. But since it is an expansion team, for the Blue Jays in its early years there will be additional costs.

The biggest burden is the $7-million expansion-fee tab charged by the American League to its two newest members, Toronto and Seattle. (The Blue Jays will have paid off this substantial debt by May 31, Bavasi says, but the Seattle Mariners will have paid only $200 000.)

The greater part of the expansion-fee payment, $5.4 million, gave the Blue Jays the right to select 30 players from other clubs and valued by those clubs at $175 000 each, in a special intra-league expansion draft. The payment, however, does not include the cost of the contracts of each player. The rest of the payment, 1.6 million, is paid directly to the league and is channeled toward membership dues.

In addition, the Blue Jays are faced with capital start-up costs, which Bavasi estimates at least $2 million. The reason for this hefty payout is that the Blue Jays literally started from scratch. Besides the obvious cost of temporary and permanent office space, which represents 25% of this sum, the Blue Jays had to dole out $50 000 for balls and bats alone. But Bavasi says the greater part of the $2 million will go for advertising and promotion.

"In our early years, we will assume additional costs we feel are calculated expenses necessary to absorb in building a tradition," he says.

Buying a tradition may be more appropriate phrase.

For example, the Blue Jays will be flying full charter to and from road games. This will cost the club an additional $35 000, or 16% more than it would to fly commercial. And at the CNE Stadium, there will be a special lounge for the players' wives and children.

"Our best publicity in the early spring is going to be the Blue Jay players and their families," Bavasi says. "The message they deliver to the players around the league by word of mouth may turn out to be our most effective advertising tool."

On top of the substantial expansion fee and start-up costs, the Blue Jays must also contend with annual operating costs of approximately $4.5 million which, according to Bavasi, is the current league average. Included in this figure are:

- $1.7 million for salaries, wages and traveling.
- $1 million for player development (scouting, farm teams, and so on).
- $1 million for general administration and part-time help.

- $800 000 for maintenance, including staffing.

(The $4.5 million figure may be somewhat out of date because of the recent draft, and subsequent signing, of free agents. In 1976, for example, Joe Rudi, Bobby Grich and Don Baylor of the Oakland A's received a combined salary of about $175 000, not including bonuses. This year, since playing out their options and signing with the California Angels, their combined salaries total more than $500 000. Add another $1 millon in total signing bonuses and these three players alone take a substantial chunk out of the $4.5-million operating expense budget Bavasi cites.)

In total (expansion fee, start-up costs, operating expenses), it will cost close to $14 million for the Blue Jays to operate this year. However, since half this amount represents the expansion payment and may be amortized over several future accounting periods, the Blue Jays must, in fact, generate $7 million to break even.

That's what goes out. What comes in? Bavasi says league statistics show the average yearly revenue per team in the American League (based on one million attendance over a season) is $4.6 milion — $3 million from ticket sales, $900 000 from radio and television contracts, $600 000 from concessions, novelties, and publications, and $100 000 from promotional sponsors, scoreboard advertising, and so on.

Included in this $4.6-million figure are revenues from the sale of beer and from scoreboard advertising — both prohibited in Toronto by provincial law. Nevertheless, the Blue Jays will not suffer particularly: even without these sources of revenue, the team should have little trouble generating $7 million–$8 million this year.

The Blue Jays have already sold more than 8000 season tickets, putting the club second only to the Boston Red Sox in that department. With 77 home dates, and with an average ticket price of $4.25 (the sixth-highest ticket average in all of baseball), the Blue Jays already have banked $3 million from advance season-ticket sales.

Judging by the overwhelming success at the gate chalked up by Toronto's football Argos and the Maple Leafs of the National Hockey League, the Blue Jays hope to average at least 15 000 paying customers a game in the CNE's 40 000-seat stadium, providing the club with an additional $2 million in ticket revenue.

If a 15 000-per-game attendance is achieved, the Blue Jays would have 1.2 million attendance for the season and would pocket $5 million in ticket sales alone.

Add to that another $2.5 million in revenue from radio and television contracts, concessions, promotional sponsors, and an exclusive licensing contract with Irwin Toy Co., which Bavasi says will "yield an unspecified sum, but easily the most lucrative such contract in the history of baseball."

It's clear, then, the Blue Jays owners think they can generate the $7 million necessary to break even this year. In fact, they think they can turn a profit.

Not bad, if they're right, considering that less than 10 months ago the Blue Jays didn't even have a ball or a bat.

Disregard all possible tax considerations when answering the following questions.

a) List the costs and sources of revenue associated with the operation of a major league ball club. What is the error in including startup costs as a yearly operating expense? What is the correct way to view startup costs?

b) What is the Blue Jays' approximate annual dollar cost of capital funds (assume a 15% cost of capital)?

c) Construct a break-even chart for first-year Blue Jays' operation. The axes should be as shown below.

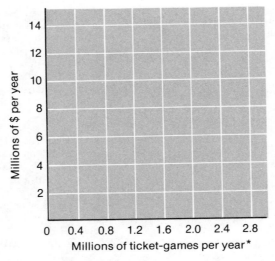

* One ticket-game represents one person's buying a ticket for one game. Therefore, for example, a season's ticket represents 77 ticket-games (as there are 77 home games) per year.

d) What is the Blue Jays' approximate break-even attendance per game?

e) Someone once said Toronto fans love losers. After 50 of 77 regular home dates, despite the worst record among the 26 major league franchises and being in last place in the American League East (44 games behind the division leader), the Blue Jays were averaging 24 000 tickets per game. On this basis (assuming this attendance figure holds true for the remainder of the season), approximate the Blue Jays' first-year accounting profit and economic profit.

f) On the basis of estimated first-year figures, what would be the approximate market value of the Blue Jays' club?

g) In February 1986, it was reported that the club "basically broke even," thanks to its participation in the American League playoffs. Its total revenues were about $35 million Canadian, and attendance for the regular season was about 2.5 million. However, the decline in value of the Canadian dollar against its U.S. counterpart hurt the club, since almost 70% of its expenses and only about 25% of its revenues were in U.S. funds. If the decline in Canadian dollar had been foreseen, how would it be reflected in the break-even analysis above?

Case 9-2

The Globe and Mail, Toronto

Lamp manufacturers brighten future by offering energy-saving products

By EDWARD CLIFFORD

Major lamp manufacturers are moving aggressively into the energy-saving field, offering offices, businesses and industries a new range of lamps and bulbs that promise both electrical and lighting efficiencies.

Their future seems bright. One of the new fluorescent lamps, for example, is rated at five or six watts less than the one it replaces. It costs about $1 more, but the light manufacturers claim that it pays for itself in lower power bills within a year to 18 months, giving it another 18 months to two years of expected life at a lower operating cost.

Management of the Toronto-Dominion Centre in Toronto was so impressed by these economics that they replaced every one of the 150 000 fluorescent lamps in the building complex last summer. Annual power consumption is expected to be reduced by about

3.5 million kilowatt hours, enough electricity to supply 450 homes for a year.

There are four major lamp manufacturers in Canada: Canadian General Electric Co. Ltd. and Philips Electronics Industries Ltd., both of Toronto; Westinghouse Canada Ltd. of Hamilton; and GTE Sylvania Ltd. of Montreal. All manufacture a line of low-energy lamps.

The typical low-energy lamp has a 35-watt rating, compared with the 40-watt lamp it is intended to replace. But it has a more efficient light output — about 81.5 lumens a watt, compared with the standard lamp's 78.75 lumens a watt. The typical contract price would be about $2.55 a lamp, compared with a standard lamp's price of $1.55, and in a typical office situation, it would consume about 96 cents less electricity in a year.

The low-power bulbs are an idea whose

time has come in most buildings since modern offices tend to be over-illuminated and a slightly lower light level is not noticed by most people. For those offices where the light level is already correct, the manufacturers produce a more expensive unit that offers the same energy savings without a loss of light.

The manufacturers also all offer such consulting services as cost analyses to customers, showing how their electrical bills can be cut by using one of the new lighting methods.

Like most equations, however, there are two sides to the calculation. If the lamp manufacturers earn more for their products and the building managers pay for them out of power savings, who then loses revenue? The answer, apparently, is the electric utilities. They advocate conservation of electricity but have high fixed costs that, in the short term, have little to do with the rate of electrical consumption.

In the most extreme case, if every electrical customer in Canada cut power consumption by 10 per cent the utilities would probably have to raise their rates by close to the same amount to compensate for lost revenue.

So, while energy-saving devices have cost benefits to the consumer, and may result in the utilities ultimately postponing system expansions, electrical rates will probably have to rise to make up for lost utility revenue.

But even this can be used as an argument in favor of installing such devices, since increased rates will be spread among all consumers. Those who have not installed energy-saving electrical equipment will be paying a penalty in the form of higher costs not offset by reduced rates of consumption.

In the case of the Toronto Dominion Centre, a switch to lower wattage lamps is expected to have another benefit — lower air-conditioning costs. Modern office buildings cost far more to cool than to heat and much of the heat that is generated in a building is from the lighting.

Changeover to the new lamps was a four-month job for a team of 20 students who worked through the nights removing the old lamps, cleaning the fixtures and lenses and installing the new lamps.

While the Toronto-Dominion will not discuss the cost of the new lamps or how long it expects to take to recover the cost of installation, it might be reasonable to estimate that it has a $70 000 labor bill and paid a $150 000 premium over the cost of regular lamps. If it pays four cents a kilowatt-hour for electricity, it would save about $140 000 a year in power, and recover its outlay within the prescribed 18-month period.

There was no waste in the installation the company said, because the building's old fluorescents had reached the end of their useful life anyway. It has always found it more efficient to replace all the lamps every three years than to send maintenance crews around replacing each lamp as it expires.

The article states that the expenditure on the new lamps will be paid back through operating savings in about 18 months. This measure of time is commonly termed the "payback period." (For part (a) include the installation costs in your calculations.)

a) Using the figures given, show how the company probably estimated this 18-month payback period.

b) The company appears to have made an error in the area of installation costs when computing the payback period. What is the evidence of such an error? Recompute the payback period excluding installation costs.

c) The trouble with the payback period method is that with it one has to judge whether 18 months is a good payback period or a poor one (in profitability terms). An alternative approach would be to estimate the net annual dollar benefit from buying the new lamps as compared with using the standard variety. If this figure is positive, it is a worthwhile investment. Estimate (i) the extra annual per lamp costs involved with the new variety, (ii) the extra annual dollar benefits per lamp in terms of less electricity used, and (iii) the net annual dollar benefit per lamp [(ii) less (i)] and the yearly savings on the 150 000 lamps.

d) Show that if the standard lights had one year left in their normal three-year life, then it would not pay to replace them with the newer variety until the end of that year.

e) Explain why most of the costs of a hydro-electric plant would be fixed.

f) The article speaks of hydro utilities having to raise rates to restore profitability if the demand for electricity falls. What assumption does the author make concerning the elasticity of demand for electricity? What does this article demonstrate concerning the short- and long-run elasticity of demand for electricity?

APPENDIX 9A: MONOPOLISTIC COMPETITION

9A-1 Long-Run Equilibrium

Monopolistic competition characterizes a market where firms produce similar goods or services, and no effective barriers exist to prevent new firms from entering the industry.

Figure 9A-1a illustrates the best output and price combination for a particular monopolistically competitive firm. As we have illustrated it, the firm's cost and demand conditions are such that the firm is able to earn an economic profit (the firm's maximum profit price (P_0) — where $MR = MC$ — exceeds the firm's average unit cost of production (AC) at that point.) Figure 9A-1b on the other hand, depicts another possibility, in which because of demand and cost conditions the best price the monopolistic competitor can charge (P_0) is below its average unit cost of production. In this instance, the firm would be incurring short-run losses.

In the long run, though, the story is different. Take, for example, the first case (Figure 9A-1a), in which the firm is earning economic profits (or in other words, where its owners are earning an above-average rate of return on their invested funds). If this was the typical case among the other producers as well, new investors would be attracted toward the industry. With reasonably easy entry, new firms would spring up. Each new firm would erode some of the market share held by existing firms. The original firm (depicted in Figure 9A-1a) would begin to find that at each price it might charge, less of its product would be demanded than before. Graphically speaking, its demand curve would shift to the left (as represented by D'). As this happened, the firm would find its profit-maximizing price falling (to P_1) — or, we might say, "It would be forced to lower its price to meet competition." However, so long as the typical firm was able to charge prices which still yielded economic profits ($P_1 > AC$), entry to the industry would continue. No further entry would

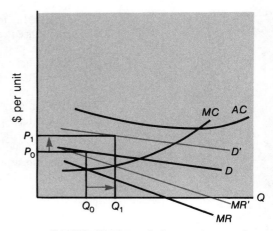

(a) **Erosion of short-run
profits by entry of other firms**

(b) **Elimination of short-run
losses by exit of weaker firms**

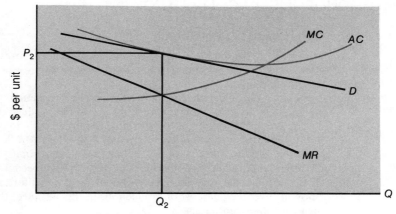

(c) **Long-run position with average firm
earning zero economic profit**

Fig. 9A-1 Short-run dynamics of monopolistic competition

(a) In the short run a monopolistically competitive firm may make economic profits. This will induce entry, shifting the firm's demand curve to the left.

(b) If, in the short run, economic losses are experienced, firms will exit from the industry, shifting the demand curve of each remaining firm to the right.

(c) Long-run equilibrium is established when firms remaining in the industry earn zero economic profits.

occur when, on average, zero economic profits were being earned. Graphically, this long-run situation is represented by Figure 9A-1c. The best price the monopolistically competitive firm can charge just covers costs ($P_2 = AC$). Economic profits are zero. The owners are earning normal rates of return on their invested funds.[1]

The opposite industrial growth pattern would occur in the case of Figure 9A-1b, where, on average, in the short run each monopolistic competitor is incurring economic losses. The owners are receiving less than they could earn elsewhere on their invested funds for comparable risk. Instead of a tide of new entrants, there would be an exit from the industry. The first firms to go would probably be those incurring the largest economic losses. As each new firm closed down, its action would increase the demand (and the market share) for the remaining ones (to D'). As Figure 9A-1b shows, this increase would encourage remaining firms to raise their prices and enable them to reduce their losses. This process would continue, until finally the remaining firms had eliminated their losses entirely. This long-run situation is depicted in Figure 9A-1c.

In the long run, a monopolistically competitive industry is characterized by firms earning, on average, zero economic profits. The industry will not be static, however. Some firms will not be as efficient (in terms of cost) or as good at product differentiation as the average firm; others will be better. Consequently, some firms will be incurring economic losses and dropping out of the industry, whereas others will be earning economic profits. Nevertheless, Figure 9A-1c might be regarded as an accurate representation of the position of the average monopolistic competitor, and should be interpreted in that way.

Monopolistic Competition and Efficiency

How can we judge whether or not monpolistic competition as a market structure is good or bad from society's standpoint? Certainly there is no reason for us to envy the position of the average owner or shareholder in a monopolistically competitive concern. The individual is earning a normal rate of return on invested funds. Put another way, considering the extra risk taken on the investment, the shareholder is doing no better than we might do by putting our funds in the local bank. However, in the long run (as well as in the short run) within a monopolistically competitive industry, price exceeds marginal production cost. This means that the value (price) consumers (society) place on the particular product is greater than the cost to society (workers and investors) of producing additional units. Monopolistic competition restricts output below the optimal level, from society's standpoint. Monopolistically competitive firms will not voluntarily produce any more (than Q_2 in Figure 9A-1c) because to do so would reduce profit. If forced to do so in the short run, firms will incur economic losses and find that in the long run it is more attractive to leave the industry and invest their funds elsewhere.

---

1. Even when zero economic profits are being earned, on average, some firms that are perhaps more efficient or innovative than others will still be earning above normal rates of return for their owners, whereas others will earn below normal rates of return.

Another source of welfare loss to society in monopolistically competitive industries is the production of output at a higher cost than under pure competition. Because monopolistic competitors face downward sloping demand curves, in the long run they produce an output level less than that required to minimize average unit costs. Therefore, everything else being equal, more resources are used up per unit of output produced in a monopolistically competitive industry than in a purely competitive one.

Perhaps some modification of our criticism of monopolistic competition is necessary. Output may not be greatly restricted in a particular monopolistically competitive industry. In other words, the demand curves facing each firm may be even more price sensitive than we have depicted them, with the result that the long-run solution may approximate the purely competitive case even more closely than we have shown it. In such an instance, efficiency losses may not be significant.

APPENDIX 9B: CANADIAN COMPETITION LEGISLATION

9B-1 History

Canadian competition legislation originated in 1889 when Parliament enacted a law making it a misdemeanour to conspire or agree to "unduly" restrict competition, output, or production and distribution facilities, to "unreasonably" enhance price or to restrain trade. In 1892 this Act became a part of the Criminal Code, and violations of its prohibitions became a criminal offence.

In 1910, a new piece of legislation, the Combines Investigation Act, established a procedure for initiating and investigating complaints of anticompetitive behaviour. This Act defined a *combine* as an arrangement designed to accomplish the various restrictions on competition listed above. The definition of combine also included *trusts, monopolies and mergers.* A new Combines Investigation Act was passed in 1923 which provided for a permanent, specialized administrative machinery for registering complaints and investigating and prosecuting offenders.

Simultaneously with these developments, a law enacted as early as 1897 gave the government the authority to reduce or remove tariffs on imports in order to counteract anticompetitive behaviour by domestic Canadian producers in specific markets. Another law made it possible to weaken or abolish patent protection if the privileges conferred by a patent were used to restrict competition unduly.

The Combines Investigation Act has been amended several times over the years. The most far-reaching overhaul of its provisions was launched in 1966 and accomplished in two steps: stage I of these revisions took effect on January 1, 1976, and stage II was enacted in June 1986. The title of the Act was also changed: it is now called the Competition Act. In total, the last reform took two decades; between 1971 and 1986 several successive drafts of the legislation were withdrawn and modified because of vigorous opposition, mainly by business interests.

9B-2 Activities Regulated by Competition Legislation

Until 1975, the Combines Investigation Act dealt only with product markets. In 1976, its jurisdiction was extended to include services, in recognition of the growing importance of the service sector in the Canadian economy. More-over, until 1975 all activities covered by the Act were subject to a criminal penalty (fine or imprisonment). The legality or illegality of the behaviour brought to the attention of the authorities had to be determined in the criminal courts, subject to the standard of proof *beyond reasonable doubt*. From 1976 to 1986 the Act incorporated a procedure for review of certain selected business practices by a nonjudicial body, the Restrictive Trade Practices Commission. If such practices were found incompatible with competition, a prohibition order was issued, but no criminal penalty was imposed.

The scope for this type of review was greatly expanded by the 1986 amendments. A new quasi-judicial body, the Competition Tribunal, replaced the Restrictive Trade Practices Commission, but also acquired significant other responsibilities. One of the most important changes made in 1986 was the "decriminalization" of the merger provisions of the Act. In other words, the Competition Tribunal, rather than criminal courts, now makes decisions as to whether a merger in progress should be allowed to proceed or whether one already consummated should be dissolved.

Offences in Relation to Competition

The business practices listed below are classified as *criminal offences* and are dealt with by criminal courts. The maximum penalties stipulated in the Act range as high as 5 years imprisonment or $5 million fine, or both. (What follows is a simplified outline of the substance of each provision. Careful study of the Act and of accumulated jurisprudence is required to establish their precise definitions and applicability to the circumstances of a particular case.)

(i) Conspiracy (agreement) to lessen competition unduly. This includes such activities as price fixing, bid-rigging, agreements to divide the market or restrict output, etc. The Act prohibits banks from agreeing upon interest rates on deposits or loans, service charges, amounts and types of loans offered, etc. Not all such agreements are illegal, however — only those that restrict competition unduly. (The courts have historically interpreted the word unduly to mean whether or not a substantial segment of the market has been affected by the conspiracy.) It is an offence simply to agree, even though the agreement may not have been carried out, or the parties may not have profited from it. Moreover, the existence of a conspiracy may be inferred from circumstantial evidence, without direct proof of communication among the parties.

(ii) Price discrimination and predatory pricing. It is an offence to engage in the practice of selling the same product at different prices to different

customers who are in competition with each other when they buy the same quantity of the product at the same time. In other words, volume discounts are permitted, but the same discount must be offered to each customer buying the same quantity. It is also an offence to sell products or services for different prices in different regions of Canada, or to sell at "unreasonably low" prices if doing so leads to lessening of competition or elimination of a competitor. Similar prohibitions apply to granting of promotional allowances to customers on other than proportional terms.

(iii) Misleading advertising. These provisions regulate a rather broad range of methods by which information about products or services is conveyed to the public: mass media, billboards, in-store displays, door-to-door selling, information printed on product containers or wrappers, etc. To qualify as an offence, such representation must be false or misleading in a material respect, i.e. must be capable of influencing consumer purchasing decisions. Statements about performance of a product which are not based on an adequate test are also misleading in this sense.

(iv) Other deceptive practices. The following offences are included in this category:
— use of testimonials about product performance, efficacy or length of life without permission of the person conducting the test;
— selling a product at a price other than the lowest price indicated on the container, wrapper, display, or advertisement ("double ticketing");
— schemes such as "pyramid selling" or "referral selling," unless they are licensed by a provincial authority;
— advertising a product at a bargain price without having a reasonable quantity available for sale ("bait and switch selling");
— sale of a product above advertised price;
— promotional contests without fair disclosure of the number and value of prizes and criteria for selection of participants and distribution of prizes.

(v) Price maintenance. This is a practice where suppliers (e.g. manufacturers or wholesalers) exert an influence on dealers (e.g. retail stores) not to sell their product below certain "suggested retail price." One method of encouraging dealer compliance is to refuse future supplies if the dealer engages in a low-price policy. Refusal to supply is a criminal offence unless the supplier can prove that the dealer made it a practice to use the product as loss-leader for purposes of attracting customers to the store, or engaged in misleading advertising of the product or provided inadequate servicing.

Matters Reviewable by the Competition Tribunal

The following are relatively new provisions of the competition legislation. They typically require some amount of economic analysis and call for assessments and evaluations of potential economic impact which may not be permissible as evidence in a criminal court. The applicable remedies are not criminal penalties, but orders to do certain things or, alternatively, to refrain from engaging in some activities.

(i) Refusal to deal. This occurs when a person is unable to obtain adequate supplies of a product because of insufficient competition among suppliers, even though the product is available and the person is willing to offer the usual price and other terms. The Tribunal must determine whether the person's business is substantially affected and may order that he or she be accepted as a customer or that import tariffs be reduced to make supplies from abroad available.

(ii) Consignment selling. In some lines of business, consignment selling is a standard practice. It means that a dealer does not buy the product outright for resale to customers, but acts only as an agent for a supplier who maintains ownership until the product is sold to final customers. However, consignment selling may sometimes be deliberately introduced by a supplier with the purpose of controlling dealer's prices or discriminating among dealers. In such cases, the Tribunal may order the practice to be discontinued.

(iii) Exclusive dealing and tied selling. A supplier may require that a customer deal only in products supplied by him (exclusive dealing) or that the customer, in order to obtain one product, must also buy another product from the same supplier (tied selling). The Tribunal may order that these practices be discontinued if they inhibit new entry into the market or introduction of a new product or otherwise substantially lessen competition.

(iv) Market restriction. A supplier may require that a dealer operate only in a specified market, perhaps so as not to compete with other dealers of the same supplier. The Tribunal may order the restriction to be discontinued if it lessens competition, either because it is practised by a major supplier, or is widespread in the market in question.

(v) Abuse of dominant position. The Act lists, as examples, several types of activities which are abuses of a dominant position. Among them are:
— squeezing, by a vertically integrated supplier, of profit margins on products supplied by an unintegrated customer who competes with the supplier;
— acquisition of a customer who would otherwise be available to a competitor;
— use of fighting brands to discipline or eliminate a competitor;
— pre-emption of scarce facilities or resources required by a competitor;
— buying up of products to prevent the erosion of existing price level;
— adoption of product specifications incompatible with other suppliers in order to prevent entry.

The Tribunal may order that these practices be discontinued if the firm(s) engaging in them dominate(s) the market and competition is lessened substantially.

(vi) Delivered pricing. Delivered pricing is defined as a practice where a supplier refuses delivery of a product to a customer in a locality where he supplies other customers whose businesses are located in that place. The Tribunal may order that this practice be discontinued if the firm engaging in it is a major supplier or if the practice is widespread in the relevant market.

(vii) The application in Canada of foreign laws and judgments. If foreign laws and regulations (directed at foreign subsidiaries operating in Canada) adversely affect competition in Canada or efficiency of an industry in Canada of international trade performance, the Tribunal may order that they not be implemented.

(viii) Specialization agreements. The Act makes it possible for competing firms to agree with each other under certain circumstances to reduce the overlaps (duplications) in their product lines. For example, one firm agrees to drop some items from its product line, in exchange for other firm(s) agreeing to allow it to specialize in items they dropped from their product lines. Such agreements must be registered and approved by the Tribunal. In making its decision, the Tribunal considers whether gains in efficiency will result (for example, from economies of scale), whether Canadian international trade performance is likely to improve, etc. The approval may be combined with a simultaneous reduction of tariffs, or licensing of patents, or divestiture of certain assets by the firms concerned. All of these actions are, of course, designed to compensate for the potential reduction in competition resulting from specialization agreements.

(ix) Mergers. The Act defines a merger as the acquisition of control over, or a significant interest in, a business of a competitor, supplier, customer, or other person. The Tribunal is given the power to order dissolution of a merger or the sale of designated assets or shares. In the case of a proposed merger, the Tribunal may order the parties not to proceed with it. A prohibition order may be issued when the Tribunal finds that the merger prevents or lessens substantially competition in the relevant market, or among the sources of supply, or among the distribution channels. In order to determine whether competition is (or may be) lessened substantially, the Tribunal examines such factors as:

— the extent of import competition
— whether a party to the merger was a failing business
— existence of substitutes for products supplied by parties to the merger
— barriers to entry into the market, such as tariffs or government regulations.

The Act stipulates, in addition, that the Tribunal should allow the merger if it is likely to yield gains in efficiency which would more than offset the consequences of lessening of competition the merger may bring about. The gains in efficiency should be reflected in improved international competitiveness. Instead of prohibiting a merger, the Tribunal may order a reduction or removal of import tariffs or a relaxation of some restrictive government regulations.

9B-3 Administration and Remedies

The Minister of Consumer and Corporate Affairs is responsible for the administration of the Competition Act. The Bureau of Competition Policy in the Department of Consumer and Corporate Affairs receives complaints about possible violations of the Act and conducts inquiries. The Bureau is headed by the Director of Investigation and Research. Subject to approval by a judge, the Director has the power to enter premises of business firms suspected of violating the Act, seize documents and examine witnesses under oath.

The Director receives a substantial number of complaints. By far the largest number of them are concerned with misleading advertising and deceptive

Table 9B-1 Operations under misleading advertising and deceptive marketing practices provisions

	1980–81	1981–82	1982–83	1983–84	1984–85
Total complaints received	9 382	9 782	11 357	11 054	10 632
Number of files opened	8 373	8 557	9 875	10 091	9 816
Number of complete investigations	2 147	2 319	24 457	2 068	2 145
Referrals to Attorney General	167	142	199	181	136
Completed cases, convictions	103	94	121	139	136

Source: Department of Consumer and Corporate Affairs, *Report of the Director of Investigation and Research. Fiscal year ending March 31, 1985* (Ottawa, 1985), pp. 81–82. Reproduced with permission of the Minister of Supply and Services Canada.

Table 9B-2 Operational activities of the Bureau of Competition Policy (excluding misleading advertising and deceptive marketing practices provisions)

	1975–76	1976–77	1977–78	1978–79	1979–80	1980–81	1981–82	1982–83	1983–84	1984–85
Number of files opened	158	143	173	205	262	238	249	256	205	256
Formal applications for inquiries	4	7	5	7	7	8	9	8	2	2
Inquiries disposed of by reports of discontinuance to the Minister	14	8	14	16	21	26	20	19	19	12
Inquiries referred direct to the Attorney General of Canada for prosecution	18	26	23	14	24	21	33	24	20	27
Inquiries closed on the recommendation of the Attorney General of Canada	2	4	6	6	3	5	6	5	6	4
Prosecutions or other proceedings commenced	12	16	24	11	21	6	24	21	16	17
Formal interventions before regulatory agencies	—	3	4	0	3	4	6	4	15	17
Other representations to bodies dealing with regulatory change	—	1	1	2	1	0	9	7	8	6

Source: Department of Consumer and Corporate Affairs, *Report of the Director of Investigation and Research. Fiscal year ending March 31, 1985* (Ottawa, 1985), p. 14. Reproduced with permission of the Minister of Supply and Services Canada.

marketing practices. As shown in Table 9B-1, in recent years these complaints have been running around 11 000 annually. In addition, well over 200 potential violations of other sections of the Act have been looked into in each of the recent years (Table 9B-2).

After a preliminary inquiry by the Director's staff, the vast majority of complaints are eliminated from further proceedings for lack of substance. Formal investigation of the remaining cases may take months, or even years, to complete. The following outcomes are possible:

(1) The Director may decide to discontinue the inquiry.

(2) The case may be referred to the Attorney General of Canada (Department of Justice) for prosecution before the courts. Prosecution may not

proceed if the Attorney General decides that the evidence would not stand up in court.

(3) The case may be referred to the Competition Tribunal (in effect only since 1986).

(4) The Director may make an intervention before other regulatory agencies.

Information about some of the ways in which complaints and inquiries have been disposed of in recent years is given in Tables 9B-1 and 9B-2. For example, while 10 000 files were opened in 1984–85 to deal with misleading advertising complaints, just over 2 000 investigations were completed, and only 136 cases were referred for prosecution before the courts. Similarly, while 256 files were opened in the same fiscal year to deal with other types of offences (Table 9B-2), only 27 cases were referred for prosecution before the courts.

The Record of Enforcement and Penalties

Historically, Canada's competition legislation has been reasonably effective in regulating some aspects of business conduct, such as misleading advertising, price-fixing conspiracies and other collusive agreements, and price maintenance. Its major failure has been in the area of monopoly and merger. For example, not a single conviction in a merger case has ever been obtained throughout the entire existence of the legislation. The probability of conviction for violating the prohibitions on price discrimination and predatory pricing has also been rather low.

Table 9B-3 provides a historical summary of the cases brought before the courts between 1899 and 1975. Table 9B-4 updates this information to 1984. Of particular interest is the increasing trend in recent years in average fines (reported in current dollars in Table 9B-4) imposed for conspiracy offences (including bid-rigging), for price maintenance and for misleading advertising.

Table 9B-3 Combines investigation activity, 1899–1975

Years	Number of cases (excluding advertising)	Conspiracy	Merger	Monopoly	Resale price maintenance/ refusal to supply	Other	Misleading advertising
1899–1960	53	43	3	1	3	3	0
1960–1975	91	41	5		34	11	573

* Penalties for conviction (approximate averages)
  Misleading advertising fines $ 700
  Other offences
    Corporate fines $6 000
    Individual fines $ 600

Source: J.R.S. Prichard, W.T. Stanbury and T.A. Wilson, eds., *Canadian Competition Policy: Essays in Law and Economics* (Toronto: Butterworths and Co., 1979)

The largest fine ever imposed for misleading advertising was $1 million (against Simpsons-Sears in 1984). In a 1985 case, three companies were convicted of conspiracy to divide the solicitation of advertising business from advertisers, to divide ownership and operation of outdoor posters and panels on a territorial basis and to set industry-wide price discounts. One of the three companies (Mediacom) received the largest fine ever imposed under the Act on a single count ($400 000).

As mentioned earlier, a major weakness of the legislation in effect until 1986 has been in the enforcement of its monopoly and merger provisions. As Table 9B-3 shows, only 9 such cases have been brought before the courts between 1899 and 1975. Yet a large number of mergers and acquisitions take place in Canada — well over six hundred in each of recent years (Table 9B-5). Some of them are horizontal mergers (among firms competing in the same market), some are vertical mergers (among firms operating in unrelated markets). Competition legislation deals almost exclusively with horizontal mergers and some consequences of vertical mergers.

Table 9B-4 **Trends in fines imposed under the Combines Investigation Act**

Period	Number of cases with fine only	Number of cases with fine & P.O.	P.O. only	Total cases	Total fines (all cases)	Avg. fine per case (all cases)*
Conspiracy						
1960–69	5	15	3	23	$1 149 800	$ 57 490
1970–74	1	7	3	11	851 950	106 494
1975–79	1	6	3	10	1 220 900	174 414
1980–84	3	4	0	7	1 483 000	211 857
Price Maintenance						
1960–69	2	5	5	12	$ 15 750	$ 2 250
1970–74	4	7	1	12	64 250	5 841
1975–79	16	13	5	34	517 500	17 845
1980–84	23	1	2	26	519 000	21 625

Period	Number of cases	Total fines	Avg. fine per case
Misleading Advertising			
1976–77	87	$ 121 687	$ 1 399
1977–78	89	142 140	1 597
1978–79	119	222 575	1 870
1979–80	102	378 380	3 710
1980–81	107	369 950	3 457
1981–82	94	225 132	2 395
1982–83	121	610 775	5 047
1983–84	139	1 654 640	11 904

* Does not include cases where only a Prohibition Order (P.O.) was issued.

Source: Department of Consumer and Corporate Affairs, *Report of the Director of Investigation and Research. Fiscal year ending March 31, 1985* (Ottawa, 1985), p. 23. Reproduced with permission of the Minister of Supply and Services Canada.

Table 9B-5 **Acquisitions recorded since 1960**

Year	Foreign*	Domestic**	Total
1960	93	110	203
1961	86	152	238
1962	79	106	185
1963	41	88	129
1964	80	124	204
1965	78	157	235
1966	80	123	203
1967	85	143	228
1968	163	239	402
1969	168	336	504
1970	162	265	427
1971	143	245	388
1972	127	302	429
1973	100	252	352
1974	78	218	296
1975	109	155	264
1976	124	189	313
1977	192	203	395
1978	271	178	449
1979	307	204	511
1980	234	180	414
1981	200	291	491
1982	371	205	576
1983	395	233	628
1984	410	231	641
1985***	466	246	712

* Acquisitions involving a foreign-owned or foreign-controlled acquiring company (the nationality of the controlling interest in the acquired company prior to the merger could have been foreign or Canadian)

** Acquisitions invoving an acquiring company not known to be foreign-owned or foreign-controlled (the nationality of the controlling interest in the acquired company prior to the merger could have been foreign or Canadian)

*** Preliminary

Source: Department of Consumer and Corporate Affairs, *Report of the Director of Investigation and Research. Fiscal year ending March 31, 1986* (Ottawa, 1986), p. 65. Reproduced with permission of the Minister of Supply and Services Canada.

Only a small fraction of the large number of mergers reported in Table 9B-5 are likely to have a significant effect on competition in the affected market. Past experience with the Combines Investigation Act, which treated mergers as a criminal offence, proved that proceedings before criminal courts are not well suited for determining the desirability of a merger from society's point of view. A major difficulty for the Crown consisted in proving that a particular merger caused a specific "detriment to the public." It is hoped that the new approach incorporated into the Competition Act passed in 1986 will lead to a more meaningful consideration of the economic consequences of a merger, not only those already observed, but also those anticipated in the future.

CHAPTER 10

Labour, Capital and Property Incomes

LEARNING OBJECTIVES

After reading this chapter you should be able to explain:

1. The connection between marginal product of labour, price of output and the demand for labour.

2. The competitive labour market, the conse-quences of minimum wage laws and the economics of labour unions.

3. Wage and salary differences among individuals, among occupations and among regions, and considerations of fairness.

4. Earnings on human capital, on financial wealth and income from land ownership.

10-1 INTRODUCTION AND PURPOSE

Most production processes require the use of three major factors of production: labour, capital goods and land. While almost every production process also requires material inputs, they have been produced by the three factors above and are not separately analyzed here. In return for their services, the owners of factors of production receive income. The determination of incomes of factors of production is the subject of this chapter.

In the absence of slavery, ownership of labour rests with the individual possessing that factor of production, and may not be transferred. On the other hand, claims on capital goods (inventories, factories, machines, buildings) and on land are represented by paper certificates. These certificates — or financial instruments — may be sold, thereby allowing an easy transfer of claims on land and physical capital between individuals.

Landowners and capital goods owners are similar, in that they may both be considered investors who have put their capital funds into different investments. Studies of aggregate income distribution therefore frequently do not distinguish between those who have debt claims on physical capital or land (such as bondholders of corporations or lenders of mortgage funds) and those who possess equity claims (for example, common shareholders of corporations, or owners of a piece of property). In each case, a physical asset, represented by the claims, provides their incomes.

In analyses of income distribution, the share of total or national income going to labour is usually compared with the share going to holders of claims on land and capital. Labour and capital shares of gross national income in Canada between 1926 and 1985 are depicted in Figure 10-1. They remained relatively constant over the period, with labour receiving slightly less than two-thirds of GNP and capital the rest. However, such figures by themselves are of limited use in judging the equity of income distribution. First, the figures are on a before-tax basis and may not give an adequate reflection of the distribution of disposable income.

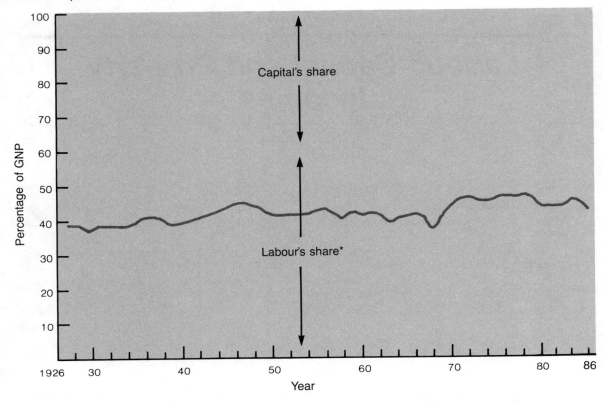

Fig. 10-1 Percentage of total economy's income (GNP) received by labour and capital owners

*Includes not only wages and salary income but also an estimate of labour remuneration received by self-employed groups (e.g. farmers, professionals, and business sole proprietors, as estimated by the authors from National Accounts data).

The division of GNP between labour and capital has remained relatively constant over the past sixty years.

Second, and more important, the figures give us no information on the income or wealth of individuals and families. For example, even though the income shares have remained generally constant, perhaps the number of people who receive labour income has increased by more than the number of people receiving nonlabour income. In this case, the share of national income received per worker will have fallen relative to the share of national income received per capital and landowner.

Further, the two groups are not mutually exclusive. Many wage and salary earners are depositors in banks, or holders of bonds, stocks, land or houses. In addition, of course, there are very few land and capital owners who are not also wage or salary earners. In short, the proportions of national income accruing to labour and capital do not really reflect how much particular individuals, or at least easily identifiable groups within society, receive for their effort and financial risk. The more interesting questions concerned with income distribution are such issues as the percentage of those who live on incomes below some defined poverty level and the reasons for this problem. Other statistics of interest are the percentage of people who are rich, or income variability between regions and occupations. Some of this information is provided in Tables 10-1 and 10-2.

More difficult questions deal with the concept of *fairness*. For example, is it fair that doctors earn

Table 10-1 **Distribution of families in Canada by income and region, 1985**

Income group	Canada	Atlantic prov.	Quebec	Ontario	Prairie prov.	B.C.
Under $10 000	5.8	7.5	6.7	4.2	5.9	6.6
10 000–19 999	18.2	25.3	19.5	15.1	18.2	18.9
20 000–29 999	18.2	21.8	19.7	16.5	18.7	16.3
30 000–39 999	18.7	17.5	20.5	18.8	18.0	17.6
40 000–49 999	14.7	12.2	13.4	15.9	14.6	16.2
50 000 and over	24.3	15.5	19.9	29.5	24.5	24.5
Totals	100.0	100.0	100.0	100.0	100.0	100.0
Average income ($)	38 059	32 127	35 068	41 775	37 996	37 968

Source: Statistics Canada 13-207

There is considerable variation in family incomes in Canada across the five main economic regions. In 1985, Ontario and Alberta were above the national average, while all the other provinces were below.

more than farmers? Should wealth be inherited, and, therefore, capital incomes be earned by heirs, who were born into their position, through none of their own doing? Internationally (or interprovincially) speaking, is it fair that people of different countries (or provinces) earn different incomes for the same work? There really are two sets of questions here: "Why?" and "Is it fair?" Economics analyzes the process by which incomes are determined and thus offer some answers to the "Why" question. Questions of justice and fairness must be decided in the light of the value systems and moral conscience of a particular society.

As to what determines the income to a factor owner in a market system, economic theory argues that the owner receives what the factor is worth. Such worth is a function of the market value of the goods or services that the factor helped to create. In the following sections we will examine this mechanism in greater detail.

10-2 LABOUR INCOME

Here, we ask why certain types of labour are paid more than others. The answer seems clear enough. Some efforts produce goods and services that people in general value more than goods and services produced by other efforts. For example, a world class boxing champion gets paid more income per hour for his work (including hours in training) than you or I, because the value of his output, which may be a world-televised fight, is considered by the public to be of greater aggregate value than our output.

However, this is really only half the explanation. Concentrating on the value of what labour efforts produce examines only the demand side of the story. That is, the fight promoters demand (want) the services of the boxer and offer him a large pay cheque because they know they in turn can package and sell the fight (through TV networks and advertisers, or through closed circuit and cable TV operators) to the public. The other half of the reason has to do with the limited supply of this type of labour. There is only one world champion, who can fight only a few fights a year at most. With demand great and supply very limited, the world champion receives a very high wage.

This is another illustration of the fact that we must always consider both demand and supply in the analysis of economic phenomena. To see how supply affects the boxer's fee, suppose there were 50 world champions for a particular weight class, each recognized by different boxing associations, which in turn were each claiming to be the authorized voice of the sport. Suppose further that the champions had roughly equal boxing ability. In this case, there could be as many as 150 announced world championship matches per year. Clearly, the

Table 10-2 Compensation by occupation, Canada, 1984

Occupation	Number	Average Income $
Self-employed:		
Doctors and surgeons	33 329	95 597
Dentists	9 091	74 665
Lawyers and notaries	20 678	65 167
Accountants	11 338	55 519
Engineers and architects	4 199	40 754
Other professionals	55 996	24 245
Investors	1 041 401	19 713
Property owners	134 321	17 370
Salesmen	35 784	17 537
Fishermen	35 439	14 487
Farmers	271 740	15 855
Business proprietors	521 641	13 534
Entertainers and artists	20 611	12 338
Pensioners	1 185 578	12 553
Others	1 858 153	4 308
Total	15 522 181	18 240
Employees:		
Teachers and professors	259 408	34 947
Federal government	327 480	27 626
Armed forces	87 304	26 192
Provincial and Municipal governments	990 736	23 810
Companies	6 821 409	20 244
Institutions	938 141	19 428
Unclassified	529 436	12 228
Total	10 312 882	21 118

* Income figures in this table consist of net income from all sources before personal exemptions, personal contributions, and standard or other deductions. Occupation in this table is determined by chief source of income. For example, a lawyer or doctor whose chief source of income is salary is classified as an employee; if investments, as an investor, etc.

Source: Revenue Canada, *Taxation Statistics* (Ottawa, 1986). Reproduced by permission of the Minister of Supply and Services Canada.

The numbers and average incomes of 22 categories of occupations as reported by Revenue Canada. Income variation is much larger within the *self-employed* category of occupations than within the *employee* category.

fee paid each champion per fight would be a great deal less than if there was only one world champion.

The above sort of analysis can be used to explain the salaries of special labour groups such as professional athletes, movie stars and daredevil stunt men. The same sort of reasoning, though, applies to the pricing of any type of labour service — connecting the demand for labour (which stems from the market value of the good or service that the labour produces) with the supply of labour. However, to gain greater insight into the determination of the wage and salary levels in more typical occupations, greater detail is required.

Demand for Labour

The demand for any product or service reflects its value to the user. As discussed in Chapter 4, the height of the demand curve represents the extra value to the user (consumer) of the last unit of the good or service consumed. The user of a good or service would be willing to pay up to, but not more than, the value expected from using it. The same principle applies in determining the **demand for labour**. Typically, though, the user of labour services is not an individual consumer, but rather a business firm (most often a corporation). In order to see the process let us follow through a numerical example involving Acme Ltd., a firm in a purely competitive athletic shoe industry.

To set the groundwork, we will consider Acme's demand for labour during 19X1. Throughout this year, the size of Acme's factory — the number of machines, supervisory personnel, and administrative and technical staff — is fixed. Depending upon the level of activity that takes place, of course, it may turn out that Acme's plant is too big or too small. Therefore Acme may wish to alter some of these fixed factors. This choice is a long-run decision, and it is going to take Acme quite some time to change its scale of operations. Therefore, for all practical purposes we may consider Acme's physical scale of operations to be fixed for the particular year in question. Among the magnitudes to be decided are: how much Acme will produce during 19X1; how much material will be used in the production process; and how many production personnel Acme will hire. We have already examined some of these questions in earlier chapters. Here, we consider how Acme decides on the amount it would be willing to pay for different quantities of production labour — that is, Acme's *demand for labour*.

The logic of the firm's decision on how much labour to hire is exactly the same as the logic followed in determining the level of output: The firm first has to establish what is the contribution to its revenues each additional unit of labour could be expected to generate. Second, this extra revenue has to be compared with the extra cost incurred as a result of hiring that labour.

As we know from Chapter 5, the relationship between units of labour employed and physical units of output produced is described by total and marginal product curves. We first briefly review this relationship and then take an extra step, from physical units of labour to dollars of revenue generated by the extra labour employed.

(i) Marginal Product of Labour Pattern

As business firms hire more and more labour, we find, as a general proposition, that over the early range of hiring the extra product obtained from adding extra units of labour increases. Then it flattens out and finally begins to decrease as the plant becomes filled up. Such a productivity pattern is shown in Figure 10-2a (much like Figure 5-1b in Chapter 5). The corresponding total product pattern is shown in Figure 10-2b (much like Figure 5-1a in Chapter 5).

This idea seems reasonable enough if we consider a plant built for, say, 35 to 50 workers. The output we obtain from hiring zero production workers will clearly be zero. The output we obtain from the first production worker will be, say, 10 units per week. The hiring of a second worker, however, should more than double total production. That is, the second worker should add more production than 10 units per week. Perhaps this worker will add 11 units per week (Figure 10-2a) so that total output is now 21 units per week (Figure 10-2b). The reason for this is that two workers can split the tasks, each operating only half the required machines. This division of labour should mean that each worker would be able to become more efficient in handling a smaller number of tasks. We should therefore observe certain productivity gains from *specialization*. The

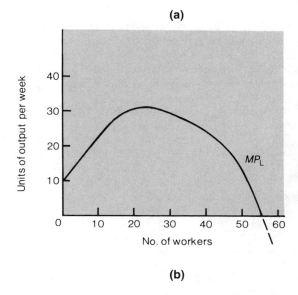

(a)

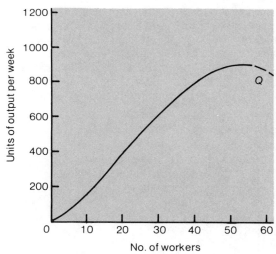

(b)

Fig. 10-2 The marginal productivity of labour pattern

A typical pattern of marginal product of labour curve (part (a)) and total product curve (part (b)). Underlying both relationships is the law of diminishing returns discussed in Chapter 5.

third worker may continue this increased efficiency of coordination and specialization and add a greater amount of production than even the second worker did. Perhaps this worker's marginal product is 12 units per week (Figure 10-2a). Total production with the three workers employed is, therefore, 33 units per week.

At some point, however, these increased efficiencies will end. In Figure 10-2, this point is shown to be reached at a work force of 20. Given the fixed space and number of machines within the plant, hiring additional workers will still increase total output (Figure 10-2b), but at a slower rate. This means that the extra or marginal product of each successive worker is declining with the hiring of more than 20 workers (Figure 10-2a).

Finally, we suppose there is just nothing for the 55th worker to do that could possibly increase output. Therefore, this person's marginal product is zero (Figure 10-2a). The 56th worker has nothing to do, and in addition gets in the way of the other workers, thereby reducing their output. As a result, the hiring of the 56th worker actually reduces total output (Figure 10-2b), and the marginal product is negative (Figure 10-2a).

Of course, the precise shape of the marginal product of labour curve for any given firm depends on many factors, including the type of product or service the firm produces and the existing size of its plant. If, for example, the size of fixed plant increases, the effect on marginal product may be as shown in Figure 10-3.

For the usual size of drive-in hamburger outlets, marginal productivity would probably fall off at far fewer than 20 employees per shift, and probably become negative well before 50. However, for large manufacturing concerns, marginal productivity would not decline until much higher employment levels were reached. The important point, though, is that for any fixed plant base, beyond some employment level, marginal productivity will fall as more and more labour is hired. Consequently, additional labour adds less new output for the firm and is therefore worth less to the firm.

(ii) The Marginal Revenue Product

In making its hiring decisions, a firm compares the cost of the last unit of labour just hired with the extra revenue that unit could be expected to generate. This *extra revenue* is the product of (i) the amount of extra output produced by the addition of one more unit of labour and (ii) the extra revenue obtained from the selling of each extra unit of output. Thus we can write

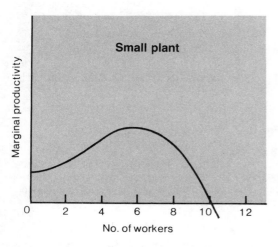

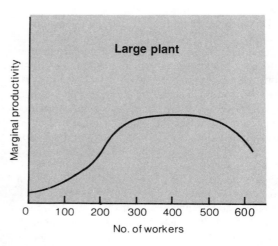

Fig. 10-3 Size of fixed plant base and marginal productivity of labour pattern

As the plant size increases, the quantity of fixed factors of production becomes greater, and the marginal product of labour curve shifts to the right.

The extra revenue to the firm from an additional hour of labour (marginal revenue product)		The extra output obtained from an additional hour of labour (marginal product of labour)		The extra revenue obtained from each extra unit of output (marginal revenue)	
MRP	=	*MP*	×	*MR*	(10-1)

Therefore, in deciding how much it will pay for a given quantity of labour, a firm must estimate both the marginal product of labour and the marginal revenue figures. (The terms **marginal revenue product** and the **marginal product of labour**, otherwise known as the *marginal physical product* or just *marginal product*, are common terms used by economists. We have used some of these terms before because they abbreviate our writing, but it may be necessary to refer again to their definitions from time to time.)

For example, suppose that by the hiring of one more hour of labour, six more pairs of athletic shoes could be produced (*MP*), and each pair sold for $35 (*MR*). In this case, the extra revenue to the firm of the additional hour of labour (*MRP*) would be $210 (that is, $35 × 6).

If the firm is in a purely competitive market, then as we showed in Chapter 5, the extra revenue the firm gets from selling an additional unit of output is simply the market price. Because the firm in such a market is so small that its output cannot significantly affect the market price, it gets the same price for every extra unit it produces and sells. Therefore, regardless of how much labour the firm hires and how much output it produces and sells, it receives a marginal revenue equal to the market price for each extra unit sold.

On the other hand, suppose the firm is an imperfect competitor and can sell more output only by reducing its price (that is, the firm faces a downward sloping demand curve for its output). As the firm hires another production employee, not only may the extra output it obtains (*MP*) be less than it got from the previous employee hired, but also the firm will not be able to get as much extra revenue from each unit of this production as it obtained from the units produced by the previous employee. For both these reasons the firm will tend to reduce the wage rate it is willing to pay for labour as additional workers are hired (beyond very low employment levels, at which rising marginal productivity may initially outweigh falling marginal revenue).

The Material Inputs

Usually (and this can be a source of confusion), economists assume that additional amounts of production labour may be fruitfully employed (can produce additional output — that is, have a positive marginal product), not only without expanding plant facilities or nonproduction personnel (as assumed above), but also without increasing material inputs. In precise economic terms, the marginal productivity of any factor input is defined as the extra output that can be derived from the addition of one more unit of the particular factor — *without a change in the quantity of any other factor used in the production process.* For example, the marginal productivity of labour within an automobile plant is the extra output due to the addition of one more hour of labour — but with no increase at all in the amount of material (steel, rubber, glass and so on) used in the plant. For instance, up to a point, less wastage may occur as more workers are hired.

An alternative but reasonable approximation for many businesses might be that a particular amount of material input is required for each unit of output (for example, 1½ tonnes of steel for each car, or 0.06 square metres of cloth for each athletic shoe produced). As more labour is hired, more output is produced — and for each additional unit of output, the necessary amount of material is used. This case approximates the actual production process for many firms and fits in with our earlier treatment of marginal costs for goods-producing firms.

This additional complication suggests only a slight modification of the marginal revenue product expression above, as follows:

The extra net revenue to the firm from an additional hour of labour, allowing for the addition of other necessary variable inputs (modified marginal revenue product)		The extra output obtained from the additional hour of labour plus the other necessary inputs (modified marginal product of labour)		The extra net revenue obtained from each extra unit of output sold (marginal revenue)	
MMRP	=	*MMP*	×	*MR*	(10-2)

For instance, suppose that in the previous example $33 worth of additional cloth, heat, light and power was also required for each extra unit of output produced as Acme contemplated hiring another hour of labour. One more hour of labour was expected to produce 6 more pairs of shoes, and thus the firm would have been willing to pay a maximum of $12 (that is, $35 × 6 − $33 ×6) for it. In what follows, we will be using the traditional expressions, given in Equation 10-1, but the entire discussion could just as easily be carried out with the expressions in Equation 10-2.

The Demand Curve

The demand curve for labour will generally slope downward to the right as shown in Figure 10-4, because as more and more labour is employed by a firm (given the size of the plant and other inputs as fixed) the extra value to the firm of additional hours of labour falls. Inasmuch as $MRP = MP \times MR$, a decline in MRP as more and more labour is hired must be the result of either (i) *declining marginal productivity* or (ii) *declining marginal revenue* (or both).

A diagrammatical illustration of the two ways in which marginal product of labour is converted

from physical units into dollar terms is given in Figure 10-5. When the firm sells its output in a perfectly competitive market, MP is multiplied by $MR = P$. However, when output is sold in an imperfectly competitive market, MP is multiplied by $MR' < P$.

Industry Demand for Labour

Just as total industry or market demand for a consumer good or service at a given price is the total of all individual consumer demands at that price, so the demand for labour at any given wage rate is the total of all individual firms' demands at that wage rate.

A profit-maximizing firm makes its decisions concerning the employment of labour by comparing the cost of the last unit of labour just hired with the extra revenue that unit could be expected to generate. The exact shape and position of a firm's demand for labour curve depends on its marginal product pattern and on the nature of competition in the market for its output.

Supply of Labour

A firm's supply of any good or service depends on the costs of that good or service — because the firm attempts to make as much profit as possible. In the same way, an individual's supply of labour depends on a perceived net cost of supplying the labour effort — as the individual attempts to allocate time so as to maximize his or her satisfaction. The individual has two choices in the use of time: work or leisure. If the individual works, payments received will enable him or her to purchase goods and services. This is a primary benefit from work. The cost of working is the sacrifice of the leisure time the individual could have had. In fact, we can think of work as giving up one good, leisure, in order to earn income for acquiring other goods. Even though leisure is not a physical good, it is certainly a good thing to most people in that it is desirable.

One question to consider here is whether more or less labour is offered as the wage rate increases. It may help in this regard to study two separate impacts of higher salary or wage rates on an individual's labour-leisure choice.

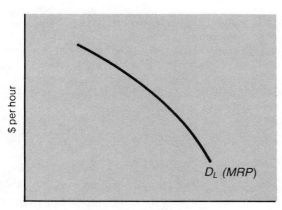

Labour (hours per year)

Fig. 10-4 Demand for labour

Demand for labour curve is downward sloping, because of declining marginal product of labour and also, if the firm operates in imperfectly competitive output markets, because of declining marginal revenue.

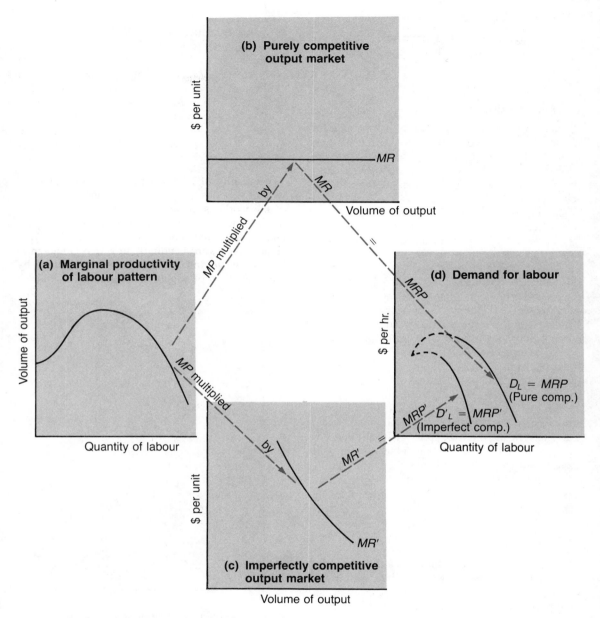

Fig. 10-5 Derivation of the demand for labour curve

A firm's demand for labour curve (panel (d)) derives its shape from the marginal product of labour curve (panel (a)). The exact shape and position of the demand for labour curve depend on whether the units of marginal product of labour are multiplied by output price $MR = P$ in a purely competitive output market (panel (b)) or by $MR' < P$ when the firm operates in an imperfectly competitive output market (panel (c)).

(i) Price Effect

As the wage rate offered increases, leisure becomes more expensive. That is, the worker sacrifices more goods and services for each hour not worked.[1]

(ii) Income Effect

As the worker's income increases, the demand for leisure as a good could be expected to increase, along with the demand for all other goods and services. Leisure becomes more attractive to most people if they have a greater income to spend on leisure time activities.

Consequently, when the offered salary or wage rate is increased, two opposing tendencies emerge. The higher price of leisure tends to lead to a reduction in its consumption, in other words, to an increase in the amount of labour offered. Offsetting this tendency, however, is the fact that higher wage rates imply a higher income for the present number of hours worked and may increase the individual's demand for leisure, in other words, reduce the amount of labour offered. It appears that in practice — at lower incomes at least — the former influence outweighs the latter, with the result that the quantity of labour increases as the wage rate is increased.

The market supply of labour is, as usual, the sum of individual supplies at various wage rates. The shape of the market supply of labour curve is depicted in Figure 10-6, in which the possibility of a backward-bending portion has been indicated by a broken line. The backward-bending portion suggests the possibility of higher wage rates reducing the quantity of labour supplied.

Industry Wage Rates

In the absence of market blockages (interferences with labour markets), wage and salary rates in the economy would be determined by the equilibrium of supply and demand for each type of labour, as shown in Figure 10-6. Employment in the particular industry illustrated would be 160 million

hours per year, at a wage rate of $8 per hour. At this rate, the extra revenue (*MRP*) to the employers from hiring the last hour of work would just equal the extra cost to the employees of working the last hour. (Instead of hours of employment per year, we could have used number of workers per year. For example, if the average work week was 35 hours for 50 weeks per year, the number of workers hired would be about 91 429 — that is to say, 160 million hours per year ÷ [35 × 50] hours per worker.)

The quantity of labour supplied by an individual worker depends on the wage rate and on the level of the worker's income. At higher income levels, the income effect may offset the wage rate effect, and a part of the supply curve may be negatively sloped (backward-bending). In a free labour market, the wage and salary rates are determined by the interaction of supply and demand.

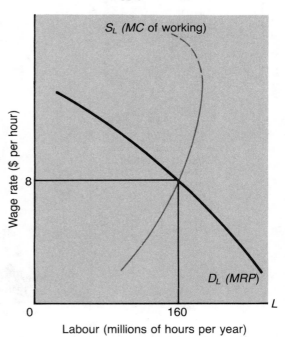

Fig. 10-6 Free market determination of labour compensation and employment

In a labour market without interference, wage rates and employment levels are determined by interaction of supply and demand.

---

1. Economists often refer to this price effect as a *substitution effect*. For example, considering the demand for a good or service, demand usually falls if the market price rises, because people substitute similar goods or services, which now have become relatively cheaper.

10-3 FURTHER LABOUR MARKET CONSIDERATIONS

In the above section, we assumed that the labour market was *purely competitive*. Even though some firms may have had monopoly power in their product markets, we assumed that there were many bidders for labour services. No one firm was large enough to materially influence the wage rate through its own actions, either by bidding for more labour or by withholding its demand for labour services. Similarly, it was assumed that no one seller of labour (worker or group of workers) could materially influence the wage rate by offering more or less labour. Within this competitive context, wage rates and employment are determined by the free interplay of supply and demand. Let us now examine some important exceptions to this situation. In particular, let us consider government or union enforced minimum wage rates, first within the context of an otherwise purely competitive labour market and then within the context of an *employer dominated* labour market.

Minimum Wage Laws

A **minimum wage law** puts a **floor** on wage rates. The possible effects of such legislation in a competitive labour market may be seen by reference to Figure 10-7. The reason for passing minimum wage legislation is to raise the wage rate in certain industries and for types of labour in which supply and demand conditions would otherwise determine a lower wage rate. In a labour market where the equilibrium wage is above the minimum wage, the minimum wage is irrelevant (as shown in Figure 10-7a). However, in an industry where the equilibrium wage is below the minimum wage, employers will hire fewer people at the minimum wage than they would if there was no minimum wage (see Figure 10-7b). In industry *B*, for example, at the minimum wage rate of $5 per hour, 10 000 people are willing to work and are seeking employment (see curve *S*). This number of people will not be hired, though, because at that level of employment the extra $3 revenue per hour received from the output produced by the 10 000th

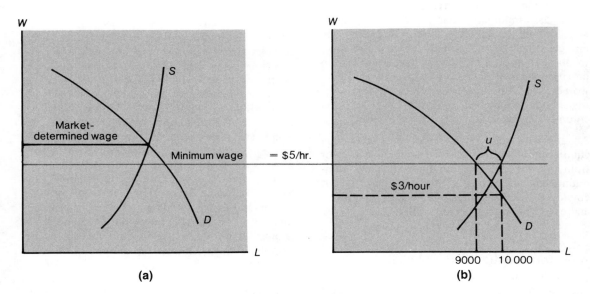

Fig. 10-7 Effect of a minimum wage on the labour market

(a) A legal minimum wage set below the market equilibrium has no effect on the labour market.

(b) A legal minimum wage set above the market equilibrium reduces the quantity of labour employed and causes excess supply of labour.

worker (from curve D) is less than the minimum wage that the firm would be forced to pay. In fact, this is the case for all employees beyond 9000. Where the minimum wage rate has some impact, it raises the wage rates of those lucky enough to remain working, but causes some unemployment within the industry. In Figure 10-7b, the amount of unemployment (as measured by u) in this case equals 1000 workers.

Union Enforced Wage Rates

One of the prime objectives of unions is to raise wage rates (including fringe benefits) of their members. Every year, or perhaps every two or three years, union leaders bargain with employers for a wage package better than they think the workers would otherwise be offered. Generally, if a union is successful in raising its members' wage rates above the level that would otherwise prevail (the equilibrium level), the effect on the labour market is the same as that of a minimum wage rate. For example, suppose in Figure 10-7b the $5 per hour minimum wage represented a union-negotiated (minimum) wage rate rather than a legislated minimum wage level. Once again, in this case there would be induced unemployment within the industry. Employers would not wish to hire more than 9000 workers because all additional workers would be anticipated to create less additional revenue than their additional cost (the union enforced wage rate).[2]

An effective wage floor (wage rate higher than equilibrium) may result from a union action or from government legislation imposing a legal minimum wage. In both cases, the quantity of labour employed is reduced below the equilibrium level, and excess supply of labour results.

A Monopsonistic Labour Market

In some labour markets, it sometimes happens that three or four larger firms are almost the sole em-

ployers of certain types of specialized labour services. In such cases the above analysis must be altered. Further, in this regard we must modify our earlier conclusions that minimum wage laws or union enforced wage rates necessarily reduce employment.

To examine an extreme but clear-cut case, let us suppose that there is a single employer of a certain type of labour. A single buyer of any good or service is called a **monopsonist**. Figure 10-8 illustrates the market for this particular type of labour. The demand for labour is represented by the D curve and the amount of labour that would be willingly offered at various wage rates by the S curve. This diagram is similar to Figure 10-6 except for one important thing. The market demand curve is not the (horizontal) sum of the demand curves of a large number of firms. Instead, it is the marginal revenue product curve of a single firm.

The presence of a single employer for a whole class of labour means that the employer's actions alone influence the wage rate. For example, at a wage rate of $8 per hour and an employment of 100 workers, management may wish to offer a higher wage rate and employ more workers. Suppose it raises the wage rate to $9 per hour and attracts 100 more workers. For a total of 200 workers hired, each hour will now be costing the employer $9 × 200 = $1800, as opposed to $8 × 100 = $800 for the original 100 workers. The extra cost of employing the second 100 workers is, then ($1800 − $800) / 100 = $10 per hour. The extra or **marginal labour cost** (*MLC*) exceeds the wage rate paid, because when the wage rate is raised the firm has to pay this new rate to all its employees. Here, for example, it costs $9 per hour for each new employee. In addition, the firm must pay $1 per hour more to its original 100 employees.

A monopsonist would be increasing its profit as long as the extra revenue obtained from hiring another employee exceeded the extra cost. The firm therefore determines the optimal quantity of labour it should hire by equating marginal labour cost (*MLC*) with the marginal revenue product (*MRP*) of that labour. In this case, the management would continue to hire additional personnel up to L_0, for which it would have to pay a wage of W_0 (since the market supply of labour curve indicates that quantity L_0 will be forthcoming at wage W_0 per hour).

---

2. This brief discussion hardly does justice to the union movement. See Chapter 15.

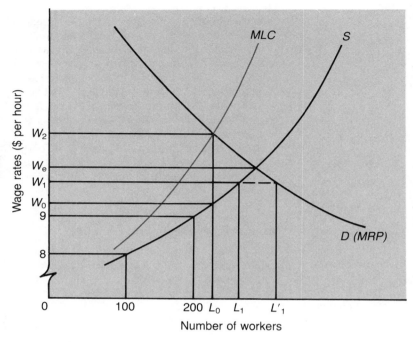

Fig. 10-8 A monopsonist employer

A monopsonist determines the optimal quantity of labour hired (L_0) by equating marginal labour cost (*MLC*) with marginal revenue product of labour (*MRP*). The wage rate (W_0) required to attract L_0 of labour is indicated by the supply of labour curve (*S*). A minimum wage or a union contract setting the wage rate at W_1 in this case raises both the level of employment and the wage rate.

Enforced Wage Rates

Let us now suppose there is either a government minimum wage or a union wage rate of W_1 (in Figure 10-8). This being the case, the monopsonist cannot offer a wage below W_1 but can hire as many as it likes at this rate. In this instance, then, the cost of hiring each new worker up to L_1 is W_1. It does not entail a raise for any previous workers because they would already be earning W_1. Under these circumstances, the upward sloping *MLC* curve is irrelevant and the monopsonist would be quite willing to employ L_1 workers at the enforced wage W_1. Actually, the monopsonist would be willing to employ more workers (L') at the given wage rate W_1, but the market would not supply L'_1 workers at this wage rate. The point, though, is

that in this case an enforced minimum wage rate above that which the employer would freely pay leads to a *greater* rather than a smaller, amount of employment, and this would be the case for all such wage rates up to W_2, though for all such wage rates in excess of W_e there would be some unemployment ($D < S$).

In the presence of monopsony in the labour market, hiring decisions consistent with profit maximization require that firms equate marginal labour cost (*MLC*) with marginal revenue product (*MRP*). In such markets, minimum wage laws or union wage agreements may raise both the wage rate and the level of employment above the monopsony equilibrium.

Wage Differences and Fairness

In the Canadian economy, there are considerable differences in wages and salaries between various occupations, and even within the same occupation but between different regions. What are the reasons for these differences? Are these differences *fair*?

Let us first examine these questions assuming competitive labour markets with no blockage (unions or minimum wage rates). The annual wage or salary compensation for each occupation would depend on the particular supply and demand conditions in each labour market. For example, suppose the market for two different types of work is as shown in Figure 10-9. Because the supply and demand conditions in the two markets differ, the salary of one occupation is $15 000 per year whereas that of the other is $75 000 per year. Let us ask ourselves why workers in occupation A do not switch and move into occupation B since the salary there is so much greater. Or, if they cannot switch, because of lack of appropriate training and

education, why is it that young people do not all train for those professions with the highest salaries? If they did so, in time the number training for an entering occupation B would increase (the supply curve would shift to the right), and the annual compensation would eventually become equal to that of A, as shown in the figure. All occupations would, therefore, eventually provide the same monetary remuneration. The reason for this levelling would be an adjustment in the supply of workers within each industry. In reality, of course, wage and salary differentials persist. There are many reasons for this, and some of these are now discussed.

Nonmonetary Costs and Benefits

Money income is not the only form of compensation from employment. Each job carries with it various *nonmonetary rewards*. Further, each job entails different *nonmonetary hardships* or *costs*. For example, maximum security prison work in-

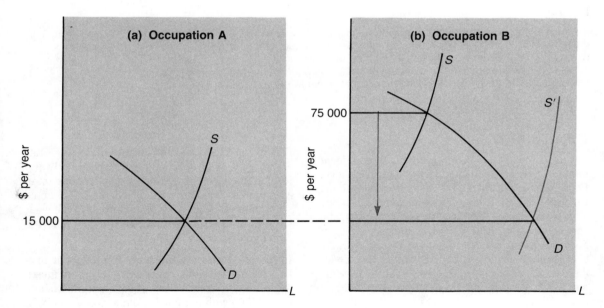

Fig. 10-9 Occupational wage differences

(a) A combination of low demand and large supply of labour in occupation A results in low annual wage.

(b) A combination of high demand and limited supply of labour in occupation B results in high annual wage.

volves certain risks that other occupations do not. In this case, therefore, extra compensation would be required relative to some safer jobs (requiring the same skill and education) to keep labour in this occupation. To be a tennis coach for seven hours a day at a private tennis club generally entails less unpleasant effort than seven hours of work on the production line of a manufacturing plant. Therefore, many tennis coaches would not switch to working in a manufacturing plant even though wages might be higher in the latter occupation.

This means that if we wish to compare *total compensation* between different jobs properly we must not forget to add in nonmonetary benefits and subtract nonmonetary costs. Doing so would significantly reduce some apparent differences in salaries between different occupations. This is also part of the explanation of regional salary differences. Salaries in a desirable part of the country (from most people's viewpoint) tend to be lower for the same occupations than those in less desirable regions.

However, after adding in all nonmonetary costs and benefits for each occupation there would still be significant differences in total compensation between occupations. Why, then, over time, does labour not leave those occupations whose total compensation is the least and move into those occupations where total compensation is the greatest? There are a number of possible reasons.

Ability Differences

A nuclear physicist may not easily be able to switch jobs and become a mechanic or a physical education instructor, just because the individual perceives better total compensation (after adding in all nonmonetary costs and benefits) in the latter occupations. The physicist may never have had the ability to become a mechanic or a physical education instructor. Similarly, the young student who may be eyeing the career and compensation of a nuclear physicist may not have the mathematical aptitude necessary for that type of work. Certain natural abilities and aptitudes (mental and/or physical) are required for different occupations. Therefore, certain differences between total compensation are likely to persist for this reason (that is, the supply curve of labour for the $75 000 a year figure occupation of Figure 10-9 may not easily shift to the right). If this is the case, the difference in salaries between occupations can only be

reduced in a free market by demand shifts. For example, if the general public became fed up with hockey, refusing to watch it on TV or pay admission to the games, a drop in demand for hockey players would occur, consequently lowering hockey salaries.

Incomplete Labour Information

Some differences in wage rates between occupations and different regions occur because there is a *lack of information* concerning the higher paying jobs. Also, some people who are willing to accept lower paying jobs in particular regions of the country rather than move to areas where the pay is better may incorrectly overestimate the nonmonetary value of living in their particular region relative to that of others merely because they have not experienced living elsewhere. A great deal of information concerning nonmonetary costs and benefits can be discovered only as the particular jobs or regional locations are experienced.

Artificial Occupational Blockages

Even though there are many reasons for the fact that free entry to occupations would not remove all monetary income differentials, differences in *total compensation* would tend to be eliminated (except for differences attributable to misinformation and different levels of natural ability, which may still be significant).

As we argued above, it is very difficult to measure precisely total occupational compensation. Nevertheless, there is a way to discover whether a particular occupation offers greater total compensation than normal. If there are eager potential entrants, capable of adequately performing the usual tasks required of the occupation, and yet these people are for some reason prevented from entering the field (either directly or at the apprenticeship or training program level), this occupation must be offering more attractive returns than normal. Further, there must be some artificial blockages to entry, imposed either from within by existing members of the occupation or, perhaps, externally by government authorities. Some examples of such barriers to entry include restrictions on enrolment in training institutions, prior residence or citizenship requirements and nonrecognition of qualifications obtained in other jurisdictions.

Human Capital

Sooner or later, our discussion of income compensation must get around to the fact that some occupations require a great deal of educational or apprenticeship training at little or no pay. For example, lawyers must spend six to seven years in university, a year articling and a year preparing for bar examinations. Plumbers must spend about five years in apprenticeship training. This time represents an *occupational investment*, the dollar value of which is roughly the cumulative salary foregone over the training period (plus the dollar value of any extra effort during the training period).

The average annual salary earned from such occupations must therefore be higher than that earned from jobs requiring similar effort, risk and nonmonetary costs and benefits, but without the long training period. In fact, if the salaries were not higher, few potential candidates would be willing to make the human investment in time, energy and lost income in training to be lawyers or plumbers. This reluctance would reduce the supply of new entrants into these occupations, and without a corresponding reduction in demand for their services, would raise wage or salaries to levels that candidates would once more find attractive.

Just as real investment adds to a company's stock of physical capital, so may we consider a person's investment in training and education as a building up of **human capital**. A rough monetary measure of the rate of return to an investment in human capital for a particular occupation can be calculated as follows:

Rate of return to an investment in human capital consisting of specialized education and training for a particular occupation $\simeq$ $\dfrac{\text{Average annual increase in salary that the occupation offers over and above that of occupations without the training but with similar risk and effort}}{\text{Total lost income experienced during the training program}} \times 100\%$

In practice, however, it may be difficult to find occupations differing only in salary and training time. Therefore, it may be necessary to attempt to place a value as well on such things as greater prestige, job security and reduced human effort associated with an occupation. The dollar equivalent of these attributes would be added to the numerator. On the other hand, the dollar equivalent of such job characteristics as danger or increased pressure from additional responsibilities attached to the occupation would have to be subtracted from the numerator.

For example, suppose one estimates the extra cost of a longer training program required to become a medical specialist rather than a veterinarian, plus the lost income of the extra years of training, to be $60 000. The average extra annual dollar income is expected to be, say, $50 000; the extra prestige is worth $5000 a year, but the extra responsibility is worth $-$15 000 per year. Finally, suppose the individual (from a personal viewpoint) views all other factors as being roughly equal in both professions. The rate of return offered to an individual contemplating investing in a medical rather than a veterinary career would, therefore, be roughly:

$$\frac{(\$50\ 000 + \$5000 - \$15\ 000)}{\$60\ 000} \times 100\% = 67\% \text{ per annum}$$

If this sort of rate of return was offered to many of those contemplating entering the medical profession, there would be a great demand by prospective students for medical programs. This increased attempted entry into the medical profession would only stop if the rate of return was bid down to levels that could be earned elsewhere for similar risk.

Earnings of Doctors: An Illustration

Many people think the earnings of doctors are quite high (see, for example, Table 10-2). This has come about partly because there is limited entry into the medical profession as a result of the high standards that must be met by prospective entrants (a supply-limiting factor) and also partly as a result of the value we place on medical care and the presence of universal medical insurance (demand factor). Some argue that doctors earn fair wages for their efforts; others vehemently disagree. Nevertheless, every year a considerable number of young people attempt to get into the medical profession in order to partake of these high earnings. Therefore it would appear that, at least in the minds of many of those contemplating a career, when all costs and benefits are weighed the medical profession offers positive inducement over many others.

Some argue that restricted entry into the medical profession should be relaxed — that standards need not be as high as they are. The medical profession for the most part, however, disagrees. Others argue that an increase in the long-run supply of doctors would not necessarily lower doctors' earnings anyway. The argument used here is that because patients are unable to evaluate accurately the need for many types of services the doctors supply, the doctors may compensate for erosion in their fees — which might otherwise come about — by convincing the reduced number of patients per doctor that each should visit more often, have additional tests, additional operations and so on. This idea in effect argues that the medical profession can shift the demand curve to the right to maintain fees and incomes should the profession face an increase in the supply of doctors.

One problem facing governments which attempt to hold down medical costs by restricting doctors' fees and incomes is that doctors who feel that they can earn a sufficiently higher income elsewhere may leave the province or country, thereby reducing supply.

Fairness

Whether or not differences in total compensation for different jobs and regions are fair is a difficult question indeed. First of all, it is necessary (as discussed above) to estimate the nonmonetary costs and benefits associated with each job and each region of the country in order to detect actual differences. This task would be difficult if not impossible by itself. You and I, for example, may disagree about the value of working and living in a small town in the Maritimes relative to a large city in Western Canada, let alone the many other factors that have to be taken into consideration. These differences in opinion as to the appropriate nonmonetary costs and benefits occur because we all have different tastes and preferences. Further, our different philosophical viewpoints would probably keep us up all night arguing about what is fair and unfair in the first place. Chapter 13 considers

the question of government involvement in attempting to provide a fair distribution of income.

The observed substantial differentials in earnings among occupations and among regions within an occupation can be attributed to a variety of factors. They include nonmonetary aspects of work, ability differences, incomplete information, labour market policies and inter-occupational differences in the level of human capital. Some government policy measures are designed to modify these differentials in accordance with the current understanding of the notion of fairness.

10-4 EARNINGS ON FINANCIAL WEALTH

Financial wealth may consist of deposits in banks or trust companies, accumulations in pension funds, life insurance contracts, bonds or common stocks. There is a whole spectrum of financial assets, each carrying its own peculiar risk characteristics and consequently offering its own particular rate of return.

The income from financial wealth stems from the dollar amount invested multiplied by the average **rate of return** (yield or interest rate) that the owner receives on it. The amount invested is either inherited or accumulated from past savings of labour income. The remaining factor that determines financial income is, therefore, the average rate of return on invested funds. It is of some interest, then, to examine what factors influence the actual average rate of return earned on invested funds.

As it turns out, government spending, taxation and the Bank of Canada all play significant roles in the determination of the level of interest rates. However, a treatment of these aspects cannot be presented without a lengthy discussion of various macroeconomic concepts. As a result, our discussion below will be deficient at least to this extent.

Capital Productivity

If financial yields rise, investors holding bonds, stocks and all other financial instruments will earn higher rates of return on their financial wealth and, consequently, higher incomes. On the other side of the coin, business firms will now have to earn more to cover the higher cost of capital (funds).

We are led, therefore, to consider the **productivity of real capital**, because real capital is what the capital funds are being used to finance. The investment in plant, machinery and inventories must provide a rate of return sufficient to cover the cost of capital funds used to finance them. We have, in fact, already examined in some detail the connection between real investment and the cost of capital in Chapters 8 and 9.

Suppose a particular firm (Co. A Ltd.) at a given time considers the investment projects indicated in the top half of Table 10-3. The estimated rates of return are calculated after all nonfinancial costs, but before the cost of necessary capital funds. The projects have been arranged by expected rate of return, from highest to lowest. As usual, this information may be depicted graphically — as in Figure 10-10. All business firms would face similar schedules of possible investment projects during the year. For example, we have also depicted a schedule for another firm, Co. B Ltd.

These schedules represent the demand by the two businesses for investment funds. For example, if the annual cost of capital funds to Co. A Ltd. is 12%, because projects 1, 2 and 3 — but not the rest — are expected to provide at least this great a return, Co. A Ltd. would demand $270 000 (that is $50 000 + $100 000 + $120 000) of new capital funds during the year. Similarly Co. B would demand $185 000 of funds if the cost of capital is 12%. We can arrive at the total demand for investment funds for both companies by adding the amounts demanded by Co. A and Co. B, as has been done in the third part of Figure 10-10. As we can see, the "step" curves lose a lot of their "lumpiness" when combined. In fact, the total business sector's demand for capital funds in a given year would be a smooth curve, as shown in Figure 10-11.

Private Investment Funds

What appears as a *cost* to the management of business firms is a *rate of return* to the lenders of capital funds (the bondholders and stockholders of the firm). Therefore, the **supply of savings funds** (or, one could say, the supply of investment funds or capital funds) to be used by the firm for investment

Table 10-3 Determination of business demand for capital funds

Project	Expected annual rate of return (before financing costs) (% per year)	Investment funds required to undertake each project ($)
Company A		
1	21	50 000
2	17	100 000
3	15	120 000
4	11	80 000
5	7	40 000
6	3	75 000
7	−2	60 000
Company B		
1	18	65 000
2	14	120 000
3	5	80 000
4	−6	20 000

Potential investment projects of two firms (Co. A and Co. B) are ranked according to the expected rate of return. Comparison of the expected rate of return with the cost of capital funds determines which projects will be accepted or rejected.

purposes would be greater, the greater the annual yield offered. In other words, the supply of investment funds would slope upward, as shown in Figure 10-11.

Given the supply and demand of investment funds as shown, the cost of capital (funds) would be about 10%, and the total amount invested during the year within the economy, $40 billion.

Let us now examine the effect on the cost of capital (or rate of return on investment funds) of two economic shocks.

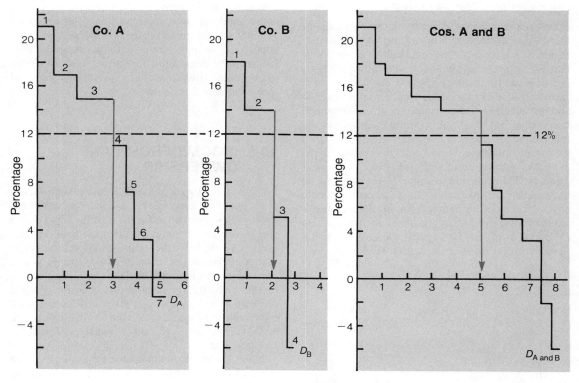

Volume of investment (00 000s of $ per year)

Fig. 10-10 **Determination of business demand for capital funds**

Graphical representation of data from Table 10-3. The assumed cost of capital funds of 12% implies that only projects with an expected rate of return above the dotted line will be accepted.

(i) The Impatience of Savers

If individuals within the economy suddenly increase their desire to consume now rather than save now and consume in future years, this event would cause a reduction in the willingness of households to supply investment funds. They would choose to buy few corporate bonds and common stock at each offered rate of return. In Figure 10-11, this change is shown by a shift to the left in the supply of investment funds' curve. At 10%, for example, as represented by the *S* curve, savers are not willing to lend to firms as much as before. The effect of this reduction in thriftiness of households would be to increase the cost of capital funds to firms (and simultaneously to lower the level of investment).

(ii) Expected Rate of Return

Economic conditions affect business estimates of the expected rates of return from capital investments. If businesses foresee a healthy economy — that is, little unemployment and strongly increasing demand for their goods and services — such factors lead them to predict higher sales revenue and profitability (after covering all nonfinancial costs) than in periods of economic slump. On the other hand, if the economy suddenly goes into a downturn, business would adjust downward the expected returns from each of their investment projects. This adjustment would lower the demand by business for investment funds at each possible cost of capital (the demand for investment funds would shift to the left as shown by the broken line D' curve in Figure 10-11, and the cost of capital (and return on investment funds) would fall.

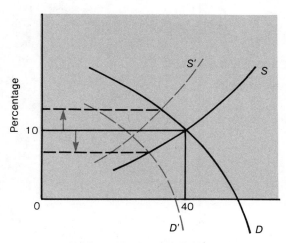

Fig. 10-11 Market demand and supply for investment funds

Market demand for investment funds shifts to the left as a result of an increased public desire to consume, rather than to save. Market supply of investment funds shifts to the left as a result of a downturn in the economy and expected reduction in the productivity of real capital.

The relationship between the productivity of real capital and the cost of capital funds influences investment decisions of business firms as well as the supply of savings funds to them. Among other factors to be considered are the public's propensity to consume (or to save) and expectations about future economic conditions.

10-5 INCOME FROM LAND OWNERSHIP

Land is a factor of production along with labour and capital. Unlike labour and capital, however, the total quantity of land is *fixed*. If land had only a single use, say, agriculture, its price would be determined strictly by the value of agricultural goods that could be produced on it. For example, with a particular productivity of land and a particular market price for agricultural products, the demand for land might appear as shown in Figure 10-12. Given the fixed quantity of land available as S, the annual *rental price of land* would be $50 per hectare per year.

Note that in the diagram we have specified the price of land in terms of the rent per year that an owner would require to lease the land to a farmer rather than in terms of the purchase price of land. Both ways of specifying land prices are actually equivalent. An illustration follows.

Suppose we own 100 hectares of property worth $100 000 on the open market. If the going interest rate is 20%, the annual rental market value of our land would be $20 000 (in other words, $100 000 × 20%). This must be so, since if the annual rent asked was more than $20 000 — say $25 000 — it would be cheaper for a farmer to borrow $100 000 at 20% and purchase our land outright, since the annual interest costs would only be $20 000 per year.

Given an interest rate (or cost of capital), the following direct connection exists between annual land rents and purchase values:

$$\begin{array}{ccc} \text{Annual land} \\ \text{rental value} \end{array} = \begin{array}{c} \text{market value} \\ \text{of land} \end{array} \times \begin{array}{c} \text{interest} \\ \text{rate} \end{array}$$

For purposes of illustration we will depict the price of land as its annual rental value rather than as the market (purchase) price.

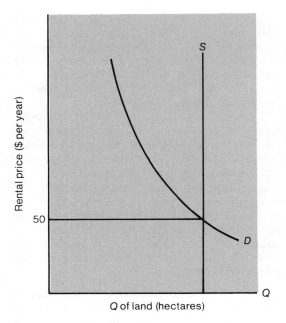

Fig. 10-12 Market determination of the price of land

A representation of the market for land with a single use (the total quantity of such land is fixed).

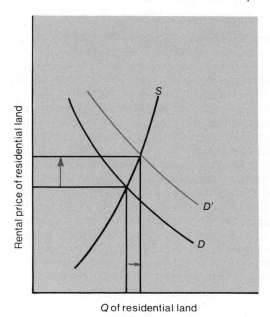

Fig. 10-13 Determination of the price of residential land

A representation of the market for land with multiple uses. The supply of land for a particular use varies with the market price.

Multiple Purpose Land

In practice, land does not have a single use. It may be used for many purposes, including agriculture, industry, recreation and housing. Therefore, whereas land in total is fixed, the amount used in any one industry — for example, agriculture or housing — is not. If families are willing to pay higher prices (in terms of annual rents or purchase prices) for land used in residential construction than farmers are willing to pay for land used in agriculture, some farmers will sell their land to developers. Whereas total land supply may be completely price insensitive, land supply in any of its particular uses is not.

For example, the market for housing land in all of Canada might appear as shown in Figure 10-13. If demand for land to be used in residential construction increased (to D'), the price of residential land would increase. However, so would the quantity supplied, as farmers within or near residential areas found that by selling their farms and investing the funds received they could earn a higher interest income than the annual return they were making from farming.

On the other hand, the supply of residential land within a 20 km radius of the centre of Vancouver, for instance, is for practical purposes a fixed quantity (unless someone fills in part of the Pacific Ocean) and completely price insensitive — as the S curve in Figure 10-12 illustrates.

Demand-Determined Value

Even though the allocation of land among its various uses may change, the total supply of land is for practical purposes a fixed, price-insensitive quantity, as shown by Figure 10-12. Therefore, the average value of land in all its uses is strictly *demand determined*. The demand for land in turn is determined, as in the case of all factors of production, by the value of the goods or services the land can provide.

The quantity of land available for its present use would remain constant at S even if, for example, the demand curve in Figure 10-12 shifted to the right and the payment for the use of the land increased above \$50 per hectare per year. Conversely, if the demand curve shifted to the left and the payment for the use of land dropped (perhaps even close to zero), the quantity of land available would remain constant at S since, as postulated above, the land has only one single use — in this case agriculture — and would not be withdrawn in response to a reduction in payment.

In general, whenever a change in the payment to the owner of a factor of production does not alter the quantity of the factor available for its present use, such payment is called **economic rent**. Economic rent must be distinguished from rental payments for the lease of an apartment or a car, or rent for a parcel of land when the quantity available changes as rent changes, as for example, in Figure 10-13, where land has multiple uses. Economic rent is that portion of a payment received by the owner of a factor (input) which is in excess of what is required to keep the input in its present use.

For example, most of the salary of an outstanding hockey player or basketball or baseball player is economic rent: there will always be only one Wayne Gretzky, no matter how high a salary the NHL may offer. Similarly, natural resources also generate economic rent. Thus, the amount of electricity obtained from a given hydro site will not change appreciably as prices of electricity fluctuate. The same holds true for mineral deposits, commercial fish stocks, and so on.

Economic rent represents a transfer of wealth from users to owners of the factor (input) in question. It does, however, have an allocative function as well — it rations the available supply to those who are most willing and able to pay for it. Since quantity supplied is insensitive to the amount of economic rent collected, most (or all) of the rent may be taxed away by the government without affecting supply. In the long run, of course, the quantity of many "fixed" factors may change; hence, the imposition of a tax on economic rent may make a difference.

Land is a unique factor of production in that its total amount is fixed. However, the allocation of land among its various uses responds to changes in relative prices.

CONCLUDING REMARKS

In a market economy, the income paid to a factor is determined by the value to the economy of what the factor produces (demand aspect) and the relative abundance of the factor (supply aspect). This tendency sometimes results in what many people regard as an unfair distribution of income. For this reason, we allow our governments to attempt redistribution of income through taxes and expenditures. As we will see later on, sometimes this attempt is successful and sometimes it is not.

KEY TERMS AND CONCEPTS

demand for labour	marginal labour cost
marginal revenue product	human capital
marginal product of labour	rate of return
minimum wage law	productivity of real capital
wage floor	supply of savings funds
monopsonist	economic rent

PROBLEMS

Problem 1

a) What factors determine the demand and supply for a particular type of labour?

b) If an individual's wage rate was increased, what factors would determine whether the individual would like to work more or less?

c) Generally speaking, why would higher wage rates tend to reduce the number of workers a firm is willing to hire? Explain.

Problem 2

Explain why legislated minimum wage rates or union-enforced wage rates in a particular industry can give rise to unemployment within the industry.

Problem 3

a) A given firm experiences roughly constant nonlabour variable costs of $2 per unit of output over a wide production range. Show that the following is a correct expression for the firm's marginal costs:

$$MC = \$2 + \frac{\text{wage rate}}{\text{marginal product of labour}}$$

(Hint: Write out the meaning of the numerator and denominator of the second expression, perhaps utilizing a numerical example.)

b) Assuming the wage rate is set by industry-wide bargaining for a two year period, explain the expected shape of the above firm's marginal cost curve as typically plotted on a diagram such as the one below.

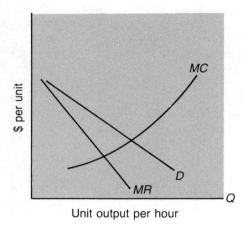

Unit output per hour

c) Using the diagram of part (b) as an aid, explain in words why the quantity of labour demanded by a firm is lower, the higher the wage rate is.

Problem 4

a) Explain why people in different occupations earn different wages and salaries.

b) Explain why some differences in wages and salaries are not eliminated over time by people's moving out of poor paying jobs and into the well paying ones.

Problem 5

a) Define what is meant by monopsony power.

b) Explain, with the aid of a diagram, why either a legal minimum wage rate or a minimum enforced wage rate (above that which a firm with monopsony power would otherwise offer) might not reduce employment.

Problem 6

a) Estimate from your own perceptions (and with whatever information you may be able to obtain) the rate of return on human capital from being a lawyer rather than a public school teacher (include your personal evaluation of perceived nonmonetary costs and benfits of each profession in the calculations).

b) Would you expect widely differing answers from any group answering the (a) part of this problem? Why? Explain what this finding has to do with Problem 4(b).

Problem 7

Company A Ltd. is in the process of evaluating six investment proposals put forth by its planning department. The results are shown directly below.

Project #	Expected annual rate of return (before financing costs) (% per year)	Investment funds required to undertake each project ($)
1	23	75 000
2	6	100 000
3	-2	80 000
4	15	200 000
5	13	90 000
6	10	125 000

a) Plot Co. A Ltd.'s demand for investment funds on a diagram such as the one below.

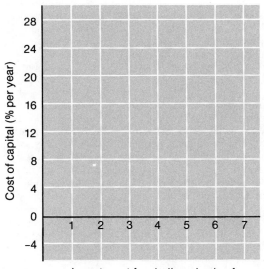

b) If the cost of capital facing Co. A Ltd. is 11%, which projects would the firm plan to undertake? What total investment? Depict the situation on the diagram drawn in part (a).

Problem 8

Explain the effects of rapid urban growth within an agricultural area on the prices of (i) residential land, (ii) farmland, (iii) the cost of wheat production.

CASES

Case 10-1

The Financial Post

Disrespect for capital may lower standard of living

By JOHN S. McCALLUM

PROSPEROUS economies throughout history have generally had a deep respect for capital. Those involved in the Canadian policy community should give this serious thought. Over and over again we make decisions that show a disrespect, often bordering on contempt, for capital.

Capital comes in three forms: human, financial, and physical. *Human capital* is the skills an individual — such as a doctor, mechanic or engineer — possesses as a result of training, experience and natural gift. *Financial capital* is a paper claim, such as a bond or mortgage, that obligates one party to make payments to another party. Often, financial capital is secured by a claim on *physical capital*, such as a house or land.

As a community, we show disrespect for capital in numerous ways. Each, however, is a play on the same theme: an actual or implied term of the capital being committed is violated by some level of government.

Examples abound:

• The Manitoba government recently joined Saskatchewan in introducing legislation which would permit a *moratorium on farm foreclosures*. The affront to capital: financial capital was advanced on the condition that foreclosure was an option of the lender should contracted obligations not be honored.

• The Ontario government, along with others, has *outlawed extra-billing by doctors*. The affront to capital: human capital was committed to accumulating medical skills on the expectation that doctors had latitude in billing.

• Between 1976 and 1984, *the federal gov-*

ernment conducted its financial affairs imprudently. The affront to capital: large unanticipated financial losses for many holding Canadian securities.

The historical link between respect for capital and prosperity is not coincidental. *Where capital is systematically not respected, people become unwilling to invest*; instead, they either increase their consumption or do their investing in more hospitable jurisdictions.

Consider some of the long-term implications of the aforementioned specific examples of how we affront capital:

• Are financial institutions likely to be enthusiastic about *new agricultural lending in areas that change the foreclosure rules* after the fact? Is this in the best interests of the capable and solvent farm operators, who depend on credit? Is it in the best interests of an agricultural industry with a greater need for capital today, than at any time since the 1930s, because of extraordinary advances in genetic and other farm technologies?

• Does Ontario's move on extra-billing *inspire young people* to make the financial and other sacrifices involved *to become a doctor*? Are doctors in practice not inspired to work less, or elsewhere? In time, does this not lead to reductions in both health-care quantity and quality?

• Aren't *real interest rates high*, and *real investment rates inadequate*, at least partly *because we have managed the C$ and inflation* to the obvious detriment of capital?

If we are to continue to be a high-standard-of-living economy, we must show more respect for capital than we have shown of late.

a) Give your interpretation of the government motivation for each of the three policy actions discussed in the article.

b) Draw a separate supply-demand diagram for each of the following: (i) the market for agricultural loans, (ii) the Ontario medical services market, (iii) the Canadian securities market.

Show the impact of each of the three "affronts to capital" in the diagrams and explain the consequences.

c) How would you illustrate, in the appropriate diagram in part (b), the effect of each of the following: (i) extraordinary advances in genetic and other farm technologies, (ii) growing "financial and other sacrifices involved in becoming a doctor," (iii) anticipated improvement in the prospects of the Canadian economy.

Case 10-2

The Financial Post

Construction workers lead labor's retreat

By JAMES BAGNALL

IN A bargaining calendar dominated this year by civil servants, meat packers and construction workers, it is the construction workers who stand out.

Across the country, nearly a quarter of a million building tradesmen are renegotiating contracts against the backdrop of an industry taking decentralized bargaining to extremes.

In Alberta and Saskatchewan, contractors are setting wage rates unilaterally for individual jobs. B.C. builders are threatening to do the same if this April's bargaining sessions don't give them the kind of flexibility they're looking for.

Proof of the hardness of the line being taken by contractors is the fact that building trade unions in the two Prairie provinces are still renegotiating contracts that expired in 1984. At the time, a sharp building recession throughout the West has forced employers to take drastic action. Unable to pay the $19–$25 an hour wages they had agreed to during the 1982 bargaining round, industry leaders, aided by favorable labor board rulings, simply proceeded as though the contracts did not exist.

"It's absolute chaos out here," says Raymond Gall, Canadian director of the Sheet Metal Workers' International Association.

"Employers still have the right to set wages wherever they want."

The Alberta Construction Labor Relations Association, a management group, doesn't see it in that light. "The bargaining relationships still exist," says George Akins, the association's vice-president in charge of negotiations, "but unless wages are competitive, there's just no work."

Union members, as well as former union members, have been taking work wherever they can find it, with the result that roughly 90% of construction in the province is now done at nonunion rates. In Saskatchewan, about 85% of the work is nonunion vs 40% in British Columbia and 25% or so in Quebec, where a growing black market in construction labor is making inroads in an industry that is, by law, 100% union.

The temper of this spring's negotiations differs wildly by region — ranging from a potentially explosive showdown between B.C. building trades unions, against the backdrop of Expo 86, to the more businesslike pace of talks in both Manitoba and Ontario.

Talks in Manitoba are a remarkable contrast to those taking place elsewhere in the West. Even though contracts don't expire until the end of April, the provincial employers' association has already reached agreement with key trades, including electricians, carpenters, sheetmetal workers and bricklayers. (The pattern is 1%–2% annually.)

Robert Glass, head of the association, says: "In the 1984 round, we didn't want to get into the same dustup they had in Alberta so we made a tradeoff with the unions — we didn't kill them on money but we got good concessions on work rules. Now we're holding our own against non-union labor."

Quebec presents the most unusual scenario this year, in part because industry-wide negotiations in 1982 and 1984 both ended with a government-imposed contract. As a result, there is a lot of pent-up frustration on both sides in this spring's round, which will involve more than 90,000 workers.

Franco Fava, president of the Association of Building Contractors of Quebec, says: "Most of the problems we've had come from government-imposed contracts, legislation and bylaws. But there's also the political problem of whether anybody is going to permit an industry-wide strike. If you need a strike to solve a lot of these problems, then maybe there should be one."

A minor building boom in Ontario is fueling some speculation about a wage push from the unions. But, so far, neither side is anticipating a repeat of the 1982 strike-plagued bargaining round. A spokesman for the influential electricians' union says: "There's all kinds of work in this province right now, but that doesn't mean we're going to go after high wages because these would kill us in the long run."

Revisions

That's a lesson that came hard after the 1982 round of talks, when many construction unions across the country struck their way to 10% average annual wages while the bottom was falling out of the economy. In the 1984 round, the same unions were forced to accept wage freezes and substantial revisions to work rules.

In many areas, they're still looking at employer demands for wage cuts and more changes to work rules. In Nova Scotia, for example, several key groups — including operating engineers — have recently agreed to revise wage rates down a few notches in mid-contract. Also voluntarily reopening a four-year wage contract is the same plumbers' local that caused such big headlines in 1983 when it negotiated 11% average annual wage raises in defiance of Ottawa's 6/5 wage restraint program. Nova Scotia building contractors are trying to negotiate a freeze as part of a contract extension.

The relatively low construction settlements may help drive national average annual wage raises downward. They are already running at the historically low level of 3.5%–3.8%. But even these numbers are starting to look good to about 8,000 workers in the meat-packing industry, where key companies such as Canada Packers are seeking to continue a wage freeze that unions agreed to in 1984.

Public service unions in British Columbia, Alberta, Ottawa and Quebec, for their part, are preoccupied with trying to fend off government attempts to increase productivity and eliminate positions.

The most interesting talks involve the latter two jurisdictions because they're going in totally opposite directions. At the federal level, Treasury Board President Robert de Cotret is conducting government-wide negotiations for the first time in an effort to standardize general working conditions for 200,000 civil servants and to make some sense of the 40-plus different bargaining units.

Since each unit retains the right to strike over key monetary issues, consistent contracts remain a long way off. However, the federal unions are moving closer to the experience of Quebec's common front of teachers, hospital employees and public sector workers — which, until this year, have negotiated contracts alongside each other.

However, a split developed in the various Quebec union groups three years ago when the teachers tried to defy the government's attempt to impose wage cuts in the public service. Although the unions are now separately trying to make up some of that lost ground, it's widely believed they don't have the stomach for another confrontation so soon.

a) Show diagrammatically what kind of developments in the relevant markets could have led to the situation where "unions were forced to accept wage freezes and substantial revisions to work rules."

b) The article suggests that collective bargaining is becoming decentralized (in some cases to the point where "contractors are setting wage rates unilaterally for individual jobs"). Assuming the construction industry is a monopsony, compare the wage and employment levels arrived at in decentralized bargaining with those arrived at in industry-wide contracts.

c) What are some of the advantages of centralized industry-wide (government-wide) negotiations?

d) In your diagrams, show the impact of competition from nonunionized labour.

CHAPTER 11

Microeconomics of International Markets

LEARNING OBJECTIVES

After reading this chapter you should be able to explain:

1. Absolute advantage, comparative advantage, and benefits from international trade.

2. The potential costs of international specialization.

3. Popular misconceptions about, and objections to, international trade.

4. Tariffs, quotas, subsidies and other protectionist policy measures.

5. Dumping in international trade.

6. Multinational enterprises, foreign investment and Canadian government policies limiting foreign ownership.

7. The benefits and costs of freer trade between Canada and the U.S.

11-1 INTRODUCTION AND PURPOSE

Canada is a very open economy, which means that international transactions are an important part of our economic life. In fact, approximately 40% of our economic activity is connected with selling or buying goods and services abroad.

There are two types of international markets: (a) goods and services, and (b) financial. This chapter seeks to investigate the costs and benefits of dealing in these international markets. By and large, we will focus on international trading in goods and services. However, the latter part of the chapter does examine some of the costs and benefits of foreign investment. Other international financial topics are considered within the subject of macroeconomics.

A breakdown of our international trade in merchandise by commodity and area is contained in Tables 11-1 and 11-2. From Table 11-1, approximately 52% of our exports are seen to be in the form of natural resource and semiprocessed products while about 48% consist of manufactured goods. Of our imports, approximately 30% are of the natural resource and semiprocessed variety while about 70% are manufactured goods. From Table 11-2, it is clear that the United States is our largest trading partner, accounting for about three-quarters of our foreign merchandise exports (sales) and imports (purchases).

Table 11-1 **Canadian foreign trade, by commodity, 1986**

Exports	Billions of $	Percent of total
Farm and fish products	11.3	9.4
Forest products	17.6	14.6
Energy materials	11.3	9.4
Other minerals and metals	15.4	12.8
Chemicals and fertilizers	5.0	4.1
Motor vehicles and parts	34.3	28.4
Other manufactured goods	23.5	19.5
Other exports	2.2	1.8
Total merchandise exports	120.6	100.0

Imports		
Food	7.6	6.9
Energy materials	5.1	4.6
Industrial and construction materials	20.2	18.3
Motor vehicles and parts	33.4	30.2
Producers' equipment	31.2	28.2
Consumer goods	12.0	10.9
Total merchandise imports	110.5	100.0

Source: *Bank of Canada Review*, March 1987

The composition of Canadian exports is dominated by natural resources and resource-based products. The bulk of imports, on the other hand, consists of manufactured goods.

11-2 BENEFITS OF INTERNATIONAL TRADE

We read and hear about so many problems concerned with international trade that we must often wonder if it is all worth it. On the other hand, when we vacation in Hawaii, Florida or Europe, or perhaps buy a foreign car, foreign stereo equipment or foreign TV set, we must think that there are some benefits to foreign trade.

All imports must eventually be paid for with goods and services either now or in the future. For this reason, the following question is important: *Can we obtain an imported good or service from*

Table 11-2 **Canadian foreign merchandise trade, by area, 1986**

	Exports to (billions of $)	%	Imports from (billions of $)	%
U.S.A.	93.6	77.6	76.8	69.5
U.K.	2.7	2.2	3.6	3.3
Other (EEC and OECD)	7.5	6.2	11.8	10.7
Japan	6.1	5.1	7.6	6.9
Other countries	10.7	8.9	10.7	9.7
Total	120.6	100.0	110.5	100.0

Source: *Bank of Canada Review*, March 1987

The U.S. is Canada's main trading partner; trade with the U.S. represents about three-quarters of the value of Canada's exports and imports.

foreigners at lower cost — in terms of other goods or services given up in exchange — than we would have to sacrifice by attempting to produce the particular good or service ourselves? If the answer is yes, then this means that by importing the good instead of trying to produce it ourselves we could have more of all goods and, therefore, be better off. Some goods cannot, of course, be produced in some countries if the necessary ingredients are lacking (for example, minerals found only in certain areas of the world). International trade therefore occurs simply for reasons of lack of availability of such ingredients. In other cases, however, countries trade with each other in order to take advantage of differences in production costs.

Absolute Advantage

A country (or region) *A* is said to have an **absolute advantage** in the production of a particular good or service relative to another country *B* if country *A* can produce the good or service with less resource input (for example, labour, capital, land, energy) than country *B*.

It is technologically possible to produce heated man-made lakes enclosed by protective bubbles in the winter so that tropical holiday environments can be created in any part of Canada. The resource cost per tropical vacation, however, would be prohibitive. Likewise, wheat and newsprint could be produced in the Caribbean under controlled environmental conditions. The resource cost per tonne of grain or newsprint would, however, be very high. The Caribbean thus has an absolute advantage in the production of tropical holidays relative to Canada, and Canada has an absolute advantage in the production of wheat and newsprint relative to the Caribbean. In a similar fashion, we could say that the Caribbean is at an absolute disadvantage relative to Canada in the production of wheat and newsprint, whereas Canada is at an absolute disadvantage relative to the Caribbean in the production of tropical vacations.

It is not difficult to understand, therefore, why Canadians are better off not producing their own tropical vacations but instead importing them (that is, travelling to the Caribbean), and why Caribbeans are better off not producing their own wheat and newsprint but instead importing these products from Canada.

Comparative Advantage

Suppose now that one country, A, is more efficient (uses less resources) than another country, B, in the production of every good and service. Does this mean that country A has nothing to gain by trading with country B and should become self-sufficient in the production of all goods and services it wishes to consume? As we will now demonstrate, the answer is *no*. Even if one country has an absolute advantage in the production of every possible good and service its population might want, it will generally be the case that this country will find its standard of living increased by producing less of some things and instead importing them from other countries. Let us now demonstrate this point by means of a numerical example.

We will assume that payment for imported goods takes the form of exports to the trading partner in the same year. Suppose there are two countries, A and B, each with the same population (of, say, ten million people) and the same quantity

of capital. Figure 11-1 depicts the production possibilities (capabilities) of each country.[1]

The figure shows, for example, that if country A put all of its workers and factories into the production of automobiles, it would be able to produce nine million cars per year — but no food. By shifting resources out of the automobile industry and into the food industry, it could get more and more food at the expense of fewer and fewer automobiles. Finally, if it chose to put all of its resources into food production, it could produce nine million metric tonnes per year — but no auto production. (We can, if we like, think of automobiles as representing luxury goods and food as necessity goods in these economies.)

Country A can produce much greater output of either good per unit of input resources than country B. Country A therefore has an absolute advantage (relative to country B) in the production of both goods.

Production and Consumption Patterns before Trade

What each country actually chooses to produce and consume without international trade depends both on its productive capabilities (production possibilities) as depicted in Figure 11-1 and the tastes or preferences of the population. Suppose, to be specific, that tastes are such that the population of each country wants to consume three million tonnes of food per year and then have as many luxuries (cars) as possible. Country A would therefore produce and consume at point A on its diagram and country B at point B on its diagram. Both countries' consumption patterns before trade are outlined in Table 11-3.

Country A is *better off* at present, in the sense that its population — even without international trade — enjoys the higher material standard of living (consuming the same amount of food, but more cars than the population of country B).

---

1. Note that the production possibilities curves in Figure 11-1 are straight lines, unlike the curves in Figures 1-5, 1-6 and 1-7 in Chapter 1. Recall that the curvature (concavity) of the production possibilities curves in Chapter 1 describes the rising opportunity cost of a good as more of it was produced with the country's resources. The straight lines in Figure 11-1 reflect the assumption, made for ease of numerical calculations, that all resources are equally suitable for production of both goods and the opportunity costs remain constant.

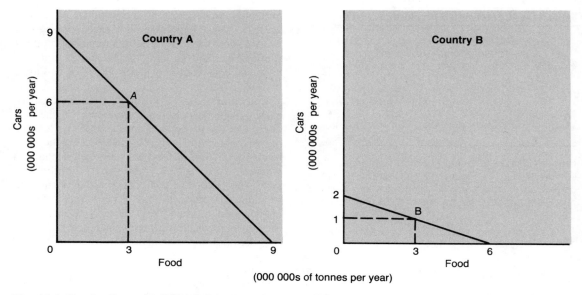

Fig. 11-1 Production possibilities for countries A and B

Both countries have identical resources, yet country *A* is capable of producing more food and cars than country *B*. Country *A* therefore has absolute advantage in the production of both goods. Consumption patterns (points *A* and *B* on the curves) are determined by preferences of the population.

Table 11-3 Production and consumption patterns before trade

Country	Food (000 000s of tonnes per year)	Cars (000 000s per year)
A	3	6
B	3	1
Total	6	7

Numerical representation of patterns described by points *A* and *B* in Figure 11-1. Without trade, the consumption of each good in each country must equal production.

Real Domestic Production Costs

In order to see whether or not it would be worthwhile for either country to engage in international trade, we must first examine domestic production costs. In Table 11-4, we have tabulated the costs of producing one more unit of each product for both countries. For example, to go from producing no food per year to nine million tonnes of food per year would cost country *A* nine millions cars per year; the cost per tonne of food production per year, therefore, is one car per year. Note that car production is less costly, in terms of the quan-

Table 11-4 Comparative production costs

Country	Cost of producing one more tonne of food per year	Cost of producing one more car per year
A	1 car per year	1 tonne of food per year
B	0.33 cars per year	3 metric tonnes of food/year

Numerical representation of production possibilities curves shown in Figure 11-1. Country *A* has a comparative advantage in car production, while *B* has a comparative advantage in food production.

tity of food given up, in country *A* than country *B*, but in the case of food production the situation is just the opposite (it is less costly in country *B*).

If one country can produce a particular good *relatively* more cheaply in real terms than another country (that is, in terms of the quantity of other goods that must be sacrificed), we say it has a **comparative advantage** in the production of this particular good. Notice that since the figures in one column are reciprocal of the figures in the other column, if one country has a comparative advantage in the production of one good, the other country must have a comparative advantage in the production of the other good.

Trade Benefits

If country *A* is willing to export one car to country *B* for, say, 2 tonnes of food (or any other amount less than 3 tonnes), it would be cheaper for country *B* to import cars than to attempt to produce them itself (since, from Table 11-4, domestic production by *B* of cars costs 3 tonnes of food for each one). Also, since it only costs country *A* 1 tonne of food to produce a car, the 2 tonnes of food (or any other amount greater than 1 tonne) it receives for the car export would mean that country *A* would also have benefited from the exchange. (The same information is conveyed in the "Cost of producing one more tonne of food per year" column.)

Suppose each country chooses to specialize in the production of that product which it can produce more cheaply than the other country, and an in-

ternational price of 2 tonnes of food for each car is agreed upon. Then, assuming each country still wants to consume only 3 million tonnes of food per year and as many cars as possible, the production, trade and consumption patterns would be as shown in Table 11-5.

Entries of Table 11-5a follow from the fact that each country has chosen to specialize in the production of the particular goods as shown. Comparing this table with Table 11-3, we see that the combined production of food has remained unchanged whereas that of cars has increased by 2 million per year. This is because each country is now engaged in its most efficient line of production, having abandoned the product it produced less efficiently. Resources released from the abandoned inefficient activities are now employed elsewhere more productively. This is the key to understand the concept of **gains from trade**. Our example has the production of only one product increasing, but in a more general case the combined production of the other good may also increase.

In practice, world tastes and production possibilities (that is, world demand and supply conditions) would determine international prices and hence the price ratio between food and cars. Further, the tastes of each country's population would determine the total amount it would wish to consume of each good. In this example, we arbitrarily supposed that international prices would be such that 2 tonnes of food would trade for 1 car. It should be emphasized, however, that the fact that *specialization in production* has increased combined outputs of the two countries does not depend on this arbitrary assumption. The effect of the choice of a particular price ratio is merely to distribute the gains from trade in a different way between the two countries than with some other price ratio.

Since country *B* produces 6 million tonnes of food per year, but only wants to consume 3, the remaining 3 million tonnes would be exported each year to country *A*, which conveniently wants to import 3 million tonnes of food per year. In return for the 3 million tonnes of food exported to country *A*, country *B* receives 1.5 million cars (see Table 11-5b). We have supposed in this example that with food and car prices such that 2 tonnes of food trades for 1 car each country would want exactly the amount of imported goods that the other wishes to export. If instead, country *A* wanted only 2 million tonnes of food while country *B* wished to export 3 million tonnes, there would be a surplus

Table 11-5 Production, trade, and consumption pattern after specialization

(a) Production pattern

Country	Food*	Cars†	Gains from specialization (in 000 000s of cars per year)
A	0(3)‡	9(6)	Not applicable
B	6(3)	0(1)	Not applicable
Total	6(6)	9(7)	2

(b) Pattern of international trade

	Country A	Country B	Total
Exports: Food*	0	3	3
Cars†	1.5	0	1.5
Imports: Food*	3	0	3
Cars†	0	1.5	1.5

(c) Consumption pattern

Country	Food*	Cars†	Distribution of specialization gains (in 000 000s of cars per year)
A	3(3)‡	7.5(6)	1.5
B	3(3)	1.5(1)	0.5
Total	6(6)	9 (7)	2

* Millions of tonnes per year
† Millions of cars per year
‡ ( ) indicate before-trade figures from Table 11-3

With access to international trade, each of the two countries will specialize in the production of one of the two goods. The combined production of the two countries will increase as a result (part (a)). Each country will export the excess of its production over its consumption of one good and import the excess of its consumption over production of another good (part (b)). Assuming that tastes in both countries leave the after-trade consumption of food unchanged, the gains from trade take the form of increased consumption of cars (part (c)).

of food on the international market. If prices were allowed to fluctuate freely, this surplus of food would force food prices downward until the surplus disappeared. For example, this might be the case when prices had adjusted to levels such that 2.5 tonnes of food traded for 1 car. At these prices desired exports would again equal desired imports.

The entries of Table 11-5c follow directly from Table 11-5a and 11-5b. For example, country B produces 6 million tonnes of food and exports 3 million tonnes for 1.5 million cars. Its population, therefore, has for consumption purposes 3 million tonnes of food, which it produced and did not export, together with the 1.5 million cars it imported. This constitutes a net benefit to country B of 0.5 million cars per year over and above what it could have produced itself without specialization and international trade. Similarly, it turns out that country A receives a welfare gain as well, represented by 1.5 million cars per year in this example. The numerical results of Table 11-5 are summarized diagrammatically in Figure 11-2.

In reality, access to international trade does not necessarily lead to complete specialization; that is, in our example both countries might produce some cars and some food. One reason for incomplete specialization, of course, is that there are many types of food and many models of cars, and specialization takes place within the broad product categories. Another reason may be that countries do not want to abandon the production of some "vital" goods and services (see next section). Transportation costs may also be a factor: Canada, for example, exports oil from Alberta, but imports oil for consumption in the East. Finally, the pattern of increasing opportunity costs (concave production possibilities curve discussed in Chapter 1) also leads to incomplete specialization for a wide range of international price ratios.

Trade among countries takes place either because of unavailability of some products in some of the countries or because of differences (advantages) in production costs between countries. A country may have an absolute advantage in trade if it produces a good or service with a smaller amount of resources than another country. Countries can, however, benefit from trading even if one of them has an absolute advantage in each good. It is sufficient that one country have a comparative advantage in the production of a good; that is, the ability to produce it relatively more cheaply than another country.

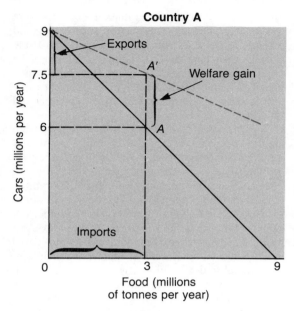

Country A

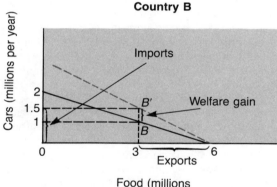

Country B

Fig. 11-2 Production and consumption patterns after trade

Graphical representation of data from Table 11-5. The international price ratio of 1 car for 2 tonnes of food is indicated by the downward sloping dotted line. With trade, country A produces 9 million cars and no food, whereas country B produces 6 million tonnes of food, but no cars. The after-trade consumption points are A' and B'. It is assumed that access to international trade does not affect the consumption of food in either country. The gains from trade take the form of increased consumption of cars.

11-3 COSTS OF INTERNATIONAL TRADE

The fact that countries have comparative advantages in the production of particular goods and services leads them toward specialization in production and international trade. This specialization causes resources to be allocated more efficiently and is the source of a higher standard of living than could be attained by domestic production alone. This is why Canada produces wheat and forest products rather than pineapples. It also explains why we take trips to California, Hawaii and Florida rather than heating Canadian lakes and enclosing them in bubbles. There are, however, some potential costs of specializing in production as suggested by comparative advantage considerations. We will now examine some of these.

Vital Goods and Services

Suppose that after production specialization, country B, knowing that country A cannot obtain food within a short period of time except by importing it from B, decides to prevent any food exports at a price less than four times the previous one. That is, instead of 1 car for each 2 tonnes of food, the price becomes 2 cars for each tonne of food. Assuming no military force is utilized, country A has no choice but to pay the price demanded. It would do country A no good to threaten retaliation by withholding its car exports, since country B could do without cars longer than A could do without food.

In that year, the consumption pattern and gains from specialization and trade would not be as reflected in Table 11-5c but instead as shown in Table 11-6. Country A might have been better off it if had not specialized completely in the production of automobiles, or if it had at least stockpiled some food.

The food industry is certainly *vital* in that we could not survive very long if its products were withheld from us. However, there are other industries for which domestic control is normally regarded as essential, *regardless of comparative costs*. For example, military services might be more efficiently provided by one's foreign neighbour, but most countries would be unwilling to allow complete foreign provision of such services.

Table 11-6 Consumption pattern with a price ratio of 2 cars for 1 tonne of food

Country	Food*	Cars†	Distribution of specialization gains (in 000 000s of cars per year)
A	3(3)‡	3(6)	−3
B	3(3)	6(1)	5
Total	6(6)	9(7)	2

* Millions of tonnes per year
† Millions of cars per year
‡ ( ) indicate before-trade figures from Table 11-3

After country *A* completely specialized in the production of cars, country *B* quadrupled the price of food. While the combined production and consumption remain the same as in Table 11-5, all gains from trade accrue to country *B*. Country *A* is worse off than before trade.

A Narrow Industrial Base

Another possible problem is that comparative advantage considerations alone may give rise to a country specializing in the production of a very narrow range of goods and services. There might be two basic difficulties with this.

First, fluctuations in world demand and supply conditions for these few products may give rise to a very *unstable pattern* of real income (GNP) and employment — with economic booms followed by deep recessions. For this reason, it may be perfectly rational to want to widen one's industrial base even though it goes somewhat against comparative advantage. The decision would then be to accept a lower level of real GNP on average over time but benefit from a more stable economy.

Second, some people like to see their country producing a wide range of goods and services (especially manufactured goods), rather than specializing to too great an extent in resource industries. For example, these people might like to see themselves or their children having a wider choice of industries in which to work, even though the real wage rates would on average be lower. People might then rationally choose to accept a lower

material standard of living than that which could be had by greater specialization in production, in favour of the nonmaterial benefits they see associated with a greater variety of industry. Remember, nonmaterial aspects of life are very important to most people. Canadians have very often indicated their dislike of being strictly "hewers of wood and drawers of water."

Infant Industry

It is possible that a small but growing domestic industry (an infant industry) may currently have high costs relative to foreign producers but that these current high costs are not indicative of its long-run cost structure. As a new industry, it may be operating well below its minimum efficient scale of production. It is possible that when it reaches the minimum efficient scale its costs would compare very favourably with foreign costs. Learning-by-doing cost reductions may also be possible as the industry gains cumulative production experience. In such instances the domestic industry usually pleads for some type of *temporary protection* against foreign producers. This protection means that Canadians pay more for the particular product than for a comparable import. The relevant question is thus, "Will the industry sometime in the future be able to compete without protection?" The total cost to Canadians during the anticipated protection period must then be weighed against the savings made when the industry is finally able to provide products at lower prices than those of foreign producers.

Costs of Adjustment

When foreigners are willing to sell products to us at lower prices than many of our domestic producers can charge and still earn a normal rate of return on investment, we are receiving information that such foreign producers have a comparative cost advantage in these product lines. In the absence of market interference, the high cost domestic firms would be driven out of the industry, since competition from lower foreign prices would reduce their profits and shareholders' rate of return below that which could be earned elsewhere.

Although this would cause an overall increase in the standard of living of the average Canadian (by forcing our land, labour and capital into more productive uses), it would, nevertheless, impose serious **adjustment costs** on the industry subject to foreign competition. For one thing, shareholders of the dying firms face a capital loss on their shares of stock. In addition (and this fact generally appears to have more political impact), the workers within the displaced firms would have to find other jobs, perhaps be retrained or possibly have to move to other regions of the country.

Such costs are sometimes taken into consideration by government, which may pay retraining and relocation costs to ease the burden of those affected. In other cases (and some people say all too often), the government may give tax relief or subsidize the ailing industry and region so that the relatively inefficient domestic firms can continue to compete with the foreign firms. This, of course, thwarts comparative advantage and leads to a lower overall material standard of living for Canadians. But whether the government should or should not do this sort of thing all depends on how we see the particular costs and benefits involved.

Participation in international trade according to the principle of comparative advantage generally improves a country's welfare. However, it may also bring about excessive specialization and adjustment costs. In the case of infant industries, the present as well as future costs and benefits must be taken into account.

11-4 INVALID ARGUMENTS AGAINST INTERNATIONAL TRADE

Because of the complicated nature of international trade and financial transactions, some apparently sensible notions on the subject may not appear quite so sensible upon further investigation. Let us now examine a number of invalid propositions advanced from time to time concerning international trade.

Exports are Good; Imports are Bad

Some people mistakenly believe that a prime goal for a country should be to export as much and import as little as possible. The reasoning is that exports stimulate employment for the exporting

country whereas imports reduce employment. This may be true, but other things, such as tax reductions, increases in government spending or expansionary monetary policies may be used in place of export demand or to offset the employment effects of imports. Further, whereas these other expansionary measures increase the goods and services available for consumption or investment in Canada, an increase in exports per se merely increases our production of goods and services for foreign consumption.

To examine this assumption further, suppose we decide to aim for a continual surplus of exports over imports. This means that we are proposing to produce with Canadian land, labour and capital more goods and services for foreign countries each year than we receive from them. Clearly, in such an instance, we would be enhancing foreign standards of living at the expense of our own. We would do the work and others would enjoy the fruits of our labour.

What is good about exports is not the exports themselves — foreigners get those to consume — but, *the fact that in exchange we get imported goods more cheaply than if we produced them ourselves.* Exporting more than is imported is only a good idea if a country wants to increase its claims on foreigners (its accumulated investment abroad). Importing more than is exported on average is good, apart from the usual gains in production specialization, in that it enables the country so doing to enjoy a *temporary* greater material standard of living by using foreign production as well as its own.[2] But the cost of an import surplus is more and more foreign claims on domestic real assets and future production.

Keeping the Goods and Money

One argument to "buy Canadian" rather than foreign goods and services is that when we buy foreign goods, we get the goods but foreigners get our money. On the other hand, when we buy Canadian goods, we get the goods and also keep

---

2. Exports represent domestic production sent abroad. Imports represent foreign production received by the domestic economy. Total output in any year available for present or future consumption is, therefore, domestic production minus exports plus imports, which is greater the fewer the exports and the greater the imports.

Table 11-7 Exchange rates and international competitiveness

	International price per unit			
	£1 = $1		£1 = $1.5	
Country	Food	Cars	Food	Cars
A	$9 000 (£9 000)	$9 000 (£9 000)	$9 000 (£6 000)	$9 000 (£6 000)
B	£2 000 ($2 000)	£6 000 ($6 000)	£2 000 ($3 000)	£6 000 ($9 000)
	cheaper	cheaper	cheaper	same price

The currency of country *A* is $, the currency of country *B* is £. Originally, with the exchange rate of £1 = $1 (left half of the table), country *B*'s food and cars are cheaper and are imported by country *A*. Demand for *B*'s goods (and currency) bids up the exchange rate to £1 = $1.5. As a result, the prices of cars are now equal in both countries, while the price of food remains cheaper in country *B* (right half of the table).

our money in Canada. However, this is not a sensible argument against importing. Let us run through an example.

Suppose a Canadian buys a crate of oranges from an American, who accepts Canadian currency as payment. If the American is satisfied with holding our Canadian money indefinitely, what a tremendous deal we have struck! We received a crate of oranges from the United States and managed to "con" the American into accepting a piece of paper in exchange. We could do with a lot more of such transactions.

Unfortunately, however, the American will not hold our currency indefinitely. What is more likely is that the American will use it either to buy a Canadian product or sell the Canadian currency to another American, who wants to buy a Canadian good or service. Typically, therefore, we will be getting our currency back in exchange for some Canadian good or service, which we can produce more efficiently than they can in the U.S. Let us suppose that this leads to a shipment of Canadian metal of some kind. Eventually, the money comes back to us — since it cannot be spent abroad — and the net result is that we trade Canadian goods or services for foreign goods or services. In our example, it is Canadian metal for U.S. oranges. Or, it may be an exchange of Canadian natural gas for trips to Florida. We benefit because we end up

being able to consume more things than we could have otherwise. If we had produced Canadian oranges by shifting resources from metal production to orange groves in greenhouses, it would have cost us a lot more sacrificed metal production than by trading metal for U.S. oranges.

Cheap Labour Countries Can Undersell

It is not possible for a country to undersell another in every possible industry. In order to see this, let us re-examine our earlier example. In country *A* of Table 11-4, the cost of producing 1 car is, in real terms, 1 tonne of food. Therefore, without international trade, the prices in country *A* would reflect this ratio.[3] That is, one car would be priced the same as one tonne of food, say, at $9000. For the same reason, suppose that in country *B*, without international trade, each car was priced at £6000 while each metric tonne of food sold for £2000, that is, the cost of producing one car is 3 tonnes of food. These figures are summarized by the unbracketed numbers of Table 11-7.

---

3. There are two reasons, however, why this may not be true. Relative prices of two goods may not properly reflect relative costs if a significant degree of monopoly power exists or if there are short-run adjustments going on in at least one industry.

Each worker in country *B* would be receiving a lower real wage per year than each worker in country *A* since *B*'s productivity is so much lower. Disregarding land and capital inputs, Table 11-3 shows that the average yearly real wage in country *A* would be 3 million tonnes of food plus 6 million cars divided by 10 million workers — or .3 tonnes of food plus .6 cars per worker. In country *B* it would be .3 tonnes of food plus .1 car per worker. In monetary terms, using country *A*'s prices and currency, country *A* workers receive an average annual wage of $8100 (that is, $9000 × .3 plus $9000 × .6), whereas the workers of country *B* get an average of only $3600 per year ($9000 × .3 plus $9000 × .1). In any case, we have a situation whereby the labour in country *B* is very cheap relative to the labour in country *A*.

Now, suppose we open up international free trade. At an exchange rate of £1 = $1, in country *A*'s currency, country *B*'s cars and food would cost $6000 each and $2000 per tonne respectively. On the other hand, country *A*'s production in country *B*'s currency would be priced at £9000 a car and £9000 per tonne of food. The prices of each country's goods in the other country's currency are shown by the bracketed numbers in Table 11-7. Clearly, at the exchange rate of £1 = $1 the demand for country *B*'s currency by country *A* importers would be great because both *B*'s food and cars are very cheap relative to those of country *A*. But there would be no demand by country *B* for the currency of country *A* because *A*'s goods are more expensive than *B*'s. The price of country *B*'s currency would, therefore, be *bid up* relative to country *A*'s.

When the exchange rate had become as high as £1 = $1.50, the price of *A*'s and *B*'s cars would be equal at $9000 or £6000 each. But the price of *B*'s food would still be cheaper than *A*'s, in either currency. Food importers in country *A* would still be trying to buy pounds (£) while as yet no one in country *B* would want dollars. The price of pounds would, therefore, be bid above $1.50. As this happens the price of *A*'s cars would become cheaper than *B*'s. At this point, there would be some demand for *A*'s currency by country *B* car importers and trade would begin. Although *B*'s food is still cheaper than *A*'s, *A*'s cars have now become cheaper than *B*'s (even though *B*'s workers are only paid a fraction of *A*'s). Consequently, demand for

A's food by *A* residents will slacken while demand for *A*'s automobiles increases. The opposite will be happening in country *B*. As a result, there will be a movement toward specialization in the production of those products in which we had previously shown each country to have a comparative advantage (Table 11-4). And, the high wage country will be able to sell its cars abroad.

Some popular arguments regarding the undesirability of imports, "buy Canadian" policies and our so-called inability to compete with cheap labour countries do not stand up to close examination. Longer-term consequences and exchange rate adjustments are important and should be included in the analysis.

11-5 PROTECTIONISM

If the above costs and benefits of completely free trade have been evaluated and the decision has been taken to limit the amount of international trade, there are a number of possible methods. They are generally classified into **tariffs** and **nontariff barriers** to trade. The former are gradually being reduced. The latter are more difficult to detect and remain an important obstacle to international trade.

Tariffs

The government may choose to limit the flow of imported goods by imposing a duty or tax on the foreign items as they enter the country. Such taxes are called *tariffs*. If the government wishes to limit the flow of exported goods for some reason, an export tariff may be imposed. Import tariffs are, however, far more common.

After the Second World War, countries organized in GATT (General Agreement on Tariffs and Trade) negotiated a series of *tariff reductions*. The latest round of tariff cuts (the Tokyo Round) was scheduled to be phased in by 1987. At the end of the phase-in period, the average weighted Canadian tariff on dutiable imports was expected to be about 9 or 10 percent. When duty-free imports are taken into account, the overall level of Canadian tariff protection in 1987 is estimated at 4 percent. The magnitudes of specific tariff reductions on selected categories of imports from the U.S. are illustrated in Table 11-8.

Table 11-8 Average Canadian tariff on industrial imports from the U.S.

Commodity	1987	1979
Clothing	24.4%	25.4%
Footwear	22.3%	24.8%
Primary textiles	19.1%	22.7%
Furniture	14.3%	19.3%
Plastics	13.4%	17.2%
Drugs	9.0%	15.0%
Synthetic resins	8.9%	11.2%
Chemicals	8.4%	14.7%
Musical instruments	8.3%	17.0%
Nonelectrical machinery	8.1%	14.8%
Earthenware/stoneware	8.0%	13.1%
Electrical apparatus	7.9%	15.2%
Paper	7.8%	14.9%
Rubber products	7.6%	13.8%
Iron & steel	7.1%	10.6%
Photographic equipment	7.0%	14.8%
Wood products	7.0%	14.0%
Consumer electronics	6.7%	14.7%
Nonferrous metals	3.1%	9.2%
Office equipment	2.5%	13.1%

Source: *The Financial Post*, November 10, 1984

An illustration of tariff rates before and after the Tokyo Round of GATT negotiations. Some Canadian industries remain highly protected, and the tariff reductions affecting them have been relatively modest.

Quotas

Another method of restricting imports or exports (again, more typically imports) is to assign **quotas**, which arbitrarily restrict the volume of particular foreign goods entering or leaving Canada.

Subsidies

Goods are imported because foreigners can produce them more cheaply than we can. In order to stem the flow, the government may give tax relief or direct subsidies to particular domestic industries, which effectively lower their costs and enable them to charge lower prices and compete with foreign producers.

Government Procurement

Many countries, including Canada, make it difficult for imported goods and services to compete in supplying the public sector. In Canada, for example, most provinces give preference to goods manufactured in the province (or at least in Canada) in their government purchasing. In some cases (for example, in Quebec) only firms operating in the province are allowed to bid on certain contracts; in other cases, firms located in the province get the contract even when their bid is a higher price than that of an out-of-province competitor (say, up to 10 percent higher, as in Ontario government purchasing).

Red Tape

There are more subtle ways of reducing imports — for example, excessive quality specifications imposed by governments (which would be costly for foreigners to meet), intentional administrative delays for processing documents accompanying foreign shipments and so on. For example, in 1982 when Japanese auto manufacturers would not agree to limit their exports of cars to Canada voluntarily, the Canadian government intentionally slowed down the processing of documents, a tactic which forced thousands of Japanese cars to sit idly on the docks in Vancouver.

Controls designed to inhibit imports are typically referred to as methods of **protectionism** in that they protect higher cost domestic firms from foreign competition. The costs and benefits of protectionism, or the opposite — free trade — have already been discussed.

One point that perhaps deserves emphasizing is that often the choice is not between having a protected industry or having no industry at all (although in some instances this may exactly be the case). More often, it is a choice between an efficient industry and an inefficient one. We mention this here partly because some protected industry spokesmen would have us believe otherwise and partly because our earlier simplified example of Table 11-5 treated a case in which each country under a system of free trade would completely specialize in one industry and get completely out of the other.

In protected industries, domestic prices are higher than they otherwise would be. This allows less efficient producers to remain solvent and earn a normal rate of return on invested funds, but it also allows potentially more efficient firms to either dissipate their efficiency advantages in higher costs or earn above normal profit rates of return. In the absence of protection, the resulting lower domestic prices forced upon producers to match foreign competition will cause the marginal firms to suffer losses and leave the industry. But for other firms the lower prices will serve either to rekindle the drive for higher efficiency, of which they are capable, or reduce abnormally high profits. These firms will, however, remain within the industry.

Import tariffs have been the target of several international negotiations and are gradually being reduced. Nontariff barriers to trade, however, remain an important source of friction among countries engaged in international trade.

In the next section we examine the issue of *dumping*, which has given rise to many pleas for domestic industry protection.

11-6 DUMPING: INTERNATIONAL PRICE DISCRIMINATION

When a supplier sells an identical good or service in two or more different markets at different prices that do not reflect differences in costs, this action is known as **price discrimination**. Many examples of price discrimination exist. For example, eggs are sold to the consumer and industrial user at different prices. Lawyers, accountants, tax advisers, realtors and home decorators often gear their fee to a client's income or property value. There are generally different prices charged children, young adults and senior citizens at places of entertainment and on public transportation.

For effective price discrimination to exist, the product in question must be of such a nature that it cannot be easily resold by the lower price customer to the higher price customers. In the case of services, resale is generally an impossibility. In the case of goods, the markets must usually be physically separate.

Consider as a specific example a movie theatre charging different prices to adults under the age of 65 than to senior citizens. Figure 11-3 illustrates the two market segments. Of these two classes, we

suppose that senior citizens are more sensitive to the price of movie tickets than are younger adults. For simplicity, we also suppose that the theatre faces constant marginal costs over the relevant range of total sales volume.

Suppose for the moment that the theatre disregards the senior citizen audience entirely. The profit-maximizing price to charge younger adults is P_y. At such a high price, we have assumed that no senior citizens would attend the theatre (Figure 11-3b). If, however, the movie theatre is permitted to charge a lower price to senior citizens and is at the same time not obliged to lower its prices for younger adults, the theatre will earn a greater profit by doing so. For all movie tickets sold to senior citizens up to a volume of Q_s, the additional revenue (MR) from each ticket sold exceeds the added cost (MC) of providing the service. Under price discrimination, the profit-maximizing prices to charge younger adults and senior citizens are P_y and P_s respectively.

Since the average price sensitivity of both audiences together lies between that for the younger adult and senior citizen groups alone, if the movie theatre is not allowed to price discriminate, the single profit-maximizing price is somewhere between P_y and P_s. Price sensitive consumer classes (here, senior citizens) thus benefit from price discrimination at the cost of relatively price insensitive consumer classes. Since lower income groups tend to be more price sensitive than higher income groups, price discrimination can act as an implicit method of *income redistribution*.

Where a seller engages in voluntary price discrimination, the tactic must be more profitable than charging a single price, since the seller always has the option of charging a single price. The source of increased profit from being able to charge a lower price to price sensitive consumers comes from picking up the extra sales that the firm would not get at a single higher price. Further, the supplier under a two-price strategy obtains these extra sales without having to lower the price (and thus without losing any revenue) in a price insensitive market.[4]

International price discrimination is otherwise known as **dumping**. Although dumping may in-

---

4. It is not always the case that price discrimination results in greater profit. Consider, for example, the case where one consumer group is so price sensitive that there is no price above marginal cost that would attract any sales at all from this group.

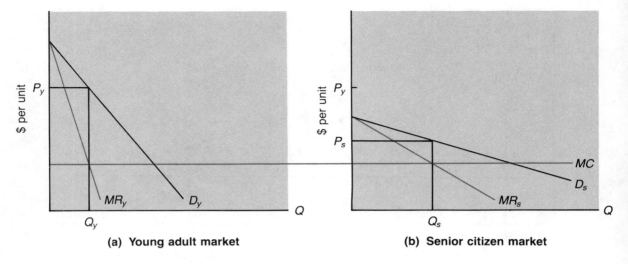

(a) Young adult market   **(b) Senior citizen market**

Fig. 11-3 Price discrimination at movie theatres

An illustration of price discrimination in domestic markets for services. The profit-maximizing price is higher in the market with lower price elasticity of demand (part (a)) than in the market with more elastic demand (part (b)).

volve both goods and services, most discussion about dumping has been concerned with international price discrimination for goods (merchandise). Markets separated by territorial boundaries and often great distances yield potential situations for price discrimination. Usually, the foreign supplier engaging in price discrimination has a greater degree of monopoly power in its home market than it does in its foreign market. Since there is less competition (fewer substitute brands available) in the home market than abroad, the supplier faces less price sensitive consumers at home than in the foreign market. Consequently, a two-price strategy will mean greater profits than a single-price strategy. In particular, the supplier will charge a higher price in its domestic market than it will in its foreign market. Figure 11-4 illustrates this situation graphically.[5] The supplier assumed to be engaging in dumping is a Japanese firm. Its foreign market is assumed to be Canada.

Winners and Losers in Dumping

Competition generally lowers profit regardless of the head office location of the competitors. Consequently, Canadian producers suffer reduced rates of return on investment. This result may be evidence that these Canadian producers do not have a comparative advantage relative to the Japanese in the production of the good in question. Everything else being equal, investment funds and Canadian workers employed in such firms could be more fruitfully employed elsewhere. The same qualifications hold for this conclusion as were made in Section 11-3.

Canadian consumers benefit by being able to acquire products at lower prices than would be present if foreign competition did not exist.

Lobbies against dumping are therefore likely to come from Canadian producers, whose profits are eroded, as well as from Canadian workers who see (at least temporary) dislocation and unemployment costs. There may also be complaints to the Japanese government by Japanese consumers, who may be unhappy with having to pay higher prices than Canadians for Japanese products.

---

5. Of course, in practice we would expect marignal costs to be greater in the foreign market if transportation costs are important. Even so, if the foreign market (Figure 11-4) is price sensitive enough, a lower profit-maximizing price will be warranted.

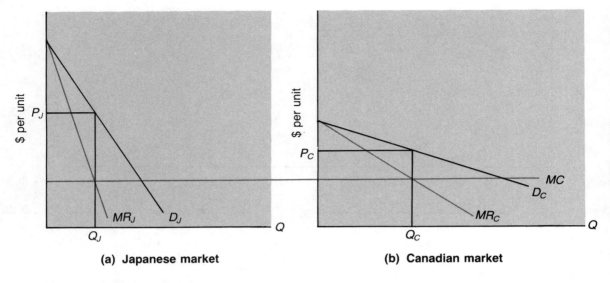

(a) **Japanese market**   (b) **Canadian market**

Fig. 11-4 International price discrimination

An illustration of price discrimination between two national markets. A Japanese firm is assumed to face a less elastic demand in its domestic market than in its export market (Canada). Hence the profit-maximizing price charged in the Japanese market (part (a)) is higher than in the Canadian market (part (b)).

Predatory Dumping

As long as the dumping situation is permanent, the winners and losers are as discussed directly above. This is not the case, however, with *predatory dumping*. Predatory dumping is a temporary low-price strategy by a supplier trying to increase the degree of long-run monopoly power in a foreign market. For instance, suppose that the Japanese producer actively seeks to eliminate competition in the Canadian market by undercutting Canadian producers. The long-run objective of this strategy is to eliminate substitute brands and thereby reduce the price sensitivity of the Canadian market. If accomplished, this would enable the Japanese producer to obtain a higher long-run price for its product in the Canadian market and extract greater long-run profit. Since greater long-run profit comes out of the pockets of Canadian consumers who must pay the higher long-run prices, in this instance there would be no Canadian winners.

Naturally, Canadian producers and workers,

when faced with stiff foreign competition, very often charge that foreign suppliers are following a predatory pricing policy to the detriment of all Canadians. It is often difficult for the government to know when dumping may be deemed predatory and when it is simply evidence of a lack of comparative advantage (or inefficiency) on the part of Canadian producers.

Government Policy against Dumping

In the face of suspected dumping, Canadian producers, under the Anti-Dumping Act of 1968, may make formal complaint to the federal government. If dumping seems to be occurring and if such dumping is felt to be inconsistent with the long-term viability of a Canadian industry and long-run healthy competition, a temporary tariff may be placed on the foreign imports. The matter is then referred to the Canadian Import Tribunal (formerly known as the Anti-Dumping Tribunal) for greater study. If, in fact, injurious competition is confirmed, tariffs or import quotas may be instituted on a longer-term basis.

New legislation, the Special Import Measures Act, passed in 1984, makes it easier for the federal government to impose contingency protection measures. The Act includes provisions on countervailing duties (designed to offset the effect of subsidies made available to foreign exporters by their governments), emergency safeguard measures and other nontariff barriers. It also makes it easier for the industry to prove that dumping causes injury to domestic producers.

It is inevitable that various political factors enter the decision whether or not to protect particular segments of Canadian industry. For example, imagine what might happen if, without long-term antidumping levies, a factory would have to close down in the riding of an influential Member of Parliament.

Business firms frequently charge different prices for the same product or service sold in different markets. Such price discrimination is a profit-maximizing strategy when the price differentials reflect differing elasticities of demand. Dumping is a form of price discrimination employed in international trade. Most countries, including Canada, have in place policy measures designed to protect their domestic industries from potential damage caused by dumping.

11-7 FOREIGN INVESTMENT

Either directly or indirectly through corporations, Canadians own land, buildings and other real assets within foreign countries. This is called Canadian **direct investment abroad**. In addition, Canadians own financial claims against such assets in the form of foreign stocks, bonds and bank deposits. These holdings are referred to as Canadian portfolio investment abroad (if the common stock ownership constitutes a *controlling interest*, it is classified as *direct* investment rather than portfolio investment). Similarly, foreigners own or have financial claims against Canadian real assets.

Figure 11-5 indicates the extent of Canada's **net indebtedness** to foreigners, its composition and the extent to which it has grown over the years from 1945 to 1984. "Total Liabilities" indicate accumulated amounts of past foreign direct and indirect investment in Canada, while "Total Assets" indicate the direct and portfolio claims that Canadian residents have upon foreign real assets as a result of accumulated past investments. The difference between liabilities and assets (what we owe foreigners less what foreigners owe us) reflects our net indebtedness to them. As of the end of 1984, this figure stood at roughly $153 billion.

The United States is our largest foreign creditor, while at the same time the largest amount of investment that we undertake in foreign countries is accumulated in the U.S. Figure 11-6 summarizes the geographical distribution of our net foreign indebtedness.

To the extent that we import more than we export in any given year we must undertake new foreign borrowing to make up the difference. Such new foreign borrowing increases our net (accumulated) foreign indebtedness. This is not the only reason our net foreign indebtedness increases each year. The other major reason stems from foreign corporations investing in Canada as well as earning yearly profits that are reinvested in Canada. Of course, Canadian corporations abroad are doing the same thing, but such amounts are smaller.

Inducement for Foreign Investment

(i) Direct Investment

A foreign citizen or corporation will seek to acquire a factory, store, oil well or perhaps buy a controlling interest in an existing Canadian company for the same reason that a Canadian investor would — because the perceived rate of return is expected to be greater than that which could be earned elsewhere for a similar risk.

If Canada experiences economic hard times, which have the effect of reducing investor expectations of future profitability, then investment in Canada — both domestic and foreign — will decline. On the other hand, the Canadian government may, by imposing additional taxes on foreign profits or other controls, reduce the profitability of foreign investment without affecting profits of domestic investors. In such a case, only foreign investment would decline.

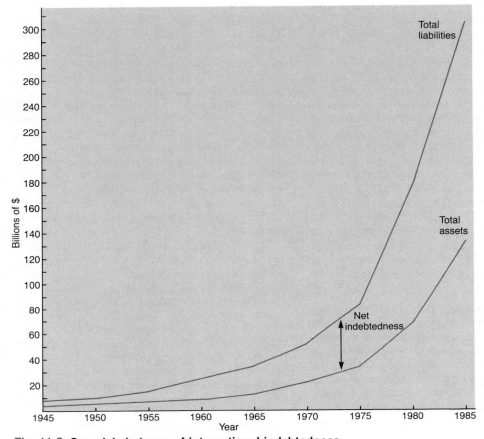

Fig. 11-5 Canada's balance of international indebtedness

Source: Statistics Canada 67-202

Canada's foreign liabilities have grown faster than foreign assets, causing an increase in net international indebtedness.

(ii) Portfolio Investment

As we might expect, the same profit motive influences foreign portfolio investment. If interest yields or rates of return are more attractive on Canadian financial instruments than on foreign financial instruments with similar risk elements, foreigners will be enticed to purchase these Canadian financial instruments. Most foreign portfolio investment is undertaken by foreign financial institutions and other foreign business firms.

To Have or Have Not?

Typically, Canadians declare that they prefer domestic ownership of Canadian resources to foreign ownership. Of the two types of foreign investment — portfolio and direct — the greatest debate concerns the latter, especially with regard to the *multinational enterprise*.

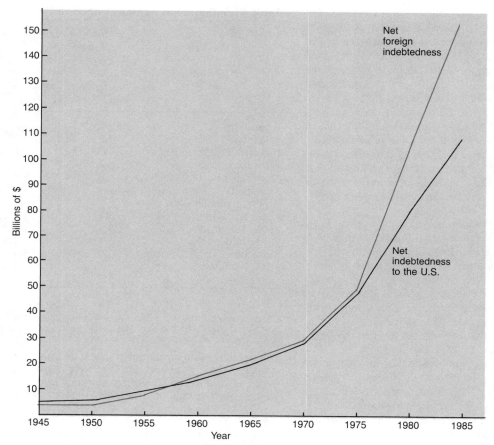

Fig. 11-6 Canada's net indebtedness to all foreigners compared with Canada's net indebtedness to the U.S.

Source: Statistics Canada 67-202

Canada's net indebtedness to the U.S. has become a smaller portion of its total international indebtedness.

The Multinational Firm

As we saw in Chapter 7, the very nature of oligopoly suppresses competitive actions that might rock the boat. Actions by a major oligopolist that are seen as an attempt to erode the market share of other major firms usually provoke fierce reaction. Occasional price wars are evidence of such reactions. One way of using oligopoly power without severely upsetting one's rival has historically been to expand sales through foreign markets.

Sales abroad can either take place by producing domestically and then exporting or by physically locating one's production facilities in the foreign market. The choice between these two actions is largely a matter of cost considerations. If transportation costs to foreign markets are high, foreign wages are low, or foreign countries place tariffs or other barriers against imported goods, the cheaper option may be to physically locate abroad. If the product being sold is a service (for example, engineering consulting, accounting services or banking), then location abroad may be a necessity. In the case of goods, if after-sale service is important (as it is, for example, with automobiles and home appliances), physical plant location in foreign markets may be important from a potential sales (demand) standpoint. Sometimes foreign governments offer subsidies to firms that will locate in depressed areas. For these and other reasons, numerous companies have found it to their advantage to physically locate in foreign countries. The investment of these companies is referred to as foreign direct investment and such firms are known as **multinational enterprises**.

Typically, multinational enterprises are large firms and have some degree of monopoly power in their home country. These firms generally have a differentiated product: the differentiation is based on potential technological advances or on product reputation and consumer goodwill developed in their home market. Often such multinational firms enjoy economies of scale and learning by doing cost advantages relative to other firms in the (host) foreign market.

Canadian-owned multinationals include Inco, Alcan, Northern Telecom and Massey Ferguson, which among them own subsidiaries in such countries as the United States, England, Ireland, Brazil, Turkey, Malaysia, Guatemala and Indonesia. Some of these Canadian multinational subsidiaries were set up not to sell output abroad but instead to acquire raw material inputs from the parent company. A number of Canadian banks, including the Royal, Commerce and Bank of Nova Scotia have also long had sizeable foreign operations.

Far more numerous than the Canadian-owned multinationals operating abroad are the foreign-owned multinationals operating in Canada. Examples of the latter group include: Shell, Goodyear, Greyhound, Readers' Digest, Coca-Cola, General Motors, Ford and Chrysler. In fact, relative to other developed countries Canadian industry has a very high proportion of foreign ownership and control. Table 11-9 shows the approximate degree of **foreign control** in the Canadian economy. Roughly speaking, a company is said to be foreign controlled if 50% or more of its common stock (actually, voting rights) are held outside of Canada. We note that overall foreign control has been

Table 11-9 Degree of nonresident control

Industry	Assets of foreign controlled corporations as a percentage of industry assets		
	1967	1979	1984
Agriculture, forestry and fishing	8.2	4.8	3.3
Mining	60.0	49.7	35.1
Manufacturing	56.7	49.3	44.3
Construction	14.0	10.7	9.8
Transportation, storage, communication and public utilities	6.2	5.5	3.3
Wholesale trade	28.5	25.7	21.9
Retail trade	20.4	13.2	12.6
Services	17.3*	14.9	15.4
Total, nonfinancial industries	38.0	28.5	24.2

* 1967 figure excludes finance

Source: Royal Commission on Corporate Concentration; Statistics Canada 61-210. Reproduced with permission of the Minister of Supply and Services Canada.

The degree of foreign control in almost all Canadian industries has gradually declined. By 1984, all major sectors of the Canadian economy had less than 50 percent foreign ownership.

declining and is now below 50% in both the mining and manufacturing industries.

Table 11-10 illustrates the connection mentioned earlier between foreign ownership and oligopoly. By examining the figures of Table 11-10, we can see that foreign ownership is more important in the more concentrated industries. Further, within 12 of the 33 major industries surveyed the largest firms were foreign controlled in 1984.

Potential Costs and Benefits

The question of potential costs and benefits flowing to a host country from direct investment through the multinational corporate firm is a hotly

Table 11-10 Foreign control in 33 major industries, 1984

Industry	% of sales accounted for by largest four firms	% of foreign control	Highest ranking Canadian firm	Industry	% of sales accounted for by largest four firms	% of foreign control	Highest ranking Canadian firm
Tobacco products	90.7	100	6	Chemicals and chemical products	23.3	70	4
Communications	67.6	12	1	Other mining	20.6	35	1
Transport equipment	70.4	74	8	Printing publishing & allied industries	25.2	11	1
Petroleum and coal products	67.9	59	2	Miscellaneous manufacturing	12.6	37	3
Rubber products	60.8	92	8	Wood industries	18.4	13	1
Storage	90.8	5	1	Food	17.7	31	1
Primary metals	60.4	18	1	Furniture industries	10.1	20	1
Metal mining	46.1	24	1	Knitting mills	18.8	21	2
Public utilities	51.9	0	1	Leather products	17.6	19	1
Transportation	47.1	4	1	Metal fabricating	13.7	30	1
Beverages	46.8	28	1	Retail trade	11.1	13	1
Textile mills	38.6	49	2	Clothing industries	6.1	10	6
Paper and allied industries	33.8	25	1	Services	9.8	15	2
Mineral fuels	36.0	39	2	Wholesale trade	9.5	22	1
Electrical products	33.8	48	1	Agriculture, forestry and fishing	4.3	3	1
Nonmetallic mineral products	27.0	70	5	Construction	4.1	10	1
Machinery	16.1	44	1				

Source: Statistics Canada 61-210

A disaggregation of major sectors into more narrowly defined industries shows that the degree of foreign ownership in some segments of the manufacturing sector remains substantial. In the majority of industries listed here, however, the largest firms are Canadian owned.

debated issue. There are both winners and losers. In the short run, the multinational may increase the demand for skilled personnel, unskilled workers and managerial talent of the host country, thereby increasing the wages of these groups. Host country consumers may receive products that were not available as cheaply from domestic producers. The host country also benefits from the supply of foreign entrepreneurship and access to foreign capital at lower cost than available at the domestic market. On the other hand, in the long run, the multinational may, through merger, takeover or cutthroat competition, eliminate some domestic producers and then seek to exploit its resulting market power through output restriction and monop-

oly prices. This action could hurt consumers and limit overall demand for workers.

In the short run, the host country benefits from the technological advancements that the foreign firms bring to the host country. In the longer run, the acquisition of new technologies through foreign firms may limit the amount of research and development expenditure undertaken domestically. This fact does not mean that such technologies as were received via multinationals could have been more cheaply developed domestically, but some people believe that domestic research and development activity is important for its own sake.

Others argue that multinational firms often locate in a host country merely to get behind tariff walls, and in so doing end up producing for the host market in relatively small, inefficient plants. The multinational then produces for the world market from its parent operations. It has been commented that the presence of foreign multinationals in Canada has had some effect in limiting the growth of rival Canadian companies, which then have difficulty approaching world-scale size and a position to effectively compete in world markets. Some Canadian industries have also been characterized as branch-plant operations, where the foreign-owned subsidiaries perform only a truncated set of activities in accordance with the global plans of the parent companies.

Another difficulty with multinationals is their ability to apply imaginative accounting techniques and divert recorded profit for tax purposes from the host country to the country of the parent, which may have a lower tax rate. For example, the multinational subsidiary may purchase component parts or consulting advice from the parent company at intentionally inflated prices. Such action reduces the apparent profit of the subsidiary and increases the apparent profit of the parent.

Some of the most important concerns of host countries with respect to the presence of foreign-owned multinationals are social and political in nature, though this does not mean that they are any less important. Economic power to some extent implies political power. Large multinational corporations can be so important for various regions of the country that they may significantly influence certain government actions regarding things like pollution control, taxation, subsidies and regulations. Employees of foreign-owned firms, as voters, may find it to their advantage to put the interests of multinationals ahead of national interests.

Finally, there is the danger that the national government of the multinational parent may attempt to impose behaviour on the subsidiaries that is at odds with policies of the host government. This phenomenon is known as **extraterritoriality**. For instance, during the 1960s, U.S.-owned subsidiaries in Canada were prohibited from trading with Cuba. Such a prohibition was contrary to Canadian law. In the 1970s, Gulf Canada took part in a worldwide uranium cartel that the Canadian government apparently encouraged as being in the Canadian interest. However, since Gulf Canada's action was deemed to be in violation of American law, the United States government took action against Gulf Oil Inc. In the 1980s, some Canadians voiced concern over the manufacture by U.S.-owned subsidiaries in Canada of various components of military hardware which they viewed as incompatible with Canada's foreign policy position.

Government Policy toward Multinationals

Canadian government policy toward foreign direct investment has taken two main forms:

(1) exclusion or limitation of multinational activities in sectors of the economy deemed critical in relation to public policies or the development of a distinctive Canadian culture;

(2) screening of foreign investments in other sectors of the economy according to a set of criteria intended to assess their benefit to Canada.

Federal and provincial governments have passed legislation that either excludes or limits foreign ownership in various industries, including: transportation, finance, telecommunications (including broadcasting) and natural resources. In certain sectors of the resource industries, governments have bought outright the subsidiaries of foreign multinationals. Examples include the Saskatchewan government (potash), the Quebec government (asbestos) and the federal government (petroleum). The most significant direct criticism of these government takeovers has come from those who believe the government to be a less efficient manager of resources than the private sector.

The practice of screening foreign investments in Canada was implemented following the passage of the Foreign Investment Review Act in 1973. The Act established the Foreign Investment Review Agency (FIRA) and charged it with the responsibility of determining whether a proposed foreign investment would confer significant benefits on Canada. The criteria employed in such assessments were concerned with the impact of the investment on job creation, technology, innovation, export performance and its compatibility with Canadian industrial policies.

Between 1973 and 1985, FIRA rejected about 7% of foreign investment proposals. (This figure does not, of course, say anything about the proposals which were never made because of the deterrent effect of FIRA.) Over the years, this approach toward foreign investment was subjected to a number of criticisms, among them the vagueness of the screening criteria, the secrecy with which decisions were made, and inadequate accountability of the Agency to the politicians. Above all, however, critics noted that FIRA discouraged foreign investment in Canada at a time when most countries of the world competed for foreign capital in an attempt to enhance their employment prospects and international competitiveness.

In 1985, the government passed the Investment Canada Act, which replaced FIRA with a new agency, **Investment Canada**. It considerably relaxed the rules for admitting foreign investments into Canada. Since 1985, foreign investments creating new business (as opposed to foreign takeovers of existing businesses) have been practically exempt from regulation. At the same time, many smaller foreign takeovers which were subject to review under the previous legislation are no longer regulated. Finally, the applicants are not required to show that the foreign investment will result in *significant* benefit to Canada (*net* benefit is sufficient.)

The degree of foreign ownership in Canada is among the highest in the world. Foreign investment provides access to sources of foreign capital, technology, entrepreneurship and managerial skills. In part, however, it also places control over Canada's economic future in the hands of foreigners, potentially restricts the range of activities of firms operating in Canada, and introduces the possibility of extraterritorial application of foreign laws. The Canadian government policies toward foreign invesment have evolved from prior screening of potential investments for significant benefit to Canada into a more accommodating approach.

11-8 FREER TRADE BETWEEN THE U.S. AND CANADA

The problem of economic relations with the U.S. is as old as Canada itself. The narrower issue of free trade between the two countries loomed large in the 1911 Canadian elections and has occupied the attention of academic economists for some time. A major impetus to the public debate was the 1985 *Report of the Royal Commission on the Economic Union and Development Prospects for Canada* which recommended that this policy initiative be pursued.

Background

After the formation of the European Economic Community and the European Free Trade Association, Canada remains one of the very few industrialized countries whose firms do not have guaranteed access to a market of at least 100 million consumers. Only in selected sectors have steps been taken to enlarge the market available to Canadian producers. The best known example is the Canada-U.S. Automotive Products Trade Agreement (Auto Pact) signed in 1965. The Auto Pact is a bilateral trade agreement which led to the integration of the North American production and sales of automobile products into one market. The "safeguards" built into the Auto Pact ensure that the production of cars in Canada must not drop below a certain proportion of cars sold in Canada. The agreement has worked well and is viewed by many as a model for similar arrangements in the future.

As indicated in Section 11-5, Canada has also actively participated in several rounds of tariff cuts in the framework of GATT. Further reductions of trade barriers within GATT are certainly a possibility, but it is a slow process with uncertain payoffs. The Royal Commission therefore recommended that priority should be given to bilateral negotiations with our main trading partner — the U.S. — while simultaneously maintaining interest in the GATT efforts.

A major incentive for Canada to pursue free trade negotiation with the U.S. is the growing protectionism in that country. In the mid 1980s, the U.S. government, anxious to reduce the growing merchandise trade deficit, has been increasingly ready to interfere with the flow of imports into the U.S. The policy measures available for this purpose included countervailing duties against imports believed to be subsidized by the country of origin, antidumping duties, preferential government procurement such as "buy American" requirements, and retaliation against "unfair" trade practices in exporting countries. Canada has felt the impact of these measures a number of times. One example was the U.S. threat of a countervailing tariff on Canadian softwood lumber at the end of 1986. The U.S. government justified this action by arguing that Canadian provinces — owners of the forests — did not charge sufficiently high "stumpage fees," that is, the payment for trees the logging companies were allowed to cut. (The problem was resolved when Canada imposed a 15% export tariff on lumber exported to the U.S.)

In its analysis, the Royal Commission considered three possible forms of a free trade arrangement between Canada and the U.S. First, a **common market**, which calls not only for free movement of goods and services within the member countries, but also a free movement of labour and capital and common tariff and trade policies with respect to the outside world. Second, a **customs union**, which calls for free movement of goods and services and common tariff and trade policies with respect to the outside world (but not free movement of labour and capital). Third, a **free trade area**, where the movement of goods and services would be free, but each country would be able to impose its own restrictions on the movement of labour and capital within the area as well as its own tariffs and trade policies with respect to the outside world. The Royal Commission rejected the first two options and recommended the *free trade area* arrangement as the most practical and acceptable to both countries.

Potential Benefits

The benefits of freer trade are expected to come from two main sources. One is the cost reductions derived from *economies of scale* Canadian producers will realize once they gain access to the large U.S. market. The other are the efficiency gains from *increased competitiveness* within the Canadian economy as it becomes more open to import competition.

Both concepts are easier to understand with the help of a diagram. In Figure 11-7, we show the long-run average cost curve (*LAC*) of a typical Canadian industry analogous to the *LAC* curves introduced in Figure 9-5 in Chapter 9. With only limited access to the U.S. market, the demand curve facing this industry is D_0 and the largest

plant size compatible with this size of market is SAC_2. Some firms, however, manage to operate with plants as small as SAC_1 and still survive. This is possible because of Canadian import tariffs (and nontariff barriers) which, when added to the U.S. export price (P_{US}), raise the Canadian market price to P_{CAN}.

Most Canadian industries are oligopolistic (see again Table 7-1 in Chapter 7); this market structure makes it relatively easy for Canadian firms to collude and charge uniform prices equal to P_{US} plus Canadian import tariff. The quantity demanded at this price is Q_0. (In some industries, though, the $MR = MC$ rule prevails instead and joint industry profits are maximized at a price which is lower than the U.S. price plus the Canadian tariff. In yet another group of industries, competition may prevail and disrupt joint profit maximization altogether.)

If Canada decided to remove tariffs and nontariff barriers *unilaterally* (that means other countries, including the U.S., would keep their tariffs and nontariff barriers in place), the domestic Canadian price would drop from P_{CAN} to P_{US}. Quantity demanded would increase to Q_1 and all plants with *SAC* curves above P_{US} would be eliminated. These gains from eliminating small inefficient plants plus the benefits from increased consumption and increased competitiveness and rationalization of Canadian industries would, according to some estimates, raise Canadian GNP by about 3.5 percent.

Suppose now Canada's trading partners also remove their tariffs and nontariff barriers, that is, a *multilateral* free trade agreement is implemented. Now, in addition to the gains available from unilateral tariff removal, Canadian producers obtain access to a larger market. Consequently, the demand curve in Figure 11-7 shifts to the right, to $D_{FREE\ TRADE}$. As a result, plants as large as SAC_3 become viable, and the associated economies of scale can be exploited. Estimates of the benefits to Canada from this type of trade policy range as high as 7–10 percent increase in GNP.[6]

---

6. *Report of the Royal Commission on the Economic Union and Development Prospects for Canada*, Vol. 1, p. 329.

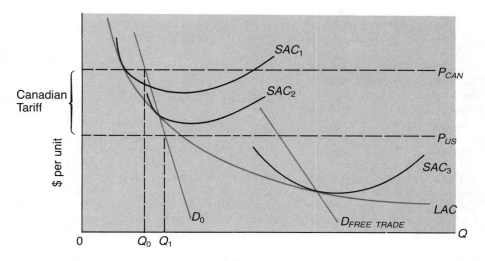

Fig. 11-7 Impact of free trade with the U.S. on a Canadian industry

Before free trade, the industry faces demand curve D_0 and can charge prices as high as P_{CAN} (which is the U.S. price P_{US} plus Canadian tariff). Removal of Canadian tariffs drives industry prices down to P_{US} and forces elimination of plant sizes with SAC curve above P_{US}. Removal of U.S. tariffs shifts the demand curve to $D_{FREE\ TRADE}$ and makes possible production with plant sizes as large as SAC_3.

Potential Costs

The effort to form a free trade area between Canada and the U.S. has been the target of two sets of objections. On the *economic* side, such a policy move inevitably imposes substantial adjustment costs. These would disproportionately affect some regions of the country, some sectors of the economy and some segments of the labour force. The potential *noneconomic* consequences of a move toward free trade have been at least as hotly debated. For example, fears have been expressed of further erosion of Canadian national identity, potential loss of some uniquely Canadian cultural and social values, threat to some components of Canadian social policy, including unemployment insurance and medicare, etc.

One could compile a long list of Canadian economic policies designed to protect some industries, regions or groups in society. These policies typically work through some kind of restric-

tion on competition and thus on free flow of goods, services and factors of production. We have already encountered rent controls (in Chapter 2), agricultural policies (in Chapter 4), marketing boards (in Chapter 7), minimum wage legislation (in Chapter 10) and foreign investment controls (in the previous section), to name just a few. Yet more of such policies are discussed in Chapter 12. Since many of them affect not only domestic, but also foreign, markets (more precisely, Canada's competitiveness in foreign markets), it was inevitable that their form and continuing existence should become a part of the debate on freer trade.

One question which requires special attention is the impact of free trade on the location of foreign-owned subsidiaries in Canada. After all, why did they come here to start with? Frequently, the answer is "to jump over the Canadian tariff wall," that is, to manufacture here rather than having to import the same goods from abroad and pay tariff duty. If this is so, would they not pull up their stakes, manufacture in the U.S. and ship the goods to Canada duty free once the free trade area is established?

Economists answer "not necessarily," for several reasons. First, as access to larger markets makes Canadian plants larger and more efficient, the productivity of investments in Canada will rise and thus the theory predicts that *more*, not less, investment will be made. Second, if initially a withdrawal of foreign investments should occur, the selling of assets denominated in Canadian dollars would depress the exchange rate so that eventually manufacturing in Canada would become cost competitive. (Recall again, the relationship between exchange rate and international competitiveness, discussed in Section 11-4). Third, large-scale sales of manufacturing assets would depress their prices and make it profitable for some investors to buy them and continue manufacturing in Canada.

A free trade area with the U.S. would benefit Canada by making possible gains from economies of scale, increased competitiveness and rationalization of Canadian industries. Potential adverse effects include the economic adjustment costs as well as risks to certain uniquely Canadian political, social and cultural values.

After a period of intensive negotiations during 1986 and 1987, representatives of the U.S. and Canadian governments signed a draft agreement on October 4, 1987. During the following weeks the negotiating teams worked out precise details, and the agreement was tabled in the House of Commons on December 11, 1987. Approval by the Parliament of Canada and by the Congress of the United States was scheduled for the summer of 1988.

CONCLUDING REMARKS

Perhaps one of the most important aspects of international trade and investment involves vested interests and the power that vested interests may have in influencing government policy. For example, if we produce shoes for the domestic market and have to compete with foreign shoe manufacturers, it would certainly be in our interests, even if not in the Canadian consumer's best interest, to lobby Ottawa for some measure of protection from foreign competition. We could quite easily demonstrate that if the protective measures were stiff enough we would not only enhance our profit position but also increase employment in our industry. It may be interesting, however, to ask ourselves the following questions in this regard:

(a) Who pays for the higher industry profits and higher wages necessary to attract the new employees?

(b) If this was done with every industry in Canada, what would be the costs and benefits?

(c) If higher employment was judged to be a benefit in (b), why could not this higher employment be attained instead by stimulating demand in other sectors of the economy?

KEY TERMS AND CONCEPTS

absolute advantage	dumping
comparative advantage	direct investment abroad
gains from trade	net indebtedness
adjustment costs	multinational enterprises
tariffs	foreign control
nontariff barriers	extraterritoriality
GATT	Investment Canada
quotas	common market
protectionism	customs union
price discrimination	free trade area

PROBLEMS

Problem 1

a) What are the advantages of engaging in international trade?

b) What are some costs and benefits of trade liberalization (freer trade than we have at present between Canada and other countries)?

c) What are four types of protectionism?

d) Would you advocate completely free trade for every good and service? Explain.

Problem 2

The production possibilities of two countries are shown below. Suppose that country *A* desires 0.5 million tonnes of wheat per year and after that, as much oil as possible. Country *B* wants 0.4 million tonnes of wheat per year, and after that, as much oil as possible.

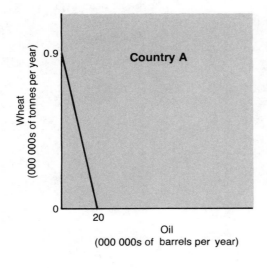

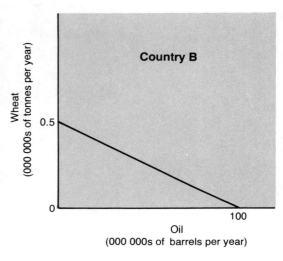

a)   What would be the production and consumption pattern of each country without international trade?

b)   What are the costs of oil and wheat production for each country?

c)   Suppose money prices implying a ratio of 1 tonne of wheat for 30 barrels of oil are agreed upon. What would be the production and consumption patterns after specialization and trade?

d)   Country *B* suddenly forces a higher price for oil, so that now 1 tonne of wheat trades for 10 barrels of oil. What would be the production and consumption patterns afterwards?

e)   With the new price of oil would country *A* be wise to seek to become self-sufficient in oil production? What costs are involved in attempting this? What if there was some question as to whether the price of oil would soon fall from the level announced in (d)?

Problem 3

a)   Can you explain why the Japanese are on average more efficient manufacturers than agricultural producers relative to Canadians?

b)   Explain why a drastic reduction in Canadian labour productivity in the resource industry would reduce the wages in both the Canadian resource sector and the manufacturing sector and allow Canada to compete more effectively with the Japanese for manufactured goods.

c) Even though Japanese agriculture is very inefficient due to lack of suitable farmland, the Japanese government heavily subsidizes farming so that Japan is approximately 75% self-sufficient in agricultural products. Explain briefly the logic of this policy.

d) What are the pros and cons of Canada having a policy self-sufficiency in shoe or automobile production, or say, 50% self-sufficiency in these products.

Problem 4

Some groups argue that we should impose quotas or heavy tariffs on manufactured clothing from low-wage countries because multinational corporations operating in such countries are exploiting the foreign workers by paying pitifully low wages.

a) Explain briefly which groups would gain and which groups would lose from a policy designed to block a significant portion of goods coming from low-wage countries.

b) What sort of domestic immigration policy would be consistent with concern for pitifully low-paid foreign workers?

c) Explain briefly how you might be able to check on the sincerity of those groups who advocate protectionism on the basis of concern for foreign workers.

Problem 5

a) What distinguishes direct from indirect (portfolio) foreign investment?

b) For each event on the list below state what the expected effect would be on foreign direct or portfolio investment and why.

  (i) a sudden increase in Canadian interest rates
  (ii) an announcement by the Canadian government of an increase in corporate taxes
  (iii) a sudden increase in U.S. interest rates
  (iv) political instability in Canada

c) Explain why the existence of tariffs tends to encourage direct foreign investment.

d) In Chapter 9 we spoke of the move toward rationalization of certain sectors of Canadian industry, which involves a movement on the part of companies toward the production of a narrower range of products. *World product mandating* is an example of product line rationalization involving multinational corporations. A successful example in Canada has been the case of Black and Decker, whose Canadian subsidiary was granted world rights to produce and market the company's orbital sander. What are the potential benefits of a domestic branch plant of a foreign multinational receiving a world product mandate from its parent? If the Canadian government seeks to *force* foreign multinationals to give world product mandates to Canadian subsidiaries, explain briefly how this might affect foreign direct investment in Canada.

CASES

Case 11-1

The Globe and Mail, Toronto

Shoe quotas no longer fit in Canada

By DAVID STEWART-PATTERSON

The federal government has decided to end most quotas on imported shoes Dec. 1, to the dismay of domestic manufacturers and the delight of consumers.

The Shoe Manufacturers Association of Canada said as many as 16,000 of the 20,000 jobs in the industry could disappear and its share of the Canadian market could drop to about 20 per cent from 40 per cent.

And Liberal industry critic Lloyd Axworthy said the government has broken a campaign promise made by Prime Minister Brian Mulroney in Quebec's Eastern Townships region during last year's election to keep the quotas.

"The workers of the shoe industry can now call the Prime Minister the Pinocchio of Sherbrooke," Mr. Axworthy said.

However, International Trade Minister James Kelleher said quotas have been in place for almost eight years and have forced Canadians to pay between $450-million and $500-million more for their shoes than they would otherwise have.

The new shoe policy follows closely the recommendations of a lengthy study completed last summer by the Canadian Import Tribunal. Quotas on imported women's and girls' shoes will be phased out over three years.

The quotas on those products will rise by 6 per cent next year, 8 per cent the next year and a further 10 per cent in the third year before being lifted altogether.

Quotas and high tariff walls may provide temporary shelter from international competition, but "experience has taught us that they are counterproductive in the long run," Mr. Kelleher said.

"They can have the effect of isolating the industries they were meant to protect, of making them less able rather than more able to stand on their own."

The bottom line is that while the Conservative Government faces strong pressure to continue the quotas from domestic manufacturers, the tribunal's report meant that an extension would have been almost impossible to justify under international trade rules.

Quotas are only allowed if a country can prove that imports are hurting its domestic industry, and must be temporary and intended to give the industry time to adjust.

Even then, affected countries can demand compensation in the form of easier access for other goods they make and, if they are not satisfied, may retaliate by penalizing Canadian exports.

The European Community threatened to impose punitive duties on a wide range of Canadian exports worth $150-million after the quotas were extended last year, and eventually settled for a deal to reduce Canadian duties on a variety of European goods that Mr. Kelleher said cost the federal treasury $12-million.

And while domestic shoe makers predicted a gloomy future for their industry in the wake of the government's announcement, a spokesman for the EC in Ottawa said the community will probably be forced to retaliate anyway.

Women's and girls' shoes account for about 60 per cent of EC shoe exports to Canada, and the new Canadian policy therefore discriminates unfairly against European producers, the spokesman said.

The extension of the quotas is "completely unjustified" under the terms of the General Agreement on Tariffs and Trade, and the EC "will make full use of its GATT rights against what it considers to be a protectionist measure."

The community would be allowed to retaliate by raising its tariffs within 30 days of publishing a list of products to be affected. The spokesman said he expects either a compensation package or retaliatory measures to be in place by year-end.

Even without the quotas, Canadian shoe makers will remain protected by a 23 per cent rate of duty on imports, far higher than the average Canadian tariff.

Although the end of quotas may seem like a Christmas present for consumers, Jack Shand, president of the Canadian Shoe Retailers Association, said it is one that they may not get until next year.

Orders for shoes are usually made months in advance, and retailers and importers are now considering their purchases for the fall and winter of 1986. There could, however, be increased imports by new players in the market, especially of cheaper shoes from Third World countries, which are less dependent on fashion trends.

John Tyhurst, a lawyer with the Consumers Association of Canada, said the decision feels like a victory for consumers, but he is worried

that the industry might use the phase-out period as an excuse to renew protection.

A spokesman for the Canadian Importers Association said he is afraid that the government may have a hidden agenda that will see the inevitable surge in imports following the end of quotas used as an excuse to slap them on once again.

However, Mr. Kelleher said the government expects the surge and believes that the shoe market will stabilize within 12 to 18 months. Canada will also talk to major exporting countries and warn them that it would be in their best interest to ensure the surge does not become an uncontrolled flood.

He also promised an adjustment program to help affected companies and communities, but these were quickly denounced by opposition politicians. "It's a program to help people get out of town when the industry fails," Mr. Axworthy said.

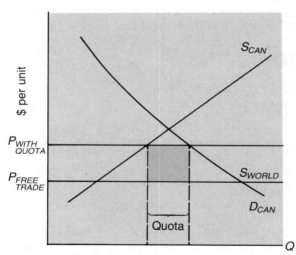

a) With the help of the above diagram, show how one might arrive at an estimate of the cost of quota to Canadian consumers (such as the $450 million–$500 million cited in the article).

b) Show, in your diagram, the impact of quota removal. What attitude toward the quota removal would you expect from each of the following: (i) Canadian shoe manufacturers, (ii) foreign shoe manufacturers, (iii) Canadian shoe wholesalers and retailers, (iv) Canadian consumers, (v) foreign consumers.

c) Explain the meaning of Mr. Kelleher's statement that quotas "can have the effect of isolating the industries . . . making them less able . . . to stand on their own."

Case 11-2

The Financial Post

Stopping countervail key to forging free-trade deal

By DUNCAN CAMERON

AMBASSADOR Simon Reisman has recently made it clear that without some concessions from the U.S. on the use of trade remedy legislation against Canadian exports, there will be no bilateral trade agreement with the Americans. As chief Canadian free-trade negotiator, he is not prepared to recommend a deal to cabinet without some commitment by the U.S. to limit the application of countervailing duties on Canadian exports.

On the American side, incoming Senate finance committee Chairman Lloyd Bentsen, while anxious to see talks with Canada given a high priority, has made it equally clear that the U.S. is not prepared to negotiate away its power to impose countervailing duties on imports deemed by the U.S. to have received Canadian government subsidies and to have caused injury to American industry.

Thus the outcome of free-trade talks seems to depend upon differences over countervail/subsidy being resolved.

Rodney Grey, fresh from his experience negotiating for Canada during the Tokyo Round, was the first to sound the alarm about U.S. contingency protection and its potential impact on Canada. Grey pointed out that as a result of post-Tokyo tariff reductions, Canada could expect to develop industries that were fully competitive on a North American scale.

The implication is that, for these firms, as much as 90% of production would be shipped to the U.S. If, following a ruling in the U.S., such an industry were deemed to have received a subsidy from the Canadian government, the industry could be hit by an American countervailing duty that rendered its production noncompetitive in the U.S. Such a ruling by the U.S. authorities would destroy the Canadian industry.

From the other side, a North American competitive industry based in the U.S. might export 10% of its production to Canada. If that industry were deemed by Canada to benefit from subsidies, and a Canadian counter-

vailing duty imposed as a result, the impact on the U.S. industry would affect only 10% of production. Thus, the use of countervailing powers is asymmetrical: Big countries, such as the U.S., can hurt small countries, but small countries, such as Canada, can not hit back with anything like the same effect.

For a free-trade agreement that has as an objective the assured access by Canadian industry to the American market, this becomes the crucial issue. If, at great cost, Canadian industry restructures to benefit from the advantages of free trade, only to find that the price of its success is being shut out of the newly developed American market, what is the point of a free-trade agreement?

From the American perspective the issue is a broader one. The U.S. Congress is concerned about the U.S. trade deficit of more than US$150 billion. Rightly or wrongly, the American attitude is that unfair trade practices by overseas competitors have undermined the U.S. trading position on a worldwide basis. Getting Congress to exempt Canada from legislation that allows the U.S. to deal with government-subsidized exports would set a precedent that could be used by others in negotiations with the U.S.

In the legalistic environment of trade remedy disputes, no such precedent would be envisaged without a most significant undertaking by Canada to restrict the use of *industrial policies*. Not only would this require agreement from the Canadian provinces, any Canadian commitment would have to be measured against the requirement under the Canada Act to reduce regional disparities. This constitutional provision implies the use of industrial policies that might be countervailed by the U.S.

In the light of the importance of countervail/subsidy, one idea is that a framework agreement could be negotiated between Canada and the U.S. that would create a supranational trade disputes agency to investigate national trade grievances. This agency's objective would be to see that each side looked at the same factors when determining criteria for trade remedy action, and that each side adopted similar standards for measuring the degree of injury — the basis for determining the level of protective duty to be applied.

Unequal impact

The agency would have the advantage of encouraging two unequal countries to apply equal rules in dealings with each other. But it could not offset the unequal impact that follows when "equal" rules are applied by a big country against a small country. Moreover, the harmonization of trade remedy practices between Canada and the U.S. may not please those who fear that Canada would inevitably adopt more American practices, thus eroding Canadian sovereignty.

The alternative would be to negotiate the countervail/subsidy issue through the new GATT round. Since many industrial policies permitted under GATT can also be countervailed under U.S. trade remedy legislation, the problem can be seen, in part, as the need to harmonize U.S. law and GATT rules. In this respect, Canada is likely to find allies with similar concerns, if it is prepared to work through the long, difficult process of reaching agreement in mutilateral talks.

a) Illustrate the impact of both the U.S. and the Canadian countervailing duties in a diagram similar to Figure 11-7 in the text.

b) Among the Canadian "industrial policies" mentioned in the article are subsidies given to firms operating in designated regions of the country, support for research and development, industrial training assistance, etc. Show, in your diagram, the effect of their removal (perhaps under U.S. pressure) on a typical Canadian industry. How does this effect compare with the impact of potential U.S. countervailing duty? What are some of the broader considerations in this policy decision?

c) What, in your opinion, might be some of the possible consequences if Canada did not negotiate a freer trade deal with the U.S.?

Government Microeconomic Policy

12-1 INTRODUCTION AND PURPOSE

In this chapter, we wish to examine the justification for government microeconomic policy. For example, what is the reasoning behind such government-sponsored efforts as subsidies for particular industries, laws governing pollution, government-sponsored marketing boards for agricultural products and price controls for public utilities? All of these things affect the workings of a free market and in turn influence price, sales volume and employment levels in such industries.

There are two generally recognized objectives of

possible government intervention within individual markets. These are **economic efficiency** and **social equity**. We will first discuss the meaning of these terms and then examine how politics affects government intervention in the market system. Though governments may rationalize their actions solely in terms of efficiency and equity, much of what dictates government intervention within markets is of a *political nature*. We cannot hope to understand government economic policy unless we recognize this fact.

Chapter 13 continues the development begun in this chapter and also considers the topic of *government (public) finance*.

12-2 ECONOMIC OBJECTIVES OF GOVERNMENT

Most of us would probably like to think that governments interfere with the free workings of a market only in order to make things in some sense better than they would otherwise be. But what are the criteria for "better"?

Pareto Optimum

One way of making things better is to take actions that would make some people better off (happier) without making anyone else worse off. When all such actions have been taken, a *Pareto best* (or **Pareto optimum**) position for the economy is said to exist.[1] Typically, we expect the government to do more than this.

Maximum Total Welfare

Another concept of making things better is to take actions that will increase *total welfare* (happiness or well-being) within the economy. Suppose, for example, the government reduces your taxes and increases those of someone else by an equal dollar amount. If, as a result, your happiness increases by more than the reduction in happiness of the other person (perhaps because that person values material goods that the income commands less than you do), the total welfare of society as a whole will increase. But in practice, just how is the government to measure total happiness within the economy? How, for any particular policy decision can a government measure the amount of happiness lost by those adversely affected and compare it with the amount of happiness gained by others? This is a difficult task indeed.

The two broad objectives of government intervention in the economy are improved economic efficiency and social equity. One criterion of economic efficiency is Pareto optimality, that is, an allocation of resources such that a change from Pareto optimality will make someone worse off without making someone better off. Maximization of social welfare is a more meaningful criterion. However, its applicability is limited because it is difficult to compare the changes in welfare of individuals.

---

1. Named after Vilfredo Pareto (1848–1923), a well-known economist and sociologist.

12-3 ECONOMIC RULES FOR EFFICIENCY

As mentioned briefly in Chapter 6, economists have attempted to develop tests for efficient allocation of resources (land, labour and capital). We argued that one test is to see whether, in every industry, **price equals marginal cost**. We noted, though, that this rule would not guarantee efficiency in every case. Now, we would like to elaborate on this qualification.

First of all, a more general rule for economic efficiency is that in every industry *price should equal both long-run marginal cost and long-run average cost*. To understand this rule, let us examine Figure 12-1, which depicts a purely competitive industry and a representative firm.[2] Initially, let us suppose that the market price is P_0. The representative firm would take this price as given and produce volume q_0. At this volume, the extra cost (LMC) of producing the last unit of output is exactly equal to the extra value that consumers derive from its production (P_0) (as measured by the height of the market demand curve).

It would seem, therefore, that the welfare of society has been maximized. The extra cost to society of producing the last unit is just equal to the extra benefit that this last unit provides to society. However, economists would not regard the situation described in Figure 12-1 as depicting an efficient allocation of resources, since owners of firms would be earning higher rates of return than could be earned elsewhere for comparable risk. In other words, the firms would be more than covering the cost of capital funds — and would be earning *economic profit*.

Remember, the annual dollar cost of capital funds used to finance the firm's assets includes the annual accounting profit required to provide the owners with a normal rate of return on their invested funds. Further, as an important economic cost, the annual dollar cost of capital is included as part of total and average cost. As a consequence, any firm which sells at a price exceeding average cost earns economic profits. For our representative firm

---

2. The concept of the long-run cost curves, remember, assumes that the firm and the industry have enough time to adjust all inputs as production volume is varied — that is, not only the amount of labour and materials used but also the number of machines and size and number of plants. Long-run marginal costs, therefore, include the extra cost of capital funds needed to change the scale of plant, whereas such costs are not included in short-run marginal costs (since in the short run the firm must operate within its given physical facilities).

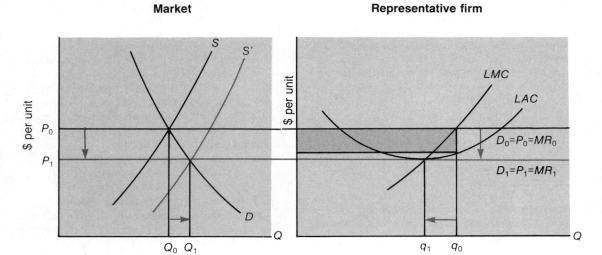

Fig. 12-1 Improvement of resource allocation by industrial expansion

In original market equilibrium, with price P_0 and quantity Q_0, a typical firm max-imizes profit by producing q_0. At this level of output, $P = LMC$, but social welfare is not maximized, since economic profit is made. As a result of entry, market supply curve shifts to S', price is driven down to P_1, and a typical firm reduces output to q_1. This outcome maximizes the firm's profits as well as social welfare, since $P = LMC$. Economic profit is zero and each firm produces at minimum LAC.

of Figure 12-1, total annual economic profits are depicted by the shaded area.

Because economic profit represents *excess* (accounting) profit — that is, above the normal profit which could be earned in other industries at similar risk — there is at present a poor allocation of economic resources (land, labour and capital). In fact, unless there are barriers to entering the in-dustry, new firms would come into existence, financed by investors attracted by the above normal rate of return. The industry would expand. As the expansion takes place, a greater volume of output would be offered at each and every possible market price. As Figure 12-1 shows, the industry supply curve would shift outward and the market price would fall to P_1. At P_1, the representative firm's production would be lowered to q_1. At q_1, the value to consumers of the last unit produced (P_1) again just equals the additional cost of resources needed to produce the last unit (LMC). In addition, economic profits have been elimi-nated. Since price now just covers average cost (LAC), owners of the firm receive only a normal rate of return on their invested funds.

Another way of thinking about the situation is as follows. Originally, at Q_0 (in Figure 12-1) margin-al costs were not as low as they could have been. The representative firm was producing beyond the most efficient scale of production (beyond the minimum long-run average cost volume). Entry by new firms in effect forces additional efficiencies on the industry by inducing each existing firm to pro-duce at a scale at which marginal and average costs of production are lower.

Resources are efficiently allocated if in each in-dustry $P = LMC = LAC$. The extra value to society of the last unit of ouptut is just equal to the extra cost to society of its production ($P = LMC$). As well, economic resources are efficiently alloca-ted here because the market is calling for neither an increased nor a decreased investment of land, la-bour and capital in the industry; it is allowing just the normal rate of return on such investment for the risk undertaken ($P = LAC$). Further, output is produced with the least possible use of inputs (that is, at minimum LAC).

12-4 EFFICIENCY AND MARKET FAILURES

In a purely competitive economy with no block-ages preventing entry to or exit from the industry, an efficient allocation of resources would be attained. Firms would tend to price at a level equal to marginal cost. In the long run, industrial expansion or contraction would take place so as to minimize average cost and allow business owners to earn only a normal rate of return on invested funds. This is why economists hold up the purely competitive model as a standard by which to judge any particular industry. However, there are many instances in which a free market would not bring about economic efficiency as defined above. We shall now consider some cases of such **market failures**.

Imperfect Competition

Even though the purely competitive model is generally the economist's ideal, few markets in the economy actually achieve this ideal (refer once more to Table 7-2). The Canadian economy is characterized by imperfectly competitive market structures, which do not meet the long-run criteria for allocative efficiency.

Take, for example, a firm selling any differenti-ated product or service. Suppose long-run demand and cost data are as represented by Figure 12-2. Whether by a cost markup procedure or any other means, if the firm is attempting to be as profitable as possible it will produce volume Q_1 (where $LMR = LMC$) and charge a market price of P_1. Because price exceeds marginal revenue for an im-perfect competitor (see Section 6-2), price also ex-ceeds marginal cost. This means that in an im-perfectly competitive market, the price society is willing to pay for additional output is greater than the additional cost to society of resources that would be used in its production. Therefore, more inputs should be devoted to production of this particular good or service, and in this sense economic resources (land, labour and capital) are not efficiently allocated.

In an imperfectly competitive industry, free market forces will not automatically allocate resources in such a way that the best output level for society as a whole is produced. But why? Does

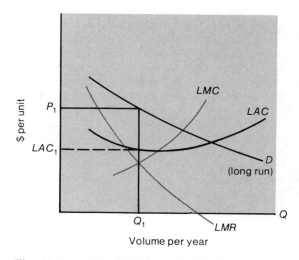

Fig. 12-2 Inefficient resource allocation in an imperfectly competitive market

Profit-maximizing behaviour requires that an im-perfectly competitive firm produce output Q_1 for which $MR = MC$. This level of output is sold at price P_1. Since $P_1 > LMC$, profit maximization under imperfect competition leads to sub-optimal allocation of resources from society's point of view.

society not know what is best for itself? The problem is that in the market place there are dif-ferent groups, each acting in its own best interest, which does not necessarily coincide with that of society as a whole.

In our imperfectly competitive example of Figure 12-2, we can identify at least two major groups (consumers and firm owners), each of which will be acting in its own self-interest. Even though society would benefit by a production in-crease beyond Q_1, all this benefit would accrue to consumers as a result of the lower prices. The firm's owners would become worse off by increas-ing production beyond Q_1, because their profit would be less. Therefore, in such a market profit-maximizing firms would not willingly increase output beyond Q_1.

The welfare loss due to such output restriction is, however, only a part of the social cost of im-perfectly competitive market structures. Some economists argue that the costs of product differentiation typically associated with imperfect competition are substantial. Since the Canadian market is relatively small, most Canadian industries are populated by plants which produce many product lines with short product runs. Because of this extensive product differentiation, economies of scale in production are often not realized. Moreover, competition by means of product differentiation, rather than by price, is costly to the consumers. For example, it entails relatively high per unit costs of promotion and distribution, including excess capacity in retailing.

Natural Monopoly

In some industries, the production technology dictates that the whole market be served by a single firm (or perhaps only a small number of firms). Typical of these industries are public utilities (electricity generation, telecommunications, etc.). For example, to provide telephone service, even to a sparsely populated geographical area, a heavy investment in sophisticated plant and equipment is required. There is also, of course, a considerable need for engineering, maintenance and supervisory personnel to service this fixed plant base. However, should the population of the area double, for example, the need for new fixed plant, equipment and connected personnel would increase by a far smaller amount. This means that because of the technological requirements inherent in the production of telephone services, there are considerable economies of scale.

To see what sort of economic industrial structure this implies, let us follow through a short example of two equal-size telephone companies which have identical long-run cost structures, as represented in Figure 12-3.

We have depicted falling (long-run) average costs per call as average annual output increases because technological considerations imply that a given percentage increase in volume requires less than the same percentage increase in plant, equipment and associated personnel.

Small Scale Inefficiency

Suppose 800 million telephone calls were to be made during each year. Regardless of the market shares held by each single telephone company, the economy as a whole would be more efficient if one telephone company was allowed to expand and take over the whole market. For example, with two companies, each holding 50% of the business, the volume done by each would be 400 million calls per year at a cost per call of $0.25. With a single firm, the cost per call would be only $0.15. This means that whereas two firms would use up economic resources totalling $200 million (800 million × $0.25) per year to supply telephone services, a monopoly would only use $120 million (800 million × $0.15) per year to supply the same volume of telephone services. In this case, $80 million worth of resources (land, labour and capital) would be released to produce other goods and services.

An industry where technological considerations imply falling average unit costs over the entire range of feasible output is called a **natural monopoly**. In such an industry, if there are a number of smaller firms in the market they will generally find it profitable to merge or otherwise combine in order to take advantage of the *economies of scale*. Smaller firms will then generally not be able to compete with the larger low-cost enterprises. One way or another, they will be forced to sell out to the larger firms, leave the industry entirely or become government subsidized because they may provide services in areas where larger firms would not find it profitable to operate (for example, in sparsely populated rural areas). As a result, such industries tend to be dominated by very large firms. With regard to telephone services, each Canadian company like Bell Canada, British Columbia Telephone, or the provincially owned telephone companies of Manitoba, Saskatchewan or Alberta is, for all practical purposes, a monopoly within the geographical area it covers.

As we saw in Chapter 6, though, another type of economic inefficiency tends to appear in a monopolized market. This inefficiency arises because it is profitable for a monopoly to price its output higher than marginal production costs.

Consider the case of a telephone monopoly, whose cost data are represented by Figure 12-3. If the demand and marginal revenue data are as shown on the figure, a profit-maximizing monopoly would price its services at $0.24 per call. Given this price and demand, 770 million telephone calls would be made each year. However, at

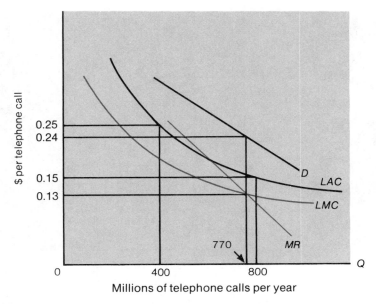

Fig. 12-3 Economies of scale in the telecommunications industry

If 800 million telephone calls are required, in the presence of economies of scale a single firm can provide this number of calls at $0.15 per call, while two competing firms would require $0.25 per call. Demand curve *D* and marginal revenue curve *MR* suggest a profit-maximizing price of $0.24 per call and quantity of 770 million calls per year. This is not socially optimal since price ($0.24) exceeds marginal cost ($0.13).

this volume, the value placed by consumers on additional telephone calls — represented by the price they would be willing to pay ($0.24) as reflected by the demand curve — is greater than the cost (*LMC* = $0.13 per call) to the economy of the extra required resources to produce additional telephone service. That is, we have the familiar monopoly case of restricted output (in this case, restricted output of telephone services).

Destructive Competition

It is sometimes argued that industries with a heavy proportion of fixed costs are vulnerable to **destructive** (predatory) price **competition** which would result in waste of resources if unchecked by some type of government intervention. For example,

railroad companies require heavy investment in fixed plant and equipment and have sizeable economies of scale. Once this equipment (rails and rolling stock) is in place it lasts for a long time and is not readily resalable. This means that at relatively low operating levels, fixed costs are a very high proportion of total costs, and variable costs (and marginal costs) are very low in comparison. For trucking, on the other hand, even at low levels of operation the extra costs (marginal costs) of transporting one tonne of freight one kilometre in distance are high relative to the railroads. Further, trucks have a readily available North American resale market.

To see what the above factors might mean for railroad-trucking competition, examine Figure 12-4. The cost structures of the trucking industry and

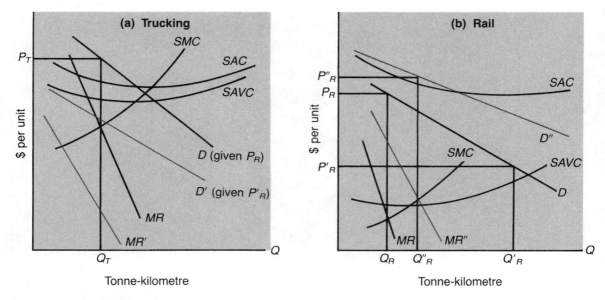

Fig. 12-4 An example of predatory pricing possibilities

The railway industry (part (b)) faces demand curve *D* and average cost curve *SAC*. Its optimal price P_R results in economic losses. A price reduction to P'_R makes the losses even larger in the short run. However, the increased demand for rail transportation causes a shift to the left in the demand curve for trucking services (to *D'* in part (a)). Consequently, some trucking firms suffer economic losses and exit from the industry. As a result, the demand curve for rail services shifts to the right (to *D''* in part (b)).

the railroads have been depicted to fit the above description. Demand data have also been illustrated. An important point to remember is that the demand facing each industry will depend vitally on the price that the other industry is charging for transport services because transportation by road is a substitute for transportation by rail (at least for many commodities and shippers). This is not true, of course, for a few geographical areas where one or the other carriers may be absent.

If both industries priced in a short-run profit-maximizing fashion, initially the prices per tonne-kilometre would be P_T and P_R, as shown. The way the diagrams have been drawn, the price of trucking (P_T) would be greater than average short-run costs per tonne-kilometre, whereas the price of rail services (P_R) would be below short-run average

costs. Investors in the trucking industry would be earning an economic profit (above normal rates of return on invested funds); those in the railroad industry would be earning economic losses (below normal rates of return).

Next, suppose the railroads decided to attempt to increase their share of the transportation business by the strategy of sacrificing additional short-run profits now for possibly greater short-run profits in the future (in other words, greater average annual profits in the long run). They may lower their prices per tonne-kilometre temporarily to P'_R, which would stimulate the tonne-kilometre volume of business (to Q'_R), but cause even greater annual losses in the short run — because the price is now even further below the average cost of providing the service (that is, they have strayed from the $MR = MC$ point). The large magnitude of the price cut is made possible by the wide gap between SAC and $SAVC$. Even at the drastically lower price P'_R, variable costs are still covered and a contribution to fixed costs is made.

The impact of these reduced railway rates would be significantly felt in the trucking industry. Demand for trucking services would fall drastically. For example, it may now be represented by D'. We have admittedly depicted a drastic case, but in this instance even the best short-run trucking price could not match the railroad's, nor even cover the short-run variable costs of operating — let alone provide the owners with a normal rate of return on invested funds. This action would therefore cause many trucking firms to sell some of their rolling stock and others to go out of business entirely.

As a result, the railroads would then experience an increase in demand for their services, possibly to D'' in Figure 12-4b, enabling them now to charge a profit-maximizing price P''_R, which would be high enough to cover all operating costs and earn more than a normal rate of return for the shareholders ($P''_R > SAC$). Such a strategy of undercutting competition in the short run to gain more monopoly power and greater profits in the long run is termed *predatory pricing*.

With the prevailing price P''_R, the railroad now makes economic profit and the trucking firms may once again consider entering the market to take advantage of the new high prices and profits. This potential cycle of exit and re-entry of firms might constitute a waste of resources. It is therefore sometimes viewed as a case of market failure and a rationale for government intervention.

Externalities

Externalities — or third party effects — occur when the process of production or consumption confers benefits or costs on economic agents other than the producers or consumers of the product or service.

Private and Social Value

Market demand indicates how much consumers are willing to pay for goods and services and therefore reflects the value they place on the goods and

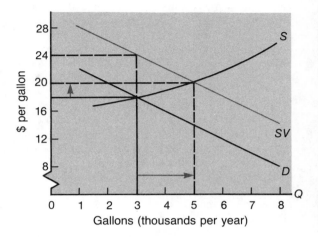

Fig. 12-5 Private and social value

Demand curve D describes the private valuation of the various quantities. Demand curve SV takes into account the benefits some individuals derive from consumption by others. Interaction of the supply curve S with the two demand curves shows that socially optimal consumption exceeds privately optimal consumption.

services. This value, because it reflects each buyer's own preferences, is called **private value**. In some instances, there are not only benefits to the purchaser of a good or service but also benefits to outsiders. For example, suppose Jones, who lives across the street from me, is contemplating whether or not to paint his house. I and the other neighbours think it certainly needs painting. But Jones is not so sure. He has other things to spend his money on, and he never liked painting. As it turns out, Jones is willing to do his house only if he can get paint for $16 a gallon or less. Sixteen dollars per gallon is consequently the private value (to Jones) of the paint.

Suppose the market demand and supply curves for paint are as shown in Figure 12-5. From the figure, it appears as though there are others who are willing to pay more for the paint than Jones (though others still are only willing to pay less). At present, the market price for paint, based on demand and production costs, is shown by the figure to be $18 per gallon. Because the paint is not worth $18 per gallon to Jones, he would decide to let the painting go by for at least one more year. However, being Jones's ten immediate neighbours, we desperately want him to spruce up his house. A new paint job on his house would be a relief to the eye and increase the value of our homes. In fact, if we could do it without hurting Jones's feelings, we might be willing to chip in as much as $3 each to see his house painted. That means we perceive the pleasure and increased market value that would result as being worth roughly $3 to each of us. Of course, if Jones let his house go unpainted for another four or five years, we might be willing to up this amount considerably as Jones's house becomes a real eyesore and begins to affect the market value of our properties.

Though the private value to Jones of each gallon of paint is only $16, the total **social value** to the neighbourhood (including Jones and his neighbours) is somewhat greater. If, for example, we assume five gallons of paint would do Jones's house, the total social value per gallon would be the $16 that Jones would pay plus the neighbours' willing contribution, which is $6 per gallon — ($3 per neighbour × 10 neighbours) ÷ 5 gallons. The total social value per gallon is $22.

In Table 12-1 we have reported in the first two columns the demand information reflected by the *D* curve of Figure 12-5. At $16 per gallon, five of the 4000 gallons demanded represents Jones's demand. Alternatively, we could argue that the 3995th to the 4000th gallon of paint demanded represents that which Jones would be willing to buy of his own volition — and he values these five gallons at $16 each. The social value of each of these five gallons (including the value to the neighbours of Jones's paint) is $22 a gallon. Similarly, there are probably other neighbours surrounding other houses in need of paint. These people, too, would perhaps be willing to contribute toward their neighbours' cost of paint. In other words, the private demand data in Table 12-1 and the demand curve in Figure 12-5 do not accurately reflect the total value to society of the paint. These social values have, however, been depicted in Table 12-1, and the curve reflecting them is represented by *SV* in Figure 12-5.

Table 12-1 Private value (as reflected by market demand) and social value

Gallons demanded per year	P Private value of last gallon ($)	Social value of last gallon ($)
8 000	8	14
7 000	10	16
6 000	12	18
5 000	14	20
4 000	16	22
3 000	18	24
2 000	20	26
1 000	22	28

Numerical representation of information from Figure 12-5. For each market quantity demanded, the social value of the last unit exceeds the private value by $6.

In a market where the social value of production is greater than the private value, the actual demand curve usually reflects only private value and underestimates the social worth of the product or service. The reason is that other people affected by the outcome of the purchasing decision usually do not offer to subsidize the purchaser, and so the purchaser buys solely on the basis of personal values. In this situation, therefore, even a purely competitive market would underproduce and not allocate resources efficiently.

In this example, the appropriate price and output combination for economic efficiency is $20 per gallon and 5000 gallons annually. At this production level, the extra cost to society of the resources used in making the last gallon of paint is just equal to what society as a whole would be willing to pay for the last gallon. However, in actual fact, the purely competitive market volume would be only 3000 gallons. At this volume, the value to society of the next gallon of paint is $24, whereas the cost to society of the next gallon is only $18. Therefore, production would not be at the best level for society as a whole.

A slight modification of this example illustrates another important category of situations where a free market, left to its own devices, would not provide the socially optimal amount of goods or services. This is the case of **public goods**. To be specific, consider, for example, the benefits all members of society derive from provision of national defence or street cleaning or control of infectious diseases. As in the house-painting case, some members of society would be willing to contribute only a little (or not at all) to such activities. They might argue, perhaps, that they do not wish to be protected by the armed forces or by health authorities or that they actually enjoy messy streets. Some citizens, of course, might make these statements merely to disguise their true preferences, in the hope that others will take care of the problem anyway and *all* will enjoy the benefits.

In the economist's jargon, consumption of public goods is *nonexclusive* (once I pay for the cleaning of the street, I cannot prevent my neighbours from enjoying the benefits). This presents an opportunity for some members of society to act as **free riders**, that is to contribute less to the provision of public goods than the value they derive from their consumption. As a result, the amount of such goods provided by a free market would be smaller than socially optimal.

Private and Social Costs

Now let us consider the case in which **social costs** of output are greater than **private costs**. For example, take the use of aerosol spray cans. Suppose that the gas emitted from such cans causes potential harm to the atmosphere, thereby increasing health hazards for all of us. This increased health risk must certainly be treated as a cost of the production and use of these products. Actually, we may think of this aspect as a reduction in the social value of the product (from the demand side) rather than an increased cost (from the supply side) if we like. This cost of production is not accounted for by the producing firms, and is not reflected in marginal production costs. Further, each consumer typically will not think about the extra cost imposed on society from use of the product. Therefore, these additional pollution costs are not reflected in the private demand and supply curves.

Suppose now that the relevant demand and supply information is as shown in Figure 12-6. If the industry is purely competitive, the market price

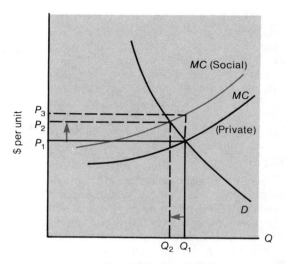

Fig. 12-6 A divergence between social and private costs

The production (and use) of a product imposes costs on society which are external to the producer (user). As a result, social marginal cost exceeds private marginal cost, and the socially optimal quantity (Q_2) is lower than the privately optimal quantity (Q_1).

and volume produced would be P_1 and Q_1, as shown. However, including the cost of the fluorocarbon emissions, the social marginal costs are higher than private costs. Suppose that these social marginal costs are represented by the broken line curve as shown.

Again, we see that a purely competitive market would not allocate resources in an economically efficient manner. The Q_1th unit (spray can) yields a social value of P_1 (if it is assumed that the market demand curve reflects social value), whereas the additional cost to society of the last unit produced is greater, at P_3. Therefore, this last can should not have been produced. In fact, output should be cut back to Q_2 on economic efficiency grounds.

In the above examples of market failure we have seen that the free market solution may not allocate resources in the most economically efficient fashion. The extra cost to society of producing the last unit of output does not equal the extra benefit to society of the use of the product, once produced. These situations, consequently, provide an economic rationale for possible government interference in the free market system.

Equity

Another reason for government interference in the free workings of demand and supply is *equity* or *fairness*. For instance, many think it is fair that the rich should be taxed more heavily than the poor or that farm incomes should be increased and stabilized. These are clearly value judgements, and the relevant decisions cannot be made on the basis of economic reasoning alone. The political process, social values, ethics and philosophy play an important role.

Market mechanism guarantees efficient allocation of resources only under a very restrictive set of conditions. Most real-life markets are subject to the possibility of market failure and misallocation of resources. Examples of market failure include imperfect competition, natural monopoly, destructive competition and externalities.

12-5 METHODS OF GOVERNMENT INTERFERENCE

There are many ways in which governments interfere with the working of the market mechanism in order to remedy the perceived cases of market failure. We will now discuss a few of these, roughly in the order in which they were presented in the previous section.

Competition Policy

Competition policy is a government policy designed to improve the efficiency of allocation of resources in industries characterized by imperfect competition. The Canadian version of this policy — the Competition Act — is discussed in detail in Appendix 9-B.

Regulation of Public Utilities

The provision of such goods as electricity, gas and telecommunications services can often be handled efficiently by one company over sometimes wide geographical areas. In order to obtain economies of scale, the government often permits a monopoly to be set up — but under regulated conditions.

Unregulated, normal managerial activities of a monopolist, acting in the shareholders' interests to maximize profits, would lead to too low a volume of services. Remember, a monopolist producing where $LMR = LMC$ causes an output at which $P > MC$, that is, where the value to society of the last unit of service offered is greater than the extra cost to produce it. The government seeks to remedy this situation by forcing lower prices than the monopolist would freely charge.

To see more clearly what the government might try to do here, examine Figure 12-7. Long-run market demand, marginal revenue and marginal costs that a monopolist might face in the absence of regulation are indicated in the figure. If the firm tried to choose a price close to that which would provide the greatest profit, it would charge P_M. At this price, too little service (Q_0) would be offered to the public (since $P_M > LMC$). Further, the firm would be earning economic profits (since $P_M > LAC$). For these reasons resources would be misallocated.

Suppose a government-appointed regulatory body decided to impose a maximum regulated price on the market. Suppose they choose P^1_{reg} as shown in Figure 12-7. The company would now know that price is beyond its control but that it could still manipulate output to attempt to maximize profits within this government constraint. This action would put it in the same position, with respect to price-output decision, that a pure competitor would be in. The extra (marginal) revenue obtained for each additional unit of service no longer varies but is instead constant at P^1_{reg}.

In this instance, to maximize profit the company would offer Q_1 units of service at the price P^1_{reg} (where $MR = MC$). Though at this output and price the monopolist would now be restricted to only a normal return on invested funds (because $P^1_{reg} = LAC$), resources would still be inefficiently allocated. The value to society of the last unit produced (as reflected in the height of the demand curve) would still exceed the extra cost of production (MC). A further symptom of this remaining inefficiency would be the shortage of service at the regulated price P^1_{reg}. The firm would voluntarily produce Q_1 but demand at the regulated price would be greater than Q_1 at Q'_1.

As another option, the regulatory body may choose P^2_{reg} as its regulated price. At this price, to maximize profits the firm would voluntarily produce Q_2, a volume which would equal demand at this price. There would be no shortage and the

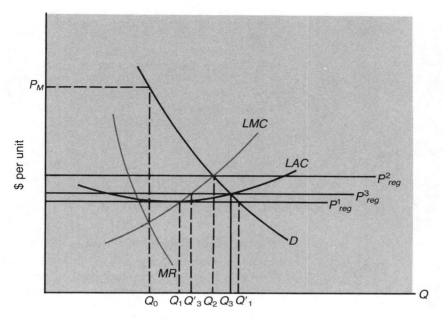

Fig. 12-7 Regulating a monopolist

In an attempt to improve efficiency of resource allocation, the regulatory agency requires the firm to charge a price different from the monopoly price P_M. If P^1_{reg} is imposed, no economic profits are made, but only Q_1 is produced. At this level of output, $P > LMC$ and demand exceeds supply. If P^2_{reg} is imposed, then Q_2 is produced, $P = MC$ and demand equals supply, but the firm makes economic profits. If P^3_{reg} is imposed, then Q_3 is produced, no economic profits are made and demand equals supply. However, $LMC > P$.

value to society of the last unit produced would just equal its extra cost of production (because the demand price equals MC at Q_2). However, here the firm would be earning economic profits (since $P^2_{reg} > LAC$); resources would still be poorly allocated.

A third option — and as it turns out one followed in practice by Canadian regulatory agencies — is to fix a regulated price of P^3_{reg} and attempt to force the monopolist to produce at Q_3. At this point, the firm would be earning just a normal return on invested funds and there would be no shortage of service. However, there would still be inefficiency because for all units of output

produced beyond Q_2, the extra cost of production (MC) exceeds the value to society of service units provided. Further, in this instance the monopolist would be involuntarily producing all units beyond Q'_3, which is the output level that would maximize its profit at a regulated price of P^3_{reg}. The life of a regulator is not an easy one.

Another type of regulatory problem arises in situations where economies of scale prevail throughout the relevant range of output levels (within the limits of the market size as described by the market demand curve). Suppose, for example, that government regulatory bodies attempt to set the price charged for telephone calls at a

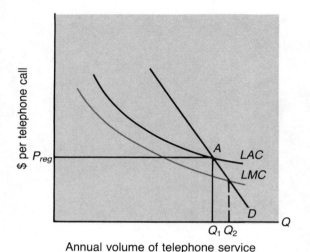

Fig. 12-8 Regulation of a natural monopoly

The price chosen by regulatory authority (P_{reg}) covers long-run average cost and demand is met. However, allocative efficiency is not achieved since $P > MC$.

prices below LAC, and because LMC is below LAC it will not voluntarily produce at a price which equals LMC.

For this reason, most government regulation of natural monopolies attempts to set the rate so that when taken in combination with demand it leads to companies' covering long-run average costs. This situation enables such monopolies to just cover their cost of capital funds and, if privately owned, provide their shareholders with a normal rate of return on investment. The regulatory agencies then take solace in the fact that though the other criterion of economic efficiency ($P = LMC$) is not quite met, at least it may be better approximated than in the unregulated case.

Regulation of Telephone Services

Federally incorporated telecommunications companies are regulated by the Canadian Radio-television and Telecommunications Commission (CRTC). Such companies include Bell Canada and B.C. Telephone. Provincially incorporated companies are regulated by government public utilities commissions in their respective provinces, except in Alberta, Saskatchewan and Manitoba, where the telephone companies are provincial Crown corporations.

The exact nature of the regulation differs slightly in each case, but by and large it proceeds as follows. The commissions make sure that the companies live up to their charters. For example, the companies must generally provide telephone service in their areas "on demand," with the latest improved design in use in the locality at that time. This requirement is part of the price the companies must pay for their monopoly privileges. Either the company or the regulatory commission may request a rate hearing, at which time evidence (estimates of cost and demand) is presented for or against a change in rate schedules. The prime objective of the rate hearings is always to allow rates at which the company covers reasonable long-run average costs. That is, the commission desires that the approved schedule, combined with an efficient operation, will enable the company to cover its operating costs and provide a fair (normal) rate of return for its shareholders. The industry will then be able to acquire new funds for expansion if necessary to meet increasing demand.

level such as that indicated by P_{reg} on Figure 12-8 and at the same time force the telephone company to meet demand. In such a case as that shown in Figure 12-8, the telephone company would provide Q_1 telephone services per year and just cover its long-run costs — that is, the common shareholders would receive a normal rate of return on their invested funds.

Unfortunately, as shown in Figure 12-8, such a regulated rate does not quite achieve the efficiency objective $P = LMC$. In fact, it would be the case that the amount of resources in the industry is still too small (output is still too low). The market value of additional telephone services sold is greater than the value (LMC) society puts on the extra resources needed to produce the extra output. However, the company will not voluntarily increase its services to Q_2. To do this, it would have to lower its price below P_{reg} and in fact below its average cost per unit (LAC). Consequently, it would not be able to cover the cost of capital funds necessary for such an expansion to Q_2. The company cannot cover the cost of capital if it

Regulation of Transportation

Until 1986 the transportation industry was highly regulated and did not operate in a freely competitive market framework. The rate schedules (prices) particular transportation companies set were carefully scrutinized by government appointed bodies, as was the entry or exit by any firm to or from the industry.

The Canadian Transport Commission, a federal body, regulated interprovincial rail, air, water and road transport of solids by pipeline. Oil and natural gas pipelines are also a federal responsibility and are regulated by the National Energy Board. On the other hand, regulation of transportation strictly within a province is the responsiblity of provincial authorities.

The basic objectives of the 1970 National Transportation Act were roughly as follows:

(a) to encourage an efficient use of transportation by all available modes at the lowest total cost (or lowest average cost per unit of transportation, that is, per tonne-kilometre);

(b) to see that each mode of transport bears a fair proportion of the real costs of the resources, facilities and services provided to each mode of transport at public expense;

(c) to see that each mode of transport receives compensation (subsidies) for the services it is required by the Canadian Transport Commission to provide as a public duty.

In July 1985, the federal government released a document entitled *Freedom to Move*, which proposed a reform of the regulation of transportation. In June 1986, the government tabled in the House of Commons two bills based on this document: the National Transportation Act, 1986 and the Motor Vehicle Transportation Act, 1986. The main thrust of the legislation was to encourage greater price competition and generally reduce the regulatory restrictions. It also established a new regulatory body, the National Transportation Agency, which would replace the Canadian Transport Commission.

In air transportation, the legislation proposed gradual elimination of the regulation of passenger fares and air cargo tariffs. Entry into the airline business would be made easier; all carriers which meet national safety standards (are "fit, willing and able" to operate) will be given a licence. A special regulatory regime is envisaged for northern and remote areas of Canada to ensure that essential services will be maintained. The National Transportation Agency will have the right to examine fare levels and increases and disallow those deemed unreasonable.

In rail transportation, shippers will be allowed, for the first time, to negotiate better rates and services with the railways. "Captive shippers" (those with access to only one railway) will be given opportunity to negotiate competitive rates for shipment on two railways. Competing railways will no longer be permitted to agree together on rates.

Trucking is regulated by provinces. However, following an agreement with the provinces, the Motor Vehicle Transportation Act of 1986 establishes a uniform nation-wide entry test for extraprovincial trucking. Regulation of trucking rates and regulatory restrictions on the routes a particular trucking company can serve or the type of commodities it can carry will be phased out.

Taxes and Subsidies

In order to correct underproduction, which occurs when the social value of output is greater than private value, the government has to stimulate greater output. It can do this either by subsidizing purchasers (as could have been done by Jones's neighbours in the house-painting example) or by subsidizing producers. The subsidy to producers could be given either on a per unit produced basis (like a negative excise tax), which would lower their marginal costs of production; or on the basis of income tax relief to encourage new entrants into the industry and thereby greater output in the longer run.

In the case of industries in which there are external costs such that social marginal costs exceed the market price, the objective of government policy is to reduce production to the point where social marginal value equals social marginal cost. To reduce output, a tax can be levied either directly on the purchaser of the good or service, or indirectly on the producer. The net effect of such measures is shown in Figure 12-9.

For simplicity only, we have supposed that the industry is purely competitive. In the absence of

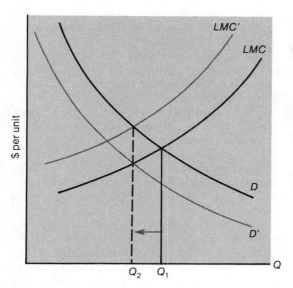

Fig. 12-9 A case in which social costs exceed private costs

Because of the excess of marginal social cost (*LMC'*) over marginal private cost (*LMC*), the industry output (Q_1) is larger than is socially optimal. A tax on producers makes private marginal cost equal to social marginal cost, and output level drops to socially optimal quantity Q_2. The same outcome can be achieved by a tax on consumption, shifting the demand curve from *D* to *D'*.

taxes, output would be at Q_1, reflecting only private costs and benefits. Social marginal costs, on the other hand, are depicted by the broken line *LMC'* curve. This curve implies that an efficient allocation of resources from society's standpoint would be at Q_2. This level can be attained by a tax on producers, to raise long-run marginal costs to *LMC'* or on consumption of the good (say by licence fees), to lower net private valuation of the product's consumption down to *D'*.

Taxes are also used to finance the provision of public goods. The coercive power of the state is employed to overcome the free rider problem — that is, all members of society must contribute, regardless of their stated preferences as to the

desirability of consumption of public goods. While financing is the responsibility of government, the actual provision of public goods may be contracted out to the private sector. Typically, a mixture of the two is the norm. Thus, we have public and private schools, hospitals, garbage collection firms, etc. The recent trend toward **privatization** and **contracting out** of government operations is based on the belief that private sector firms, as a rule, can do the job at lower cost than government agencies.

A whole range of government policies are in place to remedy the various forms of market failure. Competition policy, direct government regulation of selected industries, and taxes and subsidies are some of the government policy instruments. A recent trend in Canada is toward less regulation and greater reliance on competitive market mechanism.

12-6 PROBLEMS OF PRODUCT INFORMATION

One of the more controversial reasons for government interference in the market place is the difficulty an individual consumer may have in judging product quality. If I am to have a brain operation, how can I judge in advance whether the doctors who will perform the operation are competent? How can I know whether my new automobile has a design feature that will make it difficult to handle under critical driving manoeuvres? Does my favourite ice cream contain an ingredient that will increase my risk of early death?

We can be quite sure that most suppliers will point out the good features of their goods and services, and we will, of course, be aware of some of the bad features. However, to the extent that we may not be aware of some of the bad features, the perceived value of the product will be overestimated by us as consumers. Exaggerated perception of product quality leads to a higher level of market demand than would prevail if the true quality of the product was known. Figure 12-10 illustrates this point graphically. *Misperceived product value* leads to market demand (*D*), which is greater than it would be (*D'*) if the *true product quality* was known. As a consequence, a competitive market

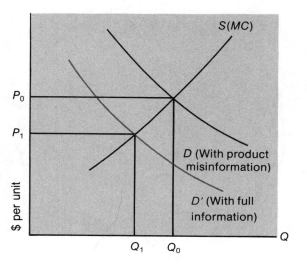

Fig. 12-10 Effect of product misinformation

When consumers overestimate the product quality, the market demand curve is further to the right than would be the case if consumers had correct information. As a result, the output level (Q_0) is higher than the efficient level (Q_1).

that the secret ingredient XS-75 in a cold medicine is useless. With consumers having learned of a product's true quality, market demand would reflect this information. In Figure 12-10 market demand would eventually gravitate to D', and with *full information* the long-run market price and quantity would tend toward P_1 and Q_1 respectively. At Q_1, economic efficiency prevails, with the value to consumers of the last unit produced equal to its marginal cost of production.

Unfortunately, in practice, we might never get to this long-run situation. As, or even before, market demand for the cold medicine with XD-75 begins to slip, the same company under the same or different brand might come out with a new improved formula, QM-19, "shown to be effective." Continual adaptation of products and the creation of "new" products can maintain *information gaps* between perception and experience.

Learning through experience can also be a very costly way of acquiring information. Purchasing home insulation that causes sickness and eventually has to be removed at a cost of thousands of dollars is an expensive way for a consumer to discover product quality. Driving a car that may explode in low speed rear end collisions is another example of costly information gathering through actual consumption experience.

with misinformation leads to a higher price (P_0) and output level (Q_0) than should prevail for economic efficiency. At the free market output quantity Q_0, the marginal cost to society of the last unit produced ($MC = P_0$) exceeds the unit's true benefit to society (consumers), a benefit which is only discovered through actual consumption.

Information Acquired through Experience

Since by experience consumers do discover the true quality of the products that they buy, any divergence between believed and actual product quality can only be temporary. For example, through experience consumers eventually discover

Government and Consumer Protection

In order to overcome informational deficiencies concerning product quality, the government acts both as an information gatherer and as an enforcer of minimum product standards. For example, the provincial governments through departments such as the Ontario Ministry of Consumer and Commercial Relations attempt to ensure that businesses conduct fair practices toward the consumer, while the federal government regulates products which may be sold nationally. Federal product regulation comes under the jurisdiction of the Bureau of Consumer Affairs within (the department of) Consumer and Corporate Affairs Canada.

The following are some of the federal acts under which Consumer and Corporate Affairs Canada attempts to protect the consumer.

Hazardous Products Act — Purpose: To prevent products with hidden hazards from reaching the consumer. Examples: potentially harmful children's toys and furniture; nonsafety glass on shower doors; certain highly flammable textile products; and hockey helmets that do not meet prescribed safety standards.

Consumer Packaging and Labelling Act — Purpose: To require prepackaged consumer products to display certain basic product information.

Textile Labelling Act — Purpose: To require proper labelling of the fibre content and identity of manufacturer.

Food and Drug Acts — Purpose: To protect the consumer from risk to health, fraud and deception in relation to food, drugs, cosmetics and therapeutic devices. Examples: food additive clearance; pesticide, chemical and microbiological hazard control; establishing standards of safety and purity for foods; testing of new drugs and the requirement of licensing of such drugs.

Some people criticize the government's role in **consumer protection**. Those critics suggest that the existence of government enforced standards for some goods and services leads us to become even less careful consumers. We take the attitude that "the government wouldn't let the product on the market if it didn't perform"; or, "they (the advertisers) couldn't say if it wasn't true." Since government protection is not complete, and would be prohibitively costly if it was, this attitude is dangerous and leads to some consumer mistakes that would not be made if the consumer assumed a greater responsibility for self protection.

There are those who would do away with all government departments of consumer protection and rely instead on the normal legal remedies against fraud and misrepresentation. If a product proves not to perform as one might reasonably expect, or in fact causes harm, the consumer can sue the producer. This remedy is only feasible, of course, when the damage being sought is a large sum of money, but not otherwise. If a shirt shrinks badly when washed or if one gets a stomach upset from a meal prepared in an unsanitary fashion at a highway rest stop, court action is often impractical, since the cost of such action would exceed the damage being sought.

Some critics charge that government product standards often go too far. Meeting high quality

"Not only do they not make 'em like this any more, it's ILLEGAL to make 'em like this any more!"

GRIN AND BEAR IT by George Lichty: © Field Enterprises, Inc. Courtesy of Field Newspaper Syndicate.

standards raises costs and prices. Consumers may thus be forced to buy a high-priced, high quality product when they would have preferred to purchase a lower quality product at a lower price.

Of those who support government market intervention in the name of consumer protection, some accept the validity of the above criticisms but then argue that there is also an equity consideration at issue. The line of reasoning is as follows. Those consumers who regularly do comparative shopping, subscribe to independent consumer information magazines and are aware of their legal rights probably need very little additional protection from the government and are also likely to be middle or high income earners. At the other end of the spectrum, there are people who do need the protection afforded by government consumer legislation, and a high proportion of these people are likely to be low income earners.

One of the characteristics of purely competitive markets is that both buyers and sellers are perfectly informed about the quality of products or services. If this assumption is not satisfied, market failure may occur. Government policies attempt to remedy the problem either by forcing the provision of additional information or by keeping some products or services out of the market altogether.

12-7 EFFICIENCY AND SOCIAL WELFARE

To say that one is against a policy action that would lead to greater economic efficiency sounds silly. In fact, though, one may not be able to prove that a particular action that moves in the direction of economic efficiency as defined earlier (with price equal to long-run social marginal cost and also equal to long-run social average cost) actually increases social welfare. For example, in the case of monopoly regulation, a government wants to encourage output beyond the profit-maximizing level and toward the point where social marginal value equals social marginal cost. The government regulatory body would thus cause the profit of the monopolist to fall, and thereby make the owners of the corporation worse off. For example, if the monopoly has its shares publicly traded on the stock exchange, the share prices will fall as a result of the lower profit, and the shareholders will take a capital loss. Therefore, though consumers are made better off by the government's actions, shareholders are made worse off. It may be argued, in some instances, that the harm done to shareholders outweighs the benefit brought to the consumers as a result of the regulatory action. If that belief is true, the regulations would then be reducing total social welfare.

Total Social Happiness

Because most government intervention in the market place typically benefits one group and harms another, the rationale for undertaking such action is either (i) that the benefits are expected to outweigh the harm, with the result that total social welfare is expected to increase; or (ii) that the total harm is expected to outweigh the benefits, with the result that total social welfare will fall but the benefiting group for some reason is given prefer-

ence over the group harmed. Some may say that (ii) should never be the case, and that the only reason for government intervention should be to increase *total social happiness*. Others argue that groups such as the elderly or infirm should be helped by a tax on the rest of society even if the total happiness the rest of society would have derived from its tax money is greater than the induced happiness received by the former groups. This question, like most important philosophical questions, cannot be settled by logical argument alone. Instead, the answers are matters of personal taste, opinion and moral conviction.

Political Motivation

To maximize economic efficiency is one possible criterion of government policy. To maximize social welfare by taking into consideration economic efficiency on the one hand, and the welfare of groups hurt by otherwise economically efficient action on the other, is another possible motive. In addition, the aiding of specific groups of people, even at the cost of economic efficiency or a reduction in total social welfare, may be another possible rational course of action for governments to take. Some of these actions we as voters may or may not like, and we have the option of voicing our displeasure at the ballot box. In fact, in a democratic system, there is one more strong possible motive for specific government action. We now discuss this.

Maximization of Votes

As voters, we cannot count up the total amount of happiness created by the party in power, compare it with the total amount a new government would create and then vote in a party with the highest score. Even if we could compare total happiness creation in an approximate fashion, it is not clear that we would vote for parties on this basis. Instead, and what is far more likely in practice, we can examine what the party in power has done for us (and others in the country) lately and formulate our beliefs of what the other parties might do for us and others if elected.

Exactly how each person decides to vote is up to that person. Some may be influenced by religious or moral commitments to vote for the party that can be expected to do the most for poor Canadians at the expense of the rich, or for the party that will probably do the most for third-world nations — and so on. Others may vote solely on the basis of which party they think will do the most for themselves, individually. In a democracy, we do not ask that voters state why they make their particular choices. Because each vote counts equally, we implicitly count each person's reasoning process equally. Whichever party gets the most representatives (Members of Parliament) voted in is elected.

Because of the way parties get into power government certainly has, as one of its criteria for undertaking economic policy, the acquisition of votes. Some go so far as to say that in practice, the only objective for any government policy — economic or otherwise — is **the maximization of votes**, to get into and stay in power, not the maximization of total social happiness or anything else like it. These people argue that if playing up to business, unions or civil servants is good for votes, this will motivate government policy. It seems an exaggeration to suppose that economic policy is carried out solely to get the most votes. By the same token, it is ridiculously naïve to suppose that no government policy is carried out primarily for the purpose of getting votes, or that vote getting is not at least a consideration in most economic actions by the government.

The question is, of course, "what should be the criteria for government economic policy?" The answer depends on our beliefs. We may think that the total welfare of society should be maximized, even though this requires us to make judgements about how much one group is hurt in favour of another and how much the other group gains. Alternatively, we may think that the democratic basis for economic decisions is best. In this case, perhaps the government should in fact make each economic decision on the basis of what is best for the maximum number of people (or voters). Again, we may think that economic efficiency should be the primary consideration of government economic policy.

If we allow a complete laissez-faire economic market system, this means that we let the free working of supply and demand within each market allocate our resources (land, labour and capital) among competing forms of production. In a purely competitive market system without externalities, the resulting allocation of resources would seem to

be quite desirable. From a static perspective, given each consumer's income, society's welfare would be maximized. The extra social value created by the last unit of output produced (P) would just equal the extra social cost (LMC) of producing the good, and average production costs would be minimized.

However, it is doubtful that within such a system we would be completely satisfied with the resulting distribution of income, because there is not an equal dealing out of wealth, intelligence and talents at birth. Therefore, even in such an idealized purely competitive environment it is likely that many would opt for at least some government intervention in the form of taxation and redistribution of income and wealth.

Further, in reality some markets have externalities, others contain monopoly power and the gathering of product information in certain instances may be very costly. Because these cases create a divergence between social marginal costs and social marginal benefits, a completely free market allocation of resources may not maximize economic efficiency. This fact, therefore, may give rise to some warranted government intervention, involving perhaps the creation of taxing and subsidy-granting government agencies, regulatory bodies and other government departments.

Costs of Bureaucracy

In a particular instance, it may turn out that even though one does see a deficiency within a particular market it might not be wise to advocate government intervention. Though the government action may eliminate the market deficiency, the resulting resource costs from the added government bureaucracy may outweigh the benefits.

First of all, the added labour (civil servants), land and capital for government buildings is a cost, because these resources could be used to produce other goods and services. In addition, because it is difficult to accurately estimate marginal social costs and benefits it is difficult for the government to know exactly how much to control industries in which it is believed that such divergences exist. Therefore, there will be many *government mistakes* resulting in shortages or surpluses of particular goods and services. These must also be looked on as *real costs* to society of government control.

The net benefits from government control of a particular industry are the gross benefits expected as a result of improved resource allocation in the economy less the cost to those who may be harmed by the reallocation (shareholders and possibly others) — and also less the costs of bureaucratic mistakes, civil servants' salaries, land and capital used in the control process. To advocate government control of an industry while neglecting these real costs is folly.

Another Cost of Controls

There is one more cost of government intervention and control of the market system that deserves mention. If the government intervenes and seeks to exert some sort of control over a market, this means some group or groups are forced to act in a way that they would not act if given their free choice. This fact is prima facie evidence of a cost to this group. The natural reaction of such a group is to minimize its losses under such controls. This reaction may consist of *attempting to get around the controls* somehow. At the very least, it involves an attitudinal and motivational change which should not be neglected. For example, if a public utility has its pricing structure regulated, the company knows that the regulatory body is watching its profit pattern as part of its consideration in setting new rates. That is, the regulatory body will not allow the company's rate of return on some base to exceed a particular limit. Knowing this, there is less motivation to maximize profits. Why should managers strive to maximize profits, when making larger profits will only lead to lower regulated rate structures — thereby making it harder for the company to make normal accounting

profits in the future? Therefore, there is a tendency under such control for managers to devote less effort to reducing costs. Such inefficiency leads to more resources being necessary to produce the same amount of goods. Also, accountants may be instructed to devote more time and effort to hiding revenue and enlarging costs wherever possible, thereby showing an apparent lower profit. These costs must also be taken into consideration before one advocates government intervention within a particular market.

One model of the behaviour of governments asserts that the primary objective of governments is to maximize votes rather than social welfare. Even if governments attempt to maximize social welfare, their interventions in the market may be costly or create additional distortions, with the possible result that the overall efficiency of the economy does not improve.

CONCLUDING REMARKS

In a market economy, there are various rationales for government intervention at the micro level. These include monpoly power, possible divergences between social and private costs and benefits, product information problems and the possibility that the government may better understand what is good for a particular group within society than that group itself. The government corrective devices include taxes, subsidies and regulation. An ongoing debate concerns whether or not the government oversteps its bounds in using these devices and in some instances creates more inefficiencies than it eliminates.

KEY TERMS AND CONCEPTS

economic efficiency
social equity
Pareto optimum
the "price equals marginal
    cost" rule
market failure
natural monopoly
destructive competition
externalities
private value
social value

public goods
free rider
private costs
social costs
regulation of public utilities
regulation of transportation
privatization
contracting out
consumer protection
maximization of votes

PROBLEMS

Problem 1

a) Define what is meant by a Pareto optimum situation.

b) Do you think governments should do more than gear their economic policies to a Pareto optimum position for the economy? If so, what should be the broad objective(s) of such policies?

Problem 2

a) What economic rationales are there for government interference within a free market?

b) In each case mentioned for part (a), suggest appropriate government policy action.

c) Before market intervention is undertaken, what sort of cost-benefit analysis should the government perform?

Problem 3

Suppose the diagram below represents a particular industry at a given point in time.

a) Assume the firms within the industry are approximately in their best long-run position. Indicate on the diagram the market price and output that would prevail if the industry was (i) purely competitive, (ii) monopolistic.

b) In each case in part (a), would the firm's shareholders be earning abnormally low or abnormally high rates of return on their invested funds? Explain.

c) From your answer to (b), what would you expect to happen to the number of firms in the industry? Show on the diagram the effect of movement into or out of the industry.

d) Can new competitors always be expected to enter an industry where economic profits are being earned? Explain.

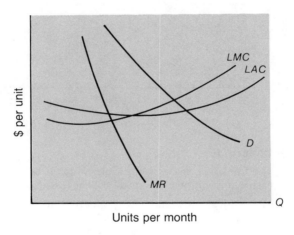

Problem 4

a) Discuss any externalities connected with the following goods and services: (i) alcohol, (ii) education, (iii) cigarettes, (iv) home insulation.

b) For each of the items listed in part (a), state whether social cost exceeds private cost or social benefit exceeds private benefit.

c) Would you advocate taxing or subsidizing any of the above?

Problem 5

Suppose a government felt that economies of scale in a particular industry were such that a single firm would be most efficient in terms of lowest average cost of production.

a) What other inefficiencies might then occur in terms of resource allocation?

b) Suppose that a monopoly to be regulated has the cost and demand pattern shown below. What if any undesirable features might be connected with a regulated price of either P_1, P_2, P_3, or P_4? If you were head of the regulatory agency, at which price would you regulate the company and how might you attempt to overcome any resulting difficulties?

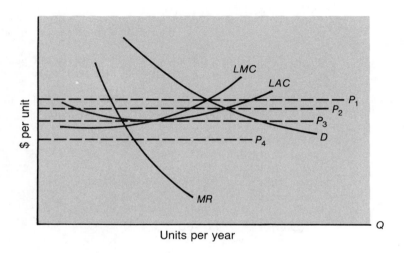

Units per year

Problem 6

The Canadian Broadcasting Corporation (CBC) is different from other broadcasting institutions in Canada in that it is entirely government owned.

a) Why do breweries tend to sponsor CBC television sports programs instead of opera, drama and ballet?

b) Do you think CBC television should finance programs such as opera and the ballet out of public tax revenue if no sponsors can be found? Discuss briefly.

c) If nonsponsored programming is to be carried out by the CBC, who should decide what programs to air — a football coach, a ballet director, a veteran civil servant with an engineering background, a veteran civil servant with a liberal arts college education or a committee? Discuss.

d) You may very well disagree with others who may have answered parts (b) and (c). Does this agreement involve differences in economic principles or differences in personal taste and philosophical conviction?

CASES

Case 12-1

Sulfur and nitrogen oxides are pollutants sent into the atmosphere primarily through emissions from transportation, smelting and coal-fuelled electricity generation. Such pollutants may travel thousands of kilometres through the air. Precipitation transforms these pollutants into acidic form — hence the term "acid rain."

Acid rain attacks forms of life, paint and other protective coverings, fabrics, building materials, electrical components, paper, leather, plastics and works of art.

Canadian Business

Counting the cost of acid rain

By ROSS HOWARD and MICHAEL PERLEY

To date almost the only discussion of acid rain in economic terms has focused on the cost of turning it off. In surprisingly short order, governments and industry have been able to project frightening multibillion-dollar expenditures needed if acid rain sources are to be curbed in North America. One recent prediction runs close to $5 billion over a decade for Canada alone.

There's much to suggest that such sums are exaggerated, based as they are on traditional technology and corporate analyses, but much more important, these costs are grossly deceptive. They loom as large as they do — casting shadows of galloping inflation, corporate bankruptcy, job loss and skyrocketing consumer prices — because they stand alone. The other cost of acid rain — economic damage — has been left unconsidered.

The task of calculating acid rain damage is admittedly far more intricate than the abatement estimates, and governments and decision-makers have so far chosen to ignore the question because they don't know its exact dimensions. But there is already some evidence that the cost of acid rain is so enormous that it could undermine the financial stability of entire regional and national economies. And while the detailed damage reports are still unavailable, there is much to gain by recognizing the enormity of what it at stake.

• • •

To mid-1980 there were no Ontario government studies on the financial impact of dead lakes. In fact, it wasn't until early 1980 that the first such study was commissioned, and it could take two years or more to complete. Fortunately, to the south in the six-million-acre Adirondack state park in New York, where equally intense acid rain is monitored, there are indications of what Ontario may find. The park lies only a full day's drive away from more than 55 million Americans, and each year, until recently, at least 1.7 million fishing trips were registered in the park, generating an estimated $16 million in the local economy. But in 1976, after the confirmation of more than 100 acid-dead lakes, state park researchers estimated that nearly $1.5 million in fishing expenditures had been lost. As parks commissioner Anna La Bastille told a Toronto conference on acid rain in late 1979, fishermen don't spend money to dabble in dead lakes. A more detailed study in 1978 based just on the dead lakes — the total had risen to 170 — showed a direct annual loss of

$370 000. Applied to all 3000 lakes in the park, the economic loss was estimated at "probably much higher than $1.7 million a year," the commissioner reported. "We've turned that park into a national acid cesspool, and now we in the area are paying for it," she added.

• • •

Ontario's environment minister, Harry Parrott, once tossed off an unexplained estimate of $500 million a year as a possible acid rain damage cost, when he spoke before the legislative committee. But the economic effects of acid rain on tourism could, almost like the physical effects of acid rain, begin unnoticed and be attributed to something else. Ontario tourism operators objected to newspaper reports about acid rain in the late spring of 1978, calling it the worst possible publicity for the beginning of the tourist season. Who can blame them? And yet, future seasons may never happen if the conspiracy of silence continues. Dr. David Schlinder of the federal Freshwater Institute feared the worst when he told the committee in early 1979: "There's been much talk of the jobs lost if major polluters are forced to curb their emissions. But I hope somebody is thinking of the thousands of tourist operators who will be out of business in 10 to 15 years if there are no controls on emissions."

• • •

At a UN conference in Stockholm in 1971, the Swedes also considered the damages to forests, property and human health, in dollar terms.

• • •

Consider what is at stake in Canada alone. Trees cover 35% of the land. Directly or indirectly they provide one out of every 10 jobs in the country, $18.5 billion worth of shipped material and $9 billion in added value in 1978, a $10.6-billion net contribution to Canada's balance of payments in 1979. Canada is the world's leader in newsprint production and export (half the world's total);

second in pulp production (Sweden is fourth); and harvests nearly 5 billion cu. ft. of wood per year. That's only part of the story. After a century of uncontrolled decimation, the Canadian forest industry is now running out of trees.

• • •

More than forests are at stake. Agricultural crops are worth $8.9 billion per year in Canada. There is strong evidence that what grows in the soil is affected by the acid rainfall. The extensive experiments by the US Environmental Protection Agency (EPA) at Corvallis, Ore., and others at Oak Ridge, Tenn., Hawaii and the experimental tobacco plots north of Toronto all show damage to crops such as radishes, beans and tobacco.

• • •

There is one aspect of the damage that is clear-cut now, and enormously expensive — property damage. Long before Sweden concluded that sulphur dioxide and associated air pollutants were costing $20 million a year in metal, stone and wood corrosion, engineers and scientists around the world had charted rates of air pollution damage. To cite only one example, Cleopatra's Needle, the stone obelisk moved from Egypt to London, has suffered more deterioration in the damp, dirty and acid atmosphere of London in 80 years than it had in the preceeding 2000 years of its history. Cement concrete, metals, paints, even fabrics are victims — flags fade faster and are tattered sooner in cities such as Los Angeles or Chicago than in cities of cleaner air. In 1978 the US president's Council on Environmental Quality estimated that property damage due to acid rain is $2 billion a year. In 1977 the National Research Council of Canada reported that sulphur emissions in air cause an estimated $285 million in damage per year in building deterioration, including $70 million in exterior paint damage alone. The distinction between direct damage by air laden with local sulphur dioxide and windblown sulphuric acid from distant sources is not clear yet, but the total damage due to sulphur emissions, in one form or another, is obvious. As the International Joint Commission reported in 1979, 50% of the corrosion of cars may be due to acid rain.

And finally, there are health costs. One study estimated that at least 5000 Canadians may die each year because of acid-rain-related sulphates; other researchers put the figure at 187 000 deaths a year in the US. The dollar value of a life in North America is inestimable on an individual basis; on a national basis economists and health care professionals estimate that premature death causes an average $80 000 loss in income alone.

No one knows exactly what acid rain is already costing North America, or will cost if the problem increases. Future costs, however, go well beyond the merely economic. As biologist Tom Hutchison of the University of Toronto told the Ontario legislature committee, "Deterioration of our lake environments, of the fisheries and the recreational aspects that go with it, is going to hit a lot of people very hard. . . . If we allow our short-term solutions to problems to devastate that environment, as we are on the way to doing now with acid rain, I think we are going to have to do a lot of answering to a lot of people in 15 to 20 years' time."

Unfortunately for Hutchison and that environment, 15 years time is beyond the normal vision and term of office of those making the decisions now.

The Financial Post

Pollution busters get tough with bad guys

By ROBERT ENGLISH

FEATURING TACTICS familiar from late-night television movies, raids are being carried out against Ontario's environmental bad guys by a commando team of ex-cops-turned-pollution-busters.

A pounding *Miami Vice* soundtrack wouldn't be out of place as a high-resolution camera clatters in a Cessna high above Lake Ontario, tracking plumes of effluent.

In another part of Canada's most heavily industrialized province, a stakeout team nurses Styrofoam cups of cold coffee as it waits for an illegal truckload of deadly waste to hit the road.

In the nation's capital, municipal filing cabinets are rifled for evidence after a lightning swoop under the cover of a search warrant.

Put simply, Ontario has decided that polluting the environment is no longer just an affront to the body politic, but a serious crime. It has put teeth (some would say fangs) into environmental protection.

As proof, even the provincial government's own GO-Transit commuter operation was convicted — and fined — for a spill into Lake Ontario last year.

And last week, Ontario Environment Minister James Bradley introduced a long-awaited bill proposing stiffer fines and, for the first time, jail sentences for polluters. Included is an ill-gotten-gains clause, which allows a judge to strip a company of profits made by violating environmental laws.

Open-ended mandate

Alex Douglas, 59, a deceptively mild mannered, ex-Metro Toronto police staff sergeant with a ruddy complexion and soft Northern Irish accent, came out of retirement to spearhead the province's war on polluters.

He was named director of the new Investigations and Enforcement Branch of the Ministry of the Environment, announced by the Tory government in June, 1985.

Douglas has an open-ended mandate and has been promised a free hand to operate without interference, particularly of the political variety. Enforcement used to be carried out, often reluctantly, by abatement officers from the ministry, whose primary role was to negotiate with industry to find ways to reduce pollution. Enforcement often played second fiddle to compromise.

This conflicting approach led to the formation of a stopgap, 15-man special unit in 1981. Douglas' force (he says the branch is run like a police operation), now totals 63 people (including 42 field operators from police and scientific backgrounds), and has a $3.2-million budget.

The unit became operational in January, headed by a roving eight-member force likened by some to a SWAT (special weapons and tactics) team of ex-cops and pollution experts.

So far, the government's get-tough approach has resulted in the laying of 693 charges by the enforcement branch, resulting in $563,000 in fines in fiscal (March to March) 1985–86. By comparison, in fiscal 1983–84, 259 charges were laid and fines totalled only $91,467.

Living up to its no-nonsense billing, the force has charged big and small alike, from a Sudbury grocery store, a St. Thomas pig farm, and the town of Clinton, to Toronto Hydro, Polysar Ltd. of Sarnia and Kodak Canada Inc. of Toronto. "We're playing no favorites, and no one has suggested that we do," Douglas says.

a) From the discussion in the first article explain the effect that acid rain is expected to have on the fishing and lumber industries in terms of price, volume of output, industry profitability and the market value of (price of common stocks of) such companies as Macmillan-Bloedel and Abitibi-Price (companies heavily involved in forest products production). Explain if the effects come through the demand or supply side of the market and give as much detail as you can.

b) Do you think it is possible to place a value on human life? If we as a society think that human life has an infinite value, how much would we collectively spend on highway safety features such as median barriers? If we collectively think that human life has an infinite value, what should we do about pollution which might take 5000 lives per year?

c)   Abatement refers to the reduction of pollution. To abate acid rain would involve increasing marginal costs (*MC*) for industry and decreasing marginal benefits (*MB*) to society as abatement approached 100%. Suppose the diagram below depicts the situation. If the government prohibited all omissions of pollutants that cause acid rain would this likely be an optimal or best policy from society's standpoint? (Why or why not?) What should be the target level of abatement for government policy?

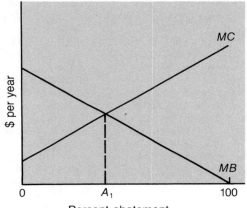

d)   Taking into account the discussions in the articles plus the fact that pollutants that cause acid ran can travel long distances, what sort of political difficulties can arise in managing the problem?

e)   In the above diagram, show the impact of criminal penalties discussed in the second article on the amount of pollution. How does the size of the penalty enter the picture? The probability of conviction?

f)   Comment on the relative merits of the type of enforcement discussed in the second article and "negotiations with industry to find ways to reduce pollution."

Case 12-2

The Globe and Mail, Toronto

Bell rate application will be challenged

By LAWRENCE SURTEES

Consumer and business associations are unanimously opposed to Bell Canada's rate rebalancing proposal, which seeks to increase local monthly telephone rates by $1.25 and to reduce long-distance costs.

Bell submitted the plan to the Canadian Radio-Television and Telecommunications Commission yesterday for approval.

Rate rebalancing involves across-the-board reductions to long-distance rates, but makes up the lost revenue through increases in the rates charged for basic monthly local service.

Interest groups, who will fight the scheme at a CRTC public hearing, think the plan is flawed and will cause many subscribers to pay more money needlessly.

No date has been set for the hearing, but it is expected to be held in the fall. Bell wants the changes to take effect in two stages: the first by July 1 and the second by Jan. 1.

To further the century-old goal of ensuring universal access to cheap telephone service, the CRTC and its predecessors have priced basic phone service below cost and allowed the phone company to make up the difference by charging more for long-distance service.

The utility arm of Montreal-based Bell Canada Enterprises Inc. is the largest domestic telephone company and serves seven million customers in Ontario, Quebec and parts of the Northwest Territories.

Bell has postponed making its application since adopting the concept in September, 1984, as a response to potential long-distance competition.

Although Toronto-based CNCP Telecommunications Ltd. lost its bid to compete against Bell in August, 1985, the CRTC said it would consider a future rate rebalancing proposal from the companies.

Bell officials cited several reasons for making the proposal: long-distance rates are overpriced and local rates are underpriced, resulting in lost revenue; the extent of the im-

balance is increasing annually; high long-distance rates will lead many business users to seek competitive alternatives; and rebalanced rates will allow Bell to compete effectively.

But the current proposal is only "the first step in a phased approach to rate rebalancing," said Gary Bray, Bell vice-president of government and regulatory affairs. He said he could not say what other plans the company has.

"It's premature to say how much further we would go, or by how much we want to alter rates. This first step will provide the opportunity to assess the impact of rebalancing and to determine the extent, pace and magnitude of further steps."

Michael Lisogurski, assistant vice-president of business development, said Bell's initial plans extend over a five-year period.

But the prospect of even more changes scares interest groups, many of which do not agree with Bell's economic forecasts or justifications for rebalancing its rates.

For now, Bell wants to make the first round of local rate increases in two stages and, similarly, will make two sets of reductions in long-distance charges. Highlights of the proposal include:

- A total increase of $1.25 a month for basic service to all subscribers (business and residential) for each single phone line. The first increase of 30 cents is proposed for July 1 and the second of 95 cents for Jan. 1, 1988.
- An average decrease of 8 per cent in long-distance rates for calls made from points in Bell's territory to points served by other domestic companies, taking effect July 1. This measure was agreed to and announced by Telecom Canada in December.
- An average reduction of 6 per cent in long-distance rates for calls made within Bell's territory, taking effect Jan. 1, 1988.
- A variety of reductions and increases in other items and services.

The cumulative effect will add $125-million to Bell's local service revenue and take the same amount away from long-distance revenue, Mr. Lisogurski said.

Bell said it made surplus revenue (after expenses) of $1.5-billion from long-distance services in 1984 — the most recent year for which such figures were kept. But, in the same year, Bell lost $1.4-billion from local services.

Bell's parent, BCE, is Canada's most profitable corporation, making a profit of $1.02-billion on revenue of $13.9-billion for the year ended Dec. 31, 1986, compared with $1.05-billion on revenue of $13.3-billion a year earlier.

"We're totally against the rate rebalancing proposal and we believe the (telephone companies) are hosing us," said Joseph Schmidt, vice-president of regulatory affairs at CNCP. "The proposal will get them ready to compete five years in advance by socking increased costs on the local subscriber.

"To the CRTC and the federal government, we say let's have competition and rivalry before we have rate rebalancing."

The Consumers Association of Canada also opposes the plan, and specifically objects to "the net effect of the changes, which is a higher phone bill for subscribers," said David McKendry, director of the CAC's regulated industries program.

He said the CAC disagrees with Bell's justifications for reducing long-distance calls. "Several recent federal-provincial studies show that there is an insignificant amount of bypass of monopoly services by business users, thus blowing away Bell's argument that high rates will force subscribers to find an alternative."

Mr. McKendry sees the scheme "as a strategic move by Bell to prepare for competition." But he said the CAC and other groups representing subscribers "will have to take on

EXAMPLES OF BELL CANADA RATES

LOCAL—TORONTO	FEB. 1987	JAN. 1988*
SINGLE BUSINESS LINE	$41.40	$42.65
SINGLE RESIDENCE LINE	11.60	12.85
2-PARTY LINE	8.30	9.10

LOCAL—OTTAWA		
SINGLE BUSINESS LINE	$34.95	$36.20
SINGLE RESIDENCE LINE	9.60	10.85
2-PARTY LINE	7.10	7.90

LONG-DISTANCE** Montreal–Vancouver	FEB. 1987	JULY 1987
Mon.–Sat. 8 a.m.–6 p.m.	$5.50	$4.70
Mon.–Sat. 6 p.m.–11 p.m.	6.49	6.72
Daily 11 p.m.–8 a.m.	6.16	5.26

LONG-DISTANCE Toronto–St. John's		
Mon.–Sat. 8 a.m.–6 p.m.	$5.20	$4.60
Mon.–Sat. 6 p.m.–11 p.m.	6.49	6.58
Daily 11 p.m.–8 a.m.	5.82	5.15

* Subject to CRTC approval

** Customer-dialled call. Examples are for calls outside Bell's territory.

the CRTC, as well as Bell," because the CRTC "opened the door for Bell's application."

Although the Canadian Business Telecommunications Alliance agrees that long-distance rates are too high, it will fight the local increases, CBTA lawyer Kenneth Englehardt [said] in a statement.

He said the CBTA has opposed Bell's economic forecasts for many years and that its demand predictions will be integral to the battle. The CBTA argues that Bell's forecast is too low, which means the company will underestimate potential revenue gains from lowering its long-distance rates. "If, as we suspect, the demand forecast is too low, then long-distance rates could be reduced without changes to local rates."

a)   The article suggests that the past policies of the regulatory authorities deliberately priced basic (local) phone services below cost, making up the difference by overcharging on long-distance calls. What groups of telephone subscribers benefited from this "cross-subsidization" policy? Do you agree with this approach to income redistribution or would you recommend a different method? Why?

b)   In the following diagrams, indicate the price-cost relationships in the two markets before the rebalancing of rates (*LMC* denotes long-run marginal cost).

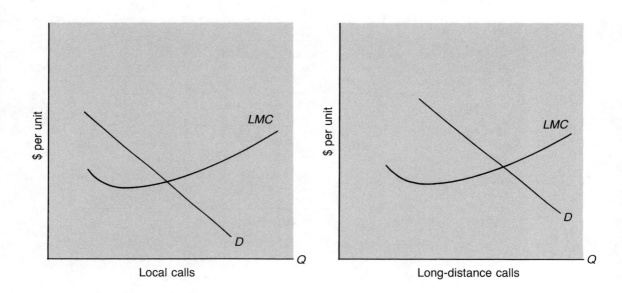

c)   An application by CNCP Telecommunications to compete with Bell in the long-distance market was denied by the CRTC in August 1985. In addition, some business users attempted to bypass the Bell long-distance service by making their connections via the cheaper U.S. route or by means of their own transmission facilities. The local service market, however, was not subject to such competition. Why?

d)   Restate the argument in the last paragraph of the article with the help of the concept of price elasticity of demand. How does the elasticity estimate by Bell differ from that made by the CBTA? Explain why, depending upon the elasticity of demand, it might be possible to cut long-distance rates without changing the local rates.

e)   Would you expect the price elasticity of demand to be greater for the local service or the long-distance service? Why? Given these elasticity differentials between local and long-distance demand curves, what rate differentials would be appropriate in view of the theory of price discrimination discussed in Chapter 11?

Government and Public Finance

LEARNING OBJECTIVES

After reading this chapter you should be able to explain:

1. The role of governments as suppliers of public goods.
2. The role of government in the redistribution of income.
3. The Canadian tax system.
4. The impact of tax changes on prices and output levels.
5. Government deficits and national debt.
6. The privatization of some activities currently performed by governments.

13-1 INTRODUCTION AND PURPOSE

In Chapter 12, we discussed various reasons for government activity within the microeconomy. These included the existence of monopoly power, possible divergences between private and social costs and benefits, product information difficulties, the notion of equity or fairness and political motivation. In this chapter, we wish to return to some of the nonpolitical rationales.

The government may influence microeconomic activity through a number of channels, including regulation of private industry, government-owned business enterprises, or direct production of a particular good or service through government departments, and taxation. Involvement of the government may influence the allocation of resources among various types of production activities, the efficiency of production, and the distribution of income.

Here, we will concentrate on the government's role as a producer of goods and services and as a redistributor of income. This will include a discussion of both government expenditure and taxation. Finally, we close the chapter with a brief look at government financing statistics at federal, provincial and local levels.

13-2 GOVERNMENT AS A PRODUCER

Federal, provincial and local levels of government provide various goods and services. In some cases, the government has a monopoly over production; in other cases it faces competition from private enterprise.

Public Goods

For the most part, goods and services can be produced in small enough units so that they may be enjoyed almost completely by the purchaser alone. This being the case, if the individual consumer values a given unit produced at least as much as it costs to produce it, a price can be established that will be agreeable both to the consumer (in that it will be less than or equal to the perceived value of the product) and to the producer (in that it will at least cover production costs, including a normal rate of return on invested funds). In such an instance, a market will be established for the production of the good in question, and it may be argued that this market will benefit both consumer and producer. If there is monopoly power in the market, external costs or benefits, or a serious consumer-information deficiency, government involvement of some kind might possibly be used to make the market more efficient — in more nearly equating marginal social costs and benefits — but otherwise, there is little economic rationale for government involvement.

On the other hand, let us now consider a good or service that cannot be packaged up so that its provision benefits only the purchaser. Take, for example, national security, which is provided by the Department of National Defence. As already alluded to in Chapter 12, if national security is to be provided at all, it by and large will protect everyone equally. Suppose, for instance, that it costs $300 per person per year to provide adequate military defence for Canada. Also, suppose that, for one reason or another, various people feel the potential benefit is not worth the price, so that if given a free choice they would opt not to buy this protection for themselves. Practically speaking, could people be given this choice? If some did not want military protection at $300 per year and therefore were exempted from payment, how could

we identify who had or had not paid, in order to know exactly which persons in Canada the military should protect and which ones it should not protect? Could any meaningful national defence be provided at all if every fourth or fifth person throughout Canada did not receive protection because that person had not paid for it? Clearly not.

In a similar fashion, weather forecasting benefits all citizens, whether or not they are willing to pay for its provision.

Such goods and services as justice, police, fire fighting, national security, penitentiary services, roads, road signs and the like are called **public goods**. The chief characteristics of public goods are as follows: (i) if provided at all, they are consumed concurrently by a large number of people,[1] and (ii) those who receive benefits cannot easily (at a low cost) be separated from those who do not. This second characteristic makes it impractical to charge each person only for the quantity that the individual may consume. As a result, a free market would typically not emerge for such goods. Public goods are therefore financed out of tax revenue and often produced by government agencies.

Even though it may be difficult to charge each individual precisely for the amount consumed, sometimes a rough separation can be made between groups of people who are likely to use the good or service more than others, and they can be charged accordingly. For example, roads are presumably used more by those who own cars; therefore, licence fees are charged to automobile owners, while those who do not own cars escape such levies. Even better, a tax on gasoline allows discrimination among different intensities of road use.

As we have argued above, one of the main features of a public good involves *externalities*; that is, the fact that even if only those who are willing to pay the price are required to do so, the provision of the public good will benefit others as well. Sometimes it is easy to determine whether a particular good or service belongs to this category — for

---

1. This characteristic means that the product is indivisible into small individual consumption units. Airplanes are divisible products, while airports are quite indivisible. Jumbo jets may be produced to carry two or three hundred people or small planes may be produced and sold for the purpose of carrying one individual or family. However, it is generally infeasible to produce single family airports.

example, police protection, weather reports, stop signs and the like. Other times it may be more difficult to judge the extent of externalities involved. For example, take the case of a commuter transit service within a city. Those who live in the city but do not take the transit service may nevertheless benefit greatly from it. The fact that many people use the service may cause the streets to become less crowded with private automobiles, thereby reducing pollution, traffic noise and congestion, and making it more pleasant for those who still choose to drive downtown. To this extent, perhaps all city residents should pay some of the cost of operating the commuter system. However, what share should be paid by the consumer, and what share by the citizens through taxes?

Natural Monopoly and Government

Another area the government has seen fit to enter is the production of those goods and services for which there seem to exist tendencies toward a *natural monopoly*. In those industries for which economies of scale are important, larger organizations have a decided cost advantage. Therefore, from the standpoint of supplying market demand with the least amount of inputs, a monopoly may be the most efficient form of organizational structure to have. On the other hand, as we have pointed out earlier, monopoly power may create other inefficiencies in the economy.

In certain industries, the government allows privately owned monopolies to operate under the watchful eye of some regulatory body (as, for example, in the case of Bell Canada, which has for all practical purposes a monopoly in the provision of telephone services in a number of provinces and is regulated by the CRTC. See Chapter 12.) In other instances, however, the government has demanded that the monopoly be government owned, as in the case of the post office (*Canada Post*), and presumably operated as close to the $P = LAC = LMC$ point as possible. Still in other instances, where there may be more than one but yet only a few producers within an industry, the government has decided to own one of them and compete alongside one or more privately owned firms (as in the case of Air Canada competing with privately owned airlines and in the case of the CNR competing with the privately owned CPR.

Types of Government Enterprise

As a producer, the government may provide a good or service (but mostly services) directly through government departments under the control of a Cabinet minister or indirectly through **Crown corporations**. Crown corporations are separate business firms, which supposedly operate in a manner similar to any other business firm, with one exception — all the shares of stock are owned by the government. The government is therefore the sole owner of these corporations and as such may exert considerable influence on their operations. Some well-known federal Crown corporations are Canada Post, Bank of Canada, Canadian National Railways Ltd. (CNR), Canada Mortgage and Housing Corporation (CMHC), Canada Deposit Insurance Corporation, Economic Council of Canada and the Royal Canadian Mint. There are over 30 federal Crown corporations. The provincial governments also have their own Crown corporations — 233 of them in 1983.[2] In 1981, the revenues of Crown corporations accounted for 13 percent of Canada's GNP and their assets accounted for 11 percent of total corporate assets.[3] The total number of public enterprises of all types (federal Crown corporations, provincial corporations and municipal commissions responsible for gas, electricity and urban transit) is about 1300, including both parents and subsidiaries.[4]

To a considerable extent, the types of goods and services provided by each of the three levels of government are dictated by the jurisdictional spheres laid out in the Canada Act, 1982. The federal government has jurisdiction over matters of a national concern and over those matters not otherwise assigned under the Canada Act to the provinces. For example, the federal government provides postal services through Canada Post, national security through the Department of National Defence and paper currency and coin through the Bank of Canada and the Royal Canadian Mint respectively.

Control of natural resources was given to the

2. *Report of the Royal Commission on Canada's Economic Union and Development Prospects*, Vol. II, p. 142.

3. Ibid., p. 169.

4. Economic Council of Canada, *Government Enterprise: Roles and Rationale*, p. 2.

provinces, as well as the power to make laws relating to property, civil rights and matters of a local nature. In turn, local governments were created by the provinces and delegated responsibility to provide services that can be more effectively carried out at a local level. Municipal governments have nine main functions, which are: police protection, transportation, environmental health, public health, welfare, environmental development, recreation, community services and education.

Though many of these services are treated as public goods and financed out of general tax revenue, some charges are made directly to users, as in the cases of transportation, recreational services and the provision of water and sewer services. Electricity and gas are provided by local utility boards in conjunction with provincial authorities. These commodities are not, of course, treated as public goods and consumers are required to pay prices that cover full costs, including a normal return on invested funds.

All levels of government in Canada provide certain goods and services either directly or through government-owned enterprises. The objectives of this policy include handling of the public-good externality and the natural monopoly problem as well as pursuits of other matters of national interest.

13-3 GOVERNMENT AS INCOME REDISTRIBUTOR

Income may be earned either from inherited wealth or by means of an individual's abilities and hard work. Clearly, we do not all receive the same amount of inherited wealth nor are we all born with equal mental or physical abilities to generate income from our own efforts. Some people argue that this is pretty much the "luck of the draw," and that we are each entitled only to the proceeds of our own good or bad fortune. For example, they argue, if you should enter a lottery and win a prize it is strictly your good luck, and we would not think of depriving you of your winnings and redistributing them among the losers.

Others say that monetary inheritances and personal characteristics acquired at birth, which subsequently lead to income inequalities, are not at all comparable to lottery winnings. In a lottery, each person has the option to buy or not buy a ticket. In other words, each individual has a *free*

choice whether or not to play the game. This is hardly the case with birth-rights. No individual has ever made a decision whether or not to be born. This event might be compared instead with a game where each of us passes through a tunnel. As we emerge, we find that several things might have happened: we might be blind or deaf, rich or poor, ugly or handsome, possess athletic prowess or be poorly coordinated. And one of the most important parts of this game is that we all *must* play.

The latter group of people argue that initial endowments of wealth or abilities raise the question of equity or fairness. To this group, it seems that as a result of an unequal distribution of these endowments at birth, there is some justification for a *reshuffling* of income between rich and poor. Presumably, people should be allowed to maintain higher incomes if they earn them with greater work or sacrifice than others, but to the extent that these higher incomes result from better initial endowments there should be some sharing of the wealth.

People who believe that income redistribution is necessary appear to be in the majority, because we do in fact give our governments the right to tax and redistribute income on the basis of equity or humanitarian reasons. However, redistribution is a difficult problem. For example, if one person earns $150 000 a year and another $25 000, to what extent is the $125 000 difference attributable to initial endowments? Some of the income difference may be accounted for by inherited wealth of course, but what if it is not? Suppose that the $150 000 income is that of a business executive and the $25 000 income that of a worker. To what extent is the income of the executive the result of studying harder and longer in school, working longer hours, having to travel more, accepting greater responsibility and work pressure? Is it possible that the worker could have studied harder in school and achieved the same or a similar income position as the executive? In other words, how do we decide to what extent income differentials arise from the result of individual choice? To what extent has an individual with a lower income voluntarily followed a career route with less work and less risk in return for less income?

Methods of Redistributing Income

Once the decision to redistribute income from high to low income groups has been made, the next question is, how to do it? There are two basic methods: a pure **income supplement** or **subsidized consumption** of specific goods or services to low-income families. There are significantly different economic implications in these two methods, which we will now discuss.

(i) Income Supplements

This method consists of allowing lower income families to pay lower taxes, or, if the incomes are below a certain level, giving direct income payments to such families. An important thing to note about this method is that it allows the family complete freedom to choose how to spend the income. The presumption here is that the family itself is best able to decide which goods and services will benefit it the most.

(ii) Subsidized Consumption

Under this method of income redistribution, the government subsidizes the consumption of specific goods and services for families on lower incomes. In Canada, a good example of this type of subsidization are the various provincial and federal housing schemes, where families receiving annual incomes lower than certain specified amounts have several options. They may rent government-owned housing at rates lower than those required to cover full cost, purchase a house at lower than market prices or borrow money for the purpose of financing the purchase of a house at less than current market interest rates.

In the case of subsidized consumption schemes, low-income families do not benefit from income redistribution unless they purchase the specific designated commodities in particular quantities. For example, the government usually allows subsidized rental and purchases only of housing which meets the government specifications of floor space, frontage, lot size and so on.

Many people argue that subsidized consumption is not an efficient way in which to redistribute income. If, for instance, the housing subsidy amounts to, say, $2500 per family per year, we would say that this is in effect the amount of the income supplement to the low-income family. However, if the family instead received a $2500 cheque each year from the government, there is a good possibility that they might spend it differently. Perhaps they would spend only an additional $1500 a year on housing and $1000 more a year on other goods and services they might prefer. In effect, the government is providing a $2500 annual income supplement that *must* be spent on housing. It restricts people's choice, and forces them to use the income supplement for housing instead of on some other goods and services from which they might derive more benefit. While the low-income recipients are better off under a subsidized consumption plan than without it, they are not as well off as they would have been under an income supplement plan which would cost the government the same amount of money.

Some dispute this view by arguing that if the low-income families received income supplements instead of subsidized consumption they would not spend it in a way so as to make themselves better off in the long run, but instead squander it on frivolous consumption. These people regard the government as being better able to decide what is good for low-income families than the families themselves.

Nonincome Criteria

Some income supplement plans are based on criteria other than low income — for example, children's allowances and old age security. The government pays so much a month per child to each family (under the Family Allowance Act), regardless of income. Similarly, it pays so much a month to people over 65 years of age (under the Old Age Security Act).[5] The idea is that people who have more children may have more financial difficulty supporting them. Similarly, people who are over the age of 65 tend to have lower incomes. Critics argue that it is not always true that those who have one, two or even more children, or those who are over the age of 65, are in need of income supplements. This is the concept of "universality" of such programs. Its validity is periodically subject to public debate. Further, some critics argue against being forced to purchase Old Age

---

5. There is also, under a 1966 amendment to the Old Age Security Act, a provision for an additional amount to be paid to pensioners with no income other than OAS. This is called a *Guaranteed Income Supplement*.

Security.[6] (We pay for old age security benefits through taxes.) Why should people not be given a free choice about whether to purchase such "old-age-income insurance" from private insurance companies instead of being forced to do so by the government? Again, the usual comeback to this criticism is that given a free choice, the public will very often not make decisions that are in its own best interest.

Negative Income Tax Proposal

Partly because of the above criticisms of existing piecemeal income supplement and subsidized consumption efforts at income redistribution, a number of people support what is known as a **negative income tax scheme**. Under this plan, it would be recognized that the essential part of various income supplements and subsidized consumption plans is, for purposes of equity, to redistribute income or at least provide for a *minimum acceptable living standard* for all people. Further, it is desirable to do this (i) with the least administrative costs and arbitrary bureaucratic decisions and (ii) still provide reasonable incentives for people to improve their living standard through their own efforts.

Suppose, for example, that $12 000 is deemed to be a minimum acceptable income for four person families including two children. This sum, then, would be the minimum income base to be provided entirely by a government income supplement (or *negative income tax*) when the gross family income from all other sources is zero (see Table 13-1). Tax is paid on income earned. In the table, we suppose that the tax rate on this income is a straight 40%. For lower income families (in this example those earning below $30 000 a year), the effect of additional income earned would be only to reduce the net income supplement received by the earner.

If, for instance, the family gross income rises from $0 to $10 000, the $4000 tax (40% of $10 000)

Table 13-1 A negative income tax mechanism

Gross (before-tax) family income	Tax or income supplement (−)	Net (after-tax) family income
$0	$ − 12 000	$12 000
10 000	− 8 000	18 000
20 000	− 4 000	24 000
30 000	0	30 000
40 000	4 000	36 000
50 000	8 000	42 000
60 000	12 000	48 000

Tax at the rate of 40% is paid on the gross family income reported in the first column. Assuming that the minimum acceptable after-tax family income is $12 000, the second column reports the net transfer between the family and the tax department, that is 40% of the figure in first column minus $12 000. The third column gives the net income, that is, gross income from first column minus net transfer from second column.

would only reduce the income supplement from $12 000 to $8000. In this manner the recipient would always be able to keep 60% of any extra earned income.

In the current Canadian political system, redistribution of income is an important function of government. It takes the form of income supplements or of subsidized consumption of specific goods and services. A negative income tax schedule is a method of redistribution which preserves individual incentives to increase earned income while guaranteeing some minimum level of family income.

13-4 GOVERNMENT TAXATION

Government taxes may be imposed to influence the allocation of resources in particular markets where monopoly elements or externalities are important — hopefully in a direction that more nearly equates marginal social benefits and costs. The more obvious use of taxes, however, is to *finance the government*, both as a producer (to the extent that such activities are not self-financed) and as a redistributor of income.

6. There is also another major plan for Old Age Pensions, and that is the Canada (or in Quebec, the Quebec) Pension Plan. The CPP (or QPP) is based on compulsory contributions from earnings as a condition for receiving a stipulated pension at age 65.

Methods of Taxation

Taxes may be placed on labour or capital income, on the production or sale of specific goods and services, or on property and wealth. **Direct taxes** are those levied directly against individuals (for example, income and inheritance taxes.) **Indirect taxes** are those levied against goods and services (for example, import tariffs, excise and sales taxes, and property taxes). Because indirect taxes are ultimately paid either by consumers of the goods and services or by shareholders, they are indirectly levied on individuals. Ultimately, of course, *all* taxes must be paid by individuals. One basic question of taxation is, how much tax should each person pay?

The more government services are provided that are not self-financed, the larger will be the necessary tax bills. Residents of communities with extensive transit service, well paved roads, good garbage collection and snow removal, well stocked libraries, and attractive community services normally expect to pay more property taxes than communities that do not have such amenities. There is, in fact, considerable agreement that taxes should to some extent be paid in relation to *benefits received*.

There is also the notion of *equal sacrifice*. For example, it is generally assumed that a dollar's tax imposed on an individual earning $200 000 a year represents less of a real cost or sacrifice than a dollar's tax imposed on someone earning only $20 000 a year. Therefore it is argued from an equity standpoint that the individual earning $200 000 a year should pay more tax than the one earning only $20 000 — but how much more? Should the wealthier person pay just a little more, twice, ten times or perhaps fifteen times as much tax?

For comparison purposes, income taxes are usually related to before-tax income on a percentage basis. If one individual pays $1000 tax on a gross income of $20 000, this represents a five percent effective tax rate. Does equity require that five percent also be paid on $200 000, which would yield $10 000; that is, ten times the amount of tax paid by the lower income taxpayer? Or should the rate be a higher or lower percentage? Does it make a difference how the income is earned? Should earnings from race tracks and lotteries be taxed in the same manner as wage earners? Many people believe that these questions have not yet been satisfactorily answered. Some believe that they cannot be satisfactorily answered.

Types of Taxation

A tax is said to be **proportional** if its payment requires the same percentage of income regardless of the income level. For example, a flat income tax rate of 25% would be a proportional tax. A tax is said to be **progressive** if its payment requires a greater percentage from high incomes than from low incomes (note here that "progressive" does not necessarily mean "good"). For example, if the effective income tax rate were, say, 18% for people earning $25 000 a year, 25% for those earning $35 000 a year and so on, income taxes would be progressive. Finally, a tax is said to be **regressive** (but not necessarily bad) if its payment requires a smaller percentage of income as income rises. If, for example, because of vast arrays of deductions and loopholes for those in higher income tax brackets the effective income tax paid as a percentage of income actually falls as before-tax incomes rise, the income tax structure could be said to be regressive.

Personal income taxes are levied in a progressive manner. The approximate pattern of personal income tax rates is shown in Table 13-2.

In a great many cases, taxation affects the behaviour of individuals and business firms in that taxpayers seek to avoid, or at least to minimize, the effect of taxation. Further, to the extent that taxes influence behaviour of individuals and firms, a large share of taxes originally imposed on one group of individuals may ultimately be paid by another group. This is the issue of tax incidence and is discussed below.

Excise Taxes[7]

Excise taxes are taxes levied on some specific goods or services but not on others — and are often not made explicit to the consumer. Whether or not they are made explicit, however, is of no consequence and will not affect the consumer's demand

---

7. The analysis for import duties and property taxes would be similar to that of excise taxes.

Table 13-2 Approximate personal income tax rates, 1986

Status	Income	Federal and provincial tax	Marginal tax rate (%)	Average tax rate (%)
Single taxpayer (no dependants)	7 500	413	12.6	5.5
	10 000	1 017	24.2	10.2
	15 000	2 322	26.1	15.5
	20 000	3 697	27.5	18.5
	50 000	15 089	38.0	30.2
	100 000	40 621	51.1	40.6
Married taxpayer (two children under 16)	7 500	—	—	—
	10 000	56	2.2	0.6
	15 000	1 139	21.7	7.6
	20 000	2 455	26.3	12.3
	50 000	13 099	35.5	26.2
	100 000	38 292	50.4	38.3

Source: Canadian Tax Foundation, *The National Finances 1986–87*, Tables 7.12 and 7.13, pp. 7:25–7:26.

Illustration of the progressivity of the Canadian personal income tax. Both the marginal and average tax rates rise as income rises and the marginal tax rate exceeds the average tax rate.

for the particular commodity. In other words, if a consumer is willing to pay a maximum price of, say, $5.95 for a particular good, the consumer is presumably not influenced by what portion of the $5.95 goes toward labour expenses, profits or the government.[8] But the producer certainly will be influenced by the taxes that must be paid out of the $5.95 collected from the consumer. If the producer

has to remit more to the government in the form of an excise tax than previously, this has the same effect as if labour or material costs had increased. Each and every unit produced will cost more than before. In other words, the producer's marginal costs of production have risen. If we suppose the excise tax has increased by, say, 40¢ per unit, to produce each additional unit will now cost 40¢ more than before.

Now let us examine who actually pays this tax — that is, on whom the *burden* of the tax really falls. Of course, the firm remits the tax to the government. Does this mean the firm pays (or its shareholders pay) the entire burden of the tax? The tax is paid out of monies collected from the consumer. Perhaps, then, the consumer really pays all the tax? The answer to both these questions is, "Probably not." In the instance of an excise tax it is likely that consumers, shareholders and even the employees of the firm will suffer somewhat and pay a portion of the tax. Figure 13-1 illustrates two possible situations in this regard.

In Figure 13-1a, demand is assumed to be quite price sensitive. This might be the case, for example, if there are close substitute goods or services available on which excise taxes have not been imposed. In this instance, the rise in excise taxes would result in only a small price increase but a relatively large fall in output. We have seen previously that with demand conditions constant, a fall in output (as a result of cost increases) means lower profits, and in fact, generally speaking the larger the fall in output, the larger the profit reduction. Further, the reduction of output implies a lower demand for labour. In this case, then, with demand relatively price sensitive, though the consumers suffer as a result of the higher prices, a large portion of the burden is pushed onto the shareholders and workers in the industry. The availability of close substitutes on which an excise tax has not been imposed has provided the means by which consumers are able to *escape* a large portion of the tax burden.

Figure 13-1b on the other hand, reflects an industry in which there are price insensitive demand conditions, perhaps arising from the limited possibility of finding reasonable substitutes for a necessary good. In this case, there would be a larger market price increase combined with a smaller reduction in market output than in industry *A* (Figure

---

8 An exceptional case might occur where the public has become so incensed at the knowledge of the amount of tax or profit in the price of a specific good or service that, even though at $5.95 they would otherwise be willing to purchase, out of spite, or in order to show their displeasure, they would refrain from buying the good. But despite the publicity such instances receive, they are the exception rather than the rule.

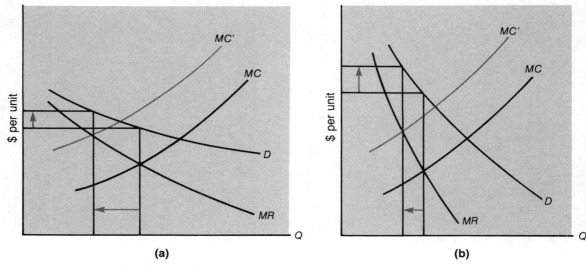

**Fig. 13-1 Incidence of an excise tax increase: short-run impact
on two firms**

An increase in excise tax shifts the marginal cost upwards, causing an increase in
price and a reduction in output.

(a) If a firm faces elastic demand, the price increase is relatively small and output
reduction is relatively large. Shareholders and workers thus bear a large
share of the tax burden.

(b) If the firm faces inelastic demand, the price increase is relatively large and
output reduction relatively small. Consumers bear a large share of the tax
burden.

13-1a). Here, consumers would suffer a larger portion of the burden than in industry *A*, and the
shareholders and employees of the producing firms
would carry a smaller portion. The lack of suitable
substitutes has, in this case, prevented consumers
from escaping a major share of the tax burden.

In summary, it will typically be the case that as a
result of the imposition of an excise tax, the burden of
the tax will be shared by consumers, employees and
shareholders. In general, the portions that producers
are able to shift *forward* to consumers through price
increases will depend on the reaction of consumers
— that is, how sensitive consumers are to price
increases, as partly determined by such factors as
tastes and the availability of close substitutes. To the
extent that consumers can find close substitutes, the
burden of the excise tax is shifted *backward* onto
employees and shareholders of the firm.

Commodity Sales Taxes

As of 1986, the federal government levied a twelve
percent sales tax applicable to most manufactured
goods, whether imported or produced in Canada.
Likewise, the provincial governments (except
Alberta) levied a retail sales tax on manufactured
goods (varying between five and ten percent,
depending on the province.) Because sales taxes
are not levied on most services, the effect of an increase in sales taxes is to raise unit costs and the
market prices of goods relative to services. This
lowers the quantity of goods demanded and increases the demand for services. Shareholders,
consumers and workers in the goods industries
therefore lose. Consumers of services also suffer
higher prices as a result of the increased demand
for services, but workers and shareholders in the
service industries gain.

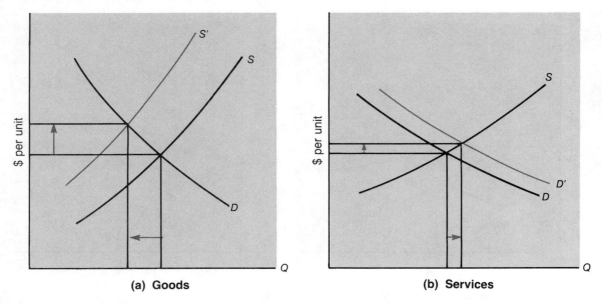

(a) Goods   (b) Services

Fig. 13-2 Effect of an increase in the federal commodity sales tax rate in two sectors

An increase in sales tax on goods shifts the supply curve in the goods-producing industry upward (part (a)). As the output of goods drops and their price rises, consumers buy more services, which are now relatively cheaper. The demand curve for services shifts to the right (part (b)).

Figure 13-2 illustrates the effect of an increase in federal or provincial sales tax rates.[9]

Governments finance their activity by direct and indirect taxes. The income tax rates in Canada rise progressively with income levels. The burden of indirect taxes is shared between consumers and firms in proportions determined by the price elasticity of demand for the product being taxed.

Corporate Income Tax

The **corporation income tax** (or *profits tax*) is levied not on economic profits but on accounting profits. This method is used strictly for convenience sake, because accounting profit figures are easier to ascertain. With regard to the income

statement of Co. *A* Ltd. for the year 19X1 (Table 13-3), the accounting profit before tax (that is, before deducting the income tax expense) was $100 000. This is the figure on which income tax calculations would be made. If the corporate income tax rate is 40%, income taxes remitted to the government would be $40 000, leaving the company an *after-tax*, or net accounting profit of $60 000 for the year. To arrive at the firm's figure for the year's economic profit, we further would have to deduct the dollar amount that could have been earned on the shareholders' funds if they had been invested elsewhere.

The important point to note, though, is that increases in corporate income taxes raise the firm's costs and reduce its profit. Let us examine the significance of this for the firm's behaviour and tax incidence. As it turns out, we would expect no change in the firm's behaviour in the short run, and the entire tax burden would be felt by the firm's shareholders. In the longer run, though, when the

---

9. Since sales tax rates are increased by "so many percentage points," based on the manufacturing or retail ticket price, the absolute dollar increases in marginal costs will be greater for higher volumes, where marginal costs are higher. The shift in supply curve is therefore not parallel.

Table 13-3 Company A Ltd. income statement for the year ended Dec. 31, 19X1

Sales		$800 000
Less expenses:		
Materials	$350 000	
Labour	220 000	
Heat, light, power	130 000	$700 000
Profit before tax		$100 000
Less: Corporate income tax expense 40%		40 000
Profit after tax		$ 60 000

Calculation of before-tax and after-tax accounting profits in a simplified income statement.

Table 13-4 Pattern of before- and after-tax profits for a 40% tax rate

Before-tax profit	Tax paid	After-tax profit
50 000	20 000	30 000
100 000	40 000	60 000
200 000	80 000	120 000

With a given tax rate, the after-tax profit varies exactly in proportion with the before-tax profit.

firm would have had time to adjust its investment activities, there would be two possible effects, depending on the degree of competitiveness of the industry. Let us now examine the difference between short-run and long-run tax incidence under varying competitive conditions.

The Short Run

In the short run, regardless of the corporate income tax rate, the firm will clearly make the highest possible profit after tax by earning the highest possible profit that it can on a before tax basis.[10] In fact, its net (accounting) profit after tax will go up or down by precisely the same percentage that its profit before tax goes up or down. See Table 13-4. As a result, for the firm to make as much after-tax profit as possible in the short run, it should focus on *before-tax profit maximization*. In other words, it may completely neglect the income tax rate in its decision making. It may curse the fact that recently announced increases in corporate income taxes will mean lower after-tax profits, but whatever output and price combination was achieving the

best after-tax profit before the announcement will still achieve the best (though a lower) after-tax profit after the tax increase.

Figure 13-3 illustrates the effect of an increase in the corporate income tax rate for a firm with monopoly power. As shown in Figure 13-3a, neither marginal revenue nor marginal cost is affected by the profits tax. As Figure 13-3b further shows, an increase in the corporate income tax rate has no effect on the ouptut level (and therefore the price level) that maximizes before- or after-tax profits, but merely reduces the level of maximum after-tax profits that are attainable.

There is, consequently, no reason to expect a change in short-run corporate behaviour as the result of a change in the corporate income tax. Because there is no change in the firm's prices or volume of output in the short run, neither consumers nor the firm's workers suffer from an increase in the corporate income tax rate.

The entire burden is shifted *backward* onto the shareholder group through a lower net profit and hence a lower rate of return on its invested funds. This fact might make it seem attractive to consumers and workers to advocate higher corporate income taxes whenever increases in government spending have to be financed. In fact, if these two groups were asked, generally their response would be that corporate income taxes are most desirable because shareholders, who may generally be better off than the average citizen anyway, pay the cost. But do shareholders pay the entire cost of corporate income taxes? Let us look at the long run.

---

10. This is illustrated in Table 13-3. The general case may be demonstrated as follows:

$$\text{After-tax profit} = \text{Before-tax} - \text{Corporate income taxes}$$
$$= \text{Before-tax profit} - \text{Tax rate (\%)} \times \text{Before-tax profit}$$
$$= \text{Before-tax profit} \times (1 - \text{Tax rate (\%)})$$

Thus, for any given percentage tax rate, the higher the before-tax profit, the higher the after-tax profit.

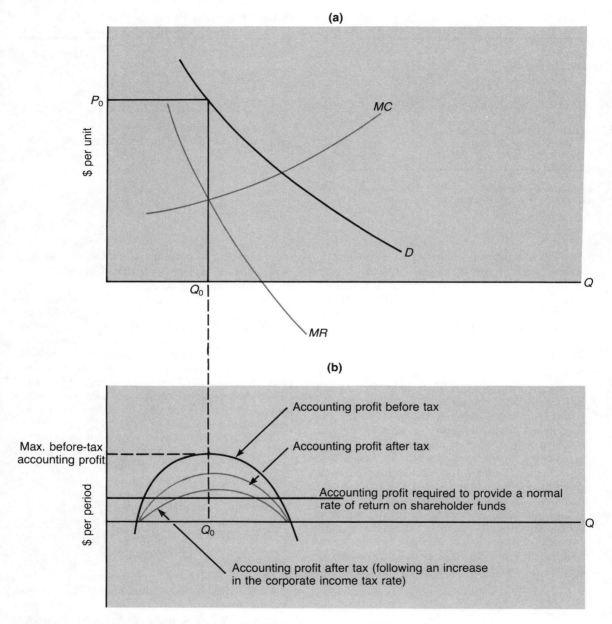

(a)

P_0

$ per unit

MC

D

Q_0

Q

MR

(b)

Accounting profit before tax

Accounting profit after tax

Max. before-tax accounting profit

Accounting profit required to provide a normal rate of return on shareholder funds

$ per period

Q_0

Q

Accounting profit after tax (following an increase in the corporate income tax rate)

Fig. 13-3 Effect of an increase in the corporate income tax rate

In the short run, an increase in the tax on profit does not affect the firm's costs or revenues. The profit-maximizing price and output therefore remain unchanged (part (a)). The accounting after-tax profit is, however, reduced (part (b)).

The Long Run

Very often in economics what is true in the short run does not hold over the long run, and this is certainly the case with respect to incidence of a corporate income tax increase. Initially, the entire burden of taxation is thrust on the shareholder group. However, the shareholders may not sit idly by and accept this unfavourable redistribution of income. Whether or not they do react depends on the degree of competitiveness of each particular industry.

First of all, consider shareholders of firms in industries that exhibit long-run economic profits — that is, persistent above normal rates of return on investment, protected by various artificial barriers to entry. If the increase in corporate tax rates does no more than reduce some of this excess profit while still leaving above normal rates of return, there may be little long-run reaction. There will be no incentive to move invested funds out of the industry because they are still earning above normal rates of return right where they are. There may only be less pressure by new potential entrants to the industry because some excess returns have been eroded. Essentially, though, long-run price and output would remain at their short-run levels.

With reference once more to Figure 13-3, there is no impact of higher corporate tax rates on long-run demand conditions or on long-run marginal costs. Remember long-run marginal costs include only a normal rate of return on investment. With neither long-run demand nor long-run cost conditions altered, and shareholders still able to earn an above normal rate of return on investment, the profit-maximizing output and price level remain unaltered. In this case, an increase in the corporate income tax does not affect the market behaviour of any group, and the entire tax burden is permanently shifted backward onto shareholders.

Next, consider the possibility that at least for some firms a corporate income tax rate increase might reduce the rate of return on shareholders' invested funds below that level which could be earned elsewhere for a similar risk. In this case, such firms would not be able to raise funds for expansion or even asset replacement because their shareholders could earn higher rates of return elsewhere. These firms would therefore be forced to close down their operations in the long run and go out of business. This action would leave fewer

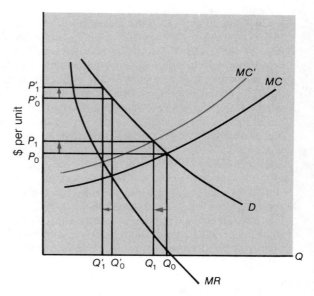

Fig. 13-4 Long-run effect of a corporate income tax increase which causes short-run economic losses

In the long run an increase in corporate income taxes may cause the exit of some firms from the industry. This causes a shift to the left in the industry marginal cost curves. If the industry is perfectly competitive, output drops from Q_0 to Q_1 and price rises from P_0 to P_1. If all firms act as a joint monopoly, output drops from Q'_0 to Q'_1 and price rises from P'_0 to P'_1.

producers in the industry selling less total output at generally higher prices. The long-run market impact is illustrated in Figure 13-4.

In the long run, as firms leave the industry there are fewer firms willing to produce output at any given price. More technically, the industry marginal cost curve shifts to the left. At one extreme, if the industry is purely competitive (in which case the industry marginal cost curve represents its supply curve), output would fall from Q_0 to Q_1 and the price would rise from P_0 to P_1. At the other extreme, if the firms collaborated so as to maximize joint profits (all firms would act together as a monopoly), output would fall from Q'_0 to Q'_1 while the market price would rise from P'_0 to P'_1.

In this situation then, the short run gives a misleading indication of the ultimate course of events. If the imposition of a higher corporate income tax reduces shareholders' returns on invested funds to below normal, the shareholders will invest elsewhere, thereby forcing a contraction within the industry. As the least efficient firms leave (such firms would suffer the greatest economic losses by the tax increase), the remaining firms will operate at higher prices. The higher prices mean that the total volume sold by the industry will be less (due to the price sensitivity of demand). Consequently, part of the corporate income tax burden is eventually shifted forward to consumers, who must pay higher prices, part of it backward to shareholders through low rates of return (ultimately reflected in falling stock prices) and part backward to workers within the industry who suffer reductions in employment.

Personal Income Taxes

In the short run, people will probably just complain about increases in **personal income tax**. Over the longer term, such increases may affect their *incentive to work*. A rise in income tax reduces the net benefit from working; and, as a result, when people have time to react, may lead them to choose less work and more leisure.

For many people — perhaps most — work is a bad rather than a good thing. Work is undesirable in itself, but is a means to an end. People work in order to acquire income to purchase goods and services. Thus, we may regard workers as giving up one "good," leisure, in order to acquire other goods and services such as food, clothing, shelter and recreation. If people are offered higher net (after-tax) wage rates for their work, they may be willing to work more. The argument here is that higher net wage rates increase the quantity of other goods that can be obtained through the sacrifice of leisure, therefore making the sacrifice of leisure more attractive. Higher taxes do precisely the opposite. By reducing the net wage rate, higher taxes reduce the benefit offered for the sacrifice of leisure (that is, work), possibly reducing the amount of leisure people are willing to give up at any given before-tax wage rate.

Income tax increases may have further consequences. If, at any wage rate, less labour is offered than before, firms will have to offer higher wage rates to hire any given amount of labour and to produce any given amount of output. The effect of this increase is to raise the unit costs (marginal and average) of production, thereby inducing firms to raise prices. Further, as we have seen earlier, higher unit costs mean less profits for shareholders. Consequently, the burden of increased personal income tax will generally be felt by consumers and shareholders, as well as by workers.

Other Effects

Taxes result in behaviour changes if they affect the *relative costs and benefits* of certain activities. For example, if personal income tax rates are raised, since leisure is not taxed, the income benefits from working are reduced, while leaving the benefits of leisure (the benefits of not working) essentially unaffected. The new cost-benefit pattern of work leads people to change their behaviour. This change, predictably guided by a desire to escape the new costs, will end up with at least part of the costs being thrust unintentionally on other groups.

To take one more example of the difficulty the government has in isolating the incidence of taxation, consider the case in which income taxes are levied. Taxes are paid, for the most part, only on monetary incomes, even though most occupations are really a mixture of monetary and nonmonetary rewards. Suppose, for example, two occupations are currently offering the same total compensation, equivalent to $30 000 a year, but that the breakdown of this total compensation between monetary and nonmonetary rewards is different. Occupation *A* offers, say, a monetary income of $15 000 and nonmonetary rewards of $15 000, while occupation *B* has monetary rewards totalling the full $30 000 a year. Because both occupations offer the same *total* compensation, people, on average, will not tend to prefer one over the other.

Now, however, suppose an income tax of 25% is imposed. The tax to be paid in occupation *A* is $3750 (that is, 25% × $15 000), whereas that in occupation *B* is $7500 (that is, 25% × $30 000). This income tax rate reduces the after-tax compensation in occupation *A* and *B* to $26 250 and $22 500 respectively. The tax, in addition to making leisure perhaps more attractive and thereby reducing the labour offered at existing levels of before-tax compensation in both industries, has also made occupation *A* more attractive than occupation *B*. This will result in more people seeking jobs in occupation *A* relative to occupation *B*, forcing the before-tax monetary wage in occupation *B* upward by more than that in occupation *A*. The cost of providing goods and services in industry *B* will rise by more than that in industry *A*. In turn, the prices in industry *B* may rise by more than those in industry *A*. Finally, as a result of the different effects on market prices in the two industries, consumers in these two industries may not share an equal portion of the tax burden.

The person who initially pays a particular tax may not necessarily bear the entire burden. In most instances, tax changes, or the imposition of taxes where none previously existed, cause changes in relative costs and benefits of specific actions, whether they be pricing and output decisions in the short run or investment and employment decisions in the longer run. Evaluation of the new cost-benefit information most often leads eventually to different pricing, output and employment decisions. These changes generally mean that consumers, workers and shareholders all bear a part of any tax burden.

13-5 TAXATION AND INCOME REDISTRIBUTION

The government attempts to redistribute income, not only through its expenditure (for example, income supplements and consumption subsidies), but also by means of taxation. Tax incidence has important implications for income redistribution efforts.

Many people, for instance, might point to apparently huge corporate profits as reported in annual reports and argue that these companies should be taxed more heavily. Perhaps they should, but we must remember a number of things before we advocate such action. First of all, what portion of the large dollar amounts of accounting profits represents merely a *normal rate of return* on invested funds? For if the accounting profit does no more than provide a normal rate of return on investment for the shareholder it is not possible to tax this profit away without placing a part of the tax burden on consumers and workers, perhaps the very groups toward which the government is attempting to redistribute income. In the short run, the shareholders will bear some of the cost as their

share prices fall in response to lower after-tax accounting profits. But if this lowers the shareholders' rate of return below that which can be earned elsewhere, they will take their funds out of the industry and invest where they can earn a normal return. The shareholders, by being able to partially escape the tax in the long run by leaving the industry, may reduce the tax proceeds. Further, the reduced supply causes higher prices and lower employment opportunities, thereby hurting consumers and workers. This would hardly be an effective way to attempt income redistribution.

Some measure of the relative burden of all government taxes (that is, including personal and corporate income taxes, tariffs, inheritance taxes, sales and excise taxes and so on) shared by various Canadian income groups is provided by Figure 13-5, which shows the approximate effective tax rate in terms of net total government taxes paid as a percentage of before-tax income.

Figure 13-5 indicates that, all in all, Canadian taxation appears to be sharply progressive up to the

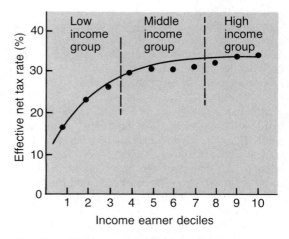

Fig. 13-5 Effective tax rate based on before-tax income (1978)

Source: Sally Pipes and Michael Walker with David Gill, *Tax Facts 3: The Canadian Consumer Tax Index and You*, 3rd edition (Vancouver: The Fraser Institute, 1982).

The effective Canadian income tax rates are sharply progressive up to the middle income level. Thereafter, however, progressivity levels off.

middle income group. However, beyond that, the degree of progressivity falls off significantly. For example, the effective net tax rate of the upper 10% of all income earners (the 10th income earner decile) is only about three percentage points higher than the low middle income group (the 4th income earner decile). These results are consistent with a number of studies done in both Canada and the U.S.

The progressivity of income tax structure is one of the policy instruments for redistribution of income. It does, however, have the potential for negative impact on incentives to work and to invest.

13-6 THE OPERATION OF GOVERNMENT

The government, in its roles as producer and redistributor of income, operates via expenditure and taxation channels as we have seen above.[11] The expenditure responsibilities and taxation powers of the federal and provincial governments are derived from the division of powers and responsibilities as set out in the Canada Act, 1982. Finally, some duties are delegated by the provincial governments to the local level.

As an example of how governments operate, it might be worth-while to examine the setup of the *federal government*, which, by any measure, is the largest single government body in Canada. Figure 13-6 is a summarized organization chart of the federal government.

The responsibility for justice in Canada is borne by the judiciary, or the **judicial branch** of government. The judiciary includes all the levels of courts in Canada and their officers. The **legislative branch**, consisting of the upper house (**Senate**) and the lower house (**House of Commons**) is where new laws are passed. These laws provide the framework for government operations, which are administered through the **executive branch**,

headed up by the Prime Minister and the Cabinet.[12] Each Cabinet minister is in charge of one or more departments, where the day-to-day government activities within the economy are managed. Under each department, there are usually several agencies and commissions (some of which may be set up as Crown corporations), each of which carries out its own specialized function. Some agencies serve to *regulate*, others act as *producers*, while still others attempt to *redistribute income*.

For example, the job of the Canadian Radio-television and Telecommunications Commission (CRTC), which comes under the Department of Communications, is to regulate broadcasters and various companies within the telecommunications industry. The job of Canada Post (a Crown corporation) is to provide mail service. The primary job of the Department of National Health and Welfare is to redistribute income. In this role, it administers such programs as the Canada Pension Plan, Old Age Security and Guaranteed Income Supplements, family and youth allowances, the Canada Assistance Plan and emergency welfare services. As one example of a department that is at once a producer, regulator and redistributor of income, the Department of Agriculture provides research and experimentation services in agriculture, regulates standards of agricultural products as well as administering programs which concern farm income security.

Members of the House of Commons are the elected officials of government. Most other government officials are appointed, including members of the Senate. After an election, the majority party forms the government executive. The leader of the majority party becomes the Prime Minister, who in turn chooses his Cabinet ministers. Each Cabinet minister receives a portfolio of one or more government departments as a responsibility to administer. The day-to-day managers of each department are nonelected government employees or **civil servants**. The most senior civil servant

---

11. In the sphere of macroeconomic policy, the government also uses expenditure and taxes to influence such vital aspects of economic activity as unemployment, inflation and foreign trade.

12. At the provincial level, the executive branch is headed by the provincial Premier and Cabinet. At the municipal level, it is headed by the Mayor.

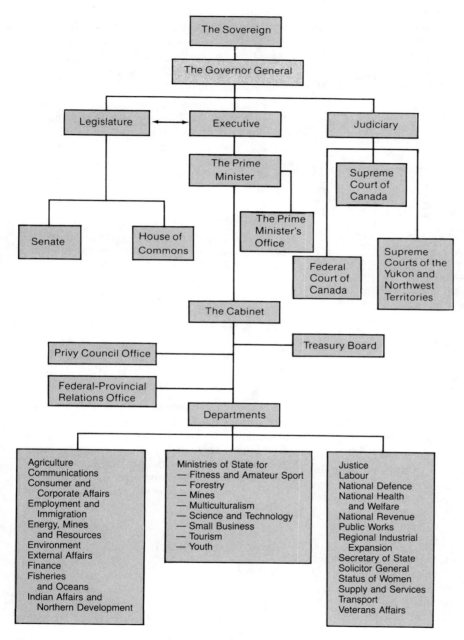

Fig. 13-6 Organization chart of the federal government

The Legislature, the Executive, and the Judiciary are the three branches of government. The executive branch is by far the largest. The numbers, names and functions of the executive government departments change more frequently than those of the other branches of government.

post in a government department is that of **deputy minister**. If the governing party loses office, the Cabinet ministers change, but generally the large body of civil servants within the departments does not change.

We now summarize the types of expenditure and taxation carried on by each level of government. The items are arranged in order of importance, from most to least important. Following this is a brief analysis of the distribution of consolidated government expenditure and revenue, together with a look at the historical pattern of government expenditure, taxation and debt.

Government Expenditures

Federal

Social Welfare. The largest federal government expenditure is for **social welfare**, accounting for roughly one-third of the entire federal budget. Such expenditures include the Canada Pension Plan, Old Age Security, veterans benefits, unemployment insurance payments, family and youth allowances and assistance to disabled and needy persons.

Protection. This includes national defence and federal police services (in particular those of the RCMP).

Health Care. This includes expenditures for hospital and physicians services, part of which are also paid by the provinces.

General Purpose Transfers. These expenditures involve monies transferred from the federal government to the provinces and municipalities in connection with the federal government's role as a redistributor of income throughout the various geographical regions of Canada.

Other Expenditures. Other federal expenditures include transportation and communications, general administrative expenditures, education, natural resources, agriculture, trade, industry, tourism, environment, foreign affairs and foreign aid, and interest on the national debt.

Provincial

Health. The largest expenditure by the provincial governments is on health, accounting for roughly one-quarter of the total provincial budgets. Such expenditures include both physicians and hospital expenses.

Education. Education takes roughly the same proportion of provincial expenditure as health care.

Social Welfare. These expenditures include such things as child welfare services, living accommodation for the elderly, welfare assistance to needy persons and rehabilitation services.

Other Expenditures. These include expenditures for such items as general government administration, police, transportation and communications, natural resources, agriculture, trade, industry, tourism, housing, interest on provincial debt and transfers to the federal and municipal governments.

Municipal

Education. Almost half of local government expenditure is made by the school board authorities for primary and secondary education.

Transportation and Communication. These services include roads, snow and ice removal, bridges, subways, tunnels, street lighting, traffic services, parking and public transit.

Other. These include police protection, sewer and water, health, social welfare services, recreation and community services, interest on municipal debt and general government administration.

Each level of government is responsible for financing certain types of economic activities corresponding to the constitutional division of powers. The largest share of federal government expenditures is taken up by social welfare. Provincial governments spend the most on health. The largest share of local government expenditures goes for education.

Government Taxation

Federal

Individual Income Tax. Every person who is resident in Canada is liable for the payment of federal income tax on earned income. Including allowances for various deductions as specified in the Income Tax Act, approximate federal rates of tax on personal income were illustrated earlier in Table 13-2.

Excise and Sales Tax. The Excise Tax Act allows the federal government to levy a general twelve percent sales tax on the selling price of goods manufactured in Canada or imported into Canada.

"Look, we only promised the voters no NEW taxes . . . nothing was said about more of the same OLD taxes!"

GRIN AND BEAR IT by George Lichty: © Field Enterprises, Inc. Courtesy of Field Newspaper Syndicate.

This tax does not apply to goods exported from Canada nor does it apply to certain other goods such as: drugs, electricity, clothing and footwear. The Excise Tax Act also imposes a number of special excise taxes in addition to the federal sales tax. Those taxes are shown in Table 13-5.

Typically, the federal sales tax is *hidden* in the ticket price of the final good, unlike provincial retail sales taxes, which are calculated and added onto the retail ticket price when the consumer pays for the item. It makes very little difference to the consumer which method is used, however, as the ultimate result is the same — a higher *final price* (where "final price" includes all taxes).

Corporate Income Tax. Federal taxes are levied on corporate incomes, as discussed earlier. In 1986, for most nonmanufacturing firms, the approximate rate of federal tax for large corporations was 36% of accounting profit (special rates applied for small businesses and some manufacturing and processing firms). This, together with provincial tax of about 15% (depending on the province), implied an overall corporate tax rate of about 50%. The effective rate of tax for manufacturers and processors was six percentage points lower than that of most other corporations. Owners of noncorporate businesses are taxed directly on their personal incomes from such businesses.

Customs Duties (Tariffs). Most goods imported into Canada are subject to customs duties at various rates as provided for by tariff schedules.

Other Federal Taxes. Other federal taxes include social insurance levies, Canada Pension Plan taxes, alcohol and tobacco taxes and nonresident taxes.

Tax Reform Proposal. In June 1987, the federal government released a white paper on taxation. It proposed a far-reaching overhaul of Canada's tax system. One major thrust of the reform proposals was a cut in personal income tax rates, beginning in 1988. However, the government also announced its intention to introduce sometime in the future a consumption tax that would increase the tax burdens of individuals according to how much they spend on goods and services. Three alternative forms of this tax were presented for discussion: (1) a single national sales tax which would combine federal and provincial retail sales taxes; (2) federal sales tax on goods and services; (3) federal value added tax which, roughly speaking, would be a percentage of the difference between a company's buying and selling prices.

The white paper also proposed a change in the treatment of many of the income tax deductions, such as the personal and married exemptions, tuition fees and charitable donations. Under the existing system, they reduce the amount of taxable incomes. For the same amount of deduction — say tuition fee payment — taxpayers with large taxable incomes and high marginal tax rates save more on taxes than taxpayers with lower incomes and lower marginal tax rates. The system proposed in the white paper would change these deductions into tax credits, which means that they would directly reduce the tax bill by the same amount for each taxpayer, regardless of his or her level of income.

The corporate income tax rates would also be reduced, but some corporate tax deductions, loopholes and methods of tax avoidance would be eliminated so that the overall corporate tax bill would increase.

Provincial

Personal Income Tax. All provincial governments levy income taxes on residents within their boundaries. Except for the province of Quebec, these taxes are collected on behalf of the provinces by the federal government. In 1985, the tax rates ranged from a low of 43.5% of federal tax in Alberta to a high of 60% in Newfoundland.

Retail Sales Tax. Retail sales taxes are levied on the final purchaser and are collected by the retailer.

Table 13-5 **Special excise taxes of the federal government**

Item	Tax, Dec. 1982
Cigarettes (per 5 cigarettes)	3.864¢
Cigars	20.5%
Pipe tobacco, cut tobacco, snuff	$2.5502
Jewellery, including articles of ivory, amber, shell, precious or semi-precious stones, clocks and watches[1], goldsmiths' and silversmiths' products, except gold-plated or silver-plated ware for the preparation or serving of food or drink	10%
Lighters	10¢
Playing cards (per pack)	20¢
Slot machines — coin, disc or token-operated games or amusement devices	10%
Matches	10%
Tobacco, pipes, cigars and cigarette holders and cigarette rolling devices	10%
Wines[2] (additional excise taxes)[3]	
Wines of all kinds containing less than 1.2% absolute alcohol by volume	1.42¢/L
Wines of all kinds containing less than 7% absolute alcohol by volume	17.03¢/L
Wines of all kinds containing more than 7% absolute alcohol by volume	35.48¢/L
Insurance premiums paid to British or foreign companies not authorized to transact business in Canada or to non-resident agents of authorized British or foreign companies	10%
Air transportation tax on tickets purchased in or outside of Canada for transportation of persons	
(a) in the taxation area[4] (including travel in Canada) (8% max.)	$23.50
(b) beginning in Canada and ending outside the taxation area[5]	$12.50
Automobiles, station wagons and vans designed for use as passenger vehicles — tax applies to vehicles which exceed the specified mass for the vehicle type[6]	
Automobile mass limit 2 007 kg	
Station wagon and van mass limit 2 268 kg	
Tax rates:	
— for the portion of the mass that exceeds the mass limit but not more than 45 kg[7]	$30.00
— for the portion of the mass that exceeds the mass limit by 45 kg but not more than 90 kg	$40.00
— for the portion of the mass that exceeds the mass limit by 90 kg but not more than 135 kg	$50.00
— for each additional 45 kg in excess of the mass limit plus 135 kg	$60.00
Gasoline for personal use[8]	1.5¢/L
Air conditioners designed for use in automobiles, station wagons, vans or trucks	$100

Almost all of the foregoing items, except insurance premiums and air transportation, are also subject to the general sales tax. Alcohol and tobacco products are subject to additional taxes under the Excise Act (referred to as excise duties).

[1]Special excise tax only applies on the amount by which the sale price or the duty-paid value of the clock or watch exceeds $50.

[2]These taxes apply only to wines manufactured in Canada. The customs tariff on wines includes a levy on imported wines to correspond to the taxes on domestic production.

[3]These taxes apply to both domestic and imported wines.

[4]Includes Canada, the islands of St. Pierre and Miquelon, and the U.S. except Hawaii.

[5]Reduced to $4 for a child under 12 travelling at a fare of 50% or more below the applicable fare; nil if the fare is 90% below the applicable fare.

[6]Excludes ambulances, hearses, vehicles for police or firefighting.

[7]The weight limit is 4425 lb. for automobiles and 5000 lb. for station wagons and vans.

[8]Reduced from 10¢ to 7¢ a gallon effective Aug. 25, 1978; the rate was converted to metric equivalent effective Jan. 1, 1979.

Source: Canada Yearbook, 1985

The federal excise taxes are hidden in the price of final goods, unlike the provincial sales tax which is added to the retail price.

In 1986, all provinces except Alberta levied this type of tax, with rates generally ranging between five and ten percent.

Motive Fuel Tax. Each province imposes a tax on the purchase of gasoline. This specific tax is a very important source of provincial revenue.

Corporate Income Tax. All provinces levy a tax on the accounting profit of corporations earned within provincial boundaries. The rates applicable are around 15%. Except for the provinces of Ontario and Quebec, the federal government collects this tax on behalf of the provinces.

Other Taxes. These include such taxes as estate and gift taxes; hospitalization and medical care premiums; amusement taxes; gasoline and diesel fuel oil taxes; motor vehicle licences and fees; taxes and royalties on mining, oil and natural gas production; land transfer taxes, taxes on premium income of insurance companies and other miscellaneous taxes. Not all provinces levy all of the aforementioned taxes, and rates vary considerably.

Municipal

Property Taxes. For more than a century, the main source of revenue of local governments has been related to real estate. Generally speaking, the two major taxes levied on property within municipalities are taxes for the provision of local government services and education taxes. The latter are established by the local school board, which is generally a governmental authority separate from the municipality in which it is situated. Typically, however, the municipality collects the school tax along with its own taxes.

Business Taxes. These are taxes levied directly on the operation of a business and related in some manner to the extent of business activity carried on.

Water Taxes. Taxes for the provision of water are typically charged either on the value of property or on the basis of water used.

Other Taxes. These include concession fees, licences and fines.

Consolidated Government Finance

In what follows we wish to examine government financing in its broader sense. As a result, we will for the most part not distinguish between the different levels of government. In this regard, all ex-

penditure and tax figures are presented on a consolidated basis with intergovernmental transfer payments netted out.

Expenditures and Sources of Revenue

Figure 13-7 shows the relative importance of the various types of government expenditures and revenue for the year 1982.

As can be seen, roughly half of total government expenditures at all levels was made in the areas of health, education and welfare. About 37% of the government's total revenue was in the form of direct personal and corporate income taxes, while indirect taxes on goods and services (**consumption taxes**) amounted to about 17%.

Table 13-6 shows the growth over the years of government expenditure and revenue as a percentage of total national income.

The first set of expenditure figures includes transfer payments from governments to individuals and businesses in the form of income supplements and other subsidies. The bracketed set excludes these transfer payments. To the extent that a portion of government spending consists of transfer payments back to other individuals and businesses, who then carry out the final expenditure on goods and services, these final expenditure decisions are made by the private sector and not by the government. Only the remaining portion (that is, 23.1% in 1985) of government expenditure is on goods and services of the government's own choosing. On the other hand, taxes for income redistribution payments (that is, the transfer payments to individuals and business firms) do reduce the private choice of those who must pay the taxes. For example, if an individual pays $3000 taxes, that person has been relieved of the ability to decide what this portion of income should be spent on, regardless of whether the government uses it for purchasing the services of civil servants or in the payment of old age security benefits.

In summary, both transfer payments and direct government expenditures on goods and services place *constraints on private decision making*, with the latter type of government expenditures placing the greater constraints. As a result, often both transfer payment-inclusive and transfer payment-exclusive measures of government spending are utilized to reflect changing degrees of government constraints on private decision making. As Table 13-6 clearly shows, both measures of government

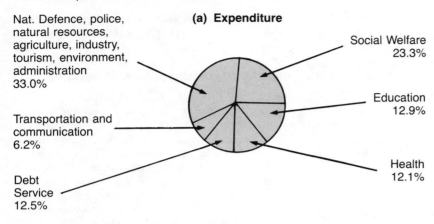

(a) Expenditure

Nat. Defence, police, natural resources, agriculture, industry, tourism, environment, administration
33.0%

Social Welfare
23.3%

Education
12.9%

Transportation and communication
6.2%

Health
12.1%

Debt Service
12.5%

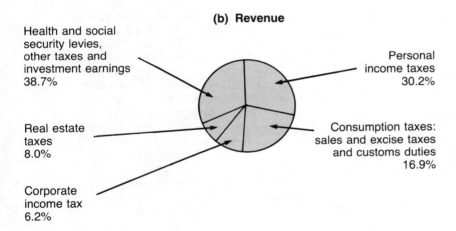

(b) Revenue

Health and social security levies, other taxes and investment earnings
38.7%

Personal income taxes
30.2%

Real estate taxes
8.0%

Consumption taxes: sales and excise taxes and customs duties
16.9%

Corporate income tax
6.2%

Fig. 13-7 Consolidated government expenditure and revenue, 1982

Source: Statistics Canada 68-202

About half of the expenditures of governments of all levels was made in the area of social welfare, education and health. The bulk of revenues came from income taxes and health and social security levies. Indirect (consumption) taxes accounted for about 17 percent of total government revenues.

Source: Statistics Canada 11-003; *Economic Review*; Department of Finance, *The Fiscal Plan*, February 1986; National Tax Foundation, *The National Finances 1986–87*. Reproduced with permission of the Minister of Supply and Services.

Table 13-6 Total government expenditure and revenue as a proportion of gross national product 1926–1985*

Years	Expenditure %		Revenue %
1926	14.5	(9.6)	16.5
1930	16.5	(12.8)	15.4
1935	25.0	(13.0)	22.2
1940	25.2	(17.1)	24.4
1945	43.2	(31.1)	29.1
1950	22.1	(13.1)	25.1
1955	26.3	(17.5)	26.1
1960	29.7	(17.7)	27.9
1965	29.9	(19.5)	30.3
1970	36.4	(23.1)	37.3
1975	41.3	(24.0)	38.9
1980	41.8	(22.8)	39.1
1981	42.6	(22.6)	41.1
1982	47.7	(24.4)	41.8
1983	47.9	(23.8)	41.2
1984	48.2	(23.4)	41.4
1985	48.2	(23.1)	41.4

* Gross National Product is roughly equal to total before-tax income of all Canadians.

The share of government expenditures and revenues in Canada's GNP has increased about three times over the past sixty years. Major growth took place during the 1960s with the implementation of a variety of important social programs. The government share of GNP has stabilized in the 1980s.

expenditures indicate government influence in economic decision making in 1985 to be roughly three and a half times what it was in 1926.

As Table 13-6 also indicates, revenue has usually fallen short of government expenditure, with the result that the government has engaged in significant amounts of borrowing over the years. Figure 13-8 shows the historical growth of **national debt** (federal government debt) and **public debt** (total government debt). Though the government has

gotten deeper and deeper into debt, the economy as a whole has also grown. As a result, interest payments required no greater proportion of total national income in 1985 than they did in 1933. However, the proportion has risen steadily since the middle 1950s and rose very sharply in the late 1970s and early 1980s, to the point where it has become a national issue.

Each level of government has available to it a series of taxes and levies as sources of revenues to finance government activities. Income taxes and health and social security levies account for the largest share of consolidated government revenues. The relative influence of governments on the economic activity in Canada has increased dramatically during the past sixty years. This is evident from such statistics as government expenditures and revenues as a proportion of GNP as well as the size of public debt and associated charges.

13-7 QUESTIONING THE GOVERNMENT'S ROLE

The benefits of most government services are more or less self evident. That is, everyone agrees it is worthwhile to have postal service, rail transportation, a military, police protection, and education. However, there are those who argue that the government has overstepped its role as a producer in the economy. Let us first of all list the two main criticisms levied against the government in this regard and then examine the reasoning behind them.

Voiced Criticisms

Firstly, the government produces many goods and services that the private sector could itself provide, and often produces these less efficiently (that is, with the use of more input resources: land, labour and capital) than would be the case if done within private industry.

Secondly, the government, in general, provides too much of those services it has taken upon itself to produce (relative to what the private sector would provide) and, as a result, wastes economic resources.

The reasoning behind the first criticism is the belief that management personnel within private industry receive their rewards (salary and prestige)

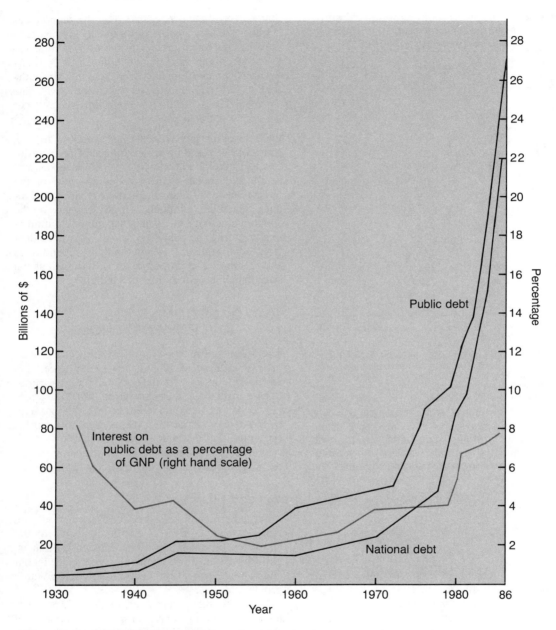

Fig. 13-8 Government debt and interest payments

Source: Statistics Canada 68-202; *Bank of Canada Review*; K.A.H. Buckley and M.C. Urquhart, eds., *Historical Statistics of Canada* (Toronto: Macmillan of Canada, 1965); Department of Finance, *The Fiscal Plan*, February 1986, and *Budget Papers*, February 1987. Reproduced with permission.

Both the public debt and national debt (measured here in current dollars) have risen rapidly during the 1970s and 1980s. Their growth has accelerated especially in the 1980s.

in direct proportion to the amount of profit they earn for the shareholders. Private sector managers thus have an incentive to produce in the most efficient manner possible. Also they are pressured into efficiency and cost minimization by competition or the threat of competition. Others argue that, while this would be true in purely competitive markets, in most markets producers have some degree of monopoly power, which lessens the competitive threat. Further, government regulations of such industries possibly lessen the incentive of many privately owned industries to strive for profit maximization and maximum efficiency. Another point made by those attacking private industry is that tariff walls and other forms of protection from foreign competition also reduce efficiency in the private sector. One reply of private market proponents is that government regulations and tariffs are established by governments in the first place and can hardly, therefore, be used as a rationale for government ownership. The debate continues.

The second criticism is that once a government has decided to provide a service below cost (in some cases free) to the public, too much will be produced. For example, suppose postal services were provided free of charge (which they are not, of course). In that case, people would overuse the post. Junk mail would be even more plentiful than it is at present, children would use the post as entertainment by sending letters and notes to friends living just down the street and so on. The situation can be analyzed with the aid of a diagram.

We suppose that the long-run demand and cost structure for postal service is as shown in Figure 13-9. The socially optimal production level is Q_1, where the marginal benefit received by society from the last piece of mail sent (P_1) would just pay for the marginal cost of sending it. The correct price for postal services, one that would yield the best usage of the post office, would therefore be P_1. On the other hand, if postal services were partly subsidized out of general tax revenue, and the price of postal service set below P_1, there would be overuse of the postal service. In the limit, if postal services were free, with all operations paid for by taxes, the volume of postal services used would be Q_2. However, for all material posted beyond Q_1, the extra cost to society per unit of mail would outweigh the extra benefit to society, with a resultant misallocation of economic resources (that is,

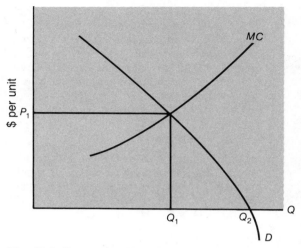

Fig. 13-9 Demand and costs in the postal service

The socially optimal quantity of service is Q_1 and the socially optimal price is P_1. If the service was provided free of charge, Q_2 would be demanded and marginal cost of the last unit would exceed its value to consumers.

too many postal workers, too many or too large post office buildings and too much mail travelling in the post).

Because many government departments do not charge for their services at all, we find in such instances overprovision of services, too many civil servants employed and too much machinery, equipment and buildings devoted to that activity. But as we said earlier, it may be impractical to charge a price for the consumption of public goods. As a result, the public may not have any idea how much it really costs to provide one more unit of a particular government service. As far as the individual consumer is concerned, it is "free." The government merely produces enough to meet this demand. Then, at the end of the year, when the public gets the tax bill for this and all the other services that have been provided, they recoil in horror.

Suggested Solutions

Most critics of the government's role as a producer will admit that there are certain goods and services that the government should continue to provide. And for some of them we may just have to live with overuse. Many argue, however, that certain services which have long been recognized as appropriate for the government to produce may in fact be more efficiently produced in the private sector. Let us examine two government services for which this solution has been suggested.

The Postal Service

Some critics point to Canada Post and wonder why the government should have the exclusive right to deliver mail. They argue that private firms should be allowed to enter the industry and compete with the government on the basis of price and quality of service. The government has always taken the position that it should handle the mail for security reasons — that is, to protect the confidentiality of public correspondence. One might argue, though, that even with privately run competition allowed, if government-provided confidentiality is important to someone, that person would still have the option of using the government mail service. Competition would be healthy, it would expand the choice available to users, and possibly lead to a more efficient, lower cost postal service. If the new entrants could not compete with the government and earn at least a normal rate of return on investment, they would leave the industry. (Another issue is whether the postal service is a natural monopoly and thus whether allowing competition may be socially inefficient.)

Education

The government has long assumed the role of providing almost universal education, for those who wish it, from kindergarten through high school. The rationale for the government providing this service has been that there are many external benefits provided by an educated populace. When individuals receive an adequate education, not only the recipients benefit directly by having gained knowledge, widened their horizons, and increased their earning power in the market place, but the rest of the citizenry also benefits by having more enlightened neighbours and co-workers and perhaps a more stable society.

Milton Friedman, while not denying these externalities, has argued that this is not a sufficient reason for the government to run schools. He and others advocate a **voucher system**, which might operate somewhat along the following lines.

Taxes for education would be paid in the normal way. Suppose the estimated education cost per child per year is $1000. Each child's parents would receive a $1000 education voucher, which could be used at any school, either government or privately run. The parent would then be able to choose freely which school's services to purchase, rather than being forced to send the child to the nearest school in the neighbourhood. The total number of vouchers a school receives would then be redeemed by the government for cash and thus determine each school's revenue. Schools that have better teachers or otherwise better programs would attract more students, hence, more vouchers and more revenue. Schools could increase their profit by offering better programs or by lowering their costs, and, if privately run, would have the incentive to do so. The argument is that an incentive would then exist for schools to offer better and lower cost programs.

Comment on Government Involvement

The public's control of what is produced in the market place is exercised by consumer *votes* in the form of dollars of expenditure. If the public is willing to purchase a good or service at the price producers are willing to sell, we take this as evidence that the value of the product to the consumer exceeds or equals the cost of its production. The public's control of government tax and expenditure actions in the pursuit of market regulation, production of public goods or income redistribution comes about through votes on election day. The public, if it does not like the way the government is doing things, can vote it out of office and vote in another party, which will presumably do things differently. Unfortunately, there are various difficulties with this system.

Out of the hundreds of things done by government, we could (if we bothered to sit down and think about it) list many as being significantly important to each of us. Our lists would differ, but there would likely be many overlapping items, things such as unemployment insurance, egg or milk marketing legislation, rent control, children's aid, minimum wages, tax deductions, sales tax rates, seat belt or speed limit legislation, defence expenditure, civil service salaries, old age security, pollution control, truth in advertising laws and so on. Next, suppose I like the way the government is handling half of these concerns and dislike the way they are handling the other half. For instance, suppose I want less government health care expenditure but favour seat belt legislation. How can my tastes be communicated through the voting system to bring me less health care expenditure but maintenance of seat belt legislation, especially since others may want just the opposite? My only consolation may be that almost everyone else will end up being just as frustrated as I am by the political process. Further, the more economic activities the government involves itself in, the greater are these sources of dissatisfaction likely to become.

The fact that different government activities are carried out at different governmental levels — local, provincial and federal — is interesting in its own right. Many people, for example, argue that (i) the public generally has more *direct control* over local governments than governments at higher levels and (ii) the interests and needs of people within a given locality are likely to be more homogeneous than those of people across the entire nation. For this reason, they argue for more government expenditure and taxation powers at the local and provincial levels and less at the federal level. Others argue, however, that if the country is to be one nation, the federal government must have broad powers of taxation and expenditure to equalize regional differences and carry out policies for the country as a whole. For example, in order to mitigate regional economic inequalities, provinces

receive taxes from richer municipalities and transfer them to poorer ones. Similarly, the federal government transfers tax revenue from richer provinces to poorer ones.

Both the extent and nature of government role in the economy have been increasingly debated. Especially prominent in recent years have been proposals for increasing the role of the private sector in the provision of goods and services presently supplied by governments or government-owned enterprises.

CONCLUDING REMARKS

The standard rationale for government involvement in the microeconomy is (i) the *control of monopoly power*, (ii) *externalities* (divergences between social and private costs and benefits), (iii) *incomplete product information*, (iv) *redistribution of income* and (v) *provision of public goods*. There is a considerable dispute as to how well the government performs its role in each of these areas. Some argue that these functions are so difficult (costly) to perform under some circumstances that they should not be performed at all, whereas others argue that the government should increase its involvement in the private economy. Unfortunately, as we each develop our own vested interests, it is hard for us not to let them override impartial economic cost-benefit analysis of the issues (even though impartial economic cost-benefit analysis may be difficult enough).

KEY TERMS AND CONCEPTS

public goods	judicial branch
Crown corporations	legislative branch
income supplement	Senate
subsidized consumption	House of Commons
negative income tax scheme	executive branch
direct taxes	civil servants
indirect taxes	deputy minister
proportional tax	social welfare
progressive tax	consumption tax
regressive tax	national debt
corporation income tax	public debt
personal income tax	voucher system

PROBLEMS

Problem 1

a) The government makes laws and acts as a regulator of the economic system. What possible justification is there for the government's acting as (i) a producer and (ii) a redistributor of income and wealth?

b) What is a Crown corporation?

c) Explain the two basic government methods of aiding those on low incomes and discuss the desirability of each method as compared with the other.

Problem 2

Explain the following terms: direct taxation; indirect taxation; proportional, progressive and regressive taxation; excise taxes; commodity sales taxes; tax incidence.

Problem 3

a) What would be the effect on consumers, workers and shareholders in the wine industry of an increase in the excise tax on wine?

b) What difference would the degree of substitutability between wine and cider make concerning tax incidence in the wine industry? (Hint: first assume cider and wine are very good substitutes and then assume that they are very poor substitutes.)

c) Analyze the effect of a general increase in provincial (commodity) sales tax rates on (i) markets for goods and (ii) markets for services. Which groups are harmed by such an action?

Problem 4

a) Discuss the following statement: "Corporate income taxes should be raised in industry X. This will hurt no one but the rich shareholders, which include some large financial institutions. This is obviously a more reasonable way of raising government funds than that of increasing personal income tax rates on a country-wide basis, which would hurt the little guy."

b) How is it possible that raising income tax rates may cause the market wage rates in different occupations to be forced upward by different amounts?

Problem 5

a) What are the main expenditure and taxation items for federal, provincial and local governments?

b) List the three most important items of total government (all three levels) expenditure and taxation.

c) Did the government involve itself to a greater degree in the economy in 1926 than it does now? What is your evidence? Compare the most recent figures on government expenditure (transfer payment inclusive and transfer payment exclusive) with those of 1985 and comment on the significance of the results. (Check with Statistics Canada publications or the *Canada Yearbook* if available.)

d) What is the difference between the terms *public debt* and *national debt*? Has the public debt become more or less onerous over the years? (Again, it would be useful to get current figures from Statistics Canada or the *Canada Yearbook*.)

Problem 6

Discuss some criticisms that have been levied against the government in its role as producer and redistributor of income. What is your personal opinion?

CASES

Case 13-1

The Financial Post

You should get what you pay for

By RICHARD M. BIRD

SHOULD THE tax system be adjusted so that an individual's taxes are more directly related to the services provided to him by the government? The Canadian Tax Foundation has just published an important study on this subject, entitled Charging for Public Services. *It was written by Richard M. Bird, professor of economics at the Institute of Policy Analysis, University of Toronto. This is a Post digest of part of that study.*

THE RESULT of distributing government services free (or at less than the marginal cost of supplying them) is to increase the apparent need to expand the supply of such services, to avert shortages and to satisfy the frustrated demand.

In short, the failure to impose correct prices on the public provision of goods and services that provide significant benefits to particular private individuals — and such activities constitute a large part of the public sector — leads inevitably to increased pressure through the political process from these individuals for more such goods and services. And what the public wants in the way of increased government spending, the politicians are usually quite happy to provide, as are the bureaucrats, whose domain thus continually expands by popular request.

Restrict demand

The natural human desire to obtain more free, or subsidized, goods thus combines with the equally natural desires of politicians to be popular (and re-elected) and of bureaucrats to be part of a growing organization to constitute a powerful upward pressure on the level of government spending. It follows from this analysis that the most important role of charging for public services in many instances is to restrict demand rather than simply to permit the expansion of supply.

The decision on the quality of service is similarly left mainly to the tender mercies of bureaucratic organizations, which have no real incentives (pecuniary or otherwise) to satisfy their customers in any but the grossest way. That usually means, for example, that everyone gets the same amount of service — whether he wants it or not.

Authoritarian egalitarians may be happy with this state of affairs, but it is hard to see why anyone else should be. It is, of course, true that the minimal standards necessary for civilized existence in a complex modern urban society require that each citizen "consume" a package of basic public services — health, education, protection, and so on — whether he likes it or not. But there seems to be no reason why those who want more than this basic package, or some variant of it, should not be entitled to express their desires and get their wishes through such quasi-market devices as public pricing.

Consider the postal service, an area of traditional government monopoly provision of an essentially private service, following basically uniform pricing rules not unlike those common in other bureaucratic settings. More thought can and should be given to the role of pricing policy in the postal service. Up to now, all attention to this question appears to have been devoted to the marginal cost of providing different classes of mail service and to the extent to which certain types of mail deserve a subsidy from the public treasury as a whole.

Less cost?

This whole area can also usefully be viewed from another angle — that of reducing costs. While there has been much effort in the postal service to reduce the major cost element — its labour-intensity — little attention seems thus far to have been paid to the possible role of public pricing in attaining this goal. For example, barring some futuristic sort of arrangement, the labour cost of sorting and, especially, delivery will likely continue to be the most intractable, and therefore rapidly expanding, part of the total postal labour bill.

To date, attempts by the Canadian Post Office to cope with this problem have been confined to reducing delivery service to everyone. No reason was really offered for this move except to save costs. But it is perhaps not unfair to infer that this path was taken also to avoid creating differentiations between the delivery service received by different classes of customers.

Such egalitarianism seems inappropriate. It would surely be possible and even profitable to offer more variety in frequency of delivery, with everyone getting some minimum (say, the present once-a-day, five days a week), and those willing to pay an annual or quarterly charge for better service — presumably, mostly businesses — being able to get it.

Similarly, delivery charges might perhaps vary with the location of the mailbox, with the lowest charge for those who have a post office box, the next lowest for those with a mail box on the street, and the highest for under-the-door delivery.

One point which emerges from the postal example is that it is not enough just to charge for public services. One must levy the *right* charges to reap the virtues of public pricing.

The prevalence of the wrong charges in those areas in which charging is used has done a good deal to discredit unduly the whole idea of charging for public services. To some extent, then, the problem is less that the principle of pricing is deficient than that its practice is faulty.

In the end, there is no question that the real obstacles to increased use of the benefit principle in public finance lie in public attitudes as to what is public and what is private, and what is sold and what is free — that is, in what one economist has labeled "philosophical and sentimental hangups against marginalism and markets." Nowhere are such attitudes clearer than in the constantly reiterated refrain that one cannot charge for health, education, or whatever, because free access to such things is a basic human right or basic necessity of existence.

If the market is so inapplicable in these areas, it is curious we employ it so widely with regard to such real basics as food, clothing, and shelter. What these examples make plain is that the real hangup is not the essentiality of the service but rather the nature of the provider — namely, a governmental organization.

a) Explain why services provided at a zero price (or in general at a subsidized price) tend to cause overutilization of such services by the general public and hence a tax bill that is unduly large.

b) What justification is there for charging a subsidized price (that is, a price lower than the full cost of providing the service), with the subsidy provided for through taxes?

c) In your opinion does the rationale of part (b) apply for (i) a city bus or subway service, (ii) postal delivery, (iii) public school education? Explain.

d) Explain how subsidized housing schemes give those who qualify not what they may want, but instead what the government wants them to have. How else could the government help them and allow them instead to get what they (the recipients) want?

e) What justification is there for a central authority's giving people not what they want but instead what a central authority wants them to have? Do you think we should base economic policy on this justification?

f) How would varying the charges for postal service directly with the convenience and quality of service provided improve the economic efficiency of postal delivery?

The Market System and Dissenting Views

14-1 INTRODUCTION AND PURPOSE

In previous chapters, we have been primarily concerned with explaining how the market system works. Our explanations comprise what may be referred to as the *orthodox*, or *mainstream view* by economists in the western world. However, there are economists who would take exception to certain important aspects of our discussions.

Almost everyone can point to defects within the present-day market system, and orthodox economists (along with those of opposing viewpoints) are continually advocating *structural change*. However, they typically emphasize changes that would strengthen the existing market system and help it to function more efficiently and, in some cases, more equitably. But there are also more radical economists who believe that the market

system is an inappropriate framework for the development of human welfare.

There are disagreements along two fronts: (i) how the market system actually operates and (ii) what is the best type of economic system. The purpose of this chapter is to investigate briefly these two areas of dispute.

14-2 ECONOMICS AND ADAM SMITH

The Nature of Wealth

Almost all the economic principles presented in this book may be found in another book written over two hundred years ago — Adam Smith's *An Inquiry into the Nature and Cause of the Wealth of*

Nations (1776). As the title indicates, Smith was attempting to explain what it was that constituted a nation's true wealth and those factors that could increase this wealth. He had a formidable task. A theory prevalent in Smith's day was **mercantilism**. According to this theory, since personal wealth could be represented in monetary terms, then a nation's wealth consisted of the amount of money — that is, gold and silver — within its borders. If a person's wealth was increased by acquiring another £100 of gold and silver, then the wealth of a nation of individuals must correspondingly increase by the same amount. One prescription for increasing a nation's wealth was that a country should seek to sell as much of its goods as possible abroad for gold and silver (money) in order that it might increase its domestic stock of wealth.

Adam Smith attempted to point out that the usefulness of money was chiefly as a *medium of exchange* and its acquisition should not be an end in itself. Smith argued that a nation's *real wealth* was reflected in its annual flow of goods and services which were available for the population's consumption. The material wealth and welfare of a nation's citizens would be enhanced by an increase in this per capita flow, not by the accumulation of foreign bank notes or pieces of gold and silver.

> The annual labour of every nation is the fund which originally supplies it with all the necessaries and conveniences of life which it annually consumes, and which consist always either in the immediate produce of that labour, or in what is purchased with that produce from other nations.
>
> According, therefore, as this produce, or what is purchased with it, bears a greater or smaller proportion to the number of those who are to consume it, the nation will be better or worse supplied with all the necessaries and conveniences for which it has occasion.[1]

The prescription stemming from this view of wealth therefore, suggests *maximizing the flow of goods and services per person*. Smith argued that this activity was the easiest part of all. The market system would do it automatically.

---

1. Adam Smith, *An Inquiry into the Nature and Causes of the Wealth of Nations* (New York: Random House, Modern Library Edition, 1937), p. lvii.

The Division of Labour

Each person is born with, or acquires, certain individual tastes, aptitudes and abilities, and can therefore perform certain work tasks more efficiently than others. Some people make good shoemakers, some good tailors, and some good farmers, computer scientists, pro golfers or teachers. It is certain that all people cannot perform all jobs with equal vigour and dexterity. A family that decides to produce the things it wants, including food, clothing and shelter, will get less of everything (including leisure) than a family that pursues only that activity for which it has the most aptitude — perhaps farming — and then trades some of its produce for the other goods and services it desires.

This is one example of the **division of labour** by occupation which Smith argued was a method of increasing the flow of goods and services per family and, hence, national wealth. Smith saw, however, that the division of labour could be taken much further than this within each industry. Efficiency might be immensely improved if the total activity connected with the production of a good was split up into a number of separate tasks. For one thing, each worker could concentrate on learning one or two tasks instead of perhaps 20, 30 or 300. In addition, the simplication of the production process into distinct repetitive processes would allow the application of machinery, which might be able to perform such tasks with more precision and efficiency.

> The greatest improvements in the production powers of labour, and the greater part of the skill, dexterity, and judgement, with which it is anywhere directed, or applied; seem to have been the effects of the division of labour. . . .
>
> To take an example . . . the trade of the pinmaker; a workman not educated to this business (which the division of labour has rendered a district trade), nor acquainted with the use of the machinery employed in it (to the invention of which the same division of labour has probably given occasion), could scarce, perhaps, with his utmost industry, make one pin in a day, and certainly could not make twenty. But in the way in which this business is now carried on, not only the whole work is a peculiar trade, but it is divided into a number of branches, of which the greater part are likewise peculiar trades. One man draws out the wire; another straightens it; a third cuts it; a fourth points it; a fifth grinds it at the top for receiving the

head; to make the head requires two or three distinct operations; to put it on is a peculiar business; to whiten the pins is another; it is even a trade by itself to put them into the paper; and the important business of making a pin is, in this manner, divided into about eighteen distinct operations, which, in some manufactories, are all performed by distinct hands, though in others the same man will sometimes perform two or three of them. I have seen a small manufactory of this kind, where ten men only are employed and where some of them consequently performed two or three distinct operations. But though they were very poor, and therefore but indifferently accommodated with the necessary machinery, they could, when they exerted themselves, make among them upwards of forty-eight thousand pins in a day.[2]

The Market System

Exchange transactions carried on through the market provide the mechanism whereby each person is able to devote energy to the production of that good for which he or she has a natural aptitude or talent. It allows a shoemaker to devote more time to making shoes, which a shoemaker can do much better than growing food or making clothes. Through the market, the shoemaker is able to sell the products of labour (shoes) for money to be used as a medium of exchange in the purchase of food and clothes, which in turn are produced by those people who have greater natural inclination to do so. To Adam Smith, the division of labour, which provides one of the greatest sources of improvement in per capita national wealth, is made possible by *voluntary market exchange*.

If a voluntary exchange takes place between two parties, it must be perceived by both parties as being to their mutual advantage. The benefit of free exchange is a most important idea of Smith's and a pivotal element in his justification for a free market system. We have often used this idea in earlier chapters, but it seems important enough to reemphasize it here.

Adam Smith argued that transactions taking place within a free market would benefit both buyer and seller, and that in such a free market, trades could take place only at prices that benefited both parties. If one good or service became valued

less in relation to other goods so that its price fell to such a level that a normal rate of return on investment could not be earned, its production would become no longer beneficial to the producers. The producers would consequently cut back their production, sell off whatever assets they could, and place their investment in the production of other goods for which the prices (which must always benefit buyers, otherwise they would not buy) would earn them at least a normal rate of return on their investment.

A free market system would in this way, Smith argued, automatically generate the production of goods and services which provide benefits to consumers, workers and producers alike — though Smith's overriding concerns appear to have been with consumers and workers.

What was true of the free market mechanism as far as goods and services were concerned, Smith said, would also hold for labour. If labour could move freely between occupations, without impediments (such as government-required licences, professional association or other union requirements), it would always move to those occupations in which it would gain maximum net benefit. If the wages in one industry or occupation were lower than those in another, labour would move to that industry or occupation which offered the higher compensation. Of course it takes time for new skills to be learned, and some would not be able to move, either because of age or other impediments, just as capital owners might take time to shift their capital funds from a declining industry to a more thriving one and consequently suffer below-normal rates of return in the interim. But the market always pointed the way for people to achieve the maximum benefit through economic transactions.

To see the benefit of market signals and the cost of not following them, consider the situation of an industry whose products are no longer desired, but which continues to produce them supported by government regulation or subsidies. For example, suppose that as the car replaced the horse as the major mode of transportation and the demand for buggy whips fell, the government prohibited companies from reducing the production of buggy whips — perhaps for fear of unemployment within the buggy whip industry. With demand falling each year, buggy whip production and sales volumes could have been maintained only at lower and lower market prices. Eventually, whatever

---

2. Ibid., pp. 3–5.

profits the industry originally had been earning would have disappeared, and large losses would develop. Finally, the various companies in the industry would have been thrown into bankruptcy. The unemployment problem, though it had been temporarily postponed, would have come about anyway. The costs of postponement in this case were forced on the industry (that is, if the industry had been allowed to ease off production and employment earlier, it would not have suffered such losses).

Alternatively, suppose that to prevent losses and ultimate bankruptcies, the government decided to compensate owners of the buggy whip firms through subsidy payments just sufficient to maintain a normal rate of return on investment. As before, the industry would have been forced to reduce prices in order to maintain production and employment in the face of declining demand. As time went on, however, the subsidy payments would have to become greater and greater. If in a given year buggy whip prices were 50 cents, and the cost of producing the last buggy whip, including a normal return on investment (long-run marginal costs, in other words), amounted to $1.50, this would necessitate a $1 subsidy to producers. Such a subsidy presumably would be paid from tax revenue collected from the public at large. The production of this last buggy whip created a good worth 50¢ to society, and society had to give up $1.50 worth of goods and services in order to get it (whip purchasers contributed 50¢ and taxpayers $1). Production of this last buggy whip consequently made society $1 *worse off*, and this amount of loss is represented by the subsidy. Similarly, the production of all those buggy whips that required a subsidy made society worse off than it otherwise would have been (*reduced national wealth*, in Smith's terminology). In a free market, with the absence of subsidies, none of these buggy whips would have been produced (because those that required a subsidy could not have earned a normal rate of return in the absence of that subsidy).

Market Imperfections

Some people who have heard of Adam Smith but have not read his *Wealth of Nations* have accused him of being too naïve — of pretending that the economy is everywhere composed of individuals freely offering to sell their labour to individual competitive producers, and that the market is not distorted by monopoly elements or imperfections of any kind. This accusation is quite wrong. Throughout all of his three volumes, Smith frequently talks of market impediments arising from government regulations against free trade (both domestic and international), licensing, artificially long apprenticeship requirements, and always, monopoly power.

It is essential, Smith argued, to allow free mobility of all resources within a nation in order to maximize the wealth of the people (national welfare). A producer must be free to establish production of any commodity the market wants. Barriers against this only serve the monopoly interests of existing producers and not the great body of the people, who were Smith's prime concern. Further, an individual must be free to offer labour in any chosen occupation, without government restrictions, artificial licensing or unreasonably long apprenticeships designed by professions as a way to get cheap labour and minimize the number who might enter the profession, thereby bidding up the price of qualified professional services.

Smith was also concerned about possible combinations of workers to raise wages and those of producers to lower them, though he believed the latter danger was greater than the former.

> People of the same trade seldom meet together, even for merriment and diversion, but the conversation ends in a conspiracy against the public, or in some contrivance to raise prices.[3]

Individual Self-Interest

An important assumption of Adam Smith, which has been debated for a long time, is outlined as follows. Smith assumed that people, by their very nature, operate in their own self-interest and in fact attempt to maximize their own satisfaction. It is not necessarily the case that they undertake all actions on the basis of self-interest, but Smith assumed that people in their economic transactions will typically follow this rule. Each person with investment funds will seek to place them in order to earn the most profit (highest rate of return). The most profit would be earned in those industries

---

3. Ibid., p. 128.

whose products were most valued by consumers. The investor would therefore purchase the necessary capital equipment and seek to attract labour from other industries for the production of these goods. In order to do this, the investor would have to offer attractive wage rates. If labour acted so as to maximize its own interest, it would therefore seek employment in the expanding industry. The goods that consumers wanted would be produced, the investor would earn an attractive rate of return and labour would benefit from higher wage rates. Smith was able to show that the market system would *harness human self-interest* and, as if by an *invisible hand*, direct it toward those actions that provide benefit for all society.

> . . . man has almost constant occasion for the help of his brethren, and it is in vain for him to expect it from their benevolence only. He will be more likely to prevail if he can interest their self-love in his favour, and show them that it is for their own advantage to do for him what he requires of them. Whoever offers to another a bargain of any kind, proposes to do this. Give me that which I want, and you shall have this which you want, is the meaning of every such offer; and it is in this manner that we obtain from one another the far greatest part of those good offices which we stand in need of. It is not from the benevolence of the butcher, the brewer, or the baker, that we expect our dinner, but from this regard to their own interest. We address ourselves, not to their humanity, but to their self-love, and never talk to them of our own necessities but of their advantages.[4]

Policy Implications

The basic policy implication flowing from Smith's view of the world was a general "hands off" approach by government (*laissez-faire*: let people do as they please, especially in commerce). Smith saw the use of most government regulations to prohibit the production of one thing or another, to grant special subsidies in one industry or another and to confer monopoly rights — either on producers or workers — as bad in that they would prevent the free mobility of resources, which is the key link in the transmission of market benefits and the correct division of labour. Smith's role for government was limited to defence, justice, public works and certain public institutions.

---

4. Ibid., p. 14.

Much of the economic theory presented in this book utilizes the concepts formulated by Adam Smith over two hundred years ago. Voluntary market exchange, based on the division of labour and guided by individual self-interest, greatly contributes to social welfare. Market imperfections as well as government intervention in the economy should be limited.

14-3 THE MARKET SYSTEM TODAY

The market system today is much different from that envisaged by Adam Smith in the *Wealth of Nations*. We do not have atomistic competition (perfect competition, as discussed in Chapter 5) as a chief characteristic of our market system. Instead, our economy is a hodgepodge of monopolistically competitive, oligopolistic and quasi-monopolistic industries, with each one in some way or another influenced by government.

Government involvement takes many forms. Some industries are protected from foreign competition by tariffs; others may be directly regulated by government commissions. In some industries, government-owned corporations may occupy a large percentage of the market. All corporations face sales and income taxes of one sort or another. Many have to meet various government product safety and pollution standards in their production activities. Some are regulated with respect to their investment, pricing and output decisions.

Products themselves are far more sophisticated and complex today than they were in Adam Smith's time. To make a rational choice today often requires a great deal more reliable information than it did two hundred years ago. Manufactured foods such as cereals, bread, fast-food hamburgers, ice cream and diet soft drinks lead to questions about the impact on our body of many chemicals that Adam Smith never ate. Does watching TV or playing video games hurt our eyesight? Is there a defective part in our new automobile? How fast will the car's body rust?

Consequently, most people argue that Adam Smith's story of how the market system operates is no longer adequate; some argue that it never was. The orthodox economic view today admits that Smith's story of 1776 is no longer an entirely accurate representation of the market system as we know it now. But the orthodox view also asserts that Smith's story contains many basic truths that are as relevant today as they were two hundred years ago.

There is general agreement that the complexities of modern goods and services and the economic system are not adequately explained by Adam Smith's theories. Economists debate, however, whether his powerful insights into the working of the market mechanism are as useful today as they were two hundred years ago.

14-4 DISSENTING OPINIONS

The preceding chapters have presented the orthodox view of how the economy works. Clearly we did not suppose for one minute that the actual economy was composed of purely competitive industries. We examined production activities under the assumption of purely competitive surroundings in Chapter 5 for two reasons — first, to develop certain general principles that carry over to other market structures; and second, to develop a *model of allocative efficiency*, which we were able to use as a standard to judge market efficiencies of more commonplace market structures. Almost all our time has been spent in examining markets with varying degrees of monopoly power and studying the influence of government market intervention of one sort or another on the determination of prices, output and social welfare.

Now, however, we wish to examine the positions taken by a number of critics of this orthodox view of microeconomics. In some cases, these different views, although qualifying our results somewhat, do not affect the basic conclusions concerning the operation of the market system. However, some of the more radical views stand in sharp contrast to what we have said so far and they have serious implications for analysis. We begin by examining the milder views opposing orthodox analysis and then proceed to discuss the more radical opinions.

Ownership, Management and Modern Objectives

One basic assumption used in our previous analysis, and one traced back to Adam Smith, is that

people are motivated in their economic actions primarily by a desire to promote their own self-interest. Consumers wish to allocate their incomes in such a manner as to maximize their satisfaction through consumption. Firms are assumed to serve the interests of their owners by attempting to maximize shareholder wealth (or profits). Of course, everyone makes mistakes, and so consumers and firms do not always achieve these goals. But the attempt is the important thing.

This is an area of some disagreement, in particular with respect to the objectives of the firm. Some people argue that the organization of production activities for the most part in large corporate concerns has led to a distinct separation of ownership from management. As a result, these critics contend, managers will be able to pursue their own objectives as distinct from those of the owners. In order to develop this argument in greater detail, let us briefly outline the type of organizational structure found in large modern-day corporations.

Corporate Structure

A large corporation may have hundreds of thousands of owners, or shareholders — each of whom owns in a general way a piece of the company. Part ownership of a corporation is represented by common share certificates. If a company has 20 000 common shares outstanding, the owner of each share is entitled to a 1/20 000 share in the company's profits. Further, if the company is sold in bankruptcy or otherwise, each share would entitle the owner to a 1/20 000 portion of the proceeds from the sale after all creditors have been paid. If a corporation decides that some of the year's profits should be given back to the shareholders, a dividend is declared. If the total dividends to be declared in a particular year are $20 000, then this would be $1 per share.

In addition to entitlement to a proportionate share of the company's profits, each share gives an owner the right to vote for members to the company's board of directors as well as on a selected number of important matters (for example, a proposal to merge with another company). The board of directors is supposed to be the *link* between the shareholders and the company's management body. The board of directors decides on major policy matters, though not on day-to-day operations, and they are the shareholders' representa-

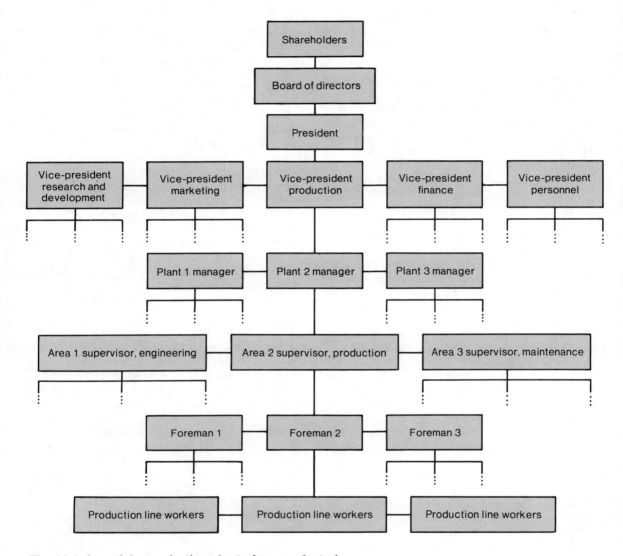

Fig. 14-1 A partial organization chart of a manufacturing company

A typical organization structure of a large manufacturing corporation. The board of directors represents shareholders and makes decisions on the most important policy matters. All other decisions are made by management, responsible to the president.

tives within the company. The board of directors is designed to protect and foster the interests of the shareholders in the pursuit of profits.

A partial organization chart in Figure 14-1 illustrates the typical sort of management setup for a large fictitious manufacturing company.

Authority and power flow from the top down,

though information flow is two-way. For instance, a decision on whether to build a new multimillion dollar plant may have to be authorized by a formal board of directors vote, but the information on costs and demand estimates will come up through the organization from the engineering, marketing and finance departments. Again, the board of directors decides on only the most important company matters involving large sums of money or significant changes in operating policy. Day-to-day operations of the company are carried on by the various department vice-presidents and other executives below the board. The senior officers within each department are responsible to the president, who is in turn responsible to the board.

A large part of a manager's job consists of co-ordinating the activities of those on a lower level who are engaged in carrying out their own specialized tasks. We may examine the organization from the production department upward. The men and women on the production line receive their day-to-day instructions from the foreman who coordinates their activities. In a large plant, there may be many subunits under one foreman. A group of foremen may be coordinated by a supervisor, the supervisors in turn by the plant manager, the plant managers (if there is more than one plant) by the vice-president of production. Just as each worker knows most about an individual specialized task and very little in comparison about those of other workers performing different functions, the same is true within levels of management. The vice-president of marketing knows most about marketing and the functioning of the marketing department but usually very little (in comparison) about the production department, personnel department and so on. To achieve the productivity gains sought from a division of labour, the marketing vice-president is expected to devote every effort to the marketing department and let the other vice-presidents do likewise. The president coordinates the separate activities of the vice-presidents toward the achievement of corporate objectives.

Shareholder Influence

In the typical modern-day large corporation, there is a certain degree of separation between ownership and management. Certainly, there is physical separation in that most shareholders are not involved in management and day-to-day control of the firm (though those on the board of directors and other chief executive personnel may be substantial shareholders). Further, it is usual that no one shareholder owns a significant number of shares relative to the total amount outstanding. As a result, each shareholder may have negligible direct control over the board of directors. This is not unlike the situation we as individual voters find ourselves in

when we elect our Members of Parliament. If we do not like the actions of our parliamentary representatives, we can suffer in the meantime and vote against them at the next election. Similarly, if actions of management do not meet with shareholders' approval, the shareholders may vote for different directors at the next annual general meeting. Finally, if shareholders do not get satisfaction they may sell their stocks. This latter remedy is not as readily available to the voter, though a similar end might be achieved by leaving the country.

Separation between ownership and management has led some people to argue that the management of a corporation, in attempting to seek its own self-interest, may be able to disregard the interests of the shareholder group — or, if not disregard the shareholders' interests entirely, at least subordinate them to its own. These people suggest that management may attempt to use the corporation as a vehicle for the attainment of the following sorts of goals: income and material fringe benefits, power, prestige and corporate growth. Because of the weak link between a widely dispersed shareholder group and corporate management, there may be little regard for profit maximization.

If the modern corporation really does attempt to maximize shareholder wealth, as we saw in Chapter 8, this implies the maximization of average annual profits for the long run — or, more briefly, the *maximization of long-run profit*. Consequently, when we compare alternative modes of management behaviour to profit maximization the latter term always refers to long-run profit maximization.[5]

In this section we do not discuss how the firm might seek to maximize its profit, but instead whether or not it does seek to maximize profit. This distinction is important. For example, as we explained in Chapter 6, there is more than one way to focus on profit maximization.

Detailed demand and cost measurement is now becoming more and more feasible for larger firms. Such measurements make it possible to apply analysis employing comparisons of long-run marginal revenue and long-run marginal cost in attempting to choose price, advertising and quality levels that

---

5. Recall that in the long run the firm is assumed to have enough time to be able to adjust all of its inputs for the production of any particular output level. This is in contrast to the short run when the firm is restricted, for example, to operate within a given physical plant size.

will maximize profits. Of course, a large portion of the data is based on estimates of future demand and is difficult to measure accurately. Hence, there will be decision errors. However, the process is nevertheless an attempt to maximize profit.

In another instance, a firm may seek to maximize its long-run profit by market experimentation with products of different quality, as well as with different levels of advertising expenditure. Such a firm may also attempt to set its prices by choosing the best markup on some cost measure — say, unit labour or average total costs. But again, as we argued in Chapter 6, there is likely only one best (maximum profit) mix of price, advertising and product quality, and therefore this latter approach is roughly equivalent to searching for that mix on a marginal cost-marginal revenue basis. The resulting configuration of such things as market price, output, advertising level and product quality under all profit-maximizing approaches is likely to be the same. Therefore, the implications for social welfare stemming from market actions are similar under all approaches to long-run profit maximization.

In this section, instead of examining various possible techniques firms might use to approximate profit maximization, we discuss whether or not firms do attempt to maximize profit in the first place.

Management Objectives and Behaviour

Those who argue that the modern large corporation does not attempt to maximize profit usually admit that even with such wide dispersion of ownership, for a corporation to continue to exist it cannot afford to neglect profitability completely. It must at least earn a *normal rate of return* on invested funds. If it does not meet this minimal profitability criterion, demand for the company's shares will drop, until eventually the market price of the corporation (as evidenced by the price per share multiplied by the number of common shares outstanding) falls significantly below the net receipts that could be realized from selling off the company's assets and paying off all debts. In such a case, it will pay an outside group to buy up all the corporate shares and liquidate the firm.

If the nonprofit maximization thesis is to be true for a particular corporation, this firm must possess some degree of monopoly power and there must exist certain barriers preventing the establishment of new firms. If, for instance, there are no barriers to entry, any potential for above normal rates of return on investment (that is, economic profits) will attract investors into the industry until this potential is eliminated. At that time, if a particular firm's management is not maximizing profits, it will be earning less than a normal rate of return on shareholders' funds. The price of its common stock will fall, and its relaxation of profit-maximizing behaviour again will threaten its very existence.

Even if the corporation has some entrenched monopoly power and there is a significant separation between shareholders and management, the corporation must at least earn normal accounting profits for its shareholders. However, within this constraint, does modern-day corporate management have some options available? Let us examine this question further.

Figure 14-2 assumes that a particular corporation has some monopoly power (reflected in the downward sloping demand curve). Remember also that economists define average cost so that when the firm just covers its cost, a normal rate of return is earned on invested funds. If the corporation operates purely in the long-run interests of the shareholders, it would produce Q_1 units at a market price of P_1. On each unit sold it would earn an economic profit of $P_1 - LAC_1$; on its output of Q_1, it would earn a total economic profit of the shaded area $((P_1 - LAC_1) \times Q_1)$.

Now suppose instead that the corporate managers want to increase their own salaries, vacations or convention activities, have plush offices and executive dining rooms or chauffeur driven limousines. They might eat up this potential economic profit by pursuing such activities, which they perceive as being more in line with their own self-interest than profit maximizing. Or instead, since to maximize profits requires close attention to costs and demand, and involves considerable effort and possibly risk taking, corporate management may decide, once normal profits are earned, to relax the drive for still higher profits and spend more time on the golf course.

Some people have argued that corporate management goals of power, prestige and monetary reward are closely associated with organizational size, and therefore, that a primary objective of

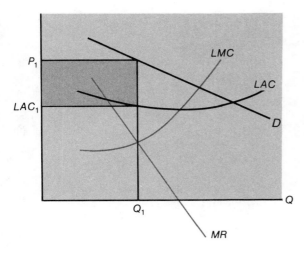

Fig. 14-2 Managing the firm and the shareholders' interests

If the objective of management is profit maximization, quantity Q_1 should be produced and price P_1 should be charged. The shaded area is the maximum profit possible with the given cost structure and demand conditions.

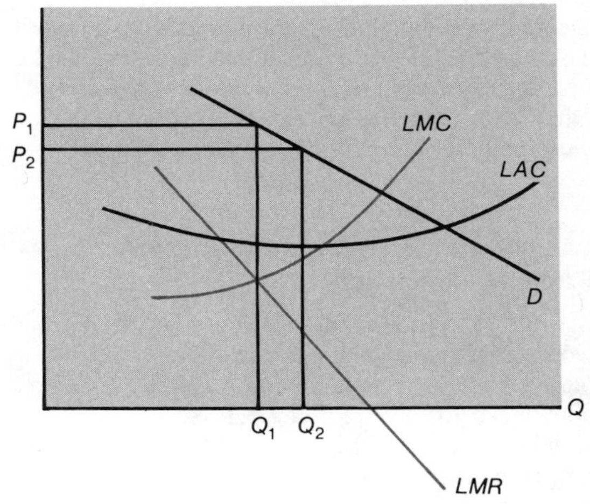

Fig. 14-3 Directing the firm toward management goals

If the objective of management is expansion of the size of the firm, quantity $Q_2 > Q_1$ will be produced and price $P_2 < P_1$ charged. The resulting profit is less than the maximum possible.

modern management is growth of the firm's sales volume. There is usually more power and prestige associated with being the manager of a large corporation than of a small one, and asset and personnel growth come on the heels of sales growth. Further, it is easier to climb the organizational ladder through internal promotion if the organization itself is growing quickly. Large organizations need more department heads and more vice-presidents than do smaller ones. This *organization-theory argument*, shown in Figure 14-3, may be contrasted with that of profit maximization.

Again the profit-maximizing output and price are Q_1 and P_1 respectively. If management pursues the objectives of power and prestige through corporate size, it may, however, operate at a greater output level than that necessary for profit maximization — for example, at Q_2. It is able to produce

at Q_2 and still earn an above normal rate of return for the shareholders (since $P_2 > LAC$).[6]

The foregoing theories may also be combined. For example, one might hold that corporate managers attempt to achieve their own self-interest, which is only consistent with that of the shareholders until enough accounting profit has been earned to provide a normal rate of return on invested funds. Earning a normal rate of return guarantees that share prices will not deteriorate and ultimately lead to a selling of corporate assets. Once

---

6. William J. Baumol advanced the hypothesis that large corporations may, in fact, attempt to maximize sales revenue, subject to the constraint that they at least earn a normal rate of return on investment (which would occur in Fig. 14-3 at the output level for which $LMR = 0$). Some people have argued that it seems more reasonable that management power and prestige would be connected with sales *volume* rather than sales revenue.

the management's continued existence has been secured by earning normal profits, it is then free to ease up on the drive to higher profits and pursue its own goals, including higher monetary incomes, other fringe benefits, power and prestige. Some of these may be linked to higher sales volume.

Welfare and Objectives other than Profit Maximization

In order to examine efficiency costs to society that would result from such corporate behaviour as that outlined above, let us again compare the results with those for a purely competitive economy (in which, remember, firms are forced to maximize profits in order to earn just a normal rate of return). Rather than treat each possible alternative type of management behaviour in turn, we will instead consider a combination of those considered above.

Suppose, for example, a purely competitive industry is monopolized overnight. Further, instead of continuing to act as profit maximizers, the managers decide to pursue their own objectives by (i) easing up on the drive for profits, (ii) increasing their own salaries and fringe benefits and (iii) striving for greater power and prestige by operating at a larger sales volume than that required for maximum profits.

With reference to Figure 14-4, the purely competitive industry would produce Q_1 units at the minimum possible unit cost. The price charged (P_1) would just cover costs, which include a normal return on the shareholders' investment. The management of the monopolized industry, acting in its own interests as argued above, would operate with higher unit costs (LAC' and LMC') as a result of the higher management salaries and fringe benefits, and at a higher sales volume than that required for profit maximization (say, Q_2 rather than Q_3). We have also depicted a situation in which the corporation is earning an above normal rate of return for its shareholders (since $P_2 > LAC'$), though the preceding arguments hold that this might not always be the case.

The efficiency implications of this sort of management controlled monopoly power are the following. For any particular volume produced, the costs of production would be greater than those experienced under pure competition. The source of

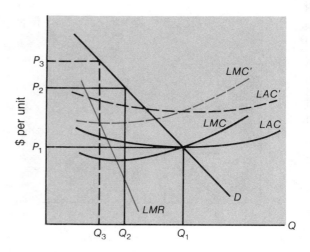

Fig. 14-4 A management-controlled monopoly

When a purely competitive industry is monopolized, the quantity produced is reduced below the original level Q_1 and price is raised above the original level P_1. If the managers of the monopoly firms pursue their own objectives, per unit costs increase and the output and price decided upon (Q_2 and P_2) differ from the profit-maximizing output and price (Q_3 and P_3).

these increased costs would be the higher management salaries, plush offices, other fringe benefits and reduced scrutiny with regard to cost control. As compared with a purely competitive industry, output would lower. At the level produced, the extra value of additional output to society (as reflected by the market price (P_2)) would exceed the extra *necessary* cost to society of resources used up in the goods' production (LMC at Q_2). This is evidence of a welfare loss to society as a whole. Additional evidence of a poor allocation of resources from such industrial behaviour is the fact (in this example) that above normal profit is being earned in this industry that should ordinarily attract investment of additional capital (that is, the construction of new physical facilities for production). This, however, is presumably being prevented by various barriers to entry.

Impact on Distribution of Welfare

If we do not differentiate between shareholders, managers or consumers, we may argue, as we have done earlier, that monopoly power creates welfare losses for society at large. Not all groups in society lose from monopoly power, however. In a profit-maximizing industry with monopoly power, shareholders are wealthier than they otherwise would be (or, saying it another way, they earn higher annual profits than they would if the industry was purely competitive).[7]

Managers are not better off than they would be in a purely competitive industry. If profits are really maximized, costs are minimized. That fact, in turn, means that managers must not be paid any more than normal total compensation (that is, what they could earn elsewhere) for their efforts. As a result, in a profit-maximizing industry with monopoly power, not only is total welfare reduced, but also welfare is transferred from consumers to shareholders.

On the other hand, in an economy made up of industries with monopoly power and controlled by managers following some sort of satisficing behaviour patterns, again total economic welfare would be reduced (as compared with that of pure competition), but in this case the management group would become better off. If the managers do a little better, in terms of profit, than earning a normal rate of return, the shareholders may also benefit. But if profit is not maximized, the shareholders will not benefit as much as they might have if managerial behaviour was geared solely to profits. As far as the consumers are concerned, they may be better or worse off than in a monopolized industry where profits are maximized. If output exceeds that required for profit maximization — which many argue would happen if certain management interests are connected with organization size — then consumers will pay a lower price for their products than they would in a profit-maximizing industry with monopoly power (though they will still be paying higher prices than they would in a purely competitive industry).

Industries with monopoly power tend to create net welfare losses for society as a whole, regardless of whether the management of such firms seeks to maximize profits or pursue its own self-interest. If profits are maximized, shareholders become better off at the expense of consumers; management is unaffected. On the other hand, if management objectives are pursued rather than maximum profits, part of the consumers' loss becomes managements' gain. The shareholders may or may not be better off than in a purely competitive industry but certainly they are worse off than if the industry was maximizing profits.

The Manager-Controlled Industry

The important qualifications we placed on our welfare analysis earlier in comparing monopoly power with pure competition under profit-maximizing assumptions (Chapters 6, 7 and 9) hold here as well. Everything else being equal, firms pursuing management objectives impose a welfare cost on society as a whole. But is *everything else equal* in practice? Is it not possible that technological developments occur more rapidly within corporations with monopoly power than in purely competitive firms because the economic profits that can result from such developments will not be so easily eroded by new entrants into the industry? It certainly is possible, though not necessarily true. If it is true, though, the cost reductions from such advancements may be enough not only to provide economic profits to shareholders and excess returns to management (if the firm is not profit maximizing) but also to allow lower prices for consumers, in which case there would be a net welfare gain to society (since all groups are better off) as opposed to pure competition. Figure 14-5 illustrates this possibility.

The figure supposes that the management incentive to search for technologically advanced production methods, enabling management to have higher salaries, fringe benefits and organizational growth, has led in the long run to a lower cost structure (LAC' and LMC') than in a purely competitive industry (with costs of LAC and LMC). The firm is assumed to choose a production level of Q_2, which is beyond the profit-maximizing level but still yields an above normal rate of return for the share-

---

7. This excludes the case of monopolistically competitive industries, remember, which are not protected by high barriers to entry.

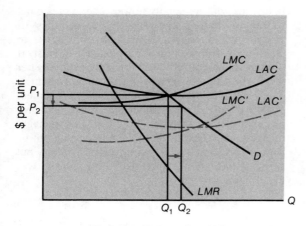

$ per unit

P_1
P_2

LMC
LAC
LMC' LAC'
D
LMR
Q_1 Q_2
Q

Fig. 14-5 Possible gains from manager-controlled monopolies

If a purely competitive industry is monopolized, it is possible that technological change implemented by the monopoly reduces per unit costs from *LAC* to *LAC'*. The management of the monopoly may then choose to produce quantity Q_2 which is larger than the competitive level and charge price P_2 which is lower than the competitive level.

holders ($P_2 > LAC'$). Further, with market prices lower than under pure competition ($P_2 < P_1$), consumers are better off.

There is an ongoing debate among economists about the relevance of this potentially important qualification.

Policy Implications

In the case of monopoly-power firms controlled on behalf of management oriented objectives, the potential welfare cost to society in terms of economic efficiency is similar to that of such firms geared toward profit maximization. The implication for government policy action, therefore, would also be similar. The objective should be to move the industry's output structure closer to the purely competitive level. This might imply stimulating competition by removing some of the bar-

riers to entry, by government regulation or even by nationalization. Again, though, the foregoing qualification and the bureaucratic cost of such government intervention must be recognized and explicitly taken into account before such action is undertaken. In certain instances, all things considered, it may be that society is deemed better off with the private monopoly situation.

Analysis of Market Shocks

The basic analysis of market shocks remains intact even if the above modifications to firm behaviour are correct. For example, let us consider the instance of a firm that has a certain amount of monopoly power and in which the separation of ownership from management enables some relaxation of profit maximization in favour of management goals.

(i) Demand Shock

Figure 14-6 illustrates the effect of a demand shock resulting for example from a change in tastes, income or population, and compares the reactions of a management-goal-oriented satisficing firm with those of a profit maximizer. Here, we take the example of a firm's management achieving its own goals by expanding to as large an organization as possible, subject only to earning at least a normal rate of return for its shareholders.

Initially, then, in Figure 14-6a the firm would produce at Q_1 and charge a price of P_1. As demand increases to D', output would expand to Q_2 and prices would rise — as would also be the case for a profit-maximizing firm under normal monopoly conditions (and oligopoly conditions too, if the demand increase is large enough — see Chapter 7). For all cases, a simple shorthand supply-demand diagram (Figure 14-6b) correctly depicts the market reaction tendencies.

(ii) Supply Shock

Figure 14-7 illustrates an adverse supply shock brought about, say, by an increase in wage rates. Again we assume the firm is managed with the objective of earning only a normal rate of return on investment and then eating up what would other-

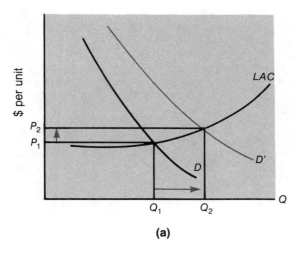
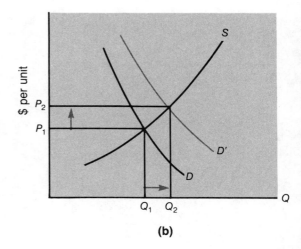

Fig. 14-6 An increase in demand

(a) As the demand curve shifts to the right, management satisfied with making only normal profit expands output from Q_1 to Q_2 and raises price from P_1 to P_2.

(b) The nature of the impact of an increase in demand can also be illustrated with a supply-demand diagram, although the magnitudes of the changes may not be precisely represented.

wise be profit by allowing unit costs to be higher than otherwise and also by operating as large an organization as possible consistent with the other two objectives. The firm would initially produce at Q_1 (in Figure 14-7a) and charge a price of P_1. An adverse cost shock would lead the firm to produce less output (Q_2) at a higher price level (P_2). Again this is the same effect that would impinge on a profit-maximizing monopolist or oligopolist (if the rise in costs were large enough). Again a simple supply-demand diagram (Figure 14-7b) captures the essence of the market reactions — that is, higher costs generally lead to higher market prices and less output.

Management objective of technological achievement may lower costs and prices in a monopoly below competitive levels and improve customer welfare. Management satisfied with the objective of making only normal profit reacts to demand and supply shocks in a manner consistent with the predictions of the supply-demand model.

14-5 THE GALBRAITHIAN VIEW

John Kenneth Galbraith, in his book *The New Industrial State*, proposed yet another theory of modern corporate management. He believes that his ideas have far-reaching implications.[8]

Galbraith says that the economy is for the most part composed of large corporations with varying degrees of monopoly power and that atomistic competition is virtually extinct. There is reasonably widespread agreement on this point. Further, Galbraith agrees with many who stress that the separation of ownership from management in large corporate enterprises may allow such management to pursue nonprofit-motivated self-interest. However, Galbraith takes this argument to a greater extreme than most others would.

8. John Kenneth Galbraith, *The New Industrial State*, 2nd edition (Boston: Houghton Mifflin Company, 1971). Copyright © 1967, 1971 by John Kenneth Galbraith. The following excerpts are reprinted by permission of the publisher, Houghton Mifflin Company.

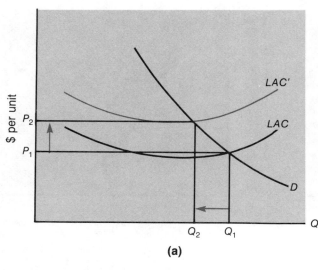

(a)

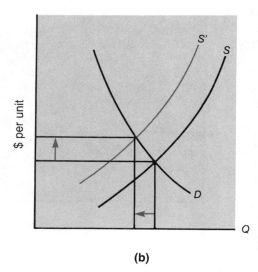

(b)

Fig. 14-7 An increase in costs

(a) As the cost curve shifts upward, management satisfied with making only normal profit reduces output from Q_1 to Q_2 and raises price from P_1 to P_2.

(b) The nature of the impact of an increase in costs can also be illustrated with a supply-demand diagram, although the magnitudes of the changes may not be precisely represented.

Technology and the Technostructure

Galbraith states that the root driving force of industrial behaviour is changing technology — *the imperatives of technology* as he calls them. The efficiency of modern-day firms has been achieved by extreme division of labour and the application of machines to simplified repetitive tasks. In order to take full advantage of those divisions of labour, large companies have sprung up. In particular, Galbraith mentions several specific ways in which technological advancements cause a need for large organizations:

(1) increased time is necessary between the beginning and completion of production

(2) large amounts of investment in physical facilities are necessary

(3) decision making becomes inflexible

(4) technology requires specialized workers

(5) there arises a greater need for organization and coordination of separate tasks

(6) there develops a need for planning.

Not all of the above reasons are independent of each other. For example, reasons (1), (2) and (3) help to explain (5) and (6). Galbraith goes on to point out that because the efficiencies available from advancing technology have given rise to large firms, this has led to monopoly power as well as to the need for long-range planning.

In meeting the first five imperatives of technology, the sixth is most important. Since there are long time spans between the initiation of production plans and the marketing of the finished product (he gives as an example the production of each new model of automobile, which may take several years from design stage to assembly line), as well as the requirement for large investment, the hiring and training of specialized workers, and an inflexibility of decisions once taken, careful planning is required to have decisions yield desirable results. This necessity for planning has led to the development of a sophisticated group of technical-managerial personnel, which Galbraith refers to as the **technostructure**.

> It embraces all who bring specialized knowledge, talent or experience to group decision-making. This, not the management, is the guiding intelligence — the brain — of the enterprise. . . . I propose to call this organization the Technostructure.[9]

Because the modern corporation has grown to possess significant amounts of monopoly power, Galbraith argues, the technostructure makes decisions in pursuit of its own self-interest. Though its general security requires that it earn a normal rate of return on shareholder investment, this constraint is easily met within these monopoly-type structures. Beyond this, the technostructure is able to satisfy its own wishes for greater identification, adaptation, security and prestige.

Persuasive Advertising

Not only can the technostructure satisfy its own needs via the corporate vehicle, but also it has little difficulty in doing this, Galbraith contends, because it controls inputs to the corporation, the price of the product, and the volume sold. The prime instrument the firm has for this control, according to Galbraith, is *advertising*. Through advertising, the firm is always able to persuade consumers to buy its products at the prices it establishes, so that it will cover its costs (including all benefits accruing to the technostructure) and provide the shareholder with a minimum satisfactory rate of return. Further, advertising convinces people that consumption is the way to happiness. Through persuasive advertising, the technostructure encourages the population to strive for a lifestyle, that involves long hard hours of work for enough income to purchase the goods and services that it has been led to believe provide happiness.

The purpose of demand management is to insure that people buy what is produced — that plans for the amounts to be sold at the controlled prices are fulfilled in practice. . . .

In the absence of the massive and artful persuasion that accompanies the management of demand, increasing abundance might well have reduced the interest in acquiring more goods. They would not have felt the need for multiplying the artifacts — autos, appliances, detergents, cosmetics — by which they were surrounded. No one would have pressed upon them the advantages of new packages, new forms of processed foods, newly devised dentifrices, new painkillers or other new variants of older products. Being not pressed by the need for these things, they would have spent less reliably of their income and worked less reliably to get more.[10]

Welfare and Market Shocks

Because Galbraith offers no explanation for the determination of prices and output, we are not able to compare the economic efficiency implications that would stem from his *technostructure*-driven firms with those following profit maximization. Further, the Galbraithian model offers no prediction as to the effect on market behaviour, prices or output of demand and supply shocks.

Policy Implications

Galbraith argues that encouraging greater competition will not work as a policy device since the imperatives of technology force the establishment of large-scale quasi-monopolistic structures. His policy recommendations are that the intellectuals of the community, especially the academics and scientists, should through the universities and colleges — which supply the human resources for the corporate technostructure — seek to alter the tastes and preferences of the technostructure toward more aesthetic things in life. Further, the intellectuals should also attempt to influence government to move society's lifestyles in a more preferred direction.

---

9. Ibid., p. 71.

10. Ibid., p. 204 and p. 210.

Friedman on Galbraith[11]

Milton Friedman has argued strongly against the propositions of John Kenneth Galbraith. Friedman asserts that Galbraith's views, apart from having little or no support from other economists, also have no empirical validity. Of Galbraith's contention that large firms cause the most technological development, Friedman says this is simply not true and quotes various studies on the matter. Of Galbraith's view that corporations manipulate people's tastes, Friedman argues that economic analysis has demonstrated first that a considerable portion of all advertising is informative rather than persuasive, and second that the most sensible thing for a corporation to do is to find out the nature of people's tastes and then try to satisfy rather than manipulate them.

Friedman also refers to studies that refute Galbraith's hypothesis that technocratically controlled large corporations tend to sacrifice profits for other goals. In short, Friedman states,

I know of no scientific studies which have validated that [Galbraith's] view of the world is meaningful and accurate in the sense that it yields predictions about the behaviour of enterprises, of industry, or of the economy as a whole that can be checked, tested against evidence, and found to hold.[12]

Friedman appears most upset concerning the philosophy of Galbraith's policy proposals. Friedman argues,

. . . Galbraith's Tory Radical position implies that the values of the masses are inferior to those of the intellectual aristocracy, and that, of course, is the theme that runs throughout his analysis. But, moreover, if the values of the masses are created by self-interested advocates in industry, then they have no claim to be considered as valid, or to be respected. Thus in order for Galbraith to strengthen his emphasis on the right of the aristocracy to shape the values of the masses, it is extremely convenient to be able to treat those values as having no validity but simply as the creation of self-interested advocates. . . .

Many reformers — Galbraith is not alone in this — have as their basic objection to a free market that it frustrates them in achieving their reforms, because it enables people to have what they want, not what the reformers want.[13]

11. This is part of the title of a book by Milton Friedman, *Friedman on Galbraith and on Curing the British Disease* (Vancouver: The Fraser Institute, 1977).

12. Ibid., p. 29.

13. Ibid., p. 32.

Galbraith's critique of the modern capitalist economy derives from the notion that the corporate technostructure manipulates consumer tastes by means of advertising so as to advance its own objectives. Large corporations are for the most part exempt from pressures of the market discipline. The countervailing power of the state, including economic planning, is needed to protect the stability of the system.

14-6 MARXIAN ECONOMICS

Karl Marx lived from 1818 to 1883. His most famous work was *Das Kapital* (Capital). The book is in three volumes, the first having been published in 1867 and the last, with the help of Friedrich Engels, in 1894. The marxist viewpoint is important today because of its profound influence on socialist and communist doctrines.

Marx argued that capitalism (private ownership of the means of production) and the ownership of private property in general are evil in that they lead to the *exploitation* of the great mass of humanity, the working class or the **proletariat**, by the owners of capital, the **bourgeoisie**.

Labour Theory of Value

A critical part of *Das Kapital* is Marx's discussion of the **labour theory of value** and so-called **surplus value** or profit. Marx argued that labour was the ultimate source of all production. There is no disagreement on this point. Even though much production activity today is carried on with the most sophisticated type of equipment, labour is the original source of all machinery. That is to say, humans made the first crude implements by hand and then used these to make more sophisticated machines and so on. The same is true of materials that become part of the production process for some particular finished good or service. We may therefore think of machinery and materials as embodying a certain amount of labour effort.

Let us now illustrate Marx's theory of value and his notion of surplus value by means of a numerical example dealing with the production of manufactured (spun) cotton yarn (to follow Marx's lead).

For simplicity, suppose it requires a negligible amount of machinery and materials to grow and harvest raw cotton. Further, suppose it takes two hours of labour to produce enough raw cotton for one unit of yarn. In addition to the production of

Fig. 14-8 The production costs of one unit of cotton yarn

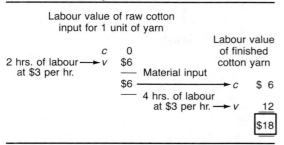

The production of cotton (left column) is assumed to require no capital or material input; that is, the amount of constant capital is zero and the value of labour embodied in it is $6. Production of 1 unit of yarn requires $6 worth of cotton raw material; that is, the amount of constant capital is $6. After $12 worth of labour input (variable capital) is added, the total value of labour embodied in 1 unit of cotton yarn is $18.

Fig. 14-9 Manufacturing costs and labour compensation under the labour theory of value

	Labour value		Labour compensation
c materials	$ 6	(2 hrs. of embodied labour)	$ 6
v labour	12	(4 hrs. of labour)	12
	$18		$18

If cotton and yarn were sold at prices identical to the value of labour embodied in them, no profit would be made.

cotton, spinning one unit of yarn requires four hours of labour. Labour is paid $3 per hour. This information is summarized in Figure 14-8 in which we have also used Marx's shorthand symbols.

The symbols *c* and *v* represent, in Marx's terms, **constant capital** and **variable capital** respectively. Constant capital is the amount of labour (or value of labour) embodied in any machinery or materials used in the production process, whereas variable capital refers to the amount of labour used up directly in the production process.

Marx held that a product is worth exactly the value of labour required in its production — no more, no less. This is the essence of the labour theory of value. According to this principle, then, the raw cotton should sell for $6 and the finished cotton yarn for $18. Using these numbers, we have constructed a cost statement for one unit of manufactured yarn based on the labour theory of value. See Figure 14-9.

If cotton and yarn sold on the basis of the labour theory of value at $6 and $18 per unit respectively, the pricing would provide absolutely no compensation to capitalists for their invested funds. Marx believed this situation would be just. In this instance, of course, the capitalists would not be inclined to

invest their capital funds in productive facilities.

Of course, as Marx pointed out (and as Adam Smith saw a century earlier), the free market for cotton and yarn would generally yield prices that would provide capitalists with some positive return on invested funds — that is, market prices in excess of those warranted under the labour theory of value. Marx referred to this excess as *surplus value*.

Where does the surplus value come from? At the core of Marx's model is the notion that labour is a very special factor of production. When a worker takes a job at the going market wage, he or she generates output of greater value than what the capitalist paid him or her in the form of wages. This excess is called surplus value and shows that workers who have no capital of their own are "exploited" by the capitalists who hire them. All other factors of production (land, machinery, material, energy, etc.) enter the value of the product at their acquisition cost and thus generate no surplus value.

Continuing with our numerical example, suppose that both raw cotton and yarn sold for 50% over materials and labour cost. This information is represented in Figure 14-10. In this case, the yarn's market value exceeds labour's total compensation

Fig. 14-10 Product value and labour compensation under market pricing

	Market value		Labour compensation
	Cotton	Yarn	
c materials	$0		
v labour	6		$ 6
s profit	3		
	$9 → c materials	$ 9	
	v labour	12	12
	s profit	10.50	
		$31.50	$18

Both cotton and yarn are sold at market prices above the value of labour embodied in them. The difference is profit and its sole source is surplus value generated by labour.

by $13.50 (that is, $31.50 − $18), which comprises $10.50 surplus value from yarn manufacturing and $3 surplus value from the growing of raw cotton.

Marx took surplus value to be evidence of *labour exploitation*. He held that because capitalists require such surplus value in order to produce at all, the capitalist mode was inherently exploitive.

Labour Exploitation

If the market value of manufactured yarn was equal to its labour value, that is, $18, to Marx this would have meant that labour was getting full compensation for its efforts. Labour's $18 income would be just sufficient to allow it to buy all the output that its work produced. In other words, labour's 6 hours of effort would have been compensated in real terms by 6 hours worth of produced goods. On the other hand, with a market price for yarn at $31.50 it would require labour to work 10½ hours ($31.50 ÷ $3 per hour) in order to buy the same amount of yarn that only took 6 labour hours to produce. In this instance, out of every 10½ hour day of work, 6 hours worth of

production would be paid to labour and 4½ hours of production would be received by the owners of capital. The 4½ hours of production (or $4\frac{1}{2} \times \$3 = \$13.50$ worth) represent the surplus value or profit to which, according to Marx, the capitalist was not entitled. Marx called the ratio $\frac{s}{v}$ the rate of surplus value and referred to the ratio $\frac{s}{c + v}$ as the rate of profit.

Marx measured the **degree of labour exploitation** not by the profit rate but by the rate of surplus value. In our example here, for cotton growing and yarn manufacturing industries combined, $\frac{s}{v} = 75\%$ (that is, $13.50/$18) and indicates that workers would have to work 75% longer than the labour time it takes to produce a unit of yarn in order to be able to buy a unit of yarn.

Marxian Dynamics and Capitalism's Contradictions

Since Marx equated profit (or surplus value) with labour exploitation, he saw the capitalists' drive for greater and greater profits as one for greater and greater labour exploitation. This problem is at the heart of Marx's view of *alienation* and conflict between the "bourgeois capitalists" and the "proletariat" (workers). Eventually this conflict, Marx believed, would lead to a final overthrow of the capitalist system by the workers. On the way to the final day of revolution, the capitalist system was doomed to experience a series of ever worsening *crises* — or what we might now call **business cycles**. These crises, Marx predicted, would arise out of the inherent contradictions of the capitalist *mode of production* (system). Let us examine this viewpoint briefly.

Figure 14-11 roughly outlines Marx's theory concerning capitalist development. The purpose of capitalist production is to earn a profit, or to earn surplus value — that is, exploit labour. Attracted by rates of profit ($\frac{s}{c + v}$), the entry of new firms and the reinvestment of profits by existing firms would lead to an accumulation of capital and a greater degree of competition among capitalists in various types of production activities. This compe-

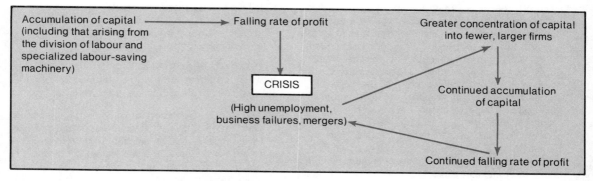

Fig. 14-11 Marx's theory of capitalist development

Competitive pressures force each capitalist to expand and invest in mechanized production. As a result, the rate of profit declines, causing periodic crises, exit of some firms, increased concentration of capital and crises at a growing scale.

tition would result in lower market prices for output and an erosion of surplus value. Further, the demand for labour would increase, thereby putting upward pressure on wage rates. Both of these events would reduce the rate of profit. To avoid these profit reductions, producers would seek to substitute labour-saving machinery and other forms of capital equipment for labour. If the degree of labour exploitation was unchanged, this substitution too would only cause further reductions in the rate of profit.

To show that an increase in capital relative to labour leads to a reduction in the rate of profit for a given degree of labour exploitation, we may rewrite the profit rate $\frac{s}{c+v}$ as $\frac{s/v}{c/v+1}$. For a given degree of labour exploitation (as measured by the rate of surplus value, s/v), the rate of profit varies inversely with the ratio $\frac{c}{v}$, which measures the extent to which "fixed capital" (materials and machinery) is used relative to "variable capital" (labour — what Marx called the **organic composition of capital**). As more fixed capital is used relative to labour (that is, as $\frac{c}{v}$ increases) for a given

degree of labour exploitation (that is, for a given $\frac{s}{v}$ value), the profit rate falls.

The falling profit rate will cause some producers in some industries to quit production altogether and will result in business failures, unemployment, and mergers of smaller weaker firms with larger ones. As the average rate of profit falls, the value of capital, as reflected in the stock market, will also fall. This is the nature of Marx's predicted crises. As a result of some producers going out of business entirely and the purchase of assets of weaker firms by larger ones, economic activity will tend to become concentrated in the hands of larger and larger firms. Further, the larger firms are the ones with greater ability to take advantage of division of labour and the introduction of more mechanized processes in order to raise their profit rates above the falling average rate and, consequently, to be able to keep their heads above water.

With the development of the capitalist mode of production, the rate of profit therefore falls, while its mass [total profit] increases with the growing mass of the employed capital. . . . Simultaneously with it grows the concentration. . . . This increasing concentration in its turn brings about a new fall in the rate of profit at a certain climax. The mass of the small divided capitals is thereby pushed into adventurous channels, speculation, fraudulent credit, fraudulent stocks, crises. . . . So long as everything goes well, competition effects a practical brotherhood of the capitalist class, as we have seen in the case of the average rate of profit, so that each shares in the common loot in proportion to the magnitude of his share of the investment. But as soon as it is no longer a question of sharing profit, but of sharing losses, everyone tries to reduce his own share to a minimum and load as much as possible upon the shoulders of some other competitor. However, the class must inevitably lose. . . .

The principal work of destruction would show its more dire effects in a slaughtering of the values of capitals. That portion of the value of capital which exists only in the form of claims of future shares of surplus value or profit, which consists in fact of creditors notes on production in its various forms [for example, common stocks], would immediately be depreciated by the reduction of the receipts on which it is calculated.[14]

With some cleanout of firms in the economy and a slowdown in the growth of capital or even a reduction in capital (some firms would not even replace worn-out equipment in the face of a falling profit rate), together with certain economy of scale improvements, which the now smaller number of larger firms may be able to make, there may be a reversal in the profit trend. Helping in this direction is the fact that the *reserve army of the unemployed* has been swelled and workers may be willing to accept lower wages.

At the same time still other agencies would have been at work. The stagnation of production would have laid off a part of the labouring class and thereby placed the employed part in a condition in which they would have to submit to a reduction of wages, even below the average. . . . On the other hand, the fall in prices and the competitive struggle would have given to every capitalist an impulse to raise the individual value of his total product above its average value by means of new machines, new and improved working methods, new combinations, which means, to increase the productive power of a certain quality of labour, to lower the proportion of the variable to the constant capital, and thereby to release some

labourers, in short, to create an artificial over-population. The depreciation of the elements of constant capital itself would be another factor tending to raise the rate of profit. . . .[15]

However, this series of events only leads to renewed capital accumulation and once more to a falling rate of profit and another crisis.

And in this way the cycle would be run once more. One portion of the capital which has been depreciated by the stagnation of its function would recover its old value. For the rest, the same vicious circle would be described once more under expanded conditions of production, in an expanded market, and with increased productive forces.[16]

Each successive crisis is likely to be more severe than the one preceding because the average size of firms is now larger as a result of producer combinations having taken place earlier. Eventually, Marx predicted, the crises would reach insurmountable proportions and finally result in a total collapse of the capitalist system.

In Marx's model, the capitalist is constantly pressured by competition to cut costs. One way of cutting costs is to mechanize production, that is, to substitute machines for workers. However, this means that the only source of surplus value (and thus profit) — the worker — is being squeezed out. As a result, the capitalist system will eventually run out of investment funds and will collapse. The successor system, socialism, is based on public ownership of *means of production* (capital). This change in ownership and the resulting changes in the class structure constitute, according to Marx, a remedy for the contradictions inherent in the capitalist system.

14-7 THE NEW LEFT

Just as one might agree with the basic principles of Adam Smith but differ on important details, so too one might be a socialist without agreeing fully with all the views of Karl Marx. Marxian ideas certainly have much to do with modern-day communism. There are some people, however, who believe that

---

14. Karl Marx, *Capital*, Vol. 3 (Chicago: Charles H. Kerr & Co., 1909), pp. 290–98.

15. Ibid., pp. 298–99.
16. Ibid., p. 299.

modern communist governments have not fulfilled the basic objectives of *Das Kapital*. One such group of radical economists regard themselves as part of the **New Left**.

The New Left sprang up as a political and social movement in the 1960s, originally over political struggles for civil rights and against the Vietnam War. In the 1970s, the New Left broadened to become a radical movement in opposition to what their members regard as imperialism, racism, sexism and other forms of social oppression.

The New Left regards those who equate social-ism with public or state ownership as the **Old Left**. For example, the New Left would point to the New Democratic Party (NDP) as reflecting the views of the Old Left in its desire to nationalize parts of the economy. Even now, of course, Canada is a mixed system of capitalism and state socialism as represented by various government-owned busi-nesses (Crown corporations) and production activi-ties flowing directly from government depart-ments, which in total account for up to 40% of the total economic activity. To the New Left, the present state-owned enterprises are not in the spirit of true Marxism.

> . . . state owned production sectors . . . tend to dif-fer only marginally, if at all, from the private sectors of the economy in as much as the state employs capitalist-oriented criteria in organizing its activities. These countries are examples of what we would call state capitalism.[17]

The New Left also rejects the centralized eco-nomic structures of the Soviet Union and other Eastern European countries.

> This system has resulted in a stratified, bureaucratic and hierarchical society in which the maximization of material goods production — subject to the constraint of preserving hierarchical control — is a primary ob-jective. Such a society might best be called state socialism.[18]

For the New Left, true socialism is more than a simple change in the legal relations of ownership.

Socialism means democratic, decentralized and par-ticipatory control for the individual: it means having a say in the decisions that affect one's life. Such a participatory form of socialism certainly requires equal access for all to material and cultural resources, which in turn requires the abolition of private owner-ship of capital and the redistribution of wealth.[19]

The capitalist market system, they argue, has certain inequities. First, private property conveys unequal benefits across the population. Those with large amounts of wealth, much of it inherited, have an unfair advantage over others. Further, private ownership of the means of production, whether on the basis of a sole proprietorship or of a shareholder in a large corporation, exploits the worker. The worker's labour is treated as a commodity sold just like any other commodity to the owners of the firm. This process in turn leads to worker alienation.

Finally, the New Left economists argue that a primary role of government in a capitalist system is as a *guarantor of a given set of property relations*. In other words, they argue that those in positions of wealth and power also have the most influence over government to uphold laws and existing institutional structures that maintain these privileged positions.

Policy Prescriptions

Because the New Left economists believe that pri-vate ownership and capitalism are the cause of the ills they identify in society — from worker, con-sumer and community alienation to racism, sex-ism, pollution and imperialism — they think the proper solution is to replace capitalism by a social-ist structured economy, but not a centralized state socialism. The New Left rejects Galbraith's notion that alienation stems essentially from the impera-tives of technology, but believe instead that it comes from centralized control.

The following statements outline what the New Left regards as the meaning of true socialism.

> . . . the aim of socialism is man. It is to create a form of production and an organization of society in which man can overcome alienation from his product, from his work, from his fellow man, from himself and from nature; in which he can return to himself and

17. R. C. Edwards, M. Reich and T. B. Weisskopf, *The Capitalist System* (Englewood Cliffs, New Jersey: Prentice-Hall, Inc., 1972), p. 4. The excerpts from p. 4 are reprinted by permission of Prentice-Hall, Inc.

18. Ibid., p. 4.

19. Ibid., p. 4.

grasp the world with his own powers, thus becoming one with the world.[20]

The ideal of "socialism" suggests an encompassing set of values: justice, equality, cooperation, democracy, freedom.[21]

As we said earlier, the New Left believes that a necessary condition for this type of socialism is the abolition of all privately held property. They perceive that small local communities of people with similar interests must form the basis for production. All production facilities should be owned jointly by all the people of the community.

These communities, it is thought, would form the basic unit for a nation of *regional commonwealths* where larger-scale decisions would be made on such matters as how much output should be devoted to consumption and how much to investment, how the population should be dispersed and how much should be allocated to prevent destruction of the environment.

Though they realize that such decentralization may cause some inefficiencies, they believe the benefits outweigh the costs.

Two Basic Disputes

Most proponents of socialism and capitalism find little disagreement on goals. Who would dispute the set of values quoted above — justice, equality, cooperation, democracy, freedom? The difference of opinion concerns the best means to obtain these ends. At the heart of the dispute are the questions of (i) private property rights and (ii) basic human nature.

(i) Property Rights

Many proponents of capitalism, including Friedman, argue that one of the duties of the government should be to decide on the meaning of property rights. The New Left argues for the abolition of private property rights. But, presumably this does not include such things as one's own bed or clothing. Well then, what about a car? A cot-

tage? The property around a house and cottage? A lake frontage? Somewhere an arbitrary line would have to be drawn. But where? This is a very difficult question for socialists.

In Marxian theory, of course, the distinction is drawn between "means of production," that is, capital, on the one hand, and consumer goods on the other. The former can be used to exploit others and thus should not be privately owned. The latter cannot become a means of exploitation. Their private ownership is therefore compatible with socialism.

The problem of property is also difficult for capitalists. Though we have settled it and allow people the privileges of their own private property — to pass most of it on to their children and to prevent others from enjoying it — the principle on which this tradition is based is difficult to enunciate and by no means an obvious truth, even to many capitalists. Early on in his *Capitalism and Freedom*, Friedman admits to the complexity of this issue.

> . . . what rights the ownership of property confers are complex social creations rather than self-evident propositions. Does my having title to land, for example, and my freedom to use my property as I wish, permit me to deny someone else the right to fly over my land in his airplane? Or does his right to use his airplane take precedence? Or does this depend on how high he flies? Or how much noise he makes? Does voluntary exchange require that he pay me for the privilege of flying over my land? Or that I must pay him to refrain from flying over it?[22]

Later on in his book, Friedman gives a very interesting example of how he believes property rights may arise in the case of four shipwrecked sailors finding themselves on four different islands. Three of the islands are very barren and the unlucky sailors must work very hard to barely keep alive. The fourth sailor, being either luckier or a better swimmer, finds himself on a larger and far more plentiful island, and is able to live quite well, presumably on abundant fruit and perhaps even small game. Suddenly, the three less fortunate sailors find out about each other and their compatriot

20. Ibid., p. 521. Quoted from Erich Fromm, *Marx's Concept of Man* (New York: Frederick Ungar, 1961, 1966). Reprinted by permission of Frederick Ungar Publishing Co.

21. Ibid., p. 524.

22. Milton Friedman, *Capitalism and Freedom* (Chicago: University of Chicago Press, 1962), p. 26. Reprinted by permission of The University of Chicago Press and the author.

on the larger island. The question is, should the three sailors be able to force the fourth sailor to share his success with them or does the fourth sailor have the right to keep them off his larger island?

Friedman argues that the fourth sailor has acquired *property rights* and should have the freedom to prevent the others from sharing in his good fortune. Socialists would certainly dispute this, and many others would as well. Numerous people who believe the market system confers many benefits on society are, nevertheless, in favour of redistribution of wealth and income, both nationally and internationally. This is an important moral question. Even Friedman himself appears somewhat uncomfortable about his position. He says,

> The fact that these [socialist] arguments against the so-called capitalist ethic are invalid does not of course demonstrate that the capitalist ethic is an acceptable one. I find it difficult to justify either accepting it or rejecting it, or to justify any alternative principle. I am led to the view that it cannot in and of itself be regarded as an ethical principle; that it must be regarded as instrumental or a corollary of some other principle such as freedom.[23]

(ii) Human Nature

Another fundamental issue that gives rise to the different suggested means of achieving desired social goals concerns basic human nature. Proponents of capitalism argue that people are basically oriented toward self-interest. With this assumption, Adam Smith showed that a competitive market system could be used to harness this self-interest for the benefit of society at large. Self-interest incentives — primarily monetary gain — drive the competitive system. Consumers seek the best bargain to maximize their satisfaction or that of their families; investors seek the highest rate of return (which can be earned only by providing goods that consumers most desire); and workers are attracted, through higher wage offers, to those industries which provide goods consumers most want. Thus all groups are made mutually better off.

Socialists of the New Left dispute the orthodox economists' assumption concerning people's basically selfish nature.

> Do not regard men and women as inherently greedy, acquisitive, selfish, competitive or aggressive. Human nature has shown enormous variation in time and space and it seems to be in part a product of the social environment. We believe that changes in the environment can interact with changes in the individual to usher in a new era of human cooperation.[24]

The importance of this view for socialists is that it allows them to argue that people can be persuaded to work for each other's benefit without the necessity of coercion by the market mechanism and its promotion of self-interest.

Some Practical Problems

The New Left shuns the centralized socialist views of the Old Left and agrees with orthodox economists that this is not a viable alternative to a market-oriented economy. They admit that they have not answered all the questions posed to them. How will prices be determined? What will be done with those who do not contribute their fair share of the workload, and how will a fair share be determined? Exactly how do we move from our present system to this ideal, decentralized socialist state? The socialists argue for experimentation on a small scale in certain parts of the economy to iron out some of these details. They point to youth communes, the Israeli kibbutzim and community cooperatives or community development corporations (CDC's). CDC's are community-owned businesses that either distribute the profits to all members or use the proceeds for community services including the provision of day-care centres and recreational programs.

Such experiments are welcomed by all liberal capitalists. As Friedman himself says,

> One feature of a free society is surely the freedom of individuals to advocate and propagandize openly for a radical change in the structure of society so long as the advocacy is restricted to persuasion and does not involve force or other forms of coercion.

> It is a mark of the political freedom of a capitalist society that men can openly advocate and work for socialism.[25]

---

23. Ibid., p. 164.

24. Edwards, Reich and Weisskopf, *The Capitalist System*, p. 4.
25. Friedman, *Capitalism and Freedom*, p. 16.

The traditional Marxist theory — especially its application in the centrally planned economies of Eastern Europe — has been challenged by some opponents of capitalism. Most thinkers of the New Left reject centralized state ownership. Some advocate the abolition of private property and the reorganization of society around local communities of people with similar interests.

CONCLUDING REMARKS

Such authors as Smith, Galbraith, Marx, Friedman and those of the New Left are very persuasive in their writings. Some, from time to time, appeal to the reader's emotional instincts. If you are at all interested in pursuing the question of what the economic system *should* be (as opposed to the discussions in this book, which centre mainly on what the economic system *is*), we urge you to seek out readings in this direction. We would also urge you to give equal time to opposing viewpoints.

KEY TERMS AND CONCEPTS

mercantilism	constant capital
division of labour	variable capital
technostructure	degree of labour exploitation
proletariat	business cycles
bourgeoisie	organic composition of capital
labour theory of value	New Left
surplus value	Old Left

PROBLEMS

Problem 1

a) How did Adam Smith's notions of wealth differ from those of the mercantilists?

b) Briefly describe Adam Smith's idea that the combination of the division of labour and voluntary market exchange could contribute toward increasing the per capita wealth of a nation — that is, the standard of living.

c) Explain what is meant by the term *market signals* and the idea that government subsidies to ailing industries would be ignoring such market signals and would cause a loss of wealth.

d) Do you believe the market system harnesses people's inherent self-interest for the good of the majority or does it create a self-interest motive within people which leads to destructive competitiveness, neighbour against neighbour?

Problem 2

a) Explain the idea that the managements of big corporations might be able to neglect shareholders' interests in favour of their own. What sort of constraints might prevent management from neglecting shareholder interests altogether?

b) Assume the accompanying diagram represents a purely competitive market. Depict (on the diagram) the output level. Would this be the output level if firms were not maximizing profits? Why would firms in a purely competitive market be led to maximize profits? What economic profits would the firms be earning on average?

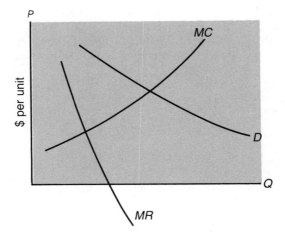

c) Assume the diagram of part (b) represents a firm with some degree of monopoly power. Depict the profit-maximizing output level. Would the firm have to produce at this level? Explain.

d) Assume the firm of part (c) wished to maximize total sales revenue. Depict the output it would produce. Why might it be led to follow such an objective? Is there any constraint on such behaviour?

Problem 3

Compare the welfare implications of (i) a purely competitive firm, (ii) a profit-maximizing firm with monopoly power, and (iii) a similar firm to (ii) but operated chiefly with management objectives in mind and leading to a higher volume of production. Look at this question from the standpoint of consumers, shareholders and society as a whole.

Problem 4

Explain the Galbraithian notions of (i) the imperatives of technology leading to large corporate structures, the *technostructure,* (ii) the technostructure's use of advertising and (iii) the responsibility of the intellectuals.

Problem 5

a) Explain Marx's *labour theory of value* and its function in demonstrating how the market system leads to exploitation of the *proletariat* by the *bourgeoisie.*

b) Explain Marx's idea that the *capitalist mode* contains inherent contradictions that will lead to ever-worsening crises and ultimate collapse.

Problem 6

a) Distinguish between the New Left and the Old Left.

b) Explain, from the viewpoint of the New Left, why the Eastern European communist economies are not examples of true socialism at work.

c) Discuss briefly the basic disputes between socialists and capitalists concerning (i) property rights and (ii) human nature.

d) Do you think Friedman's fourth sailor has the right to keep the other three sailors off his bountiful island? Why or why not?

CASES

Case 14-1

Financial Post

New view of economic theory has value

By HERBERT GRUBEL

James Buchanan, this year's Nobel prize winner in economics, is not exactly a household word in Canada, even though some will have noticed his name on the list of editorial advisers of the Fraser Institute in Vancouver. Buchanan's work has not been given wide publicity, not even after receipt of the Nobel prize. It is an interesting question why there has been this seeming conspiracy of silence.

Viewpoint

One hypothesis is that his work in the theory of public choice is too complex and esoteric. But this is not true. A much more plausible explanation is that Buchanan's ideas are highly unpopular with media people and intellectuals who would normally be discussing the ideas of Nobel laureates.

Buchanan, of George Mason University, Fairfax, Va., discovered a disturbing inconsistency in the intellectual structure that constitutes economic theory. And, of course, inconsistency is a fatal flaw in scientific work. This inconsistency arises from assumptions about the motives of people in general and politicians and bureaucrats in particular.

All of the fundamental theorems of economics are based on the assumption that people's behaviour is driven by self-interest, which is not the same as selfishness. Without the assumption of self-interest economics could not rationally explain why people buy more of a good when the price is low than when it is high. Even the effectiveness of monetary and fiscal policy in the attainment of lower unemployment in the short run is based on this assumption about behaviour.

However, this assumption does not underlie economic theories about the behavior of governments. The public sector is considered to consist of collections of individuals who, as the elected representatives of the people and as civil servants, unselfishly tax and spend money to improve the welfare of society.

Buchanan's central contribution was to suggest that these people might not behave in such a disinterested manner as to maximize social welfare. Instead, as politicians they might attempt to maximize their own election chances. As bureaucrats they might wish to maximize their own income, power and prestige by arguing for more and bigger government spending programs.

Theories and assumptions prove nothing. The astounding success of Buchanan's ideas stemmed from their ability to explain real-world phenomena that the conventional theories could not. Buchanan and a large group of disciples have documented many phenomena that are consistent with their view of the behavior of governments and inconsistent with alternatives.

In Canada, work of the Economic Council, the Fraser Institute and many individual scholars has added empirical support to Buchanan's ideas. Numerous studies have shown that marketing boards, the regulation of transportation and communication, legislation giving power to unions, professional associations and banks tend not to maximize overall social welfare, but instead serve special-interest groups that deliver votes to the politicians.

Spending on education, health care, social security, foreign aid and general administration may well have been driven to excessively high levels by bureaucrats. These individuals have great influence on these programs through their interpretation of the need for and the effectiveness of these spending programs. It is the rare social worker or CIDA official who recommends anything other than increases in expenditures on the programs of their departments.

Buchanan and his disciples from the School of Public Choice do not deny that politicians and bureaucrats have altruistic and noble motives. They merely argue that we should not be so naïve as to accept the politicians' public explanations of government activities at face value. We should remember that they are also human beings who like income, power and prestige. The relative importance and influence of these different motives is ultimately an empirical question.

Restrain bureaucrats

In the U.S., the editors of most of the influential newspapers featured articles that criticized the selection of Buchanan for the Nobel prize. These editors are known for their support of increased government spending and regulation for the benefit of the general public. It is easy to see why they would consider the award to Buchanan to be part of a conspiracy by reactionary forces to discredit the role of government in society.

In the U.S., Buchanan has a large following of people who wish to act on the implications of his ideas and findings. Foremost in this group are people who believe that politicians and bureaucrats need to be constrained by rules that limit their ability to sell votes to get elected.

This can be achieved by constitutional requirements for balanced budgets and for higher than simple majorities for the initiation of or increases in expenditure programs. I have suggested that such constraints could be written into a Bill of Economic Rights for Canadians, but there is so far no political movement in Canada analogous to that flourishing under the Buchanan banner in the U.S.

Undoubtedly, Canadians are divided in their views on the merit of Buchanan's work. However, only ideologues will deny that his ideas have stimulated a worthwhile new way of looking at the role and effectiveness of government.

Ultimately, thoughtful Canadians from all walks of life will assess the merit of the ideas. If they accept Buchanan's ideas as valid, they may have to work for the creation of restraints on the power of politicians and bureaucrats who are surely not going to volunteer them.

a) How might the discussion of managerial versus shareholder interests in Section 14-4 be helpful in providing a diagrammatical analysis of Buchanan's theory of the behaviour of politicians and bureaucrats?

b) Do you agree or disagree with Buchanan's assumption about the objectives of politicians and bureaucrats? Give examples of their behaviour supporting your position.

c) Would you support "constitutional requirements for balanced budgets and for higher than simple majorities for the initiation of or increases in expenditure programs"? Why or why not?

Case 14-2

The Wall Street Journal

Dismal science springs to life in lab

By JERRY E. BISHOP

COLLEGE STATION, Texas

On one side of the room are 14 students designated as sellers of an unnamed commodity about which they know nothing other than its cost. On the other side are 14 buyers, each of whom knows only the price at which he can resell a unit of the mysterious commodity if he buys one.

When Raymond Battalio, an economics professor, says "start," the students begin shouting out bid and asked prices, which Mr. Battalio scribbles furiously on the blackboard.

Within 30 seconds, one buyer and one seller reach a mutually agreeable price that none of their competitors are willing to match, and a trade is effected. An hour later, after dozens of trades, the students line up to collect in cash any profits that they have made in the trading.

To anyone who has watched the New York Stock Exchange in action, the "game" played by these Texas A&M students may seem familiar. But to a new breed of economists such as Mr. Battalio, it is a subject of endless fascination and months of analysis.

The students are volunteers for a laboratory experiment to test an economic theory on how prices are determined in a so-called double oral auction market, in which buyers and sellers publicly announce bid and offering prices.

Such experiments, once regarded as amusing but irrelevant to the real world, are emerging as a major tool of economic research.

More than 100 economists at a score of universities are carrying out dozens of laboratory experiments. They are raising questions about many economic theories, including some that long have guided government policies and corporate decisions.

At least one experiment has played a pivotal role in the way certain freight rates are set. Another underscored the validity of an antitrust case in the chemical industry. Experiments currently under way could influence the way governments sell offshore oil leases and the way airports sell landing rights.

"We're having a growing impact on thinking in economics," says Vernon L. Smith, the University of Arizona economist who pioneered the field.

Historically, economists' claim that their discipline is a science has stirred skepticism. Economists, like natural scientists, do go into the field to observe "natural phenomena" such as the behavior of individuals, corporations and nations in action. Like natural scientists, they formulate theories to explain what they see.

But unlike physicists or biologists, economists haven't been able to test their theories under controlled conditions. One could hardly ask the NYSE to change its rules on, say, "inside" information for a week just to test a theory on how stock prices might be affected.

The real world is far too complicated to test theories seeking to explain economic behaviour in simple ways, Mr. Smith says. "A tremendous number of assumptions must be made to deduce anything from field data," he says.

"You end up with so many hypotheses it's impossible to tear them apart" to see which are valid. Thus, economics is generally considered a non-experimental science.

Adam Smith's famous theory on free markets, for example, has been the keystone of laissez faire capitalism for 200 years. Until recently, however, it had never been tested under controlled conditions.

The Scottish economist believed that individuals, left to their own devices, would selfishly strive to exchange goods and services at the highest profit that each could attain.

Yet, without so intending, they would arrive at prices that gave the most people the most profit. Adam Smith said the traders, as if guided by an "invisible hand," would arrive at prices that produce the maximum benefits for society.

Until recently, however, there wasn't any unequivocal evidence that his assumption about free-market prices was correct. In real life, prices are affected by everything from government tax and social policies to threats of war (or peace), weather and rumors.

Neither Adam Smith nor any other economist had ever observed a "pure" free market in which traders were driven solely by the profit motive. "A lot of economists have a deep skepticism about the theory," Arizona's Mr. Smith says.

To test Adam Smith's theory, Mr. Smith, then at Purdue University, devised a laboratory experiment in 1956 to simulate trading on the NYSE.

He and other economists have repeated this experiment at least 100 times, and their awe of Adam Smith's invisible hand has grown accordingly. It is this experiment that Mr. Battalio demonstrates with 28 Texas A&M students.

Mr. Battalio first obtains the students' written consent — required by the university for any experiment involving human subjects. He then creates a profit motive.

"In this experiment you can't lose money; you can only make money," he says, displaying $600 (U.S.) in real greenbacks to be used to pay them any profits they make.

Each of the 14 student "sellers" is then handed a slip of paper disclosing the cost of each of two units of an unnamed commodity. Each student is warned not to reveal his or her costs to the others.

The costs vary from seller to seller and range from $2.40 to $5. The buyers are given similar slips stating prices at which they can resell any units they buy. Those prices range up to $5.60.

As in the real world, the higher the price, the more profit the sellers make, while the lower the price, the more profit the buyers make.

What the students aren't told is that if they consistently trade all their units at $4, they will collectively rake in more money than if trades are made at higher or lower prices.

This $4 price would be the so-called competitive equilibrium price, the price that brings supply and demand into balance and that Adam Smith predicted would be the most beneficial to society.

The trading begins as a buyer calls out: "I'll buy for 75 cents" and a seller responds: "I'll sell for $4.50." Other buyers and sellers jump in and, in a few seconds, a trade is made at $3.25.

As trading progresses, the market price begins to rise to $3.50, then $3.75. Within 15 minutes, the students are trading the units at $3.90. Then Mr. Battalio calls a halt.

Had the auction continued for another half hour, as it does in full-scale experiments, the price would have reached the $4 equilibrium price and stayed there, he contends.

The economist gives the students new slips that, unbeknownst to them, increase the buyers' demands for units. Within minutes, the students are trading units at or near the equilibrium price of $4.60.

When a third set of slips secretly increases the supply of low-cost units, the market price quickly plunges close to the $3 equilibrium price. About an hour later, the students walk out with $450 of Mr. Battalio's $600.

"It's amazing how fast (the bids and offers) converge on the equilibrium price," Mr. Battalio says.

Such experiments are starting to affect the real world. Mr. Smith and Charles R. Plott, a California Institute of Technology economist, have been experimenting to see whether, given the same supply, demand and costs, the type of market used by traders affects prices.

For instance, many industries, such as chemicals, railroads and airlines, use a posted-price market instead of a double oral auction market.

The two researchers simulated a posted-price market by having the student sellers publicly post their offering prices and stick to them for a limited time while buyers freely shop for the best price they can find.

After a while, the sellers can change their posted prices in the hope, presumably, of greater profits. The results showed that in posted-price markets, prices tend to be higher than in double oral auction markets.

This finding, in turn, led the U.S. Transportation Department to seek the experimental economists' help in a real-world problem.

In the late 1970s, the U.S. railroads asked the department to require barge companies, which compete with railroads for certain freight, to switch from privately negotiated freight rates to publicly posted rates.

The railroads contended that such public postings would protect not only themselves but small barge owners as well from unannounced price cutting by large barge owners.

When Mr. Plott and his colleagues simulated the two types of markets in the laboratory, however, they found just the opposite: price posting tended to yield higher prices than private negotiation and hurt small barge operators. The railroads dropped their request.

Oil companies that make sealed bids for offshore oil leases, meanwhile, may have more than a passing interest in some current experiments by John Kagel at the University of Houston.

The economist says he is intrigued by the notion that winners in auctions of offshore oil leases frequently seem to lose their shirts on the lease — what oilmen call the "winner's curse."

He is testing a theory that the winner's curse is more than just bad luck. All oil companies base their evaluations of a lease's potential worth on somewhat imprecise geological information.

The oil company that makes the most optimistic estimate of a lease's value rather than the most accurate one will probably bid highest and win, the theory goes. And this, Mr. Kagel theorizes, increases the chances that a bidder with an excessive estimate will win the lease and later lose money.

This theory bothers many economists, Mr. Kagel says, because it "conflicts with their notion of rational thought." After taking a few baths in offshore leases, oil companies would learn how to avoid such a pitfall, many economists contend. But Mr. Kagel's experiments hint otherwise.

In his experiments, volunteers are bankrolled and then an estimate of an unnamed commodity's value is given to each of them. As with the oil companies, each estimate is different.

The laboratory bidder knows that the true value may range from, say, $25 to $225. Only the experimenter, Mr. Kagel, knows the true value of the unit is $128. If the winning bidder offers too much for the unit, he loses money.

Among the questions the experiment seeks to answer is whether bidders in such a market can learn, after several rounds of bidding, to distrust the more optimistic estimates of value given to them.

"At first, I recruited business administration students and they all fell victim to the winner's curse," the economist said. Repeatedly, the winning bid would go to the bidders who had the highest or second highest estimates and, repeatedly, these would be overestimates.

In contrast, volunteers from the construction industry soon learned to avoid the winner's curse — but only if they competed in small groups. "In larger groups, however, there were a lot of losses and bankruptcies," he says.

Laboratory experiments are enabling economists to test ideas that might be impossible to test in the real world without disrupting an industry.

In Arizona, Mr. Smith says he is devising a laboratory experiment to see what would happen if airports sold landing and takeoff "time slots" to airlines and if airlines were allowed to trade the slots as commodities.

If such slots were tradable, he explains, prime-time slots might command premium prices. This, in turn, might push airlines to raise ticket prices for flights at those times and lower prices for less desirable flights.

"It could change the pricing structure in the airline industry," he says.

a) Why is it possible to make certain observations more clearly in laboratory experiments than in real-life markets? How useful are the experimental findings when applied in the market?

b) In what way do the experiments described here provide empirical support for Adam Smith's concept of the *invisible hand* discussed in Section 14-2?

c) What is the "winner's curse"? Is the existence of this phenomenon consistent with the assumption of rational behaviour on the part of economic agents?

d) Drawing upon your knowledge of the theory of cartels, how would you rationalize the experimental result where public posting of freight rates for barges led to higher prices than under private negotiation?

e) What do you think of the approach to airline takeoff and landing charges discussed in the last two paragraphs? Would it lead to a more efficient allocation of resources? Would it be more equitable? More just? Would you go as far as extending this notion to the pricing of the right to pollute? (This would mean those firms whose product is in demand would be able to "command premium prices" and thus be able to pay for more pollution and produce more than firms whose output is less in demand.)

CHAPTER 15

The Economic System and Group Conflict

LEARNING OBJECTIVES

After reading this chapter you should be able to explain:

1. The history of the labour movement and government legislation regulating labour relations in Canada.

2. Strikes and worker alienation in a capitalist society.

3. Centrally planned socialist economies of the Soviet type.

4. The labour-managed economy of Yugoslavia.

15-1 INTRODUCTION AND PURPOSE

In the first few chapters we spent some time describing how a completely free market system would operate under the forces of supply and demand. We saw that there were some desirable features of such markets, especially if they were highly competitive and there were only minor discrepancies between private and social costs and values. However, we also saw that there could be various reasons why free markets in each good and service may not be desirable. Some of these reasons are found in divergences between private and social costs and values, a poor distribution of income and wealth, and the desire to produce some nonmarket goods and services. Hence, there arises the possible need for government intervention in the form of regulation or government ownership.

A **purely capitalist economy** is one in which there is complete private ownership and control of the **means of production** — the factories and machines (capital) that are necessary factor inputs. All consumption, employment and output decisions are made by individuals, and there is little or no government intervention. Free markets in every commodity and service, including labour, are an essential feature of such an economy.

No economy today is purely capitalistic. The Canadian and U.S. economies, for example, represent a mixture of private and government ownership and control of the means of production. Further, governments of both countries have significant tax and subsidy arrangements that redistribute income and wealth and influence the volumes of particular goods and services that are produced. The economies of the U.S. and Canada, therefore, are a mixture of capitalistic and socialistic elements.

At the opposite end of the spectrum from capitalism is state socialism or **communism**. Communism is characterized by almost complete state or collective ownership of the means of production. One may differentiate, however, for purposes of analysis, between two types of socialist economies of today — those with a very high degree of central planning (as in the Soviet Union), and those which attempt to minimize such centralized control (as in Yugoslavia and, increasingly, Hungary).

Figure 15-1 broadly shows the relative position of a few countries along the spectrum of economic systems.

In every society there has been and probably always will be *group conflict* within which the institutional structure of the economy plays its part. Nineteenth-century laissez-faire capitalism in Europe and North America had as a rather important group conflict the working class pitted against the owners of capital (capitalists). In those days, workers received bare minimum living wages for long hours of hard, monotonous labour. Education for the children of the poor was very limited, and labouring parents could guarantee their children no better than the parents' own occupational fate in some mine or industrial sweat shop.

A basic social and economic question is, Which institutional setup is best suited to deal with and lessen group conflict while aiding in the provision of a satisfactory standard of living for all? The purely capitalist system of the nineteenth century was not the answer for many. In 1848, Karl Marx and Friedrich Engels issued their *Communist Manifesto*, exhorting, "Workers of the world unite! You have nothing to lose but your chains." And unite they did — but in different ways in different countries.

In this chapter, we will briefly compare the development of some important economic institutions in North America and Eastern Europe. More particularly, we will examine the evolution of unionism in Canada and the revolution of Soviet-style communism and worker-managed firms in Yugoslavia. Of course, these illustrate only three institutional arrangements for dealing with group conflict out of many more possibilities.

15-2 CANADIAN UNIONISM

History

To gain some historical perspective let us briefly trace the development of the **labour union** movement in Canada.

Early ninetenth-century unions attempted to organize workers of particular skills or crafts, and were known as *craft unions*. Craft unions appeared to have more potential for success in the beginning than they do now since there were fewer people to organize, and the threat to withhold services was potentially far costlier to the employer than in the case of unskilled workers, who could more easily be replaced. The objective of these early unions was primarily to improve the lot of working people by attempting to negotiate higher wages, improved safety and shorter hours of work.

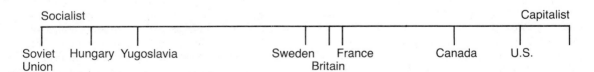

Fig. 15-1 Spectrum of economic systems

All modern economies are mixed, that is, in all of them some decisions concerning allocation of resources are made by governments and some by the market. In socialist economies, government decision-making is pervasive, while in capitalist economies the market price signals play the decisive role.

The ultimate weapon of a union is the **strike**. If negotiations break down and the union's demands are not satisfactorily met, the union may hold a **strike vote**. If successful, they "call their members out"; that is, advise them to withhold their services. Then, rotating shifts of members form a **picket line** and parade back and forth in front of the employer's gates, with placards stating their grievances. The picket line serves as notice of the strike to other unions as well as an attempt to persuade public opinion that the union's demands are fair. Very early on in the union movement it became a rule for union members not to cross their own or another's picket line to deliver materials, for example, or to provide other essential services. Unionists have given those workers who disregard the picket line and help the employer the unpleasant name of **scabs**.

Early attempts to unionize in North America faced violent opposition from business interests. Individuals attempting to organize workers were immediately fired by their employers and their names were put on employer-circulated lists, which effectively prevented them from obtaining work elsewhere. Such a tactic was known as **black-listing**.

In addition, it was commonplace for employers to hire **strikebreakers**, men who would for a fee break up a picket line by attacking and beating (sometimes to death) union leaders and strike organizers. This was very often an effective method of intimidating the other workers reluctantly back onto the job. Usually, it would be made to look as though the fight had started among union members themselves, who were often pictured as being troublemakers and communist agitators.

At other times, the employer involved in a dispute with one group of workers would send all workers home, including those who were not members of the conflicting union, in what became known as a **lockout**.

Not only were early unionists up against tough employer tactics, but the law was against them as well. Initially, attempts to unionize and withhold services for higher wages were treated by the courts as a form of blackmail or, more particularly, a *restraint of trade*.

These attempts to halt the union movement failed.

While the craft unions were trying to improve wages and working conditions for the skilled workers, the unskilled worker remained unrepresented. However, in the late 1800s the *Knights of Labour* — an American union with a Canadian affiliate — picked up the Marxian ideal and attempted to organize all workers by industry in a major class struggle against capitalism. As it turned out, though, bread-and-butter issues of various subgroups of workers within different trades and industries smothered the broader philosophical ideas of the Knights of Labour.

At the turn of the century, the most important organization of craft unions, the *American Federation of Labor* (AFL) led by Samuel Gompers, insisted on economic goals — that is, better working conditions instead of a class revolution. The objective of the AFL in the United States and of its Canadian affiliate, the *Trades and Labour Congress* (TLC), was to organize skilled workers across the country by craft. This put the TLC in direct conflict with the broader goals of the Knights of Labour and some smaller Marxist unions in British Columbia, who were advocating the overthrow of capitalism and the management and ownership of all businesses by workers. By 1930, however, the Knights of Labour and the militant unions of the West had all but disintegrated, leaving the TLC in a dominant position. Again, though, the unskilled workers were left largely unrepresented.

In 1935, the *Congress of Industrial Organizations* (CIO) was formed in the U.S. with John L. Lewis as one of its chief leaders. The objective was to organize all workers by plant and industry rather than by craft. The early Canadian affiliate of the CIO was the *Canadian Congress of Labour* (CCL). Though similar to the Knights of Labour in its all-worker approach, the CIO and CCL perceived their own goals in much narrower terms. In this respect there was philosophical agreement between the AFL and CIO, which by the 1960s were united in the U.S., as were the TLC and CCL in Canada. The latter two Canadian organizations merged and became known as the *Canadian Labour Congress* (CLC).

The Role of Government

Since corporate management is responsible for looking after the interests of shareholders (that is, owners of the means of production — capitalists) the labour-capitalist conflict often shows itself as a *labour-management struggle*. As we have seen above, early legislation, which held that organizing labour groups were using restraint of trade practices, generally did nothing to lessen this conflict. Gradually, though, the government came to believe that its role should be to improve industrial relations by enacting laws to aid the formation of unions and providing protection for the worker. As the 1975 *Canada Yearbook* states, government labour legislation is

> . . . designed to establish harmonious relations between employers and employees and to facilitate the settlement of industrial disputes. These laws guarantee freedom of association and the right to organize, establish machinery [labour relations boards or other administrative systems] for the certification of a trade union as the exclusive bargaining agent of an appropriate unit of employees, and require an employer to bargain with the certified trade union representing his employees.

The federal Department of Labour was created in 1900 under the Conciliation Act and designed to establish a climate of good industrial relations. In addition, federal legislation has been passed concerning fair employment practices (against discrimination by race, sex, religion or colour), minimum standards of work and employee safety. However, many of the federal laws apply only to federally incorporated companies. By and large, labour legislation is a provincial matter. Most of the provincial governments now have laws on their books of the following type:

(1) Strikes and lockouts may not legally take place during the term of a collective agreement, and may take place during negotiations (after expiration of an existing contract) only after **conciliation** and **mediation** procedures have been adhered to. During these procedures, a third party attempts to examine impartially the cases of the employer and employees and say what are fair and reasonable terms for a new contract.

(2) There is a maximum number of hours to be worked per day and per week (usually 8 and 40–44 respectively) before overtime pay, at the minimum rate of 1½ times the normal wage rate, must be paid.

(3) There are minimum-wage laws for most workers.

(4) There is legislation concerning minimum annual paid vacations and statutory public holidays.

(5) Employers must give reasonable notice of dismissal (the length of notice varying with the period of employment).

(6) Maternity protection is provided for female employees.

(7) All provinces have regulations for safety and protection of workers and compulsory deposits by employers into a workers compensation fund, from which workers may draw benefits if injured while on the job.

(8) All provinces have antidiscrimination laws.

In addition, the hardship of poverty from low labour income has been reduced by unemployment insurance and other social security benefits including family allowances, old age security and guaranteed income supplements, veterans' pensions and Canada and Quebec pension schemes at the federal levels, homes for the aged, child welfare services and other social assistance to persons in need and their dependants at the provincial and municipal levels.

These welfare expenditures cost the average citizen approximately 10% of total income. As usual, some argue that this is too much — others, that it is too little.

Unionism Today

Figure 15-2 sheds some light on the growth of the trade union movement in Canada. Fairly rapid growth between 1940 and 1960 gave way to much smaller increases over the next two decades. In 1986, 29.7% of the Canadian labour force were members of certified trade unions. As can be seen from Table 15-1, the degree of unionization varies significantly across industries — with almost no unionization in agriculture to over 66% in public administration.

These figures considerably understate union influence, however. Wage trends and working conditions in nonunionized firms are greatly influenced by contracts negotiated in the unionized sector. This is primarily due to the mobility of labour and the perceived threat of a company's employees joining a union, should nonunionized wages get too far out of line with those in union shops. Further, many professional groups, including doctors and lawyers,

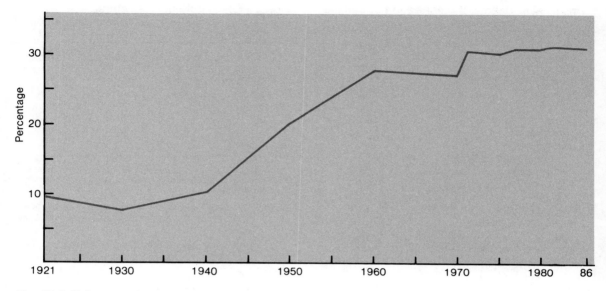

Fig. 15-2 Union membership as a percentage of the civilian labour force

Source: *The Current Industrial Relations Scene in Canada* (Kingston: Industrial Relations Centre, Queen's University, 1981 and 1987)

A major growth in unionization in Canada took place between the 1940s and 1960s. During the last two decades, the degree of unionization remained relatively constant.

have formal *associations* that establish fees for their services or negotiate with government bodies for the establishment of such fees. Since these fees are in essence members' wage rates, these associations may be regarded as unions. However, their memberships are not reflected in the statistics of Figure 15-2 or Table 15-1.

Collective Bargaining

The power of any union is directly related to the number of workers under its control. A union that has only a scattered membership of one out of every ten employees in a given factory could hardly impose great costs on the employer through a strike. On the other hand, if all the employees were members of the union, the entire plant would probably have to be closed down in the event of a walkout.

In Canada, four basic arrangements have been

worked out: (i) the closed shop, (ii) the union shop, (iii) the open shop, and (iv) the Rand formula. The first three have been listed in decreasing order of union security. That is, under a closed shop arrangement a union has maximum power, whereas under an open shop arrangement its power is minimized.

(i) *Closed Shop*
Prospective employees must join the union before they can be hired by the employer.

(ii) *Union Shop*
Nonunionized workers may be hired, but once hired, they must join the union.

(iii) *Open Shop*
An employee has the right to join or not to join the union representing his group.

The distribution of union-management contracts

Table 15-1 **Degree of unionization in Canada by industry, 1984**

Industry	Union membership (percentage)
Agriculture	2.3
Forestry	36.7
Mining	32.8
Manufacturing	45.0
Construction	38.8
Transportation, communications and other utilities	60.0
Trade	12.5
Finance	9.2
Service industries	38.1
Public administration	66.6
Average	37.2

Source: *The Current Industrial Relations Scene in Canada* (Kingston: Industrial Relations Centre, Queen's University, 1987)

There exist substantial inter-industry differences in the degree of unionization of the labour force. It is the lowest in agriculture and in the financial service sector and the highest in public administration and in transportation and communications.

Table 15-2 **Distribution of contracts concerning union security, March 1986**

Type of arrangement	Percentage of contracts
Closed shop	2.8
Union shop*	42.2
Open shop	50.7
Other	4.3
	100.0

* Includes the so-called Modified Union Shop where certain employees, for example, summer students, may be exempted from joining the union.

Source: *The Current Industrial Relations Scene in Canada* (Kingston: Industrial Relations Centre, Queen's University, 1987)

The open shop and union shop are the dominant type of collective agreement provisions regulating union security.

concerning union membership as a condition of employment is shown in Table 15-2.

(iv) *Rand Formula*

Shortly after the Second World War, Justice Ivan Rand brought down a landmark decision as arbitrator in a dispute involving the United Automobile Workers and the car companies. Under his formula, workers would not have to be members of a union to be hired, nor would workers have to join the union if hired. However, once employed, they would have to pay dues to the union that represented their group of workers. In Table 15-2, many of the open-shop contracts contain this formula.

Unions generally bargain directly with their employer (there are exceptions, such as the professional associations). A primary objective of a union is to get as great a total wage package as possible (including fringe benefits such as pensions, health schemes and the like). Because higher wage rates raise marginal costs and lower profits, employers acting on behalf of the shareholders seek to grant the lowest wage gains possible. In the actual negotiation

process, the art of *bluffing* is most essential. To see why, consider the following example.

Acme Ltd. is negotiating with its employees, who are represented by the (fictitious) United Employees Union (UEU). Acme, after judging the effect of a wage packet increase on the price of its products, the reduction in sales and loss of profits, estimates that it is willing to grant a seven percent overall increase. Unaware of the company's calculations, the UEU negotiators coincidentally feel that, everything considered, a seven percent overall increase would be a reasonable settlement. Suppose, therefore, the Acme management and the UEU negotiators both sit down at the bargaining table a day or two before the old agreement is to expire and put forth their respective offers and demands. Since offers and demands coincide, the new contract would be signed over a cup of coffee and negotiations would be rapidly concluded.

Unfortunately, management would leave the table wondering whether — since the union was so willing to accept a seven percent increase — they might have accepted six percent, five percent or even less. In fact, the board of directors may bring up that very question should profits begin to slip. Not only would management have second thoughts, but the union membership would also wonder why management was so ready to accept seven percent. Perhaps the negotiators should have asked for ten percent. It is a good bet that next year management will initially offer somewhat less than they are really willing to give and the union will initially demand somewhat more than they are really willing to accept. In other words, management must convince the shareholders that they are acting in their best interests just as the union leadership must convince its membership that they, too, are acting in their best interests.

Of course, each side soon learns that the other's first offer is actually *artificial*. Consequently, neither side takes the other's first offer seriously. The first meeting, then — in which demands and offers are laid out — merely becomes a chance to *size up your opponent* and to try to read between the lines and get subtle hints as to whether your opponent will move by one, two or three percentage points. The other half of the performance is to attempt to convince the other side that you have budgeted as far as you possibly can go. One factor that helps your case is to convince the other side that you can, at a very low cost to the group you represent, inflict serious harm should your demand (or offer) not be met. "We shall call a strike vote then," the union leader may threaten. "That's fine, we are overstocked with inventory anyway" would be a good reply by management.

Unfortunately, the bluffs are all too often called. Table 15-3 shows the annual number of work days lost per 1000 employees for various countries over a 30-year span (1955–1985). As the table indicates, relatively speaking, Canada has a lot of strike activity. Perhaps what may be even more significant is the adverse Canadian trend over time, exceeded only by the trend in Italy and the U.K.

Strike Costs

It may be worthwhile to examine briefly the economic and social cost of strikes, because they have become an important economic phenomenon in Canada over the past few years. To do this, we will take two extreme examples which we hope will cover most of the cases which occur in practice.

Table 15-3 **Strike activity**

Country	Days lost annually per 1000 employees (average for period in question)		
	1955–59	*1960–70*	*1982–85*
Canada	441	547	495
U.S.	666	591	129
U.K.	216	187	579
France	203	176	100
Germany	51	14	89
Italy	402	1185	856
Japan	262	144	11
Sweden	21	20	6

Source: *The Current Industrial Relations Scene in Canada* (Kingston: Industrial Relations Centre, Queen's University, 1982 and 1987)

Among the leading Western industrialized countries, Canada has had the third worst strike record, following Italy and the U.K.

(i) No Loss in Total Sales

First, let us suppose that companies that are hit by a strike for some period during the year are able to make up all lost sales later on in the year. In this case, because there is no permanent loss in output, one might conclude that the economic cost of the strike is quite small. However, because the output is produced over a much shorter period than originally scheduled, efficiency is likely to be lower. This means that more input resources are used in producing the same amount of output. Further, if this is the case, the shareholders will experience lower profits even with the same sales.

Consumers will experience a loss in welfare or satisfaction, since they will have preferred to have purchased the goods sooner than they were able to.

The workers may or may not benefit. They may be required to work overtime at higher rates of pay, which may or may not be to their liking. As a result of the leisure time during the strike plus the overtime requirements afterwards, they may feel better or worse off.

(ii) Permanent Loss in Sales

Often, consumers who could not purchase the good or service during the strike will not make up for this by purchasing more at a later date. For example, if there is a commuter railway strike, the loss of services during the strike is not recovered afterwards. In fact, some commuters may be so fed up that they will switch permanently to alternative means of transportation.

In this case, the company will experience a more severe profit drop. The consumers, not able merely to postpone consumption, will be forced to make more drastic adjustments in their behaviour and consequently suffer a greater welfare loss. Finally, workers will not get the overtime that was forthcoming in the previous case but are still stuck with the forced inactivity at low strike pay during the dispute. Depending upon the workers' taste for overtime, they may be better off in this case than in the previous one.[1]

Other Union Concerns

Now that most workers earn much more than a subsistence wage, union attention is being directed toward issues other than wage increases.

(i) Job Security

It is ironic in some sense that technological development, which helps to provide productivity improvements and gains in all our standards of living, should at the same time be feared by individual workers. However, this fear is quite rational. Should a labour-saving piece of automated equipment be introduced into an enterprise, it may very well make a number of workers redundant or perhaps make their learned skills obsolete and reduce their jobs to simple routine boring tasks.

As a result, more and more workers are demanding clauses in their contracts that provide for job security in the face of technological change. Unions generally prefer that, if layoffs have to occur, employees with the most seniority in terms of years employed and union membership should be favoured over employees with less seniority.

(ii) Foreign Influence in Canadian Unionism

Our brief examination of the history of North American unionism showed the parallel growth of the union movement in the United States and Canada. Many Canadian unions were established as offshoots of American organizations, and strong ties remain to this day. Table 15-4 shows, for example, that almost half of all Canadian unions have international affiliates — chiefly American. This U.S. connection bothers some Canadian unionists, who fear American domination in terms of union objectives and day-to-day control of union affairs. The tensions between a U.S. union and its Canadian affiliate occasionally lead to a separation of the two. The most recent prominent development of this kind occurred in 1986 when the Cana-

Table 15-4 Union membership by type of union and affiliate, Canada, 1986

Type and affiliate	Percentage of membership
International unions	39.4
AFL-CIO/CLC	22.9
AFL-CIO/CFL	5.6
CLC only	3.9
AFL-CIO only	3.6
Unaffiliated	2.8
National unions	57.2
CLC	30.7
CNTU (Quebec-based)	5.9
Others	4.0
Unaffiliated unions	16.6
Directly chartered local unions	0.7
Independent local unions	3.0
	100.0

Source: Labour Organizations in Canada, Labour Canada, 1986. Reproduced by permission of the Minister of Supply and Services Canada.

The majority of Canadian union membership are affiliated with national unions. The importance of international union affiliation has declined somewhat, but still remains considerable.

---

1. Another possible effect of strikes is that, to the extent that they succeed in raising wage rates above the competitive level, there will be a loss of jobs. The job loss will be evidenced either in the form of layoffs of existing workers and union members or the hiring of fewer new workers in the future. (See, for example, Section 10-3.)

dian members of the United Autoworkers Union broke off their affiliation with the U.S. counterpart and formed an autonomous Canadian union.

(iii) Worker Alienation

One union issue may not have surfaced as often as that of wages; nevertheless it has always been present and may become more important in the future for Canadians. That issue is **worker alienation** (misunderstanding, distrust or indifference by employees toward their employers and jobs).

Machines often reduce labour tasks to the simplest level, replacing painstaking labour skill and craftsmanship with single-step tasks, whose speed is governed by how fast an engineer sets the speed of a machine or conveyor belt. Industrial engineers are well known for their time-motion studies which analyze how quickly an average worker should be able to move the right hand and wrench 40 cm forward and down, turn a nut three revolutions and return 40 cm to the rest position. Workers, knowing these time-motion people are about, may attempt to prove that they cannot work any faster than what the workers regard as a comfortable pace. Intentionally slowing down in order to pace the normal speed to one's liking has become known as *feather-bedding* or *sand-bagging*.

This distaste for one's work and lack of pride and purpose is part and parcel of worker alienation. Some Western European countries, in order to try and overcome this and give workers a feeling that they have some say in their own destiny, have experimented with worker participation in management. Some Canadian companies are also experimenting along these lines. Industrial democracy may in the future become an even more important factor in labour-management relations.

The basic idea of this participation is to make the objectives of labour more consistent with the objectives of the firm as a whole by having the worker become involved in formulating these objectives. The hope is that this will increase labour-management harmony, reduce worker alienation, improve productivity and profits and establish wage rates that firms can afford while remaining in business. Fully worker-managed firms in Yugoslavia are described later in this chapter. Now, however, let us turn our attention to the economic system that has developed in the Soviet Union.

Attempts to organize workers into unions in Canada date back to the late 1800s, typically in conjunction with parallel developments in the U.S. At present, labour-management relations are regulated by a system of federal and provincial labour laws. The overall degree of unionization of labour in Canada has remained roughly constant since the early 1970s. It varies considerably from industry to industry.

15-3 THE SOVIET ECONOMY

During the nineteenth century, Eastern Europe was experiencing the same sort of class conflict as that referred to earlier with respect to North America. However, whereas socio-economic institutions and laws (for example, labour unions, labour laws, welfare legislation) have grown to mitigate this conflict by evolution in North America, in Russia change occurred by bloody revolution.

Though the Russian Revolution took place in 1917, it may help to understand the Soviet political-economic system by examining summarized excerpts from the 1936 Constitution.

> The political foundation of the USSR is the Soviet of Working People's Deputies. . . .
>
> The economic foundation of the USSR is the socialist system of economy with no private ownership of the means of production. Property is owned by the state or co-operatively. Personal property rights are limited to houses, personal and domestic belongings, personal wages, savings from work, and inheritances of personal property. . . .
>
> Work in the USSR is a duty in accordance with the Marxian principle, "he who does not work, neither shall he eat."

Central Planning

One of the most important aspects of Soviet communism is the degree of **central planning**. The government is all powerful in deciding what shall be produced, who shall get it and at what price. For this complicated task, the Soviets operate on *five-year economic plans*, supplemented by annual production targets for each good and service produced. The first plan was from 1928 to 1932; the most recently completed plan from 1981 to 1985. Over the years, these plans have by and large sought rapid industrialization and growth, which has necessitated great emphasis on investment and the accumulation of capital goods at the expense of consumer goods.

In North America, people save if they want to, and generally the rate of return they are offered on their savings is an important consideration in this decision. They will receive whatever rate of return the invested funds can earn, which, as we have seen in earlier chapters, depends crucially on business providing goods and services that are wanted (valued) by consumers. Therefore, it is said we have a consumer-oriented society (consumer sovereignty). We do, however, allow government to provide certain goods and services, which also may be consumer oriented. Parks, health services, education and protection are examples. If we think the balance between consumption and saving is not correct — that is, if at the going rate of interest we would rather consume more and save less — we do so. Also, if we do not like the amount the government is spending, through our vote we can put the government out of office and, we hope, elect another one that has policies more in line with our thinking.

In the Soviet Union, though, consumer choice has generally been given little weight. Over the years the government has geared production plans primarily for capital goods industries, while allowing only residual resources to be devoted to the production of consumer goods. The result has been a generally acknowledged *involuntary* high rate of growth in total industrial output. These rates are involuntary in that the average Soviet citizen would rather have slower growth but more consumer goods along the way.

The bureaucratic structure necessary to administer the Soviet central plan is as follows. At the top is the *Council of Ministers*, which decides on the central plan with advice from numerous state planning committees. The most important of these planning committees are the *State Planning Committee (Gosplan)*, the *State Science and Technology Committee* and the *State Construction Committee*.

In direct line between the Council of Ministers are industrial ministries, whose responsibility it is to see that the central production plan is carried out in each particular industry.

At the level of the individual firm, Soviet managers are responsible for meeting their own separate output targets in line with the directives from the industrial ministries. Traditionally, Soviet managers have been engineers with no distinct management education. With no production or pricing decisions to make, their functions are to insure the necessary material inputs can be procured smoothly in meeting production targets.

The task of the Gosplan is to translate the advice of other committees into a detailed plan, specifying how much of each good is to be produced, by whom it is to be produced and how it will be used. In order to accomplish this immense task of coordination, an economic tool known as an *input-output table* is utilized. Since this is discussed in some detail in the next chapter, for now we will illustrate the basic input-output planning problem by means of a short numerical example, but without the use of an actual input-output table.

Suppose the central plan calls for an output of 100 units of steel during the coming year. One input of steel making is electricity. Perhaps one unit of steel output requires 0.1 units of electricity. Then, the Gosplan will have to plan for 10 (that is, 100×0.1) units of electricity in the coming year just for steel production. However, this is not quite right because to produce 10 units more electricity may require 5 units more steel for generating plants, which would require 0.5 (that is, 5×0.1) more units of electricity and so on. It takes little imagination to understand the possibilities for errors in coordinating production plans for thousands of inputs and thousands of outputs.

Pricing and Money

Under early Soviet plans, the resource allocation function of prices was not recognized. That is not surprising, since in the early days after the revolution market mechanism was regarded as a fixture and tool of capitalism. The problem was only to translate inputs into outputs in the most efficient manner — clearly a job for engineers.

However, prices were used to provide a common monetary denominator for transaction purposes and cost analysis. Enterprises made transactions with one another for their materials and equipment and recorded their costs, revenues and profits in money terms. Prices were set not by supply and demand forces but by state central planners at the level of economic ministries or, sometimes, by local authorities. Prices were supposed to be roughly equal to the cost of production. In practice, however, prices of some goods reflected considerable subsidies while others indicated large profits. In addition, a hidden sales tax (**turnover tax**) imposed at the wholesale level for most goods made retail prices about twice as high as before-tax production and distribution costs; that is, about half of the retail price went as a tax to the state. This turnover tax took the place of an income tax.

Use of the turnover tax is the means by which the state can direct the desired portion of output into investment. For example, suppose the total income from production is 100 billion rubles, but that the state plan has caused only 50 billion rubles of consumer goods to be produced (when priced by the state at production cost without tax). If consumers attempted to spend all their income on consumer goods, they could not do so. There would be a 50 billion ruble shortage. Eager buyers queued at the shops would find empty shelves. In fact, for particular goods, such shortages have been one of the problems in Soviet planning. However, it did not take the Soviets long to realize the economic effectiveness of price hikes in eliminating queues. For example, to bring the market prices of available consumer goods in line with consumer incomes, a 100% turnover tax could be placed on the goods, thereby doubling their prices so that the market value would become 100 billion rubles.

If the Soviets want more investment they can merely instruct the appropriate industries to produce more capital goods, using up more inputs and hence lowering the output of consumer goods. This would again cause a gap between ruble income and market value of consumer goods, which again could be eliminated by an increase in the turnover tax.

Thus the first economic lesson learned by Soviet state planners concerning the price mechanism was that appropriate prices can be used *to bring supply and demand into balance*.

Pricing Techniques and Resource Allocation

The turnover tax can be used to eliminate consumer goods shortages, but it has not, over the years, reduced Soviet dissatisfaction with the government's allocation of resources between investment and consumer goods. There seems to be little

Table 15-5 Per unit production costs in rubles (neglecting the cost of capital)*

	Product 1	Product 2
Labour	12	8
Capital	0	2
	12	10

* Based on one unit of output per year.

Product 1 requires only labour for its production; product 2 requires both labour and capital. The Soviet pricing system, based on the Marxian labour theory of value, recognizes only those capital costs which represent depreciation and wear and tear of capital equipment (2 rubles). The opportunity costs of capital resources tied up in the production process are not included.

doubt that under free consumer choice fewer resources would have been devoted to capital and more to consumer goods over the first fifty years of communism. Some people, of course, argue that the state knows better than the average citizen what is in the citizen's long-run best interest. Typically, we assume the opposite.

The Value of Capital

Marx argued that interest and profit on capital funds represent evidence of labour exploitation by capital.[2] Marx referred to the excess of market price over labour cost (including the labour cost component of materials) as "surplus value." There was no place, therefore, in Soviet economies for a cost of capital concept. **Capital** was, originally assigned a **zero cost** in the formulation of prices by the state. This policy, however, became a serious source of resource misallocation and lost welfare for the Soviets. To see this, we briefly examine the Soviet pricing method based on Marx's labour theory of value.

Suppose there are two products that require inputs for their production as shown in Table 15-5. Each unit of product 1 requires 12 rubles worth of

---

2. Marx's concept of the labour theory of value is discussed in Chapter 14.

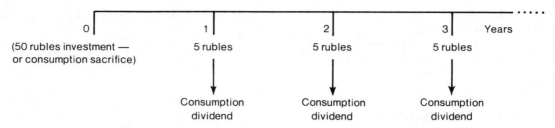

Fig. 15-3 State investment and the cost of capital

Illustration of the opportunity costs of capital tied up in the production process. It is assumed here that 50 rubles worth of investment could have generated 5 rubles of annual consumption dividend if it were not employed as capital equipment.

labour and no capital input (the production process is entirely manual). Each unit of product 2, on the other hand, requires only 8 rubles worth of labour but 2 rubles worth of capital in the Marxian sense. That is to say, the 2 rubles of capital input each year represent the depreciation or wearing out of capital equipment. Suppose, for example, that a 2 ruble new investment in machinery has to be made each year just to maintain the overall capital stock in good working order. The original investment in equipment for product 2 might have been, say, 50 rubles. Each year 2 rubles worth wear out, requiring 2 rubles worth of replacement machinery and parts to maintain the equivalent capital base at 50 rubles.[3] Marx would have recognized these two rubles as a cost of producing product 2 because labour effort would have to be expended to produce the machinery replacements. Marx did not, however, assign any value to having resources tied up in physical capital, since in his system labour alone is the source of surplus value. That is, Marx would not recognize any form of interest cost on the 50 rubles continuing fixed capital base.

As a result of this pricing method followed by the Soviets, product 2 would be assigned a lower price than product 1. If they were similar products, for example, soon only product 2 would continue to be produced since consumers would find it cheaper.

However, the costs in Table 15-5 do not reflect the total costs of production for the Soviet people. In order to produce product 2 year after year, not only does 2 rubles worth of possible consumer output in the form of sweaters, television sets or hockey sticks have to be diverted into the production of replacement machinery — which is accounted for — but also the Soviet people must permanently sacrifice 50 rubles worth of consumer goods, which they could have had if they had not produced the 50 rubles worth of machinery and equipment necessary for the production of product 2 in the first place. This is a sacrifice that would not have to be made if product 1 was produced, but was not accounted for by the Soviet-Marxian pricing formula. This sacrifice is the nature of the economic cost of capital, which Marx refused to recognize and the Soviets thought would evaporate along with capitalism in 1917. Though capitalists can disappear, real economic costs, which are of no political or philosophical persuasion, cannot. How then could this cost of capital be accounted for by the Soviet central planning authority?

If the central planning authority wishes to maximize the welfare of the average citizen, it must attempt to evaluate the cost to the average citizen of foregone consumption. This is not an easy task. However, let us at least examine the problem conceptually.

Suppose the average Soviet citizen would, if asked, be willing to postpone his or her share of 50 rubles worth of consumer goods and services *now* for investment in machinery and equipment if such an investment could provide in total 55 rubles worth of potential consumption one year from

3. Two rubles worth wears out, bringing the overall worth from 50 to 48 rubles. But 2 rubles of replacement machinery re-establishes the machinery value back up to 50 rubles.

now. Presumably, if asked again at that time, the citizen would again be willing to vote for reinvestment (postponement of consumption) of 50 rubles if within another year it could provide in total 55 rubles of potential consumption — and so on. This, as Figure 15-3 shows, indicates that the average Soviet citizen would be willing to postpone 50 rubles worth of potential consumption indefinitely for a 5 ruble annual consumption dividend. This fact would mean that in addition to covering all other production costs connected with product 2, the average Soviet citizen would charge 5 more rubles before considering the price received sufficient to justify the investment. The appropriate cost of capital is thus 10% (that is, 5/50 × 100%).

Using the above information, we may properly recalculate the costs for products 1 and 2, as shown in Table 15-6. Pricing product 2 at 15 rubles rather than at 10 would mean that if it was bought, the Soviet consumer would value the product at least at 15 rubles, which is equal to the total cost of sacrifice to the Soviet people in its production. Pricing product 2 at 10 rubles would result in units being produced whose sacrifice to the Soviet people (15 rubles worth) was greater than the value received by the Soviet people from its production (10 rubles). Consequently, there would be a misallocation of resources and too much of product 2 produced.

But this is precisely the same sort of development we went through in Chapters 8 and 9. In other words, these economic principles and the notion of a cost of capital are applicable to the entire spectrum of economic systems, regardless of who owns or controls the means of production.

Problems with the Economy

First of all, the complexities of planning production volumes and coordinating input supplies for thousands of products entail large bureaucratic costs as well as many mistakes. *Bottlenecks* often develop in the Soviet sytem, where plants run out of particular supplies and targets are missed. The early cavalier attitude toward pricing and charging an appropriate cost of capital also led to many problems of resource misallocation.

After the death of Stalin in 1953, growing allocation inefficiencies resulted in a more concentrated effort on economic analysis. At about the same time, Evsei G. Liberman, an active Soviet economist, started to work on measures of profit and profitability. During the reform period of the 1960s,

Table 15-6 Per unit production costs in rubles (including a ten percent cost of capital)*

	Product 1	Product 2	
Labour	12	8	2 Depreciation
Capital	0	7	+
	12	15	5 Cost of capital

* Based on one unit of output per year.

Cost of production figures from Table 15-5 are amended here to include the economic cost of capital. The ratio of per unit costs of the two products changes considerably when capital cost is correctly accounted for.

he made his work public. He strongly advocated the idea that profit and profitability are in no way elements applicable only to capitalistic systems, but are instead merely economic devices with practical applications. He argued that appropriate cost of capital measures must be applied within Soviet pricing formulas. Experimentation was carried out in the early 1960s, and full use of cost of capital and true economic profit measures were incorporated in 1965. This represented a deviation from Marxian philosophy. Now, capital — along with labour — is regarded as a valuable economic resource, for which charges must be made.

Included in the 1965 reform debate were suggestions for a greater emphasis on consumption, a reduction of discrimination against some domestic private enterprise, greater industrial cooperation with foreign capitalist firms, abandonment of the labour theory of value and rehabilitation of economic profit as a measure of enterprise performance.

Despite some rather innovative theoretical thinking, the **Soviet economic reform** never really got off the ground. It was stifled by the massive planning bureaucracy committed to the old ways of doing things and by the Communist party leadership fearful that decentralization in economic life might encourage calls for more political democracy. As of 1986, however, there were indications that the new Soviet leadership under Mikhail Gorbachev was embarking upon a series of far-reaching reforms. The proposals under discussion included granting greater autonomy to the enterprises, allowing limited price flexibility and responsiveness to demand and supply conditions and even permitting limited private enterprise, especially in the notoriously inefficient Soviet distribution and service sectors.

Comparisons of the standard of living in the Soviet Union with the Western countries are not easily made, since the Soviet price structure is artificially manipulated by the state (some goods are heavily subsidized, others heavily taxed). Also, the proportions of public and private goods consumption vary greatly from country to country. The Soviet Union, for example, has not only free medical and dental care and prescription drugs, but also tuition-fee university education. Nevertheless, most indicators suggest that the average Soviet worker is still very much worse off than a Western counterpart. Table 15-7 illustrates the comparative standards of living in the Soviet Union, Britain and the United States and several Western economies based on carefully documented information for a few consumer goods. The table indicates the amount of worktime required to acquire basic necessities and luxuries of life. In a rough manner, we may take the U.S. figures as comparable to those in Canada.

Table 15-7 **Retail prices of selected goods and services expressed in units of worktime:* Washington (D.C.), London, Munich, Paris, and Moscow, October 1986**

	(Worktime is in minutes, unless otherwise stated)				
Commodity	Washington	London	Munich	Paris	Moscow**
Milk fresh (1 litre)	4	6	6	8	20
Hamburger meat, beef (1 kg)	30	38	30	75	72
Sausages, most common (1 kg)	50	29	84	70	153
Potatoes, old (1 kg)	9	3	5	9	11
Apples, eating (1 kg)	18	14	16	16	28
Sugar (1 kg)	6	8	8	11	52
White bread (1 kg)	6	11	25	20	17
Eggs, large (10)	5	13	16	17	75
Vodka (0.5 litre)	78	78	61	97	569
Cigarettes (20)	7	25	17	12	14
Weekly food basket for four people	16 hrs.	17.7 hrs.	21.3 hrs.	24.9 hrs.	51.2 hrs.
Soap, toilet (150 gram)	3	4	6	8	17
Panty hose	16	14	16	17	279
Men's shoes, black, office	6 hrs.	6 hrs.	11 hrs.	8 hrs.	37 hrs.
Men's office suit	18 hrs.	16 hrs.	33 hrs.	34 hrs.	118 hrs.
Bus fare (3 km)	7	9	7	5	3
Regular gasoline (10 litres)	17	64	47	66	167
Men's haircut, dry, no extras	62	61	75	92	34
Refrigerator, small (120 litres)	44 hrs.	30 hrs.	31 hrs.	30 hrs.	102 hrs.
Colour TV set (61 cm screen)	30 hrs.	75 hrs.	54 hrs.	106 hrs.	669 hrs.
Small car	5 mths.	8 mths.	7 mths.	8 mths.	45 mths.

* The worktime requirement is based on average take-home pay of male and female manufacturing workers. Income taxes, social security taxes, unemployment insurance and health insurance premiums have been deducted from wages; family allowances have been added. A worker is assumed to have three dependants. In dollars, hourly take-home pay in January 1986 was $6.77 for U.S. workers, $5.00 for British workers, $6.49 for German workers, $5.04 for French workers and $1.59 for Soviet workers. No allowances have been made for income from the black or grey economy or for income from rent, interest or dividends.

** The survey has been limited to goods and services that can be purchased in all five cities (this excludes, for example, many convenience and frozen foodstuffs which have not yet been introduced on a wider scale in Moscow). Every effort was made to match the goods and services priced in the five cities. However, there exist substantial differences in quality, appearance, packaging, and durability. In addition, there are frequent shortages of certain goods in Moscow.

Source: *Radio Liberty Research Bulletin*, Supplement (January 21, 1987)

The Soviet economic system is characterized by central planning of production, investment, consumption, as well as other aspects of economic life. In addition, indirect taxes are employed to manipulate consumption patterns. Bottlenecks and inefficiencies have been pervasive; periodic attempts to reform the system have considered allowing a limited role for the price mechanism, increasing the autonomy of state enterprises and even permitting private enterprise on a small scale.

15-4 THE ECONOMY OF YUGOSLAVIA

A different attempt at removing labour-management conflict and worker alienation is exemplified by Yugoslavia. Though also a communist state with central control, Yugoslavia has attempted to *decentralize* in order to become more flexible and raise worker incentives. Since some West European countries have attempted this same sort of process on a limited scale and Canadian firms are also experimenting by giving labour more participation in management, it may be useful to examine the situation in Yugoslavia.

In 1950, Yugoslav legislation transferred ownership of enterprises from the state to employees. At the same time, there was a relaxation of reliance on the state and its bureaucracy for management directions. Instead, they would depend more on worker initiatives. However, in the early fifties, reforms were not completely implemented. Strong central controls and administration remained intact. Various reforms in the late fifties and early sixties finally gave way to the dissolution of central control and more and more power was assigned to workers through various management organs. At the same time, more and more freedom was given to enterprises for the distribution of their funds. We will briefly examine these events.

In 1965, socio-economic reform brought Yugoslavia relatively close to being a market economy. As a consequence, there was gradual replacement of state-controlled prices by free market prices with the objective of reaching a totally free price system for all but a few commodities by 1970. Therefore, most prices are now determined by the interaction of supply and demand. Also, under the 1965 reforms, **state planning** was to become **indicative** rather than compulsory. One important result of the 1965 reforms is that, unlike in the Soviet Union, management became less of a purely engineering problem. Prices have to be decided on — as well as investment and output plans — by the individual enterprise themselves.

The Structure for Self-Management

The philosophical theme of self-management in Yugoslavia is perhaps best revealed in article excerpts from the constitution, which may be summarized in the following manner:

> The basis of the social economic system of Yugoslavia is free associated work with socially owned means of labour and self-management of the working people in production and in the distribution of the social product in the working organization and social community. . . .
>
> Every working man acquires equal rights of management by joining a working organization, regardless of rank and executive function in the production process. . . .
>
> The working people manage the working organization directly, or through the organs of management which they themselves elect. . . .

At the top level of management for all firms with more than 30 employees is the compulsory *Workers' Council*, which consists of a minimum of 15 members elected by secret ballot for two-year terms. To provide continuity, only one-half of the committee retires each year. All workers may vote and are eligible to be elected to the Workers' Council. This body corresponds roughly to the board of directors of a Canadian corporation in that it is responsible for broad policy strategy concerning such decisions as production, price, distribution, employment and dismissal of workers.

Beyond the Workers' Council, each enterprise may organize its management however it sees fit. Typically, though, the Workers' Council appoints a director responsible for overseeing the organization in light of council policies. This position may be compared with that of a company president. However, for various functional areas of the firm, rather than have a vice-president in charge of each — as would likely be the case in a North American corporation — *section workers' councils* are in charge. These section councils decide on operational policies of their areas of responsibility, the use of resources controlled by each section, rules, regulations, budgets and wage scales.

In addition to a director, each firm will usually have a very powerful management committee or *Business Board* consisting of technician specialists and managerial people. The director is automatically a member. As well as making suggestions with regard to policy, the Business Board interprets the Workers' Council decisions and sends directives to the section workers' councils for day-to-day action.

Wages

Approximately 70% of each firm's income after nonlabour costs is at the disposal of the workers with no control from the state. The other 30% goes for various taxes and into common funds among enterprises to help workers who might lose their jobs. This is comparable to our unemployment insurance program. The higher the firm's income, the greater will be the income to be split among employees. Therefore, one of the basic ideas of worker-owned firms is that all employees are supposed to feel as though they are working for themselves and, therefore, should have more incentive and perhaps be more productive and more satisfied. The 70% of income going to the workers is split by the Worker's Council into personal income and a common consumption fund, and the remainder is reinvested in the business. The common consumption fund covers social welfare of employees, housing, holidays and social facilities. There is also provision for a guaranteed minimum annual income supported by state subsidization should the income of a particular firm not be sufficient to generate it.

Problems with the System

One obvious difficulty with the Yugoslav system is that there may be considerable lack of managerial qualifications among the workers. Theoretically, this is not supposed to matter. The technical staff, through the Business Board, are supposed to lay out for the Workers' Council alternative decision plans in terms of costs and benefits. The Workers' Council members are not expected to be able to understand the technical or managerial economic aspects and are merely to choose the alternatives with the highest excess of benefits over costs. But actual decisions are never that black and white.

Typically, managers have to be able to use their judgement and at least understand the economics of each decision, if not the engineering aspects. In order to attempt to correct this deficiency, workers' colleges have been set up in which these management skills are taught.

Even though there are worker colleges, there is still the feeling among many workers that the Workers' Council decisions are rather bewildering. As a result, the better educated skilled workers, technicians and management trained employees have disproportionate representation on the Workers' Council. Even where this is not the case, the Business Board — with its superior understanding of the complexity of various decisions — can have considerable manipulative power over the Workers' Council in the achievement of the Board's own ends. One survey showed that only 60% of the workers participated in the collective meetings, and that among this 60%, the skilled workers were overrepresented. It also turns out that a high proportion of Workers' Council members are elected more than once. This is perhaps good in the sense that it provides for better management but it is not consistent with the philosophy that each worker should be equally represented.

Since one of the purposes of worker participation in management is to remove the misunderstanding of work purpose and the feeling of alienation toward their tasks, management and owners, it might be useful to examine whether the Yugoslav experience sheds any light on this problem. Though hardly definitive by any measure, it would appear that symptoms of such alienation remain for many Yugoslav workers. Many of them are not perfectly aware that they are the managers of the firm or do not care about the financial results. Absenteeism for some firms on some days can be as high as 30%. This suggests that if a job is boring it remains boring regardless of the system of management.

A rather unique feature of the Yugoslav economic system is group ownership of the means of production and labour management of the enterprises. In practice, worker participation in management has proven to be narrowly based and without individual incentives adequate enough to overcome worker alienation and inefficiencies in the workplace.

CONCLUDING REMARKS

The existing institutional economic arrangements have often been looked on as evolutionary solutions (albeit perhaps only temporary ones) to conflict among groups within society. The conflict involving labour is referred to these days as a labour-management dispute, though in other times (and in other countries) it has been referred to as a labour-capitalist or worker-bourgeoisie struggle. Various countries have dealt with this problem in different ways. Canada has passed legislation allowing labour to form monopoly associations or unions and bargain with employers, whereas the Soviet Union and other countries have followed markedly different routes. But we are all still searching for an institutional setup with the least conflict.

It might be interesting to imagine the type of group conflict for income shares that might arise as the percentage of retired people over the age of 65 increases significantly in relation to the working population, whose output must support them and to speculate on how society might deal with that problem.

KEY TERMS AND CONCEPTS

purely capitalist economy	lockout
means of production	conciliation
communism	mediation
labour unions	worker alienation
strike	central planning
strike vote	turnover tax
picket line	zero cost of capital
scabs	Soviet economic reforms
black-listing	indicative planning
strikebreakers	

PROBLEMS

Problem 1

a) What is meant by the following terms: craft union, strike, black-listing, strikebreakers, scabs, lockouts, closed shop, open shop, union shop, Rand formula?

b) Examine the figures in Table 15-1. In what industries do unions seem to have made (i) the greatest inroads and (ii) the smallest inroads?

Problem 2

Discuss briefly the welfare costs of strikes.

Problem 3

a) Discuss how the Soviet turnover tax may be used to eliminate shortages of consumer goods.

b) Explain briefly how the application of Marx's labour theory of value led to the overuse of capital equipment and machinery in the Soviet Union.

c) Briefly contrast the method by which Canada has attempted to mitigate the worker-capitalist struggles of the 1800s and early 1900s with the methods of the Soviet Union and Yugoslavia.

CASES

Case 15-1

Here is a quick trot through some of the economic thinking which underlies the world we live in, by one of Canada's leading and most respected senior economists, Vincent Bladen. Professor Bladen also gives his own assessment of the hard choices facing society now.

The Financial Post

Don't be fooled by 'new era choices': no work — no money, no leisure

Though "Full Employment" is, of course, the thing,
It's not a bell that has a cheerful ring.
I find I cannot get my blood to boil
For universal and continual toil.

Is there no statesman in the land, not one,
To cry, "We came into the world for fun!
"Though work is well, in reasonable measure,
"The highest aim is More and Better Leisure.
"There shall be flags, and flowers, all the year,
"Wine on the table, nothing on the beer.

"We give you work: and work, we hope, you will.
"But Full Enjoyment is the target still."

— A.P. HERBERT,
"MANIFESTO"

By VINCENT BLADEN

THERE IS, of course, no conflict between A.P. Herbert's Manifesto and the program of Maynard Keynes — for Keynes was concerned with *involuntary* unemployment; with the plight of those who wanted to work, but could not find a job.

The highest aim might still be more leisure; and Keynes might well have argued that more people could have more leisure if so much production was not being lost by the involuntary idleness (leisure, if you like) of so many who wanted to work. Nor did full employment mean that we would work all day; indeed, the less involuntary idleness, the

shorter might be the average length of the working day, the fewer the working years in the average man's life.

But let us not forget that there is work to be done, if we are to enjoy the "necessities and conveniences" of life. We can reduce the amount of that necessary work by increasing productivity, or by decreasing our wants. Historically, production has been increasing, but so have wants.

"Poverty and want," said Thomas Mun, "do make a people wise and industrious." And Arthur Young, as late as 1771, said: "Everyone but an idiot knows that the lower classes must be left poor or they will never be industrious." It was one of the great contributions of Adam Smith that he preached the doctrine of the economy of high wages, in contrast with this defense of poverty as a condition of wealth.

Adam Smith's plea was partly one of equity: "No society can be flourishing and happy, of which by far the greater part of the members are poor and miserable. It is but equity, besides, that they who feed, clothe, and lodge the whole body of the people should be themselves tolerably well fed, clothed, and lodged."

His plea was also one of expediency: "That men in general should work better when they are ill-fed than when they are well-fed, when they are disheartened than when they are in good spirits, when they are frequently sick than when they are generally in good health, seems not very probable."

Finally, notice Adam Smith's argument that high wages resulting from increasing productivity of labor did not raise prices: "There are many commodities, therefore, which . . . come to be produced by so much less labor than before, that the increase in its price is more than compensated by the diminution of its quantity."

John Stuart Mill argued that the incentive to work lay in the consequent satisfaction of want: "To civilize a savage, he must be inspired with new wants and desires, even if not of a very elevated kind, provided that their gratification can be a motive to a steady regular bodily and mental exertion."

But if the savage needed to be "inspired with new wants," the English needed to be taught "not the desire of wealth . . . but the use of wealth . . . Every real improvement in the character of the English, whether it consists in giving them higher aspirations, or only a juster estimate of the value of their present objects of desire, must necessarily moderate the ardor of their devotion to the pursuit of wealth."

This recognition that we may want too much, and work too much, is interesting — but in 1848, it was surely a very narrowminded middleclass view.

Mill was obsessed with the vulgarity of the extravagances of the well-to-do, but the mass of the people wanted, and quite properly wanted, more of "the conveniences of life," more "wine on the table," more sanitation in their cities, etc. Even if the rich consumed

Fear of being fired and ending up in the workhouse has been replaced as the chief incentive to work by . . .

more sensibly, there was need for continued work for "steady and regular bodily and mental exertion." Leisure for the masses and shorter working hours could only be achieved as productivity increased, so that the provision of "conveniences" increased to the point where a little more leisure seemed more desirable than the little more of the "conveniences" that might have been otherwise enjoyed. Mill's contemporary, Karl Marx, had no illusions about the need for greater productivity. In the Communist Manifesto, he proclaimed the need for the proletariat to wrest all capital from the bourgeoisie, and "to increase the total of productive forces as rapidly as possible."

Mill examined the problem of the incentive to work when writing about communism.

"No reasonable person can doubt," he said, "that a village community, composed of a few thousand inhabitants . . . could raise an amount of production sufficient to maintain them in comfort; and would find the means of obtaining, and if need be, exacting the quantity of labor necessary for this purpose, from every member of the association who was capable of work."

. . . the desire to acquire more material possessions. But acquisitiveness may be giving way to . . .

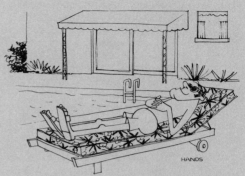

. . . a longing to ease up and enjoy a more reflective and tranquil life.

He noted the objection usually made: "that each person would be incessantly occupied in evading his fair share of the work." To this, he replied that the "factory operative has less personal interest in his work than a member of the Communist association."

But the worker had a very personal interest in keeping his job. In the factory, "they are watched, and superintended" by "salaried officials." "Though the 'master's eye,' when the master is vigilant and intelligent, is of proverbial value, in a socialist form or manufactory, each laborer would be under the eye, not of the master, but of the whole community."

When discussing the discipline of the factory, Mill referred to the "power of dismissal," and said: "Even the laborer who loses his employment by idleness or negligence has nothing worse to suffer, in the most unfavorable case, than the discipline of a workhouse." Mill had never experienced that discipline; and let us remember the "less eligibility" principle on which they operated in his day.

What I think is important in estimating the personal interest in a job, the personal incentive to work hard enough to hold that job, is the width of the gap between the standard of living of the employed and the unemployed. As wages rose, and the discipline of the workhouse remained more or less harsh, the gap widened, and the incentive to work was greater. This gap obviously depends on the movement of two elements. If it widens as the standard of living of the employed improves, that of the unemployed remaining unchanged, so it narrows if the standard of living of the unemployed improves while that of the employed remains unchanged. Since neither is likely to be unchanged, this should be stated rather in terms of the relative rates of improvement in the standard of living of these two groups.

The discipline of the workhouse has been replaced by rates of pay to the unemployed which, in some jurisdictions, almost eliminate the gap, having in mind the deductions from earnings for various taxes, and the costs of transportation to and from work.

George Bernard Shaw, in his Intelligent Woman's Guide to Socialism, argued for equality of income, but he also argued for equality of effort!:

"It is desirable that the burden of work, without which there would be no income to divide, should be shared equally by the workers. If those who are never happy unless they are working insist on putting in extra work to please themselves, they must not pretend that this is a painful sacrifice for which they should be paid. On the other hand, there are people who grudge every moment they have to spend on working. That is no excuse for letting them off their share. Anyone who does less than her share of work — and yet has full share of the wealth produced by the work — is a thief, and should be dealt with as any other sort of thief is dealt with. Weary Willie may say that he hates work, and is quite willing to take less. But that cannot be allowed — voluntary poverty is just as mischievous, socially, as involuntary poverty: decent nations must insist on their citizens leading decent lives, doing their full share of the nation's work, and taking their full share of its income."

The remainder of his chapter is concerned with the incentive to do the "dirty work." To maintain equality of income, yet to induce workers to undertake the less pleasant jobs, Shaw proposed that such workers be given "more leisure, earlier retirement, more holidays. They do not want more work and more money: they want more leisure for the same work . . . money is not the only incentive to work, nor the strongest."

Even if it were true that they generally prefer more leisure to more money (which is not consistent with the amount of "moonlighting" that is undertaken), there remains the problem of the treatment of the "thieves" who will not do their share of the work, dirty or clean. What sanctions must be imposed if persuasion and pecuniary incentive fail?

One is back to Mill: how will society "exact" the necessary labor from its citizens? From persuasion, through incentive, to compulsion. Not a cheerful note.

Maynard Keynes, writing "Economic Possibilities for our Grand-Children" in 1928, argued that "assuming no important wars and no important increase in population, the economic problem may be solved, or be at least within sight of solution, within a hundred years."

Nearly half that period has passed, and the solution is not within sight. There have been important wars, and there is a continuing drain of resources into national defense; there

has been a population explosion, and there remains the Veblenian sin of competitive consumption, or "conspicuous waste"; finally, there is an international responsibility: the economic problem must be solved not just for England, or for Canada and other highly developed countries — it must be solved for the world, not least for the "third world."

So now, as Keynes then said in 1928, "avarice and usury and precaution must be our gods for a little longer still. For only they can lead us out of the tunnel of economic necessity into daylight." Not for a "little longer," but for the forseeable future, there will be much labor to be done, and pecuniary incentives, pecuniary emulation, will play a major part in ensuring that it will be done.

As Keynes foresaw a period when little labor would be required, he speculated on the problem of adjustment to an era of leisure:

"To those who sweat for their daily bread, leisure is a longed-for sweet — until they get it. For the first time since his creation, man will be faced with his real, his permanent problem — how to use his freedom from pressing economic cares, how to use the leisure which science and compound interest will have won for him, how to live wisely, agreeably, and well. For many ages to come, the old Adam will be so strong in us that everybody will need to do some work if he is to be contented . . . Three-hour shifts, or a fifteen-hour week, may put off the problem for a great while. For three hours a day is quite enough to satisfy the old Adam in us."

I have a good deal of sympathy with this worry — but I am not convinced that this need for work is universally recognized by the workers, and that it is not a middle-class view of what they need, and ought to want. It is not the fear of leisure, but desire for material goods, that will dictate labor beyond 15 hours a week. Society will require longer hours if social objectives are to be met, and individuals will have to be induced to work long enough hours to meet those objectives. The problem is how we will be induced to work, and whether we will continue to react to pecuniary incentive: can we be persuaded by appeal to public spirit? May it be necessary, in Mill's word, to "exact," and if so, how?

I cannot answer these questions, but I want to draw attention to some features of the modern world that constitute the context in which an answer must fit. First, I state my belief that, even in the affluent society of the Western world, we are very far from that "plenty" which Keynes foresaw for his grandchildren. The affluence is not general: a very large proportion of the people live in poverty, that is, at an unacceptably low standard of living.

One must consider, too, how much is needed for the cleaning of our environment, water, and air; for the beautification of our cities; for the improvement of educational facilities for people of all ages; for the proper provision of health services; and for the support of artistic endeavor.

Second, all these programs involve either "transfers" of income, or expenditure on "public" goods. And both involve taxation. Now, an individual might voluntarily contribute to charity, and may well accept taxation, to improve the conditions of life for the poor without losing incentive to work and earn. But when the goods he enjoys come to be, in ever-larger proportions, public goods rather than private goods, the incentive may be reduced.

May he not begin to recognize that he is paying for goods to be enjoyed by others, and that he can enjoy those goods without paying for them? When the marginal rate of tax becomes very high, will public spirit, or the spirit of emulation, induce people to work for the common good, for income to be transferred to others, and for income to be taxed, to provide "public" goods for the enjoyment of all and sundry? How high is "very high"?

Thirdly, the gap between the incomes of the employed and the unemployed has widened. When, as in some jurisdictions, the unemployment pay is not taxed, and the wages of the employed are subject to many tax deductions, and where the cost of transportation to work is high, the unemployed may, for a considerable period of time, be better off than the employed worker. But even if the gap has not closed, it has generally been narrowed, and the incentive to work a 48-week year has been reduced. One might expect that the market would operate to restore the incentive: a reduced supply of labor might be expected to raise wages and thus widen the gap and increase the incentive, ultimately increas-

ing the amount of work.

The gap would be widened further by the rise in prices likely to be associated with the rise in wages. But in our day of "indexing," unemployment benefits would rise. Now that they are related to earnings, they would rise still further. To meet the increased cost of unemployment, the contributions of the employed would probably rise. The gap would be closing: the market would be thwarted.

If, with Keynes, we look forward to the "possibilities" for our grandchildren, there seems to me to be another feature to be noted. With the probability of zero population growth, and the possibility of declining population, in most Western countries the age composition is likely to change. The proportion of the aged is likely to be much greater than now. If, at the same time, the trend to early retirement continues, the proportion of pensioners would be still greater. If the trend to more generous provision for pensioners (which I detect) continues, the burden of provision for the pensioners might become heavy — so heavy that the employed would have so little incentive to work that the problem I have been discussing would become more serious.

Perhaps our grandchildren will decide that their grandparents should be induced to continue in employment as long as their physical and mental health permits, and that the gap between the earnings of the aged employed and the income of the pensioners should be adequate to induce many to seek such employment. Curiously enough, this might well prove a boom to the aged for many of whom "leisure is a longed-for sweet — until they get it."

The choice of more leisure, and less goods, seems to me a wise choice. But a desire for leisure and a disinclination to work while expecting no reduction — indeed some continuing increase — in the goods available, forces one to consider how the work required to provide that flow of goods is to be induced. If we in the aggregate want more leisure than is consistent with satisfaction of our want for goods, enjoyment of our increased leisure depends on a decrease in the leisure of others. The problem of equality of income leads on to problems of equality of work, equality of leisure.

a) Briefly provide support for or disagreement with A.P. Herbert's "Manifesto."

b) Indicate agreement (A) or disagreement (D) with the following statements made in the article and where feasible briefly state reasons.

   (i) "production has been increasing, but so have wants"

   (ii) "poverty and want do make (a) people wise and industrious"

   (iii) "It is but equity [fair], besides, that they who feed, clothe, and lodge the whole body of the people should be themselves tolerably well fed, clothed, and lodged."

   (iv) Adam Smith's argument that high wages resulting from increasing productivity of labour did (do) not raise prices

   (v) John Stuart Mill's argument, "To civilize a savage, he must be inspired with new wants and desires, even if not of a very elevated kind, provided that their gratification can be a motive to a steady regular bodily and mental exertion"

   (vi) Marx's statement that the proletariat (workers) should "increase the total of productive forces as rapidly as possible"

   (vii) "each person would be incessantly occupied in evading his fair share of the work"

   (viii) George Bernard Shaw's statement, "It is desirable that the burden . . . and taking their full share of its income" (the entire paragraph)

   (ix) Keynes's statement that "assuming no important war and no important increase in population, the economic problem [unsatisfied wants] may be solved, or be at least within sight of solution, within a hundred years [from 1928]."

c) Do you think that the gap between incomes of the employed and unemployed is an important economic factor? Why or why not?

d) Discuss the problem raised by Bladen concerning the incentive of people in the future to work and support payments for such things as pollution control, educational facilities and pension benefits to the aged.

CHAPTER 16

From Micro to Macro

LEARNING OBJECTIVES

After reading this chapter you should be able to explain:

1. The representation of inter-industry linkages by means of an input-output table.

2. The distribution of economic activity among the major economic regions of Canada.

3. Canadian government policies designed to alleviate regional economic disparities.

16-1 INTRODUCTION AND PURPOSE

Up to this point, we have studied how the economy functions by examining its individual parts. In particular, we have seen how output, prices, employment, wages and rates of return on investment are influenced by individual buyers and suppliers. The broadest view we have taken has been that of an industry or a consumer group within a single market. This is the nature of microeconomic analysis. In macroeconomics, we step back from our scrutiny of micro units and instead examine the behaviour of very broad sectors within the economy and the behaviour of the economy as a whole. The idea is to see what influences the average price level and volume of output, not of a single good or service, but of all various goods and services produced in the economy. Correspondingly, in macroeconomics we are interested not in the level of employ-

ment or wage rates within any particular industry or occupation but rather in the determination of the level of total employment and average wage rates in the entire economy.

This chapter is designed to bridge the gap between micro and macro analysis. We attempt to do this along two dimensions: (i) *by industry* and (ii) *geographically*. The Canadian macroeconomy may be thought of as a conglomeration of all the various markets or industries for goods and services produced in Canada. Alternatively it may be regarded as the sum total of all the various geographical regions of economic activity. For example, the labour market in Canada may be viewed as the sum total of the labour markets within each industry or region.

To begin with, we develop the concept of a macroeconomy along the industrial dimension. Later in the chapter, we turn to the geographic or regional dimension.

16-2 INTER-INDUSTRY RELATIONS AND TOTAL ACTIVITY

In microeconomics, we recognize that each market is really only one part of the many markets for different goods and services which together constitute what is termed *the macroeconomy*. In macroeconomic analysis, though we often neglect to say so explicitly, we are aware that whatever the economic shocks may be — from an increase in government expenditure to a poor growing season in agriculture — they have to work their way through the microeconomic reactions of individuals, firms and industries. This has to be so because the entire (or macro) economy is simply an aggregation of individual firms, consumer units and governments.

In this chapter we wish to give specific recognition to the position of each industry with respect to other industries and to the macroeconomy. We wish to analyze, for example, the effect on a particular industry of an economic shock that may initially hit some other industry. As we will see, the effect on our chosen industry will be transmitted through linkages between that industry and the industry initially affected. Further, the initial impact on our industry may affect other industries, whose linkages with ours can cause additional feedback effects — and so on. So far, we have ignored such feedback effects as being of secondary importance. (In other words, we have engaged in what economists refer to as **partial equilibrium analysis**.) But if one is concerned with effects on the macroeconomy — or if one is attempting to forecast with some accuracy the trends in any industry — such feedback effects may have to be considered. (An analysis which accounts for all possible feedback effects is termed a **general equilibrium analysis**.)

Input-Output Analysis

One form of general equilibrium analysis was developed by Wassily W. Leontief in the 1930s and was partly the reason for his winning the Nobel Prize in economics. The analytical device is called an **input-output table**. This construct, which has been used in centrally planned economies for years, is becoming more and more widely used by Western governments for national and regional development as well as by businesses for sales forecasting. Therefore it is worthwhile to examine this technique. In addition, the input-output table provides a *quantitative* description of the linkages between various industries in the economy and the macroeconomy itself.

Because input-output tables can be somewhat confusing at first, we will proceed with an example of such a table for a simplified two-industry economy (Table 16-1).

The two industries are agriculture and manufac-

Table 16-1 Hypothetical input-output table for year 19X1 (in billions of $)

Inputs supplied by \ Outputs bought by	Agri-culture	Manu-facturing	Macro (total) demand for final products	Gross output
	(Used in the production process)			
1 Agriculture	8(0.08)	18(0.09)	74	100
2 Manufacturing	30(0.30)	44(0.22)	126	200
3 Factor inputs (Labour and capital)	62(0.62)	138(0.69)	200*	
4 Gross input	100	200		300

* Total value of output always equals incomes of factor input owners

In this two-industry economy, agriculture sells $8 billion of its output to itself, $18 billion to manufacturing and $74 billion to final consumers. Manufacturing sells $30 billion of output to agriculture, $44 billion to itself and $126 billion to final consumers. The third row shows that agriculture utilizes $62 billion worth of labour and capital inputs and manufacturing $138 billion worth of inputs. The numbers in parentheses show the same concepts, but expressed as per unit of gross output in each industry.

turing. Each industry produces **intermediate** (or partly finished) **goods** that are used by the other industry as material input for its production process. In addition, each industry produces finished or **final goods** that are used by various groups in the economy as a whole. The entries in the table show how much of each industry's output is purchased by itself and by the other industry as inputs for their production processes. For example, reading across the first row we see that agriculture supplied $8 billion in output to itself (in the form of feed grain, seed, fertilizer and so on) and $18 billion in output to the manufacturing industry (the processed foods segment). The third entry in the first row indicates the total demand for agricultural finished products (fresh fruit, vegetables, milk, eggs, meat and so on). The last entry in the first row is the sum of all preceding entries and indicates, therefore, the total output of the agriculture industry, including both finished output and intermediate output used by both industries. The row for manufacturing is read in a similar manner.

The first two entries of the third row indicate the total dollar value of capital and labour inputs utilized by agriculture and manufacturing respectively, while the third entry (200) reflects the total income which also equals the market value of all finished goods produced in the economy. To see why it must always work out this way, examine the following simplified income statement for a fictitious firm, Company A Ltd. (Table 16-2).

If we add up total costs plus the accounting profit as the payment to capital (some of this may be excess or economic profit — but that does not matter for this purpose), we arrive at the sales figure ($276 + $24 = $300). But, if the above table represented a consolidated income statement for all firms in our two-industry economy, the $300 sales figure would include the $100 materials figure twice — once when sold as intermediate goods and once when sold as part of finished products. To eliminate this double counting and arrive at the market value of finished production, we could either subtract the $100 materials from the gross sales figure ($300 − $100 = $200) or merely add up just the payments for labour and capital inputs ($176 + $24 = $200).

In order to see how input-output tables may be used for planning and forecasting by government and industry, it is useful to express the entries of

Table 16-1 on a *per unit of gross output* (or per unit of gross input) basis. These numbers have been placed in parentheses beside the original entries. For example, in year 19X1, $200 billion in gross output in the manufacturing industry used $18 billion in agricultural output, $44 billion in manufacturing output, and $138 billion in labour and capital services. In other words, each $1 billion in gross manufacturing output used approximately $0.09 (that is, 18 ÷ 200) billion in agricultural output, $0.22 (that is, 44 ÷ 200) billion in manufacturing output, and $0.69 (that is, 138 ÷ 200) billion in labour and capital services. Similarly, each $1 billion of gross agriculture output required $0.08 billion in agricultural output, $0.30 billion in manufacturing output and $0.62 billion in labour and capital services as inputs for the production process.

Though this information is quite useful, it is not yet in the form necessary to answer a question such as, "How much extra manufacturing output or how much extra labour and capital is required to produce $1 billion more in agricultural output for final consumer demand?" The figures in parentheses in Table 16-1 illustrate only the *partial* or *direct effects* in each industry of an increase in final demand. They do not show the *total effects* including *inter-industry feedbacks*. For example, suppose total consumer demand for final agricultural output increases by $1 billion. The direct effect on the manufacturing industry would be a requirement of

Table 16-2 Income statement for Company A Ltd.

Sales		$300
Costs:		
Materials	$100	
Labour	176	276
Profit		$ 24

The sum of payments to labour and capital inputs ($176 + $24) represents the market value of finished production, after the sales of intermediate goods are netted out. It is identical to gross sales minus the cost of materials ($300 − $100).

Table 16-3 Total increased input requirements per $1 billion increase in final demand

	Nature of final demand	
	Agriculture	Manufacturing
Agriculture	1.13	0.13
Manufacturing	0.43	1.32
Labour and capital	1.00	1.00

Input-output coefficients for the two-industry economy illustrated in Table 16-1. For a $1 billion increase in final demand for output of an industry in the column heading, the entries in the table show the extra output of industries in each row as well as the value of input services required to bring about the $1 billion demand increase.

$0.30 billion in output. But this $0.30 billion increase in manufacturing output itself requires an additional $0.22 × 0.30 billion in manufacturing output, which itself would require an additional $0.22 × (0.22 × 0.30) billion in manufacturing output and so on. Further, the original $1 billion in new demand for agricultural output will create a requirement for another $0.08 billion in agricultural output, which will have a further requirement for manufacturing output of $0.30 × 0.08 billion and so on. The total effect — including the direct and indirect (feedback) influences — can be calculated with matrix algebra. The results of such calculations are shown in Table 16-3.

The entries in Table 16-3, known as **input-output coefficients**, are read as follows. A $1 billion increase in final demand for agricultural products leads to a necessary $1.13 billion increase in total agricultural production, a $0.43 billion increase in manufacturing output, and a $1 billion requirement for labour and capital services.

Use of Input-Output Analysis

A table of input-output coefficients may be used for national economic planning or regional development in the following way. Suppose, for example, the government wishes to stimulate economic activity in a particular province of Canada. If Table 16-3 has been derived from a provincial input-

output table, increasing government spending in the province's manufacturing industry by, say, $1 billion would increase manufacturing and agricultural production by $1.32 billion and $0.13 billion, respectively. In addition, more capital and labour inputs would be required to the tune of $1 billion. In fact, with a more detailed input-output table — such as those actually estimated for the Canadian economy — the new demand for different types of labour and capital equipment could be forecast separately.

Predicting Industrial Bottlenecks

In order to get the results predicted in Table 16-3, all the feedbacks discussed earlier must occur. These come about, remember, by one industry's output increasing, which in turn increases the output of another, which then feeds back and further increases the output of the first industry as well as others, and so on. But suppose the manufacturing industry, for example, could not increase its output beyond $1.1 billion. If this was the case, following the government's $1 billion expenditure, manufacturing output would create a blockage or bottleneck for further industrial expansion. As a result of the manufacturing industry's stalled expansion, there would not be as much demand by manufacturing for agricultural output, or for capital and labour in either industry. The feedbacks also would be correspondingly weakened.

Since an input-output table can be used to estimate the effect of a particular industrial expansion on all industries, such information, together with a knowledge of output limits of the various industries, can be used to highlight possible bottlenecks caused by an industrial expansion that is too fast in any one direction. Alternative policies may then be prepared to head off such problems.

Business Forecasting

Input-output tables are being increasingly used by business for sales and profits forecasting. The basic methods often employ mathematical models. The approach is, however, broadly outlined in a schematic manner by Figure 16-1.

First of all, a forecast is made of important macroeconomic variables which affect industry demand. From this, further forecasts are generated

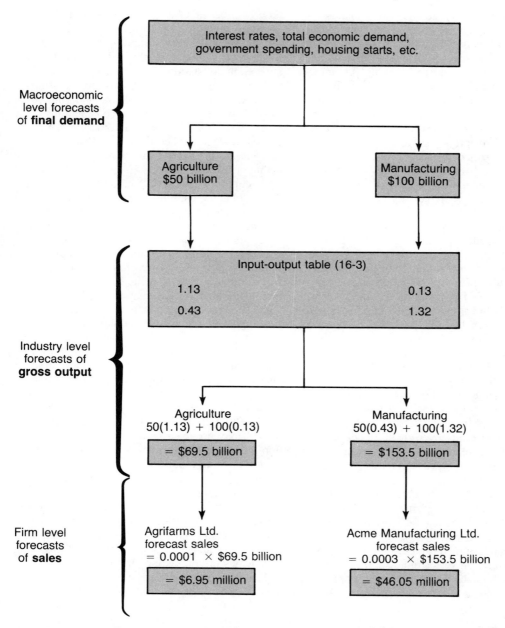

Fig. 16-1 Business forecasting with the use of an input-output table

The macroeconomic forecasts of $50 billion of final demand for agriculture and $100 billion for industry, when combined with input-output coefficients, yield industry forecasts of gross output of $69.5 billion for agriculture and $153.5 billion for manufacturing. Individual firms derive a forecast of their sales by assuming a specified market share of the industry demand forecast.

that predict demand (or changes in demand) for each industry. Once final demand for each industry's output is estimated, information from an input-output table may be used to forecast the gross output of each industry. Finally, this information may be utilized by each business firm to forecast its own sales for the coming year. In this example, it has been assumed that the two firms taken for illustrative purposes simply use a constant market share projection for their sales forecasts. **Market share** means percent of industry sales. Agrifarms Ltd. believes that it will receive a constant 0.01% of industry sales, whereas Acme Manufacturing Ltd. believes its share will be 0.03%.

In Figure 16-1 it has also been assumed that macroeconomic information leads to final demand forecasts of $50 billion and $100 billion in the agriculture and manufacturing industries respectively. This, together with the input-output coefficients of Table 16-3, leads to a total sales forecast of $69.5 billion in agriculture and $153.5 billion in manufacturing. Finally, the two firms, Agrifarms Ltd. and Acme Manufacturing Ltd. — using their notions concerning their particular market shares — would forecast their sales to be $6.95 million and $46.05 million respectively.

Typically, large macroeconomic forecasting models are too expensive for most business firms to develop themselves. Therefore, the standard practice is to rely on a government model or perhaps a model developed by a consulting firm, which would then supply its forecasts for a fee. National and regional input-output tables have been developed and used by numerous government departments. In practice, an individual firm may decide to develop an economic model of its own operations to tie in with the gross industry sales forecasts coming from the input-output tables or instead it may rely on very simple approximate relationships such as the constant market share idea used above.

Problems with Input-Output Tables

First of all, the data-gathering and analytical procedure involved in the construction of input-output tables is relatively expensive. For this reason, they are not constructed each year. As time goes on, therefore, changes in production methods may ma-

terially affect input-output coefficients reflected in an "old" table.

Another problem with input-output tables is that they are (by nature of the data available) constructed in dollar values rather than in physical volume terms. But technically, it is more reasonable to relate volumes of industrial output to volumes of inputs. For example, technical considerations may mean that to produce one automobile, so many tonnes of steel, rubber, cloth and glass are necessary. It is unreasonable to think that production techniques dictate that so many dollars worth of cars require so many dollars worth of materials. Also, dollar expenditure will be a poor approximation for volume if relative prices in the economy change. Therefore, as relative prices change over time, old input-output tables lose their accuracy.

One more limitation of input-output tables is the implicit assumption of *constant returns to scale*. For example, Table 16-1 indicates that each additional billion dollars in manufacturing output requires a fixed amount of inputs (material inputs from agriculture and manufacturing as well as labour and capital inputs), regardless of the amount of expansion. If manufacturing output grows by $1 billion, the direct need for agricultural input increases by $0.09 billion; if the expansion is $2 billion, the direct need for agricultural products is assumed to increase by $0.18 (that is, 2×0.09) billion — and so on. Since constant returns may not even be a reasonable approximation in some cases, this is a further source of inaccuracy in using input-output tables.

Though there are one or two other implicit assumptions in input-output analysis, the basic problems with them are the same limitations discussed above. The probable accuracy of input-output analysis declines with the age of the estimated table entries and with the magnitude of projected expansions or contractions in final demand.

The input-output table is a form of analysis that may be used to give useful results concerning the approximate effect on industrial output of shocks that may hit the economy. However, the input-output form of analysis is limited in that it abstracts from price considerations and does not enable one to examine what gives rise to macroeconomic or total economy shocks in the first place. For this reason, other frameworks for macroeconomic analysis have been devised.

Since the basic form of economic analysis is *supply and demand*, any microeconomic or macroeconomic analysis involves these two aspects. In fact, since macroeconomic activity is the outcome of individual economic unit behaviour, any explanation of macroeconomic causes and effects must have at its root micro supply and demand considerations. In macroeconomics, therefore, it is necessary to develop an *aggregate* (or *total*) *supply-demand framework* for analysis along similar lines to those followed in microeconomics.

The input-output table is a form of general equilibrium analysis that provides a quantitative description of the linkages among the various industries in the economy. It is used for forecasting, both at the level of the whole economy and at the level of individual firms. Among its limitations are somewhat restrictive assumptions about technology and lack of sensitivity to changes in relative prices.

16-3 REGIONAL ANALYSIS AND THE MACROECONOMY

An entire economy may be considered not only as the total of all its industries but also as the total of all its regions. Canada could, for purposes of analysis, be divided into a number of appropriate areas. For convenience let us consider the following four regions from east to west: (i) the Atlantic (comprising Newfoundland, Prince Edward Island, Nova Scotia and New Brunswick), (ii) Quebec, (iii) Ontario and (iv) the West (comprising Manitoba, Saskatchewan, Alberta and British Columbia). Table 16-4 indicates the distribution of population among these regions. Notice that over the 1976–1987 period there was a noticeable population shift from central and Atlantic Canada to the West. This has, however, slowed down with the fall of resource prices in 1986 and a boom in the economy of Ontario.

Regional Industrial Structure

In order to compare the industrial structures of these four regions we have prepared two related figures, Figures 16-2 and 16-3.

Figure 16-2 shows the proportion of total Canadian industrial activity carried out within each region. As we might expect, because of its smaller popula-

Table 16-4 **Distribution of population in Canada, 1987**

	Percent	
Region	1976	1987
Atlantic	9.6	9.0
Quebec	27.1	25.9
Ontario	36.2	36.0
West	27.1	28.8
	100.0	100.0

Source: Statistics Canada, 11-003

Over the past ten years, there has been a shift of population from Atlantic and Central Canada to the West.

tion, the Atlantic region has the smallest proportion of all types of industrial activity. The West is dominant in agriculture and forestry and mining, with Ontario and Quebec sharing a roughly equal second place in these areas. However, Ontario clearly dominates in all other areas of industrial activity except transportation and communications.

Figure 16-3 goes a little further than Figure 16-2 in highlighting internal structural differences between the four regional economies. By reflecting the *proportion* of each region's labour force engaged in the nine indicated industries, Figure 16-3 accounts for differences in population whereas Figure 16-2 does not.

As Figure 16-3 indicates, the sharpest differences in economic structure come in agriculture (1) and manufacturing (3). The West has almost twice as large a percentage of its labour force employed in agriculture as compared with the Canadian average, whereas the other three regions are each well below average in this regard. As far as manufacturing is concerned, Quebec and Ontario are the most industrialized regions; the Atlantic and Western regions are the least industrialized.

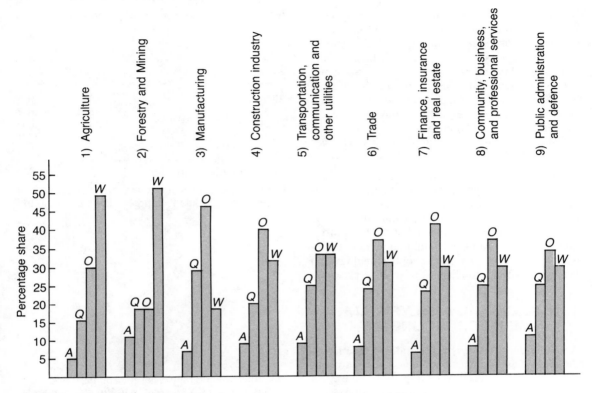

Fig. 16-2 Regional concentration of economic activity (based on 1981 Census of Canada labour employment data)

Distribution of employment in each of nine industry groups among the four major economic regions of Canada. The West dominates in agriculture and in forestry and mining; Ontario has the largest share of employment in all of the remaining industry groups.

Standard-of-Living Differentials

One recurring policy problem of a national government is the difference between the "have" and "have not" regions — as measured by, say, per capita income or unemployment rates. The first difficulty is to judge the extent of real differences in satisfaction or welfare terms between regions, since economic factors represent only one dimension of total living standards. For example, if a worker in Charlottetown, P.E.I. receives $2000 a year less income than a worker in Toronto, Ontario, and was given the opportunity to move to Toronto and obtain a higher paying job, the P.E.I.

worker may be unwilling to do so if in the worker's opinion the quality of life in Charlottetown is worth more than $2000 a year extra income. This is the same difficulty we encountered in Chapter 10 when attempting to judge the differences in total compensation between different occupations.

Let us suppose, however, that it is clear that some people would be better off if they had been born and raised in more prosperous regions of the country. The question then comes up, "Why do they not move?" Some of course do. Typically, there is net migration from the poorer regions of the country to the richer ones. The 1976–1987

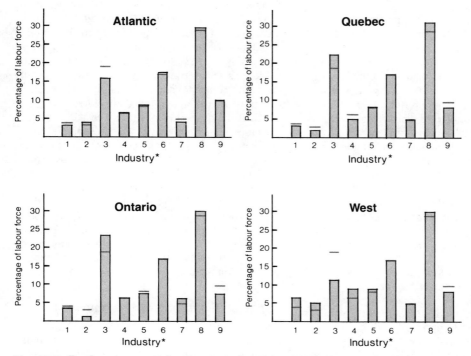

Fig. 16-3 Regional economic structure (based on 1981 Census of Canada employment data)

* Industries in same order as in Fig. 16-2. The symbol — indicates Canadian average.

Distribution of employment among nine industry groups in each of the four major economic regions of Canada, compared with the national average.

swing in population distribution from East to West, illustrated earlier in Table 16-4, reflects the better employment and income opportunities that developed from the resource industries' boom of the late 1970s. Many people, however, do not move. This is either because they feel that the non-material benefits of the region make up for a lower material standard of living or because they perceive the difference as not being worth the costs of moving and adjusting to a new environment. Some may feel it is better to be unemployed among friends and relatives than to be possibly better off financially among strangers.

Government Regional Policy Alternatives

Suppose a federal government believes it has identified serious regional income or unemployment disparities which it wishes to mitigate. This essentially means that the market system is not willing to pay high enough prices for whatever goods and services are produced in the depressed region so that a sufficient rate of return on investment can be earned, which would, in turn, lead to sufficient employment and wage rates equivalent to those in wealthier regions. This can result from the demand or supply side of the market.

From the demand side, it may be the case that

the products indigenous to the region, and which the labour force is trained to produce, are no longer attractive to the market. From the supply side, the particular commodities of the region may be getting harder — that is, more costly — to produce. This would be the case, for instance, if the seas off the Atlantic coast become overfished, a problem resulting in more work hours required than before to net any given quantity of fish. This means a productivity drop, an increase in the unit cost (marginal cost) of fish production, higher fish prices, less fish bought, lower profitability and less employment in the industry. Higher transportation costs to central Canadian markets would also bring about similar results for Atlantic coast fishermen.

On the other hand, *regional disparities* may emerge because of a sudden surge in demand for one particular region's products. This was the case for Alberta during the 1970s as a result of growing demand for that province's energy resources.

One possible policy choice for the central government is to do nothing concerning regional disparities. Those who believe that the overall benefits are better in other regions will migrate to such regions. Older people might not, but their children will. In this sense, one might say that regional disparities are always only temporary and that labour mobility will eventually remove them. But labour mobility may be sluggish. During the adjustment period we may have to allow a generation or more to suffer considerably because, owing to nonmaterial reasons or adjustment costs, they will not move.

An alternative is to help speed up labour mobility by paying moving and relocation expenses or establishing retraining programs — the objective being a reduction in adjustment costs to those who might be encouraged to move.

A third possibility is to subsidize those in relatively depressed regions so that the hardships of living there would be reduced. **Regional development subsidies** may take the form of (i) greater welfare aid, lower personal taxes and more generous unemployment insurance benefits to workers or of (ii) lower taxes and subsidies to producers. Under (ii), firms may then be able to generate a reasonable profit by investing in depressed areas and employing labour where they could not have otherwise done so.

In the short run, the cost of policy (i) to the

population outside of the depressed regions is the amount of additional welfare aid not paid for by local taxes. The cost of policy (ii) to the external population is the amount of subsidies not paid for by local taxes less the amount by which federal welfare and unemployment benefits are reduced by the induced employment. An additional benefit is that most of the unemployed would regard themselves as being better off employed.

In the long run, however, if such subsidies under either policy remain, there is a permanent net cost to the country as a whole in terms of lost output resulting from having more production activities located in regions that cannot provide rates of remuneration on labour or capital as high as those which could be earned elsewhere. Nevertheless, one might argue that there are social or political benefits from having people live in such areas and that these benefits more than make up for the net material long-run costs of subsidization.

Canadian Government Programs

In order to promote Canadian national identity, the federal government has, over the years, attempted to stimulate east-west trade across Canada rather than the more natural north-south trade flows with adjacent regions of the United States. Partly to accomplish this *trade diversion*, Canada has created tariff barriers against foreign goods.

As a result of the induced east-west flow of goods, central Canada (in particular Ontario) has become a natural region for manufacturing establishments to be set up in order to minimize total transportation costs to both eastern and western Canadian markets. Over the years, this policy has been partly responsible for making central Canada an industrial hub. Further, it has hampered industrialization in the Maritimes and on the West coast by making transportation costs to the rest of Canada prohibitive. It is not surprising, therefore, that transportation policy and freight rates have from time to time been tinkered with by the Canadian Transport Commission in order to make central Canadian markets more accessible to Maritime products.

The Department of Regional Economic Expansion (DREE) was set up in 1969 to integrate and coordinate federal programs to remove regional economic disparities. Under the Regional Development Incentives Act (1969), the Department operated programs of industrial incentives to encourage manufacturing and processing industries to establish and expand in designated regions. The designated areas included the Atlantic region, Quebec (excluding the Montreal-Hull corridor) and Northern Ontario. These, as well as various other regional plans, generally provided outright grants and forgivable loans, which were sometimes tied to the number of jobs created by the industrial development in question.

In 1973, DREE designed a General Development Agreement (GDA) to implement its programs and coordinate federal-provincial development activities. Ten-year GDAs were signed in 1974 with all provinces except Prince Edward Island, which was covered under a similar 15-year agreement signed in 1969.

In 1982, the federal government reorganized the administration of regional economic development initiatives. A new Department of Regional Industrial Expansion (DRIE) amalgamated the regional programs of DREE with the industry, small business and tourism components of the Department of Industry, Trade and Commerce. The objective was to enable the government to pursue balanced industrial growth on a national basis. Yet another reorganization took place in 1987 when new regional agencies were formed in Atlantic and Western Canada to manage the development of depressed areas. The rest of DRIE became part of the newly formed Department of Industry, Science and Technology.

During the last decade, there occurred a shift in economic activity toward Western Canada; it has, however, slowed down with the fall of oil prices in 1986. The four main economic regions of Canada exhibit significant differences in their industrial structure. Ontario and Quebec dominate in manufacturing, while the West has the largest share of agricultural and resource industries.

CONCLUDING REMARKS

In going from microeconomic analysis of a single consuming unit or a single producer to the economy at large, we may proceed by adding up economic activity by region or by industry. Quantitative inter-industry and inter-regional analysis is aided by the use of input-output tables, which nevertheless have some limitations. The next logical step for economic analysis is the study of *macroeconomics*.

KEY TERMS AND CONCEPTS

partial equilibrium analysis	final goods
general equilibrium analysis	input-output coefficients
input-output table	regional standard-of-living differentials
intermediate goods	regional development subsidies

PROBLEMS

Problem 1

a) Explain two ways of looking at the total (or macro) economy.

b) Table 1 (below) is an incomplete input-output table for a hypothetical two-industry economy. Complete the table by filling the encircled spaces.

Table 1 **Input-output table ($ billions)**

Inputs supplied by \ Outputs bought by	Used in the production process — Coal	Used in the production process — Electricity	Macro final demand	Gross output
1 Coal	4	( ) 25 ( )	◯	43
2 Electricity	◯	( ) 5 ( )	41	◯
3 Factor inputs (labour and capital)	◯	( ) 23 ( )	◯	
4 Gross input	◯	◯		◯

Table 2 **Total input requirements per $1 billion in final demand**

	Nature of final demand — Coal	Electricity
Coal	1.2	0.6
Electricity	0.22	1.2

c) Fill the six parenthetical spaces in Table 1 by converting the input requirements of each industry to a percentage of gross output.

d) Table 1 indicates only the direct input requirements for each $1 billion in industrial output. From the data in this table show that the total (direct and indirect) requirements per $1 billion increase in final demand are as given in Table 2. (This question is quite difficult. Remember, total (gross) output in coal = coal output required to operate the coal industry itself + coal output needed to fill final demand.)

e) If the final demand for coal and electricity is expected to be $16 billion and $45 billion respectively, what will be the total (gross) output needed from each industry?

f) Briefly mention some drawbacks to input-output tables that tend to introduce inaccuracies into their application.

CASES

Case 16-1

The Financial Post

GM loan moves spark furor over plant's future

By ROBERT ENGLISH

Federal and Quebec government plans to provide General Motors Corp., one of the world's largest and richest corporations, with an interest-free loan worth more than $200 million has created the predictable furor.

But the cheap financing might be a small price to pay to keep GM's Ste-Thérèse, Que., plant running, even if it continues for only a few more years.

If GM pulls the plug on Ste-Thérèse:

• An estimated $155 million in annual salaries to its 4,000 employees disappears from the Quebec economy.

• Unemployment insurance payments to those employees in the first year alone could amount to $60 million.

• Federal, provincial and municipal taxes amounting to $240 million a year are lost.

• Fourteen hundred companies that supply everything from fan belts to paper clips can forget about $270 million a year in business, which could easily cost an additional 4,000 jobs. This would bring the total cost of a plant shutdown as high as 30,000 jobs or more.

Suppliers from Ontario would also feel the pinch.

• Quebec loses the linchpin of the auto industry it has struggled so hard to create, to be left with only the questionable benefits from Hyundai Motor Co.'s $325-million, yet-to-be-built Bromont assembly plant.

"In terms of unemployment benefits alone, the payback period is probably only a couple of years," says Toronto auto-industry analyst Dennis DesRosiers, of DesRosiers Automotive Research Inc.

Until a few weeks ago it looked like General Motors' problem-plagued Ste-Thérèse assembly plant was going to disappear along with the outmoded rear-wheel-drive car — the Oldsmobile Cutlass — it's been producing for the past few years.

Top of list

But mammoth GM is being prodded sharply by both the federal and Quebec governments to give the plant a new lease on life. It has been reported Ottawa and Quebec will pitch in with $110 million each in interest free loans to help GM refurbish the facility. GM would have to commit itself to spend $450 million on the plant by 1991.

A total of more than $500 million would be required to update the plant to build a new car line. The most likely choice to replace the geriatric Cutlass would be GM's A-series cars, such as the Pontiac 6000 now built in Oshawa.

However, at the top of GM's list of needed investments before a new model could be built at Ste-Thérèse is a new clear-coat/base-coat paint line that could easily cost $250 million. Footings for such an addition have already gone in, but GM spokesman Nick Hall says this doesn't commit the company to anything.

All GM will admit is that financial discussions are being held with the governments involved. Hall stresses that no final decision on the plant's future has been made. It does hope to make an announcement before Christmas however.

Federal Industry Minister Michel Côté and Quebec Industry Minister Daniel Johnson are both keen to save the plant. Their proposals aren't without precedent. The federal government had tried to entice GM into setting up an aluminum foundry in Quebec in the late 1970s with a $60-million subsidy offer; and along with the Ontario government, has chipped in $100 million to help GM and Suzuki set up an Ontario plant. American Motors Corp. is also receiving $120 million in Ontario and federal assistance.

Quebec and Ottawa are already spending about $100 million to help Hyundai, and in the past the province lured a GM bus plant to St. Eustache with a $100-million order for 1,200 vehicles.

Various U.S. states have enticed Japanese investors with even larger cash incentives.

Cost-effective place

For General Motors Corp., which is investing more than $5 billion in its Canadian assembly operations in Ontario, the deal presents more than a few problems.

On one hand, the reason GM is investing heavily in Canada — at Oshawa and in the new joint venture with Japan's Suzuki in Cambridge, Ont. — is that it makes sense to build cars here. Thanks to currency, wage and social cost benefits, Canada is a more cost-effective place to build cars than the U.S.

As well, threats to close Ste-Thérèse have brought a number of factors nicely into line, including a chastened work force (the plant was listed near the bottom of a worldwide ranking of GM plants a few years ago). Canadian Auto Workers boss Bob White apparently read the riot act to the Ste-Thérèse union local earlier this year, and now workers (and management) seem ready to do their all to change the plant's reputation for shoddy work and absenteeism. There's also a new labor agreement to go along with the offer of government assistance.

The negatives are that GM is in the midst of a major North America-wide rationalization that will see 11 of its older, outdated plants (of which Ste-Thérèse is a prime example) closed and some 29,000 workers laid off in the U.S., with the promises of further cuts to come. Explaining to the United Auto Workers in the U.S. why some 4,000 Canadian jobs were being saved amid this carnage could be sticky. In particular, GM can't be seen to be robbing U.S. programs to spend additional money in Canada.

'Timing is bad'

There are also concerns that Canada's actions will turn up the heat under already-inflamed protectionist sentiment in the U.S. at a time when bilateral trade talks are in progress. With Canada's duty-remission schemes already under attack, the auto pact itself could become a target.

"There's going to be a price extracted from the American United Auto Workers union and the Congress," says a Canadian auto company insider. "I wonder if anybody's thought through whether that price is going to be worth it. The timing is incredibly bad. Six months ago this could all have happened without a great deal of problems."

While a case can be made for short-term benefits in providing monetary assistance to GM, according to DesRosiers, "it isn't simply a matter of spending money."

He feels significant commitments in terms of labor relations and retraining, and further development of the Quebec supplier base (perhaps with government help), are key elements to long-term success at Ste-Thérèse.

The wild card, however, remains the auto market. With annual overcapacity in North America expected to reach three million units within a few years, further plant closures are inevitable.

For a domestic auto industry united in calling for "a level playing field," the potential infusion of government funds into a GM operation raises some hackles.

Most of Ontario's assembly plants, for instance, also lack clear-coat paint lines. "Does this mean they are going to give $200 million to anybody who wants to install one?" asks one industry source. "I could run up $1 billion in this sort of thing, each instance being critical in terms of jobs.

"It's one of those things I would have hoped somebody would have had the wisdom not to offer. Now that they have, I hope others have the wisdom not to accept."

a) What kind of "market failure" (if any) can you identify here? How would you characterize the rationale for the type of government intervention discussed in the article? Distinguish between economic and political motivation.

b) What would be some of the costs of the proposed government intervention? What would be the benefits?

c) Discuss briefly the impact of such policies on competition in the Canadian car industry.

d) The article mentions concerns that the proposed actions "will turn up the heat under already inflamed protectionist sentiment in the U.S." Explain why this might be viewed as a protectionist move on the part of Canada.

e) Various provincial governments offer financial incentives to multinational corporations in order to entice them to locate in a particular province. In your opinion, what is the impact of such policies on the regional economic inequalities within Canada? Should they be pursued by the federal government instead? Why or why not? Or should industry decisions on the location of manufacturing activity be left free of government interference? Why or why not?

SOURCES OF PRESS ARTICLES

Case 2-1: "GM plans to halve its production rate for Chevette model," *The Wall Street Journal* (April 21, 1976). Reprinted by permission of The Wall Street Journal, © Dow Jones & Company, Inc., 1976. All Rights Reserved.

Case 2-2: Green, Carolyn. "Rent curbs upheaval," *The Financial Post* (November 30, 1985). Reprinted by permisson of The Financial Post.

Case 3-1: Bowen, Beverly. "Lured by recruiters, teachers head to U.S. as shortage predicted," *The Globe and Mail* (February 25, 1986). Reprinted by permission of The Globe and Mail, Toronto.

Case 3-2: Paris, Ellen. "Hippocrates meets Adam Smith," *Forbes* Magazine (February 10, 1986). Excerpted by permission of *Forbes* Magazine. © Forbes Inc., 1986.

Case 4-1: Couch, Brian. "Sales thermostat set at 'warm'," *The Financial Post* (May 15, 1976). Reprinted by permission of the author.

Case 4-2: Bowen, Beverly. "Return of vanishing foreign students sought," *The Globe and Mail* (September 13, 1986). Reprinted by permission of The Globe and Mail, Toronto.

Case 4-3: Observer News Service. "Europeans advised to burn surplus food," *The Globe and Mail* (September 16, 1986). Reprinted by permission of The Observer.

Case 5-1: Hubbard, Jaimie. "Price wars could bring shakeup in video stores," *The Financial Post* (July 12, 1986). Reprinted by permission of The Financial Post.

Case 5-2: Cluett, Jim. "Market crisis deepens amid potato squabble," *The Financial Post* (January 18, 1986). Reprinted by permission of the author.

Case 5-3: "Oil prices taking toll on U.S. rigs," *The Globe and Mail* (April 29, 1986). Reprinted by permission of Reuters.

Case 6-1: Hubbard, Jaimie. "The cola wars," *The Financial Post* (December 15, 1986). Reprinted by permission of The Financial Post.

Case 7-1: Williamson, Robert. "Car rental war means prices cut to 1¢ a day," *The Globe and Mail* (February 10, 1979). Reprinted by permission of The Globe and Mail, Toronto.

Case 7-2: Malarek, Victor. "Petrocan triggers 2-cent cut in gas price," *The Globe and Mail* (March 27, 1986). Reprinted by permission of The Globe and Mail, Toronto.

Claridge, Thomas. "Petrocan leads way as gasoline prices climb," *The Globe and Mail* (April 25, 1986). Reprinted by permission of The Globe and Mail, Toronto.

Case 7-3: Platiel, Rudy. "Farmer scrambles to beat egg quotas," *The Globe and Mail* (February 10, 1979). Reprinted by permission of The Globe and Mail, Toronto.

Case 8-1: Pritchard, Timothy. "What has made profit into a dirty word?" *The Globe and Mail* (November 13, 1976). Reprinted by permission of The Globe and Mail, Toronto.

Leduc, Lawrence; and J. Alex Murray. "Survey finds public believes profits are excessive," *The Globe and Mail* (May 27, 1976). Excerpts reprinted by permission of the authors.

Case 8-2: Bloomfield, Patrick. "OSC to review Grandma's reporting," *The Financial Post* (April 10, 1982). Reprinted by permission of The Financial Post.

Case 8-3: Wells, Jennifer. "The big chill," *The Financial Post* (October 26, 1987). Reprinted by permission of The Financial Post.

Case 9-1: Wayne, Jamie. "Blue Jays fly with financial firepower," *The Financial Post* (April 9, 1977). Reprinted by permission of the author.

Case 9-2: Clifford, Edward. "Lamp manufacturers brighten future by offering energy-saving products," *The Globe and Mail* (January 10, 1979). Reprinted by permission of The Globe and Mail, Toronto.

Case 10-1: McCallum, John S. "Disrespect for capital may lower standard of living," *The Financial Post* (August 9, 1986). Reprinted by permission of the author.

Case 10-2: Bagnall, James. "Construction workers lead labor's retreat," *The Financial Post* (March 1, 1986). Reprinted by permission of The Financial Post.

Case 11-1: Stewart-Patterson, David. "Shoe quotas no longer fit in Canada," *The Globe and Mail* (November 21, 1985). Reprinted by permission of The Globe and Mail, Toronto.

Case 11-2:   Cameron, Duncan. "Stopping countervail key to forging free-trade deal," *The Financial Post* (January 26, 1987). Reprinted by permission of the author. Duncan Cameron, a political economist at the University of Ottawa, is editor of *The Free Trade Papers* (Toronto: James Lorimer & Co., 1987).

Case 12-1:   Howard, Ross; and Michael Perley. "Counting the cost of acid rain," *Canadian Business*. From *Acid rain: the North American Forecast* by Ross Howard and Michael Perley (Toronto: House of Anansi Press, 1980). Reprinted by permission.

English, Robert. "Pollution busters get tough with bad guys," *The Financial Post* (November 1, 1986). Reprinted by permission of The Financial Post.

Case 12-2:   Surtees, Lawrence. "Bell rate application will be challenged," *The Globe and Mail* (February 4, 1987). Reprinted by permission of The Globe and Mail, Toronto.

Case 13-1:   Bird, Richard M. "You should get what you pay for," *The Financial Post* (March 12, 1979). Reprinted by permission of the author.

Case 14-1:   Grubel, Herbert. "New view of economic theory has value," *The Financial Post* (January 12, 1987). Reprinted by permission of the author.

Case 14-2:   Bishop, Jerry E. "Dismal science springs into life in lab," *The Wall Street Journal* (November 25, 1986). Reprinted by permission of The Wall Street Journal, © Dow Jones & Company, Inc., 1986. All Rights Reserved.

Case 15-1:   Bladen, Vincent. "Don't be fooled by 'new era choices': no work — no money, no leisure," Cartoons by Marie Hands, *The Financial Post* (April 17, 1976). Reprinted by permission of the author and the artist.

Case 16-1:   English, Robert. "GM loan moves spark furor over plant's future," *The Financial Post* (December 15, 1986). Reproduced by permission of The Financial Post.

INDEX